AF690968

Nikola Balvin • Daniel J. Christie
Editors

Children and Peace

From Research to Action

Editors
Nikola Balvin
UNICEF Office of Research-Innocenti
Florence, Italy

Daniel J. Christie
Department of Psychology
Ohio State University
Delaware, OH, USA

https://doi.org/10.1007/978-3-030-22176-8

"The open access publication of this volume was made possible by financial sponsorship from the UNICEF Office of Research-Innocenti. *The statements in this publication are the views of the author(s) and do not necessarily reflect the policies or the views of UNICEF.*"

Foreword

Violence takes many forms but affects children everywhere, shaping their lives and futures in profound and lasting ways. As we approach the 30th anniversary of the Convention of the Rights of the Child (CRC), which includes every child's right to protection from violence and abuse, the world is only beginning to understand both the pervasiveness of different forms of violence experienced or witnessed by children and the long-term social and psychological impacts.

Data and evidence are accumulating to provide a more solid basis for advocacy, policy and action. Violence against children (VAC) surveys and other data sources, learning initiatives such as "Know Violence in Childhood", WHO's INSPIRE strategy and the launch of the Global Partnership to End Violence Against Children are a few of the sources of knowledge and potential responses.[1]

Such initiatives serve to better inform us about the forms and faces of violence in childhood and to help frame violence within an ecological framework, where a child may be affected directly and indirectly by violence within her immediate home, school and immediate community, as well as through more macro institutional and structural conditions – including armed conflict. The media reminds us constantly of diverse forms of violence – abuse within the home; bullying and corporal punishment at schools; sexual abuse perpetrated by trusted members of institutions such as the church; neighbourhood gang violence; armed conflict and wars in which children are always victims but are also turned into combatants and perpetrators of violence; and the new and disturbing forms of violence affecting children and young people occurring in the digital space as well as in very real contexts of insecurity, conflict and crisis.

Responses are forthcoming – from law and policymakers to state institutions including police and judiciaries as well as health, education, social and protection services and through public awareness and community or civil society organizing. Nonetheless the problems are persistent, and those concerned with protection even

[1] For further information, see https://www.togetherforgirls.org/violence-children-surveys/; http://www.knowviolenceinchildhood.org/; https://www.who.int/violence_injury_prevention/violence/inspire/en/; and http://www.end-violence.org/.

in wealthy, stable and peaceful societies are severely challenged as they attempt to penetrate the institutional structures and digital landscapes where perpetrators may be hidden. In countries with weak institutions and few mechanisms of protection, countries ravaged by poverty, humanitarian crisis or armed conflict, where even the basic material needs of the child may not be met, the challenges of achieving peace and protection are incredibly daunting.

While there is still much to learn about violence and its consequences for children and a need to keep pushing forward the evidence agenda, the urgent imperative is to identify appropriate evidence-based actions and interventions – those that serve to prevent acts of violence against children, intervening at the level of drivers and working to break cycles of violence, as well as those that address the serious and lasting consequences of violence on children, their families and communities.

This volume offers some exciting directions in this search: it contributes unique insights from interdisciplinary perspectives, with a particular emphasis on what researchers studying peace psychology can bring to our understanding of violence, violent behaviours, the effects of violence including armed conflict and the ways to overcome these effects. The authors cover a broad range of issues – from those with direct relevance to current debates on violence at home and in schools and communities to the experiences of refugee and migrant children, or children in conflict, to structural forms of violence associated with extreme poverty, conflict over resources and the long-term issues of intergenerational justice associated with environmental degradation and climate change.

The papers were initially presented at the 15th International Symposium on the Contributions of Psychology to Peace hosted at UNICEF's Office of Research-Innocenti in Florence and co-organized with the Sapienza University of Rome under the title "Bridging across generations: turning research into action for children and families". The symposium brought together researchers from diverse disciplinary perspectives, particularly from Psychology and the Social Sciences, with the purpose of deepening our understanding of the issues and consequences for children of peace and violence in various contexts. It also engaged policymakers, advocates and practitioners with the intention of facilitating dialogue between the academic and policy/practice communities on issues of children and peace. Taking place at the height of the European migration crisis, when Italy was receiving unprecedented numbers of refugees, including minors, fleeing violence, conflict and despair, this discussion had particular resonance for the immediate setting but was global and cross cultural in its ambition and scope.

As Director of UNICEF's Office of Research-Innocenti in Florence at the time, I was delighted that we could support and host this symposium. The themes covered resonated with many areas of research at Innocenti – including, for example, work to understand drivers of violence against children (represented here by Maternowska et al.), bullying, protection of migrant and refugee children in both sending and receiving areas, the implication of digital technologies on child rights and protection, the link between cash transfers and other social protection programmes and mental health and violence and protecting children in humanitarian crisis or conflict settings.[2] The event also reflected a core commitment of the Office of Research-Innocenti in promoting dialogue among different stakeholders on key issues of concern for children, using research and evidence to shape public and policy debates in support of UNICEF's global normative, advocacy and programme roles.

Being part of this interdisciplinary and global dialogue among diverse stakeholders was an exceptional learning opportunity. The value of such cross-disciplinary and multi-stakeholder collaboration, also reflected in many of the papers in this volume, lies particularly in how it informs the ways in which knowledge and evidence can be translated into policy and practical action. The application of a peacebuilding perspective brought by those in the area of peace psychology to the development and implementation of programmes and policies affecting children opens scope for innovative approaches to both development and humanitarian programming relevant to the work of Innocenti and of UNICEF. It should lead us to question and challenge our own perspectives and practices as we seek to develop interventions and approaches in the best interests of the child – today and into the future.

UNICEF Office of Research-Innocenti
Florence, Italy
Sarah Cook

[2] Further information can be found at https://www.unicef-irc.org/.

Acknowledgements

This book comes together as a result of the contribution from over a hundred authors, reviewers, advisers and editors over a period of 2 years. Its roots stem from the 15th International Symposium on the Contributions of Psychology to Peace, which was co-hosted in May 2016 by the UNICEF Office of Research-Innocenti in Florence and Sapienza University of Rome, in Rome, Italy. We wish to thank our collaborators from Sapienza for believing in the necessity to discuss and study issues surrounding children and peace and strengthening the contributions made by peace psychology and other peace-oriented disciplines to this important theme. Special thanks are due to Mauro Sarrica, Giovanna Leone and Bruno Mazzara for enabling the Symposium to take place and laying the foundations for this book.

The UNICEF Office of Research-Innocenti in Florence, Italy, not only co-hosted the Symposium but also provided the motivation and financial support to publish this volume under an open access license. We thank Kerry Albright, Chief of Research Facilitation and Knowledge Management at the Office of Research-Innocenti, for her vision and strong commitment to making evidence on children publicly accessible and for being a pioneer of effectively using evidence to improve the lives of children. Her dedication to this endeavour inspired the subtitle of this volume, *From Research to Action*. We also wish to thank the former Director of the Office of Research-Innocenti, Sarah Cook, for encouraging the important dialogue between researchers and practitioner around children, conflict and violence with her support of the Symposium and this volume. Her eloquent foreword not only outlines the importance of this collaboration but also encourages the many contributors to this book to continue to address the well-being of children through their research and engagement with key stakeholders.

The chapters in this book underwent a double-blind peer review by both academics and practitioners. We sincerely thank all the reviewers – listed at the end of this section – for shaping the content of this book and making it accessible to a wider audience.

We wish to thank all the authors of book chapters who patiently wrote and revised several drafts of their manuscript, responding to our feedback with an open mind and working hard to align their work with the objectives of this volume.

Finally, we thank the team at Springer Nature for giving us the opportunity to enrich the Peace Psychology Book Series with a volume focusing on children in extremely vulnerable conditions and promoting the knowledge shared by the contributors via their vast communication networks. We especially thank Morgan Ryan for her hard work, support and perseverance to publish this body of work.

Nikola Balvin and Daniel Christie, Editors

We are grateful to the reviewers listed below in alphabetical order for helping to shape the chapters in this book under double-blind conditions:

Craig Anderson, Luca Andrighetto, Boyka Bratanova, Diane Bretherton, Christia Brown, Andy Dawes, Jo de Rivera, Michelle Godwin, Nicolas Haslam, Christine Hansvick, Ilse Hakvoort, Linda Heath, Joanna Huxster, Daniel Kardelfelt-Winter, Kathleen Kostelny, Sandy Lazarus, Joseph Lo Bianco, Cecilia Martinez-Torteya, Ersilia Menesini, Laura Miller Graff, Sarah Meyer, Cristina Montiel, Linden Nelson, Anne Pedersen, Alina Potts, Fatima Sajjad, Ann Sanson, Mauro Sarrica, John McConnell, Romana Morda, Adrian Stanciu, Shahnaaz Suffla, Luanne Swart, Laura Taylor, Barbara Tint, Angela Veale, Gabriel Velez, Loris Verzali, Mike Wessells and Ibrahim Yakubu.

Introduction

As this book goes to press, child rights activists around the world prepare to celebrate the 30th anniversary of the 1989 Convention of the Rights of the Child (CRC). Ratified by 196 State Parties, the CRC is the most endorsed convention of the United Nations (UN), holding its signatories accountable to protect and care for children affected by armed conflict and to the maximum extent possible ensure their survival and development. Yet, warring parties continue to commit grave violations against children, including using them as human shields, killing or maiming them or recruiting them to fight. In some settings, such as Syria, Yemen, the Democratic Republic of the Congo (DRC), Nigeria and Myanmar, rape, forced marriage and abduction of children are frequent conflict tactics (UNICEF, 2018a). The civil war in Syria is raging for the eighth consecutive year, continuing immense suffering to children and their families. A 2018 overview by OCHA reported 5.6 million children in need, 2.6 million displaced and 1.2 million in hard-to-reach areas (cited in UNICEF, 2018b). In 2017, the war killed 910 children inside of Syria, and instead of alleviating suffering and bringing hope, the situation deteriorated further in 2018, with 870 children killed in the first 9 months – the highest number since the war began in 2011 (UNICEF, 2018a). While well-known due to frequent reports in the international media, the conflict in Syria is by no means the only one, and as this book was written, many protracted conflicts continued and new ones emerged. In Afghanistan, violence against children occurs daily, with around 5,000 killed or maimed in 2017 and the first 9 months of 2018. In the Central African Republic, two out of three children are in need of humanitarian assistance, while in the DRC, an Ebola outbreak is further compounded by ongoing violence, preventing the necessary response and putting an estimated 4.2 million children at risk of severe acute malnutrition. The conflict in eastern Ukraine continues to have a devastating effect on children's education, while in Somalia children are abducted and recruited into armed forces. The more recent conflict in northern Rakhine State of Myanmar is responsible for violations of the rights of Rohingya children with thousands seeking refuge in Bangladesh (UNICEF, 2018a).

This brief summary of ongoing armed conflicts is by no means exhaustive – there are other countries where children suffer and where their rights to survival, protection, recovery and development are not upheld. Yet, even in countries without armed conflict, children experience violence, abuse, exploitation, discrimination and other grave violations of their rights. The Violence Against Children Survey (VACS) reports that over half of all children aged 2–17 years experience violence each year (Hillis, Mercy, Amobi, & Jress, 2016). In numbers, this accounts for around one billion children worldwide. A 2017 report published by UNICEF, using the most recent available data sources from different countries, corroborates the severity and extent of violence against children, stating that violence affects children in different settings during all stages of childhood and adolescence and is often inflicted by trusted individuals, including parents, caregivers and peers (UNICEF, 2017). Violence against children also needs to be viewed through a gender lens, with the type of violence inflicted, and its effects, often different for boys and girls. For example, girls experience higher rates of sexual violence, their first sexual intercourse often forced or coerced, leading to outcomes such as unwanted pregnancy. Boys experience lower rates of sexual violence than girls but with equally detrimental consequences including mental health issues and becoming the perpetrators of violence against their partner later in life (Together for Girls, no date). External factors, such as conflict settings, poverty and migration – an experience to which much of this book is dedicated – increase children's vulnerability to violence (Maternowska, Potts, & Fry, 2017). The consequences of violence are incredibly harmful, not just to individual children but to the communities and societies in which they live. They reflect a failure of adults to protect children.

Arguably the most influential report on violence against children in conflict settings is *The Impact of Armed Conflict on Children* (United Nations, 1996), authored by Mozambican educator and child rights activist Graça Machel. In her personal note introducing the report, she wrote: "I come from a culture where traditionally, children are seen as both our present and our future, so I have always believed it is our responsibility as adults to give children futures worth having" (UNICEF, no date). This groundbreaking report which unveiled the atrocities children in armed conflict suffer was published in 1996, but many of the violations it reported continue to destroy childhoods today.

The responsibility that adults have to protect children and give them worthwhile futures that Machel talks about is the foundational motivation behind this volume: a small contribution from peace psychologists and educators, both from academic and practitioner backgrounds, to not only document the evidence of how different forms of conflict and violence affect children in diverse settings but to provide practical suggestions and showcase successful examples of programmes and interventions for preventing, reducing and reversing the impact of direct and structural violence on children.

The Partnerships Behind This Book

Published as a volume in the Peace Psychology Book Series, this book is a contribution to and from the subfield of Peace Psychology in an effort to create a more peaceful world. This particular volume stems from one of the Symposia on the Contributions of Psychology to Peace, organized biennially by the Committee for the Psychological Study of Peace (CPSP).[1] CPSP is an international network of psychologists researching and practising peace and conflict resolution using a bottom-up approach which "respects different cultures and learns from local peoples" in order to mitigate and prevent destructive conflict (Wessells, 1999). The network's symposia enable scholars to present their current scholarship in Peace Psychology. Additionally, symposia provide a platform for the mutual exchange of ideas and experiences across cultures. Participants engage in intensive intercultural dialogue aimed at reducing cultural bias and ethnocentrism in Peace Psychology research and practice. The symposia typically examine a mix of topics traditionally studied in Peace Psychology such as nonviolence, conflict management, peace education, social justice movements, post-war reconstruction and sustainable development. Symposia sites are carefully selected to allow the study of local issues of peace and conflict and learn from the local context.

The 15th International Symposium on the Contributions of Psychology to Peace was co-hosted in May 2016 by the UNICEF Office of Research-Innocenti and Sapienza University of Rome, in Florence and Rome, Italy. Titled "Bridging Across Generations: Turning Research into Action for Children and Families", it captured research topics and priorities not only of Peace Psychology but also of the host country, Italy, and its convening partner, the United Nations Children's Fund (UNICEF), the world's largest child rights organization. Having UNICEF as one of the hosts and taking place in Italy, a country that has pioneered many of the ideas in the Convention on the Rights of the Child, the focus on children and youth emerged naturally. The program examined pressing issues for children and families, especially those manifesting strongly in Italy and its neighbours, including the European "refugee crisis", changing intergenerational relationships, emerging citizenship and the cultural narratives that emerge in the face of a growing multicultural society. In addition to having a focus on children and families, the symposium programme was unique in its focus on examining how to leverage findings to make the most of them in programming, policy and advocacy – as suggested by its subtitle. The aim was to go beyond exchanging interesting findings to turning research into outputs and actions that have the potential to positively impact the lives of children, their families, communities and societies.

It is from this symposium that the current volume stems, maintaining the focus on children and keeping the "research to action" orientation to provide practical,

[1] Committee for the Psychological Study of Peace (CPSP) recently changed its name to International Network for Peace Psychology. However, the old name is maintained in this introduction as the new one was not yet launched when the book manuscript was prepared.

solutions-focused conclusions from the presented studies. The book's contributors include researchers and practitioners who were urged to write for one another and make their chapters useful as a reference guide for those who wish to design programmes or develop policies that impact on the well-being of children and youth. They were also asked to situate their research in a wider body of evidence and, rather than focus on single studies, to broaden their chapters into review articles, contextualizing the findings in time and place and critically examining their applicability to practice. The aim to make this book available to a wide audience is further underscored by publishing it as the first open-access volume in the Peace Psychology Book Series, which was made possible by the generous sponsorship of UNICEF.

A Brief Overview of the Content

To examine contemporary issues of children, conflict and peace, this book is broken down into four parts: (I) addressing the well-being of refugee and migrant children, (II) children growing up in violent geopolitical contexts, (III) promoting peace and well-being of children and (IV) children and the survival of the species. Reflecting present-day challenges of the symposium's host country, Italy, and its neighbours, Part I examines the experiences of migrant children from diverse angles. Many of the Italian authors contributing to this part of the book explore factors related to the changing nature and identity of their country as a result of a steadily increasing migrant population. They present research on promoting tolerance among non-migrant children towards migrants (Mazzoni et al., Chap. 6), as well as examining possible ways for more positive integration experiences of migrant youth into Italian culture (Marzana et al., Chap. 7). Other chapters investigate migration status as a risk factor for children becoming victims of violence (Milani et al., Chap. 1) or being in conflict with the law (Meringolo & Guidi, Chap. 3). Grounded in social identity theory, the chapters by Haji and Noguchi (Chap. 4), Glen et al. (Chap. 5) and Bigazzi et al. (Chap. 8) discuss interventions to promote harmonious relations between children and youth from different cultural backgrounds, while Veale et al. look at the importance of the role of fathers in building the resilience of Syrian refugee children in Lebanon.

Part II of the book examines the effects of violence and armed conflict on children growing up in a range of sociopolitical contexts, including Colombia (Lopez et al., Chap. 13), Northern Ireland (McKeown et al., Chap. 12), Peru, Vietnam, Zimbabwe and Italy (Maternowska et al., Chap. 9) and the mafia stronghold of Naples in Italy (Bacchini & Esposito, Chap. 10). The chapters complement one another well, with the opening chapter examining the drivers of physical, sexual and emotional violence against children (Maternowska et al., Chap. 9), while the second chapter focuses on the detrimental effects of early exposure to community, family and school violence on a wide range of developmental outcomes (Bacchini & Esposito, Chap. 10). They reveal that although there are factors which make children more vulnerable to violence, it is a violation that affects children in all countries, across all socio-economic groups. McKeown and colleagues (Chap. 11) return to social identity theory to examine how the expression of social identities can be both a source of conflict and peace among youth in Northern Ireland and among ethnic minority youth in England. Their theoretical work is complemented by the two remaining chapters in Part II, one which discusses the reproduction of conflict narratives from one generation to another in Italy and the feelings new generations are confronted with when they learn that the narratives they had inherited are factually incorrect (Leone & Sarrica, Chap. 11). Another chapter focuses on children's conceptualizations of forgiveness, reconciliations and peacebuilding in relation to the internal armed conflict that plagued Colombia for more than 60 years (Lopez et al., Chap. 13). Together the chapters in this part of the book outline not only the immediate consequences of violence against children but the psychological effects that linger for generations to come. They offer practical suggestions on how to prevent violence in the first place, build more peaceful identities in conflict and apply a range of interventions to facilitate peaceful coexistence between children from different conflict backgrounds.

After exploring the vulnerabilities that conflict and violence expose children to, Part III of the book is more solutions-focused, presenting examples of peacebuilding programmes and long-term effects of civic engagement and more directly examining the subtitle of the book *From Research to Action*. Affolter and Azaryeva Valente share examples from "Learning for Peace" – one of the largest peacebuilding initiatives for children globally, in which education and other social services were used as a platform for leveraging social cohesion (Chap. 14). Guetta's chapter builds on this comprehensive overview to zoom in on a peace education programme delivered as part of a high school curriculum to young people in Italy (Chap. 16), while Pagani presents a body of research examining children's attitudes towards migrants to argue that complexity, diversity, education and conceptualization of peace are intimately linked (Chap. 16). The innovative research by Shani and colleagues (Chap. 17) combines Developmental and Peace Psychology to explore pathways to political orientations and activism from adolescence to adulthood using a longitudinal survey. They conclude that opportunities for constructive youth activism are likely to contribute to community empowerment and sustainability in the long term. Although presenting research from different countries, the last three chapters in Part III (Kostelny, Chap. 18; Balvin & Miletic, Chap. 19; and Wessells, Chap. 20) provide evidence for the importance of community-led, cooperative approaches to programming and research, including the use of research findings to influence policy and practice.

Finally, Part IV contains a forward-looking chapter (Sanson & Burke, Chap. 21) on children and climate change, a topic which despite its urgency is rarely covered in Peace Psychology. The authors argue that climate change is an issue of structural violence, disproportionately affecting people living in low- and middle-income countries. Climate change is also a matter of intergenerational justice because future generations are likely to be harmed by climate change more than the present generation. However, rather than getting lost in the bleakness of the situation and its outlook, the authors offer hope by providing suggestions for parents, schools, policymakers and other duty-bearers to help children develop coping strategies to adapt to life impacted by climate change and view the problem of climate change as an opportunity for promoting peace and equity in human relations.

Conclusion

The brief summary of the book's content clearly underscores the horrendous violations of children's rights, that it covers and the reader may wonder why the title is "Children and Peace" and not "Children and War". The underlying philosophy for the chapter on climate change (Sanson & Burke, Chap. 21) described above – to remain hopeful in the face of adversity and seek ways of turning a conflict situation into an opportunity to promote peace and equity – also underpins this book. As this book was written, too many children around the world suffered from direct and structural violence, but there were also those who benefitted from research-informed prevention and response interventions. While tracking the impact of Peace Psychology studies on the lives of children is rare (see Chaps. 19 and 20 for a discussion), by pushing contributors to reflect on the applicability of their work and make practical recommendations for practitioners and policymakers, the editors hoped to encourage stronger collaborations between researchers and research stakeholders, as well as the use of participatory approaches for engaging children and youth.

Despite the extreme suffering inflicted on children that her book unveiled, Graça Machel concluded her personal note with a hopeful and determined call to action, stating that "We must do anything and everything to protect children, to give them priority and a better future". No matter how large or how small, this is the responsibility of everyone (UNICEF, no date). The present book is a contribution to this mandate and reiterates the imperative that adults must do more to protect children and uphold the rights granted to them under the Convention of the Rights of the Child, 30 years ago.

Florence, Italy — Nikola Balvin
Delaware, OH, USA — Daniel J. Christie

References

Convention on the Rights of the Child [CRC]. (1989). Available online at: https://www.ohchr.org/Documents/ProfessionalInterest/crc.pdf

Hillis, S., Mercy, J., Amobi, A., & Kress, H. (2016). Global prevalence of past-year violence against children: A systematic review and minimum estimates. *Pediatrics, 137*(3), 1–13.

Maternowska, M. C., Potts, A., & Fry, D. (2017). *The multi-country study on the drivers of violence affecting children. A cross-country snapshot of findings*. UNICEF Office of Research –

Innocenti. https://www.unicef-irc.org/e-book/THE-MULTI-COUNTRY-STUDY-PAGER/HTML/files/assets/basic-html/page-4.html#

Together for Girls. (no date). *The Issue – data from Violence Against Children Surveys*. Available online at: https://www.togetherforgirls.org/the-issue/

UNICEF. (no date). *Impact of armed conflict of children: A personal note from Graca Machel*. Available online at: https://www.unicef.org/graca/graca.htm

UNICEF. (2009). *Machel study 10-year strategic review: Children and conflict in a changing world*. New York, NY: UNICEF. Available online at: https://childrenandarmedconflict.un.org/publications/MachelStudy-10YearStrategicReview_en.pdf

UNICEF. (2017). *A familiar face: Violence in the lives of children and adolescents*. New York, NY. Available online: https://www.unicef.org/publications/files/Violence_in_the_lives_of_children_and_adolescents.pdf

UNICEF. (2018a). *World has failed to protect children in conflict in 2018: UNICEF*. A Press release. Available online at: https://www.unicef.org/press-releases/world-has-failed-protect-children-conflict-2018-unicef

UNICEF. (2018b). *Syria Crisis: October 2018 humanitarian results*. Available online at: https://www.unicef.org/appeals/files/UNICEF_Syria_Crisis_Humanitarian_Situation_Report_____October_2018.pdf

United Nations. (1996). *Impact of armed conflict on children: Report of the expert of the Secretary-General, Ms. Graça Machel, submitted pursuant to General Assembly Resolution 48/15'*, UN document A/51/306, New York, 26 August 1996.

Wessells, M. (1999). *Report of the IUPsyS Committee for the Psychological Study of Peace (CPSP)*. International Union of Psychological Science: Archives. Available online at: http://www.iupsys.net/about/archives-and-documents/report-of-the-iupsys-committee-for-the-psychological-study-of-peace-cpsp.html

Contents

Author Biographies

Friedrich W. Affolter EdD is an Education Expert for Risk-Informed Programming at UNICEF NY Programme Division. He also serves as Secretary of the Early Childhood Peace Consortium (ECPC). Until June 2016, Friedrich Affolter served as the Manager of UNICEF's Peacebuilding, Education and Advocacy Programme (PBEA), which designed education programmes that contribute to the mitigation of drivers of conflict in 14 fragile and post-conflict countries. Earlier UN assignments include Sudan, South Africa, Angola and Afghanistan.

Cinzia Albanesi is Associate Professor of Community Psychology at the University of Bologna. Her research interests concern participatory practices, including participatory action research, community health promotion, coalitions and university-community partnership. Her interest in Peace Psychology is connected with her interest in social justice and emancipatory approaches.

Sara Alfieri is a Psychologist and PhD in Psychology, currently a Research Fellow in the Sacred Heart Catholic University Faculty of Psychology. She is working in Social Psychology with particular interest in familial relationships in families with adolescents and young adults: transmission of attitudes, at-risk behaviour and social engagement and teaches "Interview and questionnaire methods and techniques" at the Sacred Heart Catholic University of Brescia. Member of the Family Studies and Research University Centre's Advisory Board, she collaborates with the Istituto Giuseppe Toniolo di Studi Superiori, contributing to "Youth relations", and with numerous Italian non-profit organizations. Among her publications are *La natura familiare del pregiudizio* (*The Familiar Nature of Prejudice*) (Vita e Pensiero, 2013); *Mi impegno in tutte le lingue del mondo. L'attivismo dei giovani immigrati come promotore di benessere e integrazione* (*I engage all the languages of the world. Activism of young immigrants as promoters of well-being and integration*) (Rubettino, 2015); and *Empatia e Altruismo* (*Empathy and Altruism*) in collaboration with Elena Marta (2017).

Anna Azaryeva Valente is a Programme Specialist at UNICEF Headquarters focusing on fragility and peacebuilding. She has over 14 years of experience with national and international organizations in youth participation, education in emergencies and peacebuilding, child protection and data and analytics. Between 2012 and 2016, Anna supported implementation of the UNICEF's Peacebuilding, Education and Advocacy Programme including design of country-level conflict analyses, programme design and evidence-building across the participating 14 countries, including Burundi, Chad and Liberia among others. Anna also supported development of global guidance and capacity building on conflict analysis and conflict-sensitive and peacebuilding programming. Anna holds a Master's degree in Political Economy of Violence and Conflict from the School of Oriental and African Studies in London and a BA in Economics and International Relations from Wellesley College in Massachusetts. She is currently pursuing a Doctorate at Columbia University Teachers College in International Comparative Education.

Dario Bacchini is Full Professor of Developmental Psychology at University of Naples "Federico II".

His scholarship focuses on the development of antisocial behaviour in youth, with an emphasis on how family, neighbourhood and peer contexts contribute to or protect against these outcomes. More specifically, he examines how the exposure to violent contexts (neighbourhoods, family, school, media) influences moral cognitions and aggressive behaviour. He coordinates programmes of research and intervention aimed to prevent and contrast bullying at schools. He is a Consultant Researcher in the cross-cultural research projects "Parent Behavior and Child Adjustment across Cultures" and "Decision Making in everyday life".

Nikola Balvin PsyD, is a Peace Psychologist who works in international development. She has held several research and evaluation roles with the United Nations Children's Fund (UNICEF) since 2010. Currently she is the Research and Evaluation Specialist at the UNICEF Country Office in India, where she manages a large portfolio of studies spanning a range of sectors/disciplines. Prior to joining the India office, she was the Knowledge Management Specialist at UNICEF Office of Research-Innocenti from 2013 to 2018, and prior to that, she worked as a Research Officer on UNICEF's flagship publication *The State of the World's Children* at the New York headquarters. Before joining UNICEF, Nikola held a number of research positions in peace and conflict centres in Australia, including the Australian Centre for Peace and Conflict Studies (ACPACS) at the University of Queensland and the International Conflict Resolution Centre at the University of Melbourne. In 2011, she edited – with Di Bretherton – her first volume in the Peace Psychology series titled *Peace Psychology in Australia*.

Sara Bigazzi is a Social Psychologist and a Lecturer at the University of Pécs in Hungary. Her research interests focus on intergroup relation with focus on minority-majority issues, potential conflicts, their resolution, values and collective actions. She obtained her Doctoral Degree tutored by Serge Moscovici from the European

PhD on Social Representations and Communication. Currently, she has a research scholarship in the Hungarian Academy of Science and leads a granted research project on "The influence of social identity on intergroup prejudice and collective action". For the last two decades, she is involved in field interventions and community development, in which she translates theoretical reflections and research results in practical resolutions. She considers the holding role of communities, dialogue, the necessity to negotiate aims and values and believing that diversity, its acceptance and valorization are a basic need for any kind of human development.

Klaus Boehnke is Professor of Social Science Methodology at Jacobs University Bremen. Since 2017, he also is Deputy Head of the International Scientific-Educational Laboratory for Sociocultural Research at the Higher School of Economics in Moscow. He received his PhD in Psychology from Berlin University of Technology in 1985 and held assistant and associate professorships at the Free University of Berlin. In 1993 he became Professor of Socialization Research at the Department of Sociology of Chemnitz University of Technology, from where he moved to Jacobs in 2002. He is President-Elect of the International Association for Cross-Cultural Psychology (IACCP) and was President of the Division of Political Psychology of the International Association of Applied Psychology (IAAP) from 2004 to 2010. He is affiliated to the Committee for the Psychological Study of Peace (CPSP) as member and Senior Advisor since its inauguration in 1988. His main research interest is in political socialization.

Ildikó Bokrétás is a Social Psychologist, practical expert. She works with Roma people and socio-economically disadvantaged persons (e.g. in integration projects in urban slums at Order of Malta Foundation, Hungary, and local community development projects at countryside of South Hungary), chronically ill children and youth (Camp of Courage Foundation). She also worked at UNICEF Hungary as a fundraiser. Currently she is a Research Assistant and writing her PhD thesis at the Social Psychological Doctoral School of the University of Pécs and conducting researches on intergroup relations, values and representations of the socio-economic order.

Susie E. L. Burke is a Psychologist looking at ways of using psychological knowledge to enhance community well-being. A key interest is how to promote the role that psychology plays in helping us understand the causes, impacts and solutions to climate change and other environmental threats, including natural disasters. She runs webinars and workshops and writes articles, tip sheets and other resources on these topics. Her present interests are on coping with climate change and raising children to thrive in a climate-altered world. She is a Fellow of the Australian Psychological Society, Chair of the Australian Psychological Society Climate Change Reference Group, an Al Gore-trained Climate Reality presenter and a past National Convenor of Psychologists for Peace. She regularly consults as a mediator and facilitator for groups. Susie lives in a low-energy house and is currently bringing up bike riders and fruit trees and trying to get her local council to declare a climate emergency.

Myriam Carmenza Sierra-Puentes has PhD in Gender Studies and is Master in Gender and Equality Policy from the Universitat de Valencia (Valencia, Spain) and Master in Social and Educational Development from the National Pedagogical University of Colombia and International Center for Education and Human Development (CINDE; Colombia). He has research experience in social issues at national and international levels and is dedicated to the study of issues in the framework of the armed conflict in Colombia, especially with displaced population, peace scenarios, networks that women build, gender violence, equality policies and discourse analysis. She is currently a Professor at the Fundación Universitaria Konrad Lorenz in Colombia and leads a line of research with displaced population in the context of the armed conflict.

Tabitha Casey is Project Manager for Preventing Violence in Childhood Research and the Safe Inclusive Schools Network at the University of Edinburgh. She has coordinated research projects on international child protection spanning across Latin America, Africa, Europe and Southeast Asia and has co-authored a number of peer-reviewed articles, reports and a book on child protection and disability. Tabitha also has experience working on disability rights in the United States and Ireland and on peace and security issues at an NGO to the United Nations (UN) in New York. She has an MPH from New York University and a Master's in Disability Studies from Trinity College Dublin.

Pablo Castro-Abril is a Colombian Psychologist from the Pontificia Universidad Javeriana. He works in peace and armed conflict, specifically the relation and importance of forgiveness and reconciliation in victims, victimizers and the general population for the construction of peace culture. His undergraduate thesis was published as "Implicit Attitudes of University Students in Regard to Forgiveness in the Colombian Armed Conflict". He is currently doing a research Master at the University of Basque Country and is part of the research group of social psychology in the same university. For the postgraduate degree, he is preparing an experimental research about attitude changes in the general population regarding emotion and transcendent emotions.

Duygu Cavdar is a PhD candidate in Education at the University of Bristol. She has a strong interest in the area of Developmental and Social Psychology, and her particular research interests are adolescence and identity formation, ethnic identity development, acculturation and ethnic discrimination, gender issues and LGBT+ minorities, psychological well-being and mental health. She has published several peer-reviewed articles on the moral development, developmental needs in boarding schools and gender issues and LGBT+ youth in Turkey. She is currently conducting her mixed-methods research (utilizing a self-report survey and semi-structured interviews) and looking at how young second-generation people of Turkish heritage develop their ethnic identity in the United Kingdom and how this aligns with different acculturation strategies, perceived discrimination and mental health outcomes.

Elvira Cicognani is Full Professor of Social and Community Psychology at the University of Bologna and Coordinator of the CATCH-EyoU project. Her research interests concern the psychosocial factors and processes influencing civic and political engagement and participation, particularly among youth, interventions aimed at enhancing youth engagement and active citizenship, psychosocial factors in health behaviours and community health promotion interventions.

Daniel J. Christie is Professor Emeritus of Psychology at Ohio State University. His scholarship and activism focus on peace psychology with emphasis on initiatives and social movements that create a more just and humane world. He is the Editor and founder of the Peace Psychology Book Series and Editor-in-Chief of *The Encyclopedia of Peace Psychology*.

Sarah Cook is the former Director of UNICEF's Office of Research-Innocenti Research Centre in Florence, Italy. She was the Director when the symposium on which this volume is based took place in Italy. She recently joined the University of New South Wales, in Sydney Australia, as inaugural Director of its Institute for Global Development. She has a decade of experience in research leadership roles within the United Nations, both in UNICEF and UNRISD. She was previously a Fellow, IDS, Sussex. Her research has covered areas of social and economic policy, gender and sustainable development, with a particular focus on China.

Andrea Correa-Chica is a Social Psychologist and Researcher who works on issues of peace construction, armed conflict and political behaviour. She is a Magister and Consumer Psychology Specialist at the Fundación Universitaria Konrad Lorenz (Colombia) with experience in university teaching, design and execution of research projects in political participation and scenarios of armed conflict with qualitative and quantitative methodologies. He is currently beginning his doctoral studies at the University of Santiago de Compostela in Spain in relation to populist movements and their behaviour through digital social networks.

Jocelyn B. Dautel is a Developmental Psychologist in the School of Psychology at Queen's University, Belfast. Her scholarship focuses on the development of social cognition, or in other words, how young children think about the world around them and navigate their social relationships. Her research uses experimental methods from cognitive and social development to understand the processes underlying children's thinking about social groups, with a particular emphasis on how intergroup conflict influences these processes. Her research on the nature of social categorization is critical to understanding and preventing prejudice and intergroup conflict.

Maria del Rosario Durán Jaramillo is a Psychologist from Pontificia Universidad Javeriana who works at the Commissariat for Family. She is currently doing a specialization in forensic and juridical psychology at Santo Tomas University. She also has knowledge in psychological measurement instruments due to her diplomat at Konrad Lorenz University.

Paola Di Blasio PhD, is a Full Professor in Developmental Psychology, Head of the Department of Psychology and Director of the Centre of Research in Developmental and Educative Dynamics (C.Ri.D.E.E.). She is Editor-in-Chief of the peer-reviewed journal *Maltrattamento e Abuso all'Infanzia*, Franco Angeli, MI, and founder in 1984 of the Child Abuse Centre of Milan (CBM). Her research interests include (a) psychological trauma and distress linked both to childbirth and perinatal mental health and early mother-child interactions; (b) interpersonal violence and its consequences in different aspects (peer violence and bullying, child abuse and neglect, family conflict, parenting stress, testimony by children who are victims of violence); and (c) the impact on cognitive, emotional and psychopathological interaction with new media technologies and communication. She has 155 publications.

Concetta Esposito is a PhD candidate in Developmental Psychology at the University of Naples "Federico II". Her doctoral dissertation investigates the psychological and behavioural correlates of exposure to community violence in adolescence, including an examination of the desensitization hypothesis as a mechanism linking violence exposure and aggressive behaviour. Prior to beginning her doctoral studies, she earned an advanced Master's degree on the evaluation and management of child abuse and neglect at the University of Modena and Reggio Emilia, completing her internship at SOS Il Telefono Azzurro, an Italian non-profit organization working to promote the rights of children and teenagers in compliance with the principles enshrined in the 1989 UN Convention.

Gabriela Fernández Miranda is a Psychologist from the Pontificia Universidad Javeriana. She has interests in the study of psychological trauma in victims of the armed conflict in Colombia. At this moment, she is about to start her Master's in Investigation in Psychology at the Andes University.

Deborah Fry (Senior Lecturer in Child Protection) leads the Preventing Violence in Childhood Research work at Moray House School of Education, University of Edinburgh. Deborah undertakes primary research in three main areas: (1) to understand and unpack the drivers of violence against children, (2) to measure and develop regional and global estimates on the burden of VAC and case for investment in prevention and (3) to develop, test and evaluate interventions to prevent VAC. To date, she has collaborated with partners in 28 countries, and the research has had wide impact at national levels, including changes to national legislation and improvements to child protection systems in six countries. She has comprehensive experience in researching issues of violence within school settings and co-leads the Safe Inclusive

Schools Network, which is part of the UNESCO Platform for the Monitoring of School Violence and Bullying, to better understand the links between violence in childhood, teacher practices and learning outcomes for children. Deborah has a PhD by Research Publications from the University of Edinburgh, an MA from Syracuse University and an MPH from Columbia University. Deborah was also a Fulbright Research Scholar from 2001 to 2002 and a Marie Curie Fellow from 2012 to 2015.

Juan Gabriel Castañeda Polanco is a Psychologist and leader of the research group "Conocimiento en Contexto – CONENCON – Corporación Universitaria Minuto de Dios". He is a Specialist and Magister in Clinical Psychology at the Universidad Católica de Colombia, with professional experience as Research Director, Coordinator of a Psychology program and Professor. He is currently studying a PhD program, in which his research field is about complexity of the rural territory after the Colombian internal armed conflict.

Catherine Glen is a Visiting Research Associate in the Centre for Evidence and Social Innovation at Queen's University, Belfast, and a Rotary Scholar in the area of Peace and Conflict Prevention. Her scholarship focuses on the promotion of positive outcomes for young people impacted by developmental trauma with a specific emphasis on the incorporation of trauma-informed practices, children's rights-based approaches and the empowerment of young people as social actors. Catherine's research is shaped by her fieldwork with young people in the United States, Japan and Kenya and, most recently, with newcomer children in Northern Ireland. Through her research, fieldwork and activism, she aims to improve the lives of young people in challenging circumstances and facilitate the move towards more peaceful and fair societies.

Serena Grumi MSc, is a PhD Student in Psychology, Collaborator at C.Ri.D.E.E. (Centre of Research in Developmental and Educational Dynamics), Department of Psychology, Catholic University of the Sacred Heart. Grumi is a Psychologist and Anti-violence Worker at Casa delle Donne CaD-Brescia. Her research interests include intimate partner violence, parenting skills and mother-child relationship, professionals' decision-making about out-of-home placement in cases of child maltreatment, problematic Internet use/Internet gaming addiction and maladaptive developmental trajectories in childhood and adolescence.

Antonella Guarino is currently a PhD candidate at the University of Bologna and is a member of the Italian research team of CATCH-EyoU project. Her PhD dissertation in Social and Community Psychology focuses on the topic of youth active citizenship and its promoting factors, processes and practices. Her research interests also include the promotion of empowering processes in youth contexts and in mental health services. Her interest in Peace Psychology is concerned with the promotion of peaceful contexts through qualitative and creative methodologies.

Silvia Guetta PhD, is Associate Professor in the Department of Science of Education and Psychology at the University of Florence, Italy. She teaches Peace Education as well as Intercultural Education. Her fields of research focus on the history of Jewish education in Italy and Holocaust education. She is member of the Transdisciplinary UNESCO Chair "Human Development and Culture of Peace", of INEE (International Network Education Emergencies) and IHRA (International Holocaust Remembrance Alliance). She was a Fellow at the International Institute for Holocaust Research at Yad Vashem in Jerusalem.

Elisa Guidi Psychologist and PhD, she is currently the Vice President of the spin-off LabCom and a Lecturer in the School of Psychology of the University of Florence. She was a Research Fellow in PROVA Project (University of Florence) and winner of the 2017 Doctoral Thesis Award on the themes of the Istanbul Convention, promoted by the Italian Delegation at the Parliamentary Assembly of the Council of Europe. She carried out – by virtue of this award – an internship at the Violence against Women Division (GREVIO – Council of Europe). She worked at the Council of Europe with the Education Department – Education Policy. Her recent research interests are gender-based violence, violent radicalization, resilience and impact evaluation with a community psychology approach.

Reeshma Haji is Associate Professor of Psychology at Laurentian University in Sudbury, Canada. She is a Social Psychologist whose research focuses on intergroup attitudes in multicultural societies, with a particular interest in interreligious attitudes. Her research has been published in various peer-reviewed journals and book chapters. She created the course on the psychology of intergroup relations at Laurentian and has supervised numerous undergraduate and graduate thesis projects in this area. Dr. Haji is co-Editor of *Understanding Peace and Conflict through Social Identity Theory*, a volume from the Peace Psychology Book Series. She received a Social Sciences and Humanities Research Council of Canada (SSHRC) grant for her postdoctoral fellowship at University of Kent in Canterbury, UK. She was also awarded SSHRC funding for her doctoral studies in Social and Personality Psychology at York University in Toronto, where she also completed her Master of Arts.

Alaa Hijazi holds a PhD in Clinical Psychology from Wayne State University in Michigan, USA. She is currently a licensed Psychologist in independent practice. She previously served as an Assistant Professor in the Department of Psychology at the American University of Beirut. She also served as the mental health technical Advisor for Medecins Du Monde, Lebanon, a French NGO serving Syrian refugees. Her clinical and scholarly interests include issues related to trauma, gender, sexuality and social justice.

Daniel Horn is a Social Policy Specialist in the field of democratic participation, social protection and its financing. He received his PhD in Political Science from the Bremen International School of Social Sciences (BIGSSS) in 2015 and has an

MSc in Public Policy from the United Nations University Graduate School of Governance. He has extensive experience in the design, administration, analysis and diagnostics of qualitative and quantitative research, particularly in developing countries. He focusses on contributory and non-contributory income security policies, economic multiplier effects of cash transfers for development and taxation policies for social protection. Being an Advisor to the Global Coalition for Social Protection Floors, he has been involved in the Social Protection Inter-Agency Cooperation Board (SPIAC-B), African Union Special Technical Committee (STC) Meeting, EU Social Protection Systems Programme. Daniel Horn has worked with government agencies and international development organizations across low- and middle-income countries.

Kathleen Kostelny is a Senior Researcher at the Columbia Group for Children in Adversity, where her research is focused on child protection and children's psychosocial well-being in armed conflicts and disasters. Her research includes an ethnographic study of child protection harms and protective factors in Somalia, the effectiveness of child-centred spaces on young children's well-being in internally displaced person camps in northern Uganda following armed conflict and the impact of the Israeli military attacks and blockade on the education system in Gaza. She is currently Lead Researcher for a multistage action research programme in Kenya, involving national and international humanitarian organizations and the Kenyan government on strengthening community-based child protection mechanisms.

Giovanna Leone is Associate Professor of Social Psychology at Sapienza Università di Roma, Italy, where she teaches Social Psychology and Communication, Political Psychology and Community Psychology. She previously acted (1980–1994) as a Psychologist and a Psychotherapist at the S. Spirito Hospital in Rome. Subsequently (1994–2005) she was a Researcher and then an Associate Professor of Social Psychology at the University of Bari, Italy. She is a reviewer and Editor of international journals and MC member of Italy in the COST European action IS1205 "Social psychological dynamics of historical representations in the enlarged European Union". Her main research interests include social and collective aspects of autobiographical memory; ambivalent effects of over-helping, as observed in multicultural classrooms; relationships between intergenerational historical narratives on past intergroup violence and reconciliation; and emotional and cognitive effects of truth-telling. She has more than 120 publications.

Wilson López López is Professor in Universidad Javeriana. He earned his PhD (thesis Summa Cum Laude and extraordinary award) in Basic and Social Psychology from the University of Santiago de Compostela, with a distinguished thesis entitled "Mass Media, Conflict and Peace: Psychosocial Framing of Conflict and Peace in Colombia". He is also Associate Professor of Javeriana University, Editor of Universitas Psychologica, leader of the "Social Links and Peace Cultures" Research Group and member of the "Learning and Information Society" Research Group at the same University. He is Winner of the 2017 Interamerican Psychology Award and Winner of the Javeriano prize of investigation to the best work in the 2015 and 2017 editions and of the National Prize of Psychology in 2017; has two lines of research and publication, on the one hand social psychology (social conflicts and peace) and on the other hand scientific communication; and has published more than 100 articles in journals included in the Web of Science – SCOPUS. In addition to chapters in books and books, he has been an opinion columnist in mass media of his country as the week magazine and the newspaper the viewer. He is Board of Advisors member of the Reconciliation Barometer of the Alliance for Reconciliation Program. As a researcher, he has carried out various studies on mass media and conflict and associated topics such as forgiveness, legal issues and even drugs. He also has a line of research in Science Communication and Scientometrics. He also serves as an Advisor on International Relations and Publications for the Colombian College of Psychologists (Colpsic). He founded and is the Permanent Secretary for Latin America of the Iberoamerican Federation of Psychology Associations (FIAP) and he is President of ABA Colombia and ABAI full member; President- Elect of the Political Psychology Division International Association of Applied Psychology; member of the International Advisory Committee of the Journal Network of Spain, Latin America and Portugal (Redalyc); Codirector of the International Scientific Psychology Network; and invited Professor in several universities in Ibero-America.

Shelbi Macken is a Psychology Researcher and graduated from University College Cork with a Master's in Applied Psychology. With a focus on creative methods and participatory action research, her research interests are in understanding developmental transitions and identity shifts as a result of transnational migration.

Elena Marta is Full Professor of Social Psychology at the Catholic University of Milan. She is President of the Italian Society of Community Psychology (SIPCO) and was one of the founders of the European Association of Community Psychology (ECPA). Her current memberships include Scientific Committee of the "Osservatorio per il territorio" (Observatory for the Territory) (2017–2020) Università Cattolica, Brescia, in collaboration with CSV-Brescia; Scientific Committee of Rapporto Giovani, Istituto Toniolo-Università Cattolica Milano; and Scientific Board of Athenaeum Centre for Family Studies and Research. She was the Scientific Supervisor of the research project "Lifestyle in mobility" – granted by Erab, in collaboration with the University of Cardiff and AEGEE (2015–2017) – and has coordinated diverse national studies (promoted by the Università Cattolica del Sacro Cuore) on the topic of volunteerism and prosocial behaviour.

M. Catherine Maternowska is the data, evidence and solutions Lead within the Global Partnership to End Violence Against Children. She has extensive field experience in socio-medical research, evaluation and programming. Trained in economics, public health and medical anthropology, she has published extensively including a book on population and poverty in Haiti. She has also published in the popular press on public health and children's issues. Her experience managing donor-financed national, regional and global health programmes has focused on child protection and sexual and reproductive health with expertise in building violence policy, prevention, care and treatment. She held a faculty position at the University of California, San Francisco, for 10 years until 2010. From 2012 to 2017, she led a multi-country study on the drivers of violence affecting children at UNICEF Office of Research-Innocenti. In the Partnership she works on building political will, accelerating action and equipping practitioners to use data and generate evidence for the field of violence prevention globally. She has a PhD from Columbia University and a MPH from the University of Michigan.

Daniela Marzana is a Psychologist, as well as individual and group Psychotherapist, has a PhD in Psychology and is a researcher in the Catholic University of Milan Faculty of Psychology. She is working on Social and Community Psychology with particular interest in action research, community development and youth social involvement topics, from active citizenship to political and volunteer engagement. She teaches "Institutional Analysis" and "Psychology of Community" at the Catholic University of Milan and Brescia. Among her publications are "Social action in young adults: Voluntary and political engagement" (*Journal of Adolescence*, 2012); "Young Adults and Civic Behavior: The Psychosocial Variables Determining It" (*Journal of Prevention & Intervention in the Community*, 2012); "Volontari si diventa" (Becoming a Volunteer) (Vita e Pensiero, 2011); and "Mi impegno in tutte le lingue del mondo. L'attivismo dei giovani immigrati come promotore di benessere e integrazione" (I engage all the languages of the world. Activism of young immigrants as promoters of well-being and integration) (Rubettino, 2015).

Davide Mazzoni is Research Fellow at the University of Milano-Bicocca and was part of the Italian team of the project CATCH-EyoU. His primary scholarly interest concerns the processes of people's empowerment and its possible outcomes at individual and collective level. In particular, he is interested in examining why disadvantaged people decide to join together with the aim of producing a social change. He is strongly interested in methodological issues related to the adoption of qualitative and quantitative approaches, online and offline, in social research. In 2012 he received his PhD in Social Psychology with a dissertation focusing on collective action processes in defence of the "right to water". His main interest for Peace Psychology is through the lenses of Social Community Psychology.

Patrizia Meringolo Psychologist, is Professor in Community Empowerment and Qualitative methods of research in the School of Psychology of the University of Florence. She was in charge for International agreements with Faculties of Psychology of Belarusian State Pedagogical University, Minsk (Belarus); University

Alexandru Ioan Cuza, Iasi (Romania); Universidad de la Frontera, Temuco (Chile); and University of Lima (Peru).

She has carried out studies and action research, asked by local authorities, the European Union, Health Public Services and NGO. Her recent interests concern the quality of life in local communities, health promotion, gender differences and gender violence, juvenile justice, psychosocial problems in migrations and intergroup conflicts, young people's risky behaviours and substances use. She was Coordinator of PROVA Project.

Shelley McKeown Jones (PhD) is a Senior Lecturer in Social Psychology in the School of Education at the University of Bristol. Her research focuses on how social psychological theories, such as intergroup contact theory and social identity theory, can be applied to understand and improve intergroup relations among youth in diverse and conflict settings. Shelley's research has implications for youth social outcomes as well as policy and practice. She works with stakeholders, including teachers, to design and implement research-informed interventions, drawing on small- and large-scale quantitative research projects. Shelley has published a number of journal articles on the nature of contact in everyday spaces and the effects of contact experiences and conflict exposure on youth prosocial and antisocial attitudes and behaviours. She has also published a book on identity, segregation and peacebuilding in Northern Ireland and a coedited volume on social identity peace and conflict with Reeshma Haji and Neil Ferguson.

Luca Milani PhD, is Associate Professor in Developmental Psychology, member of the Centre of Research in Developmental and Educative Dynamics (C.Ri.D.E.E.), member of the Editorial Board of peer-reviewed journal *Maltrattamento e Abuso all'Infanzia*, Franco Angeli, MI. He serves in the Executive Board of the Italian Association of Psychology (AIP) – Section of Developmental and Educational Psychology – and in the Executive Board of Italian Association of Traumatic Stress Studies (SISST). His research interests include prevalence of PTSD in high-risk samples, child protection services and procedures, violent videogame use and maladaptive developmental trajectories in childhood and adolescence, problematic Internet use/Internet gaming addiction, identity formation in adolescence and new technologies and new technologies, flow and creativity. Milani has authored more than 50 peer-reviewed papers, books and book chapters.

Tania Miletic is a Peace and Conflict Studies Academic and Practitioner from Melbourne, with extensive research, programme and teaching experience on peacebuilding in the Asia Pacific region. Tania is currently with the Melbourne School of Government at the University of Melbourne where she engages in policy research on conflict prevention and peacebuilding in Australian foreign policy. Tania has taught related postgraduate courses in Australia, Cambodia and China. She previously worked with the Alliance for Conflict Transformation and then the Centre for Peace and Conflict Studies in Cambodia and is a visiting Researcher on a conflict resolution programme in Mainland China. Tania has consulted for a range of international organizations focused on peacebuilding and is locally engaged with community-led initiatives. She has an interdisciplinary background holding a Postgraduate Diploma in Psychology, Master's in Public Administration and a PhD in Political Science, specializing in peace and conflict.

Sarah Miragoli , PhD, is Assistant Professor of Developmental and Educational Psychology and has a PhD in Psychology of Communication and Language Processes. She is Researcher at C.Ri.D.E.E. (Centre of Research in Developmental and Educational Dynamics), Department of Psychology, Catholic University of Milan (Italy). Her fields of research include child abuse, traumatic narratives, child testimony, legal involvement of children as victims in court proceeding, processes of resilience (individual and familial factors) and sexualized behaviours. Her research projects include fragmentation in traumatic narratives of children sexually abused, marital conflict and co-parenting, PTSD cognitions in children and fears in children.

Hiromi Noguchi is a Japanese Writer and Translator. Her publication includes *TORJA Japanese Magazine* (Toronto) and *Montréal Bulletin* (Montréal). She studied and gained research experience under Dr. Reeshma Haji at Laurentian University. She also obtained her Master of Arts in Communications at York University, where she conducted in-depth interviews and captured the long-silenced voices of immigrant women in order to reveal the impact of immigration and transnational divorce on their social locations. This study was awarded many prestigious awards including Joseph-Armand Bombardier Canada Graduate Scholarship (SSHRC) and Michael Smith Foreign Study Supplements. In 2014, she founded the not-for-profit organization, Association of Post-divorce Japanese Women (APJW), a peer-support organization for separated and divorced immigrant Japanese women. APJW provides monthly workshop and court support to its members. She is currently a Licensed Paralegal of the Law Society of Upper Canada (Ontario), assisting immigrant Japanese women with their family law matters.

Ken Ondoro has been the national team leader for the interagency action research on strengthening community-based child protection research in Kenya. His prior work has included research in Puntland on community-based child protection and in Kenya with different international and national organizations, including work on Youth Environmental Learning and Agency in Conflict Management and the Health Education Research Project in Teacher Training and research on Behaviour Change Communication on HIV/AIDS. He received his MA in Sociology from the University of Nairobi.

Zenia Osman is a Social Researcher specializing in Social and Economic Development. She holds an MPhil in Social Anthropology from the University of Cambridge. She is currently an Anthropology Instructor at the American University of Beirut and the Director of Social Research at Q Perspective, Lebanon, a consultancy firm based in Beirut. Her work and research interests include anthropological approaches to childhood and adolescence, evaluation and social impact analysis of humanitarian response and development interventions and social protection policies for rural populations.

Camilla Pagani is an Associate Researcher at the Institute of Cognitive Sciences and Technologies (ISTC) of the Italian National Research Council. As Head of the Project "The sense of diversity and its psychological implications", she was mostly involved in the following research areas: youth's attitudes towards multiculturalism; the perception of threat in cross-cultural relations; the role of knowledge, fear, hate, anger, resentment and envy in youths' racist attitudes; empathy in cross-cultural relations; empathy and complex thinking; child-animal relationships with special reference to empathy and violence; and the relation between animal abuse and interhuman violence. Within her project "Diversity and Complexity", she is presently addressing the study of humans' relationship with diversity within a theoretical framework where principles from Socio-cognitive Psychology and complexity theory are especially considered. She is the Italian representative of CICA (International Colloquia on the Brain and Aggression) International Foundation and Head of its Scientific Committee.

Alina Potts is a Research Scientist with a focus on gender, violence and humanitarian assistance at The Global Women's Institute, George Washington University, where she leads participatory action research in Lebanon, Uganda and Bangladesh to mitigate the risk of sexual exploitation and abuse in the way humanitarian aid is distributed. Prior to that, she coordinated the Multi-Country Study on the Drivers of Violence Affecting Children at UNICEF Office of Research-Innocenti and provided technical advice on applied research examining the intersection between intimate partner violence and violence affecting children in emergencies, led by UNICEF and the CPC Learning Network. Alina has also led gender-based violence programming for the International Rescue Committee in a number of humanitarian responses over the last decade, conducted field research on grave violations against children in conflict and worked with refugees and asylum seekers in the United States, the United Kingdom and Ireland. She holds an MPH from Columbia University in Forced Migration and Health and BA in Anthropology and International Development from Boston University.

Ann V. Sanson is an Honorary Professorial Fellow at the University of Melbourne, Australia. Her research has principally focused on understanding the role of child, family and community characteristics in the development and well-being of children, adolescents and young adults. She is a principal investigator on two major Australian longitudinal studies tracking cohorts from infancy to adulthood (https://www.melbournechildrens.com/atp/about/; http://www.growingupinaustralia.gov.au). Ann's ongoing engagement with the contributions of Psychology to social issues includes her role as the inaugural Director of Social Issues of the Australian Psychological Society (APS) and active membership of the APS's Psychology for Peace Interest Group since the 1980s. She is Co-Chair of the Committee for the Psychological Study of Peace. Her current focus is on psychological factors relevant to addressing the climate change crisis. She is a Fellow of the Australian Psychological Society and the International Society for the Study of Behavioural Development and has over 200 publications.

Mauro Sarrica PhD, is an Associate Professor of Social Psychology and of Peace Psychology at Sapienza University of Rome. His research interests include social construction of knowledge, energy transition and ICT4D and particularly how normative and technological shifts are intertwined with modifications in reified and consensual universes of knowledge. The studies he conducts in Peace Psychology investigate the social and cultural dimensions of pacifism and reconciliation processes. A first line of research investigated social representations of peace and war at the beginning of the 2000s and the role of peace activism and training with young people. Studies on reconciliation processes concern effects of different rhetoric strategies conveying evidence of war crimes committed by the in-group after a long lasting social denial.

Sára Serdült is a Social Psychologist currently teaching at the University of Pécs. Her fields of research are intergroup relations and identity processes. She is writing her PhD on prejudice focusing on the interrelations between the target and source of it. As she finds essential to integrate practice and theory besides her academic work, she is involved in applied projects like mentoring underprivileged first-generation intellectuals, keeping trainings on conflict resolution with diverse methods. She also participates in local community development initiatives with the aim to create more diverse, inclusive, sustainable and liveable spaces.

Maor Shani is a Social Psychologist and an Evaluator in the field of Informal Education. He received his PhD in Psychology from the Bremen International Graduate School of Social Sciences (BIGSSS) in 2015. BIGSSS is the collaborative school of Doctoral Education of the University of Bremen and Jacobs University Bremen, Germany. His dissertation examined the long-term psychological impact of encounters between Jewish and Palestinian youth. He previously earned an MA in Sociology and Comparative Politics from Jacobs University and a BA in Sociology from the Hebrew University of Jerusalem. His main research interests are in the field of Political and Peace Psychology and include peace education, intractable conflicts and contemporary antisemitism. He has presented his work at several CPSP Symposia.

Laura K. Taylor PhD, is a Lecturer (Assistant Professor) in the School of Psychology at Queen's University Belfast. Her research is framed by an intergroup developmental approach to study risk and resilience processes for youth in settings of protracted conflict. Her work has implications for youth outcomes, such as aggression, prosocial behaviours and social identity, as well as broader psychosocial processes, such as shared education and intergroup relations, which may fuel or constrain conflict. Towards this end, she studies how and why violence affects behaviours and attitudes related to conflict transformation, primarily during adolescence. Through teaching and mentoring, she engages undergraduate and graduate students in research that is sensitive to the psychological needs of individuals and communities, particularly in divided societies. Taylor has published over 36 peer-reviewed articles in journals such as *Child Development*, *Developmental Psychology*,

Development and Psychopathology, *Political Psychology* and *Social Development*, in addition to a co-authored book on youth and political violence.

Iana Tzankova is a Postdoctoral Fellow at the University of Bologna and is a member of the Italian team of the project CATCH-EyoU. Her PhD dissertation in Social Psychology focused on the topic of youth civic and political participation and its contextual influences in youngsters' lives. Her interest in Peace Psychology is concerned with the psychosocial conditions in sustaining a peaceful intercultural society.

Angela Veale PhD, MMedSc Psych, is a Lecturer in Applied Psychology at the University College Cork and a child and adolescent Psychotherapist. Her research interests include post-conflict social reintegration of children and families; children, globalization and "new migrations" and psychosocial interventions. She was partner to the NORFACE-funded Transnational Child-Raising between Europe and Africa project and Co-director of the Provictimus/Oak Foundation-funded project on the social reintegration of young mothers formerly associated with armed groups in Sierra Leone, Liberia and Northern Uganda. She is a former Fulbright Scholar. She is currently working with the Health Services Executive in Ireland on the resettlement of Syrian refugees.

Michael Wessells PhD, is Professor at Columbia University in the Program on Forced Migration and Health. A long-time Psychosocial and Child Protection Practitioner, he is former Co-Chair of the IASC Task Force on Mental Health and Psychosocial Support in Emergency Settings. He has conducted extensive research on the holistic impacts of war and political violence on children, and he is author of *Child Soldiers: From Violence to Protection* (Harvard University Press, 2006). Currently, he is Lead Researcher on inter-agency, multi-country research on community-driven interventions for strengthening linkages of community-based child protection mechanisms with government-led aspects of national child protection systems. He regularly advises UN agencies, governments and donors on issues of child protection and psychosocial support, including in communities and schools. Throughout Africa and Asia, he helps to develop community-based, culturally grounded and resilience-oriented programmes that assist people affected by armed conflict and natural disasters.

Bruna Zani is Professor of Social and Community Psychology at the University of Bologna. She is member of the Italian team of the project Catch-EyoU and she was leader of the Italian team of the project PIDOP. Her main research interest are risk behaviours in adolescence, civic engagement and political participation in adolescents and young people, service-learning methodology in higher education, evaluation of community interventions on health promotion and representations of mental health. One current theme is the fight against any form of stigma and hate speech. Her recent book is *Political and Civic Engagement: Multidisciplinary Perspectives*, Routledge, London (Barrett M. & Zani B. (2015)).

Part I
Addressing the Well-Being of Refugee and Migrant Children

Chapter 1
A Multi-method Assessment of Risk and Protective Factors in Family Violence: Comparing Italian and Migrant Families

Luca Milani, Sarah Miragoli, Serena Grumi, and Paola Di Blasio

1.1 Introduction

Child abuse and maltreatment are serious developmental adversities in the short and long term for children and adolescents. International reviews highlight the enormous developmental, social, and economic costs of child abuse and maltreatment (Autorità Garante per l'Infanzia e l'Adolescenza, CISMAI, & Terre des Hommes, 2015; Bunting et al., 2018; CISMAI, Terres des Hommes, & Bocconi, 2014; Di Blasio, 2000, 2005; Di Blasio, Camisasca, & Procaccia, 2007; Fry et al., 2018; Gallo, Munhoz, de Mola, & Murray, 2018; Kimber, Adham, Gill, McTavish, & MacMillan, 2018). Research has led to improvements in knowledge about intervention strategies to buffer negative consequences of child maltreatment and abuse (cf. Masten, 2001; Masten, Cutuli, Herbers, & Reed, 2009; Ozer, Best, Lipsey, & Weiss, 2003). In this light, the concept of resilience has proved to be very useful to describe those developmental trajectories that lead to positive adaptation notwithstanding serious adverse conditions (Masten et al., 2009). Resilience is a key construct for scholars and professionals in the field of Child Protection Services (CPS), as it is the very foundation of the possibility of changing maladaptive developmental trajectories into more positive ones. Thus, professionals and practitioners in CPS are often required to make decisions about the best intervention to protect minors at risk, often with limited time and resources to collect the information needed for such a resolution.

Moreover, CPS professionals often deal with referred families that fall into "gray areas" of family functioning: they appear to be not completely dysfunctional – nor are they completely functional – but are characterized by (acute and/or chronic) difficulties and adversities that impact day-by-day functioning and parenting. In these instances, it is very important to assess the risk of harm/maltreatment in a

L. Milani (✉) · S. Miragoli · S. Grumi · P. Di Blasio
Catholic University of the Sacred Heart, Milan, Italy
e-mail: luca.milani@unicatt.it

N. Balvin, D. J. Christie (eds.), *Children and Peace*, Peace Psychology Book Series, https://doi.org/10.1007/978-3-030-22176-8_1

timely manner, in order to implement effective protective measures and to avoid recidivisms. A key element in the decision-making process is for CPS to be able to rapidly discriminate situations that need a more decisive plan of intervention (e.g., removing the child from the family) from those that require a more cautious approach. However, Italian professionals cannot rely on national documents and manuals on assessment and decision-making process when dealing with at-risk families but only on local guidelines and on their professionalism and training. As a result, in many instances, decisions are made through intuition and not informed by evidentiary information.

Migrant families are often a challenge to CPS personnel because of the difficulty in gathering relevant information, assessing the residual capital in family resources (both from a material and social point of view) and gauging the potential for repairing/enhancing family functioning (cf. Milani, Grumi, Gagliardi, & Di Blasio, 2016). Moreover, some studies have highlighted that migrant families have both a higher risk of referral to CPS and risk of maltreatment (cf. Alink, Euser, van Ijzendoorn, & Bakermans-Kranenburg, 2013).

Our Research Centre is trying to provide an assessment protocol and other useful tools to assist professionals and operators in CPS and in the judicial system in the complex decisions they face when working with at-risk families. To our knowledge, this is the first attempt at proposing a specific assessment system for this purpose in Italy, given the fact that – among the limitations previously cited – the Italian CPS system is still lacking a unified registry about allegations and management of child maltreatment. The lack of uniformity in assessment protocols hinders the possibility of comparison between methods of assessment and case management across different locals.

As concerns the international literature, research on decision-making systems in CPS is steadily shifting toward the aim of helping professionals and operators rely less on intuition and more on objective indicators when planning interventions (cf. Bartelink, van Yperen, & ten Berge, 2015, for a review). However, there is a paucity of objective indicators with the exception of the "California Family Risk Assessment": an instrument designed to help practitioners in the decision-making about at-risk children and families, focusing on the strengths and needs of caregivers, children, and family resources, via different checklists and guidelines[1] (Barlow, Fisher, & Jones, 2012).

Our assessment system is conceptually similar – albeit less detailed – than the British Framework for the Assessment of Children in Need and their Families (FACNF), a set of guidelines and indications aimed at helping CPS professionals to assess complex situations of children and families (cf. Léveillé & Chamberland, 2010). To assist professionals in this task, our framework contains some standardized checklists focusing not only on risk assessment but also on strengths and resources. We believe our assessment protocol meets operators' and professionals' requirements in terms of comprehensiveness, modularity (e.g., selecting single or multiple modules to focus on specific areas of assessment), and scientific validity.

[1] Cf. https://www.nccdglobal.org/assessment/structured-decision-making-sdm-model

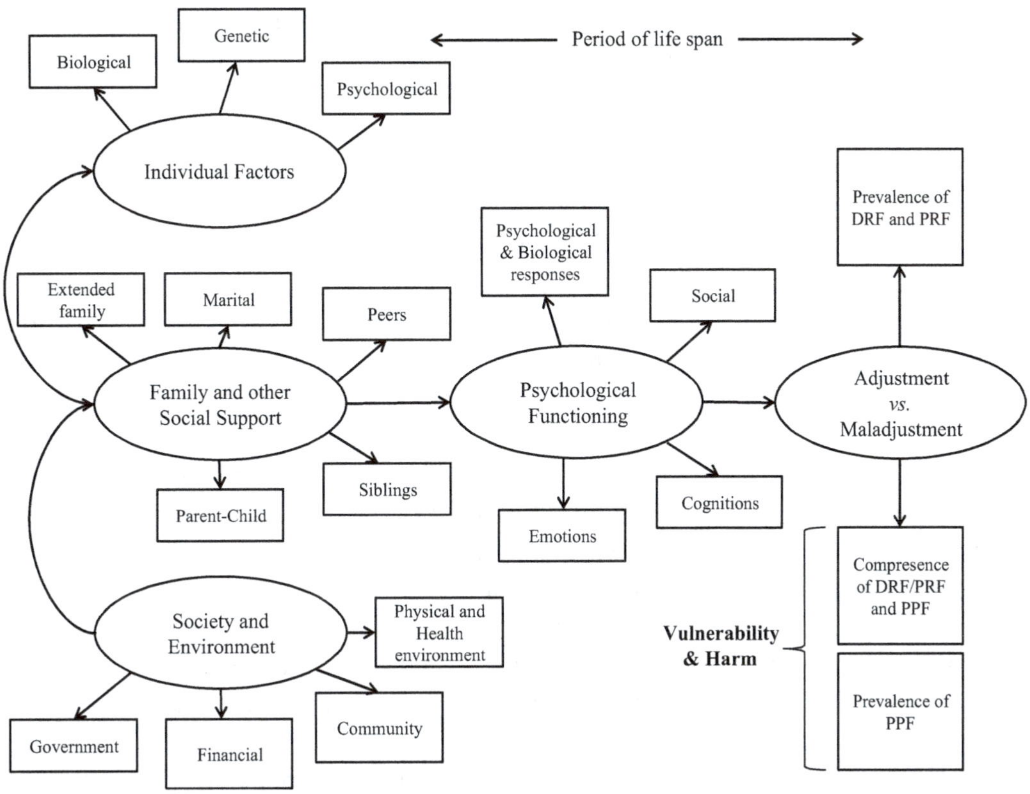

Fig. 1.1 Process-Oriented Model (Di Blasio, 2005; modified from Cummings, Davies, & Campbell, 2000)

In particular, the system presented herein can be defined as a risk assessment tool (cf. Bartelink et al., 2015) based on an array of psychological instruments and measures that can be used to offer an accurate assessment of at-risk families. It is grounded in four pillars: (a) a process-oriented model; (b) clinical expertise of our Research Centre[2] in terms of child maltreatment and abuse; (c) extensive research efforts to validate and refine the assessment system; and (d) constant interaction with field knowledge (CPS professionals and Italian judicial system).

1.1.1 The Process-Oriented Model

Our assessment system is grounded in the "process-oriented model" of developmental trajectories and children adjustment (cf. Cummings, Davies, & Campbell, 2000), which posits that human development is characterized by mutual influences between different factors and environments, which lead to adaptive or potentially maladaptive patterns. This model has been modified and articulated to fit the clinical literature on risk assessment in CPS work (cf. Cirillo & Di Blasio, 1989; Di Blasio, 1997; 2000). The final model is presented in Fig. 1.1.

[2] Centre for Research in Developmental and Educational Dynamics (C.Ri.d.e.e.) – Department of Psychology, Catholic University of the Sacred Heart, Milan, Italy.

The left side of the model highlights the contribution of genetic, biological, and psychological factors of individuals, which interact with familial functioning and environmental affordances into determining parental attitudes toward offspring. The central part of the model focuses on the "here-and-now" psychological functioning that mediates between contextual factors and adaptive/maladaptive trajectories. The right side of the model presents the outcomes of this process: social competence on one side and maladjustment on the other. In our vision, social competence can be thought as a developmental outcome related to those families where there is a preponderance of proximal protective factors (PPF). In these instances, parents are able to express positive parenting and to buffer the impact of eventual negative events (e.g., loss of job, death of a relative) by tapping into personal and contextual resources.

On the other hand, maladaptive outcomes can be characterized by those instances when parents are not able to buffer the effects of negative events – or of personal difficulties and inabilities – and expose their children to situations of vulnerability or clear harm via a significant prevalence of distal and proximal risk factors (DRF/PRF). These can take the form of a sporadic, infrequent parental inadequacies that last for a limited period of time and can be addressed by "lower-impact" interventions, such as parental monitoring or training, or can take the form of a chronic impairment that poses a serious threat to children and that needs to be tackled with more impactful interventions such as limiting parental responsibility or removing the child from the family.

1.1.2 Distal and Proximal Factors

In our opinion, the most appropriate way to conceptualize and to address potentially maltreating parents and sub-par parenting skills is an examination of risk and protective factors (cf. Camisasca & Di Blasio, 2002; Di Blasio, 2000; Di Blasio, Camisasca, Procaccia, & Verrocchio, 2005). In this light, high-risk conditions are characterized by (chronic or acute) exposure to adversities that can slowly (or swiftly, in case of traumatic events) erode, consume, and ultimately deplete physical and psychological resources of individuals and families. However, high-risk conditions are *not necessarily equivalent* to maladaptive outcomes. In fact, it is often difficult to assign a "clear-cut" score of damaging potential to many life events, due to the complexity of the mutual interaction of the factors in play. Thus, to better discriminate those factors that exert a direct influence on developmental trajectories in at-risk families and those that are indirect, we refer to the distinction by Baldwin, Baldwin, & Cole (1990) between *distal* and *proximal* factors. The term "distal" is used because these factors are supposed to have an indirect effect on children and can be thought of as a *humus* on which more proximate events and factors build their influence. Proximal factors have a direct influence on family processes and can overturn frail points of balance, often exacerbating covert tensions and conflicts. Distal risk factors can lead a given family to a condition of vulnerability; however their mere presence does not equate to harm or damage to children. Nonetheless, when distal risk factors are intertwined with proximal risk factors, the situation is very likely to evolve into a clear harm for children. For example, literature shows that maternal lack of knowledge or interest relating to child development (distal risk factor) is associated with worse health outcomes in children due to difficulties in understanding medical prescriptions. However, a lack of knowledge or interest alone is seldom related to maltreatment; other proximal factors such as family conflict and difficult temperaments in children need to be present in order to generate harm. It should be noted that proximal factors include *both* risk and protective factors. Protective factors are those proximal instances and resources that have the power – if recognized and adequately taken into consideration when implementing an intervention – to reduce the negative impact of distal and proximal risk factors. When a protective factor comes into play, if services are able to turn it into a resilience process via work with the family, it is possible that a maladaptive trajectory's likely negative outcomes will be buffered and will not cause harm to the child.

1.2 C.Ri.d.e.e. Multi-method Assessment System

In our experience, in order to sustain and mobilize residual resources in families at risk, it is important to not only focus on risk factors but also on personal, familial, and social strengths. Our proposal of a multi-method assessment system is specifically tailored to help professionals of CPS and judicial systems to promote resilience processes by identifying areas of vulnerability and areas of strength in the families at risk. The general aim of our assessment system is to integrate the specific know-how and guidelines of social workers, psychologists, lawyers, and professionals involved in the decision-making process in order to protect children at risk of abuse/maltreatment/neglect due to parenting deficits in families referred to CPS/judicial system. Thus, the different modules of our assessment system focus mainly on parenting skills and the resources in the family/social environment.

The assessment system is comprised of six stand-alone modules: one in-depth protocol for identifying proximate and distal risk and protective factors of maltreatment and recidivism against children; one explorative tool for assessing the (residual) social capital in an at-risk family; and four screening surveys for assessing parenting stress, parental child abuse potential, parents' resilience, and traumatic symptoms (in children).

As regards the surveys, three have been validated by *C.Ri.d.e.e.* research team (PSI-SF, CAPI, and TSCC), and one is a well-known measure for resilience (RSA) that we recommend for its reliability and accuracy.[3] Each of the six modules can be

[3] Operators need to contact the original authors of the RSA (Oddgeir Friborg or Odin Hjemdal) requesting their permission to use the scale.

applied alone or in conjunction with the others, and each of them provides information about one key area of family functioning:

- The Risk and Protective Factors Protocol and Graph can assist in collecting information about several aspects of family functioning and can help operators focus on risk factors as well as potential resources of the family. The array of risk and protective factors can be arranged as a list or as a graph, and it can be used to assess a single parent or the whole family. In this case, our recommendation is to assign the presence of a given factor to the whole family even if it is reported only for one parent (e.g., parental psychopathology reported for the mother only but assigned to the whole family). The rationale is that the presence of a risk and/or protective factor influences not only a given parent but also the whole family.
- The Todd Map can assist in detecting social capital of a given individual/family and deepen the knowledge about relational bonds between individuals. As in the case of the Risk and Protective Factors Protocol and Graph, the Map can be used to assess an individual or a family.
- The four screening instruments can be used to obtain quantitative data about the level of stress related to the parenting role, the risk of maltreatment/abuse by a parent, resources that can lead to resilience in parents, and the eventual traumatic consequences on the child. The precise indications about how to use each instrument can be found in the validation papers.

In our proposal, professionals should aim to assess all of the above areas as a rule of thumb, as the array of information gathered could help in subsequent decision-making. However, the modularity of the system allows professionals to arrange and personalize the assessment in order to meet time constraints and priority. In this light, some indications may be helpful:

- The Risk and Protective Factors Protocol and Graph can be completed in different sessions and can be updated as the knowledge about the family increases. Indications are to use this module whenever possible, as it is also a useful tool to monitor progress.
- The Todd Map can be used as a "resource-oriented" tool to complete the representation about the social capital of the family. As such, it can be of invaluable help to gain a broader picture of the resources that can be engaged in a support system for the family. As for the Risk and Protective Factors Protocol, it can be completed in different sessions and can be used as a monitoring tool.
- We think of the four instruments as sort of practical "alarm tools" to be administered when the operator suspects the presence of:
  - Deep parental strain that may impact child-rearing or lead to increased risk of maltreatment (PSI + CAPI + RSA)
  - Risk of parental maltreatment (CAPI + TSCC to child)
  - Risk of psycho-traumatic damage to the child (TSCC to child)
  - Need for understanding resilience resources in parents (RSA)

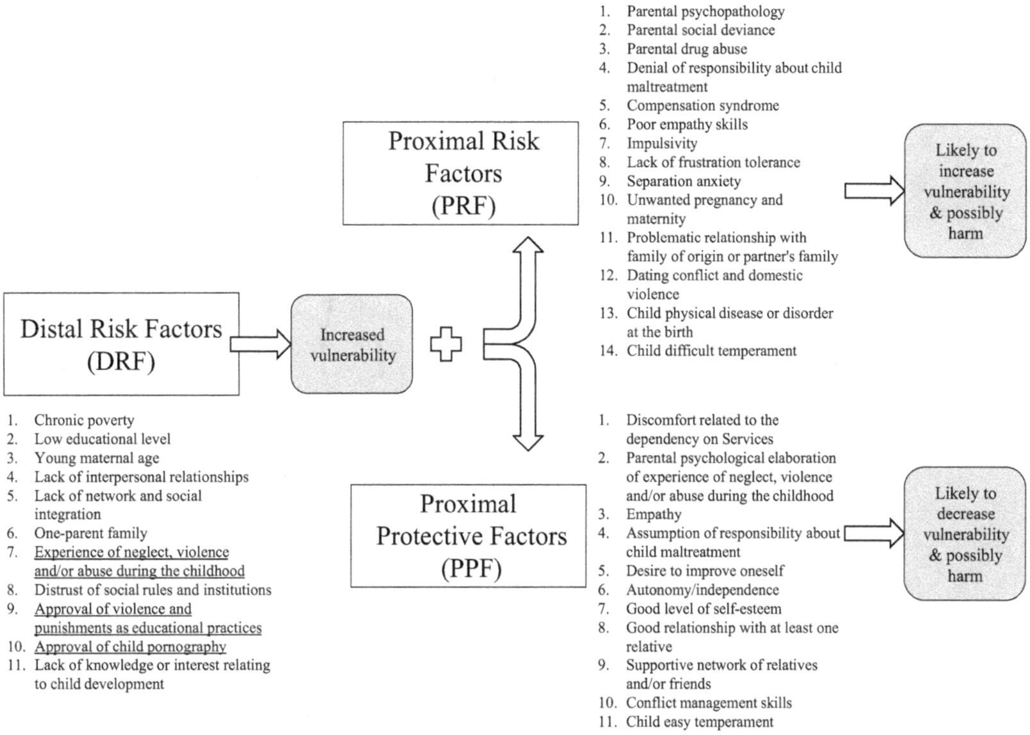

Fig. 1.2 Risk and protective factors Protocol

1.2.1 Risk and Protective Factors Protocol and Graph

The Risk and Protective Factors Protocol is a theoretically grounded instrument that consists of 36 factors. The aim of the Protocol is to help professionals evaluate individual, familial, and contextual factors that come into play when parents are at risk of not attending to their children needs or becoming maltreating/abusive.

As it is clear from Fig. 1.2, distal risk factors mostly concern context, values, and resources that exert an influence on parenting activities and raise the level of vulnerability of families. Some of them are non-specific in terms of child maltreatment and abuse (e.g., chronic poverty, young maternal age, etc.). Three are *very specific:* Experience of neglect, violence, and/or abuse during the childhood; Approval of violence and punishments as educational practices; and Approval of child pornography. These are underlined in Fig. 1.2.

Proximal factors have a direct influence on children and can overturn a frail relational balance in the family (risk factors) or ameliorate the situation by adding resources and buffering conflicts (protective factors). The 36 factors can be thought of as contributing to 4 areas of family functioning (refer to Figs. 1.2 and 1.3):

A. *Children*: Lack of knowledge or interest relating to child development, child physical disease or disorder at the birth, child difficult temperament, child easy temperament.

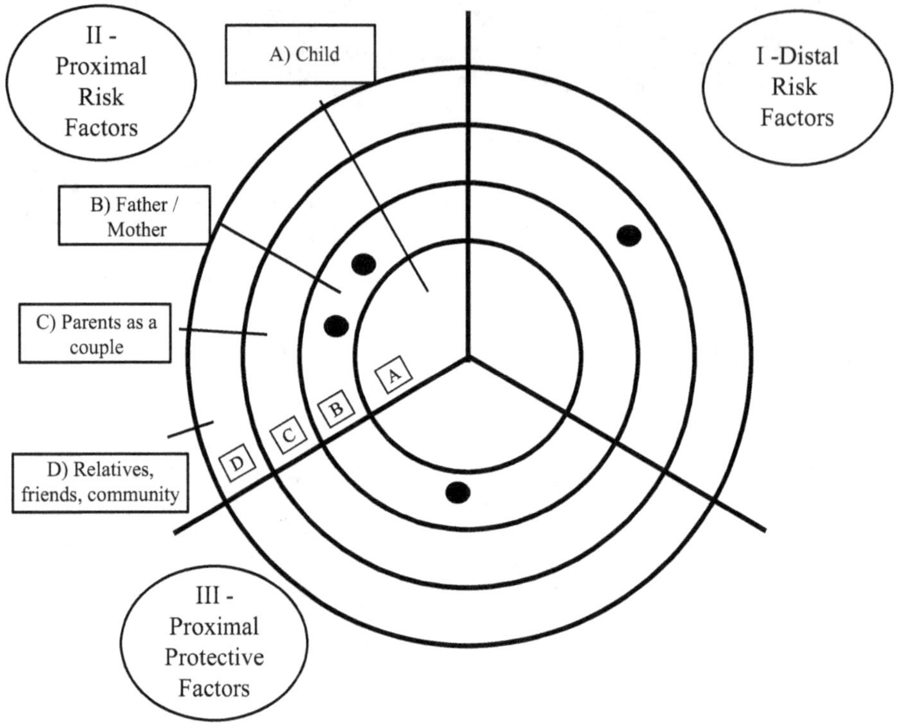

Fig. 1.3 Risk and protective factors Graph

B. *Mother/father*: Young maternal age, experience of neglect, violence and/or abuse during the childhood, parental psychopathology, parental social deviance, parental drug abuse, denial of responsibility about child maltreatment, compensation syndrome,[4] poor empathy skills, impulsivity, lack of frustration tolerance, separation anxiety, parental psychological elaboration of experience of neglect, violence and/or abuse during the childhood, empathy, assumption of responsibility about child maltreatment, desire to improve oneself, autonomy/independence, good level of self-esteem.
C. *Parents as a couple*: Chronic poverty, low educational level, one-parent family, approval of violence and punishments as educational practices, approval of child pornography, unwanted pregnancy and maternity, dating conflict and domestic violence, discomfort related to the dependency on services, conflict management skills.
D. *Relatives, friends, community*: Lack of interpersonal relationships, lack of network and social integration, distrust of social rules and institutions, problematic relationship with family of origin or partner's family, good relationship with at least one relative, supportive network of relatives and/or friends.

[4] "Compensation syndrome" can be defined as a parental attitude in which the parent expects some sort of psychological compensation for experiencing adverse growing conditions as a child, and this compensation is expected from a third person (usually his/her child) or an institution (e.g., CPS, judicial system, social welfare, etc.).

A useful complement is the risk and protective factors graph (see Fig. 1.3) that explodes the Protocol on a 2-dimensional space in order to help professionals quickly assess whose areas of family functioning are more worrying or needing attention. The operator may use it as a graphic representation of the array of risk and protective factors assessed in the family, by recording in the appropriate area the presence of a given factor. For example, a family characterized by Chronic poverty (DRF 1), Parental psychopathology (PRF 1), Separation anxiety (PRF 9), and Empathy (PPF 3) will have one note in the quadrant I-C, two in quadrant II-B, and one in quadrant III-B. This notation system allows the professional to quickly be aware of those areas that are more at-risk or more resourceful in a given family.

1.2.2 Todd Map

The Todd Map (1979) is a sociological instrument to assess relational capital in individuals. It allows the operator to measure with a graph the density and the rank of social capital of individuals, in different environments and contexts.

It can be represented as a series of concentric circles segmented in different sectors, while the parent under assessment is placed in the center of the graph. The operator should trace a dot for each person the parent is in relation with for the four relevant environments reported: family, friends, work, and public services. The distance from the center indicates how relationally close that person is to the parent: one is the most important (a close relative), while four is the least important (an acquaintance).

The Todd Map allows the operator to understand, with a quick glance, how dense the support system of a parent is in terms of proximity and distribution in the four environments. For example, a parent may have many contacts in the "work" subsystem but way less in the "friend" subsystem, signaling a potentially unbalanced distribution of social capital (as illustrated in Fig. 1.4).

The Todd Map allows also a "qualitative" assessment of the relations between the parent and his/her social capital. The operator may ask the parent to draw lines that connect the most relevant relations between him/her and the persons drawn on the map, or to differentiate the relations in terms of quality (e.g., positive relations -> solid lines; negative relations -> dotted lines, etc.). The social capital is considered a very important buffering factor in at-risk families, decreasing the likelihood of child maltreatment and abuse (cf. Fujiwara, Yamaoka, & Kawachi, 2016; Zolotor & Runyan, 2006). In this regard, we assess both a sense of community and cohesion in the neighborhood and the availability of friends, relatives, and close relationships in the family. The Todd Map can help assess how many resources the parent/family has and how close they are.

The following paragraphs will focus on four quantitative measures, aimed at providing professionals with some "alarm checks" about key areas of parenting that

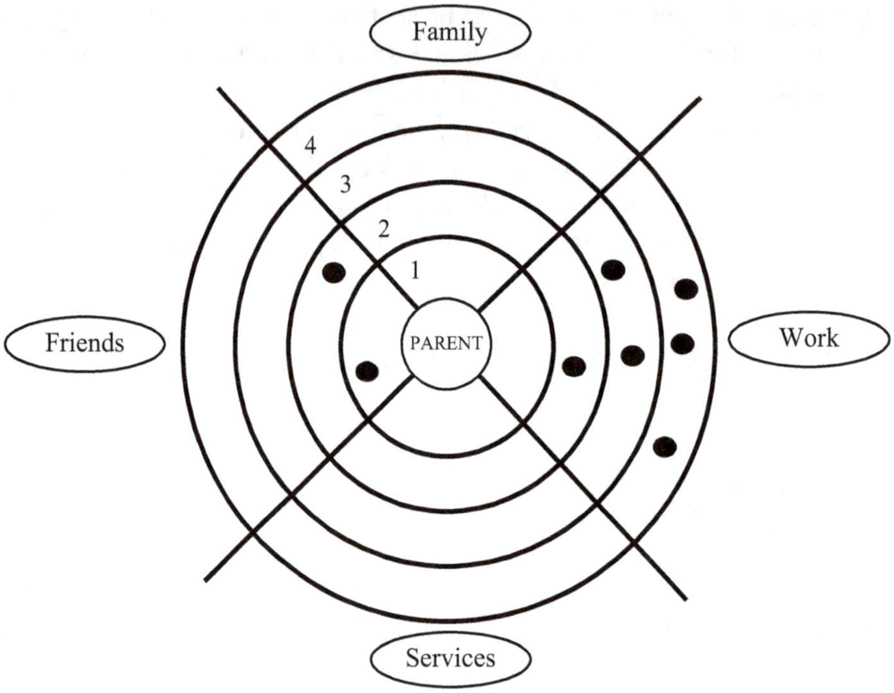

Fig. 1.4 Todd Map

need immediate attention. In particular, we assess both parenting issues and children outcomes via four measures: one about parental stress, one about parental disposition to become maltreating or abusive toward their children, one about resilience resources eventually present in parents, and finally one about eventual psychotraumatic damage to children. As previously stated, *C.Ri.d.e.e.* research team has extensively validated three of them (PSI-SF, CAPI and TSCC), while the other is a very well-known measure for resilience (RSA) that we recommend for its reliability and accuracy.

1.2.3 Parenting Stress Index Short Form (PSI-SF)

The Parenting Stress Index Short Form (PSI-SF; Abidin, 1995; Italian validation by Guarino, Di Blasio, D'Alessio, Camisasca, & Serantoni, 2008) is a self-report measure of 36 items with answers on a Likert 5-point scale (from 1 = strong disagreement to 5 = strong agreement) suitable for evaluating the stress level in the relationship between caregiver and child. The measure can be answered by each of the parents independently. The measure provides professionals with a score about a clinical level of parental stress and can be administered in about 10 minutes.

The Italian version of PSI-SF consists of three subscales such as Parental Distress (PD, 12 items; e.g., "Many things in my life disturb me"), Parent-Child Dysfunctional

Interaction (P-CDI, 12 items; e.g., "My child seldom does things that gratify me"), and Difficult Child (DC, 12 items; e.g., "My child does some things that annoy me a lot") as well as a defensive responding subscale that consists of 7 items drawn from the PD subscale. The defensive responding subscale evaluates parental bias in reporting by quantifying the desire of parents to present a favorable impression of themselves and minimize problems in the parent-child relationships. The PD subscale focuses on the sense of competence/incompetence in rearing the child, marital conflict, lack of social support, and stress associated with the restrictions deriving from the role of parent. The P-CDI subscale measures parents' perceptions of the emotional quality of their relationship with their children. Finally, the DC subscale focuses on the parent's perception of the child in terms of temperament, hostile, non-collaborative, and provoking behaviors. The sum of the scores of the three subscales (PD, P-CDI, and DC) leads to the Total Stress score, which gives an indication of the overall level of the parental role-specific stress, not deriving from other roles or other events. The 90th percentile of the total PSI-SF score represents a "clinically significant" level of parenting stress (Abidin, 1995) and can be used as an indicator that counseling or other supports are required. The values of internal consistency of the Italian validation of the PSI-SF (Guarino et al., 2008) correspond to a $\alpha = 0.91$ for the Total Stress scale, a $\alpha = 0.91$ for the PD subscale, a $\alpha = 0.95$ for the P-CDI subscale, and a $\alpha = 0.90$ for the DC subscale.

1.2.4 Child Abuse Potential Inventory (CAPI)

The Child Abuse Potential (CAP, Milner, 1986; Italian validation by Miragoli, Camisasca, & Di Blasio, 2015; Miragoli et al., 2016) is a self-report inventory of 160 items with a forced-choice format ("agree" vs. "disagree"), and it includes the Abuse scale (77 items) that is widely used as a child physical abuse screening tool. As regards the purpose of risk assessment about the physical potential abuse, only the Abuse scale (77 items) is habitually used (Milner, 1986). An even briefer version of the scale was developed for the Italian population (CAPI, 17 items; Miragoli, Traficante, Camisasca, & Di Blasio, 2017). Items were selected to maximize (a) discriminative function referred to the abuse condition; (b) predictivity of the Abuse scale on the total score; (c) factor stability; and (d) clinical validity of the selected items. A similar international brief version of the CAPI can be found in Ondersma, Chaffin, Mullins, and LeBreton (2005). The CAPI in full form can be administered in 15 minutes. The original CAP Inventory (Milner, 1986) contains a total of ten scales. The primary clinical scale is the 77-item physical child abuse scale. This Abuse scale can be divided into six factor scales: Distress (e.g., "I often feel very frustrated"), Rigidity (e.g., "Children should always be neat"), Unhappiness (e.g., "I am an happy person"), Problems With Child and Self (e.g., "I have a child who is slow"), Problems With Family (e.g., "My family fights a lot"), and Problems From Others (e.g., "Other people have made my life hard"). In addition, the

CAP Inventory contains three validity scales: Lie Scale, Random Responses Scale, and Inconsistency scale.

The factorial structure of the Italian version of the CAP Inventory presents factors consistent with the original version (accounting for 31% of the variance): "Loneliness and Distress" (16 items; e.g., "I often feel alone"; "People do not understand me"); "Rigidity" (10 items; e.g., "Children should always be neat"); "Impulsiveness and Anxiety" (13 items; e.g., "I find it hard to relax"; "Sometimes I fear that I will lose control of myself"); "Unhappiness" (7 items; e.g., "I do not laugh very much"); "Problems with Self, Child, and Family" (10 items; e.g., "I have a child who is bad"); and "Interpersonal Difficulties" (6 items; e.g., "People expect too much from me").

The Abuse scale of the Italian version of CAP Inventory shows adequate internal consistency ($\alpha = 0.87$) and, with the cut-off of 166 as suggested in the original version of the CAP Inventory (Milner, 1986), when abusive and non-abusive groups are compared, it correctly classifies 70.3% of the abusive parents and 100% of the non-abusive parents. The cut-off of 166 derives from the scoring procedure of the CAP Inventory, which involves a series of weighted items ranging from 1 to 23 (cf. Milner, 1986).

1.2.5 Resilience Scale for Adults (RSA)

The Resilience Scale for Adults (RSA) is a self-report screening instrument used to determine the ability to overcome stress and hardships while maintaining positive psychological functioning. It is based on the work of Friborg, Barlaug, Martinussen, Rosenvinge, and Hjemdal (2005) and has been validated in Italian by Capanna, Stratta, Hjemdal, Collazzoni, and Rossi (2015). RSA is comprised of 33 items on a 7-point semantic differential scale that provides a measure on six resilience factors and a total score. The scale can be administered in about 15 minutes. The six factors identified by the authors are as follows: Perception of self (e.g., confidence in own abilities); Planned future (e.g., positive attitude toward future); Social competence (e.g., confidence in own abilities to create and maintain social bonds); Family cohesion (e.g., positive attitude toward own family shared values and support); Social resources (e.g., availability of positive social capital outside family); and Structured style (e.g., ability to self-direct and plan goal-oriented actions).

In the Italian validation of Capanna et al. (2015), the structure of the test proved to be good for five factors out of six while only adequate for the "Structured style" factor. Research papers indicate that a mean total score of the RSA higher than 6.0 can be thought as "high resilience" (cf. Friborg et al., 2006) and a score below 3.5 may be correlated with problems of adaptation like substance use disorder (cf. Bonfiglio, Renati, Hjemdal, & Friborg, 2016).

1.2.6 *Trauma Symptom Checklist for Children (TSCC)*

The Trauma Symptom Checklist for Children (TSCC; Briere, 1996; Italian validation by Di Blasio, Piccolo, & Traficante, 2011) is a self-report questionnaire designed to assess posttraumatic stress, dissociation, anxiety, anger, sexual concerns, and depression in children and adolescents (separately normed for boys and girls ages 8–12 and 13–16 years), who have been traumatized and/or abused. Children indicate on a 4-point scale (0 = never to 3 = almost all of the time) how often experiences such as "Feeling nervous or jumpy inside" happen to them.

The Italian version of TSCC is a self-report of 54-item questionnaire and consists of two validity scales, Underresponse (UND, 10 items) and Hyperresponse (HYP, 8 items), as well as six clinical scales: Anxiety (ANX, 9 items; e.g., "I feel scared"), Depression (DEP, 9 items; e.g., "I feel sad and unhappy"), Posttraumatic Stress (PTS, 10 items; e.g., "I can't stop thinking about something bad that happened to me"), Sexual Concerns (SC, 10 items; e.g., "I touch my private parts too much"), Dissociation (DIS, 10 items; e.g., "I feel I'm not in my body"), and Anger (ANG, 9 items; e.g., "I feel furious"). Each clinical scale yields subscale raw and T-scores, and higher scores designate a greater number of symptoms.[5] The clinical cut-off score is set at $T = 65$ for all subscales except sexual concerns where the clinical range is set at above $T = 70$. All components of the TSCC show good reliability and validity in the Italian population (ANX: $\alpha = 0.72$; DEP: $\alpha = 0.77$; PTS: $\alpha = 0.79$; SC: $\alpha = 0.80$; DIS: $\alpha = 0.71$; ANG: $\alpha = 0.81$). It can be administered in about 15/20 minutes.

1.3 Research Data on the C.Ri.d.e.e. Multi-method Assessment System

In order to improve the Protocol of risk and protective factors (Di Blasio, 2005) and to test its applicability, a series of empirical studies were conducted. Studies adopted the "judgment analysis" approach (Stewart, 1988) to investigate association between the Protocol's factors and the level of minors' safety. This methodology requires retrospectively analyzing information cues, content, and characteristics of referred case files and to test their correlation with CPS workers' assessment and intervention (Benbenishty & Chen, 2003). In the following paragraphs, we summarize research data about the Risk and Protective Factors Protocol.

[5] T-scores are a conversion of individual scores into a standard form (based on the reference values of the Italian population), shifted and scaled to have a mean of 50 and a standard deviation of 10.

1.3.1 Exemplary Data on Italian Sample

The first preliminary study performed by Miragoli and Verrocchio (2008) focused on the collection of data on an Italian sample to verify the applicability and the discriminative power of the Protocol's risk and protective factors. The evaluation of factors' presence or absence was performed through the retrospective analysis of 400 referred families' social records. The most frequent maltreatment was neglect (35.8%), followed by physical maltreatment (15.0%). The sample was split up on the basis of the CPS workers' intervention, operationalized as child out-of-home placement (*high risk*) or monitoring and parental abilities support (*low risk*). Results showed that several factors, in particular distal factors, emerged as good predictors of workers' assessment for both mothers and fathers. In particular, it emerged that all distal risk factors but "One-parent family" and "Low educational level" were significant predictors of a *high-risk* intervention by CPSs. The most relevant proximal risk factors in predicting *high-risk* intervention were "Parental social deviance," "Parental drug abuse," "Denial of responsibility about child maltreatment," "Poor empathy skills," and "Unwanted pregnancy and maternity." Some factors were found significant only for mothers ("Parental psychopathology" and "Problematic relationship with family of origin or partner's family") and some only for fathers ("Impulsivity" and "Lack of frustration tolerance"). Regarding the interplay between distal and proximal risk factors, it is possible that the former shows more discriminant power because they have more objective indicators (e.g., poverty can be gauged with monthly wage of parents) and are consequently easier to detect.

1.3.2 Research Data on Comparisons Between Italian and Migrant Families

The risk and safety assessment could be more complex for CPS workers who operate in a context characterized by high rates of migrant families, and who often show a higher level of vulnerability (Milani, 2013). In fact, literature confirmed that the multiple challenges faced by migrant parents may negatively affect their level of well-being and the quality of their family relationships (Valtolina, 2013; Yu & Singh, 2012). Moreover, several studies identified the overrepresentation of migrant children in the rates of the cases reported to CPSs (Alink et al., 2013; Autorità garante per l'infanzia e l'adolescenza, Terre des homes, & CISMAI, 2015). This overrepresentation seems to be partially explained by socioeconomic disadvantage; however, literature did not provide univocal results about which factors predict the workers' safety assessment (LeBrun et al., 2015).

Considering this gap in the literature, a series of studies about the Protocol's application was investigated with two questions (Grumi, Milani, & Di Blasio, 2017a; Milani et al., 2016; Milani & Gagliardi, 2013):

- What are the differences in the prevalence rates of distal and proximal risk and protective factors between Italian and Migrant families?

Table 1.1 Significant differences in the prevalence of risk and protective factors between Italian and migrant families

Factors	Migrant families	Italian families	χ^2	*p*
DRF Chronic poverty	67.2%	44.7%	16.73	<0.001
DRF Low educational level	70.3%	54.6%	7.3	<0.01
DRF Lack of network and social integration	65.5%	47.7%	10.39	<0.01
DRF Experience of neglect, violence, and/or abuse during the childhood	49.7%	61.9%	4.44	<0.05
DRF Approval of violence and punishments as educational practices	58.3%	39.9%	11.07	<0.01
PRF Parents' psychopathology	36%	57.5%	15.21	<0.001
PRF Compensation syndrome	28.2%	38.6%	3.98	<0.05
PRF Separation anxiety	22.0%	39.9%	12.31	<0.01
PRF Problematic relationship with family of origin or partner's family	55.6%	72.2%	9.33	<0.01
PRF Dating conflict and domestic violence	69%	80.9%	6.11	<0.05
PPF Discomfort related to the dependency on Services	35.8%	47.7%	4.66	<0.05
PPF Elaboration of experience of neglect, violence, and/or abuse during the childhood (parents)	7.5%	15.2%	4.27	<0.05
PPF Supportive network of relatives/friends	58.7%	78%	12.37	<0.001

- Which risk and protective factors significantly influence CPS workers' removal decision in case of Italian and migrant families?

About the first aim, results are consistent with previous studies and confirmed the vulnerability of migrant parents in many areas. Table 1.1 shows that migrant families are characterized by a higher prevalence of distal risk factors related to their socioeconomic status and by a lower prevalence of protective factors compared to Italian parents (Grumi et al., 2017a). Migrant families show lower prevalence than Italian families in many indicators: parental experiences of maltreatment, psychopathology, compensation syndrome, separation anxiety, problematic relations with family, and domestic violence. We attribute these counterintuitive results to two processes: (a) migrant families could be characterized by some resilience (they accept the risk of moving from their home country to gain better living conditions); and (b) migrant families could be more "under the spotlight" of social services due to their socioeconomic condition (as the higher prevalence of distal risk factors shows) and hence taken into care before proximal risk factors appear (or worsen).

About the second point, studies demonstrated that migrant and Italian families are characterized by two different patterns of factors (Tables 1.2 and 1.3),[6] with the exception of *lack of knowledge or interest relating to child development*, which con-

[6] Regressions were performed inserting as predictors those factors that were significant to a preliminary Chi square analysis, in order to reduce the number of factors in each model and avoid any collinearity.

Table 1.2 Predictive factors of CPS workers' removal decision relative to migrant families – logistic regression model

Predictors	B	*p*	OR (95%CI)
DRF Experience of neglect, violence, and/or abuse during the childhood	0.907	<0.05	2.47 [1.05–5.84]
DRF Lack of knowledge or interest relating to child development	1.115	<0.05	3.05 [1.18–7.85]
PPF Good level of self-esteem	−1.896	<0.001	0.15 [0.06–0.36]

$\chi^2 = 37.5$; $p < 0.001$; R^2 *Nagelkerke* = 0.34

Table 1.3 Predictive factors of CPS workers' removal decision relative to Italian families – logistic regression model

Predictors	B	*p*	OR (95%CI)
DRF Lack of knowledge or interest relating to child development	3.42	<0.001	30.31 [4.55–201.79]
PRF Parents' psychopathology	2.222	<0.01	11.08 [2.51–48.93]
PRF Parents' social deviance	1.18	<0.05	3.26 [1.02–10.44]
PFF Discomfort related to the dependency on Services	−3.083	<0.001	0.44 [0.01–0.19]
PPF Autonomy/independence	−1.783	<0.01	0.22 [0.06–0.70]

$\chi^2 = 88.91$; $p < 0.001$; R^2 *Nagelkerke* = 0.66

stitutes a significant predictor for both groups. In particular, for Italian families the lack of knowledge or interest related to child development enormously increases the risk of child removal, and even though it exerts an indirect impact, it is linked to critical variables like parental monitoring and unrealistic expectations (Milner & Chilamkurti, 1991). Migrant and Italian families are characterized by a clear difference between Odds Ratio regarding this factor: we argue it could be possibly due to a sort of differential perception of its relevance by CPS personnel. It is possible that CPS professionals tend to overreact when this factor is detected in Italian families due to cultural reasons (i.e., "Bad parenting") while attributing it to cultural reasons when found in migrant families (i.e., "Different parenting"). Other relevant factors for migrant parents were *past experience of neglect violence and/or abuse during the childhood* that may affect parental well-being and quality of parent-child relationship and attachment (Ionio & Mascheroni, 2014) and the *good level of self-esteem* that supports change and allows migrant parents to ask for help in case of need, without denying obstacles and limits (Milani & Gagliardi, 2013). For Italian families other significant predictors were the *parents' psychopathology* and the *social deviance*, while *discomfort related to the dependency on services* and a good level of *autonomy/independence* reduced the level of risk perceived by social workers.

1.3.3 Decision Trees

A second set of studies used a decision tree analysis (CHAID) in order to identify the most relevant factors for the assessment of migrant and Italian parents (Grumi, Milani, & Di Blasio, 2017b; Milani, Di Blasio, & Grumi, 2017). The CHAID algorithm (Chi-squared Automatic Interaction Detector, Kass, 1980) is a form of recursive partitioning that begins with the "parent node" which is subsequently split into subgroups, "child nodes," by a predictor variable. The predictor variable at each stage was selected on the basis of *Chi-square tests*, and splitting continued until predetermined stopping criteria were met. The final nodes identify subgroups defined by different sets of independent variables.

This data analysis approach addresses issues related to the high number of risk and protective factors included in the assessment and the small sample size of our study. Moreover, it allows us to identify multiple profiles of high and low risk that are associated with a specific outcome (child-out-of-home placement decision vs. monitoring and support). We maintain that this methodology and the results it has provided could be of use to professionals in order to have some landmarks to prioritize some factors over others when acquiring information on the case they handle.

In particular, two decision trees were performed separately for migrant (n = 177) and Italian (n = 163) families. As shown in Fig. 1.5, the decision tree for migrants was estimated to correctly classify 77.4% of the cases and identified 2 high-risk parental profiles (see nodes 3 and 12) and 2 low-risk parental profiles (see nodes 6 and 7), while one node is not sufficiently discriminative at this level of split. In particular, the *good level of self-esteem* acts as a protective factor reducing the risk of child removal, but it is not sufficient when risk factors, *impulsivity* and *young maternal age,* are present.

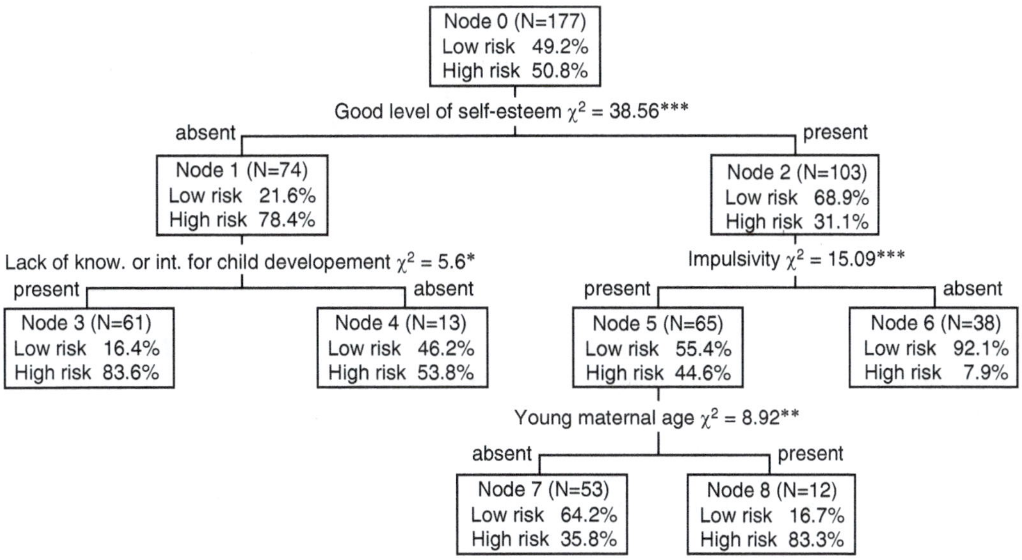

Fig. 1.5 Decision tree about migrant families' high- and low-risk profiles

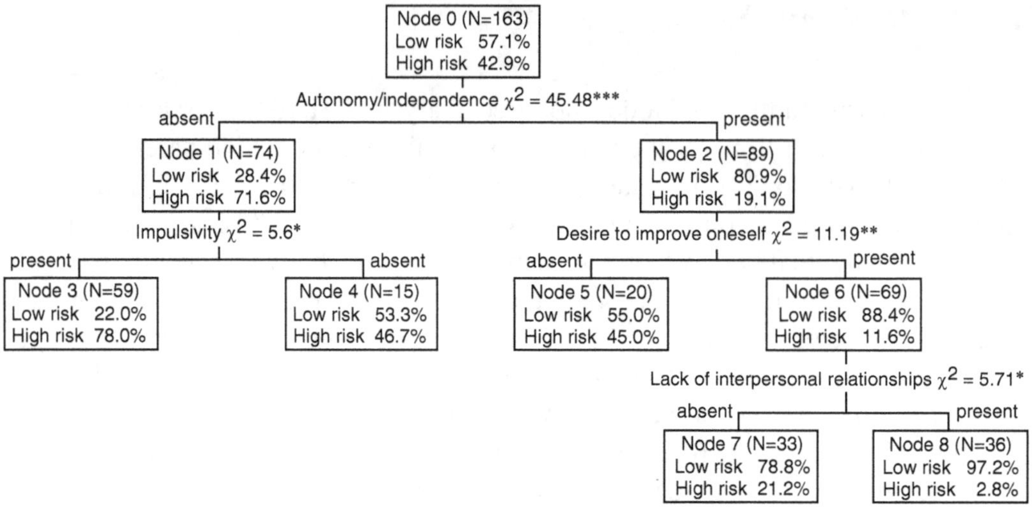

Fig. 1.6 Decision tree about Italian families' high- and low-risk profiles

As shown in Fig. 1.6, the decision tree for Italian families correctly classified 73.3% of the cases. It identified one high-risk parental profile (see node 3) and two low-risk profiles (see nodes 7 and 8), while two nodes (4 and 5) were not sufficiently discriminative at this level of split. In particular, the absence of *autonomy or independence* combined with *impulsivity* emerged as the pattern with the highest probability of child removal, while a good level of autonomy together with the *desire to improve oneself* characterizes parents evaluated as low-risk, even if they have *scarce interpersonal relationships*.

To sum up, two different patterns of predictors – except for *impulsivity* – emerged for migrant and Italian parents, suggesting that CPS workers focused on different indicators when they are asked to assess parents with different sociocultural backgrounds. However, in line with previous results, distal risk factors that are overrepresented among migrants (as *chronic poverty* and *lack of network and social integration*) did not constitute significant predictors of the safety assessment.

References

Abidin, R. (1995). *The parenting stress index* (3rd ed.). Charlottesville, VA: Psychological Assessment Resources.

Alink, L. R. A., Euser, S., van Ijzendoorn, M. H., & Bakermans-Kranenburg, M. J. (2013). Is elevated risk of child maltreatment in migrant families associated with socioeconomic status? Evidence from three sources. *International Journal of Psychology, 48*(2), 117–127. https://doi.org/10.1080/00207594.2012.734622

Autorità garante per l'infanzia e l'adolescenza, Terre des hommes, & CISMAI. (2015). Indagine nazionale sul maltrattamento dei bambini e degli adolescenti in Italia. Retrieved from http://www.garanteinfanzia.org/sites/default/files/documenti/Indagine_maltrattamento_TDH_Cismai_Garante_mag15.pdf.

Baldwin, A., Baldwin, C., & Cole, R. (1990). Stress resistant families and stress resistant children. In J. Rolf, A. S. Masten, D. Cicchetti, et al. (Eds.), *Risk protective factors in the development of psychopathology*. New York, NY: Cambridge University Press.

Barlow, J., Fisher, J. D., & Jones, D. (2012). *Systematic review of models of analysing significant harm*. Oxford, UK: Oxford University Press.

Bartelink, C., van Yperen, T. A., & ten Berge, I. J. (2015). Deciding on child maltreatment: A literature review on methods that improve decision-making. *Child Abuse & Neglect, 49*, 142–153.

Benbenishty, R., & Chen, W. (2003). Decision making by the child protection team of a medical center. *Health & Social Work, 28*(4), 284–292. https://doi.org/10.1093/hsw/28.4.284

Bonfiglio, N. S., Renati, R., Hjemdal, O., & Friborg, O. (2016). The resilience scale for adults in Italy: A validation study comparing clinical substance abusers with a nonclinical sample. *Psychology of Addictive Behaviors, 30*(4), 509.

Bornstein, M. H. (1995). *Handbook of parenting*. Mahwah, NJ: Lawrence Erlbaum Associates.

Briere, J. (1996). *Trauma symptom checklist for children (TSCC) professional manual*. Odessa, FL: Psychological Assessment Resources.

Bunting, L., Davidson, G., McCartan, C., Hanratty, J., Bywaters, P., Mason, W., & Steils, N. (2018). The association between child maltreatment and adult poverty–a systematic review of longitudinal research. *Child Abuse & Neglect, 77*, 121–133.

Camisasca E., Di Blasio P. (2002), "Una Ricerca di Follow-Up su Famiglie Maltrattanti e Abusanti. Fattori di Rischio e di Protezione", Età Evolutiva,72, pp. 89–96.

Capanna, C., Stratta, P., Hjemdal, O., Collazzoni, A., & Rossi, A. (2015). The Italian validation study of the resilience scale for adults (RSA). *BPA-Applied Psychology Bulletin (Bollettino di Psicologia Applicata), 63*(272), 16–24.

Cirillo, S., & Di Blasio, P. (1989). *La famiglia maltrattante*. Milano, Italy: Cortina.

CISMAI, Terres des Hommes & Bocconi. (2014). *Studio nazionale "Tagliare sui Bambini è davvero un risparmio?"*, research report: http://cismai.it/wp-content/uploads/2015/02/6261_Tagliare_sui_bambini_studioTDH_Bocconi_Cismai.pdf

Cummings, E. M., Davies, P. T., & Campbell, S. B. (2000). *Developmental psychopathology and family process*. New York, NY: Guilford Press.

Di Blasio, P. (1997). Abusi all'Infanzia: Fattori di Rischio e Percorsi di Intervento. Ecologia della Mente, 20, 2, 13–37.

Di Blasio, P. (2000). *Psicologia del bambino maltrattato*. Bologna, Italy: Il Mulino.

Di Blasio, P. (Ed.). (2005). *Tra rischio e protezione: La valutazione delle competenze parentali*. Milano, Italy: Unicopli.

Di Blasio, P., Camisasca, E., & Procaccia, R. (2007). Fattori di mediazione dell'esperienza traumatica nei bambini maltrattati. *Maltrattamento e abuso all'infanzia, 9*(2), 33–56.

Di Blasio, P., Camisasca, E., Procaccia, R., & Verrocchio, M. C. (2005). Children's resilience, protective and risk factors in therapy with abusing families. *Maltrattamento e Abuso all'Infanzia, 7*(3), 89–104.

Di Blasio, P., Piccolo, M., & Traficante, D. (2011). *TSCC - Trauma Symptom Checklist for Children. Valutazione delle conseguenze di esperienze traumatiche*. Trento, Italy: Erickson.

Friborg, O., Barlaug, D., Martinussen, M., Rosenvinge, J. H., & Hjemdal, O. (2005). Resilience in relation to personality and intelligence. *International Journal of Methods in Psychiatric Research, 14*(1), 29–42.

Friborg, O., Hjemdal, O., Rosenvinge, J. H., Martinussen, M., Aslaksen, P. M., & Flaten, M. A. (2006). Resilience as a moderator of pain and stress. *Journal of Psychosomatic Research, 61*(2), 213–219.

Fry, D., Fang, X., Elliott, S., Casey, T., Zheng, X., Li, J., … McCluskey, G. (2018). The relationships between violence in childhood and educational outcomes: A global systematic review and meta-analysis. *Child Abuse & Neglect, 75*, 6–28.

Fujiwara, T., Yamaoka, Y., & Kawachi, I. (2016). Neighborhood social capital and infant physical abuse: A population-based study in Japan. *International Journal of Mental Health Systems, 10*(1), 13.

Gallo, E. A. G., Munhoz, T. N., de Mola, C. L., & Murray, J. (2018). Gender differences in the effects of childhood maltreatment on adult depression and anxiety: A systematic review and meta-analysis. *Child Abuse & Neglect, 79*, 107–114.

Grumi, S., Milani, L., & Di Blasio, P. (2017a). Risk assessment in a multicultural context: Risk and protective factors in the decision to place children in foster care. *Children and Youth Services Review, 77*, 69–75. https://doi.org/10.1016/j.childyouth.2017.04.009

Grumi, S., Milani, L., & Di Blasio, P. (2017b, October). Identifying relevant factors for the risk assessment of children referred to child protection services: A judgment analysis approach. *Poster session presented at the 15th ISPCAN European regional conference*, The Hague, Netherlands.

Guarino, A., Di Blasio, P., D'Alessio, M., Camisasca, E., & Serantoni, G. (2008). *Parenting stress index – short form*. Firenze, Italy: Organizzazioni Speciali.

Ionio, C., & Mascheroni, E. (2014). L'impatto delle esperienze di vita negative della madre sul bambino. *Maltrattamento e abuso all'infanzia, 16*(3), 87–104. https://doi.org/10.3280/MAL2014-003006

Kass, G. V. (1980). An exploratory technique for investigating large quantities of categorical data. *Applied Statistics, 29*, 119–127. https://doi.org/10.2307/2986296

Kimber, M., Adham, S., Gill, S., McTavish, J., & MacMillan, H. L. (2018). The association between child exposure to intimate partner violence (IPV) and perpetration of IPV in adulthood—A systematic review. *Child Abuse & Neglect, 76*, 273–286.

LeBrun, A., Hassan, G., Boivin, M., Fraser, S. L., Dufour, S., & Lavergne, C. (2015). Review of child maltreatment in immigrant and refugee families. *Canadian Journal of Public Health, 106*(7), eS45–eS56. https://doi.org/10.17269/CJPH.106.4838.

Léveillé, S., & Chamberland, C. (2010). Toward a general model for child welfare and protection services: A meta-evaluation of international experiences regarding the adoption of the Framework for the Assessment of Children in Need and Their Families (FACNF). *Children and Youth Services Review, 32*(7), 929–944.

Masten, A. S. (2001). Ordinary magic: Resilience processes in development. *American Psychologist, 56*, 227–238.

Masten, A. S., Cutuli, J. J., Herbers, J. E., & Reed, M. J. (2009). Resilience in development. In R. Snyder & S. J. Lopez (Eds.), *Handbook of positive psychology* (pp. 117–131). New York, NY: Oxford University Press.

Milani, L. (2013). Differenze cross-culturali nell'orientamento alle punizioni fisiche e nella valutazione delle competenze genitoriali. *Maltrattamento e abuso all'infanzia, 1*, 7–10. https://doi.org/10.3280/MAL2013-001001

Milani, L., Di Blasio, P., & Grumi, S. (2017, May). *Risk and protective factors in family violence. Bridging across generations: Turning research into action for children and families.* Presentation conducted at the 15th Symposium on the Contributions of Psychology to Peace, Florence and Rome, Italy.

Milani, L., & Gagliardi, G. (2013). Fattori di rischio e di protezione nella valutazione delle competenze parentali di famiglie italiane e famiglie immigrate (Risk and protective factors in the evaluation of parenting skills: A comparison between Italian and immigrant families). *Maltrattamento e abuso all'infanzia, 1*, 59–80. https://doi.org/10.3280/MAL2013-001004

Milani, L., Grumi, S., Gagliardi, G., & Di Blasio, P. (2016). Famiglie italiane e immigrate: identificare fattori di rischio e di protezione nella valutazione delle competenze genitoriali (Italian and immigrant families: Assessing risk and protective factors in the evaluation of parenting skills). *Psicologia della salute, 1*, 67–89. https://doi.org/10.3280/PDS2016-001008

Milner, J. S. (1986). *The child abuse potential inventory: Manual* (2nd ed.). Webster, NC: Psytec.

Milner, J. S., & Chilamkurti, C. (1991). Physical child abuse perpetrator characteristics: A review of the literature. *Journal of Interpersonal Violence, 6*(3), 345–366. https://doi.org/10.1177/088626091006003007

Miragoli, S., Camisasca, E., & Di Blasio, P. (2015). Validation of the child abuse potential inventory in Italy: A preliminary study. *SAGE Open, 5*(3), 1–11. https://doi.org/10.1177/2158244015597044

Miragoli, S., Camisasca, E., Di Blasio, P., Milani, L., Ionio, C., Gizzi, N., … Malagoli Togliatti, M. (2016). Child abuse potential inventory in Italy: A comparative study of abusive and non-abusive parents. *Journal of Child Custody, 13*(4), 289–306. https://doi.org/10.1080/15379418.2016.1250145.

Miragoli, S., Traficante, D., Camisasca, E., & Di Blasio, P. (2017). Child abuse potential inventory short form: Sviluppo e validazione italiana (child abuse potential inventory: Development of a short form). *Maltrattamento e abuso all'infanzia, 19*(3), 69–85. https://doi.org/10.3280/MAL2017-003005.

Miragoli, S., & Verrocchio, M. C. (2008). La valutazione del rischio in situazioni di disagio familiare: fattori di rischio e fattori di protezione. *Maltrattamento e abuso all'infanzia, 3*, 25–43.

Ondersma, S. J., Chaffin, M. J., Mullins, S. M., & LeBreton, J. M. (2005). A brief form of the child abuse potential inventory: Development and validation. *Journal of Clinical Child and Adolescent Psychology, 34*(2), 301–311. https://doi.org/10.1207/s15374424jccp3402_9

Ozer, E. J., Best, S. R., Lipsey, T. L., & Weiss, D. S. (2003). Predictors of posttraumatic stress disorder and symptoms in adults: A metaanalysis. *Psychological Bulletin, 129*, 52–71.

Stewart, T. R. (1988). Judgment analysis: Procedures. In B. Brehmer & C. R. B. Joyce (Eds.), *Human judgment: The SJT view* (pp. 41–74). Amsterdam, The Netherlands: Elsevier Science Publishers B. V.

Todd, D. (1979). Social networking mapping. In W. R. Curtis (Ed.), *The future use of social networks in mental health*. Boston, MA: Social Matrix Research, Incorporated.

Valtolina, G. G. (2013). Contesto culturale, controllo genitoriale e punizioni fisiche. *Maltrattamento e abuso all'infanzia, 15*(1), 11–35. https://doi.org/10.3280/MAL2013-001002

Yu, S. M., & Singh, G. (2012). High parenting aggravation among US immigrant families. *American Journal of Public Health, 102*(11), 2102–2108. https://doi.org/10.2105/AJPH.2012.300698

Zolotor, A. J., & Runyan, D. K. (2006). Social capital, family violence, and neglect. *Pediatrics, 117*(6), e1124–e1131.

Chapter 2
Engaging Men to Support the Resilience of Syrian Refugee Children and Youth in Lebanon

Angela Veale, Alaa Hijazi, Zenia Osman, and Shelbi Macken

2.1 Introduction

Conflict damages the social ecological systems that sustain children's resilience such as the capacity of parents and communities to provide safety and basic needs and of the state to provide education and health services. In contexts of war and displacement, children's responses and experiences are most immediately mediated by their parents who play a fundamental role in regulating their exposure to risk and in protecting their mental health (Borowski, Ramey, & Bristol-Power, 2001; Garbarino & Kostelny, 1996; Masten & Obradovic, 2008; Murphy, Rodrigues, Costigan, & Annan, 2017; Panter-Brick, Grimon, & Eggerman, 2014; Punamäki, Samir, & El Sarraj, 1997, 2001; Qouta, Punamäki, & El Sarraj, 2008; Smith, Perrin, Yule, & Rabe-Hesketh, 2001; Thabet & Vostanis, 2000; Williams, 2010). The experiences of refugee men as parents are one of the least explored areas of psychosocial interventions with refugee families, necessitating greater engagement with men, including in their role as fathers (Panter-Brick et al., 2014).

Engaging men in gender-based violence prevention programming has emerged as a promising response in development contexts (Casey, Carlson, Two Bulls, & Yager, 2018). "Engaging Men" programs seek to challenge the social norms, attitudes, and practices that increase the risk of gender-based violence against women and girls while also harnessing positive male power to prevent violence and promote safety (Carlson et al., 2015; Ricardo & Barker, 2008). Most "Engaging Men"

A. Veale (✉) · S. Macken
University College Cork, Cork, Ireland
e-mail: A.Veale@ucc.ie

A. Hijazi · Z. Osman
American University of Beirut, Beirut, Lebanon

N. Balvin, D. J. Christie (eds.), *Children and Peace*, Peace Psychology Book Series, https://doi.org/10.1007/978-3-030-22176-8_2

programs are primary prevention initiatives that aim to identify and address underlying causes of violence and minimize the likelihood of violence occurring in contrast with secondary prevention that aims to support gender-based violence survivors (Storer, Casey, Carlson, Edleson, & Tolman, 2016). An examination of the research literature on "Engaging Men" as a gender-based violence prevention intervention shows that children, if considered at all, are at a step removed, that is, in relation to women's roles as caregivers, while men in their role as fathers rarely figure (Abramsky et al., 2016; Hossain et al., 2014; Stern, Pascoe, Shand, & Richmond, 2015). Children may be considered as direct beneficiaries in terms of delaying girls' early marriage (Casey et al., 2018) or in engaging men to overcome barriers to girls' education (Jamal, 2014). Increasingly, it is recognized that violence against women and violence against children cannot be treated as distinct issues (Fry & Elliot, 2017). Targeting men in their role as fathers within "engaging men in gender-based violence prevention" interventions is under-explored. Yet an ecological framework for understanding the origins of gender-based violence, such as that proposed by Heise (1998), supports an argument for this linkage. In her ecological model, the first level is personal history including witnessing intimate partner violence as a child or experiencing abuse; the second level is the microsystem of family relationships and in particular the importance of addressing marital conflict; the third level is the exosystem comprised of the formal and informal social structures that impact people's lives, such as community structures that can create social isolation as a risk factor for interpersonal violence following forced migration; and the fourth level is the macrosystem whereby social and cultural norms can create a climate where masculinity is linked to dominance and violence is a socially accepted dominance strategy. Many "Engaging Men" interventions are conceptualized within an ecological model. In their work with Promondu, Ricardo and Barker (2008) argue that interventions should work at three levels: face-to-face awareness-raising; community-level efforts including community-level mobilization, advocacy, and targeting of male leaders that can mobilize change; and collaborations with organizations whose focus is broader than gender-based violence. Yet most models do not consider the intersectionality between violence against women and girls and violence against children as a social category more broadly. The World Health Organization, (2016) identified strategies for ending violence against children including strengthening norms and values that support gender-equitable relationships for all children; challenging harmful gender and social norms of boys; reductions in early and forced marriage of young girls; more favorable attitudes to non-violent approaches to parental discipline; and greater recognition of what constitutes abusive behavior toward intimate partners and children – not just girls. This would mean an opportunity to broaden the remit of "Engaging Men" programs where appropriate to include consideration of men in their role as fathers and also to give more consideration to boys under 18 years. The Interagency Gender-Based Violence Case Management Guidelines (2017) recognize that boys also face risks of sexual violence. Furthermore, structural violence faced by boys such as gender-based norms that force them into child labor where a male head of household is incapacitated or absent is not generally regarded as a form of gender-based violence and therefore not considered.

This chapter presents the findings of an intervention evaluation that aimed to engage Syrian refugee and Lebanese men in Lebanon to address the main protection concerns for Syrian refugee women and children – including those related to domestic violence, sexual harassment and exploitation, and early marriage and child labor – by engaging Syrian refugee and host community men to promote safety in their communities and by increasing their capacity to use prosocial coping. The main findings have been described elsewhere (Veale, Hijazi, & Osman, 2016; Veale, Shanahan, Hijazi, & Osman, 2019), allowing this chapter to focus on the impact of the intervention on the lives of children and adolescents.

2.1.1 *Syrian Refugees in Lebanon*

The Syrian crisis has had a profound effect on children's lives and over half of Syrian refugees in Lebanon are children. Their families have experienced a steep decline into poverty as access to livelihood and income opportunities have diminished. In 2016, 70–80% of Syrian refugees did not have the necessary income to afford the survival minimum expenditure basket. A United Nations High Commission for Refugees (UNHCR, 2016) vulnerability assessment of Syrian refugees in Lebanon in 2016 found that 95% of visited households had borrowed money in the previous 30 days to purchase food, pay their rent, and access healthcare. A key reason for these extraordinarily high levels of deprivation was found to be a lack of access to work opportunities. Political factors have placed significant restrictions on Syrian men's traditional role as breadwinners for their families. Policies issued by the Lebanese government in 2015 tightened regulations over Syrian refugees, significantly restricting their mobility and their access to work opportunities. While Syrian nationals are allowed work permits in restricted labor markets (agriculture, construction, and cleaning services), in practice, work in the informal sector is restricted for men due to fear of crossing checkpoints, roundups, detention, and threat of deportation. Overall, 41% of Syrian refugees are without a legal residence permit. Unregistered refugees are ineligible for United Nations High Commission for Refugees (UNHCR) funded services or Government public services including health care. Families survive by relying on UNHCR funds, but the eligibility criteria are continuously reassessed which generates ongoing anxiety. They also rely on cash grants from the Lebanese cash consortium, World Food Programme (WFP) food vouchers, and in some cases, the labor of family members including women and children in the informal sector.

2.1.2 *Early Marriage*

As a protective strategy, Syrian refugees have resorted to early marriage of their daughters in order to help protect them from sexual harassment and risk of sexual abuse or to help with financial security (Hassan et al., 2015; Yasmine & Moughalian, 2016). Although this practice was common in Syria before, early marriage is believed to be happening at higher rates due to the belief that marriage offers increased protection (Cherri, Rodriguez-Llanes, & Guha-Sapir, 2017). Child marriage in Syria would also typically happen within communities where families knew each other and protective social connections were well established. In displacement, families are marrying young girls to men with whom there is no pre-established connection, who may have a significant age gap, or who have multiple wives, increasing the risk of DV and IPV (Boswall & Akash, 2015; Cherri et al., 2017; Mourtada, Schlecht, & DeJong, 2017; Wells, Steel, Hassan, & Lawsin, 2016; Yasmine & Moughalian, 2016). Early marriage has other negative consequences for young girls. While lack of educational opportunities can be a contributing factor to early marriage (Cherri et al., 2017), early marriage also can limit continuing education for girls. Syrian women in Lebanon reported that they thought the acceptable age for a woman to get married was 18 so that she would be able to at least complete primary education and, in the past in Syria, she would be able to complete higher education while she was married. However, in the current situation, girls who are being married early are not continuing their education (Charles & Denman, 2013), limiting their opportunities to gain skills outside of the home. Mourtada et al. (2017) reported that there were differing perceptions on the acceptable age for a young woman to be married in displacement. Most young women thought that, even in displacement, the earliest a woman should be married is 20 years old. Mothers thought that this should be lower in displacement (around 16–17 years old) and fathers thought that an acceptable age was 15 years, as long as the potential husband was deemed acceptable. Early marriage can also have negative health outcomes. Becoming pregnant at an early age, where a girls' pelvic region is too small, can lead to higher rates of both infant and maternal mortality. Girls may also not have received education around reproductive and sexual health, leading to increased prevalence of reproductive health issues among young Syrian females (Mourtada et al., 2017). Syrian families in Lebanon have reported that early marriage practices are a way to ensure that their daughter is protected by a man from sexual harassment and financial burdens (Anani, 2013).

A recent study completed by Bartels et al. (2018) tried to gain a deeper understanding of what was contributing to early marriage among Syrian refugees in Lebanon. Their methodology included asking participants to tell an anonymous story about Syrian girls living in Lebanon. Although they were not asked to share stories specifically about early marriage, many of the stories shared by participants contained elements pertaining to early marriage. After participants provided the story, they would then be asked to interpret the story using an app on a tablet. The study highlighted some differences between male and female perspectives on girls' protection as well as reasons that people resort to early marriage. It was found that while males in the community felt that females were under-protected, many females felt that they were overprotected. This male perspective of girls being under-protected is important to note as they are traditionally the head of the household and typically have the final say on family decisions. This means that even if females feel that they are overprotected, the male perspective will most likely be a major factor in decisions on early marriage or female mobility. Many females interpreted their early marriage stories to be issues of access to education, lack of security, and lack of financial resources, as well as societal expectations. Men interpreted their early marriage stories to mainly be about physical and financial protection. While this study does not provide any new information of the contributing factors to early marriage among Syrian refugees in Lebanon, it does provide an interesting insight into perception differences between genders on early marriage reasons and female protection levels, and how increased early marriage prevalence could be driven by male perspectives on women being under-protected both physically and financially.

In Lebanon, UNFPA (2017) found that child marriage rates of Syrian refugees are four times higher than among Syrians before the crisis. At a microlevel, Schlecht (2016) reported young girls sought out marriage to meet their basic needs as they knew their parents could not provide for them, while Syrian parents sought marriage for their young daughters to protect their honor due to the uncertainty of their future. At a macrolevel, displacement-related security issues, deteriorating economic conditions, and disrupted education for adolescent girls were attributed to be drivers of a reduced age of marriage among Syrian refugees in Lebanon (Mourtada et al., 2017).

2.1.3 Child Labor

According to the UNICEF Baseline Survey, (2016), approximately half of nearly half a million school-aged Syrian children in Lebanon are out of school and growing up without access to education. Syrian "out of school" children accounted for 35%, 40%, 45%, and 44% of Syrian 8-, 9-, 10- and 11-year-old children, respectively. Of children aged 12 and 13 years, 52% and 64% were out of school. This proportion increased further for older adolescents. In total, 75%, 83%, and 93% of 15-, 16-, and 17-year-olds were out of school, respectively. This highlights a particular vulnerability facing adolescents. Child labor is a major barrier to school enrollment and attendance as many families rely on their children to work instead of attending school (Lebanon Crisis Response Plan, 2017–2120; Human Rights Watch, 2016). In cases where the father cannot find work, has a disability, or is absent, adolescent males in the family may become the sole bread winner, prioritizing their responsibility of generating income over their education (DeJong et al., 2017). Another reported barrier to education for male refugees is fear of bullying and physical or sexual abuse from peers in attending school (Hassan et al., 2015). Al Ganideh and Good (2015) examined the treatment of Syrian refugee children involved in child labor in Jordan compared to Jordanian child laborers. Unstable family structures contributed to children working longer hours and the likelihood of experiencing physical abuse. While Syrian refugee children had better prior schooling than their Jordanian counterparts, they were paid much less indicating greater vulnerability to exploitative practices.

2.2 The Intervention: "Engaging Men to Promote Resilient Communities"

In 2013, the implementing organization carried out an assessment of the protection concerns and needs of Syrian refugees in Akkar District, Lebanon (Concern Worldwide, 2013). It found that women and girls reported an increased incidence of intimate partner violence and early marriage since arriving in Lebanon. It also noted high school drop-out rates of Syrian children due to costs and security concerns and the use of child labor for the economic support of families. Gender-based violence referral pathways and case-management structures had been established for all areas in Lebanon hosting refugees, yet reporting of gender-based violence cases was low, because it was a culturally sensitive topic. The assessment identified a gap in agencies working with men in protection programming. This led to the development of a community-based protection program entitled "Engaging men to promote resilience communities," with the specific objective of addressing the protection needs of conflict-affected Syrian refugee and vulnerable Lebanese children, youth, and women in Akkar. A program handbook entitled "Facilitator's Handbook: Engaging Men to Promote Resilient Communities" (Concern Worldwide & Irish Aid, 2013) was developed on the basis of a number of resources, including "Change-Maker Training Facilitator Handbook" developed by Men's Resources International; Promundo's "Programme H"; Save the Children's "Child Protection Sessions for Parents and Caregivers"; and the Centre for Interfaith Action on Global Poverty's "The Faith Effect." The "Engaging Men" program utilized a 12-week training course structure with four core objectives: promoting peaceful interactions with others, reducing violence and gender-based violence, enhancing child protection and caregiving, and increasing community safety and harmony through a community project. In a 1-year period of September 2015–September 2016, participants were 1469 Syrian and Lebanese men (70% Syrian; 30% Lebanese) across 62 groups. An examination of group composition showed that groups were predominantly Syrian or Lebanese. They undertook a 12-week course aimed at understanding issues of gender-based violence (GBV) and child protection by engaging men to promote safety in their communities and increasing their capacity to use prosocial coping and to mitigate conflicts peacefully. Topics covered included understanding gender roles and relations, the cycle of violence, non-violent communication, men as caregivers, child development, education on child labor, and early marriage. The program hypothesized that men who have been trained on these topics will be less likely to engage in gender-based violence and other forms of violence and women and children were conceptualized as the primary beneficiaries. In addition, each men's group was expected to identify, design, and implement a community project that increased the protective capacity of the community, particularly for those who were vulnerable. Two sessions focused on child-specific topics. Session ten examined the impact of caregiving and explored the stages of child development and how adult nurturing can reduce stress and promote development of children. Session eleven addressed protecting children with the aim of promoting understanding of the risks of child labor and early marriage (see Concern Worldwide & Irish Aid, 2013 for further details).

2.3 Method

Focus group discussions were conducted with ten "Engaging Men" groups selected randomly from a total of 56 groups to gather a range of views and experiences of the impact of the intervention. In total 130 men participated in the focus group discussions, of whom 80% were Syrian refugees, and 20% were Lebanese community members. Groups were predominantly composed of either Syrian or Lebanese participants. All participants had completed the 12-week "Engaging Men" training program within the previous year. A semi-structured focus group discussion schedule explored men's motivation to join the group, a free listing of the problems they faced, their experience of participation in the group, changes in coping strategies, gender-equitable attitudes and attitudes with respect to gender-based violence, attitudes to early marriage, and child labor and changes in inter-community relations. Focus group discussions were conducted in Arabic by two of the authors (Hijazi and Osman) who were female, while a third author (Veale) worked with female independent translators.

Five focus group discussions were carried out with 28 wives of Syrian refugee men participants, and two separate focus group discussions with 11 adolescent sons and 6 adolescent daughters of male participants aged 13–17. These focus groups explored questions about who is the main breadwinner in the house; main difficulties; observed impact being a member of the group had on male participants, on prosocial coping, on roles or relationships within the home, and on community relationships; and if items bought for the household instead of implementation of a community project made a difference in the life of the family.

In addition, ten family visits were conducted and the researchers met with former male participants and their wives separately, but the questions were similar to those above. There was no stipend or reward provided for participation in the focus group discussions. Peer researchers (two male and two female) linked to the "Engaging Men" intervention were selected through a recruitment and interview process. Selection criteria were that the men had participated in the program during the evaluation and the women were wives of other men who had participated in the program. They also had to be motivated, relatively educated, able to read and write in Arabic, and good communicators. They conducted ten interviews with former participant Syrian refugee and Lebanese men. Peer research triangulates "outsider" knowledge gained by researchers with "insider" knowledge gathered by those who have relationships of trust, connectedness, and empathy with study participants (Ryan, Kofman, & Aaron, 2011). All participants completed a detailed informed consent sheet in Arabic which outlined issues of confidentiality, the right to withdraw, to refuse to answer particular questions, and to cease participation at any time. For children aged 13–17 years, written consent was obtained from parents and written assent from children. Boys and girls were interviewed separately. If participants experienced any distress, the protocol stipulated they would be referred for psychosocial support using the organization's existing referral structures. One man indicated that the focus group discussion caused him considerable distress as it reminded him of events that happened in Syria. During the discussion, proper ethical procedures were followed and later followed up with the organization's protection team. Ethical approval was granted by the Ethics Committee, School of Applied Psychology, University College Cork. All data was taped and transcribed. Qualitative data were read and reread to identify if and how the "Engaging Men" intervention achieved the expected outcomes listed above. This was a form of thematic analysis (Braun & Clarke, 2006), an inductive approach where the themes identified emerged from the data. The following section presents the key findings related to family relations and protection issues affecting children.

2.4 Key Findings

2.4.1 Family Atmosphere and Emotional Regulation

Participation in the "Engaging Men" programs was identified as an important source of psychosocial support for all participants and in particular for Syrian refugee men. Engagement in the group appeared to reduce men's irritability in two ways: (i) by providing a space with other men for emotional release; and (ii) through a very explicit focus by the group facilitators on teaching men to reduce irritable behavior and engage in calmer communication. One man noted:

> It has been difficult dealing with the teenagers. My son was changing physiologically as he hit puberty and he was becoming more difficult to deal with. I used to yell at him a lot and I could see him sinking into a depression. The training helped me to treat my son better, and understand the difficulty of our situation from my family's perspective. We live in a one room house; this is where we sleep, eat and sit. No one has privacy. This is difficult for our teenagers as well as it is difficult for us.

An adolescent boy provided the following anecdote of his father:

> My father used to scream at my mom and not explain what's the matter with him, but after the sessions he became more flexible and he explains to us. For example, he says to my mom, my darling I have a headache, please can you bring to me some Panadol.

Similarly, the daughter of one of the men noted that one visible improvement in men's treatment of their wives is through taking them to an evening social visit or to visit their families. Participation in the groups led to improved patterns of interaction communication and increased openness, empathy, and perspective taking; children said some men have learned to generally become more "flexible," open-minded, open to discussion, and more accepting of others' ideas. However, given the ongoing daily stressors, some wives questioned how sustainable the observed changes could be expected to be.

2.4.2 Men as Fathers and the Impact on Their Children

The main positive outcome that was spontaneously and nearly unanimously reported across groups and interviews with men, women, and children was men's improved engagement with their children. This raises a hypothesis that attitudes towards child rearing and interactions with children may be more malleable than attitudes towards gender and interactions with wives.

2.4.3 Reduction in Yelling at and Beating Children

Various men, women, and children reported that the men used to be much more irritable with their children (e.g., frequently yelling) prior to the groups and that their interactions with them have become much calmer. One woman noted that prior to the groups, her children would ask "why is dad always irritable?" Many men reported learning to reduce their use of harsher methods (e.g., beating) to discipline children, particularly since they learned that this could have adverse impact on the children psychologically and developmentally. Some women noted that their husbands started discouraging them from beating their children as well. One man, for example, stated that he learned to instead withhold a toy if a child is not studying. Peer researchers noted that, for most respondents, the area where participants changed most was in their treatment of children and this seemed to be sustained a year after the training. As noted by one male participant to a peer researcher:

> We talk to them more, consult them more often. We have developed new relationships with our children because we feel they need it more. These are children who have lived the crisis in their formative years. Their futures have been completely upended. If we do not develop relationships with them - if they do not learn to trust our opinions, they will be completely lost.

A wife of one of the participants reported to a peer researcher:

> I used to argue with my husband all the time about how to dress our daughter. He used to insist that she wear clothes that cover her body despite the fact that she is only six. After the sessions, he changed and now allows her to wear what she likes.

The following was noted by another woman in discussion with a peer researcher:

> Before [the training], my husband was often verbally abusive to me and he would hit our children. After the [12] sessions, his treatment of the children improved and to some degree, he was less violent. But this did not last very long. After a while, he went back to the way he used to be.

2.4.4 Increased Dialogue and Positive Time Spent with Children

One outcome noted by men was that they tried to calmly dialogue with their children about something they did wrong rather than yelling at them. Some adolescents reported that their fathers now listened and talked with them more and explained their financial situation in a way they could understand. A number of fathers reported that they spent more time with their children and played with them more often. One male adolescent shared that his "...father used to spend all night outside the house, but that after the sessions he now spends an hour or two and returns to home to spend the rest of the time with the family." This was consistent with some women's reports who praised their husband's increased patience and openness with their children. One man noted that he used to "go into the house as the head of the family" but now has softened his interactions with the children. Similarly, a woman noted that after her husband started dialoguing with their children and asking their opinion on things, she feels that her children have developed stronger characters and can assert themselves to him by saying "no". She added that the change in their father's demeanor permitted them "to open up to the world, and to think of what they want to do when they grow up." A number of fathers and children described the change in interactions, noting that the fathers have been seeking to "befriend" their children rather than act as an authoritarian father, particularly in the case of adolescents. Another girl noted that her father started taking them more on outings and walks.

It also appeared that some men took great pride in increasingly assuming the role of a transmitter of knowledge with their children. Several men noted that the groups heightened their awareness of the importance of setting up good role models for children and that they teach their children about what they learned in the groups. Examples of this type of role modelling include becoming more aware of not lying in front of children, discouraging violence by not buying children pellet guns, and not shaming boys for crying, as explained by this father:

> ...one tells boys, don't cry, it's a shame, but now, one understands that a man can cry because crying is an internal feeling, and a man may want to go out into the wilderness alone to cry, over war, need, and deprivation.

A daughter also gave an example of how her father told her older brother, who was about to beat her younger brother over smoking, to not beat him, but to guide him gently instead. Another man shared how he valued learning that mistreatment of children, including deprivation of kindness and affection, has long-term adverse effects. Hence, the participants overall appeared to benefit from the information they received about child development.

2.4.5 Child Marriage

Although reduction in child marriage was not consistently *spontaneously* reported as a benefit from the intervention, when asked, many participants noted that the facilitators educated them about the adverse effects of child marriage and expressed an understanding of a number of reasons of why it might be problematic. These included incomplete cognitive development of the girl despite physical maturation, possibility of adverse health outcomes, increased risk of marital problems, divorce and the girl returning to her family, inability of such a young girl to tolerate the poverty of her husband, how marriage may prevent a girl from education, and the inability of a "child to raise a child."

One participant framed his increased awareness about the problem of child marriage through the lens of religious guidance. In that participant's focus group, participants also noted that:

> We agreed that the girl has to be above 18, and there should be no more than six years' difference between them, and that there needs to be compatibility in the education level between the girl and her husband. We learned that marriage could end up being unjust to the girl, it might not work out, and then she'd return to her family.

Another participant noted, for example, that he has two daughters of marriage age but that he was not going to marry them until they continued their education, no matter the financial difficulty. Another participant described how a fellow group member had a 13-year-old girl he wanted to marry but that he gradually listened to others' arguments about how his child might want to play and doesn't yet have the capacity to take care of children.

Some participants noted that there has been increased general awareness about child marriage, including in the media, and it has become a familiar and discussed concern. Most participants seemed to agree that young age of marriage is problematic. However, it was difficult to ascertain whether the endorsement of unfavorable attitudes towards child marriage among participants was representative. For example, one man noted that in his group, 3–4 men continued to believe in child marriage and planned on going ahead with it. It was similarly quite difficult to ascertain if these opinions actually trickled down to shape behavior. A peer researcher recounted the story of one participant who had a young daughter and wanted to arrange her marriage. The facilitator discussed this with him, convincing him against it, but after the training, the man ended up arranging her marriage anyhow.

Upon probing for examples of behavior, one man shared that the group participants advised their relatives to not marry their daughters young, and another woman gave an example of a young female relative whose uncles declined a suitor for her because she was very young.

An issue that was raised in only one setting and told to a peer researcher was the issue of how to marry girls who may already have had a sexual relationship. This story involved a wife of a participant talking about her 15-year-old daughter who had a suitor. Her husband refused to allow the marriage because he felt it was wrong "in all circumstances". But his wife worried for her daughter and tried to convince him to allow them to marry, reporting she thinks "they may already have a relationship and this would be the only way to save her." The vulnerability of adolescent girls to sexual harassment was an important concern for men, but vulnerability to transactional/survival sex or rape did not arise as discussion topics.

It is worth noting that participants differed in their views toward early marriage possibly due to their cultural background, rural vs. urban location, whether early marriage has always been the local custom or was never accepted, or whether this became an issue only after the Syrian crisis. Some participants noted that people might marry their daughters early to "relieve themselves from their expenses" or "lift her responsibility off them." According to peer researchers, child marriage was raised by men as a protection response rather than as only a reaction to economic circumstances. A peer researcher explained:

> It is not about difficult economic circumstances. What fathers are worried about is that their daughters will be harassed or worse by men. In Lebanon, they are very limited in terms of what they can do to restore their honor. If they marry her off, the burden of this honor is transferred/or shared with the husband.

This was discussed in a number of focus group discussions. Another man noted that:

> They might not find a solution but to marry their children, because they would fear for their daughter that she is getting older, and her body is becoming more visible, and/or if she left school, there is no other solution but to marry her.

Peer researchers explained that daughters are married off to other poor Syrians who may not be well known to the family, and often, this new family has to depend on the daughter's biological family for support, especially when there are marital problems.

2.4.6 Child Labor

The issue of child labor was never brought up spontaneously in any groups or interviews and the researcher had to ask about it directly. Participants talked about the necessity of employing children for the livelihood of families:

> We ourselves need to work, also our kids need to work. There is a woman from the group found herself obliged to work in order to get medicine for her children. Another woman, her 10-year-old child is working for the same reason.

> Everything has changed. Whoever finds work (including children), they have to go for it; we wouldn't do this (to our children) if we didn't need this.

> In some cases it was easier for children compared to their fathers to find low level jobs, e.g., sweeping the floors at a barber shop.

Engaging men participants were also asked about child labor, and several stated that they knew or learned about adverse effects of child labor, including depriving children of the opportunity to enjoy their childhood, children being out of school, and children becoming involved in street life and being exposed to work conditions that have adverse health effects. However simultaneously many groups noted that families had to send their children to work anyway. For example, one participant noted that:

> [the facilitator] brainstormed pros and cons of children working, if I put the child for example in a workshop, if he were to lift heavy things, he'd have disc problems, or if he were to become a painter, he would become sick when he's young, he can be molested, so I wouldn't want a child to work in a car workshop, because he'd become like a street kid, he would smoke, but I could take him to work with a tailor, because it's a cleaner opportunity, the store is visible to the public, and more contained.

In a focus group taking place in a rural location, participants noted that child labor is minimal, because everyone is really poor and no one owns a craft or a business where children could work. Another participant noted that civil society and organizations should have a bigger role to play in sponsoring families with no breadwinner, particularly those with widowed women, so that children would not have to work. While participants were educated on the risks of child labor, the income earned by children was often important to the family economy and so education did not lead to a change in family practice. Some men reported that they were ashamed to see their child working, while they themselves were unable to work.

2.5 Discussion

This analysis has explored an important aspect of children's social ecology in times of conflict, that is, the role of men as fathers and as a resource for children and their family through the examination of an "Engaging Men" intervention. In terms of Heise's (1998) ecological model addressing gender-based violence, the findings showed how, through guided discussion on masculinity and gender roles, Syrian and Lebanese men talked about their own personal history and Syrian men, in particular, talked about their changed circumstances as refugee men and fathers. Through dialogue, men took a step back from their responses of anger and frustration, became more attuned and reflective on their own needs and those of their wives and children, and were better able to regulate their emotions. This facilitated changes in family relationships through a reduction of irritable behavior and calmer communication in the home. There was a reported reduction in yelling at and beating children, increased dialogue and positive time spent with children, and a change from perceiving the father figure as authoritarian to seeing them as a guide and transmitter of knowledge. At the level of the exosystem of formal and informal social structures that shape people's lives, marriage practices are one such informal structure. Findings support those of other research on child marriage among Syrian refugees that men view it as a financial and physical protection strategy in insecure displacement contexts (Bartels et al., 2017; Cherri et al., 2017). The dialoguing method brought up men's concerns that girls are out of school and as fathers, due to their low status as refugees in a host society, they are limited in what they can do to protect their daughters from harassment. However many participants noted being more aware of the adverse effects of child marriage such as incomplete cognitive development of the girl despite physical maturation, possibility of adverse health outcomes, girls dropping out of school, increased risk of marital problems, divorce and the girl returning to her family, inability of such a young girl to tolerate the poverty of her husband, and the inability of a "child to raise a child." These effects extend beyond financial and physical protection concerns to more child-centered concerns. Labor practices are another part of the exosystem. Structural inequalities in the labor market and security concerns excluded male refugee parents to a significant extent from engagement in livelihood opportunities. On the basis of self-report through focus group discussions, men reported little attitudinal change with respect to child labor.

In Heise's (1998) model, the macrosystem level refers to social and cultural norms. Many interventions which seek to engage men to address gender-based violence use community mobilization approaches through public theatre and media (Abramsky et al., 2014), but this was not a feature of this intervention. One interesting finding was that dialogue about child marriage in men's groups was supported by a broader public discourse in the media, suggesting that interventions that address a topic from different starting points may have a multiplier effect. Discourse in the public space seemed to facilitate more critical reflection in the private space of the men's groups and some attitudinal change. Typically, a medium-to-large change in intention results in only a small-to-medium change in behavior (Webb & Sheeran, 2006), and it is less clear if the intervention produced behavioral change in the context of ongoing insecurity for Syrian families.

A limitation of the intervention was that it did not engage with the issue that was the greatest source of frustration for Syrian refugee men, that of exclusion from livelihood opportunities which impacted their capacity to provide economically for their family. A recommendation was to developed integrated programming that could create linkages to livelihood programming or employment programs. The findings raised a question about the sustainability of reported changes in emotional regulation, family relations, and attitudes around early marriage if there is no change in the significant external stressors that impact on men's daily lives. As noted in the introduction, men may conceptualize problems differently to women and girls. A recommendation is that women and girls are included as stakeholders in planning and program implementation and that program aims are accountable to them.

This chapter draws attention to the intersection between violence against women and violence against children including the impact of yelling and beating in the home and structural violence against boys in the form of child labor. This is an under-considered relationship in many "Engaging Men" programs. A limitation of the reported intervention was that the program was overambitious and lacked a clear theory of change and causal pathways to achieving and measuring change. It sought to provide psychosocial support to men, including stress management and coping, promote gender-equitable attitudinal change, and address gender-based violence, child development, and protection. However, the findings point to the value of focusing more on the intersection between gender-based programing that considers women and girls and to include a focus on violence against children as a social category more broadly. These topics were of interest to men and addressed a priority of theirs in their role as fathers. This intersection should be considered in the design of larger, multilevel, multi-stranded, systemic strategies over an extended period of time.

A further limitation of the intervention was that of blurred boundaries between primary prevention and engaging with perpetrators to reduce gender-based violence, with the intervention lacking a mechanism for addressing perpetrator accountability including violence against children in the form of beatings. The research raised the importance of clearly defining the focus, aims, and scope of interventions such as this.

2.6 Conclusion

This chapter reviewed how programs which seek to engage men can also support men in their role as fathers. The analysis found that, through dialogue, a safe emotional space was created for men to meet collectively to talk about their problems, to become more attuned and reflective about their relationships with their wives and children, and to engage in better emotional regulation. Discussions on gender created a framework for talking about the stresses of their daily life, the changed gender roles and child roles in their families as a result of their displacement to Lebanon, and their feelings and reactions to these changes with the help of skilled and sensitive facilitators. The key impact, psychosocial support, emerged from the process of talking about gender and improved the quality of life of women and children through improved family relationships. It offered an example of a space in which the theories and methodologies of peace psychology such as dialogue (Tint, 2017), and the future use of emancipatory and participatory methodologies (Seedat, Suffla, & Christie, 2017) to engage women and girls as well as men as stakeholders, may have a particular contribution to make to enhance the capacity of refugee men in their role as fathers.

References

Abramsky, T., Devries, K., Kiss, L., Nakuti, J., Kyegombe, N., Starmann, E., … Watts, C. (2014). Findings from the SASA! Study: A cluster randomized controlled trial to assess the impact of a community mobilization intervention to prevent violence against women and reduce HIV risk in Kampala, Uganda. *BMC Medicine, 12*(1), 122.

Abramsky, T., Devries, K., Michau, L., Nakuti, J., Musuya, T., Kyegombe, N., & Watts, C. (2016). The impact of SASA! A community mobilization intervention on women's experiences of intimate partner violence: Secondary findings from a cluster randomized trial in Kampala, Uganda. *Journal of Epidemiological Community Health, 8*, 1–8.

Al Ganideh, S., & Good, L. (2015). Understanding abusive child labor practices in the shadow of the Arab Spring. *Journal of Children's Services, 10*(1), 76–91.

Anani, G. (2013). Dimensions of gender-based violence against Syrian refugees in Lebanon. *Forced Migration Review, 44*, 7–10.

Bartels, S., Saja, M., Roupetz, S., Garbern, S., Kilzar, L., Berquist, H., …& Bunting, A. (2017). *BMJ Global Health, 3*, e000509. https://doi.org/10.1136/bmjgh-2017-000509

Bartels, S., Michael, S., Roupetz, S., Garbern, S., Kiltaz, L., Bergquist, H., … Bunting, A. (2018). Making sense of child, early and forced marriage among Syrian refugee girls: A mixed method study in Lebanon. *BMJ Global Health, 3*(1), e000509.

Borowski, J., Ramey, S., & Bristol-Power, M. (Eds). (2001). *Parenting and the child's world: Influences on academic, intellectual, and socioemotional development.* New York: Psychology Press.

Borkowski, J. G., Landesman, S., & Bristol-Power, M. (Eds.). (2009). *Parenting and the child's world: Influences on academic, intellectual, and socioemotional development.* New Jersey: Taylor & Francis.

Boswall, K., & Akash, R. (2015). Personal perspectives of protracted displacement: An ethnographic insight into the isolation and coping mechanisms of Syrian women and girls living as urban refugees in northern Jordan. *Intervention: Journal of Mental Health and Psychosocial Support in Conflict Affected Areas, 13*(3), 203–215.

Braun, V. & Clarke, V. (2006). Using thematic analysis in Psychology. *Qualitative Research in Psychology, 3*(2), 77–101.

Carlson, J., Casey, E., Edleson, J., Tolman, R., Walsh, T., & Kimball, E. (2015). Strategies to engage men and boys in violence prevention: A global organizational perspective. *Violence Against Women, 21*, 1406–1425.

Casey, E., Carlson, J., Two Bulls, S., & Yager, A. (2018). Gender transformative approaches to engage men in gender-based violence prevention: A review and conceptual model. *Trauma, Violence & Abuse, 19*(2), 231–246.

Charles, L., & Denman, K. (2013). Syrian and Palestinian Syrian refugees in Lebanon: The plight of women and children. *Journal of International Women's Studies, 14*(5), 96–111.

Cherri, Z., Rodriguez-Llanes, J., & Guha-Sapir, D. (2017). Early marriage and barriers to contraception among Syrian refugee women in Lebanon: A qualitative study. *International Journal of Environmental Research and Public Health, 14*(8), 836.

Concern Worldwide. (2013). *Assessment on the protection concerns and needs of Syrian refugees in Akkar District, Lebanon.* Dublin, Republic of Ireland: Concern Worldwide.

Concern Worldwide, & Irish Aid (2013). *Facilitator's handbook- engaging men to promote resilience communities.* Dublin, Republic of Ireland: Concern Worldwide.

DeJong, J., Sbeity, F., Schlecht, J., Harfouche, M., Yamout, R., Fouad, F., … & Robinson, C. (2017). *Conflict and Health, 11*(23). https://doi.org/10.1186/s13031-017-0128-7.

Fry, D., & Elliot, S. (2017). Understanding the linkages between violence against women and violence against children. *The Lancet, 5*(5), 472–473.

Garbarino, J., & Kostelny, K. (1996). The effects of political violence on Palestinian children's behavior problems: A risk accumulation model. *Child Development, 67*(1), 33–45.

Hassan, G., Kirmayer, L. J., Mekki-Berrada, A., Quosh, C., el Chammay, R., Deville-Stoetzel, J. B., … Ventevogel, P. (2015). *Culture, context and the mental health and psychosocial well-being of Syrians: A review for mental health and psychosocial support staff working with Syrians affected by armed conflict.* Geneva, Switzerland: United Nations High Commission for Refugees.

Heise, L. (1998). Violence against women: An integrated ecological framework. *Violence Against Women, 4*(3), 262–290.

Hossain, M., Zimmerman, C., Kiss, L., Abramsky, T., Kone, D., Bakayoko-Topolska, M., … Watts, C. (2014). Working with men to prevent intimate partner violence in a conflict-affected setting: A pilot cluster randomized controlled trail in rural Côte d'Ivoire. *BMC Public Health, 14*, 339.

Human Rights Watch. (2016). *Growing up without an education: Barriers to Education for Syrian Refugee Children in Lebanon.* https://www.hrw.org/report/2016/07/19/growing-without-education/barriers-education-syrian-refugee-children-lebanon. Retrieved 24 February 2018.

Inter-Agency Gender-Based Violence Case Management Guidelines. Providing care and case management services to gender-based violence survivors in humanitarian settings. https://reliefweb.int/sites/reliefweb.int/files/resources/interagency-gbv-case-management-guidelines_final_2017_low-res.pdf. Retrieved 12 December 2017.

Jamal, A. (2014). Engaging men for gender justice: Overcoming barriers to girls' education in the Pashtun tribes of Pakistan. *International Journal of Social Welfare, 24*(3), 273–286.

Lebanon Crisis Response Plan. (2017–2120). Government of Lebanon, UN Resident and Humanitarian Coordinator for Lebanon. https://reliefweb.int/report/lebanon/lebanon-crisis-response-plan-2017-2020-enar. Retrieved 24th February 2018.

Masten, A., & Obradovic, J. (2008). Disaster preparation and recovery: Lessons from research on resilience in human development. *Ecology and Society, 13*, 9.

Mourtada, R., Schlecht, J., & DeJong, J. (2017). A qualitative study exploring child marriage practices among Syrian conflict-affected populations in Lebanon. *Conflict and Health, Suppl 1*(11), 27–27.

Murphy, K., Rodrigues, K., Costigan, J., & Annan, J. (2017). Raising children in conflict: An integrative model of parenting in war. *Peace & Conflict: Journal of Peace Psychology, 23*(1), 46–57.

Panter-Brick, C., Burgess, A., Eggerman, M., McAllister, F., Pruett, K., & Leckman, J. (2014). Practitioner review: Engaging fathers- recommendations for a game change in parenting interventions based on a systematic review of the global evidence. *Journal of Child Psychology and Psychiatry, 55*(11), 1187–1212.

Panter-Brick, C., Grimon, M. P., & Eggerman, M. (2014). Caregiver—Child mental health: A prospective study in conflict and refugee settings. *Journal of Child Psychology and Psychiatry, 55*, 313–327.

Punamäki, R., Samir, Q., & El Sarraj, E. (1997). Models of traumatic experiences and chldren's psychological adjustment: The role of perceived parenting, children's resources and activity. *Child Development, 68*, 718–728.

Punamäki, R., Samir, Q., & El Sarraj, E. (2001). Resiliency factors predicting adjustment after political violence among Palestinian children. *International Journal of Behavioral Development, 25*, 256–267.

Qouta, S., Punamäki, R. L., & El-Sarraj, E. (2008). Child development and family mental health in war and military violence: The Palestinian experience. *International Journal of Behavioral Development, 32*(4), 310–321.

Ricardo, C., & Barker, G. (2008). *Men, masculinities, sexual exploitation and sexual violence: A literature review and call for action* (pp. 1–55). Promundo & Men Engage.

Ryan, L., Kofman, E., & Aaron, P. (2011). Insiders and outsiders: Working with peer researchers in researching Muslim communities. *International Journal of Social Research Methodology, 14*(1), 49–60.

Schlecht, J. (2016). *A girl no more: The changing norms of child marriage in conflict*. New York, NY: Women's Refugee Commission.

Seedat, M., Suffla, S., & Christie, D. (2017). *Emancipatory and participatory methodologies in peace, critical and community psychology*. Cham, Switzerland: Springer International Publishing.

Smith, P., Perrin, S., Yule, W., & Rabe-Hesketh, S. (2001). War exposure and maternal reactions in the psychological adjustment of children from Bosnia- Hercegovina. *Journal of Child Psychology and Psychiatry, 42*(3), 395–404.

Stern, E., Pascoe, L., Shand, T., & Richmond, S. (2015). Lessons learned from engaging men in sexual and reproductive health as clients, partners and advocates of change in the Hoima district of Uganda. *Culture, Health & Sexuality, 17*(2), 190–205.

Storer, H., Casey, E., Carlson, J., Edleson, J., & Tolman, R. (2016). Primary prevention is? A global perspective on how organisations engaging men in preventiong gender-based violence conceptualise and operationalize their work. *Violence Against Women, 22*(2), 249–268.

Thabet, A. A., & Vostanis, P. (2000). Post traumatic stress disorder reactions in children of war: A longitudinal study. *Child Abuse & Neglect, 24*(2), 291–298.

Tint, B. (2017). *Diasporas in dialogue: Conflict transformation and reconciliation in worldwide refugee communities*. Hoboken, NJ: Wiley-Blackwell.

UN High Commissioner for Refugees. (2016). *Vulnerability assessment of Syrian refugees in Lebanon*. Retrieved from *https://reliefweb.int/sites/reliefweb.int/files/resources/VASyR2016.pdf*

UNFPA. (2017). *New study finds child marriage rising among most vulnerable Syrian refugees*. http://www.unfpa.org/news/new-study-finds-child-marriage-rising-among-most-vulnerable-syrian-refugees. UNFPA. The American University of Beirut and Sawa for Development and Aid.

UNICEF. (2016). UNICEF Baseline Survey for Women and Children. https://data.unhcr.org/syrianrefugees/download.php?id=11355

Veale, A., Hijazi, A., & Osman, Z. (2016). *Engaging Men to Promote Resilient Communities, Concern Worldwide, Northern Lebanon*. Final Evaluation June 2015–May 2016. Cork: University College Cork, Ireland.

Veale, A, Shanahan, F., Hijazi, A., & Osman, Z. (Forthcoming, 2019) Engaging men to promote resilience communities among Syrian refugees in Lebanon. *Intervention, Journal of Mental Health and Psychosocial Support in Conflict Affected Areas*.

Webb, T., & Sheeran, P. (2006). Does changing behavioral intentions engender behavior change? A meta-analysis of the experimental evidence. *Psychological Bulletin, 2*, 249–268.

Wells, R., Steel, Z., Hassan, A., & Lawsin, C. (2016). Psychosocial concerns reported by Syrian refugees living in Jordan: Systematic review of unpublished needs assessments. *British Journal of Psychiatry, 209*(2), 99–106.

Williams, N. (2010). Establishing the boundaries and building bridges: A literature review on ecological theory: Implications for research into the refugee parenting experience. *Journal of Child Health Care, 14*, 35–51.

World Health Organisation. (2016). *INSPIRE: Seven strategies for ending violence against children*. Geneva, Switzerland: World Health Organisation.

Yasmine, R., & Moughalian, C. (2016). Systemic violence against Syrian refugee women and the myth of effective intrapersonal interventions. *Reproductive Health Matters, 24*(47), 27–35.

Chapter 3
Promoting Civic Engagement and Social Inclusion Interventions for Minors Involved with Crimes

Patrizia Meringolo and Elisa Guidi

3.1 The Italian Law for Minors

The juvenile justice system in Italy is concerned with boys and girls aged 14–18 who have committed offences against civil or penal codes. The current system is largely informed by the theoretical debates about social rules and social opportunities that took place in the 1970s and resulted in important reforms in psychiatric health (Law 180/1978) and in penitentiary law (Law 354/1975). In addition, the Code of Criminal Procedure for Minors, enacted in 1988, provides alternative measures and inclusion strategies for youth, designed to help them avoid detention. The following are some of the specific rules for juvenile trials (DPR 448/1988): (1) avoid detention when possible by using alternative measures (probation, community work, etc.) to foster social inclusion (art.1, art.21, and 22.); (2) particular attention is paid to personality assessments, and a core goal is to take care of minors' psychological and educational development (art.8 and 9); (3) prevention of the risk of labelling minors is taken into account to avoid spreading information about their deviant behaviour (art.13, 14, and 15); and (4) finally, it is important to pay attention to preserving minors' intimate networks, if existing and reliable, and to increase their formal and informal social networks as a precondition for planning rehabilitation.

As some quantitative indicators suggest, the New Code of Criminal Procedure for Minors has largely reduced the number of minors in criminal institutions from more than 7000 entries each year before 2000 to about 500 at present. Currently, minors in social services total more than 20,000; 12% of females and 22.5% of males come from abroad.

The communities that house juvenile offenders have about 800 minors who are waiting for a judicial decision about their disposition, whereas juvenile prisons have

P. Meringolo (✉) · E. Guidi
University of Florence, Florence, Italy
e-mail: patrizia.meringolo@unifi.it

N. Balvin, D. J. Christie (eds.), *Children and Peace*, Peace Psychology Book Series, https://doi.org/10.1007/978-3-030-22176-8_3

473, of which 36 are females and 217 come from abroad. Research indicates that migrant minors, when charged, are likely to suffer more severe punishments (Dipartimento Giustizia minorile e di comunità, 2018).

Minors in juvenile jail (called *Istituto Penale Minorile* or IPM in Italy) have generally committed crimes against property (58.6%) or, to a lesser extent, against persons (14.9%), weapon-possession offences (8.3%), or drug-pushing offences (6.5%). For minors coming from abroad (females in particular), crimes against property are the main reason for detention in IPMs (about 70%).

3.1.1 Explaining Juvenile Justice Procedures in Italy

At the time of the arrest, a minor's rights have to be guaranteed: this includes a privacy policy and the presence of specialised professionals who interact with the minor and offer information about available sources of psychological support. The magistrate in charge of preliminary investigations decides if the minor may be released or sent to a community of juvenile offenders until a judicial authority's decision is made.

The centres for first reception receive minors who lack social support. Centres do not have some of the features of a prison (there are no bars, even if there are forms of control) and their purpose is to detain minors for only a few days. During their stay, minors are observed by a specialised team (a psychologist, educator, and youth worker), the members of which write the first report for the juvenile judge. These centres – which may be public, private, or managed by Non-Governmental Organisations – may also be organised as small custodial communities with a "family" structure and an educational component. After four days, the judge decides the measure to be taken for the minors based on the following considerations: no interruption of their educational process, reduction of harm caused by the proceeding, a quick judgement process, and detention as a residual choice.

When lower measures are impossible to choose, the minor may be taken to a juvenile prison (IPM) for detention. This measure is provided for offences with punishments of more than 9 years and must be justified by the risk of the minor tampering with evidence, running away, or repeating the offence. IPMs contain minors under criminal proceedings and young adults who committed a crime when they were minors, and – according to Italian law – they can stay in juvenile prison until they are 25 years old. There is a total of 17 IPMs throughout Italy, and they are located in most of the major Italian regions.

In cases of house arrest, the court requires that the minor stay at home, sometimes with limited movement, and the court may allow the minor to attend school or other educational activities. The judge, however, can adjourn the trial, begin the procedures for probation, and ask Social Services to plan an intervention after the minor's assessment. During preliminary investigations, the judge, by request of the prosecuting attorney, may decide on a nonsuit judgement if the offence has an expected punishment of less than 2 years and if criminal behaviour seems unlikely to be repeated. Instead of detention, a minor may be given substitute measures, such as part-time imprisonment or conditional release. So far, the most common alternative measure for minors under criminal proceedings is probation with conditional release.

Nevertheless, negative issues concerning alternative punishments still exist especially among minors who lack protection from social networks. This occurs among Italian minors, particularly those living in the South who are often involved in organised crime such as the *mafia* (in Sicily), *camorra* (in Campania), and *ndrangheta* (in Calabria), and mainly among migrants whose presence is considerable in juvenile jails.

3.2 About Migrant Minors

Adolescents from abroad, largely present in IPMs, are a very heterogeneous group. They are doubly vulnerable: As minors, they are unable to totally fulfil their needs, and as migrants, they are usually perceived as strangers and viewed with prejudice attitudes. Because they are forced to grow up quickly, they are often distrustful, and it is quite difficult for them to have significant relationships with Italian professionals who are sometimes perceived as the reason for their detention. Cultural mediation appears to be an indispensable means, not only to translate procedures but to truly understand adolescents' needs. However, the most serious problems appear outside the prisons or after receiving care from justice facilities. In many cases, migrant minors have more opportunities during their stay in an IPM than after their release.

3.2.1 Migration and Its Impact on Minors

The experience of migration may turn out to be a difficult event for a minor. During 2017, about 18,000 unaccompanied children reached Italy (93% males) and more than 400 of them died attempting to reach the country's boarder (Secondo Welfare, 2018). Aside from any danger that may occur during the journey, a migrant minor who survives may suffer serious consequences after the journey. Pottie, Dahal, Georgiades, Premji, and Hassan (2015) found first-generation immigrant adolescents were more likely to experience bullying, violence, and suicidal behaviors than later-generation counterparts and native-born minors.

For parents of migrant adolescents, the task of transmitting their values of origin can become difficult, especially when the host culture's values are perceived as more attractive to adolescent migrants (Phalet & Schönpflug, 2001). The issue is problematic because the transmission of cultural heritage may be a protective factor; yet some research indicates that intergenerational value discrepancy between parents and children often grows over time (Phinney, Ong, & Madden, 2000).

Surely, migrant adolescents are heterogeneous, whether from the same or different countries and continents; nevertheless, Pottie et al. (2015) observed common features in facing discrimination and adapting to new contexts and similar risks (Peguero, 2009).

Aside from the problem of value discrepancies, a large number of studies (García Coll, 2005) have demonstrated the *migrant paradox* (Marks, Ejesi, & García Coll, 2014), whereby – despite exposure to psychosocial and economic adversity – migrant youth experience better health compared to native youth. Moreover, first-generation immigrant minors often showed better adaptation compared to native and second-generation adolescents. Resilience, which is defined as an individual's ability to successfully cope with adversity (Chiodini & Meringolo, 2016), has also been examined in migrant youth. Research has examined the higher resilience of migrant youth and its association with their families' positive characteristics, such as higher levels of care for adolescents and greater control over the influence of deviant peers (Vega, Sribney, Aguilar-Gaxiola, & Kolody, 2004). However, there is a paradox: while first-generation migrants sometimes adjust well, the second generation being born in the host society is not guaranteed positive inclusion for a variety of reasons including socioeconomic conditions that often remain precarious or may even worsen (Bosisio, Colombo, Leonini, & Rebughini, 2005).

Furthermore, even though the first generation often experiences migration as emancipation, this may not be true for the second generation, which may seek to free itself from the prejudice and discrimination encountered (Santagati, 2004). The label of the second generation may be viewed as a social position that indicates a different life from that of their peers with whom they share their experience. Although their parents have invested a lot in their social emancipation, the real opportunities available to youth are unlikely to match their expectations. Even education, a central factor in the economic and psychosocial investment of any migrant family, does not seem to prepare them enough for the future (Colombo & Santagati, 2010).

The migrant paradox does not always appear to be confirmed. Santinello, Cristini, Lenzi, Altoè, and Baldassari (2008) only partially verified it because young people also seem to conform to their Italian peers. Similar results came from other international studies, which observed a prevailing trend for youth to adopt the values, norms, and risky behaviours of their non-immigrant peers, particularly if coming from families with a similar socioeconomic status (Berry, Phinney, Sam, & Vedder, 2006). In addition, the increasing complexity of international political and economic scenarios has made inclusion more difficult, meaning young people are more exposed to the risk of becoming deviants.

Studies concerning youths involved in crime (as seen in Reyna & Farley, 2006) showed that adolescents, when compared to adults, are more thrill-seeking and are likely to try maximising the short-term advantages of their actions. Such a trend is more common among youth who have to face their double identity: they live in Western countries but come from different cultural backgrounds (Doosje, Loseman, & van den Bos, 2013). When they experience deprivation, negative emotions such as anger and frustration may arise (Schils & Verhage, 2017), causing them to avoid healthy peer groups and to prefer deviant ones. Robben and Suárez-Orozco (2000) explained, in terms of "negative social mirroring", the negative image of migrant groups shared in social contexts, which has implications for the social identity and the inclusion of migrant youth (Beiser, Hou, Hyman, & Tousignant, 2002).

However, Dimitrova et al. (2017) examined the educational, psychological, and behavioural outcomes of young migrants in Europe based on 102 studies conducted in 14 European countries. The authors concluded that improving intercultural behaviours in families, schools, and neighbourhoods, the development of intercultural relationships, and policies addressing inclusion are important factors for the integration of immigrant children and youth.

3.3 Reflections About Juvenile Detention and the Development of a New Experience: The Project PROVA – Prevention of Violent Radicalisation and of Violent Actions

Detention should be a last-resort treatment by Italian law, and, in fact, we can see the low number of youth inmates in Italy. We know that having fewer prisons does not produce more deviants. Rather, more prisons may cause higher crime rates: minors with longer stays "in" prison are the perpetrators of more serious and repeated crimes, are older than the other inmates, and are more likely to demonstrate violent behaviours and radicalisation.

IPMs in Italy, although sufficient, are not well distributed. Some are overcrowded, are in unsuitable buildings, and were originally planned to be adult prisons and then readapted. When in prison, minors coming from abroad have fewer opportunities than native Italians to form relationships with significant external persons and thus cannot best plan their future rehabilitation (Meringolo, 2012). Concerning age, IPMs are not always juvenile prisons, as a considerable number of the members of the young adult population (aged 18 to 25) are carrying out their educational treatment. Nevertheless, the coexistence of persons with such different ages may cause great difficulties regarding relationships inside a prison.

Concerning employed professionals, everyday management is carried out mostly by prison officers, whereas educational staff are primarily employed outside the prisons. IPMs are thus focussed more on custodial aims than on education-based treatments. Furthermore, it is important to plan specific professional development training sessions to improve the capabilities among professionals, educators, and police officers who must cope with the difficulties migrant minors face in prison or in probation, taking into account their experiences of exclusion and their lack of opportunities and positive relationships.

The quality of treatment has been undoubtedly improved over time, even with differences among institutions and regions. When planning for release, important educational experiences are continued, with activities, such as sports or theatre created in cooperation with local communities, as well as specific treatments for young sex offenders or for those involved in mafia crimes.

Because the main aim of the law is to bring interventions to an external criminal area, it becomes necessary to integrate treatments within existing or potential resources of the local community, thus building networks with local communities and promoting the commitment of local authorities. In fact, the latter plays an important role for planning inclusion, reducing stigma, and building (or rebuilding) social connectedness.

Based on this, the community psychology team of the University of Florence coordinated a European project called the Prevention of Violent Radicalisation and of Violent Actions (PROVA, 2016)[1] which was implemented in Italy, Germany, Romania, and Spain. The PROVA project addressed the problem of violent radicalisation of juvenile offenders in prison and on probation using different activities such as research, prevention (i.e. training and workshops), and evaluation. In order to counter conflicts and the risk of violent radicalisation, one of the main focuses of the project was to have juvenile offenders use space manipulation and re-imagination (i.e. urban space of the local communities and internal space of the prison) as a tool to promote youth aggregation, social inclusion, and civic engagement. Therefore, target groups included professionals directly and indirectly involved in the juvenile justice system, stakeholders committed to inclusion policies and to urban life organisation, and minors/young adults under criminal proceedings who come from European and non-European countries. Indirect beneficiaries were university students who were involved in planned activities with minors.

As a prevention activity, *training* was addressed to professionals to improve – with participatory methods – their competences, team building, empowerment, and skills in preventing conflicts. In addition, stakeholders were involved in *discussing issues* related to the marginalisation and the risks of violent radicalisation, the "fear of others" and the creation of scapegoats as factors that influence the municipal policies, the strategies for better inclusion, and the use of urban spaces for fostering youth aggregation. Lastly, *workshops* with youth under criminal proceedings were implemented and for the purpose of re-imagining public spaces, including the inner spaces of juvenile jails, in the knowledge that civic engagement and a sense of community may be fostered by experiences that improve the quality of the living places. The PROVA project also foresaw – to better build social networks among youth and to promote intercultural dialogue – the involvement of university students attending courses in social work, psychology, and education. These activities were implemented by means of methods that were participatory and empowering.

At the end of the PROVA project, the main outcomes included the drawing up of *guidelines* for the reproducibility of an experience and to plan sustainable activities

[1] PROVA. *Prevention of Violent Radicalization and of Violent Actions in intergroup relations.* Project No. 580365-EPP-1-2016-1-IT-EPPKA3-IPI-SOC-IN

DISCLAIMER: This project has been funded with support from the European Commission. This document reflects the views of the authors only, and the Commission cannot be held responsible for any use which may be made of the information contained therein.

to systematise policies in this field. A second outcome was to develop a *Good Practices Platform* to offer an online instrument for the dissemination of best practices related to the prevention of violent radicalisation and to promote democratic values, intercultural relationships, and active citizenship.

3.3.1 From the PROVA Project's Aims: How to Cope with Youth Violent Radicalisation

This contribution shows the main findings of the qualitative research carried out during the first step of the project, called "Preparation". The data from this exploratory research have shown some similarities among the European countries, taking into account the sociopolitical and economic specificities of each one. Here, we present the Italian outcomes, which may be considered a significant source of observation in southern Europe.

Our aim was to analyse the point of views of different professionals who are directly or indirectly involved in the juvenile justice system and of stakeholders as the persons in charge of juvenile justice and the religious ministers.

We have explored the thematic areas referred to the meaning of radicalisation, the roots of violence in young people, and the interventions and policies against violent radicalisation. Based on these perceptions, we intend to design a training program for first-line professionals and for those potentially involved, along with workshops for minors and young adults under criminal proceeding. Finally, we will offer suggestions for best practices.

3.4 Methods

3.4.1 Participants and Instruments

In Italy, the total number of participants in the qualitative research was 18, including 2 key informants (i.e. a director of the Centre of Juvenile Justice and an Imam of the Islamic Community) and 16 professionals working in the Centre of Juvenile Justice, or in an IPM or in institutions/organisations for educational and social integration.

Within local organisations and social actors involved in the prevention of violent conflict and radicalisation (previously mapped by the research team of PROVA), potential participants were voluntarily recruited via emails and telephone. After introducing the main purpose of the research, all participants gave their consent to participate in our study.

We collected data from the key informants using 2 semi-structured interviews and from the professionals through 3 focus groups. The main areas explored in semi-structured interviews and focus groups are as follows:

1. Perception of the phenomenon of radicalisation and violent behaviours in young people who are offenders or at risk of becoming offenders.
2. Individuals' points of view about these issues and the underlying processes.
3. Policies and existing interventions at the local level.
4. Participants' opinions about the importance of networking (i.e. relationships with other formal and informal institutions).
5. Participants' proposals or suggestions, especially for preventive interventions or policies.

Interviews and focus groups were recorded and transcribed verbatim, guaranteeing the anonymity of the participants.

3.4.2 Data Analysis

To analyse the emerging themes, we choose to carry out a semantic analysis on the whole textual corps of interviews and focus groups. This choice was based on the possibility of drawing a picture to synthetically represent all the facets of the narratives coming from the participants. We used the software T-LAB (version T-LAB plus 2017), which represents a set of linguistic and statistical tools for content analysis and text mining (Lancia, 2004) that allows meaningful patterns of keywords (called *lemma*) and main themes to emerge.

In this chapter, we refer to a specific analysis (i.e. the Thematic Analysis of Elementary Contexts) that deals with finding patterns of keywords within the textual corpus, which allows a representation of content through a few significant thematic *clusters*, consisting of a set of elementary contexts characterised by the same patterns of words.

3.4.3 Results

The thematic clusters that have been identified include the following: Problems (24% of the total number of lemmas), Jail (25%), School (27%), and Radicalisation (24%). Figure 3.1 shows the four thematic clusters that have been identified and how they are related to the two kinds of participants: professionals involved in the three focus groups (variable "MOD_FOCUS") and key informants involved in two interviews (variable "MOD_INT").

We can see that the Radicalisation and Jail clusters are closer to the interviews with the director of the Centre of Juvenile Justice and the Imam, while the Problems and School clusters are closer to the professionals' focus groups.

By using the statistical analysis, two dimensions have been identified: Factor n. 1, named "Conflicts" (*x*-axis, eigenvalue = 0.3264, explained variance 42.6%), which represents – going from the left to the right – the higher and lower problem

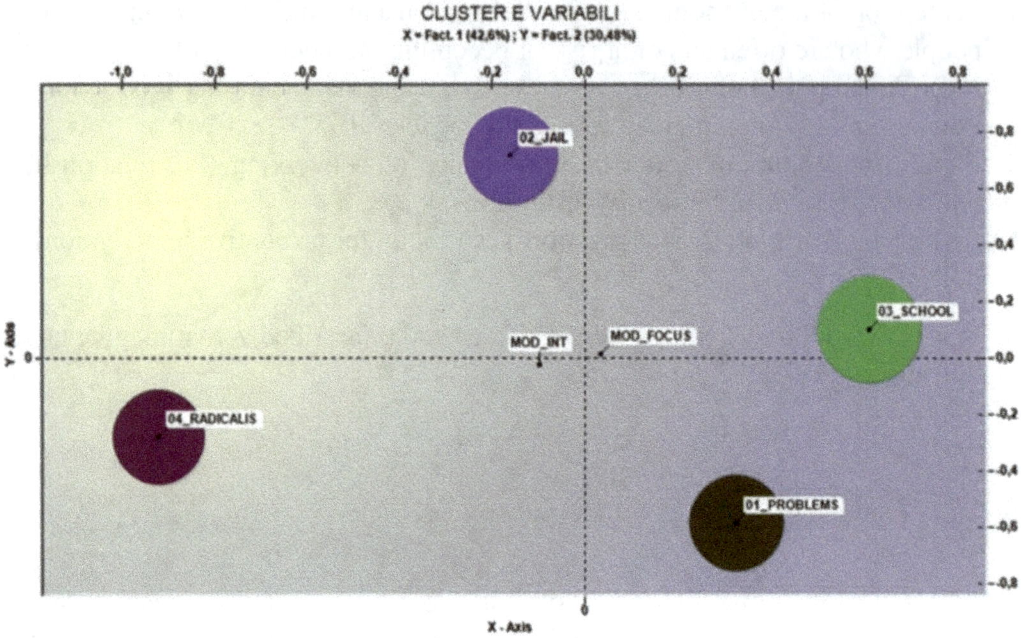

Fig. 3.1 Clusters and variables

severity, and Factor n. 2, named "Institutions" (y-axis, eigenvalue = 0.2336, explained variance 30.48%), which indicates, going from the bottom to the top, the passage from interpersonal and societal relationships leading to the institutions, both educational and judicial.

The lower quadrants of Fig. 3.1 are referred to as conflictual relationships, which are experienced in group situations or societal settings, going from the thematic clusters characterised by heavier severity on the left of the figure (i.e. violent Radicalisation) to the other thematic clusters defined as less severe (i.e. Problems) which are on the right.

The higher quadrants of Fig. 3.1 are related to institutions: the cluster related to juvenile Jail, which presents more problems, is shown on the left. The educational institutions included in the cluster School, with their positive aspects, are shown on the right.

Figure 3.2 shows the keywords belonging to each cluster in more detail, which better explain their content.

Going from the heavier situation, we may observe (in Cluster n. 4, *Radicalisation*) words like *radicalisation*, *extremist*, *violence*, and *anger* (an emotion that always emerges when talking about precursors of juvenile violence) as well as words that refer to life stories such as *memories*, *identity*, and *development*.

Some sentences coming from the participants' narratives follow:

> *Talking about ideological radicalisation… we speak about a cultural conflict that emerges from the group of angry, needy, violent people… even the graduates may be angry. There is a conflict of oriental and western culture* (Participants5, FocusGroup1).

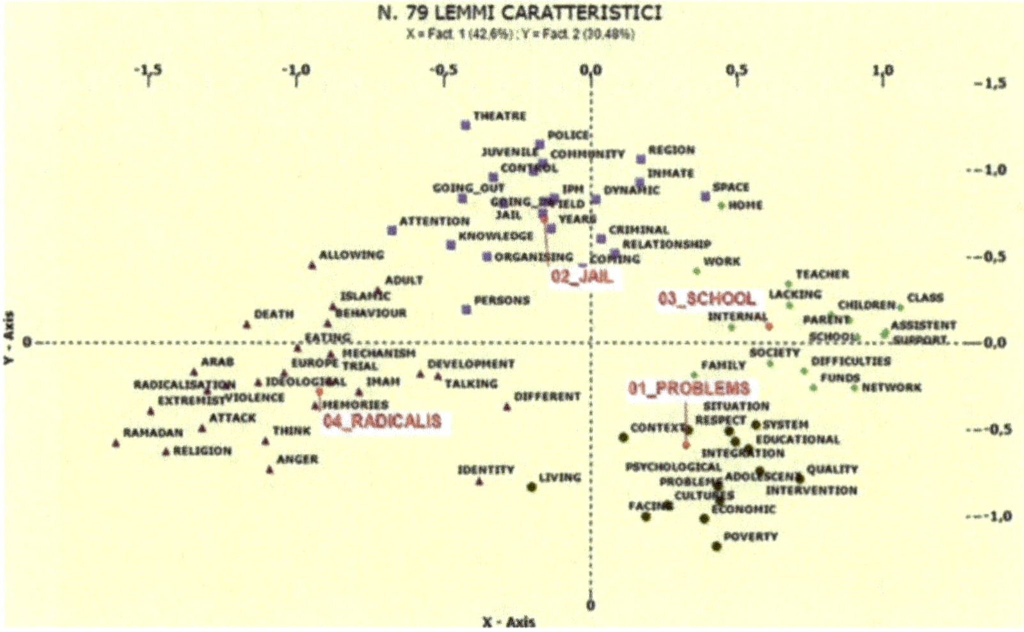

Fig. 3.2 Clusters and lemmas (keywords)

I saw that small radicalisation processes emerged not only in what we mean as Islamic or as a religion radicalisation. They were deeply rooted in breaking the rules that educators and tutors of the project have given them (Participant10, FocusGroup3).

In Cluster n. 1 (*Problems*), it is possible to see the keywords related to antecedents such as *context*, *cultures*, *family*, *facing*, *poverty*, and *difficulties*.

[...] The need to be part of a group to be strong... There were the Italian group, the Moroccan group [...]. The more people were isolated, the more they were at risk (Participant3, FocusGroup1).

In the last few years, young people have increasingly had to struggle with psychological problems, and even psychiatric disorders, due to many factors, including the use and abuse of different substances (Participant2, FocusGroup2).

What results from poverty of constructive experiences generates "poor" persons, lacking the basis to structure the idea of themselves as citizens, of people who live in accordance with the rules of the social context where they are living [...] Complex poverty creates a terrifying mix from the point of view of the final outcome (Interview I).

Cluster n. 2 (*Jail*) is characterised by both keywords related to the custodial situation (e.g. *control*, *police*, *justice*, *criminal*) and to new experiences for humanising the total institution and promoting educational measures (e.g. *theatre*, *community*, *attention*).

I do not see this problem of radicalisation within the juvenile prisons, and then I think that this problem is more present in the most deprived neighbourhoods (Participant1, FocusGroup2).

> *I think the theatre can really create a group not related to a religious or ethnic membership but creator of identity, a creator of healthy relationships, of true relationships* (Participant9, FocusGroup3).

Finally, Cluster n. 3 (*School*) gathers aspects related to inclusion and rehabilitation such as *parents*, *support*, and – above all – *networks* as well as those referring to problems such as *society*, *lacking*, *difficulties*, and *funds*.

> *Professionals should address the most deprived areas with educational projects carried out by a team of outreach educators who promote the engagement of minors and young adults in sports activities, training or education,* etc. *[...] And projects supporting their families* (Interview I).

> *Finding an international policy that guarantees a future for the [*i.e. *migrants], not to throw them anywhere but to give them a dignified future. At the end the deviance increases, and when it becomes too much to handle, it is a disaster* (Participant5, Focusgroup1).

> *In past years, the juvenile prison has built a network that, incredibly, was successful without any steady foundations in the juvenile prisons […] We met one another, and a group rose during those years. The group carried out projects and collaborated on interventions.* (Participant6, FocusGroup3).

3.5 Discussion and Conclusions

This kind of analysis provides a vivid picture of the discussions that took place in the focus groups and interviews, from which useful implications were drawn to plan preventive interventions.

By enriching data with new facets and in-depth observations in a recursive way, consistent with qualitative and participatory methods, the main theme that emerges consistently is the importance of preventive measures for inclusion (as in Berry et al., 2006). This means that the core matter is not to merely detect the symptoms of violence, as in many approaches, but rather the preconditions of conflicts, discomfort, and anger in marginalised minors, often coming from other cultures, being rootless and being actors in extreme life stories.

Therefore, at the individual level, prevention interventions – to be effective – should focus on the *early stages* of the violent radicalisation process, in its starting points such as the perceptions of exclusion and injustice (according to Doosje et al., 2016; Moghaddam, 2005, 2009) in order to counteract the risk of violent radicalisation within youth.

At a relational level, another emerging theme is the importance of planning *empowering trainings and interventions* to improve the capabilities of professionals, educators, and police officers on one hand, and minors and their families on the other. A key focus of the trainings and interventions should be how to cope with exclusion and the lack of opportunities. These new skills may enable youth to develop positive relationships with others within their social sphere and improve democratic and civic values. The involvement and strengthening of families, which is currently a weakness in the supporting network for minors (Colombo & Santagati, 2010), is a common aim of social and educational institutions as well as the juvenile justice system. It should be further exploited to ensure the sustainability of each preventive perspective and to make effective changes in the inclusion policies.

Finally, at the community level, a third and equally important theme concerns the *networking among institutions*, as recommended by the principal European agency (RAN – Radicalisation Awareness Network, 2016) that brings together practitioners from around Europe to work on the prevention of radicalisation and build local partnerships that can face societal crisis and violence. Steady networks, not only in times of emergency but also as structural best practices, seem to be the main pathway towards cultural changes that promote peace, justice, and fairness, with respect to younger and more fragile citizens.

In conclusion, these three key recommendations in the field of the prevention of violent radicalisation should also have an impact on minors and young adults involved in crimes. By focusing on the early stages of the violent radicalisation process, the empowering interventions, and the networking, front-line professionals and stakeholders who are directly and indirectly involved in the juvenile justice system may manage to involve minors and young adults under criminal proceedings in prevention programmes, to foster deeper civic education, engagement, and positive relationships in intercultural peer groups.

References

Beiser, M., Hou, F., Hyman, I., & Tousignant, M. (2002). Poverty, family process, and the mental health of immigrant children in Canada. *American Journal of Public Health, 92*(2), 220–227. https://doi.org/10.2105/AJPH.92.2.220

Berry, J. W., Phinney, J. S., Sam, D. L., & Vedder, P. (2006). *Immigrant youth in cultural transitions: Acculturation, identity, and adaptation across national contexts*. Mahwah, NJ: Lawrence Erlbaum Associate Publishers.

Bosisio, R., Colombo, E., Leonini, L., & Rebughini, P. (2005). *Stranieri & Italiani. Una ricerca tra gli adolescenti figli di immigrati nelle scuole superiori*. Roma, Italy: Donzelli.

Chiodini, M., & Meringolo, P. (2016). *Che le lacrime diventino perle: Sviluppare la resilienza per trasformare le nostre ferite in opportunità*. Milano, Italy: Ponte alle Grazie.

Colombo, M., & Santagati, M. (2010). Interpreting social inclusion of young immigrants in Italy. *Italian Journal of Sociology of Education, 2*(1), 9–48. Retrieved from: http://ijse.padovauniversitypress.it/2010/1/2

Dimitrova, R., Özdemir, S. B., Farcas, D., Kosic, M., Mastrotheodoros, S., Michałek, J., & Stefenel, D. (2017). Is there a paradox of adaptation in immigrant children and youth across Europe? A literature review. In *Well-being of youth and emerging adults across cultures* (pp. 261–298). Cham, Switzerland: Springer. https://doi.org/10.1007/978-3-319-68363-8

Dipartimento Giustizia minorile e di comunità. (2018). *I Servizi della Giustizia minorile. Dati statistici.* Retrieved from: https://www.giustizia.it/resources/cms/documents/quindicinale_15.06.2018.pdf

Doosje, B., Loseman, A., & van den Bos, K. (2013). Determinants of radicalization of Islamic youth in the Netherlands: Personal uncertainty, perceived injustice, and perceived group threat. *Journal of Social Issues, 69*(3), 586–604. https://doi.org/10.1111/josi.12030

Doosje, B., Moghaddam, F. M., Kruglanski, A. W., de Wolf, A., Mann, L., & Feddes, A. R. (2016). Terrorism, radicalization and de-radicalization. *Current Opinion in Psychology, 11*, 79–84. https://doi.org/10.1016/j.copsyc.2016.06.008

García Coll, C. (2005, April 7–10). The immigrant paradox: Critical factors in Cambodian students' success. *Biennial meeting of the Society for Research in Child Development*. Atlanta, Georgia.

Lancia, F. (2004). *Strumenti per l'Analisi dei Testi. Introduzione all'uso di T-LAB*. Milano, Italy: Franco Angeli. URL http://tlab.it/en/presentation.php, T-LAB plus 2017

Marks, A. K., Ejesi, K., & García Coll, C. (2014). Understanding the US immigrant paradox in childhood and adolescence. *Child Development Perspectives, 8*(2), 59–64. https://doi.org/10.1111/cdep.12071

Meringolo, P. (2012). Juvenile justice system in Italy: Researches and interventions. *Universitas Psychologica, 11*(4), 1081–1092. Retrieved from: http://www.redalyc.org/articulo.oa?id=64725418005

Moghaddam, F. M. (2005). The staircase to terrorism: A psychological exploration. *American Psychologist, 60*(2), 161. https://doi.org/10.1037/0003-066X.60.2.161

Moghaddam, F. M. (2009). De-radicalization and the staircase from terrorism. In D. Canter (Ed.), *The faces of terrorism* (pp. 277–292). Oxford, UK: Wiley.

Peguero, A. A. (2009). Victimizing the children of immigrants: Latino and Asian American student victimization. *Youth & Society, 41*(2), 186–208. https://doi.org/10.1177/0044118X09333646

Phalet, K., & Schönpflug, U. (2001). Intergenerational transmission of collectivism and achievement values in two acculturation contexts: The case of Turkish families in Germany and Turkish and Moroccan families in the Netherlands. *Journal of Cross-Cultural Psychology, 32*(2), 186–201. https://doi.org/10.1177/0022022101032002006

Phinney, J. S., Ong, A., & Madden, T. (2000). Cultural values and intergenerational value discrepancies in immigrant and non-immigrant families. *Child Development, 71*(2), 528–539. https://doi.org/10.1111/1467-8624.00162

Pottie, K., Dahal, G., Georgiades, K., Premji, K., & Hassan, G. (2015). Do first generation immigrant adolescents face higher rates of bullying, violence and suicidal behaviours than do third generation and native born? *Journal of Immigrant and Minority Health, 17*(5), 1557–1566. https://doi.org/10.1007/s10903-014-0108-6

PROVA – Prevention of violent Radicalisation and Of Violent Actions in intergroup relations. (2016). Retrieved from: www.provaproject.org.

RAN – Radicalisation Awareness Network. (2016). Preventing radicalisation to terrorism and violent extremism. Approaches and Practices. *Radicalisation Awareness Network.* Retrieved from: https://ec.europa.eu/home-affairs/sites/homeaffairs/files/what-we-do/networks/radicalisation_awareness_network/ran-best-practices/docs/ran_collection-approaches_and_practices_en.pdf

Reyna, V. F., & Farley, F. (2006). Risk and rationality in adolescent decision making implications for theory, practice, and public policy. *Psychological Science in the Public Interest, 7*(1), 1–44. https://doi.org/10.1111/j.1529-1006.2006.00026.x

Robben, A. C., & Suárez-Orozco, M. (Eds.). (2000). *Cultures under siege: Collective violence and trauma* (Vol. 11). Cambridge, UK: Cambridge University Press.

Santagati, M. (2004). *Mediazione e integrazione. Processi di accoglienza e d'inserimento dei soggetti migranti*. Milano, Italy: Franco Angeli.

Santinello, M., Cristini, F., Lenzi, M., Altoè, G., & Baldassari, D. (2008). Consumo di tabacco tra adolescenti immigrati e non: l'influenza di variabili familiari e socio-economiche, *Spazi interculturali: Trame, percorsi, incontri.* Incontro Tematico AIP, Roma 18–19 September.

Schils, N., & Verhage, A. (2017). Understanding how and why young people enter radical or violent extremist groups. *International Journal of Conflict and Violence, 11*, 1–17. https://doi.org/10.4119/UNIBI/ijcv.473

Secondo Welfare. (2018). *I minori stranieri non accompagnati in Italia nel 2017*. Retrieved from: http://www.secondowelfare.it/primo-welfare/inclusione-sociale/i-minori-stranieri-non-accompagnati-in-italia-nel-2017.html

Vega, W. A., Sribney, M., Aguilar-Gaxiola, & Kolody, B. (2004). 12-month prevalence of DSM-III-R psychiatric disorders among Mexican Americans: Nativity, social assimilation, and age determinants. *The Journal of Nervous and Mental Disease, 192*(8), 532–541. https://doi.org/10.1097/01.nmd.0000135477.57357.b2

Chapter 4
Indirect Contact Interventions to Promote Peace in Multicultural Societies

Reeshma Haji and Hiromi Noguchi

4.1 Introduction

As societies become more diverse through immigration and refugee settlement, promoting more favourable attitudes between groups of different cultural backgrounds is of pressing importance. An unprecedented number of 68.5 million forcibly displaced people, with more than 28 million refugees, have been reported by the UNHCR (2018). Reactions to newcomers are mixed: Western Europeans are more favourable toward a decrease in immigration than an increase (Pew Research Centre, 2018), and immigrants from North Africa and the Middle East are viewed especially negatively (Pew Research Centre, 2018). Research shows that young children learn prejudice through adults' instruction and these "social rules" shape children's understanding of their social worlds (Kang & Inzlicht, 2012). Now more than ever, it seems that an attitude of acceptance of the other, acceptance, and even the celebration of difference need to be instilled from a young age. This chapter describes some methods for fostering these favourable views of the other.

We situate this chapter within the broader context of peace psychology. Interventions aimed at promoting more favourable views of the other may help to reduce structural violence. This violence is inherent in social systems and has its effects by exposing people to inequality and injustice (Christie, Wagner, & Winter, 2001). Seeing the other as equal could enable the challenging of legitimizing myths that maintain unequal social structures. We describe interventions to be used with

Thank you to Cailynn Laprise, Rachel Vandervecht, and Burgandy Thiessen for research assistance.

R. Haji (✉) · H. Noguchi
Laurentian University, Sudbury, ON, Canada
e-mail: rhaji@laurentian.ca

N. Balvin, D. J. Christie (eds.), *Children and Peace*, Peace Psychology Book Series, https://doi.org/10.1007/978-3-030-22176-8_4

children and youth, for those who endeavour to prepare young people to confront structural violence over their lifetimes. The interventions are grounded in social psychology, specifically a key theoretical perspective known as intergroup contact.

Intergroup Contact Theory, articulated by Allport (1954), posited that bringing groups into physical contact with each other would promote more positive attitudes toward the other. This ought to be particularly the case when the interaction is marked by optimal conditions, including equal status, common goals, cooperation between the groups, and the support of authority or societal customs. This theory inspired decades of research in various parts of the globe. A very influential *meta-analysis* (statistical integration) of 515 studies found that, overall, physical interaction of groups decreases prejudice (Pettigrew & Tropp, 2006). Indeed, intergroup contact can promote more favourable intergroup attitudes even when optimal conditions are absent. Moreover, in a process called *secondary transfer*, positive attitudes developed through exposure to one group can spread to other groups not involved in the interaction (Pettigrew, 2009). For example, research with Canadian undergraduate students found that having someone from a different religious group among one's five closest friends is associated with greater openness toward other religious groups beyond the friends' (Haji & Lalonde, 2017).

Peace practitioners and scholars alike recognize bringing different groups into direct interaction with each other is not always easy. First, people may live in homogeneous societies or segregated settings. Second, the groups may be unwilling to interact with each other. Third, bringing groups together for an in-person interaction may be costly or impractical. Fourth, particularly in conflict or post-conflict societies, there is the potential for a direct interaction to go badly or for people to have anxiety about interaction. Therefore, recent research has focused on the use of indirect contact as a means of promoting positive attitudes between groups. This chapter provides (1) a description of these methods and how they have been supported by research with children and youth, (2) suggestions for optimizing these methods for practical application, and (3) future directions for research and interventions in this area.

4.2 Methods of Indirect Intergroup Contact

This section describes methods of indirect intergroup contact and evidence of their effectiveness based primarily on research with children and youth. *Indirect contact* is an umbrella term referring to methods of intergroup contact in which the *groups do not come into direct physical interaction* with each other. Three methods will be described, including extended contact, vicarious contact, and imagined contact.

4.2.1 Extended Contact

Extended contact (Wright, Aron, McLaughlin-Volpe, & Ropp, 1997) refers to the *knowledge* that someone from one's own group, the *ingroup*, has a close relationship, such as a friendship, with someone from an *outgroup*, or another group to which one does not belong. Initial research on this form of indirect contact (Wright et al., 1997) found that White American undergraduate students with close friends who had friends from other ethnic groups reported having more favourable attitudes toward those ethnic groups, even when their own friendships with other ethnic groups were controlled for statistically. This correlational research provided evidence for extended contact benefits being associated with participants' knowledge of their real pre-existing friendships, but no causal conclusions could be drawn. Therefore, the researchers also experimentally investigated the effects of extended contact on outgroup attitudes. One of these studies used an established method of creating conflict and rivalry between two groups in a laboratory setting. The groups were then separated and one member from each group was paired together. The pair engaged in a closeness-building task dubbed "the fast friends procedure", gradually revealing more information about themselves by taking turns discussing topics provided by the researchers. Then, each member of the pair was reunited with their original group and was asked to inform their group members of their experience with the member of the other group. Participants' reactions were measured on outcomes such as intergroup discrimination and perceived quality of intergroup relations at various points in the study. This experiment found that extended contact, in the form of *learning* about one's ingroup member having close contact with an outgroup member, led to decreased discrimination (favouring one's own group over the other group) and improved perceptions of the quality of intergroup relations.

Much of the research on extended contact has been carried out with children in Europe. For example, research by Lindsey Cameron and her colleagues in the UK shows that extended contact through story reading can promote more favourable outgroup attitudes. In one study (Cameron & Rutland, 2006), British schoolchildren aged 5–10 took part in a 6-week program that involved reading stories with them about children similar to themselves who had close friendships with a stigmatized outgroup (disabled children). All characters in the stories were presented favourably. After the story reading, there were small group discussions. Participants were encouraged to remember the story content and it was emphasized that the characters were typical members of their groups. These story-related activities occurred once a week for a period of 6 weeks. Participants were interviewed 1 week prior to and 1 week following the intervention, to see whether there were changes in attitudes and intended behaviour toward the outgroup. The results suggested that extended contact through story reading did indeed improve non-disabled children's attitudes and intended behaviour toward disabled children. Extended contact was most effective when the group categories (disabled and non-disabled) and the typicality of the characters (as average members of their groups) were emphasized.

Similar extended contact interventions with storybooks have been used to improve children's attitudes toward refugee children (Cameron & Rutland, 2007, Study 2; Cameron, Rutland, Brown, & Douch, 2006). For example, Cameron et al. (2006) tested the effectiveness of different variations of extended contact on British children's attitudes toward refugees. Schoolchildren belonging to two different age groups (5–8 years and 9–11 years) were exposed to a 6-week intervention involving reading and discussing stories involving friendships between British children and refugee children. Participants were exposed to one of three types of extended contact stories: (1) stories that focused on the *individual characteristics* of the British and refugee children; (2) stories that focused on the fact that the British and refugee children belonged to a *common group*, i.e. students at the same school; or (3) stories that focused on the *group memberships* (British and refugee) *but also* emphasized that the students belonged to a *common group*. Participants in the third group (called the *dual identity* group) reported the most favourable reactions toward refugee children. The study also found that this intervention was more effective for younger children than older children.

Other research has focused on existing popular books, rather than stories that have been specially designed for extended contact interventions. For example, in research conducted with elementary and secondary schoolchildren in Italy and undergraduate students in the UK (Vezzali, Stathi, Giovanni, Capozza, & Trifiletti, 2015), it was found that reading Harry Potter books improved participants' attitudes toward a variety of outgroups, such as immigrants, homosexuals, and refugees. Harry Potter books were selected because the main character, Harry, befriends characters who belong to various stigmatized groups. The researchers argued that fantasy books, such as Harry Potter, in which group memberships are fictional, offer greater potential of generalization of positive attitudes from extended contact to a variety of real-world stigmatized groups.

As another example, Vezzali, Stathi, and Giovanni (2012) conducted a study with Italian adolescents (with an average age of 12), who were given a summer reading list consisting of intercultural books (dealing with positive interaction between characters of different cultures, including a character from a culture similar to that of participants), non-intercultural books, or no summer reading list. One week after the start of the following school year, participants' reactions toward immigrants were assessed. Importantly, this research assessed not only attitudes toward immigrants, but behavioural intentions and specifically the desire to engage in direct contact with immigrants. Results indicated that students in the intercultural reading group reported more favourable views of immigrants, greater closeness to them, and a greater desire for future contact with them.

Extended contact research has also been used in segregated settings where there is a clear history of conflict, such as on the divided island of Cyprus (Husnu, Mertan, & Cicek, 2018). Intergroup violence erupted between Turkish and Greek communities in the 1970s and the result was a divided island with Turkish Cypriots residing in the North and Greek Cypriots in the South. This is a context where researchers have noted the importance of intervention at a young age, before children are exposed to considerable negative information about "the other" in stories, legends, historical accounts, and more. In one study (Husnu et al., 2018; Study 1), Turkish Cypriot children (aged 6 to 12) were assessed for both positive and negative extended contact in the form of stories heard in their families about Greek Cypriots. The researchers found that positive family storytelling about Greek Cypriots predicted children's more favourable attitudes toward them, even after the positive effects of direct contact had been taken into account.

Recently, Vezzali, Hewstone, Capozza, Giovannini, and Wöelfer (2014) published a review of the scholarly literature on extended contact, as well as *vicarious contact* (discussed in the next section), and found that many of those studies statistically controlled for direct contact. Therefore, these forms of indirect contact were associated with more favourable responses toward the outgroup, even when direct contact had been taken into account. Moreover, indirect contact effects were stronger among those with limited direct contact experience. Additionally, indirect contact was associated with more favourable outgroup attitudes in different age groups and even in post-conflict settings. This review also noted that indirect contact effects have been observed on diverse outcomes such as thoughts, feelings, and behaviours toward the other group.

4.2.2 Vicarious Contact

Vicarious contact refers to the *observation* of someone from the ingroup interacting with someone from the outgroup. It makes use of the social learning perspective and involves an ingroup member *modelling* favourable reactions toward the outgroup (Mazziotta, Mummendey, & Wright, 2011; Wright et al., 1997). Participants may observe in-person interactions or do so via some medium, such as a video or storybook.

Vicarious contact has also been used with children in post-conflict settings. In another study in Cyprus (Husnu et al., 2018; Study 2), Turkish Cypriot children (aged 6 to 11) were involved in a 3-week intervention that consisted of 30-minute sessions of having stories read to them about Turkish Cypriot children who had friendships with Greek Cypriot children. Stories were followed by small group discussions and the typicality of the characters was emphasized. This intervention improved Turkish Cypriot children's attitudes, trust, and intended behaviour toward Greek Cypriot children.

In some interventions, including the storybook methods described above, extended contact and vicarious contact can occur in parallel. The core idea of extended contact is the *knowledge* that an ingroup member has a positive relationship with an outgroup member (Wright et al., 1997). Vicarious contact goes a step beyond mere knowledge, involves the *observational learning* from an ingroup member interacting with an outgroup member, and can in some instances co-occur with extended contact. For example, anxiety may be reduced via observation of a cross-group friendship that may be afforded through extended contact. Additionally, observation of a friendly interaction between an ingroup and outgroup member provides information (knowledge) that can change negative outgroup stereotypes. Importantly, however, extended contact can occur without vicarious contact as a person may be aware of a friend's friendship with an outgroup member without having had the opportunity to observe an interaction between them.

4.2.2.1 Parasocial Contact

One subtype of vicarious contact is exposure to an outgroup member through mass media, such as television or radio, and this has sometimes been referred to as *parasocial contact*. Researchers have investigated the effects of vicarious contact through video on attitudes toward the outgroup and willingness to engage in future interactions with them (Mazziotta et al., 2011). In one study, German young adults (aged 18 to 28) were exposed to 2 video clips that showed friendly interactions between a German student and a Chinese student (parasocial contact group) or 2 video clips that showed friendly interaction between two German students (control group). Both groups also saw a neutral video clip about campus library facilities. The parasocial contact group reported more favourable attitudes and feelings about Chinese people, greater willingness to interact with them, more positive future expectations, and less uncertainty about such interactions. In a follow-up study, the researchers demonstrated that their effects were not due to mere exposure to the outgroup. Only video exposure to intergroup contact with a Chinese student, and not mere video exposure to a Chinese student, produced the more favourable reactions toward Chinese people.

In this research, it was also demonstrated that the parasocial contact made use of two different forms of social learning: (1) Observational knowledge about how to behave appropriately with the outgroup and (2) Positive expectations regarding future interactions with the outgroup (*self-efficacy expectancy*). Given that interaction with a different group can be anxiety-provoking, optimistic expectations regarding direct contact with the outgroup could be learned through parasocial contact. They suggested that this was particularly the case when the role models that were being observed were similar to participants being exposed to the intervention.

4.2.2.2 Parasocial Exposure Without Cross-Group Interaction

Intervention studies with youth have found that vicarious contact with a *positive intergroup interaction* may be essential to improving outgroup attitudes in a parasocial intervention. One study investigated the effects of parasocial contact with two 13-year-old gay male characters on LGBTQ attitudes among youth aged 13 to 21 (Gillig & Murphy, 2016). Participants were exposed to a 9-minute video about the budding romance between the characters or did not view the video and then completed an attitude questionnaire. Whereas the parasocial exposure to gay youth improved

LGBTQ attitudes among LGBTQ youth, it actually worsened attitudes among heterosexual youth. Importantly, *observation of a cross-group friendly interaction*, rather than parasocial exposure to the outgroup, may be the essence of vicarious contact intervention.

4.2.3 Imagined Contact

Imagined contact refers to the mental simulation of an interaction with an outgroup member (Turner, Crisp, & Lambert, 2007). Some initial research in this area involved undergraduate students in the UK. In one study, heterosexual male participants aged 19 to 25 imagined engaging in a conversation with a gay man that they had met on a train or spent the same amount of time imagining a nature hike (Turner et al., 2007; Experiment 3). Results indicated that those who imagined the interaction with the gay man had more positive attitudes toward homosexuals than those who imagined the nature hike. Subsequent research demonstrated that in order to optimize effects of imagined contact intervention, an imagined interaction needs to be positive and mental simulation of the event should be encouraged (Crisp, Stathi, Turner, & Husnu, 2009). Additionally, a practical teaching and learning guide related to imagined contact was provided by Stathi and Crisp (2009).

There is evidence of imagined contact's effects on young people's willingness to interact with "the other". For example, research from the UK (Turner, West, & Christie, 2013) found that high school students who imagined an interaction with an asylum seeker reported greater intentions to interact with asylum seekers. Another study by the same authors (Turner et al., 2013) also found that undergraduate students who imagined an interaction with a gay person reported a stronger intention to interact with gay people and greater trust and less anxiety about interacting with the other group. Other research in the UK context involved a 3-week intervention with schoolchildren (Stathi, Cameron, Hartley, & Bradford, 2014). White elementary schoolchildren who imagined an interaction with an Asian child on a weekly basis were compared to another group who did not engage in this activity over the same period. Again, imagined contact resulted in greater willingness to interact with the other group, as well as greater perceived similarity to them.

A meta-analysis of 71 studies on imagined contact (Miles & Crisp, 2014) confirmed that imagined contact can promote more favourable responses toward an outgroup and elaboration is an important factor in imagined contact – the more detail in which participants imagined the interaction, the greater the positive effects of imagined contact. A striking finding of the meta-analysis was that although imagined contact has been effective in promoting more favourable intergroup attitudes in adults and in children, effects of these interventions are strongest with children. This may be due to the importance of imagery in children's day-to-day lives and their potentially greater facility with imagination tasks.

Furthermore, this meta-analysis confirmed that imagined contact improved attitudes, emotions, intended behaviour, and actual behaviour toward the outgroup.

Interestingly, the effect on intended behaviour was greater than the effect on attitudes. Although the effect on actual behaviour was similar to that on intended behaviour, fewer studies existed on actual behaviour. Therefore, imagined contact has the potential for improving intended and actual behaviour toward other groups, not just improving attitudes. This is encouraging, as it's often behaviour that we are actually trying to change.

Imagined contact can be used as practice or prior preparation for actual contact as research shows that imagined contact reduces anxiety about interacting with the other group. Use of imagination for anxiety reduction has long been used in clinical settings (e.g., for treating phobias), and imagination can also be used outside the clinic for intervening prejudice toward those of other cultural backgrounds (Birtel & Crisp, 2012).

4.3 Optimizing Methods for Practical Application

As described above, there is considerable evidence for the effectiveness of indirect contact in improving attitudes toward the other. Indeed, research on real-world interventions found that there was no significant difference in effect sizes of direct and indirect contact interventions (Lemmer & Wagner, 2015), though imagined contact was not included in this analysis. Meta-analyses suggest the effect size observed is a modest medium for real-word indirect contact interventions ($\mu_\theta = 0.28$; Lemmer & Wagner, 2015) and for imagined contact ($d+ = 0.35$; Miles & Crisp, 2014). There are various factors that should be considered to optimize these effects.

It is important to note that indirect contact interventions are *particularly effective among those who have had little previous contact with the outgroup*. For example, in our research (Haji & Noguchi, 2017), we found that imagined contact promoted more favourable attitudes toward East Asians among those who did not have an East Asian person among their five closest friends. Similarly, in other research (Haji, McKeown, & Stathi, 2017) that evaluated another variation of imagined contact (known as imagined contact with I-sharing, which is detailed below), we found that imagined contact with a Muslim person promoted more favourable attitudes toward Muslims among those who had not had previous contact with Muslims. Indeed, the greater effectiveness of indirect contact among those with limited direct contact experience has been noted in reviews of the literature (e.g. Vezzali et al., 2014). In a related vein, meta-analytic research has found that indirect contact is more effective in promoting favourable outgroup attitudes among majority group members, rather than among minority group members (Lemmer & Wagner, 2015). It has been suggested that one reason for this is that minority group members have more contact experience with the majority, rather than vice versa.

Regardless of methods of contact (i.e. imagined, vicarious, or parasocial), exposing children and youth to *cross-group friendship* (positive interaction of ingroup members and outgroup members) is important for enhancing effectiveness of indirect contact interventions (e.g. Mazziotta et al., 2011; Miles & Crisp, 2014; Vezzali et al., 2014).

For extended and vicarious contact, emphasizing group memberships, or making them salient, is important to augment the influence of these forms of indirect contact on outgroup attitudes (Cameron & Rutland, 2006; Vezzali et al., 2014; Wright et al., 1997).

One theme that appears to be pervasive with indirect contact interventions with children is *repeated exposure*. Imagined contact and vicarious contact interventions described above typically took place over a period of 3 weeks (e.g. Husnu et al., 2018; Turner et al., 2013) and one of the extended contact interventions took place over a period of 6 weeks (Cameron & Rutland, 2006). Whereas laboratory studies have detected indirect contact effects in a single session, it is likely the case that repeated exposure to indirect contact produces stronger or more enduring effects on attitudes and behaviour toward the outgroup. Indeed, researchers have argued that multiple sessions over a period of time may be required for lasting attitude change (e.g. Cameron & Rutland, 2006). Based on past work, our recommendation is that interventions with children take place in multiple sessions over a period of 3 weeks or more.

The meta-analysis of imagined contact research suggests that *greater elaboration of the imagined interaction* can enhance its effectiveness (Miles & Crisp, 2014). In particular, writing about the imagined interaction strengthens the effects of the intervention. For maximal effectiveness, participants need to mentally simulate an interaction, including conversations and feelings by imagining the positive traits of an outgroup member. Additionally, elaborating on the imagined interaction, such as in a writing task, can enhance the effect (Husnu & Crisp, 2010). Imagined contact can be easily applied in education systems through storytelling or role-playing and can be used as the first step of prejudice intervention (Stathi & Crisp, 2008).

Furthermore, *perspective-taking*, which refers to imagining the same scenario from different perspectives, has been explored. Prejudice-reduction effects were compared when participants imagined a positive interaction with an elderly person from a first-person perspective (through one's own eyes) or from a third-person perspective (through the eyes of an observer). The results suggested that, compared to a first-person perspective, a third-person perspective was more effective in producing the future intention of actual contact with the elderly (Crisp & Husnu, 2011).

In extended and vicarious contact interventions, research also suggests that *identification with the character* who is engaging in intergroup contact augments the effects. For example, in the research with the Harry Potter books intervention, identification with the main character, Harry, resulted in more favourable views of the real-world stigmatized groups (Vezzali et al., 2015).

Thus, a number of studies have evaluated how to optimize indirect contact effects, particularly so that they can be used in interventions in applied settings. The future directions suggested below include other possibilities for optimizing interventions as well as relatively under-explored contexts for evaluating the effectiveness of indirect contact in promoting more favourable views of the other.

4.4 Future Directions

Preliminary research suggests some promising avenues for future work on indirect contact. Some of this research has focused on how to optimize imagined contact for intervention in real-world settings to change reactions toward those who are different. One example comes from our research in Canada in which we investigated a variation of imagined contact that involved non-Asian youth (college and university students, aged approximately 18–22) imagining a close friend's friendly interaction with an East Asian person, *imagined vicarious contact* (Haji & Noguchi, 2017). This was compared to a standard imagined contact condition (i.e. imagining one's own interaction with an East Asian person) and a neutral control condition (imagining an outdoor scene). We were interested in testing the effectiveness of imagined vicarious contact in promoting more favourable outgroup attitudes, because there has been a call for further research on how to optimize indirect contact interventions and because we believed that imagining a friend's positive interaction with an outgroup member may be less anxiety-provoking for some than imagining one's own interaction. Indeed, we found that imagined vicarious contact had a stronger prejudice-reducing effect on people with high Social Dominance Orientation (SDO; Pratto, Sidanius, Stallworth, & Malle, 1994), i.e. a preference for their ingroup to have higher social status than other groups. Specifically, the result suggested that imagined contact can improve *implicit attitudes* of people high in SDO. Implicit attitudes are measured through the strength (speed) of associations with positive and negative words, rather than self-report questionnaires, and therefore can tap attitudes that people are unwilling to report (or unconscious attitudes that they are unaware they have). Those high in SDO may experience a change in their attitudes but may be unwilling to report this, possibly due to the desire to maintain their own group's social advantage. And if this is the case, imagined contact has particular relevance as a first step toward change in intergroup attitudes of those high in SDO who may be particularly resistant to change.

Other research investigating possible ways of optimizing imagined contact for intervention has used imagined I-sharing (Haji et al., 2017). In this research, we have investigated how imagining a shared experience (e.g. laughing at the same moment) with an outgroup member can be a particularly potent form of imagined contact. We have conducted studies with university students in Canada, the UK, and the Netherlands and have found that this variation of imagined contact has been particularly effective in promoting favourable attitudes toward a stigmatized outgroup (Muslims), at least among certain groups of people (e.g. those with no direct contact with the outgroup).

In addition to simply asking people about their attitudes and behaviour, as noted above, some research on indirect contact has assessed implicit attitudes – attitudes that people are unwilling to report due to concerns about portraying oneself in a positive light, or unable to report as they may be unaware that they have negative associations about certain groups. One widely used measure of implicit attitudes, the Implicit Associations Test (IAT; Greenwald, McGee, & Schwartz, 1998), assesses reaction times to associations between groups and positive and negative words, in order to assess negative automatic associations with certain groups. Studies that have investigated the effects of imagined contact on implicit attitudes assessed with the IAT (e.g. Haji & Noguchi, 2017; Turner & Crisp, 2010) suggest that imagined contact can improve these automatic associations that people have with certain groups.

It has been noted that research on indirect contact effects on actual behaviour is limited (Miles & Crisp, 2014). Similarly, most of the research on extended and vicarious contact described above looked at outcomes of attitudes and behaviour intentions. Therefore, the dearth of research evaluating actual behaviour seems to apply to indirect contact research more generally and suggests a very important avenue for future research.

Another limitation is that research to date has not typically investigated the lasting effects of indirect contact interventions beyond more than a few months (Lemmer & Wagner, 2015). Although there is evidence of the lasting impact of indirect contact a month after end of intervention, we know little about whether effects last for a year or more (Lemmer & Wagner, 2015).

Much of the research on indirect contact, particularly imagined contact, has involved laboratory research. Intervention research in educational settings is common for extended and vicarious contact, but interventions have often been conducted in multicultural societies that did not have a recent history of intergroup conflict or segregation. In a related vein, the review by Vezzali et al. (2014) noted that more research was needed on real-world interventions involving indirect contact in naturalistic settings. That being said, a meta-analysis of real-world indirect contact interventions (excluding imagined contact) has been conducted (Lemmer & Wagner, 2015) and has found that these interventions do work in the real world, including in post-conflict settings.

Among the future directions that Vezzali et al. (2014) suggested was to consider how the type of relationship between the participant and the ingroup member in the indirect interaction influenced extended and vicarious conflict effects. They also suggested that it would be fruitful to compare the forms of indirect contact in terms of their relative effectiveness. Indeed, they suggested that different forms of indirect contact may reduce outgroup prejudice via different mechanisms (i.e. changing thoughts about the outgroup vs. decreasing anxiety about interacting with the outgroup). Furthermore, they called for additional research on indirect contact through media. As media-based interventions hold particular promise for practical application, this is an area where we look forward to seeing more research.

4.5 Conclusion

Changing prejudiced attitudes represents a step toward decreasing structural violence. And promoting more favourable views of the other among children and youth can help to impact structural violence now and in the future. Taken together, the studies described in this chapter suggest that there is considerable potential for indirect contact to improve intergroup attitudes among children and youth living in diverse societies. On the whole, interventions involving indirect contact are low cost and relatively easy to implement. In some cases, they have been shown to be particularly effective among children. Moreover, it is encouraging that research has not only found effects on attitudes, but also on intended behaviour and, through more rarely studied, actual behaviour toward those belonging to other groups. Indeed, it might be the case that younger generations' direct and indirect contact experiences influence adults' attitudes and behaviours, through the increase in children's cross-group friendships and adults' consequent indirect and direct contact experiences with outgroup children, parents, and teachers. Indirect contact may increase not only the willingness for direct contact, but the likelihood of direct contact.

The first author, who grew up in the multicultural city of Toronto, Canada, recalls a high school social studies assignment in which she had an intercultural dinner exchange with another student in the class. She and the other student took turns going to each other's house for dinner to learn about each other's culture and traditions. The exchange was informative for the students and the parents and dispelled some misconceptions about the cultures. Whereas intercultural exchanges may be beneficial in promoting acceptance or friendship, the research described here suggests that even reading or watching videos about such intercultural exchanges have the potential to promote more positive views of the other. For children and youth living in settings that are less culturally diverse, infrequent opportunities for direct intergroup contact mean that there is actually greater potential for the effectiveness of indirect contact interventions. This highlights the potential power of indirect contact as a means for promoting peace in diverse and less diverse settings.

References

Allport, G. W. (1954). *The nature of prejudice*. Oxford, UK: Addison-Wesley Publishing Company.

Birtel, M. D., & Crisp, R. J. (2012). "Treating" prejudice an exposure-therapy approach to reducing negative reactions toward stigmatised groups. *Psychological Science, 23*(11), 1379–1386. https://doi.org/10.1177/0956797612443838

Cameron, L., & Rutland, A. (2006). Extended contact through story reading in school: Reducing children's prejudice toward the disabled. *Journal of Social Issues, 62*(3), 469–488. https://doi.org/10.1111/j.1540-4560.2006.00469.x

Cameron, L., & Rutland, A. (2007). Promoting children's positive intergroup attitudes towards stigmatized groups: Extended contact and multiple classification skills training. *International Journal of Behavioural Development, 31*(5), 454–466. https://doi.org/10.1177/0165025407081474

Cameron, L., Rutland, A., Brown, R., & Douch, R. (2006). Changing children's intergroup attitudes toward refugees: Testing different models of extended contact. *Child Development, 77*(5), 1208–1219. https://doi.org/10.1111/j.1467-8624.2006.00929.x

Christie, D. J., Wagner, R. V., & Winter, D. A. (Eds.). (2001). *Peace, conflict, and violence: Peace psychology for the 21st century*. Englewood Cliffs, NJ: Prentice-Hall.

Crisp, R. J., & Husnu, S. (2011). Attributional processes underlying imagined contact effects. *Group Processes & Intergroup Relations, 14*(2), 275–287. https://doi.org/10.1177/1368430210390721

Crisp, R. J., Stathi, S., Turner, R. N., & Husnu, S. (2009). Imagined intergroup contact: Theory, paradigm and practice. *Social and Personality Psychology Compass, 3*(1), 1–18. https://doi.org/10.1111/j.1751-9004.2008.00155.x

Gillig, T. K., & Murphy, S. T. (2016). Fostering support for LGBTQ youth? The effects of a gay adolescent media portrayal on young viewers. *International Journal of Communication, 10*, 3838–3850. 1932–8036/20160005.

Greenwald, A. G., McGee, D. E., & Schwartz, J. L. K. (1998). Measuring individual differences in implicit cognition: The implicit association test. *Journal of Personality and Social Psychology, 74*(6), 1464–1480. https://doi.org/10.1037/0022-3514.85.2.19710

Haji, R., & Lalonde, R. N. (2017). If a close friend is from another religion, are you more open to other faiths? In M. Seedat, S. Suffla, & D. Christie (Eds.), *Enlarging the scope of peace psychology: African and world-regional contributions*. New York, NY: Springer.

Haji, R., McKeown, S., & Stathi, S. (2017, June). *Turning a frown upside down: Imagining a shared laugh increases implicit and explicit liking*. Paper presented at the 1st international symposium on intergroup communication, Thessaloniki, Greece.

Haji, R., & Noguchi, H. (2017, May). *Social dominance and cross-group friendship: Moderators of imagined contact on implicit views of an ethnic outgroup*. Paper presented at the Biennial Symposium on the Contributions of Psychology to Peace, Rome & Florence, Italy.

Husnu, S., & Crisp, R. J. (2010). Elaboration enhances the imagined contact effect. *Journal of Experimental Social Psychology, 46*(6), 943–950. https://doi.org/10.1016/j.jesp.2010.05.014

Husnu, S., Mertan, B., & Cicek, O. (2018). Reducing Turkish Cypriot children's prejudice toward Greek Cypriot: Vicarious and extended intergroup contact through storytelling. *Group Processes & Intergroup Relations, 21*(1), 178–192. https://doi.org/10.1177/1368430216656469

Kang, S. K., & Inzlicht, M. (2012). Stigma building blocks: How instruction and experience teach children about rejection by outgroups. *Personality and Social Psychology Bulletin, 38*, 357–369. https://doi.org/10.1177/0146167211426729

Lemmer, G., & Wagner, U. (2015). Can we really reduce ethnic prejudice outside the lab? A meta-analysis of direct and indirect contact interventions. *European Journal of Social Psychology, 45*, 152–168. https://doi.org/10.1002/ejsp.2079

Mazziotta, A., Mummendey, A., & Wright, C. S. (2011). Vicarious intergroup contact effects: Applying social-cognitive theory to intergroup contact research. *Group Processes and Intergroup Relations, 14*(2), 255–274. https://doi.org/10.1177/1368430210390533

Miles, E., & Crisp, R. J. (2014). A meta-analytic test of the imagined contact hypothesis. *Group Processes & Intergroup Relations, 17*(1), 3–26. https://doi.org/10.1177/1368430213510573

Pettigrew, T. F. (2009). Secondary transfer effect of contact: Do intergroup contact effects spread to noncontacted outgroups? *Social Psychology, 40*, 55–65. https://doi.org/10.1027/1864-9335.40.2.55

Pettigrew, T. F., & Tropp, L. R. (2006). A meta-analytic test of intergroup contact theory. *Journal of Personality and Social Psychology, 90*(5), 751–783. https://doi.org/10.1037/0022-3514.90.5.751

Pew Research Centre. (2018, May 29). *Being Christian in Western Europe*. Retrieved from: http://www.pewforum.org/2018/05/29/nationalism-immigration-and-minorities/

Pratto, F., Sidanius, J., Stallworth, L. M., & Malle, B. F. (1994). Social dominance orientation: A personality variable predicting social and political attitudes. *Journal of Personality and Social Psychology, 67*(4), 41–763. https://doi.org/10.1037/0022-3514.67.4.741

Stathi, S., & Crisp, R. J. (2008). Imagining intergroup contact promotes projection to outgroups. *Journal of Experimental Social Psychology, 44*(4), 943–957. https://doi.org/10.1016/j.jesp.2008.02.003

Stathi, S., & Crisp, R. J. (2009). Teaching and learning guide for: Imagined contact: Theory, paradigm, and practice. *Social and Personality Psychology Compass, 3*, 1129–1134. https://doi.org/10.1111/j.1751-9004.2009.00230.x

Stathi, S., Cameron, L., Hartley, B., & Bradford, S. (2014). Imagined contact as a prejudice-reduction intervention in schools: The underlying role of similarity and attitudes. *Journal of Applied Social Psychology, 44*, 536–546. https://doi.org/10.1111/jasp.12245

Turner, R. N., & Crisp, R. J. (2010). Imagining intergroup contact reduces implicit prejudice. *British Journal of Social Psychology, 49*(1), 129–142. https://doi.org/10.1348/014466609X419901

Turner, R. N., Crisp, R. J., & Lambert, E. (2007). Imagining intergroup contact can improve intergroup attitudes. *Group Processes and Intergroup Relations, 10*(4), 427–441. https://doi.org/10.1177/1368430207081533

Turner, R. N., West, K., & Christie, Z. (2013). Out- group trust, intergroup anxiety, and out-group attitude as mediators of the effect of imagined intergroup contact on intergroup behavioral tendencies. *Journal of Applied Social Psychology, 43*, E196–E205. https://doi.org/10.1111/jasp.12019

UNHCR. (2018). *Figures at a Glance: Statistical Yearbooks*. Retrieved from: http://www.unhcr.org/figures-at-a-glance.html

Vezzali, L., Hewstone, M., Capozza, D., Giovannini, D., & Wöelfer, R. (2014). Improving intergroup relations with extended and vicarious forms of indirect contact. *European Review of Social Psychology, 25*, 314–389. https://doi.org/10.1080/10463283.2014.982948

Vezzali, L., Stathi, S., & Giovannini, D. (2012). Indirect contact through book reading: Improving adolescents' attitudes and behavioural interventions toward immigrants. *Psychology in the Schools, 49*(2), 148–162. https://doi.org/10.1002/pits.20621

Vezzali, L., Stathi, S., Giovannini, D., Capozza, D., & Trifiletti, E. (2015). The greatest magic of Harry Potter: Reducing prejudice. *Journal of Applied Social Psychology, 45*(2), 105–121. https://doi.org/10.1111/jasp.12279

Wright, S. C., Aron, A., McLaughlin-Volpe, T., & Ropp, S. A. (1997). The extended contact effect: Knowledge of cross-group friendships and prejudice. *Journal of Personality and Social Psychology, 73*(1), 73–90. https://doi.org/10.1037/0022-3514.73.1.73

Chapter 5
Promoting Prosocial Behavior Toward Refugees: Exploring the Empathy-Attitude-Action Model in Middle Childhood

Catherine Glen, Laura K. Taylor, and Jocelyn B. Dautel

5.1 Introduction

There are currently more than twenty-two million refugees in the world, over half of whom are school-aged children (UNHCR, 2018). Integrating these children into their new communities can be a challenging process that carries significant implications for both their personal well-being (Fazel, Reed, Panter-Brick, & Stein, 2012) and the establishment of long-term harmonious intergroup relationships (Esses, Hamilton, & Gaucher, 2017). Consequently, it is imperative that refugees enter welcoming and supportive environments. Children resettled in high-income countries tend to receive support that fulfills their basic material needs; however, there is a serious lack of provision to sustain their social-emotional well-being. One of the most important factors in promoting their social-emotional well-being is establishing supportive relationships with host-society children (Fazel, 2015). Within the broader context of peace psychology, positive intergroup relations in childhood are considered to be fundamental in the establishment of long-term peace (Christie, 2006). Despite this fact, investment in programs which prepare host-society children to engage meaningfully with their new peers is largely lacking. Although there is a widespread assumption that enhancing children's intergroup empathy could be an effective intervention strategy for promoting positive intergroup relations (Aboud & Levy, 2000; Nesdale, Griffith, Durkin, & Maass, 2005), this claim is largely unsubstantiated. This chapter aims to address this claim by outlining the empathy-attitudes-action model (Batson, Chang, Orr, & Rowland, 2002) and demonstrating

C. Glen (✉) · J. B. Dautel
Queen's University Belfast, Belfast, UK
e-mail: cglen01@qub.ac.uk

L. K. Taylor
Queen's University Belfast, Belfast, UK

University College Dublin, Dublin, Ireland

N. Balvin, D. J. Christie (eds.), *Children and Peace*, Peace Psychology Book Series, https://doi.org/10.1007/978-3-030-22176-8_5

how it can be applied through a brief pilot study in Northern Ireland that focuses on helping recently arrived refugees in middle childhood. The chapter concludes with recommendations for future research and advocates for the implementation of interventions that prepare children to engage meaningfully with incoming refugees.

5.2 Children as Social Actors and Peacebuilders

Traditionally, little emphasis has been placed on the role that children can play in fostering positive and long-lasting intergroup relations. This is partly due to previous perceptions of children as either troublemakers, victims, or passive bystanders (Cummings, Merrilees, Taylor, & Mondi, 2017). This conceptual trap overlooks the role that children can play in building peace (for exception, see McKeown & Taylor, 2017; Taylor & McKeown, 2017; Taylor et al., 2018) and the reality that the relationships built during childhood serve as the building blocks for future generations (Abrams & Killen, 2014). Reflecting these truths, there has been a call to recognize children's participation as social actors or individuals who have agency and influence (IANYD, 2016; UNICEF, 1989). An increasing body of work has started to examine factors that promote young people's cooperation between groups in contexts where intergroup relations remain tense (McEvoy-Levy, 2006; Taylor et al., 2014). Encouraging children to engage in positive behaviors across group lines may prove particularly effective in reducing forms of episodic violence such as bullying or even in consolidating long-term peace.

Participation also requires that children have an effective voice in their own lives and in the community around them. There is a paucity of research that focuses on the perspective of refugee children themselves; however, existing research finds that refugee children place a high level of importance on their peer relations. Focus groups with newcomer pupils (including refugees) in Northern Ireland primary schools found that, before resettling, children's top concern was their ability to make friends in school (Kernaghan, 2015). In Britain, refugee and asylum-seeking pupils recommended schools implement preparatory programs which educate host-society children on potential refugee experiences prior to the arrival of refugee students (Fazel, 2015). As part of the move toward enhancing children's agency, it is necessary to explore the underlying processes involved in children's development of positive attitudes and prosocial behaviors toward refugees.

5.3 Refugees as an Out-Group

A refugee is "someone who has been forced to flee his or her country because of persecution, war, or violence" (UNHCR, 2018, para. 1). After displacement, many refugees flee to neighboring countries, most commonly in refugee camps or urban settings. However, others resettle in a high-income country where the ethnic, religious, and cultural composition of the majority of inhabitants is usually vastly different from their own. Within these communities, they are an ethic out-group, that is, someone belonging to a different ethnic group (Schulz & Taylor, 2018). Moreover, refugees constitute a specific subset of the immigrant population who may be subject to particular stigmatizations, negative perceptions, or mixed emotional responses. These categorizations are critical when considering the attitudes and behaviors of host-society children toward refugees.

Ethnicity is a salient characteristic which influences children's development of out-group attitudes (Nesdale et al., 2005). By the age of 6 years old, children from the ethnically dominant group can recognize their ethnic group and may hold more positive in-group attitudes compared to other groups (Aboud, 1988). Children also demonstrate intergroup biases in their empathy and prosocial behavior toward others based upon group membership (Abrams, Van de Vyver, Pelletier, & Cameron, 2015). By the age of 7, these intergroup biases may turn to explicit prejudice and negative out-group-directed behaviors (Levy & Killen, 2008). As children enter into middle childhood, their attitudes toward ethnic groups become more nuanced and are influenced by an array of factors such as empathy, perception of out-group threat, and group norms (Nesdale et al., 2005). Given the complexity of attitude formation, it is important to consider the context in which it occurs. However, the majority of research concerning children's attitude formation toward ethnic out-groups is conducted within the context of more traditional majority/minority relations (e.g., White majority children and Black minority children in the United States). As a consequence, factors that lead to the development of positive attitudes and behaviors toward more novel out-groups, and specifically those which may be stigmatized or viewed as a threat by the broader society, are not well understood.

Children's attitudes toward ethnic out-group members are substantially shaped by the cultural contexts in which they occur (Pauker, Williams, & Steele, 2016). Thus, it is important to consider how refugees constitute a specific subset of the ethnic minority population and often face negative or mixed perceptions from the wider society. Attitudes toward refugees worldwide are worsening, with polling revealing that the majority of European adults hold negative views toward immigration (Dempster & Hargrave, 2017). While adults are more accepting of refugees than those classified as immigrants, compassion for refugees is often accompanied by anxiety (Dempster & Hargrave, 2017). In European countries, the majority of adults report feeling that refugees pose a threat to national security and experience anxiety over real world concerns when accepting refugees into their country (Wike, Stokes, & Simmons, 2016). Such "threat narratives" in the wider community shape children's attitudes toward refugees. Though the existence of intergroup biases and prejudice in childhood is well established, more specific understanding about how to promote positive out-group attitudes and behaviors toward refugees is sparse.

5.4 Previous Interventions

To date, two prominent studies have evaluated interventions targeted at improving attitudes and behaviors toward refugees. Cameron, Rutland, Brown, and Douch (2006) assessed the effectiveness of extended contact interventions in improving children's attitudes toward refugees and intended behaviors toward (hypothetical) refugee children (e.g., how much they would like to play with a refugee child or invite him/her to their house). Results demonstrated that extended contact was an effective intervention in improving attitudes toward refugees, but did not have a significant impact on children's behavioral intentions toward refugees. Thus, while benefits were seen for attitudes, those changes were not coupled with meaningful changes in behavior. Nesdale et al. (2005) note that "given that practical reconciliation between ethnic groups demands changes in behavior (e.g., a preparedness to interact, cooperate and share), there is a need for research that addresses the linkage between children's ethnic attitudes and behavior, in the context of their empathy toward ethnic minority group members" (p. 635).

Turner and Brown (2008) evaluated "Friendship Project," a school-based intervention in the UK designed to improve children's (9–11 years old) attitudes toward refugees by combining multicultural curricula, anti-racist interventions, and an empathy-based component. In the empathy-based component, children were prompted to imagine children (similar to themselves) in situations similar to those faced by refugees. Children were then prompted to think about how they may feel in this situation and how refugees might feel. Results found that the program was effective in improving children's short-term attitudes, but not long-term attitudes, and that it had no effect on children's empathy toward refugees. Though this study evaluated an existing program aimed at promoting children's empathy toward refugees, it is important to note that the empathy component used was impersonal, focused on perspective taking, and used hypothetical circumstances. Furthermore, this study did not access children's behavioral intentions toward refugees and thus did not address the link between attitudes and behaviors within the context of empathy.

Interventions aimed at reducing prejudice toward more traditional ethnic minorities tend to utilize either multicultural curriculums or anti-racist programs. These programs are based on the assumption that prejudice stems from ignorance or misinformation regarding an out-group and providing correct information will reduce prejudice. However, such programs are not widely effective. A large meta-analysis examining 122 intervention-comparisons of programs around the world designed to reduce prejudice or promote positive intergroup attitudes in children and adolescents found only low to moderate intervention effects (Beelmann & Heinemann, 2014). Interventions that promoted empathy through contact and social-cognitive programs, however, were the most effective in promoting positive intergroup attitudes. Moreover, recent studies have found that the positive effects of such contact interventions are mediated by intergroup empathy (Vezzali, Hewstone, Capozza, Trifiletti, & Di Bernardo, 2017), suggesting that promoting empathy may bolster the effects of such interventions. Thus, exploring and evaluating interventions specifically aimed at promoting children's empathy toward refugees is a logical next step. Given the lack of research, testing models shown to be successful in adults could offer insight into how to promote positive attitudes and prosocial behaviors among children.

5.5 Empathy-Attitudes-Action Model

The Empathy-Attitude-Action model (EAA) was developed to describe how empathy can promote prosocial behaviors across group lines (Batson et al., 2002). Empathy, defined as an "other-oriented emotional response congruent with the perceived welfare of another" (Batson et al., 2002, p. 1856), is an important motivator for prosocial behaviors (Batson, 2010). The EAA model asserts that the link between empathy and prosocial behavior is not a direct link, but is instead mediated by out-group attitudes. That is, inducing empathy toward one member of a stigmatized out-group (i.e., the empathy target) can improve attitudes toward that group to which that person belongs and, in turn, promotes prosocial behavior toward that group as a whole. A three-step process is described whereby (a) increasing empathy toward one member of an out-group may lead to an increased valuing of the individual's welfare, (b) this increased valuing is reflected through positive attitudes toward the out-group as a whole (Batson, Chang, Orr, & Rowland, 2002), and (c) these positive attitudes lead to an increase in motivation to help other members of that particular out-group, given that the need is salient to their group membership (Batson et al., 2002).

Evidence for a robust empathy-attitude-action model has been demonstrated in adult populations using a variety of stigmatized groups, such as individuals with AIDS, experiencing homelessness, or convicted of murder (Batson et al., 1997). Attitude change resulting from empathy induction appears to have relatively long-lasting effects, with attitude improvements being evident at even one-to-two weeks after the empathy induction. These positive attitudes, in turn, promote a willingness to engage in prosocial behaviors toward other members of that group. For example, empathy induced by listening to the story of an individual addicted to heroin led to improved attitudes toward those struggling with substance abuse and, in turn, led to participants allocating resources to help those struggling with substance abuse (Batson et al., 2002). A simplified version of the EAA mediation model is depicted in Fig. 5.1.

5.5.1 *Empathy*

While there are many conceptualizations of empathy, Batson's definition refers to empathy as a state. That is, empathy which is experienced to varying degrees depending upon the specific situation. This is in contrast to trait empathy, which is

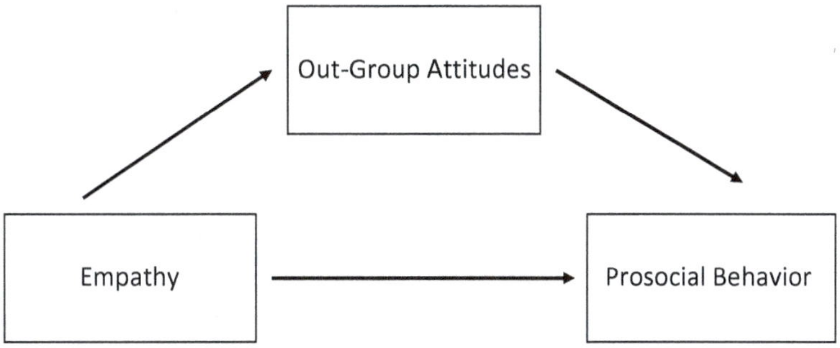

Fig. 5.1 EAA model

considered a more stable personality variable in which individuals differ in their propensity to empathize with others (Davis, 1983). State-based empathetic responses are broadly thought to have two dimensions: cognitive and emotional, or affective. Affective empathy is a subjective state that is often thought to be the result of emotional cognition, or perspective taking (Batson et al., 1997). For example, listening to the story of an out-group member first prompts cognitive empathy by allowing the listener to put him/herself in that person's position (i.e., take the perspective of that person). This cognitive process then creates an affective empathetic response in the listener. This affective empathetic response then leads the listener to become more concerned with the welfare of the out-group member.

In this assertion, cognitive awareness of another's emotional state is necessary before other-oriented and parallel emotional responses can occur. This cognitive skill emerges around the age of five and becomes more advanced as children develop. By middle childhood, occurring between the ages of seven to eleven, children display more sophisticated forms of empathy, which impact their interpersonal prosocial behaviors (Abrams et al., 2015; Eisenberg, Eggum, & Di Giunta, 2010). By focusing on middle childhood, a period when children display advanced forms of empathy coupled with more nuanced understandings of group dynamics, we now explore each pathway of the empathy-attitude-action model among children.

5.5.2 *Empathy and Prosocial Behaviors*

Prosocial behavior can be defined as a "voluntary behavior intended to benefit another" (Eisenberg et al., 2010, p.146) and is a superordinate category which includes behaviors such as sharing of resources, helping, and comforting (Schroeder & Graziana, 2015). Decades of research has identified empathy as a primary driving force for prosocial behavior, and increasing or inducing empathy has been linked to increased prosocial behavior across the lifespan (Eisenberg et al., 2010). For example, inducing empathy in children through the use of videos that portray others in need has been shown to increase children's willingness to share resources (Williams,

Driscoll, & Moore, 2014). Yet, this research has traditionally been conducted in the interpersonal domain, which does not consider the role of group boundaries. Given that group membership may shape empathetic responses, there is a need to evaluate these processes within the intergroup domain (Sierksma & Thijs, 2017).

Previous research by Abrams et al. (2015) found that when 5- to 10-year-old children were placed into minimal groups, those with higher levels of trait empathy were more willing to engage in out-group-directed prosocial behaviors. It follows that if trait empathy is predictive of out-group prosociality, increasing intergroup empathy might also promote prosocial behavior across group lines. In support of this assumption, Sierksma, Thijs, and Verkuyten (2015) found that in-group biases in children's helping intentions could be overcome by inducing empathetic understanding. In an experimental vignette, 8- to 13-year-old children were read a story about a child who was either part of their imagined friend group (an in-group member) or not (an out-group member). In the empathy induction condition, children where prompted to take the perspective of the child in need. Children in the no-empathy condition listened to the same story, but were not prompted to take the perspective of the child in need. Children in the no-empathy condition gave more resources to the in-group member and fewer resources to the out-group member. However, those in the empathy induction manipulation gave equally to in-group and out-group members. This suggests that empathy induction has specific effects on children's behavior toward out-group members. These studies provide mounting evidence that inducing empathy toward an out-group member can promote prosocial behavior toward that group.

5.5.3 *Extending Prosocial Behavior to the Group*

Batson et al. (2002) demonstrated that, in adults, empathy induced for an out-group member in need may increase readiness to help that individual. Furthermore, this readiness to help may generalize to the out-group as a whole if the individual's need is related to their group membership. Developmentally, there is evidence that by middle childhood, children's growing sense of group dynamics and moral understanding could enable them to generalize the need of one person to the group as a whole. For instance, children have the capacity to understand the concept of group-based need and inequality (Elenbaas & Killen, 2016). This understanding has been linked to prosocial behavior, as children may rectify injustices through their resource allocations (Elenbaas & Killen, 2016; Rutland & Killen, 2017). For example, 8-year-old children have been shown to give more resources to groups that have been historically disadvantaged within their society (Olson, Dweck, Spelke, & Banaji, 2011). Given that children understand and respond to group-based need, it is possible that inducing empathy for an out-group member could generalize into a willingness to help that group as a whole.

5.5.4 Empathy and Attitudes

The empathy-attitudes-action model proposes that attitudes mediate the relationship between empathy and prosocial behavior (Batson et al., 2002). The majority of research today has focused on trait empathy, rather than state-based empathetic responses which are tested in the pilot study below. Still, correlational studies between children's trait empathy and out-group attitudes suggest that empathy may play a vital role in shaping out-group attitudes.

Nesdale et al. (2005) investigated the relationship between empathy in 5- to 12-year-old White Anglo-Australian children and their attitudes toward out-group members who were either of the same ethnicity (other Anglo-Australian children) or of a different ethnicity (Pacific Islander). Children were told they were taking part in a team drawing competition against one of these groups. In this study, children's trait empathy and attitudes toward the opposing team were then assessed. The results showed that empathy predicted liking for differently ethnic out-group members. However, liking for the same ethnicity out-group was not correlated with empathy. That is, empathetic children tended to express more positive attitudes toward out-group members, but not in-group members. This differentiation may have been attributed to children's understanding of social inequities and compassion for those that have less favorable circumstances. Thus, empathetic children may be more sensitive to intergroup inequalities and may hold more positive attitudes toward members of disadvantaged groups.

Building upon these results, Vezzali et al. (2017) conducted a correlational study among Italian immigrant and nonimmigrant primary school students (ages 8–11 years old), which investigated the links between trait empathy, attitudes, and contact. In keeping with the results of previous research (Nesdale et al., 2005), the study found that intergroup empathy mediated the relationship between contact and positive out-group attitudes. As such, children with higher levels of empathy had more positive out-group attitudes. These studies hold significant implications for supporting an empathy-attitude link in children, specifically toward minority out-groups. If higher levels of trait empathy are linked to more positive out-group attitudes, enhancing intergroup empathy should promote positive attitudes toward refugees. However, changing attitudes alone is not wholly beneficial, as they may not translate into meaningful action.

5.5.5 Attitudes to Action

The final component of the empathy-attitudes-action model is the link between out-group attitudes and an increased willingness to help out-group members. A considerable body of literature has explored this attitude-behavior relationship in adults and has found that attitudes generally serve as an antecedent for subsequent behavior (for a review see Ajzen & Fishbein, 2005). However, the nature of the behavior and the contexts in which it occurs are imperative to determining attitude-behavior consistency (Ajzen & Fishbein, 1980). In addition, cost-benefit considerations play a role when deciding whether or not to engage in a specific behavior. A person may hold a favorable view of another, but chose not to offer assistance if this comes at a cost to themselves or to others (Batson, 2011). Furthermore, the group membership of the recipient is also known to be a factor in the decision to engage in helping behaviors for both adults and children (Levy & Killen, 2008; Taylor & Hanna, 2018; Taylor et al., 2014). Studies aimed at improving children's attitudes toward out-group members have often found discrepancies between improvements in attitude and increases in prosocial behavior (Aboud et al., 2012).

As with the majority of research within the intergroup domain, the attitude-behavior relationship in this context has focused almost exclusively on the link between negative attitudes and behaviors. For instance, there is a wealth of research demonstrating that negative out-group attitudes in adults and children, such as prejudice, are associated with negative intergroup behaviors including aggression or violence (Genthner, Shuntich, & Bunting, 1975; Van Zomeren, Fischer, & Spears, 2007). A new line of thinking has proposed that the decision to engage in negative or positive behaviors may develop through different processes (Aboud, 2003). Thus, a shift in the research paradigm to focus specifically on the relationship between positive out-group attitudes and prosocial behaviors is necessary. However, much of the current literature addressing this call has been conducted using cross-sectional field studies and therefore has a limited capacity to explain and unravel causal patterns. For example, following an earthquake in Italy, the majority of children with more positive attitudes toward immigrants showed a greater willingness to meet and help immigrant victims (Vezzali, Cadamuro, Versari, Giovannini, & Trifiletti, 2015). By employing a longitudinal design, Taylor et al. (2014) found that positive out-group attitudes were associated with later patterns of out-group prosocial behavior in young people living in a post-accord society. Taken together, there is converging evidence that promoting positive out-group attitudes could promote meaningful prosocial action.

5.5.6 Inducing Intergroup Empathy

Testing the empathy-attitudes-action model requires the successful induction of intergroup empathy. Narratives, presented through the use of books and storytelling, have previously been successful in inducing empathy (e.g., Sierksma et al., 2015). These approaches can be utilized in both experimental and applied contexts and are thought to induce empathy by allowing the individual to see a situation from another person's perspective.

5.6 Pilot Study

To test the empathy-attitude-action model in middle childhood in response to the refugee crisis in Europe, a pilot study was developed which induced empathy toward Syrian refugee children (Glen, 2017). Syrian refugees were selected as the target group given the United Kingdom's announcement to expand the Vulnerable Persons Relocation scheme to resettle at least 2,000 Syrian refugees in Northern Ireland (NI) and because they would represent an ethnic out-group in the NI host society.

Ninety-two children between 8 and 11 years old participated in an intervention using a realistic refugee scenario in schools across NI and were randomly assigned to an information-only (control) or a story (intervention) condition. Across both conditions, participants were first given a child-friendly definition of a refugee. Next, children were introduced to gender-matched (hypothetical) child—Mohammad or Ayesha (M/A)—and told that he/she was a refugee from Syria who was moving to NI and would soon become a pupil at their school. In the information-only condition, participants moved on to the dependent variable questions in a one-on-one interaction with a trained researcher, while in the story condition, children heard an adapted version of a published children's story book based on a true account of two Syrian children's journey to resettle in Europe. The story was "read" to children using a pre-recorded audio to ensure that each participant heard the story in an identical manner. Children then completed the dependent variable tasks, which included an empathy manipulation check, out-group attitudes toward refugees, a resource allocation task, and realistic helping opportunity directed toward M/A.

Empathy was assessed through self-report using a one-item question derived from Williams et al. (2014). Children were asked either "How did you feel while listening to the story" (story condition) or "How did you feel when learning about refugees" (information-only condition) and responses were recorded using a four-point Likert-type facial affective scale (FAC), with responses ranging from *awful* to *brilliant*. Out-group attitudes were assessed using a three-question scale created by Nesdale et al. (2010). Children were asked (1) "How much do you like Syrian refugee children," (2) "How much would you trust Syrian refugee children," and (3) "How much would you like to play with Syrian refugee children." Responses were recorded using a four-point Likert-type scale and summed to form a composite score. Consistent with Batson's model, prosocial behavior toward refugee children as a generalized out-group was assessed through a resource allocation task. Children allocated seven one-pound coins between three groups, helping either Syrian refugee children, animals, or nature.

Extending Batson's model, realistic helping intentions toward the empathy target were assessed using a two-question item from Vezzali et al. (2015). Children were asked "How much time do you want to help M/A during lunch" and "How much time do you want to help M/A after school." Responses were recorded using a five-point Likert-type scale of progressively shaded in clocks ranging from *none of the time* to *all of the time* and were aggregated to form a composite score. This extension allowed us to differentiate the role of empathy and out-group attitudes in both prosocial behavior toward the empathy target and prosocial behavior toward the empathy target's group.

The pilot study found that empathy was successfully induced in a school setting through a brief narrative intervention. That is, children in the story condition reported significantly more empathy than those in the information-only condition, echoing Batson's finding that exposure to a realistic narrative can be an effective method for inducing empathy toward a member of an out-group. It should be noted, however, that those in the information-only condition also reported relatively high levels of empathy; that is, children empathized readily with refugees, even when provided only with brief, factual information. This finding is encouraging as inter-group biases in empathy are well documented and reveal that, typically, adults and children do not readily empathize with those they perceive to be dissimilar to themselves (Chiao & Mathur, 2010; Vanman, 2016). Furthermore, other studies using more hypothetical and impersonal means of promoting empathy toward refugees failed to produce similar results (Turner & Brown, 2008). Taken together, this finding provides evidence for future studies to utilize realistic narratives as a means of empathy induction toward refugees specifically.

Furthermore, although children in both conditions were willing to provide direct assistance to M/A, children in the story condition reported greater realistic helping intentions toward the target. Regarding the other two dependent variables, there were no significant differences in children's out-group attitudes or the number of resources allocated to refugees. For each of these outcomes, children in both conditions expressed positive attitudes toward refugees and consistently allocated resources in favor of refugees in general. According to Batson, choosing to allocate resources in favor of the empathy target's group suggests a higher valuing of the out-group's welfare over that of competing groups. This is reflective of developmental research which finds that by the age of 8 years old, children's helping behaviors are significantly influenced by the perceived need and merit of the recipient (Moore, 2009; Schmidt, Svetlova, Johe, & Tomasello, 2016). Correlations for the dependent variables can be found in Table 5.1.

Next, two mediation analyses were run to test the EAA model. There was a significant link from attitudes to realistic helping intentions; however, empathy was not directly related to out-group attitudes nor to either type of prosocial behavior. Thus, the pilot study did not find conclusive evidence for the EAA model. However, within the context of empathy induction, children's out-group attitudes were highly predictive of their willingness to engage in meaningful, realistic helping behaviors toward the incoming refugee pupil. This corroborates previous research which found that young people with more positive out-group attitudes engage in more prosocial behavior toward out-group members (Taylor et al., 2014; Vezzali et al., 2015). Given the focus on specific, realistic helping intentions, this finding may provide a fairly reliable representation of *actual* future helping behavior (Ajzen & Fishbein, 2005). Furthermore, the intentions assessed were costly and required sacrifices in the form of both time and effort. As cost-benefit considerations are important in the decision to engage in helping behaviors (Batson, 2011), this is a particularly encouraging finding. As the first study of EAA in middle childhood, the successful induction of empathy and identification of the attitude-behavior link are promising directions as we begin to unravel the relations within this model.

Table 5.1 Correlation of dependent variables

	1	2	3	4
1. Empathy	–			
2. Helping intentions	0.12	–		
3. Resource allocation	0.02	0.12	–	
4. Out-group attitudes	0.10	0.58**	0.16	–

Note. Numbers are Pearson's correlations
$n = 94$
$^{**}p < 0.01$, two-tailed

However, several limitations of the pilot study should be acknowledged and addressed in future research.

5.6.1 Limitations and Future Research

First, the empathy measure used in the pilot study may not have adequately captured the level or type of empathy experienced by participants. While there are many forms of empathy, the pilot study only assessed affective empathy as this reflected Batson's original study in adults. However, Batson's study used multidimensional assessment of affective empathy that required an advanced vocabulary and ability to express complex emotions and, thus, was not appropriate for the current population. It is possible that the child-friendly, single-item assessment used in the current study did not adequately capture the complexity of affective empathy.

Future research, therefore, should use more comprehensive measures which account for multiple forms of empathy. For instance, measures which differentiate between affective and cognitive state empathy, such as the personal reactivity and empathetic concern subscales of the Interpersonal Reactivity Index (Davis, 1983), could be modified to assess out-group-directed empathy. Furthermore, future research may try to assess the degree to which trait empathy is a precursor for responding to message-induced state empathy in middle childhood. Capturing the complexity and multidimensional experience of empathy may provide a clearer picture of its role in attitude formation and out-group-directed prosocial behavior in the future.

Second, the resource allocation task may not have provoked adequate competition between groups. Factors such as fairness, recipient's need, and group loyalty play a role in children's resource allocation (Rutland & Killen, 2017), and future research should continue to explore these factors. For example, allocation benefiting refugees could be placed in direct competition with other children, such as those from the in-group, other ethnic groups, or with a serious illness.

Third, this study was limited in our ability to assess the directionality of effects. For example, future studies should assess out-group attitudes at multiple time points, such as before and after empathy induction. Moreover, while there is mounting evidence that trait and state empathy are precursors for positive out-group attitudes (Batson et al., 1997; Vezzali et al., 2017), positive out-group attitudes may be a precursor for out-group empathy. More complex designs may allow for future researchers to unravel the dynamic and multidimensional relation between empathy and attitudes.

Fourth, although random assignment was used with the empathy induction, the pilot study did not control for children's previous quantity or quality of contact with refugees or other ethnic groups. This is an important limitation as Northern Ireland is historically a homogenous society in which children may have had little experience with members of other ethnic groups. Contact is known to play a role in the formation of out-group attitudes (Aboud, Mendelson, & Purdy, 2003) and, thus, future research should assess both the quantity and quality of children's previous contact with diverse out-groups. At the same time, contact interventions should consider incorporating empathy-inducing techniques, such as narratives, to enhance the impact on positive intergroup relations (Vezzali et al., 2017).

Finally, research should strive to incorporate the views of refugee children themselves and investigate how intergroup processes may differ between majority and minority group children. Intergroup relations are by no means one-way, and research would benefit from adopting a more dynamic approach.

5.7 Call to Action

It is imperative that research not only advance theoretical understanding but also inform policy and program implementation. As highlighted in this chapter, children may actively contribute to improving intergroup relations. Although the empowerment and facilitation of children as social actors is gaining traction in research, the rhetoric of participation far outweighs its implementation.

Interventions to promote episodic peacebuilding and consolidate long-term peace often focused on fostering positive intergroup encounters (Christie, 2006). However, such efforts are often reactionary rather than preventative, intervening only after negative group dynamics have taken root. At this point, hostile group dynamics are hard to change. The relatively recent influx of refugees into high-income countries offers an opportunity to not only prevent the development of negative intergroup dynamics, but also to prepare children to build long-lasting, meaningful relationships with their new peers.

New, empirically driven models on promoting cross-group friendships place a focus on making children 'contact ready' and preparing them to engage in meaningful, sustained relationships with out-group members (Turner & Cameron, 2016). Such models advocate for socio-cognitive capacity building interventions which enhance children's empathy. On a broader scale, programs which aim to promote trait empathy and helping behaviors from a young age should be more widely implemented. For example, Roots of Empathy (Gordon, 2005) has shown some promise in cultivating children's empathy. Future research should extend these types of interventions to focus specifically on empathy in intergroup contexts.

Interventions aimed specially on preparing children to welcome refugees should consider using a socio-cognitive approach to enhance empathy toward refugees.

As demonstrated by our pilot study, exposing children to realistic narratives of refugees' experiences can be a useful form of empathy induction. Such empathy-inducing narratives could be combined with extended or imagined contact (Cameron et al., 2006; Turner & Cameron, 2016). For example, narratives could be extended to incorporate stories of friendship between refugee and host-society children. Such interventions would be relatively low-cost, logistically easier to organize than interventions involving face-to-face contact, and administered by para-professionals. Schools may be key sites to facilitate such preparatory interventions as they are often the first point of contact between host-society and incoming refugee children. Although schools are often overloaded with new agendas and policies, the interventions outlined above could be incorporated into existing curriculum and administered by teachers in the classroom.

By investing in interventions that prepare host-society children to welcome their new peers in meaningful ways, we are responding to the voices of refugee children. Preventative programs are an important long-term investment that can aid in addressing the multifaceted nature of integrating refugees into new communities (Fazel & Betancourt, 2017). Although integrating refugees into a new society is challenging, host-society children can play an integral role in establishing an environment that supports the well-being of refugees and fosters peace for generations to come.

Acknowledgments We would like to thank the many schools, parents, and children who participated in this research. In addition, we would like to recognize the contributions of Dean O'Driscoll and Lynn Muldrew who participated in the creation and data collection of this research project. The pilot research was carried out as part of the MSc dissertation project of Catherine Glen, who studied with the financial support of the Rotary International and Capital Rotary Club, Rotary District 7770 in 2016-17, with follow-up funding in 2018.

References

Aboud, F. E. (1988). *Children and prejudice*. New York, NY: Basil Blackwell.

Aboud, F. E. (2003). The formation of in-group favoritism and out-group prejudice in young children: Are they distinct attitudes? *Developmental Psychology, 39*(1), 48–60. https://doi.org/10.1037/0012-1649.39.1.48

Aboud, F. E., & Levy, S. R. (2000). Interventions to reduce prejudice and discrimination in children and adolescents. In S. Oskamp (Ed.), *Reducing prejudice and discrimination*. Mahwah, NJ: Lawrence Erlbaum Associates.

Aboud, F. E., Mendelson, M. J., & Purdy, K. T. (2003). Cross-race peer relations and friendship quality. *International Journal of Behavioral Development, 27*(2), 165–173. https://doi.org/10.1080/01650250244000164

Aboud, F. E., Tredoux, C., Tropp, L. R., Brown, C. S., Niens, U., & Noor, N. M. (2012). Interventions to reduce prejudice and enhance inclusion and respect for ethnic differences in early childhood: A systematic review. *Developmental Review, 32*(4), 307–336. https://doi.org/10.1016/j.dr.2012.05.001

Abrams, D., & Killen, M. (2014). Social exclusion of children: Developmental origins of prejudice. *Journal of Social Issues, 70*(1), 1–11. https://doi.org/10.1111/josi.12043

Abrams, D., Van de Vyver, J., Pelletier, J., & Cameron, L. (2015). Children's prosocial behavioral intentions towards outgroup members. *British Journal of Developmental Psychology, 33*(3), 277–294. https://doi.org/10.1111/bjdp.12085

Ajzen, I., & Fishbein, M. (1980). *Understanding attitudes and predicting social behavior*. New York, NY: Eaglewood-Cliffs.

Ajzen, I., & Fishbein, M. (2005). The influence of attitudes on behavior. In D. Albarracin, T. Johnson, & M. Zanna (Eds.), *The handbook of attitudes*. London, UK: Lawrence Erlbaum Associates.

Batson, C. D. (2010). Empathy-induced altruistic motivation. In M. Mikulincer & P. R. Shaver (Eds.), *Prosocial motives, emotions, and behavior: The better angels of our nature* (pp. 15–34). Washington, D.C.: American Psychological Association Press.

Batson, C. D., Chang, J., Orr, R., & Rowland, J. (2002). Empathy, attitudes, and action: Can feeling for a member of a stigmatized group motivate one to help the group. *Personality and Social Psychology Bulliton, 28*(12), 1656–1666. https://doi.org/10.1177/014616702237647

Batson, C. D., Polycarpou, M. P., Harmon-Jones, E., Imhoff, H. J., Mitchener, E. C., Bednar, L. L., … Highberger, L. (1997). Empathy and attitudes: Can feeling for a member of a stigmatized group improve feelings toward the group? *Journal of Personality and Social Psychology, 72*(1), 105–118.

Batson, C. D. (2011). *Alturism in Humans*. New York, NY: Oxford University Press.

Beelmann, A., & Heinemann, K. S. (2014). Preventing prejudice and improving intergroup attitudes: A meta-analysis of child and adolescent training programs. *Journal of Applied Developmental Psychology, 31*(1), 10–24. https://doi.org/10.1016/j.appdev.2013.11.002

Cameron, L., Rutland, A., Brown, R., & Douch, R. (2006). Changing children's intergroup attitudes toward refugees: Testing different models of extended. *Child Development, 77*(5), 1208–1219.

Chiao, J. Y., & Mathur, V. A. (2010). Intergroup empathy: How does race affect empathic neural responses? *Current Biology, 20*(11), R478–R480. https://doi.org/10.1016/j.cub.2010.04.001

Christie, D. J. (2006). What is peace psychology the psychology of? *Journal of Social Issues, 62*(1), 1–17. https://doi.org/10.1111/j.1540-4560.2006.00436.x

Cummings, E. M., Merrilees, C. E., Taylor, L. K., & Mondi, C. F. (2017). Political violence, armed conflict, and youth adjustment: A developmental psychopathology perspective on research and intervention. In *Political violence, armed conflict, and youth adjustment: A developmental psychopathology perspective on research and intervention*. Cham, Switzerland: Springer International Publishing. https://doi.org/10.1007/978-3-319-51583-0

Davis, M. (1983). Measuring individual differences in empathy: Evidence of a multidimensional approach. *Journal of Personality and Social Psychology, 44*, 113–126.

Dempster, H., & Hargrave, K. (2017). Understanding public attitudes towards refugees and migrants (Working Paper No. 152). Retrieved from ODI websight: https://www.odi.org/publications/10826-understanding-public-attitudes-towards-refugees-and-migrants

Eisenberg, N., Eggum, N. D., & Di Giunta, L. (2010). Empathy-related responding: Associations with prosocial behavior, aggression, and intergroup relations. *Social Issues and Policy Review, 4*(1), 143–180. https://doi.org/10.1111/j.1751-2409.2010.01020.x

Elenbaas, L., & Killen, M. (2016). Children rectify inequalities for disadvantaged groups. *Developmental Psychology, 52*(8), 1318–1329. https://doi.org/10.1037/dev0000154

Esses, V. M., Hamilton, L. K., & Gaucher, D. (2017). The global refugee crisis: Emperical evidence and policy implications for improving public attitudes and facilitating refugee resettlement. *Social Issues and Policy Review, 11*(1), 78–123.

Fazel, M. (2015). A moment of change: Facilitating refugee children's mental health in UK schools. *International Journal of Educational Development, 41*, 255–261. https://doi.org/10.1016/j.ijedudev.2014.12.006

Fazel, M., & Betancourt, T. S. (2017). Preventive mental health interventions for refugee children and adolescents in high-income settings. *The Lancet Child & Adolescent Health, 2*, 121–132. https://doi.org/10.1016/S2352-4642(17)30147-5

Fazel, M., Reed, R. V., Panter-brick, C., & Stein, A. (2012). Mental health of displaced and refugee children resettled in high-income countries: Risk and protective factors. *The Lancet, 379*, 266–282. https://doi.org/10.1016/S0140-6736(11)60051-2

Genthner, R., Shuntich, R., & Bunting, K. (1975). Racial prejudice, belief similarity, and human aggression. *Journal of Psychology, 91*, 229–234. https://doi.org/10.1080/00223980.1975.9923947

Glen, C. (2017). Promoting empathy, positive attitudes, and prosocial behaviours towards refugees: Exploring the empathy-attitude-action model in middle childhood. (Unpublished master's thesis). Supervisor: L. K. Taylor. Queen's University Belfast, Belfast, Northern Ireland.

Gordon, M. (2005). *Roots of empathy: Changing the world child by child*. Markham, ON: Thomas Allen & Son.

IANYD. (2016). *Young people's participation in peacebuilding: A practice note*. Retrieved from UNDP websight: http://www.undp.org/content/undp/en/home/librarypage/democratic-governance/practice-note%2D%2Dyoung-people-s-participation-in-peacebuilding.html

Kernaghan, D. D. (2015). *Feels like home: Exploring the experiences of newcomer pupils in primary schools in Northern Ireland*. Retrieved from Barnardo's websight: https://www.barnardos.org.uk/feels_like_home_exploring_the_experiences_of_newcomer_pupils_in_northern_ireland.pdf, https://doi.org/10.1044/leader.PPL.20012015.20

Levy, S., & Killen, M. (2008). *Intergroup attitudes and relations in childhood through adulthood*. Oxford, UK: Oxford University Press.

McEvoy-Levy, S. (2006). *Troublemakers or peacemakers? Youth and post-accord peace building*. Notre Dame, IN: University of Notre Dame Press.

McKeown, S., & Taylor, L. K. (2017). Intergroup contact and peacebuilding: Promoting youth civic engagement in Northern Ireland. *Journal of Social and Political Psychology, 5*(2), 415–434.

Moore, C. (2009). Fairness in children ' s resource allocation depends on the recipient. *Psychological Science, 20*(8), 944–948.

Nesdale, D., Durkin, K., Maass, A., Kiesner, J., Grif, J., Daly, J., & Mckenzie, D. (2010). Peer group rejection and children ' s outgroup prejudice. *Journal of Applied Developmental Psychology, 31*, 134–144. https://doi.org/10.1016/j.appdev.2009.11.004

Nesdale, D., Griffith, J., Durkin, K., & Maass, A. (2005). Empathy, group norms and children's ethnic attitudes. *Journal of Applied Developmental Psychology, 26*(6), 623–637. https://doi.org/10.1016/j.appdev.2005.08.003

Olson, K. R., Dweck, C. S., Spelke, E., & Banaji, M. (2011). Children's responses to group-based inequality: Percetuation and rectification. *Social Cognition, 29*(3), 270–287. https://doi.org/10.1521/soco.2011.29.3.270.Children

Pauker, K., Williams, A., & Steele, J. R. (2016). Children's racial categorization in context. *Child Development Perspectives, 10*(1), 33–38. https://doi.org/10.1111/cdep.12155

Rutland, A., & Killen, M. (2017). Fair resource allocation among children and adolescents: The role of group and developmental processes. *Child Development Perspectives, 11*(1), 56–62. https://doi.org/10.1111/cdep.12211

Schmidt, M. F. H., Svetlova, M., Johe, J., & Tomasello, M. (2016). Children's developing understanding of legitimate reasons for allocating resources unequally. *Cognitive Development, 37*, 42–52. https://doi.org/10.1016/j.cogdev.2015.11.001

Schroeder, D., & Graziana, W. (2015). *Oxford handbook of prosocial behavior*. Oxford, UK: Oxford University Press.

Schulz, M., & Taylor, L. K. (2018). The processes underlying the quality contact with the primary out-group and in-group importance on support for the Syrian resettlement in a post-accord context. *Peace and Conflict: Journal of Peace Psychology, 24*(3), 306–314.

Sierksma, J., & Thijs, J. (2017). Intergroup helping: How do children see it? In E. Leeuwen & H. Zagefka (Eds.), *Intergroup helping*. New York, NY: Springer International Publishing.

Sierksma, J., Thijs, J., & Verkuyten, M. (2015). In-group bias in children's intention to help can be overpowered by inducing empathy. *British Journal of Developmental Psychology, 33*(1), 45–56. https://doi.org/10.1111/bjdp.12065

Taylor, L. K., & Hanna, J. R. (2018). Altruism born of suffering among emerging adults in Northern Ireland. *Journal of Aggression, Conflict and Peace Research, 10*(3), 157–169.

Taylor, L. K., & McKeown, S. (2017). Youths' peacebuilding potential: Intergroup contact and civic participation amongst a post-accord generation in Northern Ireland. In K. Niven, S. Lewis, & C. Kagan (Eds.), *Making a difference with psychology* (pp. 56–62). London, UK: Richard Benjamin Trust.

Taylor, L. K., Merrilees, C. E., Baird, R., Goeke-Morey, M. C., Shirlow, P., & Cummings, E. M. (2018). Impact of political conflict on trajectories of adolescent prosocial behavior: Implications for civic engagement. *Developmental Psychology, 54*(9), 1785–1794.

Taylor, L. K., Merrilees, C. E., Goeke-Morey, M. C., Shirlow, P., Cairns, E., & Cummings, E. M. (2014). Political violence and adolescent out-group attitudes and prosocial behaviors: Implications for positive inter-group relations. *Social Development (Oxford, England), 23*(4), 840–859. https://doi.org/10.1111/sode.12074

Turner, R. N., & Brown, R. (2008). Improving children ' s attitudes toward refugees: An evaluation of a school-based multicultural curriculum and an anti-racist intervention. *Journal of Applied Social Psychology, 38*(5), 1295–1328.

Turner, R. N., & Cameron, L. (2016). Confidence in contact: A new perspective on promoting cross-group friendship among children and adolescents. *Social Issues and Policy Review, 10*(1), 212–246. https://doi.org/10.1111/sipr.12023

UNHCR. (2018). What is a refugee? Retrieved from: http://www.unhcr.org/refugee-facts/what-is-a-refugee/

United Nations Children's Fund (UNICEF, 1989). *Convention on the Rights of the Child.* Retrieved from: http://www.unicef.org/crc/

Van Zomeren, M., Fischer, A. H., & Spears, R. (2007). Testing the limits of tolerance: How intergroup anxiety amplifies negative and offensive responses to out-group-initiated contact. *Society for Personality and Social Psychology, 33*(12), 1686–1699. https://doi.org/10.1177/0146167207307485

Vanman, E. J. (2016). The role of empathy in intergroup relations. *Current Opinion in Psychology, 11*, 59–63. https://doi.org/10.1016/j.copsyc.2016.06.007

Vezzali, L., Cadamuro, A., Versari, A., Giovannini, D., & Trifiletti, E. (2015). Feeling like a group after a natural disaster: Common ingroup identity and relations with outgroup victims among majority and minority young children. *The British Journal of Social Psychology, 54*, 519–538. https://doi.org/10.1111/bjso.12091

Vezzali, L., Hewstone, M., Capozza, D., Trifiletti, E., & Di Bernardo, G. A. (2017). Improving intergroup relations with extended contact among young children: Mediation by intergroup empathy and moderation by direct intergroup contact. *Journal of Community and Applied Social Psychology, 27*, 35–49. https://doi.org/10.1002/casp.2292

Wike, R., Stokes, B., & Simmons, K. (2016). *Europeans fear wave of refugees will mean more terrorism, fewer jobs.* Retrieved from Pew Research Center website: http://www.pewglobal.org/files/2016/07/Pew-Research-Center-EU-Refugees-and-National-Identity-Report-FINAL-July-11-2016.pdf

Williams, A., Driscoll, K. O., & Moore, C. (2014). The influence of empathic concern on prosocial behavior in children. *Frontiers in Pscyhology, 5*, 1–8. https://doi.org/10.3389/fpsyg.2014.00425

Chapter 6
Civic Participation and Other Interventions That Promote Children's Tolerance of Migrants

Davide Mazzoni, Elvira Cicognani, Iana Tzankova, Antonella Guarino, Cinzia Albanesi, and Bruna Zani

> *I do not like the word tolerance, but I cannot think of a better one.*
>
> Ghandi (1869–1948). (Cited in UNESCO 1997)

6.1 Tolerance Toward Migrants

Reflecting the growing political and scholarly debates about international migration and the so-called refugee crisis in the last few decades, the research on tolerance (and more generally on attitudes toward migrants) has flourished, making tolerance one of the focal concepts in peace psychology (Noor & Christie, 2015; Rapp, 2017). A lack of tolerance implies the rejection of people whom we perceive as different, for example, members of a social or ethnic group other than ours, or people who are different in political or sexual orientation. A lack of tolerance toward foreigners is a contemporary problem in many countries, often related to phenomena like xenophobia, racism, antisemitism, romaphobia and antigypsyism. Its manifestations comprise a wide range of actions from avoidance to hate speech to physical injury or even murder. For all of these reasons, studying the factors that promote tolerance during different stages of an individual's development increasingly becomes an important issue for social science research (Côté & Erickson, 2009; Gniewosz & Noack, 2008).

In this chapter, we begin by providing a definition of 'tolerance', illustrating the wide range of attributes associated with the concept in the literature. Second, we identify some key paths through which tolerance can develop at different stages of an individual's development. Through a literature review, we will track some of the factors that can increase tolerance toward migrants during early and late stages of

D. Mazzoni (✉) · E. Cicognani · I. Tzankova · A. Guarino · C. Albanesi · B. Zani
University of Bologna, Bologna, Italy
e-mail: davide.mazzoni@unimib.it

N. Balvin, D. J. Christie (eds.), *Children and Peace*, Peace Psychology Book Series, https://doi.org/10.1007/978-3-030-22176-8_6

development. Finally, we will conclude by presenting an overview of methodological approaches that practitioners have at their disposal to promote tolerance toward migrants.

6.1.1 Defining Tolerance: Positive and Negative Connotations

In general terms, tolerance means accepting the fact that human beings, naturally diverse in their appearance, situation, speech, behaviour and values, have the right to live in peace and to be as they are. On the other hand, intolerance may take the form of marginalization of vulnerable groups and their exclusion from social and political participation, as well as violence and discrimination against them (UNESCO, 1995, see also UNESCO, 1997).

Tolerance does not require to solve all differences; rather, it entails a reciprocal respect of our rights as human beings (see Rapp, 2017). For this reason, from a certain point of view, tolerance often refers also to the ability to put up with something potentially disagreeable (Freitag & Rapp, 2015; Langerack, 1994; Rapp, 2017). The fact that the object of tolerance is something potentially disagreeable and that negative attitudes are not completely eliminated has led some influential authors to suggest that other concepts, such as 'acceptance' and 'respect' for other social groups (defined by different sexual orientation, disability, race, ethnicity, etc.), should be preferred to 'tolerance'. For example, Schirmer, Weidenstedt and Reich (2012) argue that 'being tolerated' often means 'being put up with' or 'being grudgingly ignored'. According to these authors, multicultural approaches that are based on tolerance may send misleading signals, as they implicitly state that members of ethnic and racial minorities are actually not welcome.

While acknowledging the legitimacy of the above positions, in this contribution we start from the assumption that tolerance has important consequences for democratic life. Indeed, people's effort to control prejudice (i.e. negative evaluations, beliefs or feelings directed at people because of their ethnicity) and tolerate other groups is crucial to sustaining democratic norms (Freitag & Rapp, 2015). For example, with specific reference to migration, tolerance implies the belief, based on equalitarian principles and a political conviction, that migrants and non-migrants should be treated equally (Van Zalk, & Kerr, 2014). This requires just and impartial legislation, law enforcement and judicial and administrative process. In this sense, even if a complete (i.e. without any kind of rejection) acceptance would be desirable, we emphasize here that tolerance represents a more realistic goal that helps civil societies to cope with rising levels of diversity stemming from increased migration and individualism (Rapp, 2017, p. 42).

The fact that tolerance represents not only a desirable personal value but also a democratic virtue and a necessity for a free, modern and open society (Rapp, 2017) is also demonstrated by the negative effects of intolerance. While tolerance is usually accompanied by social cohesion and non-hostility (Morley, 2003; Paluck, 2011), prejudice and intolerance are accompanied by discrimination and violence (e.g. Cabrera, Nora, Terenzini, Pascarella, & Hagedorn, 1999; Jasinskaja-Lahti, Liebkind, & Perhoniemi, 2006; Oakley, 1997). One of the consequences of intolerance is that migrant communities can become socially and economically marginalized. Examples of migrants living as marginalized groups within society may coincide with minority ethnic groups, religious groups and seasonal workers (Andersson, 2003; Eldering & Knowrth, 1998; Laverack, 2009). In a new country, migrants are often faced with restricted legal rights and lower socio-economic status which can lead to feelings of exclusion and poor physical and mental health, accompanied by a limited understanding of how to access healthcare and social services: in one word, they are powerless (Laverack, 2009).

The reasons listed above emphasize the importance of tolerance toward migrants as a necessity for peace, rather than a cherished principle (UNESCO, 1995). In the next section, we provide some insights about the factors which influence its development.

6.1.2 A Developmental Approach on the Study of Tolerance

The most important insights about the development of tolerance come from the extensive multidisciplinary research that focused on the development of national and racial prejudice. This literature showed that prejudice developed at a very young age in children, and both descriptive and experimental research has by now mapped out the changes that occur with age and the main factors that influence such changes (for a review, see: Raabe & Beelmann, 2011).

In many parts of the world, in multicultural societies, prejudice seems to begin around age 4 to 5 (Aboud et al., 2012). However, despite this growing body of research, the processes through which individuals develop tolerance (or intolerance) toward migrants remain partially unclear. For example, some findings showed a peak in prejudice in middle childhood and a slightly decreasing trend until late childhood. However, the results concerning the differences between age groups showed also significant heterogeneity, indicating that the developmental trend is not universal, reflecting the role of many coexisting factors.

Recent research has adapted an ecological approach, focusing on various influencing factors (i.e. Ashy, 2011) across individual and social-environmental levels of explanation. For example, numerous studies focused mostly on individual factors, such as cognitive or social-cognitive abilities, like classification skills, social perspective-taking abilities (Bigler, Jones, & Loblinger, 1997; Smetana, 2006), lay theories[1] (Levy, Karafantis, & Ramírez, 2008), moral development (Killen, Margie, & Sinno, 2006) and group norm understanding (Abrams & Rutland, 2008).

[1] Much literature confirms that people's perceptions are guided by their lay (naïve, implicit, folk or common sense) theories, helping them to understand, predict, control and respond to their social world.

Other approaches emphasized the role of family factors, such as having parents with negative intergroup attitudes (Miklikowska, 2016; White & Gleitzman, 2006); social-environmental factors, such as having a friendship with an out-group member (Feddes, Noack, & Rutland, 2009; Van Zalk & Kerr, 2014); or intergroup contact[2] experiences (Tropp & Prenovost, 2008). Finally, some research applied a more developmental perspective, focusing on motivational processes, such as ethnic awareness and ethnic identity development (Nesdale, 1999; Rutland, Abrams, & Levy, 2007).

It is also reasonable to assume that the effect of such factors is not the same across development stages. In other words, it is possible that a specific factor could play a key role for the development of tolerance at one developmental stage (rather than in another one). However, the evidence on this point is quite scarce and leads to conflicting results. For example, even if Tropp and Prenovost (2008) found that intergroup contact had a positive effect independently from the age of children and adolescents (i.e. contact had almost the same effect in each age group), the same researchers suggested that early contact experiences would be instrumental in nurturing the long-term development of positive intergroup attitudes. This would imply that earlier contact experiences would be more important than later ones. On the other hand, later developmental stages like adolescence and young adulthood are important periods to study attitudes toward migrants, as both social identity and peer relationships undergo crucial changes (Tajfel & Turner, 1979; Bukowski & Kramer 1986; Newcomb et al. 1999). It is especially during these stages of development that young people tend to gradually make contact with a variety of others who are different from themselves and their families. Moreover, during this period individuals increase their abstract reasoning abilities, which represent a necessary condition to understand tolerance principles (Hjerm, 2009), but which are not really consolidated before adolescence (Rydgren, 2004).

6.2 Evidence from the PIDOP and the CATCH-EyoU Projects

Past research suggests that tolerance toward migrants increases with age and that school (e.g. school climate; Gniewosz & Noack, 2008) and social and political voluntary associations (Côté & Erickson, 2009) may represent important learning contexts for democratic attitudes, favouring the development of tolerance. To test this hypothesis, and to clarify the role of different forms of participation that may involve young people at different developmental stages, we set up two studies based on two

[2] Contact between members of different groups has long been advocated as a productive means for reducing intergroup prejudice. The empirical evidence supports this notion, with hundreds of studies indicating that people (especially people from dominant groups) gain more positive attitudes toward other groups (typically non-dominant groups) by communicating with members of those groups (Harwood, 2017).

different sets of data, from the PIDOP (Processes Influencing Democratic Ownership and Participation) project and the CATCH-EyoU (Constructing Active Citizenship with European Youth: Policies, Practices, Challenges and Solutions)[3] project.

Both sets of data were collected in Italy, where the issue of tolerance/intolerance toward migrants has become increasingly more prominent in the past decade. It is a topic that has been adopted by politicians as a means to increasing their popularity (Rivera, 2012), often scapegoating migrants for the dissatisfaction and resentment many Italians feel about their social and living conditions (Bonomi 2008; Rivera, 2012).

In Study 1 we investigated the relationship between different forms of civic and political participation and tolerance toward migrants. The sample consisted of 1240 adolescents and young adults. Females were 46.5% and the mean age was 20.07 years (min. 14, max. 29). Participants completed a paper questionnaire, with the following variables considered for analysis: age, gender, migrant status, parents' education, different forms of participation and tolerance toward migrants. Participation was assessed asking if, in the last year, they took part in a list of activities. In accordance with the factor analysis, items assessing participation were grouped into 'online' (e.g. linking news or videos with a social or political content, discussing social or political questions on the net, connecting to a group dealing with social or political issues on a social network), 'unconventional' (writing political messages or graffiti on walls, political actions which might be considered illegal) and 'civic' (donating money, engaging in volunteer work, taking part in concerts or events with a social or political cause). Tolerance was assessed through four items measuring the support for some migrants' rights (for more information on the methodology, see Tzankova, Guarino, & Mazzoni, 2019). The analyses were conducted separately for adolescents and young adults using SPSS. Tolerance toward migrants was regressed on the following variables: age, gender, migrant status, parents' education and three forms of participation.

In Study 2 we investigated the relationship between different forms of participation, school climate and tolerance toward migrants and refugees.[4] The sample consisted of 1732 adolescents and young adults; 60.7% were female and the mean

[3] PIDOP (Processes Influencing Democratic Ownership and Participation) was a multinational research project which examined the processes which influence democratic ownership and participation in nine European countries. PIDOP was supported by a grant received from the European Commission seventh Framework Programme, FP7-SSH-2007-1, Grant Agreement no: 225282.

CATCH-EyoU (Constructing Active Citizenship with European Youth: Policies, Practices, Challenges and Solutions – www.catcheyou.eu) had the aim to identify the factors, located at different levels (psychological, developmental, macrosocial and contextual) influencing the different forms of youth active engagement in Europe. CATCH-EyoU was funded by the European Union, Horizon 2020 Programme, Grant Agreement number 649538. The views and opinions expressed in this publication are the sole responsibility of the author(s) and do not necessarily reflect the views of the European Commission.

[4] In the study questionnaire, the term 'refugee' was used to refer to a displaced person who was forced to cross national boundaries and cannot return home safely. The use of the term was intentionally broad and did not necessarily reflect only those persons who fit the definition of 'refugee' according to international conventions.

age was 19.73 years (min. 15, max. 30). Participants completed a paper questionnaire and the following variables were considered for analysis: age, gender, migrant status, parents' education, school climate, different forms of participation and tolerance toward migrants and refugees. Participation was assessed asking if, in the last year, they took part in a list of activities, which partially differed from study one and were grouped into online (similar to study 1), civic (similar to study 1), political (traditional political participation, like working for a political party or for a political candidate) and protest (e.g. taking part in a political event where there was a physical confrontation with opponents, taking part in an occupation of a building or a public space). The measure of school climate was assessed only in the adolescents' group and focused on perceived fairness (e.g. 'our teachers treat us fairly', 'the rules in our school are fair'). The analyses were conducted separately for adolescents and young adults using SPSS. In the main analyses, tolerance toward migrants and tolerance toward refugees were regressed on the following variables: age, gender, migrant status, parents' education, school education and the four forms of participation.

Results were largely consistent across the two studies and showed that some sociodemographic characteristics (being female, migrant and with higher educated parents) were positively associated with higher tolerance toward migrants. We also found that civic forms of participation were the most predictive of tolerance, suggesting that these forms of participation provide more opportunities of contact with 'differentiated others' in a democratic environment. Online participation was associated with more tolerance only among young adults, probably because of the differences in Internet usage between adolescents (to communicate with their own peer group) and young adults (to interact with a high number of distant people). Protest was significantly related with tolerance toward refugees (but not toward migrants) among young adults, suggesting that tolerance toward refugees would be more related to radical and manifest forms of participation (i.e. politicization of the 'refugee crisis'). School climate did not demonstrate a clear effect on tolerance. Although the correlational nature of the study design is insufficient to establish a causal relationship between variables, the findings emphasize the importance of civic and political participation as a 'school for democracy' in which young people may learn a range of civic skills and enhance their tolerance toward migrants.

6.3 Different Approaches for Increasing Tolerance

According to UNESCO, laws are necessary but not sufficient for countering intolerance in individual attitudes. For this reason, different strategies need to be developed to foster tolerance and awareness of human rights in children.

The research we reviewed when writing this chapter showed that the development of tolerance is a complex process, which is influenced both by individual and social factors. While some of them are relatively stable, many others can be modified through experience. In this regard, the Member States of the UNESCO meeting in

Paris in 1995 declared that education for tolerance 'should aim at countering influences that lead to fear and exclusion of others, and should help young people to develop capacities for independent judgement, critical thinking and ethical reasoning' (UNESCO, 1995). In the following section, we present some approaches that – consistently with this statement – can be useful for increasing tolerance toward migrants among native children and adolescents.

6.3.1 Global Citizenship Education

Global citizenship refers to a sense of belonging to a broader community and common humanity. It emphasizes political, economic, social and cultural interdependency and interconnectedness between the local, national and global (UNESCO, 2015). UNESCO has promoted global citizenship education since the launch of the UN Secretary-General's Global Education First Initiative (GEFI) in 2012, which made fostering global citizenship one of its three education priorities (UNESCO, 2015). This approach identifies specific learning objectives that should be pursued in different domains (cognitive, emotional, behavioural), at different developmental stages. In this frame, tolerance is one key learning objective that should be reached together with other values and skills that enable people to live together peacefully.

One advantage of global citizenship education has to do with its universal value, which implies that it is not restricted to a specific regional area. For example, even if there is some evidence that specific interventions may increase the feeling of similarity and tolerance toward other Europeans (e.g. Dolejšiová & López, 2009), there is also evidence that European identification can be a predictor of intolerance toward migrants, suggesting that having a more inclusive (e.g. continental) border does not equal having a more tolerant attitude toward migrants from other continents (e.g., Licata & Klein, 2002). With the adoption of a universalistic perspective, global citizenship education overcomes such limits, aiming at promoting tolerance toward all the human beings, from all regions of the world.

6.3.2 Intercultural Dialogue and Intercultural Competence Education

Cultural diversity is an essential condition of human society which brings about new social and political challenges. In this context, intolerance, discrimination and violence can threaten peace and the very essence of local and national communities. The essential objective of intercultural dialogue is to enable people to live together peacefully and constructively in a multicultural world, promoting understanding and interaction.

In 2008, the Council of Europe's White Paper on Intercultural Dialogue (2008) defined intercultural dialogue as the open and respectful exchange of views between individuals and groups from different ethnic, religious, linguistic and national backgrounds on the basis of mutual understanding and respect, arguing that such dialogue is crucial for promoting tolerance, mutual respect and understanding, preventing conflicts and achieving social cohesion.

In 2015, in light of the high numbers of refugees and asylum seekers arriving in the EU, national culture ministers agreed to create a new policy coordination group on intercultural dialogue, focussing on the integration of migrants and refugees in societies through the arts and culture (European Union, 2017). This group's report (executive summary), published in 2017, includes 46 case studies and 23 recommendations focussed on three main themes: empowerment through intercultural dialogue and the arts, intersectoral and partnership working and evaluation of intercultural dialogue objectives and projects.

Both documents observe that the competence that is required for participating in intercultural dialogue is not given to individuals by default. Intercultural competence can be described as the specific attitudes, knowledge, understanding, skills and actions which together enable individuals to understand themselves and others in a context of diversity and to interact and communicate with those who are perceived to have different cultural affiliations from their own (Spitzberg & Changnon, 2009; Huber & Reynolds, 2014). This competence needs to be learned, and providers of education (including education professionals, public authorities, civil society organizations, religious communities and the media) have a crucial role to play in equipping citizens with such competence.

In this sense, intercultural education should not be interpreted as being limited to 'formal education' (i.e. the structured education and training system that runs from pre-primary and primary through secondary school and on to higher education and lifelong learning). Intercultural learning can also occur through non-formal education (i.e. education outside the formal educational setting) and informal education (i.e. the lifelong process whereby every individual acquires attitudes, values, skills and knowledge from influences and resources in his or her own social environment) and it includes key competence areas like democratic citizenship, language and history.

For readers interested in the application of intercultural dialogue, a volume edited by Josef Huber and Christopher Reynolds (2014) presents a detailed description of how intercultural education can be implemented by actors in the formal, non-formal and informal educational spheres. This work explains the principles of pedagogical planning that should be used, relevant methods of learning and teaching, issues to consider when implementing intercultural education in each of the three educational domains and issues concerning assessment and evaluation. A wide range of approaches and concrete activities are presented, in order to promote the intercultural competence of individuals. Overall, such approaches emphasize that in the case of formal education, intercultural education cannot be a separate school subject but is instead a holistic approach which should be embedded throughout the school curriculum, with all teachers, irrespective of the age of their students and the subject they teach, having responsibility for its implementation (see also Barrett, 2018).

6.3.3 Community-Based Approach

According to our results, civic and political participation contribute to the development of tolerance; this may happen through different processes, for example, providing a context for intergroup contact, offering people from different backgrounds the opportunity to interact, sharing common goals and learning democratic values 'in practice'. Community-based approaches, even if not directly referring to intercultural dialogue, are a powerful tool for promoting tolerance between migrant and non-migrant populations by engaging them in a participative and empowering process. The process needs to be based on critical insights regarding the relationship between professionals who implement interventions, the communities with which they work and the structural and symbolic dynamics of power and privilege that operate within and between these communities (Sandler, 2007).

The literature identifies many approaches which are consistent with these premises. For example, in the field of health, stakeholders make alliances with community leaders, integrating users as active agents, promoting social participation and generating positive relations between migrant populations and other community groups, advocating and supporting migrants in their collective actions aimed at gaining equal health rights and so encouraging social justice (Balcazar et al., 2004; García-Ramirez et al., 2011). In the youth field, community-based projects are usually aimed at identifying common interests between diverse groups of young people, mobilizing peers, working collectively to address community and human rights issues in schools and communities and promoting inclusiveness (Watts & Flanagan, 2007).

In this sense 'tolerance', rather than being an object of education, represents an outcome (an achievement) of the empowerment process, which implies the recognition of migrant minorities as main actors, rather than passive objects of the tolerance (or intolerance) from the majority. To achieve true tolerance, the world views and perspectives of different individuals and groups need to be taken into account, especially the most vulnerable, who are usually also the most silenced and forgotten (García-Ramírez, de la Mata, Paloma, & Hernández-Plaza, 2011).

6.4 Conclusion

Alarmed by the recent rise in acts of intolerance, violence, racism, exclusion, marginalization and discrimination directed against migrant minorities, we opened this chapter with the UNESCO definition of tolerance and emphasizing its importance.

Tolerance means respecting the rich diversity of our world's cultures, of different forms of expression and ways of being human (UNESCO, 1995).

Starting from a similar assumption, we shed some light on the main factors which can promote tolerance, with a specific focus on childhood and adolescence, as they are key life periods in which individuals develop attitudes toward others. In line with the socioecological perspective, such factors can be placed at different levels of society and can play a different role at different developmental stages. More specifically, in regard to adolescence and young adulthood, we emphasized the importance of taking part in different forms of civic and political participation.

Moving to a more applied focus, we described two broad educational approaches, global citizenship education and intercultural competence education, which have been specifically developed for promoting tolerance and can be fruitfully applied in the migration domain. Moreover, we showed how community approaches (based on the promotion of civic and political participation) can promote fruitful interaction between migrants and receiving societies.

The content of this chapter has some important implications for the well-being of children and adolescents. First, inscribing the concept of 'tolerance' as an aim of global citizenship education and of intercultural competence education means recognizing its usefulness also for those who are usually considered as the 'advantaged' ones. Indeed, the competences that allow people to live peacefully are beneficial for all the human beings, migrants and non-migrants, who are inevitably living in a new multicultural globalized world. On the other hand, although it goes beyond the scope of this chapter, we must recognize that migrant children and adolescents are often the victims of intolerance, with serious consequences on their personal and social well-being (e.g. Hernandez & Charney, 1998; Lustig et al., 2004). The construction of a more tolerant society will thus be integral to improving their well-being.

With regard to specific interventions to promote tolerance in childhood and adolescence, we must recognize that they are not widespread, they are rarely informed by developmental theory and research (Killen et al., 2011) and previous reviews evaluating the effects of interventions in childhood and adolescence found mixed results (Paluck & Green, 2009; Aboud et al., 2012). We strongly believe that developing tolerance toward migrants should represent not only a cherished principle but also a necessity for peace and for the economic and social advancement of all peoples. In 1995, Member States of UNESCO pledged to support and implement programmes of social science research and education for tolerance.[5] In this chapter we provided an overview of the complexity of this task, illustrating some of the main resources that practitioners and policymakers have at their disposal. Future research,

[5] 'This means devoting special attention to improving teacher training, curricula, the content of textbooks and lessons, and other educational materials including new educational technologies, with a view to educating caring and responsible citizens open to other cultures, able to appreciate the value of freedom, respectful of human dignity and differences, and able to prevent conflicts or resolve them by non-violent means' (UNESCO, 1995).

accompanied by a systematic evaluation of relevant interventions, is necessary in order to provide further suggestions for more effective strategies.

References

Aboud, F. E., Tredoux, C., Tropp, L. R., Spears Brown, C., Niens, U., & Noor, N. M. (2012). Interventions to reduce prejudice and enhance inclusion and respect for ethnic differences in early childhood: A systematic review. *Developmental Review, 32*(4), 307–336. https://doi.org/10.1016/j.dr.2012.05.001

Abrams, D., & Rutland, A. (2008). The development of subjective group dynamics. In S. R. Levy & M. Killen (Eds.), *Intergroup attitudes and relations in childhood through adulthood* (pp. 47–65). New York: Oxford University Press.

Andersson, M. (2003). Migrant youth and the dynamics of marginalization. *Young, 11*, 74–89. https://doi.org/10.1177/1103308803011001077

Ashy, M. A. (2011). Ecological model. In D. J. Christie (Ed.), *The encyclopedia of peace psychology*. https://doi.org/10.1002/9780470672532.wbepp094

Balcázar, F. E., Garate-Serafini, T. J., & Keys, C. B. (2004). The need for action when conducting intervention research: The multiple roles of community psychologist. *American Journal of Community Psychology, 33*, 243–252. https://doi.org/10.1023/B:AJCP.0000027009.01838.f2

Barrett, M. (2018). How schools can promote the intercultural competence of young people. *European Psychologist, 23*, 93–104. https://doi.org/10.1027/1016-9040/a000308

Bigler, R., Jones, L., & Lobliner, D. (1997). Social categorization and the formation of intergroup attitudes in children. *Child Development, 68*(3), 530–543. https://doi.org/10.2307/1131676

Bonomi, A. (2008). *Il rancore: Alle radici del malessere del Nord*. Milano: Feltrinelli.

Bukowski, W. M., & Kramer, T. L. (1986). Judgments of the features of friendship among early adolescent boys and girls. *The Journal of Early Adolescence, 6*, 331–338. https://doi.org/10.1177/0272431686064004

Cabrera, A. F., Nora, A., Terenzini, P. T., Pascarella, E., & Hagedorn, L. S. (1999). Campus racial climate and the adjustment of students to college. *The Journal of Higher Education, 70*(2), 134–160. https://doi.org/10.2307/2649125

Côté, R. R., & Erickson, B. H. (2009). Untangling the roots of tolerance: How forms of social capital shape attitudes toward ethnic minorities and migrants. *American Behavioral Scientist, 52*, 1664–1689. https://doi.org/10.1177/0002764209331532

Council of Europe. (2008). *White paper on intercultural dialogue "living together as equals in dignity"*. Strasbourg: Committee of Ministers, Council of Europe. Retrieved from: http://www.coe.int

Dolejšiová, D., & García López, M. A. (2009). *European citizenship – In the process of construction - challenges for citizenship, citizenship education and democratic practice in Europe*. Council of Europe Publishing. https://pjp-eu.coe.int

Eldering, L., & Knorth, E. J. (1998). Marginalization of migrant youth and risk factors in their everyday lives: The european experience. *Child & Youth Care Forum, 27*, 153–169. https://doi.org/10.1007/BF02589561

Feddes, A. R., Noack, P., & Rutland, A. (2009). Direct and extended friendship effects on minority and majority children's intergroup attitudes: A longitudinal study. *Child Development, 80*, 377–390.

Freitag, M., & Rapp, C. (2015). The personal foundations of political tolerance towards migrants. *Journal of Ethnic and Migration Studies, 41*, 351–373. https://doi.org/10.1080/1369183X.2014.924847

García-Ramírez, M., de la Mata, M. L., Paloma, V., & Hernández-Plaza, S. (2011). A liberation psychology approach to acculturative integration of migrant populations. *American Journal of Community Psychology, 47*, 86–97. https://doi.org/10.1007/s10464-010-9372-3

Gniewosz, B., & Noack, P. (2008). Classroom climate indicators and attitudes towards foreigners. *Journal of Adolescence, 31*, 609–624. https://doi.org/10.1016/j.adolescence.2007.10.006

Harwood, J. (2017). Intergroup contact. *In Oxford Research Encyclopedia of Communication.* https://doi.org/10.1093/acrefore/9780190228613.013.429

Hernandez, D. J., & Charney, E. (1998). *From generation to generation: The health and well-being of children in migrant families*. Washington D.C.: National Academy Press.

Hjerm, M. (2009). Prejudice toward migrants and cross-municipal variation in the proportion of migrants. *Acta Sociologica, 52*, 47–62. https://doi.org/10.1177/0001699308100633

Jasinskaja-Lahti, I., Liebkind, K., & Perhoniemi, R. (2006). Perceived discrimination and well-being: A victim study of different migrant groups. *Journal of Community and Applied Social Psychology, 16*, 267–284. https://doi.org/10.1002/casp.865

Killen, M., Margie, N. G., & Sinno, S. (2006). Morality in the context of intergroup relationships. In M. Killen & J. G. Smetana (Eds.), *Handbook of moral development* (pp. 155–183). Mahwah, NJ: Erlbaum.

Killen, M., Rutland, A., & Ruck, M. D. (2011). Promoting equity, tolerance, and justice in childhood. *Social Policy Report, 25*(11), 1–32.

Langerak, E. (1994). Pluralism, tolerance, and disagreement. *Rhetoric Society Quarterly, 24*, 95–105. https://doi.org/10.1080/02773949409391008

Laverack, G. (2009). *Public health: Power, empowerment & professional practice* (2nd ed.). London: Palgrave Macmillan.

Levy, S. R., Karafantis, D. M., & Ramírez, L. (2008). A social-developmental perspective on lay theories and intergroup relations. In S. R. Levy & M. Killen (Eds.), *Intergroup attitudes and relations in childhood through adulthood* (pp. 146–156). New York: Oxford University Press.

Licata, L., & Klein, O. (2002). Does European citizenship breed xenophobia? European identification as a predictor of intolerance towards migrants. *Journal of Community and Applied Social Psychology, 12*, 1–15. https://doi.org/10.1002/casp.684

Lustig, S. L., Kia-Keating, M., Knight, W. G., Geltman, P., Ellis, H., Kinzie, J. D., … Saxe, G. N. (2004). Review of child and adolescent refugee mental health. *Journal of the American Academy of Child and Adolescent Psychiatry, 43*, 24–36. https://doi.org/10.1097/00004583-200401000-00012

Miklikowska, M. (2016). Like parent, like child? Development of prejudice and tolerance towards migrants. *British Journal of Psychology, 107*, 95–116. https://doi.org/10.1111/bjop.12124

Morley, K. M. (2003). Fitting in by race/ethnicity: The social and academic integration of diverse students at a large predominantly white university. *Journal of College Student Retention: Research, Theory and Practice, 5*(2), 147–174. https://doi.org/10.2190/K1KF-RTLW-1DPW-T4CC

Nesdale, D. (1999). Ethnic prejudice in children: A social identity model. In P. R. Martin & W. Noble (Eds.), *Psychology and society* (pp. 92–110). Brisbane, Australia: Australian Academic Press.

Newcomb, A. F., Bukowski, W. M., & Bagwell, C. L. (1999). Knowing the sounds: Friendship as a developmental context. In W. A. Collins & B. Laursen (Eds.), Relationships as developmental contexts. Mahwah, NJ: US Lawrence Erlbaum Associates.

Noor, N., & Christie, D. (2015). Themes in peace psychology research. In D. Bretherton & S. Law (Eds.), *Methodologies in peace psychology* (Peace psychology book series) (Vol. 26). Cham: Springer. https://doi.org/10.1007/978-3-319-18395-4_3

Oakley, R. (1997). *Tackling racist and xenophobic violence in Europe: Review and practical guidance*. Strasbourg, France: Council of Europe Publishing.

Paluck, E. L. (2011). Peer pressure against prejudice: A high school field experiment examining social network change. *Journal of Experimental Social Psychology, 4*, 350–358. https://doi.org/10.1016/j.jesp.2010.11.017

Paluck, E. L., & Green, D. P. (2009). Prejudice reduction: What works? A review and assessment of research and practice. *Annual Review of Psychology, 60*, 339–367. https://doi.org/10.1146/annurev.psych.60.110707.163607

Raabe, T., & Beelmann, A. (2011). Development of ethnic, racial, and national prejudice in childhood and adolescence: A multinational meta-analysis of age differences. *Child Development, 82*(6), 1715–1737. https://doi.org/10.1111/j.1467-8624.2011.01668.x

Rapp, C. (2017). Shaping tolerant attitudes towards migrants: The role of welfare state expenditures. *Journal of European Social Policy, 27*, 40–56. https://doi.org/10.1177/0958928716672181

Rivera, A. (2012). Il razzismo: continuità e metamorfosi. *Anuac, 1*, 1–6. https://doi.org/10.7340/anuac2239-625X-5

Rutland, A., Abrams, D., & Levy, S. R. (2007). Extending the conversation: Transdisciplinary approaches to social identity and intergroup attitudes in children and adolescents. *International Journal of Behavioral Development, 31*, 417–418. https://doi.org/10.1177/0165025407083669

Rydgren, J. (2004). The logic of xenophobia. *Rationality and Society, 16*, 123–148. https://doi.org/10.1177/1043463104043712

Sandler, J. (2007). Community-based practices: Integrating dissemination theory with critical theories of power and justice. *American Journal of Community Psychology, 40*(3–4), 272–289. https://doi.org/10.1007/s10464-007-9131-2

Schirmer, W., Weidenstedt, L., & Reich, W. (2012). From tolerance to respect in inter-ethnic contexts. *Journal of Ethnic and Migration Studies, 38*(7), 1049–1065. https://doi.org/10.1080/1369183X.2012.681448

Smetana, J. G. (2006). Social-cognitive domain theory: Consistencies and variations in children's moral and social judgments. In M. Killen & J. G. Smetana (Eds.), *Handbook of moral development* (pp. 119–153). Mahwah, NJ: Erlbaum.

Spitzberg, B. H., & Changnon, G. (2009). Conceptualizing intercultural competence. In D. K. Deardorff (Ed.), *The SAGE handbook of intercultural competence* (pp. 2–52). Thousand Oaks, CA: Sage.

Tajfel, H., & Turner, J. C. (1979). An integrative theory of intergroup conflict. In W. G. Austin & S. Worchel (Eds.), *The social psychology of intergroup relations* (pp. 33–47). Monterey, CA: Brooks/Cole.

Tropp, L., & Prenovost, M. (2008). The role of intergroup contact in predicting children's interethnic attitudes: Evidence from meta-analytic and field studies. In S. Levy & M. Killen (Eds.), *Intergroup attitudes and relations in childhood through adulthood* (pp. 236–248). New York: Oxford University Press.

Tzankova, I., Guarino, A., & Mazzoni, D. (2019). Tolerance toward migrants among Italian adolescents and young adults: The role of civic and political participation. Psicologia di Comunità, 1, 49–68. https://doi.org/10.3280/PSC2019-001005

UNESCO. (1995). Declaration of principles on tolerance (16 November 1995). Retrieved from: http://portal.unesco.org

UNESCO. (1997). *Defining tolerance*. Retrieved from: http://unesdoc.unesco.org

UNESCO. (2015). *Global citizenship education: Topics and learning objectives*. Paris: United Nations Educational, Scientific and Cultural Organization. Retrieved from: http://unesdoc.unesco.org

Union, E. (2017). How culture and the arts can promote intercultural dialogue in the context of the migratory and refugee crisis. In *Report with case studies, by the working group of EU member states' experts on intercultural dialogue in the context of the migratory and refugee crisis under the open method of coordination*. Luxembourg: Publication office of the European Union. https://doi.org/10.2766/468525

Van Zalk, M. H., & Kerr, M. (2014). Developmental trajectories of prejudice and tolerance toward migrants from early to late adolescence. *Journal Youth Adolescence, 43*, 1658–1671. https://doi.org/10.1007/s10964-014-0164-1

Watts, R., & Flanagan, C. (2007). Pushing the envelope on youth civic engagement: A developmental and liberation psychology perspective. *Journal of Community Psychology, 35*, 779–792. https://doi.org/10.1002/jcop.20178

White, F. A., & Gleitzman, M. (2006). An examination of family socialisation processes as moderators of racial prejudice transmission between adolescents and their parents. *Journal of Family Studies, 12*, 247–260. https://doi.org/10.5172/jfs.327.12.2.247

Chapter 7
Does Participating in National and Ethnic Associations Promote Migrant Integration? A Study with Young First- and Second-Generation Migrants

Daniela Marzana, Sara Alfieri, and Elena Marta

7.1 Introduction: The Challenges of Migration and the Role of Social Participation in National and Ethnic Associations

Research carried out in recent decades on the experiences of migrants in Western countries recognizes the complexity and multidimensionality of adaptive and integrative processes associated with the difficulties of living in a new sociocultural context.

Following an overview of the distinctive characteristics of different migrant generations, we present a brief review of studies that connect social participation with integration and multiculturalism. In this chapter we define social participation as the process by which individuals are "actively participating in the life of their communities" by joining associations and volunteering (Harvard School of Public Health/MetLife Foundation, 2004; Pozzi, Pistoni, & Alfieri, 2017). We then describe the results of a qualitative study that explored what integration meant for a group of young engaged migrants, how integrated they felt, and what role participation in associations, both national and ethnic, played in these young people's perception of integration. Next, we discuss our results, connecting them with the principal results found in the literature. We conclude with the implications of our research findings.

A large number of factors have been proposed as being associated with the adaptation and integration of different migrant generations. For the first generations these factors include sociodemographic variables (e.g., gender, age, length of stay in the host country, socioeconomic status), post-migration variables (e.g., acculturation factors), and social contextual variables (e.g., characteristics of the host country, perceived discrimination, social support, ethnic network) (Berry, 1997;

D. Marzana (✉) · S. Alfieri · E. Marta
Catholic University of the Sacred Heart, Milan, Italy
e-mail: daniela.marzana@unicatt.it

N. Balvin, D. J. Christie (eds.), *Children and Peace*, Peace Psychology Book Series, https://doi.org/10.1007/978-3-030-22176-8_7

Bornstein, 2017; Brubaker, 2001; Giuliani, Olivari, & Alfieri, 2017; Marzana, Alfieri, & Marta, 2016; Musterd & Ostendorf, 2009; Sam & Berry, 2006). For the second generations – that is, those that did not directly experience migration in that they are the offspring of migrants – these factors are linked to the difficulties of maintaining the culture of origin with the same intensity and frequency as their parents; furthermore, they are less influenced by the values and practices of their family's country of origin (Brambilla, Manzi, & Regalia, 2010; Crul & Vermeulen, 2003; Kasinitz, 2008).

Adaptation and integration processes take on particular significance in some phases of the life cycle such as adolescence and young adulthood, when the construction of one's personal and social identity takes place (Arnett, 2003; Arnett & Tanner, 2006; French, Seidman, Allen, & Aber, 2006; Phinney, Horenczyk, Liebkind, & Vedder, 2001). Constructing personal identity during migration is a complex developmental task because it requires the integration and involvement of at least two aspects that are prominent in first and second migrant generations: ethnic identity and national identity (Benet-Martínez & Haritatos, 2005; Berry, 1990; Brambilla et al., 2010). For young migrants, this transition to bicultural identity goes hand in hand with the typical transition of this age group, which has to do with the transition to adulthood.

Most research (Rumbaut & Komaie, 2010; Stepick, Stepick, & Labissiere, 2008) on young migrants has distinguished between two generations:

(a) First generation: those who arrived in the new country and established themselves there with their own migration project: work, study, reunification with other family members, etc.
(b) Second generation: those who were born in the host country from migrant parents.

The difference between first-generation young adults and young adults of second generations lies in the fact that the former experience, among others, problems of finding acceptance and meeting expectations related to their migratory life while the latter generations not only have to face problems of acceptance but also the challenges related to their desire of living autonomously. This latter task is often only partially aligned with the family's migratory project and is influenced by an array of cultural references (Besozzi, 2009). Moreover, young second-generation migrants define themselves as belonging to the country where they live but struggle to be recognized as such by their parents and by the society in which they grew up (Volpato, 2011).

Young adults' and adolescents' participation in the life of their society is an important factor for their growth process, in that it promotes identity construction and also contributes to the functioning of democracies (Fattori, Pozzi, Marzana, & Mannarini, 2015; Flanagan & Levine, 2010). This has been widely studied in the psychosociological field (Berkman & Glass, 2000; Jensen, 2003; Kawachi & Berkman, 2000; Lundy, 2007; Marzana, Alfieri, & Marta, 2016; Marzana, Pozzi, Fasanelli, Mercuri, & Fattori, 2016; Thoits & Hewitt, 2001; Vecina, Chacon, Marzana, & Marta, 2013; Watts & Flanagan, 2007).

In recent years we have seen this research interest broaden to include young migrants engaged in coping with a dual transition: the transition to adulthood and integration into the new society (Chiaranzola & Ardone, 2008). The research questions that guided this corpus of studies were: "Can young migrants' social participation be a strategy for creating a network of relationships, learning the culture, and redefining oneself?" and "Will participating in national and ethnic associations help migrants feel integrated into their community and society?". There are many ways that integration has been understood in the literature: for example, as work, academic, linguistic, legal integration, and so on. The meaning of integration that we use in the present paper is complex and multifaceted (De los Mozos, 2008; Penninx, 2003, 2005). It draws on aspects of identification with ethnic and national communities and includes both migrants' attitudes toward society and society's attitudes toward migrants.

Extending the concept of social participation to migrants means considering them not only in the position of "users" and receivers of services but also as activators of interventions and protagonists in solidarity movements. According to González, Martín, and de Castro Cardoso (2011), the higher the percentage of the migrant population participating in society, the higher the level of their integration into society. In this connection, Suárez-Orozco, Hernández, and Casanova (2015) carried out a study in the USA with the aim of exploring the social participation of young first- and second-generation Latino migrants in American life. The results of the study revealed a strong commitment on the part of the migrants to help others in a variety of ways: offering to be agents of change, volunteering on a regular basis, and mentoring and tutoring in order to help young people choose professions that can make a social contribution. Similar results were found in studies on other populations (Jensen, 2008; Rumbaut, 2008; Stepick et al., 2008).

In the field of migration, social participation can be an important instrument for social integration because it promotes the migrant's adaptation to the local context and allows him/her to actively express citizenship (Alarcón, 2011; Gele & Harsløf, 2012).

In 2007 Flanagan, Cumsille, Gill, and Gallay conducted a study aimed at understanding what influence social participation carried out by foreign students had on their beliefs and values. The sample consisted of 1052 students of African, Arabic, European, and Latin American origin residing in the USA. The results of the study demonstrated that, controlling for age, gender, and cultural background, the young people involved in social participation tended to appreciate the hosting society, to commit themselves to supporting the democratic values promoted therein, and to experience a sense of community. This entailed, firstly, that participants enjoyed a high level of individual health and well-being (Eccles & Gootman, 2002; Resnick et al., 1997); secondly, they felt more motivated to repay what they had received from the community through volunteerism.

Sonn and Fisher (1996) conducted a study in Australia with 23 people who were classified as colored in South Africa and were then residing in Melbourne. They were interviewed with an instrument to assess sense of community. The authors proposed that migrants' participation in intermediate structures such as school, religious groups, family bonds, and sporting and social organizations offered experiences of safety, belonging, a sense of stability, justice, and acceptance. Sonn (2002) conducted another study on South Africans who lived in Australia to try to understand the way in which a sense of community could be transferred from one context to another in the context of migration. He found that activity settings, including associations, provided migrants with the opportunity to participate in the new society and gave them a social role that allowed them to feel part of the community, generating a sense of "we-ness" and increasing well-being and quality of life.

In a qualitative study carried out in Andalusia (Taurini, Paloma, García-Ramírez, Marzana, & Marta, 2017), aimed at exploring how participation in community influenced migrants' well-being, the authors found that it (1) increased bicultural skills, (2) developed social relations with members of the host community, (3) strengthened social bonds with members of one's own cultural group, (4) increased abilities to be an active citizen, and (5) changed prejudices toward one's cultural group in the host country.

A quantitative investigation of 700 young migrants (18–33 years old) in Italy (Marzana & Alfieri, 2015; Marzana, Alfieri, & Marta, 2016) explored the connection between participation in community and the perception of integration and well-being. The authors found that socially engaged young migrants, independently of social demographic differences, presented higher levels of bicultural identity, perception of integration, well-being, and a sense of community.

Research on migrants' participation has investigated the role of social participation both in ethnic associations – those that arise from the aggregation of foreign people residing in the host nation – and in national associations created by citizens of the host nation. However, there are few studies that have investigated the possible differences between being a volunteer in a national as opposed to an ethnic association. In this connection, Handy and Greenspan (2009) noted that the outcomes of participation in ethnic associations, as opposed to organizations composed only of groups of citizens native to the country, can be very different.

According to Schoeneberg (1985), there are two factors that usually distinguish national organizations from ethnic ones: (a) the fact that the latter have a dual orientation, toward the country of origin and toward the country of residence, and (b) that they offer diversified activities rather than activities related to one interest only. Schoeneberg (1985), in a study that was among the first in the field, asserted that the type of result that could be obtained by ethnic associations (segregation vs. integration) depended in large measure on the orientation and activities that they offered members and, on the positions, that they covered in the society in which they operated.

In later years, a study was conducted in Belgium by Jacobs, Phalet, and Swyngedouw (2004) on Moroccan, Turkish, and Belgian immigrants with a low educational level. The results revealed that the Turkish immigrants showed the highest level of ethnic engagement in the community, but the Moroccan immigrants had the highest level of political involvement. Moreover, the study drew a distinction between belonging to ethnic associations, which produced ethnic social capital, and belonging to mixed associations, which produced cross-cultural social capital.

Brettell (2005) studied the organizational life of Indian immigrants in the USA, finding that belonging to ethnic associations allowed immigrants to continue to speak their mother tongue and to transmit transnational and transcultural engagement to their children. Ethnic associations thus seem to promote the development of biculturalism in second-generation immigrants.

Paloma, García-Ramírez, de la Mata, and Association, A. M. A. L. (2010) argued that ethnic organizations could help build bridges between newcomers and the receiving society and empower society (Maton, 2008). The authors analyzed the experience of an Andalusian association that influenced the construction of the self and promoted community improvement. It is thus evident that the type of association does not have a single effect on integrative processes, but is associated with them through a variety of forms.

7.2 A Study on Young First- and Second-Generation Migrants in Italy

The research project presented herein originated within a broader project (Marzana & Alfieri, 2015) of which this is a qualitative follow-up study. The present work focused on young migrants who had to cope with a dual transition: (a) becoming adults and (b) finding the best possible adaptation between the two cultures to which they belonged, that of their country of origin and that of the host country.

The original study had involved young migrants between the ages of 17 and 36; of these, 56.8% were engaged in an association (63% in Italian associations with the rest in ethnic or mixed associations), and 43.2% were not engaged. Using a self-report questionnaire, we investigated variables related to life satisfaction and self-esteem; variables of knowledge about context; perception of one's own integration, ethnic identity, and national identity; and, finally, a sense of community. Results indicated that, in all the variables mentioned above, the young migrants who participated in their community had significantly higher means than their peers who did not participate.

The aims of the present qualitative study were to explore (1) the meaning that integration had for young migrants who participate in associations, (2) how integrated they felt, and (3) the role of social participation in associations, both Italian and ethnic, in the participants' perception of their integration.

Participants were 21 young migrants from sub-Saharan Africa, 9 males and 12 females, ranging in age from 18 to 28 ($M = 22$) and residing in Italy. Sixteen of the young migrants participated in ethnic associations, while five participated in Italian associations (with 5.41 years of involvement in the association, on average).

Semi-structured interviews were used to collect data. The interview was conducted on an individual basis by an Italian researcher in the offices of the associations in which the young migrants were volunteering. The interview themes were based on the research aims. We identified a priori two thematic areas: meaning and perception of integration and the role of the Italian and ethnic associations in which the young migrants participated, exploring elements of the associative experience that promoted integration. Demographic information (age, marital status, country of birth, educational level, and profession) was also gathered. All interviews were carried out by the same researcher, lasted from 30 minutes to 1 hour, and were audiotaped and transcribed.

The transcripts from interviews were analyzed using thematic analysis, which is a method for identifying, analyzing, and reporting themes from the data (Braun & Clarke, 2006). Researchers using this method have to choose between one of two analytical levels: the semantic/explicit level vs. the latent/interpretative level (Boyatzis, 1998). The analysis in the present work was carried out at the semantic level, in other words, the level of meaning.

7.2.1 *Principal Findings and Discussion*

1. Meaning of Integration

The interviewees attributed a variety of meanings to the word "integration," independently of the typology of the association to which the participants belonged. One meaning of integration that came to light was respect and value of diversity, independently of the migrants' generation. According to the interviewees, each person's peculiarities, in both individual and cultural terms, were a source of enrichment as much for the young migrants as for the host society and must not be seen as reasons to discriminate:

> I think that we have to keep in mind that we are all different, but the point that should be emphasized is reciprocal respect. Respect for difference. We are always saying, "Human beings are all equal." No! Human beings are different and we have to respect one another's diversity. That is utopian talk, not reality, the reality is that we are all different. We have to always respect one another's diversity and value it[1] (L., male, age 22[2]).

A second meaning that emerged, independently of the interviewees' generation, was "integration as responsibility": the possibility of being active in the host society and working for the good of the country. This second meaning went beyond the idea of merely accepting rules and adapting to one's context, focusing, instead, on what one can do to be a resource for society:

> Everyone has to be responsible and aware of his or her role in society and therefore to move and want what is good for everyone and become active for the good of the country (F., female, 22).

---

[1] All the quotes are translated from Italian.

[2] The capital letter is in place of the name to guarantee anonymity.

Important distinctions were found in how integration was defined depending the interviewees' generation, however. Most of the first-generation young people believed that integration involved adapting to Italians' attitudes and ways of doing things, respect for the rules, and renouncing something of oneself. In fact, they maintained that the factors that could define an integrated person were knowledge of the host country's language and compliance with that culture's customs:

> I think about a boy or a foreign family who arrives in a country and after years they are integrated in the system, they feel part of the system, they work, respect the rules, understand that these rules are different from the ones in their own country, but they accept them and follow them (S., m, 27).

> Even if I'm a foreigner, I condemn people who go to another country and want to impose their culture and their laws. In my country we say "When you go to a country and you find everyone naked, you also have to be naked." If you come here, you have to do things like the Italians. When we go to an Islamic country, they require the women to put on a burqa, why is it that when they come here they can't do things like we do? (M., f, 24).

The second-generation youth, on the other hand, saw integration as the possibility of becoming part of a social group, of collaborating, and not only being limited to coexisting and merely tolerating one another. This suggested that integration is a reciprocal *rapprochement*, which also underscored the role of the host society. Many of the young people, in fact, believed that the task of Italians was to open up to foreigners, forcing themselves to get to know people before judging them, and they evoked the bidirectionality of the integrative process that must involve both of the interested parties:

> Integrating in the sense of sharing, being with people, talking, getting to know their culture (J.B., m, 26).

> [For me integration is] many elements put together that make an organization, in the sense that they collaborate with one another, they understand one another, they know how the group is made up, they live one with the other (N., f, 20).

As can be seen from the above, integration had to do with identification for the second-generation youth: being integrated meant feeling part of something and the ability to be oneself without being judged. It seemed that the young people who had been in Italy for a longer time cared more about the connection between integration and definition of identity. In fact, they were the ones who were driven to belong to associations by a desire for personal understanding and development, to understand who they were, and to keep together aspects of the two cultures. They were the ones who pointed out that one of the difficulties that a person can encounter after one's own or one's family's migratory process is the loss of identity, and they were the ones who maintained that belonging to an association could contribute to the definition of identity. Finally, it should be noted that two second-generation young women wished to emphasize that the word "integration" does not only refer to the modalities of reception and integration of foreigners into a new society, but that it was a theme that could also be extended to other situations and contexts:

> I don't even see it only as integration of foreigners into Italy, [...] integration is bigger than that, when, for example, you begin a new course of study and you have to enter, when I met my boyfriend, integration was going to meet the people who love him, his family and friends (P., f, 23).

> It's like when you finish a job and you have to begin a new one you feel a little uncomfortable because you don't know your colleagues and so you feel a little uncomfortable, or children when they have to change school, they have to change everything, classmates, teachers, friends (C., f, 27).

This suggests that it is impossible to avoid such an important theme, which involves and challenges all of us as people and does not only concern foreigners or the few people who are interested in it.

2. Perception of One's Own Integration

Perception of integration was very different in the generations under consideration, and those differences played out in the realm of ethnic and Italian identity. The first-generation youth admitted that they were less, or not at all, integrated compared to the second-generation youth and often defined themselves only in terms of ethnic identity ("I am Moroccan," "I am Tunisian"). Some of them emphasized the impossibility of forgetting their origins and talked about their desire to return to their place of birth. Some of them stressed that integration is a utopian idea because Italians were often more favorable to accepting people who were more similar to themselves, those who had a lighter skin color and spoke their language correctly. In most cases, an idea of partial acceptance came out, limited to the few who were already integrated because they had been born here or were already more easily integrated into society. Many of these young people, while acknowledging the positive role played by some Italians, believed that, in general, Italians as a population are closed to foreigners and not very interested in learning about differences, and they talked about the suffering caused by being always and everywhere perceived as an illegal immigrant, despite all their efforts. As stated by L., who came to Italy to take a second degree in medicine:

> If you say the word "integration," I think it remains a word because integration in itself does not exist. In theory integration should be from two sides: I as a foreigner have to try to integrate and Italians also have to let me do it, it isn't like this (L., m, 22).

The second-generation youth talked about their dual belonging (Italian and migrant), or they defined themselves as exclusively Italian, independently of how others saw them:

> Not everyone thinks about it in the same way. I can say that I'm integrated, some others will say that I'm not, the important thing is what I think. (G., f, 25).

Fokkema and de Haas (2011), in a study drawing on a dataset of four African migrant groups in Spain and Italy, demonstrated that the younger the person was when he/she migrated, the greater his/her possibilities of integrating into society were.

This latter aspect could also be connected to the fact that the second-generation youth were in the 18–27 years age bracket, with a median age of about 21 years. Many of them had just completed or were in the middle of the process of obtaining citizenship, which can be requested for the children of foreign parents after they come of age according to Italian law, but is often obtained some years later. Obtaining citizenship and the difficulty of the process certainly put the young person's belonging into question, just as this should cause us to reflect on our concept of citizenship (Granata, 2011). The tortuous process of obtaining official recognition of one's belonging to the Italian nation, or its recent acquisition, could push second-generation youth to question their own identity even more and to reshape it. Many of these young people talked about having developed a bicultural identity, and some of them made it clear that it required them to locate themselves in between two cultures.

3. Role of Social Participation in Associations in Promoting Integration

The interviewees unanimously stated that participating in associations (Italian and ethnic) enabled them to feel more integrated and that participation was very useful for young people who have recently arrived in a new country. Several studies have shown that social participation is a catalyst for the construction of identity because it spurs one to experience agency, social relatedness, moral and political awareness (Yates & Youniss, 1996), and self-efficacy and self-esteem (Born, Marzana, Alfieri, & Gavray, 2015; Marta & Pozzi, 2007). In fact, migrants require these elements in order to develop the critical thinking that leads them to comprehend the conditions of difficulty in which they are living and which help them feel that they possess the necessary means to face their life situation (García-Ramírez, Manuel, Paloma, & Hernández-Plaza, 2011). In this way, the individual develops "multiculturality" and becomes capable of maintaining one's roots as a reference point but is open to the possibility of learning new cultural elements that are useful and positive for one's own process of self-construction (Garza & Gallegos, 1985) and for the betterment of the social condition of one's ethnic group (Paloma & Manzano-Arrondo, 2011; Prilleltensky & Arcidiacono, 2010).

According to the young people interviewed, both types of associations (Italian and ethnic) promoted the host country's culture, values, and language; that is, they guaranteed the development of useful intercultural skills for relating to the native-born population. It did not matter whether one spoke or interacted with Italians or with migrants of the same or other countries: participating in associations, in the words of the interviewees, was a good method for entering into dialogue and learning which behaviors to use in specific situations in the Italian context:

> This type of group teaches you certain values and certain aspects that society does not teach you. (S, m, 23)

Moreover, all the youth who were interviewed agreed that partaking in associations allowed them to broaden their relational networks. McLaughlin and Talbert (2006) demonstrated that participants belonging to minority ethnic groups who experienced being valued by other members of the community felt more motivated to integrate into the new society; this led them to have a more positive view of other people and to feel included and safe (Zeldin, 2002; Zeldin & Topitzes, 2002).

Some activists in ethnic associations held a different opinion, however, claiming that partaking in ethnic associations risked causing more closure or the marginalization of its members rather than allowing them to integrate into the host society:

> So, remaining amongst ourselves does not allow us to integrate. I understood this after two years and I tried to separate a little because I cannot live here and be always with my countrymen (L., m, 22).

Ethnic associations also ensured that migrants could keep strong connections to their origins, remembering the traditions and customs of their homeland, as well as economically supporting their compatriots, as A. explained:

> Sometimes there are people who live in isolated places where there aren't many foreigners, and at least if they come [to our association] they can find some companionship like a family reunion. (A, m, 23).

The national and ethnic associations had very similar characteristics. Both supported social integration and intercultural exchange in that they were perceived as an opportunity to meet people from different cultures. Both of these association types were seen as opportunities to feel useful, and both promoted agency; that is, feeling that one is a resource for the country and able to improve oneself. All of these aspects were clearly summarized in this young migrant's words:

> You feel you are a part of the country, you feel you are a resource, you feel you belong, that you aren't a foreigner (H, m, 19).

7.2.2 Conclusion

The results of this study suggest that identity definition is different for each generation, ranging from ethnic identity for the first generation, bicultural identity for the generation in between and the second generation, to a concept of the self as Italian. Nevertheless, in agreement with Granata (2011), we believe that attempts to reduce identity to a single dimension are oversimplifications with the worrisome outcome of eliminating the complexity inherent in persons, each with his/her own peculiarities. In a globalized, dynamic, and fluid world, a plurality of belongings and self-definitions characterize most people and, even more so, individuals who have a migratory event in their history or family background. The young people in this study attest to this, having found a variety of ways to define themselves, carefully avoiding classifying themselves in overly simplistic ways. Some define themselves only as a person; some refer to their name to express who they are; some define themselves based on their parents; and some, finally, see themselves as global citizens or as Italians with a different origin story.

The longer young migrants live in Italy, the more their sense of belonging to the country seems to be strengthened. However, in most cases they do not seem to lose the connection to their origins. We found consensus among the participants regarding the positive effects of social participation on integration, with some differences depending on whether they participated in national or ethnic associations. It appears that ethnic associations run the risk of closing themselves off from, rather than opening to, the host society, while Italian associations allow participants to feel of use to the country, thus developing the hope for sense of civic engagement.

What seems to be missing in both the Italian and ethnic associations is the creation of a collective action that would make it possible not only to question but also to transform social structures (Moane, 2003; Paloma & Manzano-Arrondo, 2011; Pozzi, Fattori, Bocchiaro, & Alfieri, 2014; Prilleltensky, 2003, 2008). It thus seems crucial to ensure that the passage "from reflection to action" is accomplished in order to promote empowering community narratives (Balcazar et al., 2012) and to develop sociopolitical empowerment. The sociopolitical empowerment of migrants is indispensable to counter the inequality that they experience and to allow them to become politically active members of society who contribute to its development (Montero, 2009).

7.3 Implications

The "European Foundation for the Improvement of Living and Working Conditions" (2006) states that social participation is a fundamental element for fostering the integration of migrants. In the 2006 report, the authors argue that local institutions should promote this type of activity through incentives, public relations, and financial support. In particular, in order to develop an integrative process, it might be useful to support migrant associations, which are examples of self-organization and represent the roots of democracy and civil society. Further indications come from Flanagan, Gallay, Gill, Gallay, and Nti (2005) and Zeldin and Topitzes (2002), who identified another instrument of integration: teaching ethical and democratic values in schools in order to promote an interest in politics in the new generation of migrants.

Therefore, the efficacy of designing interventions for migrants that not only provide services but also allow them to take an active position is clear. The active engagement of young migrants is enriching for themselves and for the entire community, promoting dialogue and positive coexistence. Projects aimed at developing a sense of citizenship and social participation should encourage foreigners and native-born persons to join voluntary associations in order to promote integration, intercultural exchange, and active citizenship.

Traditionally citizenship is the belonging of a person to a state. Citizenship is therefore a concept that implies the belonging of the person to an institutionalized political community, the state, with the assumption of a set of rights and duties.

In Italy, for example, it is considered an Italian citizen from birth the child of a father or mother citizen at the time of his birth, wherever it takes place. The principles on which Italian citizenship is based are (a) the transmissibility of citizenship by descent "iure sanguinis," (b) the purchase "iure soli" (by birth on the territory) in some cases, and c) the possibility of dual citizenship by a formal request.

For many scholars, citizenship has been devalued as a tool of integration (Joppke & Morawska, 2014). As social and economic entitlements are legitimized not by nation-states and national policy but by the discourse of "universal personhood," international norms, and treaties, the traditional association between citizenship and rights, between the national state and the individual, has been broken David Jacobson claims in *Rights Across Borders* Jacobson (1996). We can suppose then that integration occurs independently of national citizenship. The growing number of foreigners, but especially the children of migrants present in Italy, should make us question and reflect on the inadequacy of our categories of citizenship and integration, and the phenomenon of associative engagement could certainly signal a turning point away from a type of thinking that has not kept up with the times. The person who commits to the good of his/her country is a citizen, enthusiastically donating time to make it a better place; the notion of citizenship should extend to the will to activate oneself in one's own life context. It is in this sense that the results of this study reveal interesting perspectives that are not only theoretical but also practical, demonstrating the positive implications of participating in associations for the process of integration and identity definition in young migrants in relationship with the native born for the construction of a fairer multicultural society.

References

Alarcón, V. B. (2011). Voluntariado e inmigración. Tendencias y perspectivas. In *Actas del I Congreso Internacional sobre Migraciones en Andalucía* (pp. 1251–1258). Granada, Spain: Instituo de Migraciones.

Arnett, J. J. (2003). Conceptions of the transition to adulthood among emerging adults in American ethnic groups. *New Directions for Child and Adolescent Development, 100*, 63–76.

Arnett, J. J., & Tanner, J. L. (Eds.). (2006). *Emerging adults in America: Coming of age in the 21st century* (p. 3). Washington, DC: American Psychological Association.

Balcazar, F. E., Suarez-Balcazar, Y., Adames, S. B., Keys, C. B., García-Ramírez, M., & Paloma, V. (2012). A case study of liberation among Latino immigrant families who have children with disabilities. *American Journal of Community Psychology, 49*(1–2), 283–293.

Benet-Martínez, V., & Haritatos, J. (2005). Bicultural identity integration (BII): Components and psychosocial antecedents. *Journal of Personality, 73*(4), 1015–1050.

Berkman, L. F., & Glass, T. (2000). Social integration, social networks, social support, and health. *Social Epidemiology, 1*, 137–173.

Berry, J. W. (1990). Psychology of acculturation. In J. Berman (Ed.), *Crosscultural perspectives: Nebraska symposium on motivation* (pp. 475–488). Lincoln, NE: University of Nebraska Press.

Berry, J. W. (1997). Immigration, acculturation, and adaptation. *Applied Psychology, 46*(1), 5–34.

Besozzi, E. (2009). Una generazione strategica. In E. Besozzi, M. Colombo, & M. Santagati (Eds.), *Giovani stranieri, nuovi cittadini. Le strategie di una generazione ponte* (pp. 13–56). Milan, Italy: Franco Angeli.

Born, M., Marzana, D., Alfieri, S., & Gavray, C. (2015). "If It Helps, I'll Carry On": Factors supporting the participation of native and immigrant youth in Belgium and Germany. *The Journal of Psychology, 149*(7), 711–736.

Bornstein, M. H. (2017). The specificity principle in acculturation science. *Perspectives on Psychological Science, 12*(1), 3–45.

Boyatzis, R. E. (1998). *Transforming qualitative information: Thematic analysis and code development*. Thousand Oaks, CA: Sage.

Brambilla, M., Manzi, C., & Regalia, C. (2010). Relazioni Famigliari e Benessere nelle Seconde Generazioni dell'Immigrazione: Il Ruolo dei Nonni ["Family Relations and Wellbeing in the Second Generations of Immigrants: The Role of Grandparents"]. *Rivista di Studi Familiari, 2*, 82–95.

Braun, V., & Clarke, V. (2006). Using thematic analysis in psychology. *Qualitative Research in Psychology, 3*(2), 77–101.

Brettell, C. (2005). Voluntary organizations, social capital, and the social incorporation of Asian Indian immigrants in the Dallas-Fort worth metroplex. *Anthropological Quarterly, 78*(4), 853–882.

Brubaker, R. (2001). The return of assimilation? Changing perspectives on immigration and its sequels in France, Germany, and the United States. *Ethnic and Racial Studies, 24*, 531–548.

Chiaranzola, C., & Ardone, R. (2008). Processi di adattamento in giovani albanesi immigrati. In E. Scabini & G. Rossi (Eds.), *La migrazione come evento familiare*. Milano, Italy: Vita e pensiero.

Crul, M., & Vermeulen, H. (2003). The second generation in Europe. *International Migration Review, 37*(4), 965–986.

De Haas, H., & Fokkema, T. (2011). The effects of integration and transnational ties on international return migration intentions. *Demographic research, 25*, 755–782.

De los Mozos, F. J. Á. (2008). Immigrant organizations as a factor of social integration. In *Migrations in a global context* (p. 27). Bilbao, Spain: University of Deusto.

Eccles, J., & Gootman, J. A. (2002). *Community programs to promote youth development*. Washington, DC: National Academy Press.

European Foundation for the Improvement of Living and Working Conditions. (2006). *Fourth European working conditions survey*. European Foundation for the Improvement of Living and Working Conditions.

Fattori, F., Pozzi, M., Marzana, D., & Mannarini, T. (2015). A proposal for an integrated model of prosocial behavior and collective action as the expression of global citizenship. *European Journal of Social Psychology, 45*(7), 906–917. https://doi.org/10.1002/ejsp.2154

Flanagan, C., & Levine, P. (2010). Civic engagement and the transition to adulthood. *The Future of Children, 20*(1), 159–179.

Flanagan, C. A., Cumsille, P., Gill, S., & Gallay, L. S. (2007). School and community climates and civic commitments: Patterns for ethnic minority and majority students. *Journal of Educational Psychology, 99*(2), 421.

Flanagan, C. A., Gallay, L. S., Gill, S., Gallay, E., & Nti, N. (2005). What does democracy mean? Correlates of adolescents' views. *Journal of Adolescent Research, 20*(2), 193–218.

French, S. E., Seidman, E., Allen, L., & Aber, J. L. (2006). The development of ethnic identity during adolescence. *Developmental Psychology, 42*(1), 1–10.

García-Ramírez, M., Manuel, L., Paloma, V., & Hernández-Plaza, S. (2011). A liberation psychology approach to acculturative integration of migrant populations. *American Journal of Community Psychology, 47*(1–2), 86–97.

Garza, R. T., & Gallegos, P. I. (1985). Environmental influences and personal choice: A humanistic perspective on acculturation. *Hispanic Journal of Behavioral Sciences, 7*(4), 365–379.

Gele, A. A., & Harsløf, I. (2012). Barriers and facilitators to civic engagement among elderly African immigrants in Oslo. *Journal of Immigrant and Minority Health, 14*(1), 166–174.

Giuliani, C., Olivari, M. G., & Alfieri, S. (2017). Being a "Good" Son and a "Good" Daughter: Voices of muslim immigrant adolescents. *Social Sciences, 6*(4), 142.

González, M. C., Martín, S. C., & de Castro Cardoso, D. (2011). Voluntariado e inmigración. *Revista de Teología y Pastoral de la Caridad, Corintios, 23*(139), 110–125.

Granata, A. (2011). *Sono qui da una vita. Dialogo aperto con le seconde generazioni [I have been here for a lifetime. An open dialogue with second generations]* (pp. 1–166). Roma, Italy: Carocci Editore.

Handy, F., & Greenspan, I. (2009). Immigrant volunteering: A stepping stone to integration? *Nonprofit and Voluntary Sector Quarterly, 38*(6), 956–982.

Harvard School of Public Health/MetLife Foundation. (2004). *Reinventing aging: Baby boomers and civic engagement.* Boston, MA: Harvard School of Public Health, Center for Health Communication.

Jacobs, D., Phalet, K., & Swyngedouw, M. (2004). Associational membership and political involvement among ethnic minority groups in Brussels. *Journal of Ethnic and Migration Studies, 30*(3), 543–559.

Jacobson, D. (1996). *Rights across borders: Immigration and the decline of citizenship.* Leiden, The Netherlands: Brill.

Jensen, L. A. (2003). Coming of age in a multicultural world: Globalization and adolescent identity formation. *Applied Developmental Science, 7*, 188–195.

Jensen, L. A. (2008). Immigrants' cultural identities as sources of civic engagement. *Applied Development Science, 12*(2), 74–83.

Joppke, C., & Morawska, E. (2014). Integrating immigrants in liberal nation-states: Policies and practices. In *Toward assimilation and citizenship: Immigrants in liberal nation-states* (pp. 1–36). London, UK: Palgrave Macmillan.

Kasinitz, P. (2008). Becoming American, becoming minority, getting ahead: The role of racial and ethnic status in the upward mobility of the children of immigrants. *The Annals of the American Academy of Political and Social Science, 620*(1), 253–269.

Kawachi, I., & Berkman, L. (2000). Social cohesion, social capital, and health. In L. F. Berkman & I. Kawachi (Eds.), *Social epidemiology*. New York, NY: Oxford University Press.

Lundy, L. (2007). "Voice" is not enough: Conceptualising Article 12 of the United Nations Convention on the Rights of the Child. *British Educational Research Journal, 33*(6), 927–942.

Marta, E., & Pozzi, M. (2007). *La Psicologia del Volontariato*. Roma, Italy: Carocci.

Marzana, D., & Alfieri, S. (2015). *Mi impegno in tutte le lingue del mondo. L'attivismo dei giovani immigrati come promotore di benessere e integrazione*. Soveria Mannelli: Rubbettino.

Marzana, D., Alfieri, S., & Marta, E. (2016). The multidimensional nature of young immigrants' well-being. *Rivista Internazionale di Scienze Sociali, 1*(1), 21–40.

Marzana, D., Pozzi, M., Fasanelli, R., Mercuri, F., & Fattori, F. (2016). The relation between participatory social practices and social representations of citizenship: A pilot study of Italian young adults. *Voluntas, 27*, 1152–1170. https://doi.org/10.1007/s11266-015-9607-x

Maton, K. I. (2008). Empowering community settings: Agents of individual development, community betterment, and positive social change. *American Journal of Community Psychology, 41*, 4–21.

McLaughlin, M. W., & Talbert, J. E. (2006). *Building school-based teacher learning communities: Professional strategies to improve student achievement* (Vol. 45). New York, NY: Teachers College Press.

Moane, G. (2003). Bridging the personal and the political: Practices for a liberation psychology. *American Journal of Community Psychology, 31*, 151–169.

Montero, M. (2009). Community action and research as citizenship construction. *American Journal of Community Psychology, 43*(1–2), 149–161.

Musterd, S., & Ostendorf, W. (2009). Residential segregation and integration in the Netherlands. *Journal of Ethnic and Migration Studies, 35*(9), 1515–1532.

Paloma, V., García-Ramírez, M., de la Mata, M., & Association, A. M. A. L. (2010). Acculturative integration, self and citizenship construction: The experience of Amal-Andaluza, a grassroots organization of Moroccan women in Andalusia. *International Journal of Intercultural Relations, 34*(2), 101–113.

Paloma, V., & Manzano-Arrondo, V. (2011). The role of organizations in liberation psychology: Applications to the study of migrations. *Psychosocial Intervention, 20*(3), 309–318.

Penninx, R. (2003). Immigration without integration: A recipe for disaster. In *Greek conference on managing migration*, disponible en http://www.migrationpolicy.org/pubs/EuropeanResources.php.

Penninx, R. (2005). Integration of migrants: Economic, social, cultural and political dimensions. *The new demographic regime: Population challenges and policy responses, 5*, 137–152.

Phinney, J. S., Horenczyk, G., Liebkind, K., & Vedder, P. (2001). Ethnic identity, immigration, and well-being: An interactional perspective. *Journal of Social Issues, 57*(3), 493–510.

Pozzi, M., Fattori, F., Bocchiaro, P., & Alfieri, S. (2014). Do the right thing! A study on Social Representation of Obedience and Disobedience. *New Ideas in Psychology, 35*, 18–27. https://doi.org/10.1016/j.newideapsych.2014.06.002

Pozzi, M., Pistoni, C., & Alfieri, S. (2017). Verso una psicologia della partecipazione: Una sistematizzazione teorica dei rapporti tra le azioni nel sociale [Toward a Psychology of Participation: A theoretical analysis of the relationship between actions in the social context]. *Psicologia Sociale, 3*, 253–276. https://doi.org/10.1482/87884

Prilleltensky, I. (2003). Understanding, resisting, and overcoming oppression: Toward psychopolitical validity. *American Journal of Community Psychology, 31*(1–2), 195–201.

Prilleltensky, I. (2008). The role of power in wellness, oppression, and liberation: The promise of psychopolitical validity. *Journal of Community Psychology, 36*(2), 116–136.

Prilleltensky, I., & Arcidiacono, C. (2010). Modello ecologico e migranti: Benessere, giustizia e potere nella vita degli immigrati. *Psicologia di Comunita'*. Milano: Franco Angeli.

Resnick, M. D., Bearman, P. S., Blum, R. W., Bauman, K. E., Harris, K. M., Jones, J., ... Ireland, M. (1997). Protecting adolescents from harm: Findings from the National Longitudinal Study on Adolescent Health. *JAMA, 278*(10), 823–832.

Rumbaut, R. G. (2008). Reaping what you sow: Immigration, youth, and reactive ethnicity. *Applied Development Science, 12*(2), 108–111.

Rumbaut, R. G., & Komaie, G. (2010). Immigration and adult transitions. *The Future of Children, 20*(1), 43–66.

Sam, D. L., & Berry, J. W. (2006). *The Cambridge handbook of acculturation psychology*. Cambridge, UK: Cambridge University Press.

Schoeneberg, U. (1985). Participation in ethnic associations: The case of immigrants in West Germany. *International Migration Review, 19*, 416–437.

Sonn, C. C. (2002). Understanding the process through sense of community. In *Immigrant adaptation* (pp. 205–222). New York, NY: Springer US.

Sonn, C. C., & Fisher, A. T. (1996). *Psychological sense of community in a politically constructed group*. Doctoral dissertation, John Wiley & Sons.

Stepick, A., Stepick, C. D., & Labissiere, Y. (2008). South Florida's immigrant youth and civic engagement: Major engagement: Minor differences. *Applied Development Science, 12*(2), 57–65.

Suárez-Orozco, C., Hernández, M. G., & Casanova, S. (2015). "It's sort of my calling": The civic engagement and social responsibility of Latino immigrant-origin young adults. *Research in Human Development, 12*(1–2), 84–99.

Taurini, E., Paloma, V., García-Ramírez, M., Marzana, D., & Marta, E. (2017). Effects of the community engagement of migrants on their well-being: The case of Moroccan leaders in southern Spain. *Journal of Prevention & Intervention in the Community, 45*(1), 32–43.

Thoits, P. A., & Hewitt, L. N. (2001). Volunteer work and well-being. *Journal of Health and Social Behavior, 42*(2), 115–131.

Vecina, M. L., Chacon, F., Marzana, D., & Marta, E. (2013). Volunteer engagement and organizational commitment in non-profit organizations: What makes volunteers remain within organizations and feel happy? *Journal of Community Psychology, 41*(3), 291–302.

Volpato, C. (2011). *Nuovi cittadini: I giovani immigrati tra accoglienza e rifiuto*. Milano, Italy: Unicolpi.

Watts, R. J., & Flanagan, C. (2007). Pushing the envelope on youth civic engagement: A developmental and liberation psychology perspective. *Journal of Community Psychology, 35*(6), 779–792.

Yates, M., & Youniss, J. (1996). Community service and political-moral identity in adolescents. *Journal of Research on Adolescent, 6*, 271–284.

Zeldin, S. (2002). Sense of community and adult beliefs towards adolescents and youth policy in urban neighborhoods and small cities. *Journal of Youth and Adolescence, 31*, 331–342.

Zeldin, S., & Topitzes, D. (2002). Neighborhood experiences, community connection, and positive beliefs about adolescents among urban adults and youth. *Journal of Community Psychology, 30*(6), 647–669.

Chapter 8
Empowerment of Intergroup Harmony and Equity

Sara Bigazzi, Sára Serdült, and Ildikó Bokrétás

> *Think it over my Brother,*
> *they say that you are dirty and leprous*
> *but only few of them know*
> *that my people scattered all over the world*
> *has never made a war.*
> Poem by Romeo Cizmic, 5 yrs, a Roma child living in a camp in Rome (Documentary on the housing situation of Roma people in Rome. 2003. https://www.youtube.com/watch?v=Tx-k7E40JrI).

8.1 Introduction

Actions aimed at empowering minority groups often focus on the specific target group without taking into consideration the broader social context within which these actions are implemented (Rappaport, 1981). While empowerment approaches can facilitate agency of minority group members and result in them fighting for rights and participating in governance (Batliwala, 1994; Deveaux, 1996; Kabeer, 1994; Parpart, 2004; Rowlands, 1997; Sen, 1990; Sen & Grown, 1988), these results are often short-lived because they are not anchored in the wider structural and social context (Marquand, 1997; Parpart, Rai, & Staudt, 2002). Social and psychological

Study 4 was funded by the Trust for Civil Society in Central and Eastern Europe initiated by the Pro Cserehát Association in cooperation with the Center for Policy Studies in the Central European University. Study 5 was funded by the National Research, Development and Innovation Office – NKFIH [K 119793 *The influence of social identity on intergroup prejudice and colective action]*. The first author acknowledges grant support from the János Bólyai Research Scholarship of the Hungarian Academy Sciences.

S. Bigazzi (✉) · S. Serdült · I. Bokrétás
Institute of Psychology, University of Pécs, Pécs, Hungary

N. Balvin, D. J. Christie (eds.), *Children and Peace*, Peace Psychology Book Series, https://doi.org/10.1007/978-3-030-22176-8_8

change involves diverse interests, negotiation, and struggles over meaning. These processes are deeply influenced by existing power relations rooted in structural inequalities, histories of oppression, and intergroup conflicts. This chapter argues that it is more effective to work not only with target groups, but to use a systemic approach, extending interventions to majority group members with the aim of reframing intergroup relations (Christie & Louis, 2012; Gayer, Landman, Halperin, & Bar-Tal, 2009; Snow & Benford, 1988).

In particular, the aim of the following chapter is to emphasize psychological dynamics embedded in social context, which define minority and majority relations. To illustrate our theoretical arguments, we employ examples from our field experiences working with Roma communities and young unemployed people in Hungary and Italy. These examples will demonstrate how an identification of the dynamics behind psychological and social change enable the implementation of more context-specific tools of empowerment in which context defines the starting points for conceiving implementations.

The theoretical frame for our work is social representation theory and social identity theory, which together demonstrate how ideologies and representations in a context define group members' interpretation of reality and social identity (Breakwell, 2010; Duveen, 2001; Andreouli, 2010). From our perspective, social context can be viewed as shared psychological realities and normative frames, not only delimiting individuals and groups but also giving them possibilities of agency and change (Fraser, 1989; Hartsock, 1990; Jovchelovitch, 1996). Finally, we emphasize the role of power in representational and identity processes (Foucault, 1979, 1991; Howarth et al., 2013; Jovchelovitch, 1996, 2007).

Clearly, embeddedness in social context determines both the majority and minority identification and representational processes and how varying possessions of power define different possibilities to act on and change dominant realities and self-definitions. Therefore, social change is a question of power, meaning that powerful majorities have more possibilities to create change (Howarth, Andreouli, & Kessi, 2014; Jovchelovitch, 1996). Therefore, empowerment should not be considered one-sided, in line with Rappaport's (1981) criticisms of implementing one-sided solutions for societal problems; rather, there should be a twin-track approach involving both the majority and the minority, emphasizing deconstruction of the former and power construction of the latter. Majorities should be "good enough communities" – to use Winnicott's term (1953) – to ensure a social context that enables not only their members but also minorities to change their positions and declare their interpretation of reality. Building up "good enough communities" requires majority members to recognize their dominant power positions and acknowledge minorities' subordinated statuses and a readiness to change this situation into a more equal dynamic for the benefit of both. At the same time, minorities should be empowered to articulate their own version of reality and act accordingly.

Our aim in this chapter is to highlight the psychological dynamics behind these processes and contribute to the efficacy of empowerment interventions. The theoretical propositions we advance will be supported with concrete examples drawn five studies with marginalized populations, Roma groups in particular.

Study 1 is an example of an unpublished study using participatory action research in a community development project in Rome born from a need expressed by the community of a Roma camp in Vicolo Savini. This bottom-up project is unique in that it features aspects of interculturality from its onset; Roma and non-Roma people worked together on a daily basis for two years.

Study 2 documents the Student Association of Roma at the University of Pécs (WHSZ) which empowers the small number of Roma students at the university with various strategies and means of achievement through, for example, grants, learning skills courses, language instruction, strengthening social networks, identity reinforcement, and conflict resolution training (Bigazzi, 2015a; Bigazzi & Serdült, 2015). Studies 3 and 4 are both interview studies.

Study 3 analyzes the psychological effects of segregated ethnic education of Roma youth (Bokretas & Bigazzi, 2013). While Roma students from the WHSZ in Study 2 received support, the Roma youth in Study 3 have no affiliation with or assistance through community development programs (hereinafter referred to as NACD).

Study 4 examines how governmental regulation of unemployment affected intergroup relations and vulnerable youth populations in 2014 (Bigazzi & Bokretas, 2013, 2014).

Study 5 explores the views of the non-Roma society on the Roma minority in Hungary (Bigazzi, Fulop, Serdult, Kovago, & Polya, 2014).

Although the research methods and social contexts are diverse, taken together, these studies demonstrate how representational and identity processes influence intrapersonal well-being and intergroup harmony.

8.2 Theoretical Framework: Social Representation Theory and Social Identity Theory

Two classic social psychological theories provide the foundation for understanding humans as cultural beings. One is social representation theory (SRT), which focuses on the product of culture, the *cultural object*, whether abstract or concrete, real or imagined, living or inanimate. The key issue in this theory is how people of the same social group acknowledge, understand, feel, and behave in relation to an object. The second theory, social identity theory (SIT), highlights the perspective of those, the *cultural subjects*, in relation to the object.

In regard to *cultural objects*, SRT (Farr, 1993; Jovchelovitch, 1996; Moscovici, 1961, 1988; Wagner, 1998) rewrites the universal and generalized essence of psychological processes (e.g., identification, motivation, mental health, memory, learning, information processing, decision-making), proposing that these processes are social products that emerge, live, spread, and die through communicative interactions. These products are actively constructed and include the stimuli, the others, and ourselves (Moscovici, 1972; Bauer & Gaskell, 1999; Marková, 2003). Individuals act and react according to their interpretations of the stimuli, which are more or less shared as social representations (Duveen, 1998; Harré, 1984) in the communities to which the individuals belong. Differences between interpretations of reality emerge and collide between individuals of different cultures or even within individuals; this is what the SRT refers to as cognitive polyphasia (Jovchelovitch, 2002). For example, in Study 3, Roma youngsters studying in secondary school or university cope with difficulties concerning the different interpretations of schooling and learning, setting up a conflict between their family socialization environment and the expectations of the school context:

> Because there were no examples in the family. My mother is still asking: when do you finish school? And yes, I'm 23 now, and I'm still studying. They don't understand what university is. At least my parents don't understand. (23-year-old Roma student, NACD)

In regard to *cultural subjects*, SIT provides insights into both conscious and internalized memberships and associated emotional resources and values (Tajfel, 1981). Memberships that are (or become) salient act as motivators of behavior (Haslam, 2004; Reicher & Haslam, 2006; Tajfel, 1981). Thus, fellow group members, as opposed to members of different groups, are more likely to have similar worldviews, to experience more trust with in-group members, and to cooperate with each other (Branscombe, Ellemers, Spears, & Doosje, 1999; Reicher & Haslam, 2006).

To achieve positive evaluations and distinguish themselves from others, individuals engage in social comparison. Through this process they fulfil their belonging with meaning, identifying those who are the relevant others, evaluating and enhancing the group with which they identify, and reinforcing the self through membership. Most importantly, social comparison processes make it possible for the individual to satisfy needs of positivity (i.e., being evaluated positively) and distinctiveness. In Study 5, we asked 600 Hungarians whether they agreed with the statement *One of the biggest social conflicts in Hungary is that of the Roma people*. Their answers were coded regarding the kind of distinction they used; 50% of the whole sample evaluated Roma people according to their own normative system, thereby "comparing" minority members unfavorably:

> "I agree. The reasons concern the different culture and associated lifestyle, and inherited genes, which makes it impossible for them to change their socially unacceptable lifestyle. They are not able (or don't want) to socialize. Meanwhile they commit crimes in order to survive and receive social support for children." (44-year-old female with a university degree, Budapest)

> "I agree, totally. Unfortunately I work with Gypsies, I see their behaviour, their philosophy, I see how they relate to things. It is disappointing, but things are going worse. The problem is becoming unsolvable. They don't want to go to school, to work, just to be. They are parasites on the workers, and they are comfortable with it." (28-year-old male with a university degree, town)

At times, one's membership in an identity group does not confer a positive and distinctive identity for the individual. For instance, Roma youth often face negative judgments from non-Roma majority members. The following example from Study 3 illustrates how non-Roma individuals are the main reference frame for Roma people:

> I have a lot of inhibition, internal conflicts. Recently I was on a bus and a guy started to stare at me, as if he wanted me to feel my Gypsiness. And I became paranoid that I might smell like sweat. But then I thought hey, I took a shower an hour ago, but I sniffed at myself just to make sure. (24-year-old Roma student, NACD)

According to SIT, individuals can leave the group. Mobility is an individual strategy that can be used if (a) group membership is not a core element of the identity, (b) there is no sign of visible stigma for leaving, and (c) the individual perceives group boundaries as permeable. If these conditions are not satisfied, individuals will remain in the group. For those remaining, there are two types of strategies to ameliorate a negative social identity. The chosen strategy activated depends on the perceived stability and legitimacy of the social system (Tajfel, 1981). Those groups that perceive society as unstable and/or illegitimate will act for societal change. Groups that are unable to imagine a social order change are motivated to act in ways that ameliorate the image of the group so that it will be evaluated in a more positive way.

And what about unrecognized positive memberships that exist but are not identified by the individuals? SIT does not provide an answer to this question, as it focuses on the subjective perspective of acknowledged memberships as delimited in self-categorization theory (Turner, 1985). However, we think that recognition of common interests by various individuals in a local community can be an additional direction of social change. Thus, this is a question of working with identities and creating new belongings in local contexts. This work is a political act since it implicitly includes a desired social order.

Our various possible identifications and belongings are also cultural objects. When we speak about identity, it is important to note that humans do not behave singularly and autonomously in public spaces, but they act according to their interpretations of reality. This includes self-interpretations and related possibilities that are tied to the memberships in social categories available in their respective contexts. These in turn are offered and limited by and negotiated with others in their environment (Mead, 1934; Reicher, 2004; Stryker, 1968, 1987; Tajfel, 1981; Tajfel & Turner, 1979; Vygotsky, 1978, 1979).

Identity regulation processes can be understood as coping with threat. Tajfel (1981) described efforts for achieving a positive and distinctive identity; Breakwell elaborated on this concept in her description of identity regulation processes in Western cultures. She claimed that individuals living in Western cultures aim to achieve self-esteem, distinctivity, continuity, and efficacy and that failure to achieve these characteristics results in identity threat (Breakwell, 1993; Vignoles, Chryssochoou, & Breakwell, 2002). The concept of identity threat applies mostly to the experience of stigmatized minorities, as stigmatization prevents maintaining a positively evaluated identity (Breakwell, 1986, 1993, 2010). For minority members, stigmatized identity elements are salient and form the core of identity, defining one's possibilities of existence. In study 3 we find examples of how these dynamics are rooted in the identity construction processes of Roma students. Stigmatization cannot be neglected or ignored as it is always present and identity constructions are embedded in continuous dialect with it:

> It has a deep impact on your whole life how others think about you. You start to think that you are stupid, smelly or a freak in some way (25-year-old Roma student, NACD)

> …because they try to socialize you not to cry and to be proud to be a Gypsy, especially when you are mistreated. But how can you be proud if you are Gypsy and you can hear all the time how shitty Gypsies are? How can you be proud when the word Gypsy is so negative? (24-year-old Roma student, NACD)

Identity threat can be experienced without stigmatization from the outside. In these cases, threat is rooted in unprocessed past traumas and transmitted through socialization processes resulting in the subjective perception of being targeted. In this case, the core element of the identity is the subjective experience of being a victim. Identity construction can include the need to be recognized and acknowledged as a victim, which is a vulnerable, dependent position. Although collective victimhood (Bar-Tal, Chernyak-Hai, Schori, & Gundar, 2009; Vollhardt, 2012) is often a characteristic of majorities, its psychological dynamics are similar to the threatened identity of stigmatized minorities.

What threatened identities have in common with each other are the passive and subordinated positions, implicating complex consequences. One of the consequences influencing both psychological processes and intergroup relations is that of the self/other construction, which is based on a hierarchical relationship. The activation of this hierarchical relationship system implies superior and inferior positions. Groups differing in status are associated with different rights and duties (Andreouli, 2010) and these differences not only define the group's choices of action but also have a bearing on intergroup relations. These dynamics maintain existing social orders and are strictly related to power positions.

8.3 Empowerment Interventions

8.3.1 The Role of Social Interactions

Working with others in social contexts requires a focus on ongoing interactions embedded in the larger social environment rather than focusing solely on the individuals or specificities of their groups. Without considering the broader social context, "intergroup problems" might appear to be due to isolated individuals or groups, rather than consequences of existing intergroup relations, structural inequalities, and histories of oppression that fuel intergroup conflict and dominant narratives.

Focusing merely on target groups can also lead to incorrect and/or problematic conclusions as it can contribute to the "blaming the victim" phenomenon (Ryan, 1976). Blaming the victim phenomena at an intergroup level occurs in five steps: (1) a societal problem is identified, (2) the problem is attributed to a target group, (3) differences between that group and other groups are observed, (4) causes of differences are identified, (5) and, finally, social-political interventions are implemented with the aim to change the target group without considering systemic changes (Arató, 2012).

It is paramount to prioritize the focus on interactions because through them social change can emerge. We continuously negotiate with others our conceptions of knowledge, norms, values, and who we are. Identity (*who I am*) and knowledge (*how I think about the world around me*) are formed in a continuous process of meaning construction. Others not only present their own positions, but react to and explicitly and implicitly judge ours. In Study 3, we observe examples of representation and identity negotiation from interviews with Roma high school and university students. They often report how others judge them:

> At home we do not live with Gypsies, but at the center of the village. Gypsies attack us saying that we have become Gadjos, and so on. They point at us, but it is not so funny. (23-year-old Roma student, NACD)

> They (the ethnic group in her village) insult me saying I am a slut and how I live well here because I get money. And how I dress differently from them. They still attack me like this. One of them shouted behind me on the street "[you] slut of Pécs" or "slut of Germany" because I visited Germany. (24-year-old Roma student, NACD)

> The mistress in the nursery all time put my bed in a different part, and it was viewed by all of the children (22-year-old Roma student, NACD)

Interactions in the context of economic and social relations create and recreate a cultural, political, and ideological texture of meanings. These meanings allow individuals to live in a more or less consensual world regarding visions of reality, interpretations of the past, norms and deviance, possible identification dimensions, methods of interactions, approved coping strategies, and plans for the future. New interactions, new in their structure for the participants or the role assessed, can create social change. To demonstrate this process, we draw an example from Study 1. This study documents how long-term community development processes can lead to psychological change in representations and identity constructions through new interactions.

> Shishiri, an NGO in Rome active between 2002 and 2004, was created in response to the request of S, a member of a Roma camp. S was living in the most populated camp of Europe in Rome with her husband and her nine children. S had worked with me previously in a focus group on collective memory of Roma a year before and asked that Roma and Gadjo (non-Roma) people collaborate together "to create something that will have weight, that will remain with us, with others, something new that can be pulled out only from a magic hat, a *shishiri*." Picnics were then organized in various parks all over Rome where our friends and families discussed plans for collaborations. In September 2002, 20 participants (10 Roma and 10 Gadjo) voted on our roles and on rules within our new organization and

> made closer acquaintances with each other through meetings. The group gradually succeeded in negotiating the boundaries of ethnic belonging and in resolving unavoidable conflicts necessary for dialogue. When conflicts arose, the continuously exposed common goals and the adopted problem resolution strategies requiring long hours of negotiation enhanced members involvement and investment. Over time, people began to trust each other, showed curiosity, and told about their stories and how they really felt, despite fears of public opinion. Members of this small community worked to create a shared vision of reality and Shishiri became an important part of our everyday lives. Each person changed through this process although the change was not always visible, nor under direct negotiation.
>
> An example of this effect of invisible change was an explanation made by S in front of the students of the Loyola Chicago University campus in Rome. The campus invited Shishiri to speak about Roma people and their problems in Italy. S prepared a video about housing problems and camps for the occasion. At the end of the video students asked her why Roma people had so many children if they were so poor. S explained that "dead and aborted infants will return and take revenge, biting and poisoning the mothers." In the next year Shishiri was re-invited to the campus to speak to a new student group. This time, in response to the same question, S answered differently, explaining that "Romas think about families as small economic units, an interdependent system in which elders help the youngsters for the survival of all." We listened with surprise, as we had never talked about this issue, nor did we comment on her first answer 10 months before.

There is continuous tension between stability and change in social systems – between maintaining the status quo and changing the structure. In addition, when the need for change is expressed, barriers and resistance arise as the provision of change causes psychological and social anxiety. The negotiation about good and bad directions of change among the different parties, between participants and stakeholders involved, becomes a priority. These dynamics of change often prevent the recognition of diversity either of interests or identities, which is the first step to initiate negotiation and reconciliation of values, representations, and interests, and it is also a prerequisite for active participation and involvement.

> After a while, Shishiri (study 1) decided to create a dialogue with the stakeholders in Rome in addition to everyday rehearsal and assemblies. We asked for meetings with all the existing NGOs in the field, proposing cooperation of any kind. Our project was unique as both Roma and non-Roma were participating in these meetings; afterward we interpreted and discussed what happened as a group. Very soon, all these institutions refused to cooperate either implicitly or explicitly. The head of a historical NGO, which was responsible for a major integration project with Roma youth in Rome, asked me in front of Roma members if I *really thought I could work with these animals*. The head of another NGO operating primarily in political representation tried to discredit me in front of all the Roma camp, shouting loudly that *I could not enter the camp anymore, because I was a mole from the police*. Such attacks had the opposite effect and members concluded that it was happening because we were creating something new and disturbing the old mechanisms. In this way, attacks and refusals from the outside reinforced the community and new people joined our organization. After a year, we were made up of 70 people (nearly half of them Roma) and we created a theater piece without a place and without any money. However, we were very motivated to meet and work on our project every day.

Although individuals should be free to express their own views, a few exert influence on others according to their positions of power. Often these others do not even know they should be concerned, and not being involved, they do not actively participate in the negotiation. Moreover, as Howarth and her colleagues (2014) point out, participation is not only the expression of worldviews, acceptable values, and norms, but "participation can be conceptualised as the power to construct and convey particular representations over others. In other words, it refers to the symbolic power to construct legitimate social knowledge, norms and identities, and to disregard, marginalize or silence alternative ways of knowing and being" (Howarth et al., 2014, p. 2). Beyond the recognition of diversity, involvement in societal life, and deconstruction and reconstruction of meanings, values, and norms, the issue of power remains an important consideration.

8.3.2 The Role of Power

While social change is embedded in interaction – broadening, confining, and establishing the borders of the cognitive world in social dialogue – change requires more than the process of interaction and the achievement of consensus among individuals or groups. Power differences matter. Powerful groups have the ability and opportunity to define the other as well as the whole social reality through their access to the construction and dissemination of social representations (Sarrica, Mazzara, & Brondi, 2016). Clearly, the process of representation is rooted in asymmetric social relations and embedded in contexts (Moscovici, 1988). Hence, some worldviews are overrepresented in society, while the views of minority groups lack the symbolic power of ensuring respect for their version of the world (Howarth et al., 2014; Jovchelovitch, 1996). These overrepresented or hegemonic representations of the world, including that of the social order, naturalize the existing social structure and become institutionalized through regulations and laws that support the social order. Study 4 provides an example of how different layers of communication maintain the status quo and regulate the social order.

> The Hungarian legislation passed a regulation in 2012 that reduced the monthly long-term unemployment allowance from 90 to 73 euros with the eligibility criterion to take part at least for a month per year in voluntary work (in organizations validated by the local governments, while local governments are not more obligated to provide public work opportunities). The task of finding employment becomes the responsibility of people on the periphery of society. The related political discourse sent systematic messages to everyone, the unemployed, the working poor, and the middle class, thereby redefining social relations for the whole society. Even the young unemployed could sense the different layers of the message of such a regulation.

This is how a 24-year-old young unemployed Roma woman explains these layers:

> It sends a message that Gypsies are just waiting for the allowance that the workers produce. They don't really want to work. I'm sure that people who have jobs think like this. The average person, the majority thinks like this….
>
> I think they want to frighten people into getting a job. I would work, but there is no work. Do you think that if they reduced salaries more, there would be work for people?

> …Is this money to be even poorer? Or to perish? Because it is quite a lot of money to die, but it is not very much to live on.

More important than the redefined unemployment allowance and its conditions is its effects; the unemployed became the agents of their own destiny, reframing their status in society. This had clear consequences for the social order and attitudes toward them changed in greater negativity. As Howarth (2006) said "the reproduction of power relations depends on the continuous and creative (ab)use of representations that mystify, naturalise and legitimate access to power." (Howarth, 2006: 79). Such institutionalized, hegemonic representations demark identities and transmit messages about the self, about we and the others. Who are we? Who are they? Is there any connection or just differences between us? If *us* at all exists?

These ideologically sustained social realities have significant effects from the very beginning of life. They frame the primary environment, identity development, possible coping mechanisms and later autonomy, and resilience. The environment of socialization reflects this framing of society and adapts to this constructed reality (Leman & Duveen, 1998; Sarrica, Roseti, Brondi, Cervelli, & Leone, 2016). In study 3, we asked Roma high school and university students to reflect on their childhood (under 12 years of age) experiences about being a member of a minority:

> Because my mother always told me… Nay, she didn't told me. I just know from her body language that I have to behave in a different way with Hungarians than with Roma people. (16-year-old Roma student, NCAD)

> They taught me at home that I was different. And they told me that if a white person made one step, I had to make two. And I always tried. Always more and more and more and more. (17-year-old Roma student, NCAD)

These examples present the psychological states of being in a lower status position. The psychological states become alive through the dialectic of these contents and other environmental factors, such as the coping ability of the community, the primary and surrounding environment, and characteristics of the individual. It is evident that developing identity through socialization in these cases involves a sense of being a member of a minority. Moreover, minority members' constant exposure to disparaging views conditions them to continuously compare and differentiate themselves in ways that elicit reinforcement (Clark & Clark, 1950); they develop a need for constant approval, a dynamic similar to the victim role. Here is a good example of the self-reflection expressed by a Roma high school student (study 3) on how minority membership affects identity construction:

> You have to be careful when to say this happened because I am Gypsy. Because we cause pain to ourselves if in every situation where I feel discomfort I say that's because of my origins. I try to separate these two. (22-year-old Roma university student, NCAD)

In the following section, we underscore how a well-functioning community can provide a foundation of support, giving feedback about how to rectify unfavorable situations and cope with the failures an individual encounters.

8.3.3 The Role of Communities

If power relations and dominant representations are questioned, then minorities can become *empowered.* This means that the subordinated status of minorities is recognized and minority members raise the need for change. The following example presents the actions of an empowered minority, initiated through a bottom-up process of change.

> The Wlislocki Henrik Student College (WHSZ) is a program supporting underprivileged and/or Roma students (mostly first generational intellectuals) since 2013 at the University of Pécs, Hungary. The access of Roma and Gypsy youth to higher education is currently as low as 1%. Reasons for such low enrollment are rooted in the inadequate functioning of society, including problems such as institutionalized segregation and racism. The WHSZ is focused on the empowerment of Roma intellectuals through a complex approach: although implemented in an academic milieu, its main objective is not only to support students' educational progress but to create a strong community to ground future social capital, facilitating their participation in public life and initiating dialogues between Roma, Gypsy, and non-Roma/Gypsy intellectuals, a key element for long-term success. To realize these ambitions, the multielement program aims to ensure a supportive environment which enables the students to process their failures in a constructive way and build an academic career instead of quitting the system altogether. Therefore, the WHSZ implements research projects, community weekends, foreign language courses, tutorial and mentoring systems, and volunteering initiatives to mediate a set of values and alternative representations for redefining self-interpretation and positioning processes (Varga, 2015). Although the WHSZ was organized in a top-down way, through constant interaction a strong connection developed between the members; the community started to break out beyond the formal frames of the project, and minority actions emerged in a bottom-up way. The following story is a good illustration: in December of 2014, graffiti appeared on a wall in front of the University: *Sallow skinned Gypsies, even with a diploma you won't be real Hungarians! You will still be parade-Gypsies!* This openly racist message reflects the dominant representation of non Roma people, according to which Roma people do not graduate from university because the diploma is a privilege of (white) Hungarians. Students of the WHSZ gave a quick response to the graffiti: within a single day, they organized a public event through social media inviting Roma high school students, representatives from academia, and the press to participate and give voice to their alternative representation. Students used the letters of the original message to create new words like *dialogue*, *magic*, *voice*, and *love*; they wrote these alternative words on paper and covered the racist graffiti with them. The aim of the peaceful action was not only to negate the negative and restrictive representation of the Roma people but also to express their own views and versions of how they would like to be seen. These students realized that although they worked for their personal goals, they faced the same difficulties and barriers posed by stigmatization, which they could face together as members of a community.

A basic condition for bottom-up processes is that community members realize they have common goals, interests, and shared realities. These goals may change and transform once dialogical processes start concerning how to achieve them. Through dialogue, members articulate their interests and take account of others' perspectives. Discussing common goals enables people to feel involved; this is also where differences of opinion, tensions, and coalitions may emerge.

Two essential aspects of this bottom-up process are the decentralized or horizontal partnership and the ability to engage in constructive debate. The subject of criticism is not the speaker but the contents of their proposed position. Content-focused criticism is constructive since it considers arguments for and against the communicated position. A proposal requires an underlying personal view (self-statements) and content-based arguments (embedded in perspective) in order for participants to become involved, not feel threatened, and persist in the knowledge construction process. When individuals are empowered, they are open to consider alternative positions: *this is what I think according to my knowledge; it can be questioned, refuted, and reviewed together. This is my contribution, which can be approved or contested to articulate a new position*. Horizontal partnership means there are no "misconceptions" in this process of common knowledge construction, but each party's contribution is an essential and constructive part of the outcome. Individual responsibility is replaced by responsibility taken by all participants in the dialogue. Participants' approach to conflicts and debates and their mutual trust improve. Starting a discussion is threatening for participants. The first contribution reveals the otherwise invisible individual's perspective, the way they think about themselves. This process reactivates the issues of responsibility, threat, anxiety, and self-esteem (Bigazzi, 2015b).

If community members are able to keep focused on common goals and rely on interdependence to achieve them, then the community starts to *pulsate*, generating and progressively resolving conflicts constructively, which are required to create new levels of consensual states. These dialectics provide conflicted dualism, mutual tension, creative negation, participation in a never completely resolved dispute, and partial and open conclusions. Thus, new consensual knowledge is forged through (dialectic and contrasting) dialogue. New knowledge and involvement in the process of its construction change participants' positions.

It is an objective that empowerments become independent from authorities. Activity and practice creates new identity possibilities, and alternative representations can be experienced. Intergroup conflict and intergroup harmony are rooted in the texture of context, power relations, and existing representational fields. To move conflictual relations toward harmony, stakeholders' awareness of the role of the context is fundamental. Only in this way, through deconstructing our own power positions, we can invite the other to inclusive spaces, enabling the emergence of new alternative representations, partnerships based on dialogue, and the recognition of existing diversity to foster societal development.

Developmental psychology can deepen our understanding of how members of a society learn to cope with distress and to regulate emotions that emerge from intergroup relations and how they can remain open for societal change. From the very beginning of our existence, we face overwhelming experiences and an environment that helps its members restore a sense of continuity. As Winnicott (1953) pointed out in relation to the concept of mothering and the mother's almost complete adaptation to the infant's needs in the earliest stage of development, adaptational failures emerge gradually as the infant's ability to deal with these failures increases. These failures are as important as the moments of perfect care; failures provide opportunities for the infant to experience the unknown and the unusual, giving them opportunities to practice, change, and develop. Environmental responses of acceptance are needed for the infant to experience reparation. The functionality of these failures are possibilities to experience the difference between the self and the others as well as reparation through the other's active participation. Reparation reinforces the experience of autonomy and restores the continuity of the self. In this way, confidence and trust in the world arises and self-confidence increases. This process can be seen as primary empowerment, a process that influences resilience or mentalization (Fonagy, Steele, Steele, Higgitt, & Target, 1994).

Ideally, the community later takes the role of a holding environment, fostering a sense of cohesiveness. This helps individuals face failures and remain open to new changing interpersonal, social, or societal relations. Thus, empowerment is deeply dependent on community, not single individuals. Societal change is the question of empowerment and of "good enough communities," holding environments that support adaptation to failures as the individual becomes ready to deal with them.

The development of holding or "good enough" communities needs to be facilitated by processes aimed at creating inclusive spaces for empowerment by the "elite," stakeholders, social workers, community developers, and actors of social interventions. Inclusive spaces are inclusive in both a material and a psychological sense. Achieving equality requires the elite to be aware of their superior power positions and make constant efforts to deconstruct them. Deconstruction is a prerequisite for changing the dominant forms of communication, creating inclusive space – an incubator – where new social realities and cognitive alternatives may emerge. In this space, minority groups or disadvantaged groups can elaborate their own perspectives, test the validity of possibilities, and later construct and disseminate their own versions of reality. Through this process, their positions of power also change as they reposition themselves in relation to others.

8.3.4 *The Primacy of Context*

It is also important to point out that fragmented societies with structural inequalities and oppressed communities are not functional. Unrecognized inequalities cause intergroup conflicts and over time these conflicts pose a threat to majorities. An example of this is ghettos and no-go zones where entering is impossible for outsiders; gaps in society mean the limitation of freedom for everyone. Action plans and interventions that do not address inequalities on a systemic level are dysfunctional because maintaining the existing social order reproduces the same errors. Only by accepting, understanding, and working with self-other differences can communities and societies evolve. Thus, inclusion and empowerment affect both minority groups and majority society.

The existence of diversity as a given condition is not subject to debate; the question is how society and individuals deal with it. Empowerment is also important for majorities, enabling them to develop self-confidence, perspective taking, mentalization, communication, and (create) innovation. A twin-track approach is required for intergroup harmony, one which includes empowerment for both minority *and* majority groups, albeit with different objectives.

The objective of empowering majorities is to enable them to give up dominant positions and take into account the possibility of systematic changes in order to consider minority perspectives. This can be implemented through identity reinforcement, which improves self-esteem, conditions for perspective taking, openness toward the other, and abilities of mentalization while decreasing psychological distance and depersonalization. In this way, majority members become more reflective and aware of their power and its consequences, and they are enabled to surrender their dominant positions in negotiation processes without experiencing identity threat.

By contrast, merely aiming to reduce prejudice or one-sidedly strengthening the social identity of the minority in a decontextualized way (e.g., teaching of Roma culture, language teaching in ethnic schools) does not produce inclusion or a sense of agency to create social change, nor does it create alternative/contesting representations. These faint attempts simply smooth over differences and conflicts through assimilation/integration to the extent that diversity is allowed as defined by the majority. There is no negotiation or creation of opportunity through representational change. These unfounded endeavors lead to identity crises, long-term transitional states, and feelings of abandonment. In Study 3, Roma university students who studied in a separated ethnic high school reported feelings of isolation, of belonging nowhere:

> It's very hard because my family doesn't accept me. My family tells me that I am different. Other prejudiced people and peers also tell me that I am different. Ok, I'm different. But that's because I have more opportunities and I can succeed better. But now, I don't belong anywhere (23-year-old Roma student, NACD)

By contrast, contextual empowerment guarantees and expands space for experiencing the interdependence between *ability*, *activity*, and *responsibility*. Contextual empowerment means that the instruments given to people enable them to change their knowledge concerning cultural objects and subjects rooted in their context.

> As reported by Bigazzi (study 1): S asked to create something together after an evening that I invited her to sing in my music band. That evening she arrived dressed up, chic, and elegant. A few days later she called me with her proposal and asked to meet together the officers of the City Hall of Rome who worked on Roma integration and whom she knew well. When we met there, I was surprised to see that she was dressed in a dirty yellow miniskirt and tights with obvious holes in them. She spoke with a strong Gypsy accent that she had never used with me. I did not realize in that moment that she was using a kind of role and relationing, worked out over time as a subject of *assistentialist* politics. Two years later we had an appointment with the city counselor of social policies and I noted that S was dressed quite elegantly, wearing a white blouse with a black jacket. She conversed ably without an accent; took notes in her small notepad; appeared self-confident, active, and assertive; and enjoyed the situation. She had shed the expected "Roma woman who needs help" role, repositioning herself in her political relationships over time through close and equal contact with some gadjos. This contact made her able to reposition herself, to construct and generalize alternative social representations of majority-minority relations.

The recognition and acknowledgment of abilities reinforce the identity of community members, increase their self-confidence, and enhance their activities and contributions to the community. Abilities and activities reinforce each other; as the awareness of abilities results in action, so that action, in turn, is reinforced resulting in improved abilities. In this process of empowerment people can feel their own development, and the flexibility of the boundaries of their competences, and they can recognize their shortcomings and potentials. Practice, continuous monitoring of abilities, and self-reflection and feedback from others, including both successes and failures, condition and cause the stability and complexities of our identity. Responsibility for actions and the repeatedly renewed attainment of skills depend on the perceived freedom of carrying out an action and on the increased stability of identity. Acknowledgment of a new (power) position and repositioning enables recognized membership in the community, the identification of common interests, and the establishment of organizations to represent these interests.

8.4 Conclusions

In this chapter, we outlined two main theoretical approaches of social psychology that offer the frame to understand how identity construction and representations/worldviews, subject and object, are strictly interconnected. From our perspective, working on identity and/or on worldviews is the foundation of empowerment processes.

Hence, this theoretical contribution aims to shift some of the emphasis and analytic focus of interventions regarding empowerment of minorities. Rather than focus interventions on the success of lone individuals or minorities as a target group, we discuss the importance of the interactions in the interventions or empowerment projects, rather than the success of lone individuals or demarcated minorities as target groups of the intervention. Interactions contain opportunities for social change where new interpretations of the self and reality can emerge and be shared. The possibility of active participation of individuals and their influence in these interactions depends on the acknowledgment of their diverse positions and respective forms of power in the specific context of a given interaction.

Communities also matter. Community responses to failures and needs are fundamental to a well-working empowerment strategy. We suggested that interventions can be more effective and more rooted in communities if the target group is broadened for the host community to include those who hold powerful positions. The deconstruction of power positions of the majority or its representatives (in our case primarily social workers, teachers, community developers) in contact with the minorities can give space to creating alternative social representations. To practice in a safe inclusive space ensures opportunities for expression, debate, and the creation of alternatives. In these interactions, failures – which are often delegated by the majority to the minority – need to be considered a natural part of every process and detached from the membership status.

The harder part of this process is that both the deconstruction of power positions and rise of alternative social representations can be threatening for members of the majority. Sensitization of power positions and developing self-confidence for this deconstruction may be considered basic elements in the education of professionals engaged in social service; this process might be considered as empowering the majority to be primed for inclusion.

We suggest that empowering minorities must be more context-specific, reflecting the concrete problems and needs of the community itself. This may be problematic for projects requiring hard data in order to maintain funding; traditional objective indicators are unable to detect the efficacy of context-specific initiatives despite the fact that these empowerment strategies may be more adequate in addressing systemic issues.

References

Andreouli, E. (2010). Identity, positioning and self-other relations. *Papers of Social Representation, 19*(1), 14.1–14.13. http://psych1.lse.ac.uk/psr/PSR2010/19_14Andreouli.pdf.

Arató, F. (2012). Rejtett sztereotípiák az egyetemi hallgatók körében. In A. Orsós & F. Trendl (Eds.), *Útjelzők* (pp. 24–32). Pécs, Hungary: PTE-BTK.

Bar-Tal, D., Chernyak-Hai, L., Schori, N., & Gundar, A. (2009). A sense of self-perceived collective victimhood in intractable conflicts. International Review of the Red Cross, 91(874), 229–258.

Batliwala, S. (1994). The meaning of women's empowerment: New concepts from action. In G. Sen, A. Germain, & L. C. Chen (Eds.), *Population policies reconsidered: Health, empowerment and rights* (pp. 127–138). Boston, MA: Harvard University Press.

Bauer, M. W., & Gaskell, G. (1999). Towards a paradigm for research on social representations. *Journal for the Theory of Social Behaviour, 29*(2), 163–186. https://doi.org/10.1111/1468-5914.00096

Bigazzi, S. (2015a). Önismeret – személyes és társas kompetenciák fejlesztése. In A. Varga (Ed.), *Próbatétel… a pécsi roma szakkollégiumi program értékelése* (pp. 277–287). Pécs, Hungary: PTE-BTK NTI. http://wlislocki.pte.hu/sites/wlislocki.pte.hu/files/oldal_mo/00_whsz_hun_beliv_print.pdf

Bigazzi, S. (2015b). Sing-les: Diversity, dialogue, knowledge. In A. Varga (Ed.), *Inclusive university how to increase academic excellence focusing on the aspects of inclusion* (pp. 27–43). Pécs, Hungary: Autonomy and Responsibility Study Volumes IV. http://www.kompetenspedagogus.hu/sites/default/files/arato-f-varga-a-inclusive-university-univ-pecs-2015.pdf

Bigazzi, S., & Bokretas, I. (2013). "As I see the world it seems pitch black…" A social psychological study. In K. Nagy (Ed.), *The effect of reducing the social allowance in rural Hungary* (pp. 34–49). Budapest, Hungary: Procserehát Egyesület, http://www.pillangokutatas.bffd.hu/findings/studies

Bigazzi, S., & Bokretas, I. (2014). Helyzetbe zárt mentális folyamatok és viszonyrendszerek ideológiai tükre: Elméleti és társadalmi reflexiók egy kutatás során. *Kriminológiai Közlemények, 74*, 63–76. https://www.kriminologia.hu/publikaciok/kriminologiai-kozlemenyek-74

Bigazzi, S., Fulop, E., Serdult, S., Kovago, P., & Polya, T. (2014). Collective victimhood and prejudice against Gypsies in Hungary. Paper presented in EASP Small Group Meeting on Collective victimhood. Verona. 25–27 Jun

Bigazzi, S., & Serdült, S. (2015). Nemzetközi kapcsolatok. In A. Varga (Ed.), *Próbatétel… a pécsi roma szakkollégiumi program értékelése* (pp. 157–169). Pécs, Hungary: PTE-BTK NTI. http://wlislocki.pte.hu/sites/wlislocki.pte.hu/files/oldal_mo/00_whsz_hun_beliv_print.pdf

Bokretas, I., & Bigazzi, S. (2013). A felsőoktatásban tanuló roma fiatalok pszichológiája. *Romológia, 1*(1), 86–103. https://doi.org/10.15170/ROM.2014.01.01.09

Branscombe, N. R., Ellemers, N., Spears, R., & Doosje, B. (1999). The context and content of social identity threat. In N. Ellemers, R. Spears, & B. Doosje (Eds.), *Social identity: Context, commitment, content* (pp. 35–58). Oxford, England: Blackwell Science.

Breakwell, G. M. (1986). *Coping with threatened identity*. London, UK: Methuen.

Breakwell, G. M. (1993). Social representations and social identity. *Papers on Social Representations, 2*(3), 1–20. http://www.psych.lse.ac.uk/Psr/PSR1993/2_1993Brea2.pdf

Breakwell, G. M. (2010). Resisting representations and identity processes. *Papers on Social Representations, 19*, 1–11. http://www.psych.lse.ac.uk/psr/PSR2010/19_06Breakwell.pdf

Christie, D. J., & Louis, W. R. (2012). Peace interventions tailored to phases within a cycle of intergroup violence. In L. Tropp (Ed.), *The Oxford handbook of intergroup conflict* (pp. 252–272). New York, NY: Oxford University Press.

Clark, K., & Clark, M. (1950). The Negro child in the American social order. *The Journal of Negro Education, 19*(3), 341–350. https://doi.org/10.2307/2966491

Deveaux, M. (1996). Feminism and empowerment: A critical reading of Foucault. In S. Hekman (Ed.), *Feminist interpretations of Michel Foucault*. University Park, PA: Pennsylvania State University Press.

Duveen, G. (1998). The psychosocial production of ideas: Social representations and psychologic. *Culture & Psychology, 4*(4), 455–472. https://doi.org/10.1177/1354067X9800400402

Duveen, G. (2001). Representations, identities, resistance. In K. Deaux & G. Philogène (Eds.), *Representations of the social* (pp. 257–270). Oxford, UK: Blackwell.

Farr, R. M. (1993). Common sense, science and social representations. *Public Understanding of Science, 2*(3), 189–204. https://doi.org/10.1088/0963-6625/2/3/001

Fonagy, P., Steele, M., Steele, H., Higgitt, A., & Target, M. (1994). The Emanuel Miller Memorial Lecture 1992: The theory and practice of resilience. *Child Psychology & Psychiatry & Allied Disciplines, 35*(2), 231–257. https://doi.org/10.1111/j.1469-7610.1994.tb01160.x

Foucault, M. (1979). *Discipline and Punish: The birth of the prison*. Harmondsworth, England: Penguin.

Foucault, M. (1991). In P. Rabinow (Ed.), *The Foucault reader: An introduction to Foucault's thought*. Harmondsworth, England: Penguin.

Fraser, N. (1989). *Unruly practices: Power, discourse and gender in contemporary social theory*. Minneapolis: University of Minnesota Press.

Gayer, C. C., Landman, S., Halperin, E., & Bar-Tal, D. (2009). Overcoming psychological barriers to peaceful conflict resolution: The role of arguments about losses. *Journal of Conflict Resolution, 53*(6), 951–975. https://doi.org/10.1177/0022002709346257

Harré, R. (1984). Some reflections on the concept of "social representation". *Social Research, 51*(4), 927–938.

Hartsock, N. (1990). Foucault on power: A theory for women? In L. Nicholson (Ed.), *Feminism/Postmodernism*. New York, NY: Routledge.

Haslam, S. A. (2004). *Psychology in organizations*. London, UK: SAGE.

Howarth, C. (2006). A social representation is not a quiet thing: Exploring the critical potential of social representations theory. *British Journal of Social Psychology, 45*(1), 65–86. https://doi.org/10.1348/014466605X43777

Howarth, C., Andreouli, E., & Kessi, S. (2014). Social representations and the politics of participation. In K. Kinnvall, T. Capelos, H. Dekker, & P. Nesbitt-Larking (Eds.), *The Palgrave handbook of global political psychology* (pp. 19–38). London, UK: Palgrave-McMillan. https://doi.org/10.1007/978-1-137-29118-9_2

Howarth, C., Campbell, C., Cornish, F., Franks, B., Garcia-Lorenzo, L., Gillespie, A., … Tennant, C. (2013). Insights from societal psychology: A contextual politics of societal change. *Journal of Social and Political Psychology, 1*(1), 364–384. https://doi.org/10.5964/jspp.v1i1.64

Jovchelovitch, S. (1996). In defence of representations. *Journal for the Theory of Social Behaviour, 26*(2), 121–135. https://doi.org/10.1111/j.1468-5914.1996.tb00525.x

Jovchelovitch, S. (2002). *Re-thinking the diversity of knowledge: Cognitive polyphasia, belief and representation [online].* London, UK: LSE Research Online. https://eprints.lse.ac.uk/2628/1/Rethinkingthediversity.pdf

Jovchelovitch, S. (2007). Reflections on the diversity of knowledge: Power and dialogue in representational fields. In T. Sugiman, K. J. Gergern, W. Wagner, & Y. Yamada (Eds.), *Meaning in action: Constructions, narratives, and representations* (pp. 23–37). Tokyo, Japan: Springer.

Kabeer, N. (1994). *Reversed realities: Gender hierarchies in development thought.* London, UK: Verso.

Leman, P., & Duveen, G. (1998). Representations of authority and children's moral reasoning. *European Journal of Social Psychology, 29*(5–6), 557–575. https://doi.org/10.1002/(SICI)1099-0992(199908/09)29:5/6<557::AID-EJSP946>3.0.CO;2-T

Marková, I. (2003). *Dialogicality and social representations: The dynamics of mind.* New York, NY: Cambridge University Press.

Marquand, D. (1997). *The new reckoning: Capitalism, states and citizens.* Cambridge, MA: Cambridge University Press.

Mead, G. H. (1934). In C. W. Morris (Ed.), *Mind self and society from the standpoint of a social behaviorist.* Chicago, IL: University of Chicago.

Moscovici, S. (1961). *La psychanalyse, son image, son public.* Paris, France: Presses Universitaires de France.

Moscovici, S. (1972). Society and theory in social psychology. In J. Israel & H. Tajfel (Eds.), *The context of social psychology: A critical assessment.* Oxford, England: Academic Press.

Moscovici, S. (1988). Notes towards a description of social representations. *European Journal of Social Psychology, 18*(3), 211–250. https://doi.org/10.1002/ejsp.2420180303

Parpart, J. (2004). *Gender, power and governance in a globalizing world.* Aalborg, Denmark: Institut for Historie, Internationale Studier og Samfundsforhold, Aalborg Universitet.

Parpart, J. L., Rai, S., Staudt, K. A., & University of Warwick. (2002). *Rethinking empowerment: Gender and development in a global/local world.* London, UK: Routledge.

Rappaport, J. (1981). In praise of paradox: A social policy of empowerment over prevention. *American Journal of Community Psychology, 9*(1), 1–25. https://doi.org/10.1007/BF00896357

Reicher, S. (2004). The context of social identity: Domination, resistance, and change. *Political Psychology, 25*(6), 921–945. https://doi.org/10.1111/j.1467-9221.2004.00403.x

Reicher, S., & Haslam, S. A. (2006). Tyranny revisited. *Psychologist, 19*(3), 146–150. https://thepsychologist.bps.org.uk/volume-19/edition-3/tyranny-revisited-groups-psychological-well-being-and-health-societies

Rowlands, J. (1997). *Questioning empowerment: Working with women in Honduras.* Oxford, UK: Oxfam Publications.

Ryan, W. (1976). *Blaming the victim.* New York, NY: Vintage Books.

Sarrica, M., Mazzara, B., & Brondi, S. (2016). Social representations theory and critical constructionism: Insights from Caillaud's article. *Papers on Social Representations, 25*(1), 6.31–6.42. http://psr.iscte-iul.pt/index.php/PSR/article/view/62

Sarrica, M., Roseti, A., Brondi, S., Cervelli, P., & Leone, G. (2016). Flooded by a wall of water: Parent-child reminiscing about local environment and unwanted changes. *Qualitative Research in Psychology, 13*(3), 209–230. https://doi.org/10.1080/14780887.2016.1169340

Sen, A. (1990). Gender and cooperative conflicts. In I. Tinker (Ed.), *Persistent inequalities.* New York, NY: Oxford University Press.

Sen, G., & Grown, C. (1988). *Development, crises and alternative visions: Third world women's perspectives.* New York, NY: Monthly Review Press.

Snow, D. A., & Benford, R. D. (1988). Ideology, frame resonance, and participant mobilization. *International Social Movement Research, 1*, 197–217.

Stryker, S. (1968). Identity salience and role performance: The relevance of symbolic interaction theory for family research. *Journal of Marriage and the Family, 30*(4), 558–564.

Stryker, S. (1987). Identity theory: Developments and extensions. In K. Yardley & T. Honess (Eds.), *Self and identity: Psychosocial perspectives* (pp. 89–103). Oxford, England: John Wiley & Sons.

Tajfel, H. (1981). *Human groups and social categories: Studies in social psychology*. Cambridge, MA: Cambridge University Press. https://doi.org/10.1002/ejsp.2420120209

Tajfel, H., & Turner, J. C. (1979). An Integrative Theory of Intergroup Conflict. In W. G. Austin & S. Worchel (Eds.), *The social psychology of intergroup relations* (pp. 33–47). Monterey, CA: Brooks/Cole.

Turner, J. C. (1985). Social categorization and the self-concept: A social cognitive theory of group behaviour. In E. J. Lawler (Ed.), *Advances in group processes* (pp. 77–122). Greenwich, CT: JAI Press.

Varga, A. (2015). *Challenge – Evaluation of the Roma Student College Project in Pécs*. Pécs, Hungary: PTE-BTK-NTI.

Vignoles, V. L., Chryssochoou, X., & Breakwell, G. M. (2002). Evaluating models of identity motivation: Self-esteem is not the whole story. *Self and Identity, 1*(3), 201–218. https://doi.org/10.1080/1529886029006373

Vollhardt, J. R. (2012). Collective victimization. In L. R. Tropp (Ed.), *The Oxford Handbook of intergroup conflict* (pp. 136–157). Oxford, UK: Oxford University Press. https://doi.org/10.1093/oxfordhb/9780199747672.013.0009

Vygotsky, L. S. (1978). Mind in society: The development of higher psychological processes. In M. Cole, V. John-Steiner, S. Scribner, & E. Souberman (Eds.). Cambridge, MA: Harvard University Press.

Vygotsky, L. S. (1979). Consciousness as a problem in the psychology of behavior. *Soviet Psychology, 17*(4), 3–35. https://doi.org/10.2753/RPO1061-040517043

Wagner, W. (1998). Social representations and beyond: Brute facts, symbolic coping and domesticated worlds. *Culture & Psychology, 4*, 297–329. https://doi.org/10.1177/1354067X9800400302

Winnicott, D. (1953). Transitional objects and transitional phenomena. *International Journal of Psychoanalysis, 34*, 89–97.

Part II
Children Growing Up in Violent Geopolitical Contexts

Chapter 9
Beyond Risk Factors: Structural Drivers of Violence Affecting Children

M. Catherine Maternowska, Deborah Fry, Alina Potts, and Tabitha Casey

9.1 Introduction

Over the past 15 years, studies around the globe have conclusively established that physical, sexual and emotional violence affecting children (VAC) is prevalent in all societies and across all income levels at alarming levels (Know Violence in Childhood, 2017; Hillis et al., 2016). Violence is perpetrated in all contexts where children live—in their families, schools, in the care and justice systems, workplaces, neighbourhoods and communities (Hillis et al., 2016; Le, Holton, Romero, & Fisher, 2016). The outcomes of violence in childhood are well known to have long-term consequences both for individuals and for society (Norman et al., 2012). The research and data have been powerful; discourse among policymakers is shifting from "this does not happen here!" to "what is driving this?" and "how can we address it?"

The *Multi-Country Study on the Drivers of Violence Affecting Children*[1] (hereafter, "Drivers Study") set out to answer this question, placing national teams of research practitioners in Italy, Peru, Viet Nam and Zimbabwe at the centre of our process. Increasingly, public health researchers are using a "socio-ecological framework" to understand the interplay of personal, situational and structural factors in condoning

[1] See https://www.unicef-irc.org/research/violence-affecting-children/

M. C. Maternowska (✉)
Global Partnership to End Violence Against Children, Geneva, Switzerland
e-mail: catherine.maternowska@end-violence.org

D. Fry · T. Casey
Moray House School of Education, University of Edinburgh, Edinburgh, UK
e-mail: debi.fry@ed.ac.uk; Tabitha.Casey@ed.ac.uk

A. Potts
Global Women's Institute, George Washington University, Washington, DC, USA

N. Balvin, D. J. Christie (eds.), *Children and Peace*, Peace Psychology Book Series, https://doi.org/10.1007/978-3-030-22176-8_9

or preventing abuse.[2] Although this framework has gained broad acceptance for conceptualizing violence, there have been few attempts to explore ways in which researchers, practitioners and policymakers can apply the findings from the framework to better understand how individual, community, institutional and structural level risk and protective factors relate to each other and how they influence children's (and women's) vulnerability to, or protection from, violence. The focus of most prevention efforts is too narrowly cast on interpersonal violence and the associated risk factors.

Recent evidence shows that preventing violence *is* possible, though not necessarily straightforward. To effectively address and ultimately reduce interpersonal violence affecting girls and boys, programmes must be multi-levelled working across ecological contexts. In some cases, macro-level reforms in the criminal justice system and economic development have been linked to violence reduction (Finkelhor & Jones, 2006). In other cases, evidence of reduced interpersonal violence has been linked to community-level interventions focused on health, economic support and power inequities (Abramsky et al., 2016; Kim et al., 2007). Finally, interventions targeted towards individuals and families in the areas of education, awareness raising and behaviour change have, in some cases, also shown society-wide reductions in violent crime, partner violence and negative parenting practices (Abramsky et al., 2016; Allen, 2011; Jewkes et al., 2008; Knerr, Gardner, & Cluver, 2011). Only a handful of scholars have looked at the interplay of all these levels and domains to understand patterns of violence and how best to address them. In addition, scholars also often overlook the extraordinary implications of age and its nexus with gender and power: children grow and their capacities and vulnerabilities evolve and change over time. Interventions tend to remain sector-specific—without specificity to age and gender, as if occurring in isolation from the broader structural forces that may be fueling interpersonal violence (Know Violence in Childhood, 2017). Even though promising steps are being taken to better address structural factors (Marcus, 2014; Rumble, Ramly, Nuryana, & Dunne, 2018), millions of children continue to be exposed and at risk.

The findings from the Drivers Study presented here highlight how these drivers of VAC are contextualized in specific geohistorical places (Christie, 2006). We draw on two drivers of violence common across all four countries—poverty and migration—to illustrate the power of structural factors on children's everyday experiences. We then focus specifically on our findings from Peru to show how these drivers of violence are related to a child's well-being. According to Christie (2011), one of the main challenges for peace psychology is to deepen understanding of the structural and cultural roots of violence promoting the notion of "positive peace" or the ability to promote a society that reduces social, racial, gender, economic and ecological injustices as barriers to peace (Galtung, 1985; Wagner, 1988). Our integrated child-centred framework moves this shared understanding in a common direction.

---

[2] See, for example: https://www.cdc.gov/violenceprevention/overview/social-ecologicalmodel.html

9.2 Methods and the Process

The Drivers Study utilized an integrated approach to research that relied on existing research: (1) a systematic literature review of peer-reviewed and published academic papers but also including a scoping of existing written material such as research briefs and PhD theses called "grey literature", which is often difficult to locate through conventional literature searches; (2) an initial mapping of the interventions landscape, particularly of evaluated prevention programmes; and (3) secondary analyses of existing data sets. Analysed together and working in tandem with national teams, each country plotted data against the macro, meso and micro factors of the socioecological model (in relation to children's lives) to yield hypotheses around what might be driving VAC in each country site (Maternowska & Fry, 2015). Using this approach, we analysed with our national partners nearly 500 published research studies and 10 national data sets addressing VAC across the four country sites.

We fully acknowledge the origins and evolution of the socio-ecological framework for child psychology and violence prevention work. The framework was first conceptualized to explain child development by Bronfenbrenner (1979) and later was used by researchers to elucidate the complex issue of child abuse (Belsky, 1980), sexual coercion (Brown, 1995) and domestic violence (Heise, 1998). By describing an approach for systematically mapping existing qualitative and quantitative data onto it, we offer both a new application for the field of violence prevention for children and a revised version of the framework (Maternowska & Potts, 2017).

The approach was designed to work alongside national counterparts as co-researchers, rather than passive receptors for policy recommendations. Importantly, it brought together actors from multiple disciplines—including psychologists, economists, historians, medical anthropologists, social workers and specialists in development and urban studies, with each constituency lending its own unique interpretation to the data. National ownership was built into the study design, working directly with government statisticians who conducted secondary analyses in-country rather than exporting the data or outsourcing data analysis to consultants. Data analysts and policymakers alike were provided space to pause, engage and reflect at multiple stages of the process. The human-centred approach favoured relationship-driven research processes that allowed for the time and flexibility that co-creation requires to analyse and synthesize VAC data using a national lens (for more details on the process each country undertook, see: Maternowska et al., 2018).

Figure 9.1 illustrates how patterns of violence are intimately connected to larger institutional and structural factors, referred to as the "drivers" of violence—or forms of harm that create the conditions in which violence occurs. MacNair (2015) explains "structural violence" referring to chronic forms of harm such as poverty, environmental damage, misallocated resources or dangerous working conditions. In all four countries under study, our findings support the idea that no single level within the socioecological model, and no single factor (drivers or risk/protective

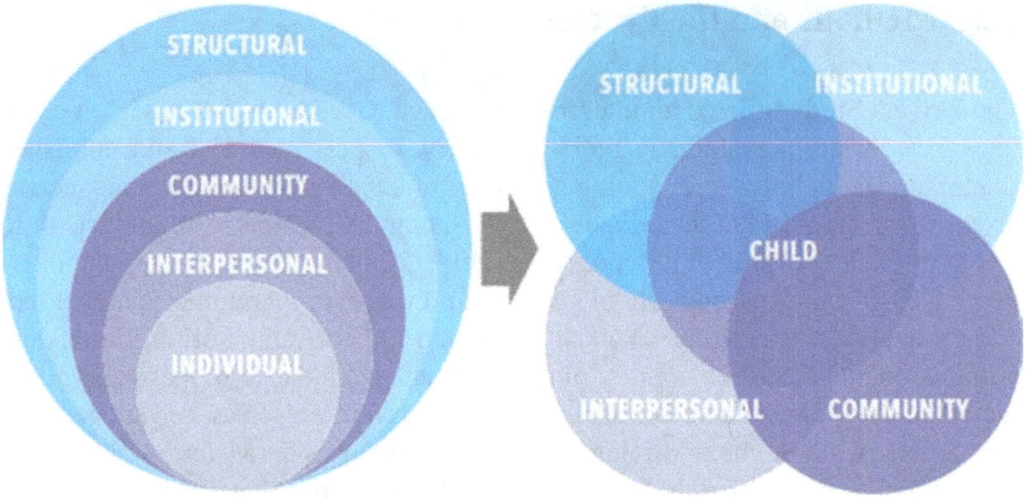

Fig. 9.1 A child-centred socio-ecological framework for violence prevention. (Source: Maternowska & Potts, 2017)

factors) within or between those levels, determines or explains an act of interpersonal violence involving a child. Instead, these factors work in multiple ways and in multiple combinations where the structural and institutional drivers of violence define and determine the changing context in which children live. The approach adds to a growing body of literature that challenges child protection narratives focused on risk factors, which tend to obscure the social ecology and particularly the determinants of much of the harm that children experience (Featherstone, Gupta, Morris, & Warner, 2016; Kumar, Sherr, Stern, & Subrahmanian, 2017; Marcus, 2014).

The integrated framework demonstrates how the structural drivers of violence, such as poverty or gender inequality, are not as distal as interpretations of Bronfenbrenner's evolving socio-ecological model suggest. Importantly, it helps policymakers and practitioners visualize and understand how context shapes children's social worlds. It shifts understandings from a seemingly hierarchical representation of the levels of the socioecological framework to one where the levels—or domains—interact. Bringing this perspective from the field of violence prevention, into the realm of peace psychology, our findings can add to the understanding of both theory and practice for preventing violence and conflict while also mitigating the effects on society. (See, for example, Christie, Wagner, & Winter, 2001.)

9.3 Linking the Global and the Local: The Structural Drivers of Violence Affecting Children

In order to re-conceptualize violence more holistically, making the important links between the global and the local, we review here how poverty and migration can co-conspire, in different ways across different contexts to create unsafe circumstances and vulnerability for some children (and not for others).

9.3.1 Poverty

Across the world, economic transformations—even those designed to address *poverty*—are often uneven and can generate increasing inequities, with unequal access to wealth and income placing considerable burdens on children. While planned structural transformations can benefit society, leading to better healthcare, increased access to education and a more vital market economy with increased opportunities for earning, they do not fully protect all citizens at all times. Inherent inequalities can reduce government's ability to react to sudden economic shifts, referred to as "shocks" (Bourguignon, 1998; Naschold, 2002). Shocks can substantially rearrange the poorest households' composition and children typically feel the reverberations. Research shows an undeniably complex, and often cyclical, connection between poverty and violence (Parkes, 2015). According to the World Health Organization's *World Report on Violence and Health* (Krug, Dahlberg, Mercy, Zwi, & Lozano, 2002), poverty increases one's vulnerabilities to exploitation in the workplace, in schools and in the home. In a review of violence against women, Jewkes (2002) observed that there are few social or demographic characteristics that actually determine risk groups for intimate partner violence, noting, however, that "poverty is the exception" (p. 1423).

Poverty and inequality—which affect children in all countries in this study—create instability in children's lives, depriving them of basic needs, and this can be linked to increased risks of violence. To develop to their full potential, children need safe and stable housing, adequate nutritious food, access to medical care, secure relationships with adult caregivers, nurturing and responsive parenting and high-quality learning opportunities at home and in school. Psychology scholars in South Africa (Seedat, Van Niekerk, Suffla, & Ratele, 2014), a country struggling with decades of violence, make clear these interconnections. Violence, the authors demonstrate, can trigger significant health, economic, and social consequences where poverty plays a central role. They cite prolonged unemployment, income and gender inequality, exposure to violence in childhood and compromised parenting, in a potent mix with access to firearms, pervasive alcohol misuse and fragilities in law enforcement, as all part of the "tangled social dynamics" of violence.

No country is immune from poverty and its threat of increased exposure to violence. As families feel pressure to cope with changing economic circumstances—in Peru, Viet Nam and Zimbabwe—children may be married early, a situation that predisposes young people to violence (Fry, Hodzi, & Nhenga, 2016; Guerrero & Rojas, 2016; Jones, Presler-Marshall, & Thi Van Anh, 2014). In Italy, Peru and Viet Nam, the poor and extreme poor tend to be concentrated among ethnic minority groups, and inevitably these groups are more vulnerable to violence (Bernacchi & Zelano, 2016; Vu Manh Loi, 2015). In Italy, the only designated "high-income" country included in the Drivers Study, levels of poverty are increasing: in fact, the number of people living in poverty hit its highest level for a decade in 2015 (Bernacchi & Zelano, 2016). In cash-strapped and impoverished Zimbabwe, the conditions that create the likelihood for violence include the intersections of poverty, urbanization and housing shortages—all drivers of violence—which directly expose women and girls to violent sexual acts including rape (Dube, 2013).

9.3.2 Migration

The effects of *migration*, from chronic poverty or low-level conflict, also permeate children's lives in all four countries of the Drivers Study: Italy, Peru, Viet Nam and Zimbabwe. Marginalization and discrimination in new places, challenges to the rights around identity, parents' economic insecurity in new market economies and social and cultural dislocation can all affect children's well-being (Bryant, 2005; Maternowska et al., 2016). Children are affected by migration when they are left behind by one or both migrating parents, migrating with parents (or born abroad) or migrating alone. While the full impact of migration on children and adolescents' development remains under-researched, it is best understood as contributing to forms of violence in childhood when situated within the broader structural context of poverty and/or conflict.

Migration as a driver of violence can have both positive and negative implications depending on its context, including whether migration is voluntary, planned in advance, and whether it is for the purposes of moving the individual and/or family to better circumstances. However, for children in Italy, Peru, Viet Nam and Zimbabwe, migration generally appeared in the literature as a factor linked with instability, due to abrupt changes in individual or family circumstances, or involuntary migration (Government Statistics of Viet Nam, 2012; Magwa & Ingwani, 2014; Yon Leau, 2013). Rapidly or abruptly changing home environments—with varying, inconsistent and often shifting parental and caretaker support—deny children the stability needed to support positive development. This, coupled with new family constellations and poor integration into new local communities, which may lack consensus around rejecting and sanctioning VAC, can make children more vulnerable to violence (Magwa & Ingwani, 2014; Strocka, 2008).

In Italy, migration is largely international in scope—while many Italians migrate abroad, more common are the children and adults entering Italy as an escape from conflict and extreme hardship in parts of Africa and the Middle East (Bernacchi & Zelano, 2016). Among migrants who have crossed the Mediterranean Sea in the last few years, children have been the subjects of attention because a large number of them are unaccompanied minors. From January 1 to November 30, 2017, over 15,500 minors arrived in Italy unaccompanied by an adult responsible; in the previous year, the number was even higher—with over 25,800 minors (Demurtas, Vitiello, Accorinti, Skoda, & Perillo, 2018).

In Zimbabwe, children, also unaccompanied, frequently move across international borders regionally (within Southern Africa) in search of economic opportunities (Save the Children Norway Zimbabwe, 2010). Factors pushing children from their homes remain understudied, but those identified include poverty and loss of family members due to HIV/AIDS (Chiliya, Masocha, & Zindiye, 2012; Save the Children, 2008; Save the Children Norway Zimbabwe, 2010). In Peru, Viet Nam and Zimbabwe, the internal migration of children from depressed rural areas to urban slum communities contributes to rapid urbanization and a host of challenges for newly settled families and children (Anderson, 2016; Bray & Dawes, 2016;

Rushing, Watts, & Rushing, 2005). Migration can also be gendered: in Peru and Viet Nam the "feminization" of migration is well documented evidenced by women seeking livelihoods both abroad and within national borders (Anderson, 2016; UNICEF Viet Nam, UNICEF Office of Research – Innocenti, & University of Edinburgh, 2017).

9.4 Understanding the Importance of Historical Inequalities to Present-Day Experiences: A Case Study of Peru

Our findings from Peru, highlighted in a nationally published report (Anderson, 2016), show how structural factors such as poverty and migration, and their linkages with larger structural factors like conflict, are difficult to separate from the everyday violence that children experience. As a middle-income country, Peru has for decades been one of Latin America's most open economies, with Peruvians overall benefitting from economic growth. According to government statistics, less than a third of the Peruvian population now live below the national poverty line, compared with around half in the early 2000s (Anderson, 2016). Nevertheless, about 8 million people remain poor, and poverty is deepest among people of indigenous origin living in remote rural areas. Although more and more Peruvians benefit from economic growth, inequality persists.

An outcome of this rapid inequality has been migration to places outside of Peru as well as from rural areas to cities within Peru (Anderson, 2016). It is estimated that nearly 10% of Peruvians are affected by international migration. Over 65% of those migrating to neighbouring countries such as Chile are women (Araujo, Legua, & Ossandón, 2002), many of whom leave their children in Peru (Illanes, 2010). This "feminization of migration" is largely driven by economic necessity as women search for better livelihoods to support their families (Araujo et al., 2002; Illanes, 2010). Even though the remittances from Peruvians who have moved overseas have enabled many families to improve their standard of living, this does not always equate improved quality of life for children. For example, having one or both parents working in another country is associated with a deterioration in personal relationships (Instituto Nacional de Estadística e Informática & International Organization for Migration, 2009).

Peru's shifting political economy and the resulting displacement of largely rural-based Peruvians has affected society as a whole. Anderson (2016) suggests that these internal movements have shifted Peruvian norms away from families and localized, community-oriented systems of protection to those based on individualism and liberal, urban values. Protection provided to children, for example, through extended families no longer functions due to increased geographical (and social) mobility. Changing family constellations under new living conditions places new demands on all household members. Mothers who once enforced norms of nurturing and care may simply not have the time, given new economic demands. The absence of extended families, usually left behind in the migratory process, may leave children bereft of the emotional support they once received from the larger family network. The Drivers Study's findings in Peru also show that rapid urbanization has contributed to communities in which diverse groups have, thus far, built little consensus concerning shared norms such as discipline, caretaking responsibilities and children's rights (Anderson, 2016).

Applying the Integrated Child-Centred Framework for Violence Prevention (Maternowska & Potts, 2017) makes visual the often complex and hard-to-grasp interactions of factors and their effects on children's well-being (see Fig. 9.2).

At the *structural level*, histories of political violence and rapid economic changes, including over-reliance on extractive industries, have influenced Peruvian policies, which impact on families and children and have also resulted in both rural to urban and international migration.

Extractive industries are a large source of government revenue and encourage foreign investment in mining and the energy sector. Peru's economy remains highly dependent on demand for these extractive metals. In the aftermath of the economic crises of the 1980s and 1990s, the country enjoyed some of the highest levels of growth in Latin America fueled by demand for copper, iron and other raw materials (Anderson, 2016). Ensuring the success of the mining and energy sector subsequently drives policy decisions around housing and community planning in communities around Peru (Anderson, 2016).

Children often migrate with their families to these mining sites in gold-extracting Amazonian basin boom town areas. Several studies highlight how children in these areas are often at high risk of labour and sexual exploitation (End Child Prostitution and Trafficking Peru, 2005; International Organization on Migration & Movimiento El Pozo, 2005). Rates of child sexual abuse are especially high in mining centres such as Cajamarca (International Programme on the Elimination of Child Labour, 2007; Mujica, 2014).

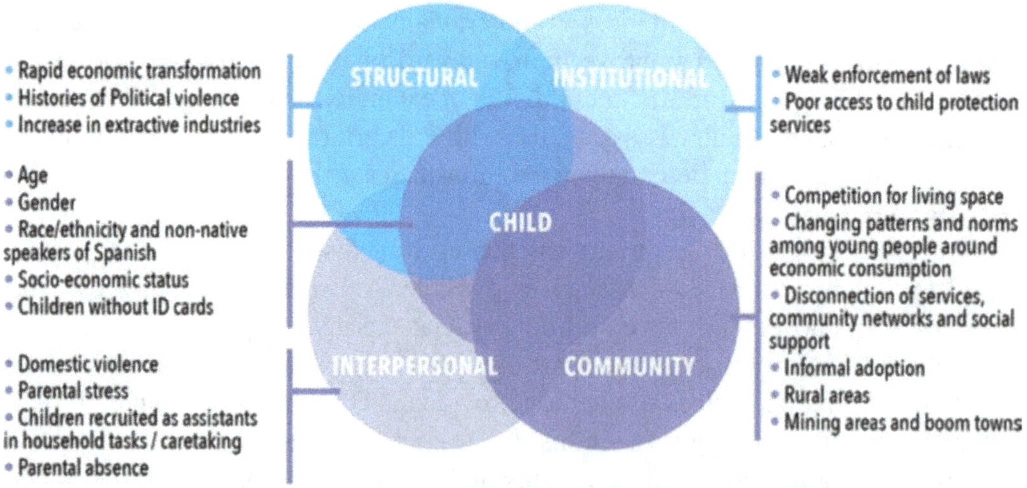

Fig. 9.2 The child-centred socio-ecological framework: exploring the underlying factors related to poverty and migration as a driver of violence affecting children in Peru

The same economic boom has led nearly 10% of the population to emigrate out of the country (Anderson, 2016). Remittances from the Peruvian diaspora abroad amount to approximately US$3 billion or about 10% of the total value of Peruvian exports (in 2008 dollars, Torres-Zorrilla, 2010, pp. 27–29). The same diaspora has also transmitted new patterns and norms around consumption and living practices. As a result of both international and rural to urban migration, many if not most children were born somewhere other than their parents' or grandparents' birthplaces (Anderson, 2016) resulting in relatively rapid intergenerational understandings of history, place and protection.

At the *institutional level*, while there is a strong legal framework in place to uphold gender equality, including the criminalization of discrimination against women, these laws and policies are not always effectively implemented, and Peruvian women still experience higher levels of poverty and unemployment than men (OECD, 2010). This may contribute to women's decisions to migrate in search of jobs in other countries or urban areas, with or without their families. Many of the boom towns built around extractive industries have poor law enforcement, another institutional driver of violence, which allows VAC and particularly sexual exploitation to continue with impunity (Mujica, 2014). In addition, child protection services are concentrated in cities and have a very meager presence in the rural, indigenous and frontier areas where some of the poorest families live and work (Anderson & Palma, 2013).

At the *community level*, rapid economic transformation leads to changes within households. Household-level poverty can be a risk factor for violence and inevitably interacts with parental stress, larger family sizes and resulting competition for living space juxtaposed against the need to recruit children as assistants in household tasks and caretaking (Nóblega, 2012). With space at a premium, poverty in Peru even influences informal adoptions among families shifting children between households and communities. When children are orphaned, even very poor relatives prefer to take them in rather than send them to orphanages or put them up for formal adoption (Anderson, 2016). Several researchers studying family dynamics have remarked on new forms of kinship where children move (or are moved) to childless couples (Anderson, Minaya, & Figueroa, 2010; Cavagnoud, 2011; Leinaweaver, 2009). More common cases include receiving a payment or gift for transferring children to households where they will become domestic servants.

Migration has also been linked to families' disconnection from services, community networks and social support (Cuenca & Díaz, 2010). This is also the case for children who migrate through formal or informal kinship networks to other areas of the country. Sometimes, the protection of the community dissipates when the victimized children are perceived as "other people's children and other people's responsibilities" (Anderson, 2016). This lack of social support is especially pronounced for poorer children who are Afro-Peruvian or mestizo—that is, children of mixed race, especially one having Spanish and American Indian parentage—or from rural origins (CHS Alternativo, 2014; ECPAT Peru, 2005).

At the *interpersonal level*, several studies point to the increased parental stress of managing large families under conditions of poverty, which has subsequently been linked as a risk factor for violent discipline, particularly by mothers (Anderson, 2016). This may be because fathers spend less time with children (Guerrero & Rojas, 2016). It may also be that a father's influence over the quality of family interactions is more indirect, for example, physical punishment may be recognized as violence while failure to provide material support is not (Cavagnoud, 2011; Yon Leau, 2013). In the household, patriarchy serves to promote violence in everyday life (See Espinoza Matos, 2000). Family members identified as "enforcers"—such as mothers or older brothers—are especially demanding of children and younger siblings as a way of maintaining peace in the family, under patriarchal structures of fatherhood.

It is also important to note the intersections between VAC and violence against women generally and specifically in the case of Peru. Intimate partner violence or "domestic violence", in which the mother is usually the victim, is not only psychologically harmful to children; it is also often associated with physical violence against children by their parents (Bardales & Huallpa, 2004; Benavides, Almonte, & de León, 2015; Guedes, Bott, García-Moreno, & Colombini, 2016). In a study on the context of poverty in Peru, scholars demonstrate how domestic violence contributes to maternal depression, in turn increasing the risk for child neglect (Benavides, León, Veramendi, & D'Azevedo, 2012). [3]

At the *child level*, markers of difference between children—such as perceived income levels or race/ethnicity through physical appearance—increase the risk for bullying in schools (INEI, 2013). According to the 2013 National Survey on Social Relations (ENARES by its Spanish acronym), about 70% of girls and boys reported ever experiencing psychological abuse such as teasing from peers, and about half reported experiencing physical violence from their peers (INEI, 2013). Comparatively, the *Young Lives* study found that about a third of students at age 15 reported they had been verbally (34%) or indirectly (32%) bullied, such as being humiliated or shamed (Pells, Ogando Portela, & Espinoza, 2016).

Lack of an identification card or "DNI" (Documento Nacional de Identidad), influenced and determined by both poverty and migration status, further increases children's marginalization and vulnerability to violence. Children without a DNI are concentrated in rural areas where not having documentation is strongly associated with the child's mother tongue not being Spanish (Jones & Villar, 2014).

[3] As Guedes et al. (2016) note, "Generally, researchers have paid less attention to poor parenting by men who abuse women, co-occurrence of child maltreatment, or batterers' use of children as weapons against female partners, especially during separation and divorce, despite the fact that using children to threaten and intimidate women has been part of conceptual models for understanding spousal abuse for more than 30 years. In fact, concern for children's safety is a reason why some women stay in abusive relationships and why others leave". *[In-text citations removed, see article for studies cited.]*

9.5 Conclusion

By plotting data across a child's social ecology, the interplay of migration and poverty as drivers of violence becomes clear. The case study from Peru demonstrates this well. Addressing violence first requires thinking about violence with a lens that spans multiple disciplines—drawing on the fields of psychology, economics, political science, history, anthropology and sociology. By plotting the data and making visual these connections, we can begin to unravel the causes and consequences of violence across time and space and ultimately use this information to design or adapt violence prevention interventions and policies. Like peace psychology (Christie, 2006; Pilisuk, 1998; Wessells, 1999), we engaged in multi-level scholarship and practice, attending to the reciprocal links between what happens to children in the home, school and community and how macro-level phenomena, most notably at the structural and institutional levels, intersects, overlaps and interacts with factors at the individual, family and community levels of the socio-ecological model.

Honouring the role of national policymakers and practitioners in data analysis was enlightening—both for the national stakeholders involved and for the larger sphere of violence prevention studies. In Peru, the process of doing this fostered communication among researchers, practitioners and policymakers working on these issues and facilitated a multi-stakeholder conversation informed by scholars and policymakers from across a range of disciplines. The insights led to documented impacts for those working to prevent violence affecting Peruvian children. Evidenced in Morton and Casey's research impact study (2017), a profound institutional normative change occurred where, over time, the Peruvian government has come to accept both that VAC occurs and, importantly, that the government is empowered and able to take the necessarily steps to prevent it. These efforts are documented in multiple forms, such as support to emerging researchers (including first authorship of peer-reviewed journal articles)[4], publication of previously unreleased VAC prevalence data by lead government ministries (see MIMP & UNICEF, 2016), and research-to-policy briefs[5] documenting these changes.

The Integrated Child-Centred Framework for Violence Prevention (Maternowska & Potts, 2017) and the approach of the Drivers Study offer insight into processes for generating evidence-informed action to tackle VAC. The framework provides an understanding of structural violence from the perspective of children's lived experiences. Peace psychology as a discipline might benefit from using and adapting frameworks such as these, working alongside other disciplines, such as public health, social work, anthropology and economics. We join Seedat et al. (2014) in suggesting that, as a discipline dedicated to non-violence, it is important for psychology to provide a relevant research response *and* to promote the transfer of theory to practice, in order to provide a safe world for children everywhere.

---

[4] See https://www.unicef-irc.org/research/pdf/433-Emerging-Researchers-.pdf

[5] See https://www.unicef-irc.org/research/pdf/430-PeruCorpPunENG02.pdf

Violence analysed, from this holistic perspective is important but so too is *addressing* these inequalities—a challenge for the field of peace psychology as much as the field of violence prevention. Recent evidence-based frameworks, now being promoted within the field of violence prevention such as *INSPIRE*: *Seven Strategies to End Violence*, are showing promising results (WHO et al., 2016). Evidence-based strategies from around the world, while still emerging, reinforce the idea that violence can be prevented but must also be simultaneously confronted at different levels, from communities in which children live through to national, regional and global systems (Fulu & Miedema, 2015). INSPIRE evidence suggests, for example, that the implementation of laws and their enforcement alone cannot be effective without simultaneous attention to safe environments, education and life skills and income generation, to name only some of the seven effective violence prevention interventions outlined (WHO et al., 2016).

The dual perspectives of peace psychology, with its emphasis on movement towards more socially just structures, and violence prevention would benefit from closer alliance to each other. No matter the discipline, the fact is that peace is a precarious notion for children growing up in this rapidly changing world. As much of the world continues to experience crises and shocks due to conflict, forced displacement, economic migration, climate disasters and disease outbreaks, it is incumbent upon us to bring our perspectives—and our applied practice—together to prevent and ultimately end violence affecting children.

References

Abramsky, T., Devries, K. M., Michau, L., Nakuti, J., Musuya, T., Kiss, L., … Watts, C. (2016). Ecological pathways to prevention: How does the SASA! Community mobilisation model work to prevent physical intimate partner violence against women? *BioMed Central Public Health, 16*(1), 339.

Allen, G. (2011). *Early intervention: The next steps, an independent report to Her Majesty's government by Graham Allen MP*. London, UK: The Stationery Office.

Anderson, J. (2016). *Multi-country study on the drivers of violence affecting children: Peru report*. Lima, Peru: MIMP & UNICEF.

Anderson, J., Minaya, L., & Figueroa, B. (2010). *Trabajo infantil doméstico. Percepciones de niñas, niños y adolescentes*. Lima, Peru: Asociación Grupo de Trabajo Redes.

Anderson, J., & Palma, H. (2013). Los ciudadanos menores del Perú. In M. Z. Lobato & S. Venturoli (Eds.), *Formas de ciudadanía en América Latina* (pp. 105–125). Madrid, Spain: Iberoamericana.

Araujo, K., Legua, M. C., & Ossandón, L. (2002). *Migrantes andinas en Chile. El case de la migración peruana*. Santiago, Chile: Fundación Instituto de la Mujer.

Bardales, O. M., & Huallpa, E. A. (2004). *Aprender sin miedo*. Lima, Peru: Ministerio de la Mujer y Desarrollo Social, Gobierno del Perú.

Belsky, J. (1980). Child maltreatment: An ecological integration. *American Psychologist, 35*(4), 320.

Benavides, M., Almonte, J. L. J., & de León, M. P. (2015). The co-occurrence of domestic and child violence in urban Peru: Evidence from three regions. *Journal of Family Violence, 30*(8), 1–9.

Benavides, M., León, J., Veramendi, M. L., & D'Azevedo, M. (2012). *Los accidentes en los niños. Un estudio en contexto de pobreza*. Lima, Peru: GRADE.

Bernacchi, E., & Zelano, M. (2016). *Multi-country study on the drivers of violence affecting children: Italian report*. Florence, Italy: Istituto degli Innocenti.

Bourguignon, F. (1998). *Crime as a social cost of poverty and inequality: A review focusing on developing countries*. Paris, France: DELTA.

Bray, R., & Dawes, A. (2016). *Parenting, family care and adolescence in East and Southern Africa: An evidence-focused literature review* (Innocenti Discussion Paper 2016-02). Florence, Italy: UNICEF Office of Research Innocenti.

Bronfenbrenner, U. (1979). *The ecology of human development: Experiments by nature and design*. Cambridge, MA: Harvard University Press.

Brown, S. (1995). *Sexual coercion and reproductive health*. New York, NY: Population Council.

Bryant, J. (2005). *Children of international migrants in Indonesia, Thailand, and the Philippines: A review of evidence and policies* (Innocenti Working Papers, no. 2005-05). Florence, Italy: UNICEF Office of Research – Innocenti.

Cavagnoud, R. (2011). *Entre la escuela y la supervivencia: Trabajo adolescente y dinámicas familiares en Lima*. Lima, Peru: Instituto de Estudios Peruanos, Instituto Francés de Estudios Andinos & Fundación Telefónica.

Chiliya, N., Masocha, R., & Zindiye, S. (2012). Challenges facing Zimbabwean cross border traders trading in South Africa: A review of literature. *Chinese Business Review, 11*(6), 564–570.

Christie, D. J. (2011). Peace psychology: Definitions, scope, and impact. *The Encyclopedia of Peace Psychology*. https://doi.org/10.1002/9780470672532.wbepp200

Christie, D. J. (2006). What is peace psychology the psychology of? *Journal of Social Issues, 62*(1), 1–17.

Christie, D. J., Wagner, R. V., & Winter, D. A. (Eds.). (2001). *Peace, conflict, and violence: Peace psychology for the 21st century*. Englewood Cliffs, NJ: Prentice-Hall.

Capital Humano y Social (CHS) Alternativo. (2014). *Explotación sexual de niños, niñas y adolescentes en la ciudad de Iquitos*. Iquitos, Peru: CHS Alternativo & Brot Fur die Welt.

Cuenca, R., & Díaz, R. (2010). *Ciudadanía de papel. La niñez indocumentada en el Perú*. Lima, Peru: CIES & Instituto de Estudios Peruanos.

Demurtas, P., Vitiello, M., Accorinti, M., Skoda, A., & Perillo, C. (2018). *In search of protection: Unaccompanied minors in Italy*. New York, NY: Center for Migration Studies. Retrieved from http://cmsny.org/publications/2018smsc-cse-uam/.

Dube, R. (2013). *She probably asked for it! A preliminary study into Zimbabwean societal perceptions of rape*. Harare, Zimbabwe: Research and Advocacy Unit.

End Child Prostitution and Trafficking (ECPAT) Peru. (2005). *¿Mercancía sexual? Cómo hemos creado la demanda para la explotación sexual de niños, niñas y adolescentes en Perú*. Lima, Peru: IDEIF, CODENI, REDES & Movimiento El Pozo. Retrieved from http://www.chsalternativo.org/upload/archivos/archivo_112.pdf.

Espinoza Matos, M. J. (2000). *Violencia en la familia en Lima y el Callao*. Lima, Peru: Ediciones del Congreso del Perú.

Featherstone, B., Gupta, A., Morris, K. M., & Warner, J. (2016). Let's stop feeding the risk monster: Towards a social model of 'child protection. *Families, Relationships and Societies, 1*(7), 7–22.

Finkelhor, D., & Jones, L. (2006). Why have child maltreatment and child victimization declined? *Journal of Social Issues, 62*(4), 685–716.

Fry, D., Hodzi, C., & Nhenga, T. (2016). *Addressing social norms that underpin violence against children in Zimbabwe: Findings and strategic planning document*. Harare, Zimbabwe: Ministry of Public Services, Labour and Social Welfare.

Fulu, E., & Miedema, S. (2015). Violence against women: Globalizing the integrated ecological model. *Violence Against Women, 21*(12), 1431–1455.

Galtung, J. (1985). Twenty-five years of peace research: Ten challenges and some responses. *Journal of Peace Research, 22*(2), 141–158.

General Statistics of Vietnam (GSO). (2012). *Exploratory research on trafficking in boys in Viet Nam*. Hanoi, Vietnam: General Statistics of Vietnam.

Guedes, A., Bott, S., García-Moreno, C., & Colombini, M. (2016). Bridging the gaps: A global review of intersections of violence against women and violence against children. *Global Health Action, 9*, 1–15.

Guerrero, G., & Rojas, V. (2016). *Understanding children's experiences of violence in Peru: Evidence from Young Lives* (Innocenti Working Paper 2016-17). Florence, Italy: UNICEF Office of Research.

Heise, L. L. (1998). Violence against women: An integrated, ecological framework. *Violence Against Women, 4*(3), 262–290.

Hillis, S., Mercy, J., Amobi, A., & Kress, H. (2016). Global prevalence of past-year violence against children: A systematic review and minimum estimates. *Pediatrics, 137*(3), e20154079.

Illanes, J. C. (2010). Migrant mothers and divided homes: Perceptions of immigrant Peruvian women about motherhood. *Journal of Comparative Family Studies, 41*(2), 205–224.

Instituto Nacional de Estadística e Informática (INEI). (2013). *Encuesta Nacional de Relaciones Sociales ENARES*. Lima, Peru: MIMP & INEI.

Instituto Nacional de Estadística e Informática (INEI), & International Organization for Migration (IOM). (2009). *Migración Internacional en las familias peruanas y perfil del peruano retrornante*. Lima, Peru: INEI.

International Organization for Migration, & Movimiento El Pozo. (2005). *Trata de mujeres para fines sexuales comerciales en el Perú*. Lima, Peru: IOM & Movimiento El Pozo.

International Programme on the Elimination of Child Labour (IPEC). (2007). *Imperdonable. Estudio sobre la explotación sexual comercial de la infancia y adolescencia en Perú: Cajamarca, Cusco, Iquitos y Lima*. Lima, Peru: Organización InternacionaI de Trabajo.

Jewkes, R. (2002). Intimate partner violence: Causes and prevention. *The Lancet, 359*(9315), 1423–1429.

Jewkes, R., Nduna, M., Levin, J., Jama, N., Dunkle, K., Puren, A., & Duvvury, N. (2008). Impact of stepping stones on incidence of HIV and HSV-2 and sexual behaviour in rural South Africa: Cluster randomised controlled trial. *BMJ, 337*, a506.

Jones, N., & Villar, E. M. (2014). Is cash the answer? Lessons for child protection programming from Peru: The Juntos (Together) program has the potential to improve children's care and protection. *Child Abuse & Neglect, 38*(3), 383–394.

Jones, N., Presler-Marshall, E., & Thi Van Anh, T. (2014). *Early marriage among Vietnam's H'mong*. ODI country report. London, UK: Overseas Development Institute.

Kim, J. C., Watts, C. H., Hargreaves, J. R., Ndhlovu, L. X., Phetla, G., Morison, L. A., … Pronyk, P. (2007). Understanding the impact of a microfinance-based intervention on women's empowerment and the reduction of intimate partner violence in South Africa. *American Journal of Public Health, 97*(10), 1794–1802.

Knerr, W., Gardner, F., & Cluver, L. (2011). *Preventing child abuse and interpersonal violence in low- and middle-income countries. SVRI Briefing Paper*. SVRI, MRC & Oak Foundation.

Know Violence in Childhood. (2017). *Ending violence in childhood. Global report 2017*. New Delhi, India: Know Violence in Childhood.

Krug, E. G., Dahlberg, L. L., Mercy, J. A., Zwi, A. B., & Lozano, R. (2002). *World report on violence and health*. Geneva, Switzerland: World Health Organization.

Kumar, A. K., Sherr, L., Stern, V., & Subrahmanian, R. (Eds.) (2017). Know violence in childhood: A global learning initiative. *Psychology, Health & Medicine, 22*, 1–122. (Supp 1).

Le, M. T., Holton, S., Romero, L., & Fisher, J. (2016). Polyvictimization among children and adolescents in low-and lower-middle-income countries: A systematic review and meta-analysis. *Trauma, Violence, & Abuse, 19*(3), 323–342. https://doi.org/10.1177/1524838016659489

Leinaweaver, J. B. (2009). *Los niños ayacuchanos. Una antropología de la adopción y la construcción familiar en el Perú*. Lima, Peru: Instituto de Estudios Peruanos.

MacNair, R. M. (2015). Theories underlying research in peace psychology. In *Methodologies in peace psychology* (pp. 19–41). Cham, Switzerland: Springer.

Magwa, S., & Ingwani, V. (2014). Exploring sexual abuse of school children in families: A case study of Masvingo District, Zimbabwe. *The International Journal of Humanities & Social Studies, 2*(9), 156–161.

Marcus, R. (2014). *Poverty and violations of children's right to protection in low-and middle-income countries: A review of the evidence*. London, UK: Overseas Development Initiative.

Maternowska, M. C., & Fry, D. (2015). *Understanding the drivers of violence. A step-by-step guide to conducting preliminary research around what drives violence*. Florence, Italy: UNICEF Office of Research – Innocenti. Retrieved from https://www.unicef-irc.org/research/pdf/440-TOOLKITstep-by-step_28Sept2016_OK.pdf

Maternowska, M. C., & Potts, A. (2017). *The Multi-Country Study on the Drivers of Violence Affecting Children: A child-centred integrated framework for violence prevention*. Florence, Italy: UNICEF Office of Research – Innocenti. Retrieved from https://www.unicef-irc.org/research/pdf/448-child-centered-brief.pdf

Maternowska, M. C., Potts, A., & Fry, D. (2016). *The multi-country study on the drivers of violence affecting children. A cross-country snapshot of findings*. Florence, Italy: UNICEF Office of Research – Innocenti. Retrieved from www.unicef-irc.org/publications/874.

Maternowska, M. C., Fry, D., Potts, A., & Casey, T. (2018). The multi-country study on the drivers of violence affecting children: Giving complexity clarity. *Vulnerable Children & Youth Studies, 13*, 1–82. (Supp 1).

Ministerio de la Mujer y las Poblaciones Vulnerables (MIMP), & UNICEF. (2016). *The multi-country study on the drivers of violence affecting children: Country peport*. Lima, Peru: Ministerio de la Mujer y las Poblaciones Vulnerables. Retrieved from https://www.mimp.gob.pe/direcciones/dgnna/contenidos/articulos.php?codigo=6

Morton, S., & Casey, T. (2017). *Changing national policy on violence affecting children: An impact assessment of UNICEF and partners' multi-country study on the drivers of violence affecting children in Peru*. Edinburgh, Scotland: University of Edinburgh. Retrieved from https://www.era.lib.ed.ac.uk/handle/1842/22063.

Mujica, J. (2014). *Elementos comparados del impacto de la trata de personas en la salud de víctimas adolescentes en el contexto de la minería ilegal de oro en Madre de Dios*. Lima, Peru: PROMSEX & ANESVAD.

Naschold, F. (2002). *Why inequality matters for poverty* (Inequality briefing no. 2). London, UK: Overseas Development Institute.

Nóblega, M. M. (2012). Risk and protective factors for physical and emotional intimate partner violence against women in a community of Lima, Peru. *Journal of Interpersonal Violence, 27*, 3644–3659.

Norman, R. E., Byambaa, M., De, R., Butchart, A., Scott, J., & Vos, T. (2012). The long-term health consequences of child physical abuse, emotional abuse, and neglect: A systematic review and meta-analysis. *PLoS Medicine, 9*(11), e1001349.

Organisation for Economic Co-operation and Development (OECD). (2010). *Peru. Atlas of gender and development: How social norms affect gender equality in non-OECD countries*. Paris, France: OECD Publishing.

Parkes, J. (Ed.). (2015). *Gender violence in poverty contexts: The educational challenge*. New York: Routledge.

Pells, K., Ogando Portela, M. J., & Espinoza, P. (2016). *Experiences of peer bullying among adolescents and associated effects on young adult outcomes: Longitudinal evidence from Ethiopia, India, Peru and Viet Nam* (Innocenti discussion paper). Florence, Italy: UNICEF Office of Research-Innocenti.

Pilisuk, M. (1998). The hidden structure of contemporary violence. *Peace and Conflict, 4*(3), 197–216.

Rumble, L., Ramly, A. A., Nuryana, M., & Dunne, M. P. (2018). The importance of contextual factors in carrying out childhood violence surveys: A case study from Indonesia. *Child Indicators Research, 11*(2), 405–421.

Rushing, R., Watts, C., & Rushing, S. (2005). Living the reality of forced sex work: Perspectives from young migrant women sex workers in northern Vietnam. *Journal of Midwifery & Women's Health, 50*(4), e41–e44.

Save the Children. (2008). *Our broken dream: Child migration in Southern Africa.* Johannesburg, South Africa: Save the Children UK.

Save the Children Norway Zimbabwe. (2010). *An analysis of irregular child migration patterns: Beitbridge Child Reception Centre report.* Harare, Zimbabwe: Save the Children.

Seedat, M., Van Niekerk, A., Suffla, S., & Ratele, K. (2014). Psychological research and South Africa's violence prevention responses. *South African Journal of Psychology, 44*(2), 136–144.

Strocka, C. (2008). *Unidos nos hacemos respetar. Jóvenes, identidades y violencia en Ayacucho.* Lima, Peru: UNICEF/Instituto de Estudios Peruanos.

Torres-Zorrilla, J. (2010). *Remesas en Ecuador y Perú.* Lima, Peru: Centrum, Pontificia Universidad Católica del Perú.

UNICEF Viet Nam, UNICEF Office of Research – Innocenti, & University of Edinburgh. (2017). *Understanding the drivers of violence affecting children in Viet Nam.* Hanoi, Viet Nam: UNICEF Viet Nam. Retrieved from: https://www.unicef-irc.org/files/upload/documents/MCSDV_Viet%20Nam_Understanding%20Drivers%20of%20VAC.PDF

Vu Manh Loi. (2015). *Data analysis of SAVY 1 and SAVY 2.* UNICEF, Hanoi, Viet Nam.

Wagner, R. V. (1988). Distinguishing between positive and negative approaches to peace. *Journal of Social Issues, 44*(2), 1–15.

Wessells, M. G. (1999). Culture, power, and community: Intercultural approaches to psychosocial assistance and healing. In K. Nader, N. Dubrow, & B. H. Stamm (Eds.), *Honoring differences: Cultural issues in the treatment of trauma and loss* (pp. 267–282). London, UK: Brunner/Mazel.

World Health Organization (WHO), Centers for Disease Control and Prevention (CDC), Global Partnership to End Violence Against Children, Pan American Health Organization (PAHO), President's Emergency Plan for AIDS Relief (PEPFAR), ... & the World Bank. (2016). *INSPIRE: Seven strategies for ending violence against children.* Geneva, Switzerland: WHO.

Yon Leau, C. J. (2013). *Sexuality, social inequalities, and sexual vulnerability among low-income youth in the city of Ayacucho, Peru.* Doctoral thesis, Department of Sociomedical Sciences. New York, NY: Columbia University.

Chapter 10
Growing Up in Violent Contexts: Differential Effects of Community, Family, and School Violence on Child Adjustment

Dario Bacchini and Concetta Esposito

10.1 Introduction

Violence is pervasive in the world, even among those who live in the most economically developed countries. In many Western industrialized cities, one in two children every year is denied his/her fundamental right to be protected from violence and to grow up in healthy and safe homes, schools, and communities, with early exposure to violence likely to be especially detrimental to the child's well-being (Margolin & Gordis, 2000).

Although it takes different forms than in war-torn areas, violence pervading Western societies affects child development and psychological functioning in many similar ways. A basic postulate is that violence breeds violence. Indeed, children exposed to a violent environment are often more aggressive and more involved in antisocial behavior than children who are not. Furthermore, children exposed to violence are more at risk for anxiety and depression, mainly due to the perception of danger in the context where they live. A violent context negatively influences also the capability of children to solve social problems and shapes a conception of the social world as hostile and dangerous. Lastly, a sudden or a chronic exposure to violence can result in post-traumatic stress disorder (PTSD) symptoms (Margolin, Vickerman, Oliver, & Gordis, 2010), such as intrusive and involuntary reexperiencing of a traumatic event, high emotional arousal, and avoidance of situations that are reminders of the event.

In this chapter we first define exposure to violence and then (a) present data from international surveys on the prevalence of violence exposure, showing that being exposed to violence is a common experience for many children in industrialized countries, and (b) discuss the main consequences associated with violence

D. Bacchini (✉) · C. Esposito
Department of Humanistic Studies, University of Naples "Federico II", Naples, Italy
e-mail: dario.bacchini@unina.it; concetta.esposito3@unina.it

N. Balvin, D. J. Christie (eds.), *Children and Peace*, Peace Psychology Book Series, https://doi.org/10.1007/978-3-030-22176-8_10

exposure, in all its forms and across contexts. Next, we will focus on the specific issue of community violence in the Neapolitan context, in the South of Italy, evidencing (c) some mechanisms through which violence might affect child development and (d) the risk and protective factors that are known to increase or reduce the likelihood of impaired child development.

10.2 Defining Exposure to Violence

One of the main difficulties when addressing the problem of violence lies in the lack of universal notions of what is acceptable and unacceptable in terms of behavior and what could be considered "harmful" over and above culture-specific social norms. In general, the World Health Organization defines violence (1996) as "the intentional use of physical force or power, threatened or actual, against oneself, another person, or against a group or community, that either results in or has a high likelihood of resulting in injury or death, as well as in psychological harm, maldevelopment or deprivation." Within this broad definition, all forms of violence against people under 18 years old are considered "violence against children." It encompasses a wide range of possible perpetrators and settings, such as parents or other caregivers in the family context, peers in the school environment and the more general peer group, or strangers while walking the streets.

Children may experience violence in multiple, sometimes overlapping, settings. In addition, the problem is complex as children may be victims ("happens to them," primary victimization) or witnesses of violence ("saw it happens to someone else," secondary victimization) within their daily life contexts. A large body of literature, especially concerning the investigation of community violence, has focused on the study of the effects related to being a victim or a witness of violence. In general, findings show that witnessing violence is linked to the acquisition of deviant social information patterns, such as selective attention to hostile peer cues, attributions that others are being hostile toward the self, rapid accessing of aggressive responses, and positive evaluations of aggressive responses, which in turn increase the likelihood of aggressive behavior (Crick & Dodge, 1994). In contrast, victimization appears to be more strongly associated with the development of internalizing symptoms (Cooley-Quille, Boyd, Frantz, & Walsh, 2001) mediated through emotional self-regulation that compromise the more general ability of individual's adaptive behavior (Schwartz & Proctor, 2000).

Although the distinction between being a victim and a witness seems to be conceptually reasonable, it is not yet clear if it always applies in reality. Understanding whether victimization and witnessing reflect two specific domains of experience, which can occur independently or co-jointly, remains an open question for future research to address.

10.3 Violence Exposure aAcross Multiple Contexts: Prevalence Estimates and Differential Effects

Violence is ever-present in the lives of children and adolescents worldwide, taking many forms and across several contexts (UNICEF; United Nations Children's Fund, 2017). Consistent with data reported in the scientific literature (Finkelhor, Ormrod, & Turner, 2007), the statistics provided by UNICEF revealed that about three in four children worldwide experience violent discipline by their caregivers on a regular basis. In terms of witnessing violence, one in four children under age five lives with a mother who is a victim of intimate partner violence. Slightly more than one in three students between the ages of 13 and 15 experience bullying. In 2015 alone, collective violence took the lives of around 82,000 adolescents worldwide. Similarly, the results from "The Multi-Country Study on the Drivers of Violence Affecting Children," led by the UNICEF Office of Research – Innocenti and involving Italy, Peru, Viet Nam, and Zimbabwe, have confirmed that physical, sexual, and emotional violence affecting children is prevalent in all societies (Maternowska, Potts, & Fry, 2016).

It is also in light of these alarmingly high numbers that considerable progress has been made on the scientific investigation of violence exposure in childhood and adolescence. An important insight offered by research over the last decades concerns the need to consider the interconnectedness of multiple contexts of violence exposure (Margolin et al., 2010) within an ecological-transactional model of development (see Lynch & Cicchetti, 1998), according to which individuals are part of multiple nested levels of environment (i.e., ecological contexts) that independently and in interaction with each other shape individual development and adaptation.

One of the major comprehensive national surveys addressing the assessment of children's exposure to multiple forms of violence is the National Survey of Children's Exposure to Violence (NatSCEV; Finkelhor, Turner, Shattuck, Hamby, & Kracke, 2015), sponsored by the US Department of Justice (DOJ) and the Centers for Disease Control and Prevention (CDC). According to the last published bulletin (Office of Juvenile Justice and Delinquency Prevention; Finkelhor et al., 2015), among all children and youth surveyed, nearly half (48.4 percent) had experienced more than one specific victimization type involving direct or witnessed victimization (out of 50 possible types), nearly one in six (15.1 percent) experienced six or more types, and nearly one in 20 (4.9 percent) had been exposed to 10 or more different forms of victimization.

Both within and outside the NatSCEV, a consistent amount of research has showed that victimization within a context may increase vulnerability to other forms and/or contexts of victimization, through mechanisms that include, but are not limited to, lowered self-esteem, distorted cognitive schemas, and lack of social support (Turner, Shattuck, Finkelhor, & Hamby, 2016). Perry, Hodges, and Egan (2001), for example, found that cognitive schemas acquired in families with aggressive interactional styles made children more susceptible to violence outside the family and, consequently, more likely to be exposed to the risk of further opportunities for victimization. Episodes of violence within the family context have been found to be associated with high levels of violence in the neighborhood (Margolin et al., 2010) or to increase child's vulnerability to school victimization (Schwartz & Proctor, 2000). In a study by Affuso, Bacchini, Aquilar, De Angelis, and Miranda (2014), Italian adolescents who scored high on family violence reported levels of violence exposure in the neighborhood and in the school as high as in the family.

Against this background, researchers have examined links between being exposed to multiple violent contexts and children's adjustment problems, hypothesizing that a cumulative experience of violent contexts increases the likelihood of developing adjustment problems. Findings have provided some support for this hypothesis, revealing that violence exposure at home, at school, and in the community is a stronger predictor of adolescents' concurrent internalizing and externalizing problems than exposure in any single setting (Mrug & Windle, 2010). Poly-victimization also seems to be a powerful predictor of current (Turner et al., 2016) and subsequent (Finkelhor et al., 2007) internalizing symptoms in children and adolescents. The results of the abovementioned study of Affuso et al. (2014) showed a similar pattern on a sample of adolescents living in the metropolitan area of Naples, indicating that the higher the number of contexts to which adolescents were exposed (ranging from 1 to 7), the higher were the levels of PTS symptoms reported by adolescents (Fig. 10.1).

Analogous to the results by Affuso et al. (2014), we found that levels of antisocial behavior and anxiety-depression increased along with the number of violent contexts to which adolescents were exposed. Furthermore, no difference due to adolescent gender has been found (Fig. 10.2).

Other hypotheses that emerging research is exploring concern the idea that some violent contexts could be more detrimental for child adjustment than others (i.e., differential effects) or the possibility that different contexts of violence may interact

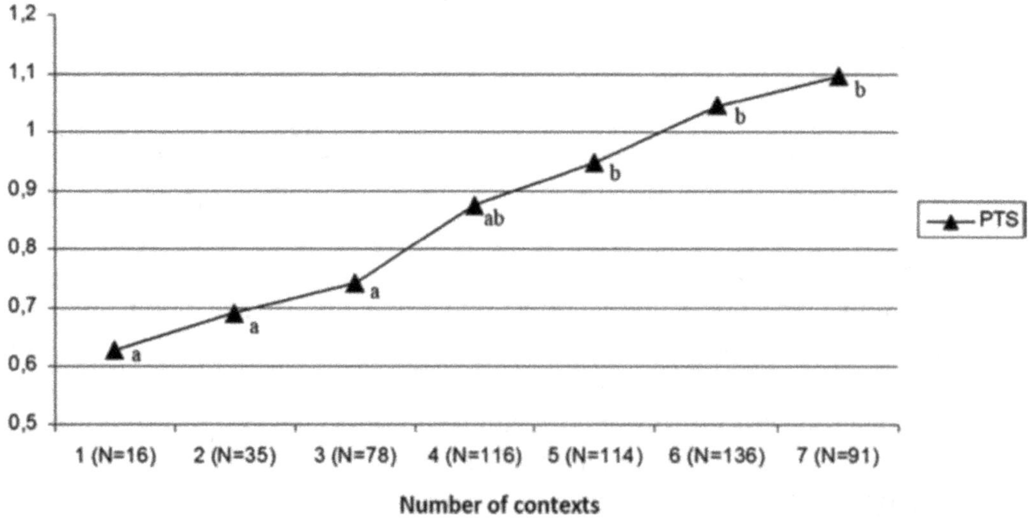

Fig. 10.1 Means of post-traumatic stress (PTS) symptoms across contexts. Sidak adjustment for multiple comparisons. (Extracted and adapted from Affuso et al., 2014)

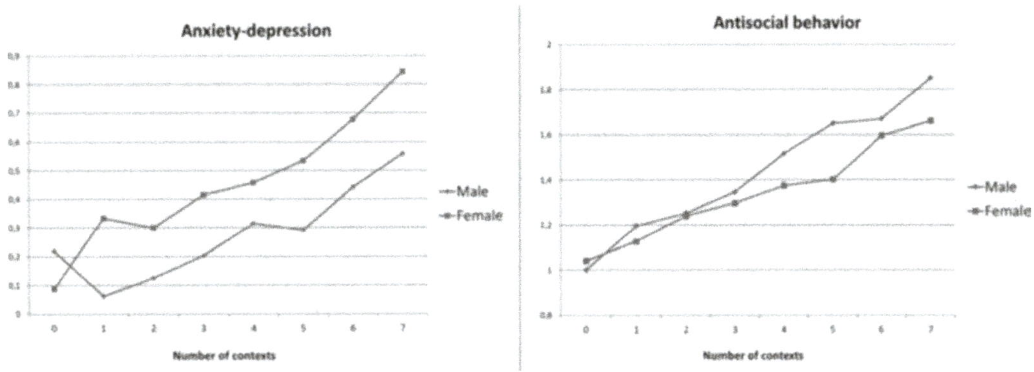

Fig. 10.2 Means of anxiety-depression and antisocial behavior scores across contexts. Data collected by Bacchini et al. on a sample of 944 adolescents living in the metropolitan area of Naples, Southern Italy. Unpublished study

with one another to amplify or attenuate their individual effects (i.e., interactive effects). In general, studies seem to suggest a sort of equifinality of violence exposure across different contexts; that is, different contexts eventuate in the same outcome. However, they also emphasize a stronger impact of exposure to microsystem violence (e.g., family and school contexts) on a wide range of developmental outcomes. This is perhaps due to the differential proximity to the child within the hierarchically ordered social ecology. Comparing violence exposure at home, at school, and in the neighborhood, for example, Mrug and Windle (2010) found that violence exposure at home and school (both witnessing and victimization) was a more robust predictor of adjustment problems (anxiety, depression, and aggression) than exposure to community violence. More specifically, witnessing violence in the community only predicted higher levels of delinquency, whereas victimization in the community was not independently predictive of any outcomes. Nonetheless, the results from Bacchini, Affuso, and Aquilar (2015) showed that witnessing neighborhood and school violence had a stronger concurrent association with antisocial behavior than witnessing violence at home. Overall, we can draw two important conclusions, albeit partial, from the results so far reported. First, although family plays a crucial role, the development of adolescents' behavior problems seems to be particularly affected also by contexts outside the family. Second, these problems are more likely to occur when adolescents experience violence as witnesses and not as direct victims, suggesting that witnessed violence does provide behavioral models for deviant and antisocial behavior, increasing the tendency to believe that such behavior is acceptable or even expected and perhaps desensitizing young people to the emotional effects of violence (Mrug & Windle, 2009). However, it is important to note that the short- and long-term consequences of poly-victimization are not completely understood because most of the studies examining poly-victimization and its consequences are based on cross-sectional data.

Other interesting issues for discussion come from the study of interaction effects between different contexts of violence. There are only a few studies addressing this question. Noteworthy is that by Mrug and Windle (2010), in which witnessing community violence attenuated the impact of witnessing domestic violence on anxiety, aggression, and delinquency. As the authors argued, the interpretation one could give is that witnessing community violence may desensitize youths to the effects of violence occurring at home, such that witnessing domestic violence had no impact on adolescents' anxiety, depression, and delinquency when youth witnessed community violence (Cooley-Quille et al., 2001). Furthermore, violence in the community may set norms or expectations for violence in other settings, so that adolescents exposed to community violence may perceive domestic violence as "normative" and be less affected by it. Regardless of these speculations, future research is needed to clarify how different contexts of violence interact with each other and what their interactions implicate in terms of consequences on child adjustment.

10.4 Youth Exposure to Community Violence: The Case of Naples

In the next paragraphs we will present some studies (published and not) based on several rounds of data collection, starting from 2006 and involving approximately 1700 adolescents. Participants aged from 10–11 to 18–19 and were drawn from several middle and high schools located in the metropolitan area of Naples. Among those, about 800 adolescents are still involved in an ongoing longitudinal research project, which is now entering its sixth year. The measure of youth exposure to community violence through witnessing and victimization has been adapted from Schwartz and Proctor (2000), where children are asked to report violent incidents that had occurred during the last year and instructed to report only serious real-life events from their neighborhoods and their communities (e.g., being or seeing someone being physically assaulted, being or seeing someone being threated, etc.).

10.4.1 Why Do We Work on Youth Community Violence in Naples?

The first thing popping up into people's head when someone says "Naples" is not the beauty of the city. Instead, people recall the stories told by the newspapers all over the world about the Neapolitan Mafia, so-called Camorra, pickpockets, drug dealing, etc.

We do not know whether Naples is more dangerous and violent than other cities in Italy and in the world, but certainly violent behavior and unemployment and school dropout rates in this geographic area are among the highest in Italy (CNEL ISTAT, 2016), sounding a serious social alarm. As reported in a recent cross-cultural study comparing the perception of neighborhood danger in nine different countries (Italy, China, Kenya, Philippines, Sweden, United States, Colombia, Jordan, and

Thailand) and including data collected in the metropolitan areas of Naples and Rome as representative of Italy, Neapolitan adolescents (10–11 years old) and their parents exhibited the highest scores (Skinner et al., 2014). The fact that Neapolitan adolescents are massively exposed to violence in their everyday life is shown also in the study of Affuso et al. (2014), in which 76% reported that they had witnessed violence or had been victims of violence in the neighborhood (assault, robbery, threats) at least one time in the last year, whereas 15% of the sample claimed to have been involved, at least once, in all contexts of violence considered in the study, that is, community, school, family, and media violence. In addition, serious concerns have been raised by the phenomena of Naples' youth gangs since 2013, approximately. Overall, our data show a consistent rate of 35–40% of adolescents reporting that they have been chased by youth gangs at least once in a year, whereas 65–70% report having seen somebody else get chased by gangs. While the problem was originally considered closely linked to the presence of organized crime, as widely chronicled in Roberto Saviano's "La paranza dei bambini" (2016), the news reported by media between 2017 and 2018 have brought to light a grave social emergency, beyond the criminal emergency. These episodes involve very young kids, not teenage "camorristi," who commit violence against other kids or adults apparently for no reason. In the wake of these events, we acknowledge the importance of deepening the possible mechanisms linking violence exposure in the community and youth gang involvement, examining how repeated exposure to violence may lead youth to be involved in delinquent peer networks, such as gangs, and/or how, vice versa, those peer associations might tend to increase exposure to community violence. The criminology literature, and in particular Gottfredson and Hirschi's "self-control theory" (1990), may represent a useful starting point for further considerations.

10.5 Linking Violent Exposure to Negative Developmental Outcomes

10.5.1 Exposure to Community Violence and the Role of Effortful Control

According to the criminology literature, self-regulating abilities seem to play an important role in adolescent involvement in violent contexts (Gottfredson & Hirschi, 1990). What we know about self-regulation in adolescence is that young people are characterized by an easily aroused reward system, which inclines adolescents toward sensation seeking, and a low ability of self-control, which limits their capacity to resist these inclinations (see Steinberg's "dual system" model, 2008). At around age 15, self-regulatory abilities may reach adultlike levels in relatively less arousing, "cool" contexts (Casey, 2015), but when tasks become more demanding or emotionally arousing, adultlike performance may not be reached until closer to the mid-20s (Shulman et al., 2016).

These considerations are fundamental when trying to explain which factors amplify the risk of adolescent exposure to community violence. As suggested by Gottfredson and Hirschi in their "self-control theory of crime" (1990, p. 157), youth with low self-control "gravitate to the street." Compared to youth with higher levels of self-control, they tend to gravitate toward activities that bring short-term pleasure and do not consider the long-term consequences of their behavior (Gibson, 2011); hence, they are more likely to put themselves in situations in which violence is likely, high-risk situations, to engage in delinquent behavior or to associate with other delinquent youth, and then to become direct victims of violence (Schreck, Stewart, & Fisher, 2006). Over the last decade, the criminology literature has encouraged researchers to incorporate neurogenetic or brain-based temperament traits (DeLisi, 2014) as an explanation of antisocial and deviant behavior (Bridgett, Burt, Edwards, & Deater-Deckard, 2015), including the tendency to be involved in violent contexts. Against this background, we recently tested a temperament-based theory of involvement in violent contexts and engagement in aggressive behavior in adolescence, specifically by examining the cross-lagged associations between temperamental effortful control, exposure to community violence (as a witness and as a victim), and aggressive behavior across four time points (Esposito, Bacchini, Eisenberg, & Affuso, 2017). The results of this study were encouraging, providing support for the hypothesis that temperamental effortful control plays a complex role in the development of violence: first, by increasing adolescents' tendency to engage in acts of aggression and externalizing behavior and, second, by increasing the likelihood that adolescents put themselves in violent contexts, both as a witness and as a victim, but only through the mediation of engagement in aggressive behavior. Overall, we concluded that the substantial relations among self-regulation abilities with aggressive behavior combined with exposure to violence within the community underscore the importance of considering interventions that target the early stages in the development of self-regulation in order to reduce juvenile aggression (DeLisi & Vaughn, 2014).

10.5.2 The Paradigm of Pathologic Adaptation to Community Violence

Repeated exposure of community violence versus one-time exposure could lead to differential outcomes. We know that community violence is linked to youths' psychological adjustment according to a dose-response mechanism, which means that as experiences of violence exposure accumulate over time, more severe psychological symptoms develop (e.g., Kennedy, Bybee, Sullivan, & Greeson, 2010). However, the impact of exposure to community violence on youths' well-being becomes more complex when considering the chronicity, or persistence, of violence exposure over time (Garbarino, 1999). Indeed, it seems reasonable to assume that witnessing or being a victim of violence repeatedly over time may have a greater or different impact than having one isolated experience of witnessing or victimization, but the research examining how repeated experiences of community violence are longitudinally associated with psychological outcomes and how this pattern of exposure may be differentially related to outcomes from one-time exposure is still needed (Foster & Brooks-Gunn, 2009).

One theory that may account for differential outcomes of repeated exposure of community violence versus one-time exposure is that youth become desensitized to violence over time. As pointed out by Huesmann (1998), children who are repeatedly exposed to violence during childhood inhabit it and experience it as less adverse. Over time, desensitization would account for a weaker association between violence exposure and emotional symptoms, such as depression, but a stronger link between violence and aggressive behaviors, indicating a greater acceptance of the use of violence as a normative problem-solving strategy (Ng-Mak, Salzinger, Feldman, & Stueve, 2004). However, less is understood about the mechanism through which desensitization develops. In their first theoretical model that they called "pathologic adaptation to violence," Ng-Mak, Salzinger, Feldman, and Stueve (2002) identified the crucial mechanism in moral disengagement processes (Bandura, Barbaranelli, Caprara, & Pastorelli, 1996): That is, chronic exposure to violence leads to a normalization of violence through moral disengagement, which in turn promotes an active engagement in future episodes of violence. However, to the best of our knowledge, no study has systematically examined how being exposed to community violence influences the development of moral disengagement. Wilkinson and Carr (2008) tried to raise this point using qualitative data from male violent offenders. They noted that individuals respond to exposure to violence in many ways, some of which are consistent with traditional concepts of moral disengagement, but also argued that those processes are not sufficient for behaving aggressively and that aspects of contingencies and configurations of situational and interpersonal factors play a powerful role in violent behavior. Thus, in a still unpublished study, we have sought to address this issue by investigating how exposure to community violence is associated with specific longitudinal trajectories of moral cognitive distortions (Gibbs, Potter, Barriga, & Liau, 1996) in a sample of 745 adolescents. Albeit partial and still processing, our findings suggest that growing up in a violent neighborhood undermines the normative process of moral development, causing delays that consolidate into self-serving cognitive distortions. Furthermore, when examining the association of trajectories of moral cognitive distortions with later aggressive behavior, the results seem to suggest that a crystallization of disengaging mechanisms and self-serving distortions legitimatizes and reinforces the recourse to aggressive and violent behaviors (Arsenio & Lemerise, 2004; Bandura et al., 1996). Based on these preliminary findings, we conclude that research on relevant environmental variables that could influence individual behaviors at several levels is necessary, both for expanding knowledge about the development and persistence of aggressive and violent outcomes and in order to design appropriate interventions aimed at preventing maladjustment in adolescence.

10.5.3 The Role of Parental Monitoring in Violent Neighborhoods

The role of parents in buffering the effects of violence exposure is well recognized in the literature. In their ecological-transactional model of community violence, Lynch and Cicchetti (1998) categorized exposure to violence in the community as an enduring distal stressor that may influence, through dynamic and mutually reinforcing exchanges, behavior and relationships within children's proximal family context; similarly, parenting and family characteristics may influence the degree to which distal stressors have an impact on children's developmental outcomes. Within this framework, many studies have focused on the moderating role of positive family characteristics, such as a supportive family environment, in buffering the negative impact of community violence exposure on poor child outcomes. An extensive review of these studies is reported in Proctor (2006), where the author points out two different moderating roles that positive family characteristics play in the relationship between exposure to community violence and negative developmental outcomes. The former is a protective-stabilizing effect, in which a factor exerts a positive effect on children's outcomes even in the presence of increasing risk, while the latter is a protective-reactive effect, in which a factor exerts a generally positive effect on an outcome, but less so at higher levels of risk (Luthar, Cicchetti, & Becker, 2000).

One of the most important family-related factors able to protect adolescents against psychological and social risk is parental monitoring. To date, researchers have found that high exposure to violence annuls the protective effects of parental monitoring not only against antisocial behavior (Miller, Wasserman, Neugebauer, Gorman-Smith, & Kamboukos, 1999) but also against symptoms of anxiety and depression (Gorman-Smith & Tolan, 1998). Based on these findings, we tested the moderating role of parental monitoring in the association of community violence, both as a victim and as a witness, with antisocial behavior and anxiety-depression symptoms in a sample of 489 adolescents (Bacchini, Miranda, & Affuso, 2011). The study showed impressive results, suggesting that different outcomes involve different mechanisms through which parental monitoring does act, or not act, as a buffer against the negative impact of violence exposure. As shown in Fig. 10.3, the linear regression analysis with parental monitoring as a moderating variable indicated that parental monitoring had a "protective-reactive" effect when the outcome was antisocial behavior, such that high parental monitoring could substantially reduce antisocial behavior only when violence exposure was low, not when it was high. Adolescents who exhibit antisocial behavior are generally also those who are more likely involved in high-risk environments, maybe due to individual factors, such as low self-control, that totally "overwhelms" the protective effect of parental monitoring. In contrast, a "protective-stabilizing" effect was found when considering anxiety-depression as an outcome, where high parental monitoring produced a reduction in depression, even when exposure to violence was high. We argue that,

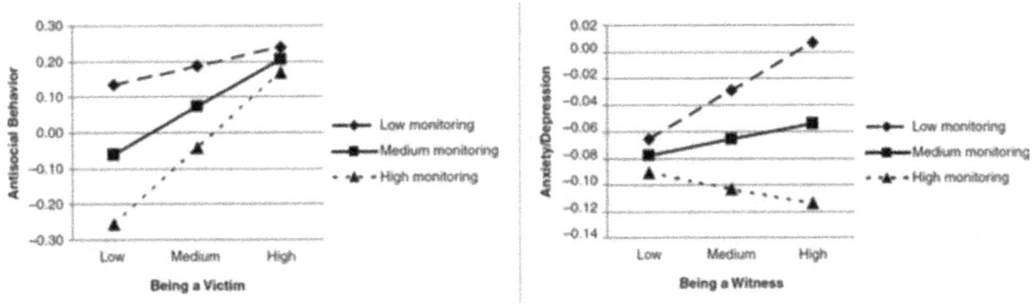

Fig. 10.3 Interactive effects of violence exposure and parental monitoring on adolescent antisocial behavior and anxiety-depression. (Extracted and adapted from Bacchini et al., 2011)

in this case, talking about these experiences with their parents, and expressing their fears, makes young people feel protected and reduces feelings of isolation and danger.

10.6 Implications for Policy and Practice

Years of research have improved our understanding of the consequences of youth violence exposure and increased our knowledge of how risk and protective factors contribute to or buffer against violence exposure. The challenge is now to develop policies that ensure the right of every child to live in a safe and nonviolent society.

We know that violence affecting youth development has many sources, and addressing this issue requires attention at all levels of the social ecology. Based on decades of experience, UNICEF (2014) has identified six key strategies to prevent violence exposure, which involve a wide range of government agencies working in the areas of education, finance, health, home affairs, justice, labor, as well as academic agencies. Those strategies include (1) helping parents to develop positive parenting skills, (2) giving children and adolescents the skills to cope and manage risks without the use of violence, (3) changing attitudes and social norms that encourage violence and discrimination, (4) providing high-quality support services for children who are victims of violence, (5) implementing and enforcing laws and policies that protect children from violence, and (6) carrying out data collection and research to plan and design intervention strategies, as well as to monitor progress and end violence.

Other preventive approaches that have been demonstrated to have a great public health impact have been promoted by the Centers for Disease Control and Prevention in USA. These programs target both youth skill development and relationships with parents, peers, and other caring adults but also use strategies influencing school and community environments (see, e.g., the program "Striving To Reduce Youth Violence Everywhere", or STRYVE; David-Ferdon et al., 2016).

However, we acknowledge that programs targeting multiple levels of the child's ecology, although optimal, require economic resources that are not always available, especially in low-income countries. In such cases, school-based programs could provide ample opportunity to reduce the costs of preventive intervention, targeting relevant factors at different levels of the child's functioning and environment, simultaneously. For example, programs like the Coping Power Universal (Lochman, Wells, & Murray, 2007) as well as the Equipping Youth to Help One Another (EQUIP; Gibbs, Potter, & Goldstein, 1995) could be easily implemented in the school setting in order to prevent violence exposure or its effects, strengthening children's moral cognition, self-regulation, and skills for social problem-solving. Further, all these abilities would promote, in the long term, the development of a nonviolent and law-abiding culture, which represents the crucial condition to ensure success in preventing and reducing children's exposure to violence.

10.7 Conclusions

Although different than in war-torn areas, violence affects children even in the most economically developed countries, breaking into their family, school, or neighborhood daily life. The reasons are complex and strictly interrelated: among all, social injustices and organized crime are two relevant contributors.

In this chapter we reviewed the empirical evidence supporting the detrimental effects of early violence exposure on a wide range of developmental outcomes. Overall, the research suggests a sort of equifinality of violence exposure across different contexts. Research indicates that, fundamentally, children need to feel safe in their daily life contexts. If they do not feel safe, they are at risk of developing internalized symptoms or eventually becoming perpetrators of violence themselves. Nevertheless, still many holes remain in our knowledge of mechanisms linking violence exposure to negative developmental outcomes, as well as of predisposing and precipitating factors that intervene in these complex relationships. Because the investment of economic, political, and social resources in deterrent strategies has been demonstrated to be not effective in reducing violence in the way that was hoped, the challenge for research in this field is to inform policies aimed at reducing the number of risk factors that, at different ecological levels, might lead children to poor developmental outcomes.

References

Affuso, G., Bacchini, D., Aquilar, S., De Angelis, G., & Miranda, M. C. (2014). Esposizione alla violenza in contesti multipli e sintomi post-traumatici da stress: uno studio con adolescenti (Exposure to violence in multiple contexts and post-traumatic stress symptoms: A study with adolescents). *Maltrattamento e Abuso all'Infanzia, 2*, 13–33.

Arsenio, W. F., & Lemerise, E. A. (2004). Aggression and moral development: Integrating social information processing and moral domain models. *Child Development, 75*(4), 987–1002.

Bacchini, D., Affuso, G., & Aquilar, S. (2015). Multiple forms and settings of exposure to violence and values: Unique and interactive relationships with antisocial behavior in adolescence. *Journal of Interpersonal Violence, 30*(17), 3065–3088.

Bacchini, D., Miranda, M. C., & Affuso, G. (2011). Effects of parental monitoring and exposure to community violence on antisocial behavior and anxiety/depression among adolescents. *Journal of Interpersonal Violence, 26*(2), 269–292.

Bandura, A., Barbaranelli, C., Caprara, G. V., & Pastorelli, C. (1996). Mechanisms of moral disengagement in the exercise of moral agency. *Journal of Personality and Social Psychology, 71*(2), 364–374.

Bridgett, D. J., Burt, N. M., Edwards, E. S., & Deater-Deckard, K. (2015). Intergenerational transmission of self-regulation: A multidisciplinary review and integrative conceptual framework. *Psychological Bulletin, 141*(3), 602–654.

Casey, B. J. (2015). Beyond simple models of self-control to circuit-based accounts of adolescent behavior. *Annual Review of Psychology, 66*(1), 295–319.

CNEL. (2016). *Bes 2016. Il benessere equo e sostenibile in Italia*. Roma: Istituto Nazionale di Statistica. Retrieved from: https://www.istat.it/it/files/2016/12/BES-2016.pdf.

Cooley-Quille, M., Boyd, R. C., Frantz, E., & Walsh, J. (2001). Emotional and behavioral impact of exposure to community violence in inner-city adolescents. *Journal of Clinical Child and Adolescent Psychology, 30*(2), 199–206.

Crick, N. R., & Dodge, K. A. (1994). A review and reformulation of social information- processing mechanisms in children's social adjustment. *Psychological Bulletin, 115*(1), 74–101.

David-Ferdon, C., Vivolo-Kantor, A. M., Dahlberg, L. L., Marshall, K. J., Rainford, N., & Hall, J. E. (2016). *A comprehensive technical package for the prevention of youth violence and associated risk behaviors*. Atlanta, GA: National Center for Injury Prevention and Control, Centers for Disease Control and Prevention.

DeLisi, M. (2014). Low self-control is a brain-based disorder. In K. M. Beaver, J. C. Barnes, & B. B. Boutwell (Eds.), *The nurture versus biosocial debate in criminology: On the origins of criminal behavior and criminality* (pp. 172–184). Thousand Oaks, CA: SAGE.

DeLisi, M., & Vaughn, M. G. (2014). Foundation for a temperament-based theory of antisocial behavior and criminal justice system involvement. *Journal of Criminal Justice, 42*(1), 10–25.

Esposito, C., Bacchini, D., Eisenberg, N., & Affuso, G. (2017). Effortful control, exposure to community violence, and aggressive behavior: Exploring cross-lagged relations in adolescence. *Aggressive Behavior, 43*(6), 588–600.

Finkelhor, D., Ormrod, R. K., & Turner, H. A. (2007). Poly-victimization: A neglected component in child victimization. *Child Abuse and Neglect, 31*(1), 7–26.

Finkelhor, D., Turner, H., Shattuck, A., Hamby, S., & Kracke, K. (2015). *Children's exposure to violence, crime, and abuse: An update*. Laurel, MD: U.S. Department of Justice Juvenile Justice Bulletin. Retrieved from http://www.ojjdp.gov/pubs/248547.

Foster, H., & Brooks-Gunn, J. (2009). Toward a stress process model of children's exposure to physical family and community violence. *Clinical Child and Family Psychology Review, 12*(2), 71–94.

Garbarino, J. (1999). The effects of community violence on children. In L. Balter & C. S. Tamis-LeMonda (Eds.), *Child psychology, a handbook of contemporary issues* (pp. 412–425). New York: Psychology Press.

Gibbs, J. C., Potter, G. B., Barriga, A. Q., & Liau, A. K. (1996). Developing the helping skills and prosocial motivation of aggressive adolescents in peer group programs. *Aggression and Violent Behavior, 1*(3), 283–305.

Gibbs, J. C., Potter, G. B., & Goldstein, A. P. (1995). *The EQUIP program: Teaching youth to think and act responsibly through a peer-helping approach*. Champaign: IL: Research Press.

Gibson, C. L. (2011). An investigation of neighborhood disadvantage, low self-control, and violent victimization among youth. *Youth Violence and Juvenile Justice, 10*, 41–63.

Gorman-Smith, D., & Tolan, P. (1998). The role of exposure to community violence and developmental problems among inner-city youth. *Development and Psychopathology, 10*(1), 101–116.

Gottfredson, M. R., & Hirschi, T. (1990). *A general theory of crime*. Stanford, CA: Stanford University Press.

Huesmann, L. R. (1998). The role of social information processing and cognitive schema in the acquisition and maintenance of habitual aggressive behavior. In R. G. Geen & E. Donnerstein (Eds.), *Human aggression: Theories, research, and implications for social policy* (pp. 73–109). San Diego, CA: Academic Press.

Kennedy, A. C., Bybee, D., Sullivan, C. M., & Greeson, M. (2010). The impact of family and community violence on children's depression trajectories: Examining the interactions of violence exposure, family social support, and gender. *Journal of Family Psychology, 24*(2), 197–207.

Lochman, J. E., Wells, K. C., & Murray, M. (2007). The coping power program: preventive intervention at the middle school transition. In P. Tolan, J. Szapocznik, & S. Sambrano (Eds.), *Preventing youth substance abuse: Science-based programs for children and adolescents* (pp. 185–210). Washington, DC: American Psychological Association.

Lynch, M., & Cicchetti, D. (1998). An ecological-transactional analysis of children and contexts: The longitudinal interplay among child maltreatment, community violence, and children's symptomatology. *Development and Psychopathology, 10*(2), 235–257.

Luthar, S. S., Cicchetti, D., & Becker, B. (2000). The construct of resilience: A critical evaluation and guidelines for future work. *Child Development, 71*, 543–562.

Margolin, G., & Gordis, E. B. (2000). The effects of family and community violence on children. *Annual Review of Psychology, 51*(1), 445–479.

Margolin, G., Vickerman, K. A., Oliver, P. H., & Gordis, E. B. (2010). Violence exposure in multiple interpersonal domains: Cumulative and differential effects. *Journal of Adolescent Health, 47*(2), 198–205.

Maternowska, M. C., Potts, A., & Fry, D. (2016). *The multi-country study on the drivers of violence affecting children: A cross-country snapshot of findings*. Florence, Italy: UNICEF Office of Research.

Miller, L. S., Wasserman, G. A., Neugebauer, R., Gorman-Smith, D., & Kamboukos, D. (1999). Witnessed community violence and antisocial behavior in high-risk, urban boys. *Journal of Clinical Child and Adolescent Psychology, 28*(1), 2–11.

Mrug, S., & Windle, M. (2009). Mediators of neighborhood influences on externalizing behavior in preadolescent children. *Journal of Abnormal Child Psychology, 37*(2), 265–280.

Mrug, S., & Windle, M. (2010). Prospective effects of violence exposure across multiple contexts on early adolescents' internalizing and externalizing problems. *Journal of Child Psychology and Psychiatry and Allied Disciplines, 51*(8), 953–961.

Ng-Mak, D. S., Salzinger, S., Feldman, R., & Stueve, A. (2002). Normalization of violence among inner-city youth: A formulation for research. *American Journal of Orthopsychiatry, 72*(1), 92–101.

Ng-Mak, D. S., Salzinger, S., Feldman, R. S., & Stueve, C. A. (2004). Pathologic adaptation to community violence among inner-city youth. *American Journal of Orthopsychiatry, 74*(2), 196–208.

Perry, D. G., Hodges, E. V. E., & Egan, S. K. (2001). Determinants of chronic victimization by peers. In J. Juvonen & S. Graham (Eds.), *Peer harassment in school: The plight of thevulnerable and victimized* (pp. 73–104). NewYork: Guilford Press.

Proctor, L. J. (2006). Children growing up in a violent community: The role of the family. *Aggression and Violent Behavior, 11*(6), 558–576.

Saviano, R. (2016). *La Paranza dei bambini*. La Feltrinelli Editore.

Schreck, C. J., Stewart, E. A., & Fisher, B. S. (2006). Self-control, victimization, and their influence on risky lifestyles: A longitudinal analysis using panel data. *Journal of Quantitative Criminology, 22*(4), 319–340.

Schwartz, D., & Proctor, L. J. (2000). Community violence exposure and children's social adjustment in the school peer group: The mediating roles of emotion regulation and social cognition. *Journal of Consulting and Clinical Psychology, 68*(4), 670–683.

Shulman, E. P., Smith, A. R., Silva, K., Icenogle, G., Duell, N., Chein, J., & Steinberg, L. (2016). The dual systems model: Review, reappraisal, and reaffirmation. *Developmental Cognitive Neuroscience, 17*, 103–117.

Skinner, A. T., Bacchini, D., Lansford, J. E., Godwin, J. W., Sorbring, E., Tapanya, S., … Bombi, A. S. (2014). Neighborhood danger, parental monitoring, harsh parenting, and child aggression in nine countries. *Societies, 4*(1), 45–67.

Steinberg, L. (2008). A social neuroscience perspective on adolescent risk-taking. *Developmental Review, 28*(1), 78–106.

Turner, H. A., Shattuck, A., Finkelhor, D., & Hamby, S. (2016). Polyvictimization and youth violence exposure across contexts. *Journal of Adolescent Health, 58*(2), 208–214.

United Nations Children's Fund. (2014). *Ending violence against children: Six strategies for action*. New York: UNICEF.

United Nations Children's Fund. (2017). *A familiar face: Violence in the lives of children and adolescents*. New York: UNICEF.

WHO. (1996). *Global Consultation on Violence and Health. Violence: a public health priority*. Geneva, Switzerland: World Health Organization.

Wilkinson, D. L., & Carr, P. J. (2008). Violent youths' responses to high levels of exposure to community violence: What violent events reveal about youth violence. *Journal of Community Psychology, 36*(8), 1026–1051.

Chapter 11
Historical Culture and Peace: How Older Generations Address the Need of Younger Generations to Learn About Their In-Group Past

Check for updates

Giovanna Leone and Mauro Sarrica

From birth to death, people are exposed to "an avalanche" (Brescó de Luna & Rosa, 2012, p. 300) of intergenerational narratives regarding the historical past of the group to which they belong. For each individual, little by little, intergenerational narratives of the in-group's past form an overall perception of "imagined communities", ranging from the small groups they belong to, such as their families, to larger groups such as their nations (Anderson, 2006). These narratives are inserted in a complex infrastructure of many different formal and informal memory devices, meant to make community members share the same historical culture (Grever & Adriaansen, 2017; Rusen, 1997).

Recent studies on history didactics carried out from an international and interdisciplinary perspective have shown how "the various informal ways of learning in traditional and new popular media – from historical novels, museum exhibitions, heritage sites, to films, television shows and documentaries, website and apps – have intensified the general attractiveness of history" (Carretero, Berger, & Graver, 2017, p. 1). It implies that currently, in many societies around the world, history – seen as a subject of formal teaching – is being conveyed in increasingly hybrid forms. Thanks to these new hybrid forms, inextricably combining both formal teaching and informal communication about the past, adult members of a community gradually scaffold the development of the historical consciousness of new born individuals, allowing them to collapse the perception of their current "we" with the historical "we" that was narrated to them. This process builds for younger generations a kind of "imagiNation" (Carretero, 2017) that ensures a sense of continuity and entitativity of nations across generational changes. Together with these in-group aims, narratives of the historical past also fulfil aims linked to intergroup relations (Mazzara & Leone, 2001). When intergroup relations are negative, intergenerational

G. Leone (✉) · M. Sarrica
Sapienza University of Rome, Rome, Italy
e-mail: giovanna.leone@uniroma1.it; mauro.sarrica@uniroma1.it

N. Balvin, D. J. Christie (eds.), *Children and Peace*, Peace Psychology Book Series, https://doi.org/10.1007/978-3-030-22176-8_11

narratives and collective memories have been largely studied as pivotal elements used to fuel intergroup hostility and distrust, to socialise new generations into an ethos of conflict and to justify the continuation of cycles of violence and of long-standing conflicts (Coleman, 2003; Tint, 2010).

Our proposal is framed in a more comprehensive description of society, focusing on societal changes rather than specific in-group or intergroup relations. Such a framework was introduced in the pioneering work of Hannah Arendt (1958, 1977). According to her unconventional and innovative lesson, societal changes are best described by taking into consideration the lifecycle of ordinary people, rather than referring to individual creativity or other special capacities of extraordinary men. By introducing the new concept of *natality* at the very core of societal changes, Arendt (1977) argued that the real source of novelty in social life is linked to the fact that each birth represents a new beginning for the community. Certainly, newborn individuals receive the world in which they live from older people; however, moving from this prearranged starting point, the *reactions* of younger individuals to the historical responsibilities of their in-group may contribute towards building and improving peaceful intergroup relations (Cairns & Roe, 2003; Kelman, 2008; Nadler & Shnabel, 2008). By introducing the concept of *natality*, and placing it at the very core of societal changes, Arendt argued, therefore, that each birth represents a new beginning for the community (Arendt, 1958, 1977).

Arendt's theoretical perspective is still innovative, since researches looking at peace building as an intergenerational task are usually aware of aspects of continuity between generations, more so than discontinuities occurring when older generations give room for change to younger ones (Leone, 2018). In fact, young citizens may use their individual historical consciousness, embedded in a larger societal historical culture (Rusen, 1997), not only to protect their positive social identity (Tajfel, 1982) but also to become more aware of moral failures and shortcomings of older generations. In this sense, the "avalanche" of intergenerational narratives may be seen not only as a source of a feeling of historical continuity with past generations but also as a springboard for change. More particularly, group-based emotions of moral shame, due to a deep understanding of historical failures of past generations, may enhance a young person's capacity to enact discontinuities and changes from old choices and habits.

The aim of our chapter is to defend the idea that, when acting in favour of reconciliation, the risk of making the descendants of groups involved in past violence deeply ill at ease, while thinking about their violent historical past, is worth taking. In order to make this point we will review classic studies which have shown that historical awareness is not only an important cultural tool but also a crucial need of younger generations, especially when they have to cope with a troubled past. Then we will describe situations in which intergenerational communication fails and silence and social denials are used instead. Finally, we will describe peace in the frame of intergenerational communication and we will draw some tentative conclusions and propose directions for research and intervention.

11.1 The Need of Young Generations to Learn About Their In-Group past

Often at times, the idea that young people are indifferent to history and are only embedded in present days is presented as common sense. On the contrary, many important classic studies have shown that learning about their in-group's historical past is a basic socio-psychological need for young people coming of age and starting to cope with their adult responsibilities in the democratic forum.[1]

A first and fundamental example on the precious contribution of history to enhance the full development of democratic societies is offered by the classic book *The Historian's Craft or Apology of History* (Bloch, 1954). Bloch wrote this unfinished masterpiece referring only to his own memory, shortly before being executed in 1944 as a leader of the French resistance. Bloch chose to build the whole of his little but classic book around a hypothetical question posed by his 12-year-old son after the sudden shock following the conquest of Paris by the Nazi troops: "What is the use of history?" Using this literary fiction, Bloch explained to his son that the function of historical accounts is not to provide advice or strategic counselling in dangerous times, but to comply with a basic law of the human mind, namely, to fulfil its "instinctive need of understanding". Especially in dark historical times, in the intimacy of their communications, families participate in a never-ending collective effort to give meaning to the historical events they have to face. Without taking into account this activity of human mind, it is impossible to understand the impact of historical facts on society. The recounting of history helps individuals assign meaning to what happened in the past and sets the stage for how they choose to conduct their lives going forward (Sweeny, 1993).

In these same dark years, another influential French scholar, Maurice Halbwachs, focused his attention on family narratives of the past. Halbwachs (1925/1992) decided to observe what happens when family members gather together to remember (*"quand la famille se souvient"*). He noted how, in the intimate setting of their face-to-face conversations, families repeatedly narrated some specific episodes, chosen from among several that had occurred in the family's past. Sometimes, shared memories would recollect specific *historical events.* At other times, these family narratives would convey to younger members recollections of *past ways of living* that had been experienced by the older generations but were subsequently gone. Although knowing them by heart, family members listened with evident pleasure to these over-narrated episodes and seemed to cherish them as a kind of family treasure. By contrast, these same memories were not shared with strangers. In his seminal books, Halbwachs (1925/1992, 1950/1980) proposed that repeated family memories *supported the personal positive identity of younger generations*. By repeatedly

[1] Interestingly, European scholars strongly addressed this point during the first decades of the past century, when they struggled to understand the dramatic social situations in which they were living. In spite of being deeply different from each other, all these scholars understood the importance of narratives of their dramatic in-group history to young individuals and the protective role that intergenerational communication play in the dark times they had to live.

sharing family memories that were not told to strangers, families were gifting to their younger members a positive image of the nucleus from which they originated and therefore of the fabric of which all of the family members were made – an "emotional armour" aimed at protecting them in the future when they needed to cope with life's difficulties.

Also in the same period, Ortega y Gasset, addressed the issue of intergenerational narratives on the in-group past in his masterpiece *The Revolt of the Masses*. He described the troubling cultural disease by which European crowds were changing into masses prone to dictatorship and pointed out that the "strange condition of human person" is "his essential pre-existence". That is that the lives of humans do not begin with their birth but are pre-shaped by the history of their community. Although being fully aware of the historicity of humans, however, Ortega y Gasset argued that the past of the community in which a person happens to be born "instead of imposing on us one trajectory . . . imposes several, and consequently *forces us to choose*" (Ortega y Gasset, 1930/1957, p. 31; emphasis added). Refusing any positivistic attitude, Ortega described therefore intergenerational historical narratives not as inescapable burdens, but as basic tools for fostering young adults' decisions, enabling them to grasp their starting points in life. According to the idea of *historical pre-existence* of the human mind (Ortega y Gasset, 1930/1957), intergenerational narratives of past historical times are offered to young people as cultural keys to understand their current social positions. By enhancing the historical awareness of the younger ones about their in-group past, older generations also allow them to better choose how to act in the social arena.

11.2 Silence and Self-Denials of Older Generations

The seminal thoughts briefly described in the previous paragraph give us an idea of the importance of young boys and girls reminiscing together with the older generation. New generations integrate single episodes into life stories and autobiographies, acquire culturally shared interpretative frameworks and master narratives and anchor individual episodes to family history and the larger sociocultural events (Fivush, Habermas, Waters, & Zaman, 2011; Reese & Fivush, 2008). Older generations, on the other hand, build a positive social identity (Tajfel, 1982) and introduce children to historical consciousness. Living with grandparents and listening to their narratives, in fact, provide children with "a rich base of information about the fundamental structures and processes of everyday life during those (past) times" (Seixas & Peck, 2004, p. 115), creating the first scaffolding for the later development of their capacity for historical thinking (Seixas & Peck, 2004; Seixas, 2017).

It is thus a puzzling experience for a young boy or a young girl to find something like a photograph of the war period, a "souvenir" of colonies, or maybe a gun well hidden in the old grandparent's closet. The old object gives a clue to instantly reconnect individuals and their close family to the major events that make history (assuming that we are in a culture where wars make history more than peace). At the same time, such discoveries create a fracture between the new generation and the previous one. Clearly, the previous generation may have decided to not share part of their history and may have wanted to create some distance between their times and the experiences of future generations.

In fact, when older generations convey to younger ones the thrust of their historical past, the acknowledgement of historical responsibilities accounting for past violence can be an important milestone in intergroup reconciliation (Vollhardt & Bilewicz, 2013). The use of conflict-driven narratives in long-standing conflicts has been largely examined: active cultivation of group perception and memories, as well as selective omissions, perpetuate emotions, keep past events alive, maintain a sense of menace to in-group survival, forge social identities and, finally, develop a conflictive ethos (Bar-tal, 2000; Tint, 2010). However, when intergroup violence comes to an end, a symbolic struggle regarding moral responsibility opens up. This struggle, which may last for a long time, aims to disambiguate, beyond all complexities inherent to any historical judgement, which role can be attributed to one's own group during aggressive incidents – be it either the role of perpetrators, or the role of victims or, finally, the less evident but very influential role of passive bystanders (Leone, in press). Although apparently protecting younger generations from group-based moral emotions – such as guilt, moral shame or social shame (Allpress, Brown, Giner-Sorolla, Deonna, & Teroni, 2014) – narratives based on silence and denial avoid conveying the crucial role played by the in-group in past violence and are important moral failures that slow down the process of intergroup reconciliation (Hameiri, Bar-Tal, & Halperin, 2017).

11.2.1 Why Do Older Generations Keep Troubled Memories Hidden?

Psychoanalytic, social cognition and constructivist perspectives, though starting from different premises, give many possible answers, which are deeply rooted in individual and group self-protective needs (Cohen, 1993). A critical approach to silence suggests linking this communicative act with power. In this regard, Fivush distinguishes between the choice of being silent and the fact of being silenced (Fivush, 2010). Whereas the first choice could be considered an expression of control and mastery of the situation – in a single phrase we may say "an act of power" – the fact of being silenced by self or others is virtually always seen as a lack of power. As Fivush (2010) underlines, silence could derive from conformity with the shared cultural scripts, which does not require justification and explanations. Silence can also be used in social interaction to impose distance, to reduce the importance of the others, to express judgement. Finally, being silent together could create a space of belonging and emotional attunement. In these three cases, silence is an expression of conformity, power and empowerment, respectively.

On the one hand, silence can be imposed on new generations as a deliberate act of power, an active choice of elites and states in constructing symbologies and technologies aimed at perpetuating cultural, structural and even direct forms of violence (Liu, Fisher Onar, & Woodward, 2014). Constructionism underlines how societies select their memories on the basis of their current needs, beliefs and goals and choose traumas and glories in order to transmit values, emotions and shared beliefs together with history (Tint, 2010, p. 242–243). Silence over human right violations committed by the in-group exemplifies this (Paez & Liu, 2009; Paez, Marques, Valencia, & Vincze, 2006).

On the other hand, imposed or self-imposed silence expresses deviation and disempowerment. These types of silencing may occur in response to violent traumas, war memories or negative events that threaten individual and social identity. Silence, in these cases, may be due to the perceived or actual lack of an audience that wants to, or can, understand stories that seem unintelligible or unbearable because they deviate so much from shared narratives. Organised manipulation of history is not even necessary when speakers perceive that their stories are too deviant to be understood and accepted by their audience or even by themselves or when they are too weak or socially isolated to have voice. Under these conditions, denial is a banal occurrence.

Psychoanalytic and social cognitive perspectives associate denial with this form of culturally self-imposed silence: a self-defensive mechanism towards threats. From a social cognition perspective, in particular, silencing is interpreted in terms of basic memory processes (e.g. forgetting, selective recall, assimilation), which contribute to self-serving and group-serving biases (Allport & Postman, 1945). Through the processes of complete denial or through more subtle omissions, individuals distance themselves or reject past events that they or their in-group can't manage. It is a non-adaptive form of coping, which fulfils the basic individual and group need to manage unbearable memories and preserve a positive identity and at the same time limit the capacity to develop more complex and critical accounts of these facts.

Together with complete silence, more subtle forms of neutralisation techniques can be used to cope with past wrongdoings. Cohen (1993) identifies five common techniques of denial that manifest in shared rhetorical discourses: "no one was affected", i.e. denial of injuries; "it's their fault", i.e. denial of the role of victims; "they are just as bad", i.e. denial of the legitimacy of judges; "we had to do it", i.e. denial of responsibility; and "it was us versus them", i.e. appeal to shared loyalty.

In order to make these techniques acceptable to audiences, narratives must refer to a "cultural pool of motivational vocabularies available to actors and observers (and honoured by systems of legality and morality)" (Cohen, 1993, p. 107), which are based on implicit disempowerment of self and others. Examples of these narratives in intergenerational communication include the need to "protect the new generations" assuming they cannot bear the truth, the idea that "time will pass and solve conflicts" implicitly accepting the fact that perpetrators and victims don't have the capabilities to solve them and the idea that "it's better to forget" because there is no other way to cope with the past.

Furthermore, these same rhetorical devices can contribute in the long term to establishing a new shared pool of vocabularies and "states of denial" (Cohen, 2001) that fulfil self-protective needs and at the same time hinder the emergence of mutual trust, acceptance and empowerment of victims and perpetrators. The literal denial ("it didn't happen") contributes to create and preserve positive social identity based on idealised historical past and social myths, like the myth of "Italian as good fellows" (Volpato, Andrighetto, Mari, Gabbiadini, & Durante, 2012). Through interpretative denial, the roles of victims and perpetrator are reframed in more acceptable ways ("… we are not responsible"), which however imposes silence on the causes and actors of wrongdoing. Lastly, the implicatory denial is a refusal to assume the consequences of one's own responsibility ("we admit our responsibilities … now you -the victim- must forget and forgive"), which, again, imposes silence on the victims who are not left free to speak for themselves and express their own needs.

11.3 Peace as an Intergenerational Task

The different forms of silence and denial of perpetrators, bystanders and victims described in the previous paragraphs are apparently functional in restoring the surface of everyday coexistence. In the long run, however, if self-protective narratives become dominant in a community, then both imposed and self-imposed choices of silence hinder reconciliation processes (Kelman, 2008). Well-known processes such as the "spiral of silence", avoidance of intergroup contact and polarisation of collective identities preserve elements that foster, beneath the surface, long-standing intractable conflict (Coleman, 2003; Halperin & Bar-Tal, 2011). Examples of these dynamics can be found in the rhetoric of Thanksgiving day (Kurtiş, Adams, & Yellow Bird, 2010), the "forgotten" Armenian genocide (Bilali, 2013; Hovannisian, 1998), the silence over collaboration during the regime of Vichy (Campbell, 2006) and the social amnesia about the Italian colonial crimes (Leone & Sarrica, 2012, 2014).

On the contrary, addressing the past and developing shared views is increasingly recognised as fundamental to reconciliation processes. According to the theoretical model proposed by Nadler and Shnabel (2008, 2015), groups involved in past violence have to face different identity threats. Perpetrators have to cope with a failure that undermines the moral image of their group and makes their social exclusion highly probable. Victims have to face their evident incapacity to control their own destiny, which is another kind of failure of their social image (Landsman, 2002). Finally, narratives of former violence can trigger serious group-based emotions in descendants of passive bystanders as well, since avoidance of solidarity towards victims implies a moral responsibility too (May, 2011). According to this theoretical proposal, for instance, a work of Wojcik, Bilewicz, and Lewicka (2010) in this somehow underdeveloped field of study has shown that descendants of bystanders born in communities where massive violence occurred were eager to learn the history of their town.

Thanks to the scaffolding of a historical culture passed from older generations to newer ones, group-based emotions of guilt, moral and social shame associated with past violence go down the generations and can also be felt by descendants born long after the end of intergroup violence (Allpress et al., 2014; Shepherd, Spears, & Manstead, 2013). This means that intergenerational recollections of past historical responsibility of one's own group for past violence – either enacted, or suffered, or indifferently witnessed – inherently produce a loss for the moral image of the group and a consequent process of social mourning (Adorno, 1986). Nevertheless, if responsibilities of one's own group are not fully and clearly stated for young listeners, intergenerational narratives about past intergroup violence cannot produce their positive effects that build and consolidate peaceful relations between old enemies (Cairns & Roe, 2003; Tint, 2010).

11.3.1 Peace as an Intergenerational Task

Surprisingly, very few studies have explored the societal struggle between the choice of silence and the decision to speak frankly about the past to new generations.

11.4 Breaking the Silence on Italian Colonialism: An Applied Example

A few studies have shown that young generations react emotionally to the historical knowledge of past responsibilities of their in-group even many years after these events and that moral emotions felt by them seem to encourage their reparative intentions towards the former victims. For instance, experimental studies were conducted to observe how Italian university students reacted when presented with either a clear and detailed or a mild historical account of violence enacted by the Italian Army during the colonial invasion of Ethiopia, which occurred during the Fascist regime. During this campaign, Italian troops used poisonous gas against the enemy, despite its prohibition by the Geneva Convention. Ethiopian resistance continued after the official end of the war, and Italian repression was cruel, particularly in response to a failed assassination attempt on Governor Graziani in 1937, when some six thousand civilians – according to Western sources – were executed, among them somewhat roughly three hundred monks of Debre Libanos.

Until recently, these crimes were socially denied. When finally proven beyond any doubt by an Italian history scholar (Labanca, 2002), they nevertheless remained silenced in social discourse. Italian history textbooks have only recently begun to explore this issue (Leone & Mastrovito, 2010; Cajani, 2013), but still present it as a short period intrinsically linked solely to the Fascist regime. Moreover, many images used in contemporary textbooks are taken from Fascist propaganda or from booklets for children (Leone, 2018). Thanks to this kind of societal self-censorships, these war crimes are still largely ignored in general social discourse (Pivato, 2011; Leone & Curigliano, 2009).

Moreover, the *Italiani brava gente* historical myth, depicting the Italian people as good and generous both in everyday life and in the military context, is still widely circulating (Del Boca, 2005). The social myth belies the brutality of Italian colonialism.

To explore how historical narratives could finally open up the Pandora box of these difficult group memories, a plan of experimental studies was set in place (Leone, d'Ambrosio, Migliorisi, & Sessa, 2018; Leone, Giner-Sorolla, D'Errico, Migliorisi, & Sessa, 2018; Leone & Sarrica, 2012; Leone & Sarrica, 2014). A part for specific aims of each experiment, all studies were conducted using a same procedure, organised into three different moments: time zero (T0), time one (T1) and time two (T2). The scheme repeatedly used for procedures ran as follows:

At (T0), each participant (young Italian university students) received a preliminary questionnaire, focused on knowledge and social representation of Italian colonialism, self-assessed emotions when thinking about this period of Italian history and assessed belief in the social myth describing Italians as good types (i.e. *Italiani, brava gente* (*IBG*): see Del Boca, 2005).

At (T1), after collecting the questionnaire, a researcher invited the participant to read the text shown on a computer screen on the desktop in front of which he/she was sitting and then to follow further instructions shown on the screen. After giving these instructions, the researcher left the room. Each participant was randomly assigned to read either an explicit ("poisonous gas" "mass killings") or implicit ("unconventional weapons" "attempts at repression") text. Participants were covertly videotaped while reading. Emotions on Italian colonialism were again self-assessed.

Finally at (T2) after a week and before receiving a debriefing, knowledge and understanding of the text was tested and the manipulation was checked. Then participants self-assessed for the third time their emotions (including moral emotions) about Italian colonialism and declared their agreement, if any, with reparative actions.

Apart from specificities linked to single studies, all the experimental evidence collected pointed to some regular patterns. Results at T0 showed that young Italian participants seemed to be unaware of Italian colonial crimes. Moreover, they expressed very low levels of intergroup emotions when thinking about Italian colonisation and declared their indifference to the social myth depicting the Italian people as good and generous types (Del Boca, 2005). Taken together, T0 results suggested that the Italian colonial past was not felt as "psychologically contemporary" by young participants (Lewin, 1943).

When experimenters analysed the facial expression of emotions shown by students covertly videotaped when reading, they observed how participants showed facial expressions of primary emotional reactions. It is interesting to stress that, being alone, their facial reactions could not be attributed to communicative intention but solely to their first appraisal of the seriousness of facts they were informed of. Emotions more often spontaneously shown by these young participants unaware of being observed were *sadness* and *contempt.*

When coming to the issue of self-assessed emotions, a comparison between T1 (immediately after reading the historical text on societally censored past colonial crimes) and T2 (a week later), all experiments showed that negative emotions significantly increased while reading the clear and detailed text on war crimes by the Italian Army. More specifically, if we take into account the self-conscious moral emotions (guilt, social shame, moral shame, pride), shown after 1 week, social and moral shame significantly increased and pride significantly decreased only for those young people receiving a clear historical narrative of the crimes committed by previous generations. These emotions, based on a change of their image of the group, could perhaps account for a moral loss of a positive idea of their historical identity, due to the awareness of past crimes that were until then kept silent in the social discourse they received about this period of the Italian national past.

Finally, and interestingly, the more recent among these researches (Leone, d'Ambrosio, et al., 2018) has shown how reparative intentions were positively associated only with the self-conscious emotions of social and moral shame, yet *not* with guilt.

Taken together, the results of this line of experimentation showed that when historical narratives break down literal social denials, only a clear account of past responsibilities of the in-group can be fully understood by young people previously unaware of this historical past and can lead to the expression of reparative intentions by young participants.

Of course, these empirical data (Leone, d'Ambrosio, et al., 2018; Leone, Giner-Sorolla, et al., 2018; Leone & Sarrica, 2012; Leone & Sarrica, 2014) also show how a clear historical narrative about the flawed moral character of one's own group that was heretofore denied or silenced can be a discomforting experience. Nevertheless, for those who are able to regulate themselves (Frijda, 1986), negative group-based emotions linked to this new awareness of moral indignities of one's own group seem to be powerful motivators of collective moral action (Smith, 1993).

In a nutshell, we can use the example of these data on societal self-censorship of Italian colonial crimes to suggest that, after a long intergenerational silence on past violence, a clear and frank account on crimes of the group formerly silenced or denied can be a way to open the Pandora's box of these past wrongdoings.

11.5 Concluding Remarks

It is possible to apply Foucault's original taxonomy of various forms of truth speaking (Foucault, 2001) to the issue of intergenerational narratives regarding the national past as well as communications about other kinds of difficult truths (a severe diagnosis, a negative law judgement, a school failure). In addition, those who speak clearly to young people on past historical responsibilities of the nation in which they happen to be born are implicitly showing their confidence in their receivers' strength and moral judgements. According to the taxonomy proposed by Foucault (2001), we may say therefore that when members of an older generation frankly narrate a shameful national history to a younger generation born after the end of these events, they are speaking to younger members with *parrhesia.* It means that, by choosing to tell them an uneasy truth, they are also showing an implicit trust in their receivers' capacity to cope with this difficult and harrowing knowledge.

Both classic theoretical models and recent experimental research suggest that this choice of *parrhesia* in intergenerational narratives of a shameful historical past may enhance reconciliation processes and peace. However, empirical research shows that different historical cultures choose to be less than completely clear about past atrocities of an in-group. It may well be that older generations could adopt this hidden communicative strategy when they suspect that descendants of the social groups that were involved will react negatively to their message (Gross, 1998).

Much more empirical research has to be done therefore to observe the way in which older generations foresee young generations' reactions to their historical accounts and choose *parrhesia* or an evasive form of communication. Research is also needed, then, to examine how young people regulate and evaluate the direct or evasive historical narratives that are passed on to them by older generations. This future direction of work could greatly add to our understanding of intergenerational processes that allow social groups to renew their relations. Nevertheless, the studies we presented in this chapter already point out a few key actions which can be considered for peace building based on the difficult intergenerational mourning for the moral losses of the past.

11.6 Application to Policy and Practice

We started this chapter noting that we all have been exposed to "an avalanche" (Bresció de Luna & Rosa, 2012, p. 300) of intergenerational narratives on the historical past of our in-groups. These narratives include formal and informal sources, memory devices, schools, media, family members, etc. which operate as interdependent components of a same societal process (cfr. Carretero et al., 2017; Grever & Adriaansen, 2017; Rusen, 1997). The following suggestions, which refer to the family, may be applied to a variety of formal and informal sources of intergenerational narratives.

- *Leverage new generations' need for knowledge.* Classic and recent studies show that learning about family and in-group historical past is a basic socio-psychological need, which allows new generations to position the self and the family group in a broader historical context. This "armour" is key to personal and social identity and to understanding current events. Following Ortega y Gasset

(1930/1957) it is important to acknowledge this *historical pre-existence* of the human mind refusing at the same time any determinism. Intergenerational narratives should be offered to young people as cultural keys, enhancing their historical awareness about the in-group's past and allowing them to better choose how to act as adults and citizens in a democratic forum.

- *Challenge conflictive master narratives*. History absorbed by children from the family (and other sources) is usually affected by self-serving bias, which forges positive social identities – and in some cases real conflict ethos – through active cultivation of memories and through forms of self-censorship and denial (Bar-Tal, 2000; Cohen, 2001; Hameiri et al., 2017; Tint, 2010). These narratives further expose new generations to a range of group emotions, including guilt, moral and social shame. Epistemic authorities (e.g. the grandparents, teachers) should thus challenge master narratives, deconstructing myths (Volpato et al., 2012) that are often based on self-indulgency. It means that intergenerational narratives, when honestly trying to inform young people about events that happened before their birth, have to strongly avoid illusions of moral superiority of the in-group and frankly speak about its historical responsibilities.
- *Regulate Group-Based Emotions*. Being exposed to previously hidden historical responsibility of one's own group for past violence – either as perpetrators, victims or bystanders – produces a loss of moral image for the group. In our research example, we have reviewed a long line of experimental studies exploring reactions of descendants of perpetrators, when becoming aware of the crimes committed by older generations. These crimes were kept silent by a massive societal self-censorship. But similar reactions could be expected also when descendants of victims are told about violence suffered by older generations. Unlike perpetrators who struggle with the difficulty of acknowledging their culpability, victims struggle to develop a sense of empowerment (Nadler & Shnabel, 2015). In both of these cases, it is essential for the younger generation to be aware of intergenerational narratives in order to proceed on the path of real intergroup reconciliation. There are risks however: When older generations are in the position of disclosing to younger people their historical past, there is the risk of producing very unpleasant effects (Leone, 2017).

The socio-psychological perspective stresses the idea that group-based emotions should not be avoided in the name of pure rationality (which is impossible). On the contrary, it is important to develop emotion regulation abilities, which permit spontaneous reactions while at the same time enhancing their positive expression and their use as a resource for cognitive processes. Formal settings, such as schools, present an opportunity for teachers to discuss sensitive issues surrounding the historical past (Brauch, Leone, & Sarrica, 2019), drawing on emotions stemming from a history of violence and encouraging young people to use this opportunity to once again hope and act for peace.

References

Adorno, T. (1986). What does coming to terms with the past mean? In G. Hartman (Ed.), *Bitburg in moral and political perspective* (pp. 114–129). Bloomington, IN: Indiana University Press.

Allport, G. W., & Postman, L. J. (1945). Section of psychology: The basic psychology of rumor. *Transactions of the New York Academy of Sciences, 8*(2 Series II), 61–81.

Allpress, J. A., Brown, R., Giner-Sorolla, R., Deonna, J. A., & Teroni, F. (2014). Two faces of group-based shame: Moral shame and image shame differentially predict positive and negative orientations to in-group wrongdoing. *Personality and Social Psychology Bulletin, 40*(10), 1270–1284.

Anderson, B. (2006). *Imagined communities: Reflections on the origin and spread of nationalism.* New York & London: Verso Books.

Arendt, H. (1958). *The human condition.* Chicago, IL: University of Chicago Press.

Arendt, H. (1977). *Between past and future: Eight exercises in political thought.* London: Penguin Books.

Bar-Tal, D. (2000). From intractable conflict through conflict resolution to reconciliation : Psychological analysis. *Political Psychology, 21*(2), 351–365.

Bilali, R. (2013). National narrative and social psychological influences in Turks' denial of the mass killings of Armenians as genocide. *Journal of Social Issues, 69*, 16–33.

Bloch, M. (1954). *The Historian's craft or apology of history.* New York: Knopf.

Brauch, N., Leone, G., & Sarrica, M. (2019). The debate almost came to a fight...'results of a cross-national explorative study concerning history teachers' shared beliefs about teaching historical sensitive issues. *Pedagogy, Culture & Society, 27*(1), 1–22.

Brescó de Luna, I., & Rosa, A. (2012). Memory, history and narrative: Shifts of meaning when (re) constructing the past. *Europe's Journal of Psychology, 8*, 300–310.

Cairns, E., & Roe, M. D. (Eds.). (2003). *The role of memory in ethnic conflict.* New York: Palgrave Macmillan.

Carretero, M. (2017). Teaching history master narratives: Fostering imagi-nations. In *Palgrave handbook of research in historical culture and education* (pp. 511–528). London: Palgrave Macmillan.

Carretero, M., Berger, S., & Graver, M. (Eds.). (2017). *Palgrave handbook of research in historical culture and education.* London: Palgrave Macmillan.

Campbell, J. (2006). Vichy, Vichy, and a plaque to remember. *French Studies Bulletin, 27*(98), 2–5.

Cohen, S. (1993). Human rights and crimes of the state: The culture of denial. *Australian & New Zealand Journal of Criminology, 26*, 97–115.

Cohen, S. (2001). *States of denial: Knowing about atrocities and suffering.* Cambridge, UK: Polity Press.

Coleman, P. T. (2003). Characteristics of protracted, intractable conflict : Toward the development of a Metaframework – I. *Peace and Conflict: Journal of Peace Psychology, 9*, 1–37.

Cajani, L. (2013). The Image of Italian Colonialism in Italian History Textbooks for Secondary Schools. Journal of Educational Media, Memory, and Society, 5(1), 72–89.

Del Boca, A. (2005). Italiani, brava gente? Un mito duro a morire. Vicenza: Neri Pozza.

Fivush, R. (2010). Speaking silence: The social construction of silence in autobiographical and cultural narratives. *Memory, 18*, 88–98.

Fivush, R., Habermas, T., Waters, T. E. A., & Zaman, W. (2011). The making of autobiographical memory: Intersections of culture, narratives and identity. *International Journal of Psychology/ Journal International de Psychologie, 46*, 321–345.

Foucault, M. (2001). *Fearless Speech.* Los Angeles: Semiotext(e)..

Frijda, N. H. (1986). The emotions. London: Cambridge University Press

Grever, M., & Adriaansen, R.-J. (2017). Historical culture: A concept revisited. In M. Carretero, S. Berger, & M. Graver (Eds.), *Palgrave handbook of research in historical culture and education* (pp. 73–89). London: Palgrave Macmillan.

Gross, J. J. (1998). The emerging field of emotion regulation: An integrative review. *Review of General Psychology, 2*(3), 271–299.

Halbwachs, M. (1925/1992). *On Collective Memory.* Chicago, IL: University of Chicago Press. (Translated abstracts from: *Les cadres sociaux de la mémoire*, Paris, Librairie Alcan.)

Halbwachs, M. (1950/1980). *The collective memory*. New York: Harper & Row.

Halperin, E., & Bar-Tal, D. (2011). Socio-psychological barriers to peace making: An empirical examination within the Israeli Jewish society. *Journal of Peace Research, 48*, 637–651.

Hameiri, B., Bar-Tal, D., & Halperin, E. (2017). Self-censorship as a socio-psychological barrier to peacemaking. In D. Bar-Tal, R. Nets-Zehngut, & K. Sharvit (Eds.), *Self-censorship in contexts of conflict* (pp. 61–78). Cham, Switzerland: Springer.

Hovannisian, R. G. (1998). *Remembrance and denial: The case of the Armenian genocide*. Detroit, MI: Wayne State University Press.

Kelman, H. C. (2008). Reconciliation from a social-psychological perspective. In A. Nadler, T. E. Malloy, & J. D. Fisher (Eds.), *The social psychology of intergroup reconciliation* (pp. 15–32). New York: Oxford University Press.

Kurtiş, T., Adams, G., & Yellow Bird, M. (2010). Generosity or genocide? Identity implications of silence in American Thanksgiving commemorations. *Memory, 18*, 208–224.

Labanca, N. (2002). *Oltremare: Storia dell'espansione coloniale italiana* (Vol. 31). Bologna, Italy: Il Mulino.

Landsman, I. S. (2002). Crises of meaning in trauma and loss. In J. Kauffman (Ed.), *Loss of the assumptive world: A theory of traumatic loss* (pp. 13–30). New York & London: Brunner- Routledge.

Leone, G. (2017). When history teaching turns into Parrhesia: The case of Italian colonial crimes. In C. Psaltis, M. Carretero, & S. Čehajić-Clancy (Eds.), *History education and conflict transformation* (pp. 147–167). Cham, Switzerland: Springer.

Leone, G. (2018). Beyond historical guilt: Intergenerational narratives of violence and reconciliation. In A. Rosa & J. Valsiner (Eds.), *The Cambridge handbook of sociocultural psychology* (pp. 458–478). Cambridge, UK: Cambridge University Press.

Leone, G., d'Ambrosio, M., Migliorisi, S., & Sessa, I. (2018). Facing the unknown crimes of older generations: Emotional and cognitive reactions of young Italian students reading an historical text on the colonial invasion of Ethiopia. *International Journal of Intercultural Relations, 62*, 55–67.

Leone, G., Giner-Sorolla, R., D'Errico, F., Migliorisi, S., & Sessa, I. (2018). It's time to be ashamed! Reactions to the breaking of a long-lasting self-censorship on ingroup war crimes. *TPM: Testing, Psychometrics, Methodology in. Applied Psychology, 25*(4), 519–535.

Leone, G., & Sarrica, M. (2012). Challenging the myth of Italians as 'good fellows': Is clarity about in-group crimes the best choice when narrating a war to its perpetrators ' descendants ? *Papers on Social Representations, 21*, 11.1–11.28.

Leone, G., & Sarrica, M. (2014). Making room for negative emotions about the national past: An explorative study of effects of parrhesia on Italian colonial crimes. *International Journal of Intercultural Relations, 43*, 126–138.

Liu, J. H., Fisher Onar, N., & Woodward, M. W. (2014). Symbologies, technologies, and identities: Critical junctures theory and the multi-layered nation–state. *International Journal of Intercultural Relations, 43*(A), 2–12.

Leone, G., & Curigliano, G. (2009). Coping with collective responsibilities An explorative study on Italian historical identity across three generations. *Journal of Language and Politics, 8*(2), 305–326.

Leone, G., & Mastrovito, T. (2010). Learning about our shameful past: A socio-psychological analysis of present-day historical narratives of Italian colonial wars. *International Journal of Conflict and Violence, 4*(1), 11–27.

Lewin, K. (1943). Defining the 'field at a given time'. Psychological Review, 50(May (3)), 292–310.

May, L. (2011). Bystanders, the rule of law, and criminal trials. *Nomos, 50*, 241–264.

Mazzara, B. M., & Leone, G. (2001). Collective memory and intergroup relations. *Revista de Psicologia Social, 16*(3), 349–367.

Nadler, A., & Shnabel, N. (2008). Instrumental and socioemotional paths to intergroup reconciliation and the needs-based model of socioemotional reconciliation. In A. Nadler, T. E. Malloy, & J. D. Fisher (Eds.), *The social psychology of intergroup reconciliation* (pp. 37–56). New York: Oxford University Press.

Nadler, A., & Shnabel, N. (2015). Intergroup reconciliation: Instrumental and socio- emotional processes and the needs-based model. *European Review of Social Psychology, 26*(1), 93–125.

Ortega y Gasset, J. (1930/1957). *The Revolt of the Masses*. New York: W. W. Norton. (Originally published as *La rebelión de las masas*.)

Paez, D., & Liu, J. H. (2009). Collective memory of conflicts. In D. Bar-tal (Ed.), *Intergroup conflicts and their resolution: Social psychological perspective* (pp. 105–124). Hove and New York: Psychology Press.

Paez, D., Marques, J., Valencia, J. F., & Vincze, O. (2006). Dealing with collective shame and guilt. *Psicologia Politica, 32*, 59–78.

Pivato, S. (2011). *Vuoti di memoria: usi e abusi della storia nella vita pubblica italiana*. Bari-Roma, Italy: Laterza.

Reese, E., & Fivush, R. (2008). The development of collective remembering. *Memory, 16*, 201–212.

Rusen, J. (1997). "Geschichtskultur" ["Historical Culture"]. In K. Bergmann (Ed.), *Handbuch der Geschichtsdidaktik [handbook of the didactics of history]* (pp. 38–41). Seelze-Velber: Kallmeyer'sche Verlagsbuchhandlung.

Seixas, P., & Peck, C. (2004). Teaching historical thinking. In A. Sears & I. Wright (Eds.), *Challenges and prospects for Canadian social studies* (pp. 109–117). Vancouver, Canada: Pacific Educational Press.

Seixas, P. (2017). Historical consciousness and historical thinking. In M. Carretero, S. Berger, & M. Graver (Eds.), *Palgrave handbook of research in historical culture and education* (pp. 59–72). London: Palgrave Macmillan.

Shepherd, L., Spears, R., & Manstead, A. S. (2013). "This will bring shame on our nation": The role of anticipated group-based emotions on collective action. *Journal of Experimental Social Psychology, 49*(1), 42–57.

Sweeny, R. C. (1993). Time and human agency: A re-assessment of the Annales legacy. *Left History, 1*(2), 63–83.

Smith, E. R. (1993). Social Identity and Social Emotions: Toward New Conceptualizations of Prejudice. In D. M. Mackie and D. L. Hamilton (Eds.). Affect, Cognition and Stereotyping (p. 297–315). San Diego: Academic Press.

Tajfel, H. (Ed.). (1982). *Social identity and intergroup relations*. New York: Cambridge University Press.

Tint, B. (2010). History, memory, and intractable conflict. *Conflict Resolution Quarterly, 27*(3), 239–256.

Vollhardt, J. R., & Bilewicz, M. (2013). After the genocide : Psychological perspectives on victim, bystander, and perpetrator groups. *Journal of Social Issues, 69*, 1–15.

Volpato, C., Andrighetto, L., Mari, S., Gabbiadini, A., & Durante, F. (2012). "Italiani brava gente." Effetti di un mito storico sulle relazioni sociali contemporanee [Italians as good fellows. Effects of an historical myth on contemporary social relationships]. In A. Miglietta & S. Gattino (Eds.), *Dietro il pregiudizio. Il contributo della psicologia sociale all'analisi di una società multiculturale [Beyond Prejudice, the contribution of social psychology to the analysis of multicultural society]* (pp. 137–150). Napoli: Liguori.

Wojcik, A., Bilewicz, M., & Lewicka, M. (2010). Living on the ashes: Collective representations of Polish–Jewish history among people living in the former Warsaw Ghetto area. *Cities, 27*, 195–203.

Chapter 12
Youth Identity, Peace and Conflict: Insights from Conflict and Diverse Settings

Shelley McKeown, Duygu Cavdar, and Laura K. Taylor

12.1 Introduction

The world is becoming increasingly ethnically diverse (Hewstone, 2015) and societies across the globe have shifted from wide-scale interstate wars to conflicts between competing groups within the same society. As a direct consequence of this changing global landscape, many of today's youth are experiencing a new social world, one which brings unique opportunities and challenges; in which young people must negotiate and develop their own sense of identity and belonging alongside historical narratives of identity.

Whilst exposure to new and different cultures can help enhance life experiences, it can also cause tensions and undermine social cohesion. Evidence for this comes from the high levels of ethnic segregation observed in spaces including schools and neighbourhoods and from across EU member states where asylum seekers, migrants and ethnic minorities are increasingly becoming targets of violence and hate speech (EU FRA, 2016). It is not surprising, therefore, that ethnic diversity and social cohesion are viewed to be at loggerheads (Putnam, 2007). Understanding how to promote better community relations amongst adolescents as the next generation of

Acknowledgements: Part of the work reported in this chapter was supported by funds from the Richard Benjamin Trust and the British Academy (BA) /Leverhulme [SG 150807]. We would like to thank the numerous school administrators, teachers and pupils for participating in this project. This work would also not have been possible without the research assistance of Jeffrey Hanna, Alexandra Kenny, Clarissa Courtney, Lauren Brown, Dean O'Driscoll, Marion Schulz, Karolina Urbanska, Lukas Horstmeier, Sofia Chirtoglou and Yangjunru (Cecilia) Li.

S. McKeown (✉) · D. Cavdar
University of Bristol, Bristol, UK
e-mail: duygu.cavdar@bristol.ac.uk

L. K. Taylor
Queen's University Belfast, Belfast, UK
e-mail: l.taylor@qub.ac.uk

N. Balvin, D. J. Christie (eds.), *Children and Peace*, Peace Psychology Book Series, https://doi.org/10.1007/978-3-030-22176-8_12

citizens is of urgent importance; but to do so, it is vital to develop a comprehensive understanding of how young people develop in such social settings and the consequences this has for community relations, both good and bad. This is because identity dynamics play a key role in societal functioning with group conflict often arising and being maintained due to competing social identities.

The aim of this chapter is to review the development of youth ethnic identity and the role of identity as a source of conflict and peace for youth growing up in conflict and diverse settings. We focus on adolescence as a critical period in which young people negotiate who they are. After outlining identity development processes, we consider ethnic identity development and how this is expressed in two case studies. First, we examine identity processes and their association with positive and negative behaviours for youth in Northern Ireland. Second, we discuss the role of identity development in light of ethnic diversity and draw on new research amongst Turkish youth in England, highlighting relevance for other contexts. We make a distinction between conflict and diverse settings as we believe that each has a unique set of circumstances that influences our understanding of adolescent identity as well as how we might best intervene to promote positive youth development. Conflict can be both violent and direct, or structural and indirect, in terms of social exclusion. When we use the word 'conflict' in this chapter, we are specifically referring to past or current political violence, whilst 'diverse' captures settings of structural violence. We conclude our chapter by outlining the possible applications of our work for policy and practice as well as highlighting suggestions for future research.

12.2 Youth Identity Development

We focus this chapter on adolescence as a critical time for identity development (Vega & Gill, 2002). This is because adolescents are not only developing the cognitive abilities that allow for identity construction, but they are also faced with a wide range of choices and increased responsibility. At this time youth have accumulated experiences from across their social ecology which encourage them to actively construct who they are (Mclean & Syed, 2015; Reidy et al., 2015; Umaña-Taylor, Quintana, & Yip, 2014). Whilst identity development is a normative process, there are important individual, group, and cultural level differences (Motti-Stefanidi, 2015) that are vital to understand if we are to develop successful policies and interventions that serve to promote positive development for youth growing up in conflict and diverse settings. In the following section, we briefly review key theories of identity development and then consider the complexity of adolescent identity development in such settings.

Whilst a number of notable theorists have attempted to explain identity development (e.g.Berzonsky, 1990 ; Erikson, 1968 ; Marcia, 1989), perhaps the most comprehensive understanding can be attributed to Luyckx et al. (2008). In their integrative identity model, Luyckx et al. (2008) propose a process-oriented approach to identity that comprises five dimensions which are divided into exploration and commitment processes. Adolescents first *explore in breadth* with different identity alternatives, make internal investment and then *explore in depth*. If they remain stuck in the early stages, they enter *ruminative exploration*, a process that might hinder the development of and identification with commitments. Adolescents then engage in commitment processes that comprise two dimensions: *commitment making* (making decisions on identity-related issues) and *identification with commitment* (identification with and emotions after commitment).

Recognising and understanding that adolescents experience these different identity development stages has implications for when and how targeted interventions may be applied. We argue that in order to best understand adolescent identity development and later consequences, we must also consider the role of social identities. Here, we focus on ethnic identity development as relevant to conflict and diverse settings.

12.2.1 Ethnic Identity Development

According to social identity theory, people categorise themselves and others into in-group and out-group members; these social categorisation processes can have an impact on intergroup attitudes and behaviours (Hogg, 2016). Ethnicity is one of the major social identities we use in our daily lives (Worrell, 2015) and is a central element of self-definition (Deaux, 2001). It is hardly surprising, therefore, that ethnic identity is particularly important for youth in both conflict and diverse settings, where perceived group differences are often exaggerated. Umaña-Taylor et al. (2014) define ethnic identity as 'a multidimensional, psychological construct that reflects the beliefs and attitudes that individuals have about their ethnic-racial group memberships, as well as the processes by which these beliefs and attitudes develop over time' (p. 23). This approach to ethnic identity focuses on the content (significance and meaning of ethnicity, such as attitudes and beliefs) as well as the process (the mechanisms by which individuals explore, form and maintain their identity) of ethnic identity formation (Schwartz et al., 2014; Umaña-Taylor et al., 2014).

Ethnic identity development can be seen as an interaction between maturation and context. Adolescents gain new cognitive capacities which give them the ability to explore what ethnicity means to them (Umaña-Taylor et al., 2014). Through exploration, youth engage in culturally specific activities, behaviours and roles. And, in turn, increased autonomy and independence, social interactions, other social demands and social contexts (such as school) can affect ethnic identity development and lead to greater *certainty* (Steinberg, 2007; Umaña-Taylor et al., 2014). This certainty can make ethnicity more salient and when ethnicity is salient, adolescents may begin to more readily integrate experiences into their self-concept, known as *identity centrality*, which indicates the durable relative importance of a particular identity component or domain for an individual (Sellers, Smith, & Chavous, 1998; Umaña-Taylor et al., 2014). Through these processes, youth develop both positive and negative feelings about their ethnic identity (Umaña-Taylor et al., 2014;

Umaña-Taylor, Yazedjian, & Bámaca-Gómez, 2004). Umaña-Taylor et al.'s (2004) model has been widely used and supported to explain ethnic identity formation among a range of ethnic groups (Brittian et al., 2013; Umaña-Taylor & Shin, 2007). Through this model, it is possible to understand how the individual interacts with the social context to develop identity; this interaction is important to consider when designing policy and practice targeted to improve individual development and cross-ethnic relations.

For adolescents growing up in conflict or diverse settings, the development of ethnic identity is arguably more complicated due to a wide range of contextual factors. In such settings, youth are likely to have complex presentations of their multiple identities than individuals who live in a monocultural society (Roccas & Brewer, 2002). Some minority youth may hold a dual identity, both the ethnocultural minority in-group and society of residence (Simon, Reichert, & Grabow, 2013), e.g. British-Asian. Further, youth growing up in conflict settings are often exposed to the categories of 'us' and 'them' from a very young age and are taught about historical and current conflicts through family narratives that influence their identity development. Recognising this complexity, in the next section we review the literature on youth identity in conflict and diverse settings drawing on examples globally as well as focusing specifically on the contexts of Northern Ireland and England.

12.3 Case Study 1: Youth Identity in Conflict Settings

Youth growing up in conflict settings face several barriers in terms of positive development. There is clear evidence for the long-lasting effects of collective violence, not only among survivors (Barel, Van IJzendoorn, Sagi-Schwartz, & Bakermans-Kranenburg, 2010), but also for subsequent generations (Merrilees et al., 2011). Given the importance of identity development for youth, it is hardly surprising that identification is associated with a wide range of negative and positive outcomes for youth growing up in conflict settings. In such settings, understanding identity processes is particularly important because conflicts are often due to and maintained by competing social identities.

Across a wide range of conflict settings, youth social identity has been examined in relation to a host of other processes. For example, a strong sense of social identity has been found to be associated with a sense of solidarity, particularly during social change, as well as a motivating factor for engaging in such change processes, particularly among minority youth such as Palestinians in Israel (Hammack, 2010). Moreover, evidence shows that social identity can act as a protective factor for youth. In particular, a strong sense of identity buffered youth Palestinians who were exposed to violence, whilst a weaker identity among Bosnia youth left them vulnerable to such exposure (Barber, 2008). A strong sense of social identity also protected adolescents in Northern Ireland from developing greater depressive symptoms

(Merrilees et al., 2014), but exacerbated aggression against the out-group over time (Merrilees et al., 2013). The trajectories of the strength of social identity have also been shown to vary based on group status (Merrilees et al., 2014). The development or maturation in the strength of social identity has also been found to be related to lower levels of insecurity in the community, or feeling threatened by out-group members (Merrilees et al., 2014). These studies suggest that understanding the role of social identity during adolescence is an important factor in conflict and post-conflict settings. They also point to the need to consider the extent to which identities should be made salient (or not) when policies or interventions are introduced; for example, evidence above shows that identity can act as a buffer as well as a negative force on individual and societal outcomes.

Although most of the intergroup conflict research focuses on maladaptive outcomes for youth in conflict settings (e.g. prejudice; see Barber, 2009), there has been a recent shift in the literature. Adopting a risk and resilience approach, which emphasises competencies rather than only pathologies (Barber, 2013; Masten, 2014), researchers have traced a number of constructive ways, such as prosocial behaviours toward the out-group (Taylor et al., 2014) and civic engagement (Taylor et al., 2017), that young people adopt when reacting to conflict and its legacy. An example of this can be found in the research on Altruism Born of Suffering (ABS) which focuses on examining the relations among risk/harm, responses, and resources that may motivate individuals to help others (Vollhardt, 2009). ABS suggest that past experiences can lead to perceived common fate, common victim identity, perceived injustice, and increased empathy with fellow sufferers (Dovidio et al., 2010); in turn, these emotional and cognitive responses may motivate altruistic outcomes, including out-group helping (Stürmer & Snyder, 2009; Taylor & Hanna, 2018). Understanding the processes underlying these positive pathways following adversity, especially among young people, may be the foundation for more constructive intra- and inter-group experiences that can help to rebuild social relations. We now turn to discussing youth identity processes in Northern Ireland as a case study that can inform understanding of identity in other conflict settings.

12.3.1 Youth Identity in Northern Ireland

Northern Ireland as a (post) conflict society provides an opportunity to understand the role of identity for youth and its implications for peace and conflict. In this context, the historical conflict (known as the Troubles) is a still deeply entrenched ethno-religious conflict between Protestants and Catholics. Despite the signing and implementation of 1998 Belfast/Good Friday Agreement among political elites (Cairns & Darby, 1998), sporadic violence between Catholics and Protestants remains (MacGinty, Muldoon, & Ferguson, 2007), and many of the communities most affected by the conflict have yet to see the dividends. Evidence for the continuing tensions between Protestants and Catholics comes from the 2016/17 hate crime statistics which demonstrate that of 2503 hate motivated incidents recorded, 42% were racist incidents and 40% were sectarian incidents (PSNI, 2017).

Today, adolescents in Northern Ireland represent a 'post-accord' generation as they were born after the 1998 Peace Agreement. Although they may be socialised by their parents and communities about the impact of the Troubles (Merrilees et al., 2011), youth are also vulnerable to the lingering, though sporadic, sectarian violence which occurs across group lines. As youth develop in this context, they are negotiating multiple social identity processes which interact with such risk factors. Yet, we also argue that it is important to recognise the potential links between social identity and the peacebuilding potential of adolescents in Northern Ireland (McEvoy-Levy, 2006; McKeown & Taylor, 2017a; Taylor & McKeown, 2017).

In terms of more positive outcomes, we found differences between Protestant and Catholic youth regarding the impact of social identity on participation in violence and civic engagement, a key factor for future peacebuilding (Taylor et al., 2017; Taylor & McKeown, 2017). In a study of 466 youth (aged 14–15), we found that for youth with a lower strength of social identity, there was no link between group identity (Catholic or Protestant) and participation in sectarian antisocial behaviours; however, when adolescents were more committed to their social group, Protestant youth reported more participation in sectarian antisocial behaviours than Catholic youth. Similarly, there was no link between group identity and civic participation at lower levels of strength of social identity; however, among youth with stronger attachment to their social identity, Catholic youth reported more civic participation than Protestant youth (McKeown & Taylor, 2017b). These findings suggest that the same intervention might not work equally well across groups when trying to decrease participation in sectarianism or increase constructive forms of engagement. These findings have implications for understanding the lingering effects of social identity for youth born after a peace agreement.

Given the history of the conflict, in this section we have focused on the strength of social identity related to Catholic/Protestant relations and interactions. However, amongst the post-accord generation there is greater endorsement and identification with a dual or joint Northern Irish identity (McKeown, 2014). Moreover, Northern Ireland is becoming increasingly diverse, and in response, future research should expand beyond traditional intergroup relations to understand the role of social identity with regards to other minority ethnic groups (Schulz & Taylor, in press), particularly among adolescents. Understanding how social identity may function beyond binary distinctions is a growing area of research; we now turn to identity processes amongst ethnic minority youth.

12.4 Case Study 2: Youth Identity in Diverse Settings

Globally, a growing number of young people are growing up in societies with increasing ethnic diversity. Understanding how these contexts shape youth identity development has implications not only for their individual outcomes, but also for more peaceful and constructive societal relations. Here, we focus specifically on first- and second-generation minority youth. On the one hand, these youth may have greater opportunities than in their country of birth or that of their parents, but on the other hand, they also often face a number of challenges (e.g. stress; Umaña-Taylor & Updegraff, 2007), disadvantages (e.g. low-income), and social difficulties (e.g. navigating a new language). For example, previous research has found a significant relationship between perceived discrimination based on ethnic identity and depression (Tummala-Narra & Claudius, 2013; Umaña-Taylor & Updegraff, 2007) and between mental distress and discrimination (Srivastava, 2012) for such youth. Similarly, Juang, Moffitt, and Whitborne (2016) demonstrated that discrimination is a risk factor for greater depressive symptoms, anxiety, and aggression among Latino and Asian-heritage college students in the US. Coupled with the stresses of being an ethnic minority, these experiences make youth vulnerable in terms of their mental health and wellbeing (Virupaksha, Kumar, & Nirmala, 2014).

At the same time, a strong connection with, and positive feelings toward, an ethnic group can result in positive youth development. For example, previous research suggests that having a strong ethnic identity has a positive effect on wellbeing, such as self-esteem (Romero, Edwards, Fryberg, & Orduña, 2014) and personal adjustment (Chae & Foley, 2010; Phinney, 1991; Smith & Silva, 2011). Moreover, if a young person attaches importance to their ethnic identity, feeling positively about their ethnic group is associated with better well-being (Brittian et al., 2013; Romero et al., 2014), and is predictive of less anxiety and fewer depressive symptoms among African American, Latino, and Asian American young adults in the US (Brittian et al., 2013). Thus, ethnic identity can have protective effects against mental health problems among minority youth, particularly when positive feelings are associated with that group.

Given the potential risk and protective factors associated with ethnic identity, young migrants (first, second and third generation), in particular, face a complex set of opportunities and challenges as they grow up and develop their own sense of self. Commentators argue that it can sometimes take years before individuals are able to adapt to their new socio-cultural environment (Berry, 2005) and this adaptation process may differ depending on migration status. For example, whilst first generation migrants typically experience a range of adaptation problems, such as learning a new language and settling into a new society, second generation migrants have a different challenge, negotiating two cultural worlds relating to the heritage culture of their parents/communities versus their society of birth (Berry & Sabatier, 2010). Balancing identification with their heritage culture whilst developing an identification with the majority society is a source of stress for second generation migrant youth (Deaux, 2001). To further illustrate the arguments above, the next section draws on research findings on Turkish minority youth in England.

12.4.1 Turkish Youth Identity in England

Turkish young people represent a minority group in Europe and the UK and yet, relatively little is known about identity processes of second generation youth in these contexts. Recent research has emphasised the need to understand multiple social identities, demonstrating that second generation Turkish young people struggle with identity construction, particularly in relation to culture, ethnicity, nationality and religion (Cavdar, 2017). The complexity of identity is demonstrated in Cavdar's (2017) interview[1] with a young person about ethnic identity formation:

> "I do not feel myself neither Turkish nor Kurdish or 100% British as well. I grew up in a Turkish/Kurdish family. But, I am living in England and my all friends and everything in British system. But, I also love the Turkish culture; it is one of my parts." (Female, 16)

Even though youth may experience conflicted feelings during the identity construction process (Brook, Garcia, & Fleming, 2008; Zevallos, 2008), attachment to their heritage culture can have a positive impact on their wellbeing. Specifically, engaging with activities related to their ethnic identity, attaching meaning to their ethnic identity and having positive feelings about their ethnic identity can be positively associated with adolescent wellbeing and mental health (Cavdar, 2017).

Yet, the impact of ethnic identity on second-generation Turkish youth is not always positive. There is evidence that young people report feeling under pressure to maintain the cultural traditions associated with their parents' heritage (Cavdar, 2017; Yaylaci, 2015). For example, in Cavdar's (2017) research participants reported being worried about using English as first language and losing communication with their parents, being unable to express their feelings properly in Turkish, having to translate for their parents (and this being a demanding duty), and the burden of having to code switch many times between Turkish and English. This demand on adolescents and young people can be a source of pressure or stress; they not only explore identity formation for themselves but must also help family and community members navigate life in the new society.

We argue that gaining an in-depth understanding of the contextual factors associated with adolescent ethnic identity formation and how these are experienced is vital if we are to develop programmes to promote minority youth development. For example, Umaña-Taylor, Kornienko, Bayless, and Updegraff (2018) found that making ethnic minority adolescents' ethnic-racial identity salient (i.e. exploration and resolution) promoted positive psychosocial functioning (i.e. higher global identity cohesion, higher self-esteem, lower depressive symptoms, and better grades). Further, Oyserman and Destin (2010) applied an identity-based motivation model, which assigns a central role to identity as it is dynamically constructed in context by using an integrative culturally sensitive framework in US schools, and found that

[1] The cited study is a part of ongoing piece of doctoral research. In this study, the author conducted an investigation on ethnic identity development of second-generation Turkish young people in the UK and how this process aligns with different acculturation strategies, perceived discrimination and mental health outcomes.

the programme improved school success and reduced risk of depression. Such programmes of research, which tackle the multiplicity and complexity of ethnic identity development, offer insights for how practitioners can improve youth outcomes.

12.5 Policy and Practice Implications

This review offers important insights that can inform the design of policies and interventions that aim to promote positive youth development and better community relations amongst youth growing up in conflict and diverse settings. Any intervention should consider the complexity of identity development, the impact of the social context, and the positive and negative outcomes associated with social identity. Based on the work presented in this chapter, we recommend that policy makers and practitioners, including those in NGOs, working with youth, consider the need to:

1. Recognise the relevant identity development stage before designing interventions. For example, whether adolescents have already crystallised their identity shapes which approach should be taken to discuss difference or promote wellbeing.
2. Consider the potential role of group social status, such as minority, historically higher power, etc. which may lead to bespoke interventions.
3. Aim for inclusive group identification. That is, given that identification can be associated with positive outcomes, allow youth to continue to identify with the relevant social or ethnic groups. Consider multiphase programmes, which first introduce adolescents to each other as individuals, followed by discussions of group differences, and ultimately potential inclusive identities.

12.6 Conclusion and Future Research Directions

In this chapter, we have applied the literature on ethnic identity development to youth in conflict and diverse settings. Drawing on a range of theories, empirical evidence and two case studies, we have demonstrated both the protective and problematic impact of identity on youth attitudes and behaviours in such settings. Complementing current research which has developed comprehensive theoretical frameworks that consider the complexity of identity processes for youth, we suggest two main avenues for future research that will inform interventions aiming to promote positive youth development.

First, we urge researchers to consider positive youth development, rather than seeing youth only as either passive victims or perpetrators of harm. For example, studies should include measures on empathy, prosocial behaviours, and civic engagement, which may all be key antecedents for later peacebuilding (McKeown & Taylor, 2017a; O'Driscoll, Taylor, & Dautel, in press). Understanding how ethnic identity development is related to these positive outcomes (moving beyond mental health and also considering behaviour), and change across adolescence, will shed new light on social identity processes. Recognising constructive youth agency will enable us to understand how to harness and promote more positive youth attitudes and behaviours.

Second, researchers should consider a social ecology approach to more fully understand how youth identity develops. Youth development is influenced by the interaction among individual characteristics (e.g. personality and political ideology), the immediate social context (e.g. peers, family, school and neighbourhood norms of interaction), and factors that indirectly influence behaviour (e.g. governmental structures, cultural patterns). Such a comprehensive approach will better inform programme development at various levels, as well as shape interventions that tackle cross-cutting issues. An integrative focus that also critically engages policymakers has the potential to have multiplicative effects beyond direct participants in such programmes. Combined with an emphasis on constructive youth outcomes, such an approach has the potential to galvanise the peacebuilding potential of adolescent social identities.

References

Barber, B. K. (2008). Contrasting portraits of war: Youths' varied experiences with political violence in Bosnia and Palestine. *International Journal of Behavioral Development, 32*, 298–309. https://doi.org/10.1177/0165025408090972

Barber, B. K. (Ed.). (2009). *Adolescents and war: How youth deal with political violence*. New York, NY: Oxford University Press.

Barber, B. K. (2013). Annual research review: The experience of youth with political conflict-challenging notions of resilience and encouraging research refinement. *Journal of Child Psychology and Psychiatry, 54*, 461–473. https://doi.org/10.1111/jcpp.12056

Barel, E., Van IJzendoorn, M. H., Sagi-Schwartz, A., & Bakermans-Kranenburg, M. J. (2010). Surviving the holocaust: A meta-analysis of the long-term sequelae of a genocide. *Psychological Bulletin, 136*, 677–698. https://doi.org/10.1037/a0020339

Berry, J. W. (2005). Acculturation: Living successfully in two cultures. *International Journal of Intercultural Relations, 29*, 697–712. https://doi.org/10.1016/j.ijintrel.2005.07.013

Berry, J. W., & Sabatier, C. (2010). Acculturation, discrimination, and adaptation among second generation immigrant youth in Montreal and Paris. *International Journal of Intercultural Relations, 34*, 191–207. https://doi.org/10.1016/j.ijintrel.2009.11.007

Berzonsky, M. D. (1990). Self-construction over the life-span: A process perspective on identity formation. In G. J. Neimeyer & R. A. Neimeyer (Eds.), Advances in personal construct psychology. Advances in personal construct psychology: A research annual, Vol. 1, (pp. 155–186). US: Elsevier Science/JAI Press.

Brittian, A. S., Umaña-Taylor, A. J., … Caraway, S. J. (2013). The moderating role of centrality on associations between ethnic identity affirmation and ethnic minority college Students' mental health. *Journal of American College Health, 61*, 133–140. https://doi.org/10.1080/07448481.2013.773904

Brook, A. T., Garcia, J., & Fleming, M. (2008). The effects of multiple identities on psychological well-being. *Society for Personality and Social Psychology, 34*, 1588–1600. https://doi.org/10.1177/0146167208324629

Cairns, E., & Darby, J. (1998). The conflict in Northern Ireland: Causes, consequences, and controls. *American Psychologist, 53*, 754–760. https://doi.org/10.1037/0003-066X.53.7.754

Cavdar, D. (2017). *Identity formation in adolescence: Mental health, acculturation, and discrimination among young immigrants in the UK (a pilot study)*. Bristol: School of Education, University of Bristol. Unpublished doctoral progression document.

Chae, M. H., & Foley, P. F. (2010). Relationship of ethnic identity, acculturation, and psychological well-being among Chinese, Japanese, and Korean Americans. *Journal of Counseling & Development, 88*, 466–476. https://doi.org/10.1002/j.1556-6678.2010.tb00047.x

Deaux, K. (2001). Social identity. In J. Worrell (Ed.), *Encyclopaedia of women and gender* (pp. 1059–1067). San Diego, CA: Academic Press.

Dovidio, J. F., Johnson, J. D., Gaertner, S. L., Pearson, A. R., Saguy, T., & Ashburn-Nardo, L. (2010). Empathy and intergroup relations. In M. Mikulincer & P. Shaver (Eds.), *Prosocial Motives, Emotion, and Behavior: The Better Angels of our Nature* (pp. 393–408). Washington, DC: APA Press.

Erikson, E. H. (1968). *Identity: Youth and crisis*. New York: W.W. Norton & Company, Inc.

European Union Agency for Fundamental Rights [EU FRA]. (2016). Current migration situation in the EU: Hate crime. Retrieved from: http://fra.europa.eu/en/publication/2016/current-migration-situation-eu-hate-crime

Hammack, P. L. (2010). Identity as burden or benefit? Youth, historical narrative, and the legacy of political conflict. *Human Development, 53*, 173–201. https://doi.org/10.1159/000320045

Hewstone, M. (2015). Consequences of diversity for social cohesion and prejudice: The missing dimension of intergroup contact. *Journal of Social Issues, 71*, 417–438. https://doi.org/10.1111/josi.12120

Hogg, M. A. (2016). Social identity theory. In S. McKeown, R. Haji, & N. Ferguson (Eds.), *Understanding peace and conflict through social identity theory* (pp. 3–19). Cham, Switzerland: Springer Publishing.

Juang, L. P., Moffitt, U., … Whitborne, S. K. (2016). Cognitive reappraisal and expressive suppression: Links to racial-ethnic discrimination and adjustment among Latino/a and Asian-heritage college students. *Journal of Adolescence, 53*, 21–33. https://doi.org/10.1016/j.adolescence.2016.08.012

Luyckx, K., Schwartz, S. J., Berzonsky, M. D., Soenens, B., Vansteenkiste, M., Smits, I., & Goossens, L. (2008). Capturing ruminative exploration: Extending the four-dimensional model of identity formation in late adolescence. *Journal of Research in Personality, 42*, 58–82. https://doi.org/10.1016/j.jrp.2007.04.004

MacGinty, R., Muldoon, O. T., & Ferguson, N. (2007). No war, no peace: Northern Ireland after the agreement. *Political Psychology, 28*, 1–11. https://doi.org/10.1111/j.1467-9221.2007.00548.x

Marcia, J. E. (1989). Identity and intervention. *Journal of Adolescence, 12*, 401–410.

Masten, A. S. (2014). Global perspectives on resilience in children and youth. *Child Development, 85*, 6–20. https://doi.org/10.1111/cdev.12205

McEvoy-Levy, S. (2006). *Troublemakers or peacemakers? Youth and post-accord peace building*. Notre Dame, IN: University of Notre Dame Press.

McLean, C. K., & Syed, M. (2015). The field of identity development needs an identity: An introduction to the handbook of identity development. In K. C. McLean & M. Syed (Eds.), *The oxford handbook of identity development* (pp. 1–10). Oxford: Oxford University Press.

McKeown, S. (2014). Perceptions of a superordinate identity in Northern Ireland. *Peace and Conflict: Journal of Peace Psychology, 20*, 505–515. https://doi.org/10.1037/pac0000105

McKeown, S., & Taylor, L. K. (2017a). Intergroup contact and peacebuilding: Promoting youth civic engagement in Northern Ireland. *Journal of Social and Political Psychology, 5*, 415–434. https://doi.org/10.5964/jspp.v5i2.769

McKeown, S., & Taylor, L. K. (2017b). *Youth social identification and participation in sectarian and civic behaviour in Northern Ireland*. Spain: European Association of Social Psychology.

Merrilees, C. E., Cairns, E., Goeke-Morey, M. C., Schermerhorn, A. C., Shirlow, P., & Cummings, E. M. (2011). Associations between mothers' experience with the troubles in Northern Ireland

and mothers' and children's psychological functioning: The moderating role of social identity. *Journal of Community Psychology, 39*, 60–75. https://doi.org/10.1002/jcop.20417

Merrilees, E. M., Cairns, E., Taylor, L. K., Shirlow, P., Goeke-Morey, M., & Cummings, E. M. (2013). Social identity and youth aggressive and delinquent behaviors in a context of political violence. *Political Psychology, 34*, 695–711. https://doi.org/10.1111/pops.12030

Merrilees, C. E., Taylor, L. K., Goeke-Morey, M. C., Shirlow, P., Cummings, E., & Cairns, E. (2014). The protective role of group identity: Sectarian antisocial behavior and adolescent emotion problems. *Child Development, 85*, 412–420. https://doi.org/10.1111/cdev.12125

Merrilees, C. E., Taylor, L. K., Goeke-Morey, M. C., Shirlow, P., & Cummings, E. (2014). Youth in contexts of political violence: A developmental approach to the study of youth identity and emotional security in their communities. *Peace and Conflict: Journal of Peace Psychology, 20*, 26–38. https://doi.org/10.1037/a0035581

Motti-Stefanidi, F. (2015). Identity development in the context of the risk and resilience framework. In K. C. McLean & M. Syed (Eds.), *The Oxford handbook of identity development* (pp. 472–489). New York: Oxford University Press.

O'Driscoll, D., Taylor, L. K., & Dautel, J. (in press). Intergroup resource distribution among children living in segregated neighborhoods amid protracted conflict. *Peace and Conflict: Journal of Peace Psychology*.

Oyserman, D., & Destin, M. (2010). Identity-based motivation: Implications for intervention. *The Counseling Psychologist, 38*, 1001–1043. https://doi.org/10.1177/0011000010374775

Phinney, J. S. (1991). Ethnic identity and self-esteem: A review and integration. *Hispanic Journal of Behavioral Sciences, 13*, 193–208. https://doi.org/10.1177/07399863910132005

Police Service of Northern Ireland (PSNI). (2017). Annual statistics of hate crimes. Available at: https://www.gov.uk/government/statistics/hate-incidents-and-crimes-in-northern-ireland-period-ending-31-december-2016

Putnam, R. D. (2007). E Pluribus unum: Diversity and community in the twenty-first century the 2006 Johan Skytte Prize Lecture. *Scandinavian Political Studies, 30*, 137–174.

Reidy, C. M., Taylor, L. K., Merrilees, C. E., Ajduković, D., Čorkalo Biruški, D., & Cummings, E. M. (2015). The political socialization of youth in a post-conflict community. *International Journal of Intercultural Relations, 45*, 11–23. https://doi.org/10.1016/j.ijintrel.2014.12.005

Roccas, S., & Brewer, M. B. (2002). Social identity complexity. *Personality and Social Psychology Review, 6*, 88–106. https://doi.org/10.1207/S15327957PSPR0602_01

Romero, A. J., Edwards, L. M., Fryberg, S. A., & Orduña, M. (2014). Resilience to discrimination stress across ethnic identity stages of development. *Journal of Applied Social Psychology, 44*, 1–11. https://doi.org/10.1111/jasp.12192

Schulz, M., & Taylor, L. K. (in press). Evaluating supplemental samples in longitudinal research: replacement and refreshment approaches. *Peace and Conflict: Journal of Peace Psychology*.

Schwartz, S., Syed, M., Yip, T., Knight, G., Umaña-Taylor, A., Rivas-Drake, D., & Lee, R. M. (2014). Methodological issues in ethnic and racial identity research with ethnic minority populations: Theoretical precision, measurement issues, and research designs. *Child Development, 85*, 58–76. https://doi.org/10.1111/cdev.12201

Sellers, R. M., Smith, M. A., … Chavous, T. M. (1998). Multidimensional model of racial identity: A reconceptualization of African American racial identity. *Personality and Social Psychology Review, 2*, 18–39. https://doi.org/10.1207/s15327957pspr0201_2

Simon, B., Reichert, F., & Grabow, O. (2013). When dual identity becomes a liability: Identity and political radicalism among migrants. *Psychological Science, 24*, 251–257. https://doi.org/10.1177/0956797612450889

Smith, T. B., & Silva, L. (2011). Ethnic identity and personal well-being of people of color: A meta-analysis. *Journal of Counseling Psychology, 58*, 42–60. https://doi.org/10.1037/a0021528

Srivastava, D. (2012). *The effects of ethnic identity, family conflict, and acculturation on racial discrimination and mental distress of second generation Asian Americans.*. PhD Dissertation. New York: Fordham University, Graduate School of Education.

Steinberg, L. (2007). *Ergenlik (Adolescence)*. Ankara, Turkey: Imge Publication.

Stürmer, S., & Snyder, M. (Eds.). (2009). *The psychology of prosocial behavior: Group processes, intergroup relations, and helping*. Chichester, England: Wiley Blackwell.

Taylor, L. K., Merrilees, C. E., Goeke-Morey, M. C., Shirlow, P., Cairns, E., & Cummings, E. M. (2014). Political violence and adolescent outgroup attitudes and prosocial behaviors: Implications for positive intergroup relations. *Social Development, 23*, 840–859. https://doi.org/10.1111/sode.12074

Taylor, L. K., Townsend, D., Merrilees, C. E., Goeke-Morey, M. C., Shirlow, P. & Cummings, E. M. (2017). Adolescent civic engagement and perceived political conflict: The role of family cohesion. *Youth & Society*. Online First. Doi: https://doi.org/10.1177/0044118X17697236

Taylor, L. K., & Hanna, J. R. (2018). Altruism born of suffering among emerging adults in Northern Ireland. *Journal of Aggression, Conflict and Peace Research, 10*, 157–169. https://doi.org/10.1108/JACPR-01-2017-0271

Taylor, L. K., & McKeown, S. (2017). Youths' peacebuilding potential: Intergroup contact and civic participation amongst a post-accord generation in Northern Ireland. In K. Niven, S. Lewis, & C. Kagan (Eds.), *Making a difference with psychology* (pp. 56–62). London: Richard Benjamin Trust.

Tummala-Narra, P., & Claudius, M. (2013). Perceived discrimination and depressive symptoms among immigrant-origin adolescents. *Cultural Diversity & Ethnic Minority Psychology, 19*, 257–269. https://doi.org/10.1037/a0032960

Umaña-Taylor, A. J., Kornienko, O., Bayless, S. D., & Updegraff, K. A. (2018). A universal intervention program increases ethnic-racial identity exploration and resolution to predict adolescent psychosocial functioning one year later. *Journal of Youth and Adolescence, 47*, 1–15. https://doi.org/10.1007/s10964-017-0766-5

Umaña-Taylor, A. J., & Shin, N. (2007). An examination of ethnic identity and self-esteem with diverse populations: Exploring variation by ethnicity and geography. *Cultural Diversity and Ethnic Minority Psychology, 13*, 178–186. https://doi.org/10.1037/1099-9809.13.2.178

Umaña-Taylor, A. J., Quintana, S. M., … Yip, T. (2014). Ethnic and racial identity during adolescence and into young adulthood: An integrated conceptualization. *Child Development, 85*, 21–39. https://doi.org/10.1111/cdev.12196

Umaña-Taylor, A. J., & Updegraff, K. A. (2007). Latino adolescents' mental health: Exploring the interrelations among discrimination, ethnic identity, cultural orientation, self-esteem, and depressive symptoms. *Journal of Adolescence, 30*, 549–567. https://doi.org/10.1016/j.adolescence.2006.08.002

Umaña-Taylor, A. J., Yazedjian, A., & Bámaca-Gómez, M. (2004). Developing the ethnic identity scale using Eriksonian and social identity perspectives. *International Journal of Theory and Research, 4*, 9–38. https://doi.org/10.1207/S1532706XID0401_2

Vega, A. W., & Gill, A. G. (2002). *Drug use and ethnicity in early adolescence*. New York: Kluwer Academic Publishers.

Virupaksha, H. G., Kumar, A., & Nirmala, B. P. (2014). Migration and mental health: An interface. *Journal of Natural Science Biology Medicine, 5*(2), 233–239.

Vollhardt, J. R. (2009). Altruism born of suffering and prosocial behavior following adverse life events: A review and conceptualization. *Social Justice Research, 22*, 53–97. https://doi.org/10.1007/s11211-009-0088-1

Worrell, F. C. (2015). Culture as race/ethnicity. In K. T. McLean & M. Syed (Eds.), *The Oxford handbook of identity development* (pp. 249–268). New York: Oxford University Press.

Yaylaci, F. G. (2015). Social communication among Turkish immigrants in Belgium. In I. Sirkeci, B. T. Seker, & A. Caglar (Eds.), *Turkish migration identity and integration* (pp. 95–108). London: Transnational Press.

Zevallos, Z. (2008). 'You have to be Anglo and not look like me': Identity and belonging among young women of Turkish and Latin American backgrounds in Melbourne, Australia. *Australian Geographer, 39*, 21–43. https://doi.org/10.1080/00049180701877410

Chapter 13
Children's Conceptualizations of Forgiveness, Reconciliation, and Peacebuilding in the Context of Armed Conflict

Wilson López López, Andrea Correa-Chica, Myriam Carmenza Sierra-Puentes, Juan Gabriel Castañeda Polanco, Gabriela Fernández Miranda, María del Rosario Duran Jaramillo, and Pablo Castro-Abril

> *"...you cannot live with grudges all your life..."*
> *"I think we can live in peace."*
> (Children in the vulnerability condition, Colombia April 2016)

13.1 Introduction

World peace is threatened. According to the Global Peace Index, peaceful coexistence deteriorated worldwide between 2008 and 2018. The Middle East and North Africa were the most affected regions (Institute for Economics & Peace, 2017,

Correspondence concerning this chapter should be addressed to Wilson López López, School of Psychology, Pontificia Universidad Javeriana, Street 5 # 39-00 floor 2, Bogotá, Colombia. E-mail: lopezw@javeriana.edu.co

W. López López (✉) · G. Fernández Miranda · M. del Rosario Duran Jaramillo
School of Psychology, Pontificia Universidad Javeriana, Bogotá, Colombia
e-mail: lopezw@javeriana.edu.co

A. Correa-Chica
Departamento de Psicoloxía Social, Básica e Metodoloxía, Facultade de Psicoloxía, Universidade de Santiago de Compostela, Santiago de Compostela, Spain
e-mail: jullyandrea.correa@rai.usc.es

M. Carmenza Sierra-Puentes
Fundación Universitaria Konrad Lorenz, Bogotá, Cundinamarca, Colombia
e-mail: myriamc.sierrap@konradlorenz.edu.co

J. G. Castañeda Polanco
Corporación Universitaria Minuto De Dios, Bogotá, Colombia
e-mail: jucastaneda@uniminuto.edu

P. Castro-Abril
Universidad del País Vasco, Lejona, Vizcaya, Spain
e-mail: pcastro008@ikasle.ehu.eus

N. Balvin, D. J. Christie (eds.), *Children and Peace*, Peace Psychology Book Series, https://doi.org/10.1007/978-3-030-22176-8_13

2018). The number and intensity of armed conflicts increased due to terrorist actions, deaths in conflict, the number of refugees, and internal displacement (Department of Peace and Conflict Research, 2017; Internal Displacement Monitoring Center, 2017; Melander, Pettersson, & Themnér, 2016; Save the Children, 2018).

International armed conflicts (i.e., confrontation between two or more states) and non-international conflicts (i.e., confrontation between government forces and nongovernmental armed groups or between those groups only; International Committee of the Red Cross, 2008) have transformed in the twenty-first century. Wars in towns and cities have increased, making streets and civilian homes battlefields where unarmed people suffer the greatest consequences (Action on Armed Violence, 2017, 2018; Human Rights Watch, 2018; Wessells, 2016).

These transformations of armed conflict create a high burden of suffering on children (Wessells, 2016). According to a recent Save the Children report (2018), one in six children worldwide lives in areas of armed conflict and is at risk of serious violations to their human rights; this statistic has increased by 75% since 1990.

13.1.1 Effect of Armed Conflict on Children

Between 2005 and 2016, armed conflicts exposed children to the following main violations: (a) murders and/or mutilations; (b) forced recruitment by armed groups to serve as combatants, spies, messengers, porters, servants, or sexual slaves; (c) sexual violence, with cases of harassment, rape, or intent (i.e., acts of nonconsensual sexual relationships), slavery and/or trafficking, prostitution, marriage, and/or pregnancy, and abortion and/or sterilization; (d) forced abduction or disappearance (either temporary or permanent); (e) attacks on schools and hospitals, including the total or partial destruction of facilities; and (f) the denial of humanitarian assistance, which implies the intentional deprivation or obstruction of the passage of humanitarian aid that is indispensable for the survival of minors (Save the Children, 2018; United Nations Secretary General, 2017).

Working with children in contexts of armed conflict is a matter of extreme urgency. In fact, at the United Nations (UN) meeting of world leaders in 2015, one of the main Sustainable Development Goals for 2030 was to work to ensure that children fully enjoy their rights of survival, development, protection, and participation (Borská, Vacková, & Small, 2016; Save the Children, 2017; United Nations, 2002). Although the most effective way to protect children from the horrors of violence is through its prevention, given the current situation, it is important to recognize that children have a great capacity for resilience and can recover from traumatic experiences of war when provided with the necessary support (Barry, Clarke, Jenkins, & Patel, 2013; Haj-Yahia, Greenbaum, & Lahoud-Shoufany, 2018; Schultz, Sørensen, & Waaktaar, 2012). However, recovery is less likely when communities and services are paralyzed by conflict and cannot guarantee the principles of provision, protection, and participation related to children's rights or when no progress is made in research or generation of intervention plans that foster the building of peaceful cultures (Fajardo Mayo, Ramírez Lozano, Valencia Suescún, & Ospína Alvarado, 2018; López & Sabucedo, 2007).

As previous investigations have reported, violations of human rights in childhood have a devastating effect because child survivors of atrocious acts are left with deep physical and emotional wounds that generate stress and trauma as well as affect their mental health and development (Fajardo Mayo et al., 2018; Haj-Yahia et al., 2018; Schultz et al., 2012; Wessells, 2016). Therefore, it is important and urgent that international communities, states, and governmental and nongovernmental institutions take practical measures aimed at the prevention of violence as well as the recovery of child victims or those in danger of becoming a victim of armed conflict to reduce the lifelong psychological and social problems associated with experiences of conflict and violence in childhood. Child victims should be supported to reintegrate into civilian life and survivors assisted to prevent them from being dragged into continuous cycles of violence (Borská et al., 2016; Save the Children, 2018; United Nations Secretary General, 2017).

Similarly, great diversity exists among children affected by armed conflict, and hence this subject cannot be addressed in a monolithic manner. It is necessary to consider their differences in terms of gender, stage of development, access to education, socioeconomic status, ethnic and cultural origins, type of victimhood (i.e., if the children are direct victims or indirect victims), and access to assistance or rehabilitative care (Haj-Yahia et al., 2018; Schultz et al., 2012). This diversity should not be avoided and when working with children affected by conflict and violence. Given that children and youth play a central role in social change, it is essential to start by answering key conceptual and empirical questions that allow adults to understand children's own perspectives across different contexts, thereby generating appropriate intervention plans (Borská et al., 2016; Wessells, 2016).

13.1.2 The Participatory Role of Children

Past research and interventions in the context of armed conflict with child victims have reported that programs which focus on the promotion and generation of hopeful scenarios that promote mental health, self-esteem, self-efficacy, and active participation help to overcome the horrors of confrontation (Barry et al., 2013; Haj-Yahia et al., 2018; Schultz et al., 2012) and demonstrate minors' high capacities for resilience, empowerment, and posttraumatic growth.

Fajardo Mayo et al. (2018) argued for the need to transform the way in which children are perceived, moving from seeing them as passive subjects to involving them as participatory actors who have a voice and the capability to respond to the violence that they have experienced. This chapter is in line with this approach, giving a voice to children as a symbol of change and allowing younger generations exposed to armed conflict to move from the role of victim to actors who transform their realities in search of building peaceful societies.

13.1.3 Multidimensional Model of Peacebuilding

The transformation from scenarios of armed conflict to scenarios of peace requires an interaction between socioenvironmental forces and individual behaviors/traits (Rubenstein & Stark, 2017). Thus, it is necessary to use an ecological framework of analysis (Bronfenbrenner, 1979) that allows for observations of change across socioeconomic, sociopolitical, sociolegal, sociocultural, socioenvironmental, and psychosocial dimensions (López López, 2017) in search of sustainable and peaceful environments.

In this regard, several studies have shown that new practices that incorporate identities, values, representations, and attitudes that promote more just and supportive intergroup relationships and break the cycle of violence are required (Jankowitz, 2017; Siem, Stürmer, & Pittinsky, 2016). It is here where children and adolescents must be considered so that they feel integrated and committed to change, resulting in processes of lasting transformation over time (Taylor et al., 2018).

13.1.4 Forgiveness and Reconciliation Related to Peacebuilding

Forgiveness and reconciliation are important aspects of peace processes because they generate positive effects at the intra- and interpersonal levels by generating new social networks, restoring others, overcoming feelings of resentment or revenge, rebuilding trust, ameliorating broken relationships, and improving coexistence in community and society (Alzate & Dono, 2017; Fehr, Gelfand, & Nag, 2010; Noor, James Brown, & Prentice, 2008).

At this point, it is necessary to clarify that although forgiveness and reconciliation are close and sometimes overlapping processes in the literature (Rettberg & Ugarriza, 2016), they are differentiated by their scopes. Forgiveness primarily involves an intra- and/or interpersonal scope (victim and/or victimizer), whereas reconciliation re-establishes the links among the victim, the victimizer, and the community to build a joint future (Castrillón-Guerrero et al., 2018).

13.1.4.1 Forgiveness

Here, forgiveness is defined as the process through which the offended person voluntarily overcomes feelings, thoughts, and negative behavior toward the offender by replacing them with those of a positive nature, thereby changing their understanding of the issue, without the need to forget (Denham, Neal, Wilson, Pickerin, & Boyatzis, 2007; Freedman, Enright, & Knutson, 2007; López López, Pineda-Marín, & Mullet, 2014; Murphy, 2007). However, it is important to clarify that the extant literature has different definitions of forgiveness that originate from different theoretical positions (Fehr et al., 2010; Rocha, Amarís, & López López, 2017; Taysi & Orcan, 2017; Worthington, 2006).

In addition, forgiveness has proven to be an important component related to children's socioemotional competence because it allows for interpersonal conflict management, anger and resentment dissipation, prosocial interaction promotion, and long-term negative outcome prevention (Denham et al., 2007).

In contexts of armed conflict (specifically, the generation of a scenario), forgiveness is more likely when the damage caused is acknowledged and accompanied by truth, empathy regarding the pain of the victims, a show of repentance, and measures of reparation (Cortés, Torres, López López, Claudia Pérez, & Pineda-Marín, 2016; López López, Andrade Páez, & Correa-Chica, 2016). Without these factors, forgiveness can be a harmful and revictimizing process (Castrillón-Guerrero et al., 2018).

13.1.4.2 Reconciliation

The study of the concept of reconciliation has increased in the literature since the 1990s, also leading to the emergence of multiple perspectives (Alzate & Dono, 2017; Bloomfield, 2015; Rettberg & Ugarriza, 2016). However, all agree that reconciliation focuses on repairing the social bonds that have been broken to build a collective future in which revenge is renounced as an option (Santa-Barbara, 2007). Ultimately, reconciliation is a process that enables the coexistence and acceptance of people and/or groups in conflict and that must be preceded by dialogue, goodwill, emotional and attitudinal change, compensation for the damage, the cessation of violence, and (in some cases) forgiveness (Bloomfield, 2015; Cortés, Torres, López López, Pérez, & Pineda-Marín, 2015; Noor et al., 2008; Rettberg & Ugarriza, 2016).

13.2 Research Context

One of the longest and most bloody internal armed conflicts in Latin America has taken place in Colombia (the context in which the research in this chapter was performed) for more than 60 years (Centro Nacional de Memoria Histórica, 2013). One of the main consequences of this conflict is its manifestation in social institutions. Furthermore, behavioral and cognitive repertoires of most members of society are linked to fear, revenge, aggressive conflict management, and legitimization of violence (Bar-Tal, 2007). The negative effects of the conflict on the youngest population of Colombia are undeniable. To counteract it, the government has adopted legislative, institutional, and social measures to improve the protection and promotion of the rights of children. However, certain deficiencies have become evident in the process (Capone, 2016).

In the midst of the bleak panorama that has led to many years of armed conflict, large mobilizations have occurred over the last decades in search of collective memories, truth, justice, reparation, negotiated solutions to conflict, and building of a collective future. In this regard, a peace agreement between the Colombian government and the Revolutionary Armed Forces of Colombia-People's Army (Las

Fuerzas Armadas Revolucionarias de Colombia-Ejército del Pueblo, FARC-EP) that seeks to consolidate peace and reconciliation was implemented in 2016 (United Nations Verification Mission in Colombia, 2018). In this scenario, the role of younger generations is fundamental. Their visions are crucial for the design and development of the country's future.

13.2.1 The Method Employed

In 2016, we explored the conceptualizations of Colombian children's forgiveness, reconciliation, and their role in building peace. Sixty-three children between 10 and 13 years old participated. One group of participants (n = 29) was composed of children directly affected by the conflict or those in situations of economic and social vulnerability residing in Soacha (close to Bogotá), an area with the greatest number of people displaced by the armed conflict. The other group (n = 34) was composed of children living in optimal (non-vulnerable) developmental conditions in Bogotá who had not directly experienced a victimizing event as part of the Colombian armed conflict. The sampling method addressed relevant aspects with regard to the diversity of these children, such as types of victimization and living condition.

To collect data through in-depth interviews, a question guide was generated and subjected to processes of cognitive and construct validation to investigate forgiveness, reconciliation, and peacebuilding in Colombia. A total of 29 questions examined the following topics:

(a) The definitions of forgiveness, reconciliation, and peace.
(b) Beliefs regarding the conditions that facilitated or hindered scenarios of forgiveness, reconciliation, and peace.
(c) Consequences that forgiveness and reconciliation have in the context of the armed conflict.

Grounded theory was used to analyze the data. As part of its inductive nature, the information collected through the interviews was coded, and an analytical interpretation was performed (Glaser & Strauss, 2009).

13.3 Results

13.3.1 Forgiveness

When the two groups of children were asked about the meaning of forgiveness, the definitions provided were (a) *strategy for conflict resolution* in which a *new opportunity* is given *to the offender*, (b) *capacity for dialogue*, and (c) *replacement of negative feelings with positive feelings*. Importantly, however, this last definition was strongly present in children in non-vulnerable conditions, whereas it was mentioned only twice in the vulnerable group. In addition, some participants considered *forgiveness and reconciliation as the same*; therefore, they answered the question "How do you understand forgiveness?" as a *reconciliation between two people or groups*. Children in non-vulnerable conditions also defined forgiveness as an *acceptance of mistakes or differences* or as a *mechanism of forgetting*. To a lesser extent, they understood forgiveness as a *strategy of war*.

The two groups of participants considered the *recognition of errors*, the need to establish a *commitment not to repeat* damage, and the *acts of reparation* by the offender as necessary to grant forgiveness. In addition, the non-vulnerable group proposed the *implementation of punishments to armed groups*, a *show of sincerity and repentance*, and an *understanding of the motives* that *the offender* had for inflicting pain as important and/or fundamental conditions for forgiveness to be generated.

The main consequences that the two groups of participants considered as generating forgiveness in the framework of armed conflict were contributions to the *re-establishment of positive interactions between enemies* to *achieve peace* by *maintaining social relationships*. In addition, the vulnerable participants proposed that forgiveness *facilitates the process of reconciliation* and *eliminates feelings of resentment*.

Finally, in relation to the impediments of forgiveness in the context of armed conflict, some participants mentioned that this process might be affected given the *difficulty* and even *impossibility for enemies within the armed conflict to forgive each other*. In addition, some of the children in non-vulnerable conditions stated that *relationships change despite forgiveness*.

13.3.2 Reconciliation

The narratives of both groups of participants defined reconciliation as a *process of acceptance and the resumption of interactions* in which *the victim and perpetrator* should *participate*. As already mentioned, however, it was common to find that some narratives did not consider a *difference between forgiveness and reconciliation*. Importantly, children in the vulnerable conditions also proposed reconciliation as a *method of union and coexistence* that contributes to the *absence of conflict*.

The main consequence of reconciliation that the two groups of participants raised was the *possibility that enemies of the armed conflict might be reconciled* to *contribute to the achievement of peace*. In addition, the participants in the non-vulnerable condition considered reconciliation as allowing for the *re-establishment of positive interactions between enemies* and the *reintegration of members of armed groups into society*.

On the other hand, in relation to the factors considered as hindering reconciliation, some of the participants in the non-vulnerable condition mentioned the *difficulty of coexistence between enemies of the armed conflict after establishing peace* and even the *impossibility that the actors could be reconciled.* The vulnerable group considered this issue as a *difficulty* but not as an impossibility.

13.3.3 Peacebuilding in Colombia

The participants defined peace in the context of armed conflict in Colombia as the *absence or reduction of conflicts* and as *union and coexistence*. Among the major differences in the definition of peace, the participants in the non-vulnerable condition stated that it was synonymous with *calmness and security as* well as with *tolerance of different points of view* and an *absence of violence*. Participants in the vulnerable condition proposed that it was a *situation in which they could live in equality* and considered this *scenario as possible in Colombia*.

Forgiveness and reconciliation were discussed as conditions that the participants believed are needed to achieve peace. Likewise the group in the non-vulnerable conditions added that it was also important to generate *a bilateral commitment* between the parties involved in the conflict.

Importantly, the group of participants in the non-vulnerable conditions stated that *peace agreements are insufficient to end conflict* and that it will *continue*, which shows the negative critical position of this group in the face of the peace treaty currently being implemented in Colombia. However, this peace was still in the negotiation phase during 2016 when these data collection was taking place (February through May).

13.4 Conclusions and Implications

Worldwide, important efforts have been made to integrate children into the building of more peaceful societies. Examples include opportunities in Chile, El Salvador, Haiti, Guatemala, South Africa, Peru, Sierra Leone, and others (UNICEF Innocenti Research Center & International Center for Transitional Justice, 2010). These instances have demonstrated that the perspectives and experiences of children are valuable resources to document the past and inform the way forward.

This chapter investigated the value of the views, perspectives, and experiences of children in the context of armed conflict. This study can help us find answers to questions such as "How can we improve the programs, services, and support that involve children?" from their perspective (Heykoop, 2018). Specifically, we sought to understand how children conceive forgiveness and reconciliation as well as the role that these processes play in peacebuilding scenarios.

Forgiveness and reconciliation are powerful tools to break the complex cycle of violence (Rocha et al., 2017). However, even if children learn that it is morally and socially important to forgive and/or be reconciled, they might not conceptually understand forgiveness or perform this action easily or well (Denham et al., 2007).

At the level of intervention, it is necessary to clarify that, in principle, forgiveness can only be granted or refused by the victim. This point is relevant when third parties (e.g., the state, church, community, and others) try to facilitate reconciliation scenarios, which might not promote expressions of forgiveness among people who are not ready to grant them (Santa-Barbara, 2007).

At the theoretical level, consensus shows that forgiveness does not mean forgetting victimization, nor does it mean reconciliation with the victimizer (Cortés et al., 2015; Rusbult, Hannon, Stocker, & Finkel, 2005; Taysi & Orcan, 2017). However, some participants stated these definitions in response to the questions "How do you understand forgiveness?" and "How do you understand reconciliation?" The implications of this confusion are potentially devastating given that children living in conflict might think that they must justify an offense or repair a relationship they actually prefer to give up (Taysi & Orcan, 2017).

Although some advanced studies have examined conceptualizations of forgiveness among children (Denham et al., 2007; Taysi & Orcan, 2017), none in the recent literature have addressed the issue specifically in the context of armed conflict. Thus, it is necessary to continue advancing this area of research using different methodologies to enable progress toward the implementation of interventions because the adult literature has demonstrated the benefits of forgiveness and reconciliation. However, it is also necessary to avoid revictimizing children by insisting on forgiveness in cases when they are not ready or by not ensuring that forgiveness is accompanied by the truth, knowledge of the motivation of the offense, a recognition of the damage, contrition, empathy, reparation, and non-repetition (Castrillón-Guerrero et al., 2018; López López et al., 2016; López López et al., 2018; López López, Pineda Marín, Murcia León, Perilla Garzón, & Mullet, 2012).

This study made progress in the investigation of interpersonal and/or intergroup forgiveness, but it did not investigate intrapersonal forgiveness. However, considering the multiple rights violations faced by children in conflict, where it is highly likely that they are involved in a victimizing act, it might also be necessary to work with interventions to positively affect the mental health of future generations.

The literature also provides reports of one-sided forgiveness processes in which there is no evidence of remorse or apology on the part of the offender (Santa-Barbara, 2007). Thus, it is relevant to continue working on the meaning of apology for both the victim and the victimizer as well as to explore when, why, and whether these apologies are important (Fehr et al., 2010). Some advances in this regard show that apologies have a liberating and repairing function that allows for personal relief, a step toward reconciliation, and the replacement of negative emotions with positive emotions. However, it is necessary to deepen studies in this regard by including perpetrators (Hareli & Eisikovits, 2006; Leonard, Mackie, & Smith, 2011; López López et al., 2016).

The main differences that were observed in the narratives of the groups of participants were (1) their visions of the negotiated exit to the Colombian armed conflict and (2) the conceptualization of peace. With regard to the first element, the group in the non-vulnerable conditions had a negative critical stance of the scope of the peace agreement and the subsequent coexistence between enemy actors, whereas the vulnerable children were optimistic, even when they stated that it was a challenging scenario. With regard to the second element, children in the non-vulnerable conditions considered peace as a concept close to security, calmness, and coexistence in pluralistic scenarios, whereas those in the vulnerable conditions focused their narratives on viewing peace as an arena of equality.

These results show that socioeconomic contexts and previous experiences in relation to armed conflict permeate the visions of the future among younger generations of Colombians. These contexts commit states and institutions to seek pluralistic intervention approaches as well as the generation of more egalitarian conditions in which the rights of children are guaranteed. These actions will help prevent new cycles of violence and build a more just future.

Acknowledgments The authors would like to thank the Fundación Alas Cinco and the Colegio Italiano Leonardo da Vinci as well as the children and families who are a part of these organizations in Colombia that allowed us to conduct the research that formed the basis of this chapter.

References

Action on Armed Violence. (2017). Explosive Truths Monitoring explosive violence in 2016. London. Retrieved from https://aoav.org.uk/wp-content/uploads/2017/05/AOAV-Explosive-Monitor-2017v9single-pages.pdf

Action on Armed Violence. (2018). The burden of harm. *Monitoring Explosive Violence in 2017*. Retrieved from https://aoav.org.uk/wp-content/uploads/2018/04/Explosive-Violence-Monitor-2017-v6.pdf

Alzate, M., & Dono, M. (2017). Reconciliación Social como estrategia para la transformación de los conflictos socio-políticos, variables asociadas e instrumentos de medición. *Universitas Psychologica, 16*(3), 1–10. https://doi.org/10.11144/Javeriana.upsy16-3.rset

Barry, M. M., Clarke, A. M., Jenkins, R., & Patel, V. (2013). A systematic review of the effectiveness of mental health promotion interventions for young people in low and middle income countries. *BMC Public Health, 13*(1), 835. https://doi.org/10.1186/1471-2458-13-835

Bar-Tal, D. (2007). Sociopsychological foundations of intractable conflicts. *American Behavioral Scientist, 50*(11), 1430–1453. https://doi.org/10.1177/0002764207302462

Bloomfield, D. (2015). Clarificando términos: ¿Qué podemos entender por reconciliación? In D. Bloomfield, C. Fernández, C. Andrés-Autor, & A. A. Novoa (Eds.), *Reconciliación: perspectivas y aportes conceptuales para su comprensión* (pp. 11–30). Bogotá, Colombia: Centro de Investigación y Educación Popular – Programa por la Paz (CINEP/PPP).

Borská, J., Vacková, J., & Small, M. A. (2016). United Nations convention on the rights of the child and its implementation in the 21st century. *Kontakt, 18*(2), e96–e102. https://doi.org/10.1016/J.KONTAKT.2016.05.005

Bronfenbrenner, U. (1979). *The ecology of human development*. Cambridge, MA: Harvard University Press.

Capone, F. (2016). Children in Colombia: Discussing the current transitional justice process against the backdrop of the CRC key principles. In *Justiciability of human rights law in domestic jurisdictions* (pp. 197–215). Cham, Switzerland: Springer International Publishing. https://doi.org/10.1007/978-3-319-24016-9_9

Castrillón-Guerrero, L., Riveros Fiallo, V., Knudsen, M., López López, W., Correa-Chica, A., & Castañeda Polanco, J. G. (2018). Comprensiones de perdón, reconciliación y justicia en víctimas de desplazamiento forzado en Colombia. *Revista de Estudios Sociales, 63*, 84–98. https://doi.org/10.7440/res63.2018.07

Centro Nacional de Memoria Histórica. (2013). *¡Basta ya! Colombia: Memorias de guerra y dignidad*. Bogotá, Colombia: Imprenta Nacional. Retrieved from http://www.centrodememoriahistorica.gov.co/micrositios/informeGeneral/descargas.html

Cortés, Á., Torres, A., López López, W., Claudia Pérez, D., & Pineda-Marín, C. (2016). Comprensiones sobre el perdón y la reconciliación en el contexto del conflicto armado colombiano. *Psychosocial Intervention, 25*(1), 19–25.

Cortés, Á., Torres, A., López López, W., Pérez D., C., & Pineda-Marín, C. (2015). Comprensiones sobre el perdón y la reconciliación en el contexto del conflicto armado colombiano. *Psychosocial Intervention*. https://doi.org/10.1016/j.psi.2015.09.004

Denham, S., Neal, K., Wilson, B., Pickerin, S., & Boyatzis, C. (2007). Emotional development and forgiveness in children: Emerging evidence. In E. L. J. Worthington (Ed.), *Handbook of forgiveness* (pp. 127–142). New York, NY: Routledge.

Department of Peace and Conflict Research. (2017). *Uppsala conflict data program*. Uppsala. Retrieved from http://ucdp.uu.se/

Fajardo Mayo, M. A., Ramírez Lozano, M. P., Valencia Suescún, M. I., & Ospína Alvarado, M. C. (2018). Más allá de la victimización de niñas y niños en contextos de conflicto armado: potenciales para la construcción de paz. *Universitas Psychologica, 17*(1), 1–14. https://doi.org/10.11144/Javeriana.upsy17-1.mavn

Fehr, R., Gelfand, M. J., & Nag, M. (2010). The road to forgiveness: A meta-analytic synthesis of its situational and dispositional correlates. *Psychological Bulletin, 136*(5), 894–914. https://doi.org/10.1037/a0019993

Freedman, S., Enright, R., & Knutson, J. (2007). A progress report on the process model of forgiveness. In E. L. J. Worthington (Ed.), *Handbook of forgiveness* (pp. 394–407). New York, NY: Routledge.

Glaser, B. G., & Strauss, A. L. (2009). The discovery of grounded theory: Strategies for qualitative research. Transaction Publishers. Retrieved from https://books.google.com/books?id=rtiNK68Xt08C&pgis=1

Haj-Yahia, M. M., Greenbaum, C. W., & Lahoud-Shoufany, L. (2018). Palestinian adolescents' prolonged exposure to political violence, self- esteem, and post-traumatic stress symptoms. *Journal of Interpersonal Violence*, 088626051878914. https://doi.org/10.1177/0886260518789144

Hareli, S., & Eisikovits, Z. (2006). The role of communicating social emotions accompanying apologies in forgiveness. *Motivation and Emotion, 30*(3), 189–197. https://doi.org/10.1007/s11031-006-9025-x

Heykoop, C. (2018). "Our stories, our way": Interdisciplinary applied research exploring the safe and meaningful engagement of young people in post-conflict truth telling in northern Uganda. In *Applied interdisciplinarity in scholar practitioner programs* (pp. 135–149). Cham, Switzerland: Springer International Publishing. https://doi.org/10.1007/978-3-319-64453-0_7

Human Rights Watch. (2018). *World Report 2018*. United States of America. Retrieved from https://www.hrw.org/sites/default/files/world_report_download/201801world_report_web.pdf

Institute for Economics & Peace. (2017). Global peace index 2017. Sydney. Retrieved from http://visionofhumanity.org/app/uploads/2017/06/GPI17-Report.pdf

Institute for Economics & Peace. (2018). Global peace index 2018. Sydney. Retrieved from http://visionofhumanity.org/reports

Internal Displacement Monitoring Centre. (2017). Global internal displacement database. Retrieved May 4, 2015, from http://www.internal-displacement.org/database/displacement-data

International Committee of the Red Cross. (2008). How is the term "armed conflict" Defined in International Humanitarian Law? Retrieved October 28, 2018, from https://www.icrc.org/eng/resources/documents/article/other/armed-conflict-article-170308.htm

Jankowitz, S. (2017). Sociopolitical implications of exclusive, intergroup perceptions of victims in societies emerging from conflict. *Peacebuilding, 5*(3), 289–304. https://doi.org/10.1080/21647259.2016.1237421

Leonard, D. J., Mackie, D. M., & Smith, E. R. (2011). Emotional responses to intergroup apology mediate intergroup forgiveness and retribution. *Journal of Experimental Social Psychology, 47*(6), 1198–1206. https://doi.org/10.1016/j.jesp.2011.05.002

López López, W. (2017). Contribuciones de Psicología de la Paz: Una Perspectiva Multidimensional. *Innovación y Ciencia, 24*(1), 100–108. Retrieved from https://innovacionyciencia.com/revista/91

López López, W., Sandoval Alvarado, G., Rodríguez, S., Ruiz, C., León, J. D., Pineda-Marín, C., & Mullet, E. (2018). Forgiving former perpetrators of violence and reintegrating them into colombian civil society: Noncombatant citizens' positions. *Peace and Conflict: Journal of Peace Psychology, 24*(2), 201–215. https://doi.org/10.1037/pac0000295

López, W. L., & Sabucedo, J. M. (2007). Culture of peace and mass media. *European Psychologist, 12*(2), 147–155. https://doi.org/10.1027/1016-9040.12.2.147

López López, W., Andrade Páez, A. F., & Correa-Chica, A. (2016). The process of asking for forgiveness as a necessary condition in order to build peace amidst the Colombian armed conflict. *Revista Argentina de Clinica Psicologica, 25*(2).

López López, W., Pineda Marín, C., Murcia León, M. C., Perilla Garzón, D. C., & Mullet, E. (2012). Forgiving perpetrators of violence: Colombian People's positions. *Social Indicators Research, 114*(2), 287–301. https://doi.org/10.1007/s11205-012-0146-1

López López, W., Pineda-Marín, C., & Mullet, E. (2014). El perdón como proceso de transformación para la paz. In J. I. R. Pérez (Ed.), *Psicología social y justicia* (pp. 225–238). Bogotá, Colombia: Editorial Universidad Nacional de Colombia.

Melander, E., Pettersson, T., & Themnér, L. (2016). Organized violence, 1989–2015. *Journal of Peace Research, 53*(5), 727–742. https://doi.org/10.1177/0022343316663032

Murphy, J. (2007). Forgiveness, self-respect, and the value of resentment. In E. L. J. Worthington (Ed.), *Handbook of forgiveness* (pp. 33–40). New York, NY: Routledge.

Noor, M., James Brown, R., & Prentice, G. (2008). Precursors and mediators of intergroup reconciliation in Northern Ireland: A new model. *British Journal of Social Psychology, 47*(3), 481–495. https://doi.org/10.1348/014466607X238751

Rettberg, A., & Ugarriza, J. E. (2016). Reconciliation: A comprehensive framework for empirical analysis. *Security Dialogue, 47*(6), 517–540. https://doi.org/10.1177/0967010616671858

Rocha, A., Amarís, M., & López López, W. (2017). El perdón como estrategia de afrontamiento. Una mirada desde el modelo de la complejidad del afrontamiento. Terapia Psicológica (Vol. 35). Sociedad Chilena de Psicología Clínica. Retrieved from http://teps.cl/index.php/teps/article/view/223

Rubenstein, B. L., & Stark, L. (2017). The impact of humanitarian emergencies on the prevalence of violence against children: An evidence-based ecological framework. *Psychology, Health & Medicine, 22*(sup1), 58–66. https://doi.org/10.1080/13548506.2016.1271949

Rusbult, C. E., Hannon, P. A., Stocker, S. L., & Finkel, E. J. (2005). Forgiveness and relational repair. In E. L. Worthington (Ed.), *Handbook of forgiveness* (pp. 185–205). New York, NY: Routledge.

Santa-Barbara, J. (2007). Reconciliation. In C. Webel & J. Galtung (Eds.), *Handbook of peace and conflict studies* (pp. 173–186). New York, NY: Routledge.

Save the Children. (2017). End of chilhood. Stolen childhoods. Washington, D.C.

Save the Children. (2018). The war on children. London. Retrieved from https://www.savethechildren.net/waronchildren/pdf/waronchildren.pdf

Schultz, J.-H., Sørensen, P. M., & Waaktaar, T. (2012). Ready for school? Trauma exposure and mental health in a group of war-affected Ugandan adolescents re-attending school. *Scandinavian Journal of Educational Research, 56*(5), 539–553. https://doi.org/10.1080/00313831.2011.621132

Siem, B., Stürmer, S., & Pittinsky, T. L. (2016). The psychological study of positive behavior across group boundaries: An overview. *Journal of Social Issues, 72*(3), 419–431. https://doi.org/10.1111/josi.12174

Taylor, L. K., Merrilees, C. E., Baird, R., Goeke-Morey, M. C., Shirlow, P., & Cummings, E. M. (2018). Impact of political conflict on trajectories of adolescent prosocial behavior: Implications for civic engagement. *Developmental Psychology, 54*(9), 1785–1794. https://doi.org/10.1037/dev0000552

Taysi, E., & Orcan, F. (2017). The conceptualisation of forgiveness among Turkish children and adolescents. *International Journal of Psychology, 52*(6), 473–481. https://doi.org/10.1002/ijop.12237

UNICEF Innocenti Research Centre, & International Center for Transitional Justice. (2010). *Children and Truth Commissions*. Florence. Retrieved from https://www.unicef-irc.org/publications/pdf/truth_commissions_eng.pdf

United Nations. (2002). Optional Protocol to the Convention on the Rights of the Child on the involvement of children in armed conflict. Retrieved October 28, 2018, from https://www.ohchr.org/en/professionalinterest/pages/opaccrc.aspx

United Nations Secretary General. (2017). Children and armed conflict. Retrieved from http://undocs.org/en/A/72/361

United Nations Verification Mission in Colombia. (2018). Report of the secretary-general. Retrieved October 30, 2018, from https://colombia.unmissions.org/en/documents

Wessells, M. G. (2016). Children and armed conflict: Introduction and overview. *Peace and Conflict: Journal of Peace Psychology, 22*(3), 198–207. https://doi.org/10.1037/pac0000176

Worthington, E. L. J. (2006). *Forgiveness and reconciliation: Theory and application*. New York, NY: Brunner-Routledge.

Part III
Promoting Peace and Well-Being in Children

Chapter 14
Learning for Peace: Lessons Learned from UNICEF's Peacebuilding, Education, and Advocacy in Conflict-Affected Context Programme

Friedrich W. Affolter and Anna Azaryeva Valente

> There is now widespread international recognition of the need for conflict sensitivity in programming and factoring in considerations of conflict and peace into programme design, implementation, and monitoring and evaluation. The need for such programme and policy guidance for administrative and social services is clear: precious resources need to be spent responsibly and wisely in peacebuilding settings to meet the panoply of recovery needs and priorities in ways that address conflict drivers and lay the conditions for sustainable peace. Failing to do this will undermine peacebuilding and statebuilding goals.
>
> (McCandless, 2012, p. 1)

14.1 Insecurity: The Primary Development Challenge of Our Time

In the second decade of the twenty-first century, a combination of several global challenges – including climate change, conflict, chronic poverty and disease, inequality and unfairness, economic shocks, and weak institutions – is creating new risks or exacerbating existing ones, including the erosion of social cohesion and peace, the reversal of development gains, and the creation of new humanitarian needs (World Economic Forum, 2018). Fragile states – where two-thirds of the worlds poor will be residing by 2030 (44% of them being youth below 20 years of age) – will be particularly affected (Office of Economic Cooperation and

Disclaimer: The views and opinions contained in this document are the authors' personal views and opinions and do not necessarily represent the positions of UNICEF or any other organization.

F. W. Affolter (✉) · A. Azaryeva Valente
United Nations Children's Fund, New York, NY, USA
e-mail: faffolter@unicef.org

N. Balvin, D. J. Christie (eds.), *Children and Peace*, Peace Psychology Book Series, https://doi.org/10.1007/978-3-030-22176-8_14

Development [OECD], 2015, pp. 13, 84). According to the World Bank Group (2011), insecurity "… is the primary development challenge of our time" (p. 1).

The costs of conflict are enormous. In human terms, vulnerable groups such as children and their caretakers pay the highest price for war and are the ones likely to benefit the most from peace. According to Save the Children, approximately 357 million children lived in countries and areas affected by war in 2016, which is 1 out of 6 of the world's children. Out of these children, 165 million were affected by high-intensity conflicts (Kirollos, Anning, Fylkesnes, & Denselow, 2018, p. 7). Around 16 million babies were born into conflict in 2015 alone (UNICEF, 2015b). A child in a fragile or conflict-affected state was nearly three times more likely to be out of primary school, two times more likely to be undernourished, and nearly twice as likely to die before his or her fifth birthday, compared to a child in another developing country (World Bank, 2011, p. 5).

Both direct and structural violence denies children their right to protection and development of their full potential and to participate freely and fully in cultural life in conditions of equality, human dignity, and non-discrimination (Dawes & van der Merwe, 2014, p. 236; Punamäki, 2014; United Nations General Assembly [UNGA], 2016; Human Rights Council, 2016, par. 41, 44). Exposure of children and young people to abuse in high-violence contexts is associated with an increased risk of impaired physical and mental development and increased chances to either transform into a perpetrator of violence or become a victim of violence later in life (United Nations [UN] & World Bank Group, 2017, p. 17). Emerging evidence suggests that both poverty and adverse life experiences may result in long-term physiological and epigenetic effects on brain development and cognition in young children (Black et al., 2017, p. 77; Punamäki, 2014; National Scientific Council on the Developing Child, 2005). War and famine experienced during early adolescence (10–14 years of age) are "even more strongly associated with a decrease in total lifespan than stressors experienced at any other age of childhood" (Falconi et al., cited in Dahl & Suleiman, 2017, pp. 22–23). Education inequality is associated with an increased likelihood of violent conflict (Omoeva & Buckner, 2015); violent conflict in return further exacerbates inequality in education and other socioeconomic outcomes (Omoeva, Hatch, & Moussa, 2016).

In economic terms, the cost of violent conflict is also astounding. Countries at war "lose an average 8.5 percentage points in economic growth in the first year of civil war and 4.5% in subsequent years. These effects persist for several years following the end of hostilities" (UN & World Bank Group, 2017, p. 1). The cost of containing violence has been estimated to be at:

> "… US$13.6 trillion a year globally, a figure … equivalent to 13.3 [percent] of world GDP or US$1,876 PPP [purchasing power parity] per annum, per person…. To further break it down, that figure is US$5 per person, per day, every day of the year. When you consider that according to the most recent World Bank estimates 10.7 [percent] of the world's population are living on less than US$2 per day, it shows an alarming market failure." (IEP, Schippa, cited in UN & World Bank Group, 2018, p. 33)

Prevention measures could safeguard between USD 5 billion and 70 billion per annum (Mueller, cited in UN & World Bank Group, 2017, p. 4).

14.2 Child Development and Protection Prerequisites for Sustainable Peace

Numerous resolutions and protocols acknowledge the importance of child protection and development programming as a prerequisite for sustainable peace. Psychological and neuroscientific evidence also stresses the importance of social support structures that protect children against excessive stress and the risks of violence.

14.2.1 UN Resolutions on Child Well-Being and Conflict Prevention

Both the United Nations General Assembly [UNGA] and the United Nations Security Council [UNSC] acknowledge the link between child protection, child development, and conflict prevention. Resolution 2427 emphasizes that:

> "… a strong focus is needed on combatting poverty, deprivation and inequality to prevent and protect children from all violations and abuses in particular in the context of armed conflict and to promote the resilience of children, their families and their communities, and the importance of promoting education for all and peaceful and inclusive societies for sustainable development." (United Nations Security Council [UNSC], 2018b, p. 1)

UNSC Resolutions 2250 and 2419 recognize how the disruption of youth's access to education and economic opportunities dramatically impacts durable peace and reconciliation while at the same time acknowledging the "important and positive contribution of youth in efforts for the maintenance and promotion of peace and security" (UNSC, 2015, p. 1).

Article 29d of the Convention of the Rights of the Child (UNGA, 1989) calls for "the preparation of the child for responsible life in a free society, in the spirit of understanding, peace, tolerance, equality of sexes, and friendship among all peoples, ethnic, national and religious groups and persons of indigenous origin." The 2030 Agenda for Sustainable Development highlights the interconnectedness between sustainable development, education, and peace (United Nations, 2015, p. 2; Goals 4.7 & 16). The twin Sustaining Peace Resolutions endorsed by both the UNGA and UNSC (2015), as well as the review of Resolution 1325 (UN Women's Organization, 2015), request that *all* UN agencies contribute to sustaining peace, for social services to be leveraged for peacebuilding, and for paying special attention to the role of women in peacebuilding.

14.2.2 Basic Human Needs, Altruism, and Aggression

Children's ability to evolve into caring, non-violent, and optimally functioning citizens depends on family, school, community, and macro-political contexts that allow for the constructive satisfaction of basic human needs – safety and security, effectiveness and control, comprehension of reality, positive identity, positive belonging, as well as independence and autonomy (Staub, 2003, pp. 52–67). "Optimally functioning persons" are children and youth who have "their basic needs fulfilled to a reasonable extent, and who have developed the capacity to fulfill needs in constructive rather than destructive ways, and who have experienced a continuous evolution of effectiveness and identity and connection as a result of the continued fulfillment of these needs" (Staub, cited in Affolter, 2005, p. 382). Although development discourse communities have historically overlooked the psychosocial relevance of their aid and development interventions (Affolter, 2004, 2005), evidence is accumulating to show that societies that offer more education, employment, livelihood, and political engagement opportunities, as well as social mobility opportunities for young people – thereby addressing both socioeconomic and psychosocial needs of populations – tend to experience less violence (Idris, 2016; Paasonen & Urdal, 2016; Staub, 2011). Some evidence suggests that the best predictor of a state's peacefulness might be "how well women are treated, rather than the status of wealth, democracy, ethnicity, or religious identity" (Caprioli, cited in UNICEF, 2016b, p. 2). Similarly, early childhood development interventions are increasingly documented to provide a potential pathway to violence reduction as well as family and community transformation (Richter, Lye, & Proulx, 2018; Leckman, Panther-Brick, & Salah, 2014).

14.3 UNICEF's Peacebuilding, Education, and Advocacy Programme [Learning for Peace]

It is in this context that lessons learned from UNICEF's 2012–2016 "Learning for Peace" programme[1] offer valuable insights on how social services – education in this case – can be leveraged to contribute to the mitigation of conflict factors, and for strengthening social integration and cohesion, while at the same time ensuring the safeguarding of children's developmental and cultural needs and rights.

UNICEF (2016c) defines social cohesion as "the quality of bonds and dynamics that exist between ... groups within a society" (p. 12). UNICEF recognizes in social cohesion one critical dimension of peace which – in order to become sustainable – must be combined with the availability and access to economic resources, information and communication, justice, security, leadership and positive governance, as

[1] "Learning for Peace" (also known as the "Peacebuilding, Education and Advocacy in Conflict-Affected Context Programme" or PBEA) was funded by the Government of the Netherlands and implemented by UNICEF from 2012 to 2016. It emerged from the "Education in Emergencies and Post-Crisis Transition Programme" whose final program evaluation called for emergency interventions that address the root causes of conflict and fragility (UNICEF, 2015a, p. 16). Research and program evaluation reports as well as education-for-peacebuilding guidance notes produced under the "Learning for Peace" programme, can be accessed on USAID's Education in Crisis and Conflict Network [ECCN] website at https://eccnetwork.net/resources/learning-for-peace/ and on the website of the International Network for Education in Emergencies (INEE) at http://www.ineesite.org/en/learning-for-peace.

well as an ability to constructively deal with conflict legacies of the past (UNICEF, 2016c; see also Pham & Vinck, 2017, pp. 12ff.). The unequitable, non-transparent, nonaccountable, or incompetent administration of social services, however, can prompt affected identity groups to suspect deliberate acts of discrimination (McCandless, 2012, p. 9; World Bank Group, 2011, p. 88), thereby fuelling resentment and aggravating "social erosion" dynamics. According to Larsen (2014, pp. 2–3), social erosion occurs when the number of citizens sharing beliefs that enable them to trust one another declines. Social erosion can be mitigated, however, whenever social service providers make use of the opportunity to design and administer service interventions in ways that facilitate "social integration," which is a precursor to social cohesion (Larsen, 2014, p. 2).

While the "Learning for Peace" interventions introduced below do not provide quantitative evidence from impact evaluations for justifying the claim that they have impacted community or national trust levels, evidence from programme monitoring, case studies, and other research designs nonetheless suggests that they contributed to facilitating social integration, cooperation, inclusion, trust, and participation among citizens and citizen groups whose relationships were previously eroded (UNICEF, 2016c). For example, in rural communities in Côte d'Ivoire where inter-ethnic relations had deteriorated as a result of decade-long electoral violence, the operationalization of inclusive early childhood development services and women adult literacy services in 16 villages succeeded in cultivating trust, solidarity, and community engagement first among women and later also fathers from diverse ethnic backgrounds. In Burundi, returnees and host communities reorganized around school social platforms. In Pakistan, Afghan refugee girls were able to access education services in neighboring host communities, and madrasa students joined extracurricular sports and arts events together with children from public schools.

An independent evaluation of "Learning for Peace" concluded that UNICEF's decision to leverage social services for peacebuilding purposes was feasible and that the initiative's "emphasis on conflict analysis based programming... leads to responsive context-specific programmes that can contribute to peacebuilding" (UNICEF, 2015a p. xiv).

"Learning for Peace" was implemented in 14 conflict-affected contexts (Burundi, Chad, Côte d'Ivoire, Democratic Republic of Congo, Ethiopia, Liberia, Myanmar, Pakistan, State of Palestine, Sierra Leone, Somalia, South Sudan, Uganda, and Yemen). It aimed, at a minimum, to make education and other social services – based on conflict analyses which incorporated a focus on the education sector – conflict-sensitive toward existing conflict factors ("do-no-harm") and where possible to contribute to their mitigation ("do-more-good").

As illustrated in Fig. 14.1, "Learning for Peace" used a systemic approach to education for peacebuilding, going beyond traditional "peace education" approaches. This could include – at the macro level – education policies and sector plans, curriculum framework development, teacher recruitment and school construction contracting policies, equitable education resource distribution, as well as institutional and staff capacity development inside ministries. In addition, it included capacity development for education agencies and religious and community organizations at the meso level, as well as parents and children at the micro level. Far from suggesting

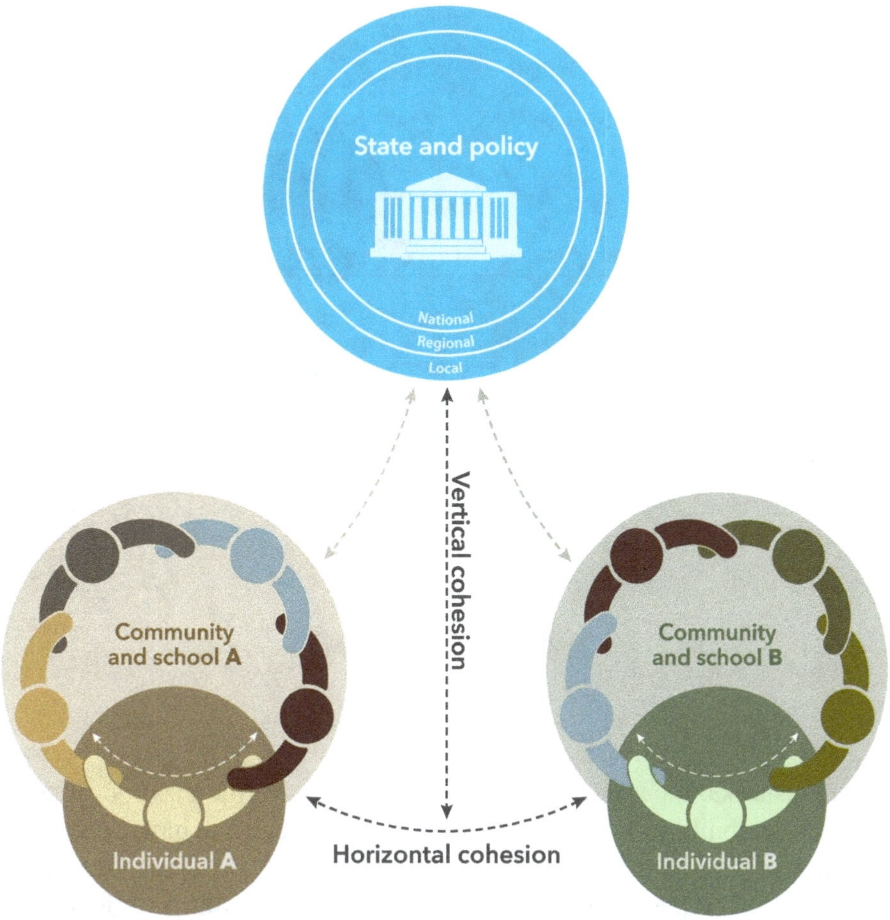

Fig. 14.1 Peacebuilding education for vertical and horizontal social cohesion. (Source: UNICEF, 2018)

that the education sector alone has the capacity to fully and independently mitigate conflict factors – this requires cross-sectoral socioeconomic and political interventions at multiple levels of the human ecology – "Learning for Peace" attempted to design education interventions to contribute to the mitigation of conflict drivers either by strengthening horizontal relationships between individuals and groups, or vertical relationships between government institutions and citizenry (UNICEF, 2016a).

14.4 Theoretical Framework for Understanding Education in Conflict and Peace and Education for Peacebuilding Programming

Education sector policies and structures can be designed to contribute to the mitigation of education-related conflict factors and for facilitating social integration. Drawing on earlier work of Nancy Frazer, Johan Galtung, and Jean-Paul Lederach – and based on additional country-level research conducted in "Learning for Peace" programme countries – Novelli, Lopes Cardozo, and Smith (2015) proposed a *4 Rs Analytical Framework* (see Fig. 14.2) for analyzing the contribution of education

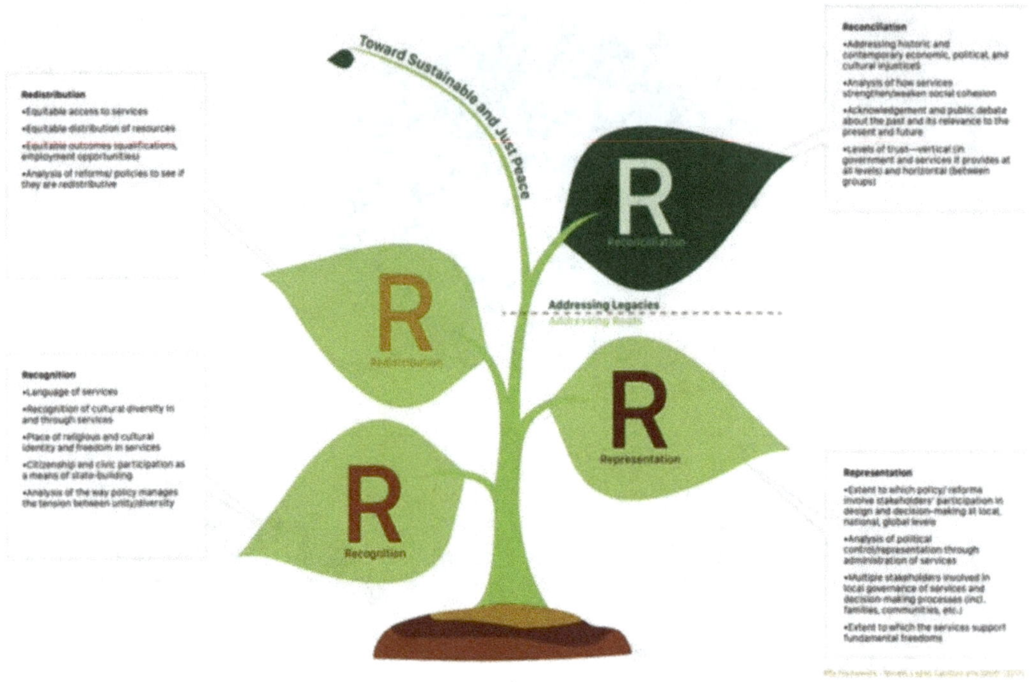

Fig. 14.2 Sustainable peacebuilding in education: The "4 Rs" analytical framework

services to sustainable peacebuilding. Although the education sector alone is not a panacea for peacebuilding – indeed, education systems can and have been "hijacked" in the past to polarize and antagonize societies (Bush & Saltarelli, 2000) – education services can be leveraged to work in tandem with other political, socioeconomic, psychological, and cultural empowerment efforts. In order to do this, governments and education actors need to ensure (a) the equitable *redistribution* of education resources and opportunities; (b) the *recognition* of the diverse education needs of identity groups; (c) the participation as well as the social and political *representation* in education decision-making processes; as well as (d) the use of education social platforms for *reconciliation* learning. The framework also recognizes the complex interaction between the "4 Rs."

In the remainder of this chapter, conflict analysis and research findings, as well as anecdotal evidence from "Learning for Peace" programme reports (peacebuilding-oriented education policies, institutional capacity development, as well as community interventions), will be presented in relation to each of the 4 R categories, thereby illustrating possibilities and limitations of education programming efforts for vertical and horizontal social cohesion and the mitigation of conflict causes.

14.4.1 *Redistribution of Education Resources: To Counter Education Inequities and Inequalities*

Poverty, low levels of development, and inequitable economic development are frequently cited as conflict factors in PBEA country conflict analyses (for conflict analysis summaries, see Learning for Peace, 2018). Frustration and tension were found to be increased by negligible economic diversification, poor infrastructure, and unfair distribution of or lack of relevant educational opportunities, particularly in the formal sector.

The link between education inequality and violent conflict has been corroborated by research conducted by FHI 360 on behalf of UNICEF. Omoeva and Buckner (2015) examined horizontal education inequality between culturally defined or constructed groups and socioeconomic divisions (e.g., ethnic, religious, etc.) by comparing education equality data and conflict data from nearly 100 countries over the past 50 years. They generated robust evidence that the likelihood of violent conflict doubles for countries with high levels of intergroup inequality in education (after controlling for known conflict risk factors such as wealth, political regime, geography, etc.). The research also suggests that greater education equality between male and female students decreases the likelihood of conflict by as much as 37%. Similarly, Omoeva et al. (2016) found that conflict widens education inequalities among groups and individuals, with lower wealth-based groups and gender disparities particularly impacted. The longer the conflict, the harder it becomes to return to pre-conflict levels of inequality, and the more relapses to the conflict there are, the more the gap widens between post-conflict inequality and pre-conflict inequality.

Under "Learning for Peace," education programs have been designed to address the mitigation of inequalities. In northern Burundi, conflict risks resulting from the arrival of returnees from the Mtabila Camps in the United Republic of Tanzania resulted in host communities' inability to provide education opportunities for all. UNICEF supported the construction of classrooms in communities predominantly consisting of returnees and where community members had provided the land or contributed labor to produce ecologically friendly materials. As a result, returnee children were able to access education alongside children of host communities, and the damaging consequences of remaining out of school were avoided. The shared school construction process also increased solidarity among returnees and community members. Conflict sensitivity principles such as respect, inclusiveness, impartiality, transparency, accountability, and ownership were applied to facilitate the involvement of community members, neighbors, and returnees and ultimately increased community cohesion. As refugee returns continued to be a source of concern in a number of provinces in Burundi – many of those returning had no meaningful connection with their communities of origin – education programs proved to be a meaningful platform to build relationships, notwithstanding austerity and distress (UNICEF Burundi, 2016).

In Pakistan's provinces of Baluchistan and Sindh, as well as the Federally Administered Tribal Areas, the UNICEF Pakistan Country Office supported Alternate Learning Programmes (ALPs) in hard-to-reach and conflict-prone areas, benefiting more than 16,000 out-of-school children (48% girls) who otherwise would have grown up without access to quality education services. A refugee inclusion project promoting interaction between children from host communities and out-of-school boys and girls from Afghan refugee camps showed a significant 25% increase in the enrolment of refugee children in public schools of Baluchistan, Khyber Pakhtunkhwa, and Sindh provinces. Enrolment of Afghan girls also increased by 17% (UNICEF Pakistan, 2016).

In the Democratic Republic of Congo, a Policy Dialogue Forum supported the development of a new Education Sector Plan that stressed the need of equity, conflict sensitivity, new citizenship, and emergency education in the government's new sectoral education and training strategy (République Démocratique du Congo, 2014). Similarly, the education sector plans of Côte d'Ivoire (République de Côte d'Ivoire - Ministère de l'Education Nationale, 2017) and Pakistan's Sindh province (Government of Sindh, 2014 p. 263) acknowledged the risk of conflict resulting from unequal access to opportunities and resources.

14.4.2 Recognition: Of Identity, Voices, and Needs

Ethnic and religious divisions – mobilized along political lines and emphasizing grievances in terms of inequalities between groups – are often also reinforced through the education sector. In Myanmar, "Burmanization" caused resentment among ethnic minority groups. In Baluchistan and Gilgit-Baltistan in Pakistan, feelings of resentment emanated from a perception of ethnic discrimination. Conflict analysis research commissioned under "Learning for Peace" also highlights the unmet needs of a growing youth population with limited prospects of employment or participation in civil society (Learning for Peace, 2018). The marginalization of youth voices, identities, and needs is also evident in education sector plans analyzed in a comparative case study analysis that included the countries of Myanmar, Pakistan, South Africa, and Uganda (Lopes Cardozo, Higgins, & Le Mat, 2016).

In the Eastern Asia and Pacific Region (Malaysia, Myanmar, and Thailand), UNICEF in partnership with the University of Melbourne launched a Language Education and Social Cohesion [LESC] initiative to study and address the risks associated with language and ethnicity issues that children face in educational and non-educational settings. A key finding of the LESC initiative is that conventional analyses of conflict have underestimated the role of language and ethnicity differences in instigating conflicts, as well as in sustaining conflicts once they have commenced. Language becomes a slow-acting conflict instigator wherever policies are used to discriminate minorities and a fast-acting instigator where it is used for exclusionary, stigmatizing, or inflammatory speech against minority groups (LoBianco, 2016, p. 14). In Myanmar, LESC's approach to leverage language policy for conflict mitigation consisted in the establishment of language planning platforms where stakeholders from both government and ethnic minority groups came together for the first time to jointly reflect and engage with critical language policy issues and to devise policy recommendations for mitigating conflict risks related to cultural rights and social identity (LoBianco, 2016). LESC also aimed to align language-related education policy with national education sector plans, since child early learning and literacy in the mother tongue is a prerequisite for the effective acquisition of other national languages (Abadzi, 2006, pp. 50–57) and thus a building block for mitigating the risks of education inequality in Myanmar:

> A high rate of functional literacy can help a child gain access to cultural capital, to material success through better skills acquisition, and to enhanced employability. It is a critical part of a quality education, and it improves children's chances of experiencing better health and social well-being throughout their lives. A well-educated child is also more likely to participate actively and constructively in decision-making processes and therefore to become an asset in national political processes. (Toole, in LoBianco, 2016, p. 1)

In Somalia, marginalization of youth has been recognized as a salient driver of conflict (Learning for Peace, 2018). Youth are frequently uneducated; excluded from political, economic, and social processes; and unable to access suitable employment for gaining an independent livelihood. As a consequence, marginalized youth may choose to join religious or freelance armed or criminal groups. In 2014, the Somali Federal Government, in partnership with UN agencies, decided to conduct a school curriculum review that would take into account the values and aspirations expressed by youth and elders of rural communities. A community-based consultative process was launched, which included 248 young Somali men and women who held focus group interviews with youth and community elders to inquire which values and competencies Somali learners should acquire across different subjects taught. The findings were presented to the government and served the purpose of developing a new curriculum framework that was more reflective of community voices as well as more context-relevant. In addition, the programme created a social platform for youth to participate in a national decision-making process that will impact education programming in Somalia for years to come. Youth researchers have been publicly valued by education officials, education stakeholders, and community leaders. The Government of Somalia recognized the education sector's potential contributions toward social cohesion and peacebuilding, in particular when it comes to issues of equity, inclusion, and livelihood opportunities for young people in Somalia (Renders & Knezevic, 2017).

14.4.3 Representation: Participation in Decision-Making

Conflict analyses across PBEA countries illustrated that weak governance – characterized by divided politics, limited policies and legislation, inadequate local capacity to guarantee for safety and security, political corruption and exclusion, as well as the centralization of power and resources – is a predominant driver of conflict (Learning for Peace, 2018). Education systems frequently reflect governance weaknesses and fail to provide social spaces for youth, teachers, and minority groups (Smith, Marks, Novelli, Valiente, & Scandurra, 2016). In Kenya's semi-arid regions, for example, education systems embedded in tribal and political power struggles are ill-prepared to assist youth from pastoralist backgrounds to develop critical thinking and leadership skills necessary for mitigating divisive identity politics. Programs that strengthen pastoralist resilience and development learning are absent. Instead, "underemployed young people often dissociate with local politics, and – feeling that they are not full citizens of Kenya – turn towards religious, martial or criminal identities that seem to be a better fit for coping with a politicized and violent society" (Scott-Villiers, Wilson, Molu Kullu, Ndung'u, & Scott-Villiers, 2015, p. 65).

Education can become a vehicle for peacebuilding when serving as a consultation platform where dialogue, participation, and representation become possible. This was illustrated in the abovementioned Myanmar example where ethnic minority groups were invited to negotiate minority language policy together with experts and government representatives, and in the example from Somalia where curriculum reform reflected community recommendations that were collected by youth action research facilitators.

In Uganda, the "Learning for Peace" programme has put in use the SMS-based U-Report technology to enable more than 300,000 youth to make their voices heard on consultation platforms dedicated to the discussion of social development issues and in which members of Parliament also did participate. U-Report enables participants to ask questions, voice opinions, and provide feedback about policy decisions, advocate for community rights, and inquire or become acquainted about the availability of social service mechanisms. When the Office of the Prime Minister initiated in 2015 a redrafting of a new peace policy for Uganda, U-Report facilitated the provision of inputs of 40,000 young people on the type of matters youth thought necessary to be addressed in the new Uganda Peace Policy. (An initial draft was prepared in 2012, where youth voices had not been consulted.) U-Report Uganda also supported the Uganda Civil Society Youth Coalition that brings together more than 375 youth-led and youth-serving community-based and civil society organizations utilizing U-Reporter feedback. For the Ugandan government, U-Report platforms provided the opportunity to "stay in touch" with youth voices and sentiments. They increased the government's appreciation of youth perspectives for policy discourse and program development and young people as potential partners in consultations relating to social services programming, as well as nation building (UNICEF Uganda, 2016, p. 22).

When it comes to gender relationships in conflict and post-conflict countries, norms that condone sexual and gender-based violence often undermine stability and present an additional security risk in communities and states – even after conflict has officially ended (Blair, Gerring, & Karrim, 2016, p. 1; UNICEF, 2016b; El-Bushra & Rees-Smith, 2016; see also von Joeden-Forgey, 2016, pp. 129–130). In Somalia and South Sudan, UNICEF's "Communities Care" project used two mutually reinforcing strategies: (1) strengthening care and support for survivors of gender-based violence, particularly survivors of sexual violence, and (2) engaging communities in collective action to prevent sexual violence.

Facilitating participatory dialogue among stakeholders was the key strategy of the "Communities Care" programme for catalyzing community-led action toward the mitigation of gender-based violence in rural communities. In this process, female and male community members, elders, religious leaders, leaders of camps for internally displaced populations, youth leaders, health workers, police, teachers, students' parents, and school administrators were involved in structured meetings that were held twice a week over the course of 15 weeks to discuss and reflect on core values such as fairness, justice, and equality. After the dialogues, Communities Care supported participants to take action, including (a) working with fathers and husbands on how to support daughters and wives who are survivors of sexual violence; (b) encouraging religious leaders to take a public stance against sexual violence with their congregants; (c) urging local officials to strengthen laws and policies to reduce impunity for perpetrators; (d) supporting girls and boys to access education; and (e) men and boys demonstrating respect for women and girls by participating in household duties.

More than 1000 people participated in "Communities Care" discussions, and more than 42,000 citizens became involved in community action and engagement events in both Somalia and South Sudan. The midline study and preliminary anecdotal and monitoring data suggest that the programme has provided a platform for identifying community-level solutions for use in conflict and post-conflict settings to address individual and collective conflict vulnerabilities and hazards while simultaneously building on their existing capacities as community leaders and activists (Read-Hamilton & Marsh, 2016).

14.4.4 Reconciliation

Societies with histories of conflict endeavoring to engage in processes of economic and social reconstruction incur the risk of conflict relapse should they choose not to address past human rights abuses or other forms of severe trauma (Ramírez-Barat & Duthie, 2015, p. 1). Transitional justice processes that promote accountability and redress for human rights violations present an essential element to prevent recurrence of violations and the integration of victims into communities and societies.

Recognizing that post-conflict development and reconstruction frameworks often ignore the role education plays in legacies of past human rights violations, the International Center for Transitional Justice [ICTJ] in partnership with UNICEF commissioned 17 case studies to determine whether and how education can play a role in a society's formulation of constructive responses to human rights violation histories. The research findings are published in the book *Transitional Justice and Education: Learning Peace* (Ramírez-Barat & Duthie, 2016). The volume documents truth commissions' efforts to illustrate how education has contributed to conflict in the past, as well as efforts to produce and educate the public by sharing transitional justice education materials and tools with schools and universities. The study furthermore contains examples of curriculum reform as well as teacher training and support for "teaching the past," examples of reparations programs that provide redress through educational assistance to victims or their family members, as well as nonformal education projects addressing the legacies of the past. The study concludes that it is possible and in specific contexts feasible to include education sector programming into a societal response to past human rights violations, as long as it is recognized that such processes must be context-specific, risk-informed, conflict-sensitive, consultative, and long-term. Efforts to leverage education for transitional justice processes need to be complemented by broad reforms in other areas, as well as investments in reconstruction and peacebuilding (Ramírez-Barat & Duthie, 2015, 2016).

Supporting reconciliation efforts through a transitional justice lens was attempted by "Learning for Peace" but – apart from the abovementioned research project – with only moderate results. Governments of fragile states are weary and often lack the resilience necessary to withstand the risks and shocks that may emanate from touching on painful memories from the past. Even if a government has come into power with a strong voter mandate, the willingness to acknowledge past injustices and human rights violations always risks the emergence of fissures within institutions and societies which could diminish the positionality of government representatives among stakeholder groups.

Notwithstanding, in Côte d'Ivoire – where political rule nurtured and exploited resentment against ethnic minorities – UNICEF and ICTJ assisted the government in the development of a safe and effective methodology for gathering statements of children and young people witnessing human rights violations. A collaborative link between the commission and the education sector, however, could not be established. UNICEF and ICTJ successfully supported youth platforms organizing truth-telling events within their existing networks and subsequently radio campaigns that highlighted how the politicization of universities and schools directly influenced conflict dynamics in Côte d'Ivoire (Ladisch & Rice, 2016, pp. 368, 372 & 375).

Also in Côte d'Ivoire, a UNICEF/CARITAS kindergarten programme accessible to families from diverse ethnic groups in conflict-affected rural communities succeeded in establishing relationships of trust between mothers from antagonized ethnic groups. A complementary literacy and livelihood project for these mothers provided additional platforms for dialogue and social exchange – first among mothers and later also among fathers, some of whom were active supporters of political parties supporting the conflict on different sides. The programme eventually cemented horizontal social cohesion in 16 conflict-affected villages where there was none previously. This case study is noteworthy because it demonstrates that early childhood development services can be leveraged to strengthen community cohesion, thereby mitigating structural violence which in return has positive implications for stress reduction and early childhood development (Learning for Peace, 2018). Morgan et al. (2014) suspect that the reduction of structural violence is possibly far more relevant for early child protection and peacebuilding and can accomplish far more than early childhood development interventions aiming to buffer the impacts of toxic stress (p. 125).

Many of the earlier mentioned "Learning for Peace" project examples – Myanmar's LESC (LoBianco, 2016), Somalia's youth supporting the development of a new curriculum framework (Renders & Knezevic, 2017), and Somalia's and South Sudan's "Communities Care" project (Read-Hamilton & Marsh, 2016) – succeeded in increasing trust between groups and institutions, however, modestly. While trust-building is a significant component of reconciliation and thus noteworthy, it remains insufficient, however, without the opening of social platforms and the facilitation of acknowledgments of injustices that have occurred in the past.

14.5 Assessing Education for Peacebuilding Interventions

Measuring changes resulting from a peacebuilding program intervention remains challenging as the desired peacebuilding change is often less tangible and long-term. In order to measure the prevention of conflict, for example, one would have to prove the causation of "non-events," e.g., the successful avoidance of something which did not occur (Menkhaus, 2004, p. 5). Chigas, Church, and Corlazzoli (2014) argue that it is:

> "… much easier to make causal linkages in short results chains—e.g., when the number steps or changes between the activities implemented and the impacts is small. The diverse types of activities conducted for peacebuilding—from dialogue and reconciliation programmes to reintegration of ex-combatants, justice, reform, infrastructure, development and livelihoods—do not all work directly on conflict and peace, but rather seek to affect conflict and peace drivers indirectly. Evaluating this impact entails examining an intervention not only in terms of its own objectives, but (also) in terms of actual outcomes as related to key drivers of conflict and peace. This creates longer and more complex causal chains and makes it impossible to make defensible judgements about sole attribution." (p. 6)

In order to assess the association of education services with existing levels of horizontal and vertical social cohesion, UNICEF partnered with Harvard Humanitarian Institute (HHI) in developing and pilot testing an Education, Peacebuilding and Social Cohesion Assessment Framework (EPSC) (Pham & Vinck, 2017; see Fig. 14.3). The Framework has six dimensions: (a) social cohesion; (b) leadership, good governance, and inclusive politics; (c) access to resources and opportunities; (d) the legacies of past conflict; (e) information and communication networks; and (f) justice and security. These dimensions were identified as relevant during scoping assessments in Burundi, DRC, Côte d'Ivoire, and Uganda where different categories of local stakeholders were queried about their understanding and awareness of social cohesion challenges and prerequisites in their own community and regional contexts. The EPSC contains contextualized specific indices to measure cohesion factors such as trust, social relationships, civic and social participation, inclusion, and attitudes toward social services, as well as constructive dispute resolution. Where possible, the EPSC measured the relationships between teachers, parents, students, and community members, as well as social cohesion factors before and after an education intervention (Pham & Vinck, 2017).

Although it is difficult to measure attribution of social service delivery (such as education) to peacebuilding – due to the fluctuation of uncontrolled elements in fragile contexts (i.e., breakout of violent conflict, changes in political regimes, natural disasters, and economic shocks, all of which co-influence causal chains) – the assessments conducted in Burundi, Côte d'Ivoire, DRC, and Uganda demonstrate

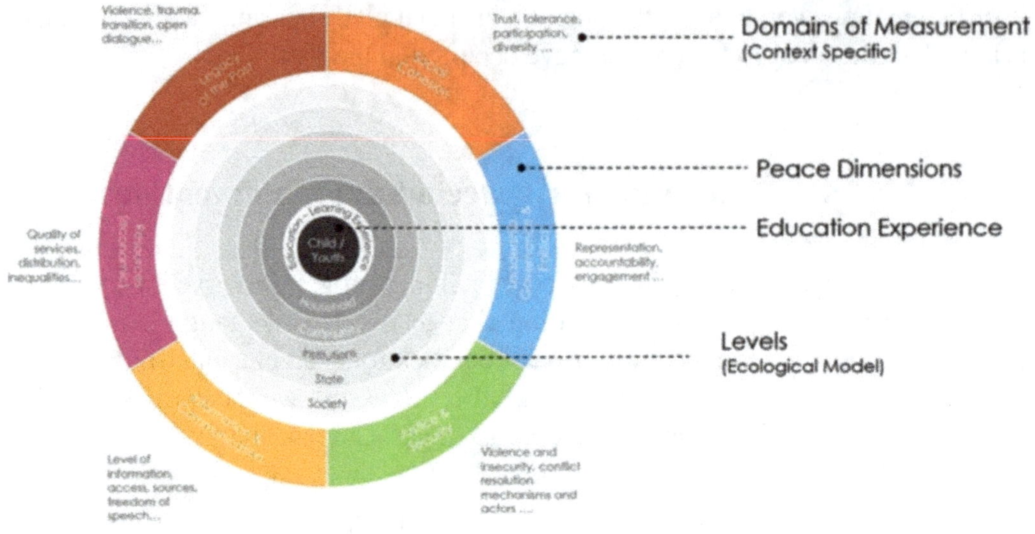

Fig. 14.3 Education, Peacebuilding and Social Cohesion Assessment Framework [EPSC] (Pham & Vinck, 2017, p. 12)

that it is possible to measure and even map an "association" of existing (or non-existing) social service components with varying degrees of social cohesion or a prevalence of conflict factors and to compare these with cohesion and social service statistics in alternative geographies (Pham & Vinck, 2017). The EPSC can serve to assess the degree of stability or fragility of relationships, and to juxtapose this analysis with the availability and quality of social services (such as education but also health, water and hygiene, nutrition, or protection services) in fragile and post-conflict settings. It can be used to determine social integration intervention priorities and to measure changes once an intervention is under implementation or at the end of an implementation phase.

One of the key takeaways from the HHI analyses and other monitoring and evaluation efforts employed by country offices is that the choice of instruments, the analysis process, and the interpretation of the results must include consultations and validation with local actors who can interpret the results, triangulate findings using qualitative data sources, and identify consistencies and inconsistencies based on contextual knowledge. For example, young people in Côte d'Ivoire, Uganda, Sierra Leone, and Burundi were assisted in using participatory video tools for the documentation of their own "Most Significant Change" experiences occurring in times of violent conflict (see InsightShare, 2018a). Together with local facilitators, young people formed evaluation teams and co-designed evaluation processes of youth-led peace and transitional justice efforts in Côte d'Ivoire; sustainable livelihood programmes for youth in Karamoja, Uganda; child-friendly schools and youth-led peace interventions in Sierra Leonean communal conflict settings; and the communication of Ubuntu values among returnees and host community members in Burundi (InsightShare, 2018b).

14.6 Conclusion: Learning for Peace

Prevention of violent conflict remains a critical challenge for progress toward sustainable development for all. Central to this is the need to address grievances around inequities and exclusion from access to power, opportunities, and security (United Nations & World Bank Group, 2018). Within this context, "Learning for Peace" presented an opportunity to better understand the complex relationship between education, conflict, and peace and reflect on possible ways forward on how education and other social services can be leveraged to better contribute to the mitigation of conflict factors.

Four main messages can be highlighted for national governments, education, and research partners moving forward. First, it is critical to prioritize investments in education and other social services before, during, and after conflict. The narrow emphasis on security, financial, and political systems – while necessary – is not sufficient to address the underlying grievances linked to exclusion and social injustice. Social services provide opportunities to begin addressing the underlying causes of conflict and building and sustaining peace. Education, in particular, is a unique vehicle to influence the growing younger generations, their caregivers, and supportive communities to collaboratively build resilient and peaceful societies.

Second, as demonstrated by education-focused conflict analyses conducted through "Learning for Peace," in societies where societal social capital is weakened by crises and violence and where trust and relationships are broken, education does not remain neutral. Education systems, institutions, and programs can either aggravate existing tensions and create new grievances or support rebuilding the social fabric and social capital. It is therefore critical to ensure that education planning and delivery recognizes and responds to the conflict dynamics and in doing so addresses the issues of equity, transparency, quality, and relevance of education services.

Third, "Learning for Peace" has demonstrated across diverse country contexts that children and young people – as well as their families, caregivers, and service providers – are critical partners and agents of change. Children and young people in particular proactively engage in building peaceful communities and can make important contributions to reconciliation and reconstruction processes when presented with participation and engagement opportunities. It is therefore important to expand the participation of the younger generations in peacebuilding efforts and processes and proactively examine how formal and nonformal education can support their agency and capacity for leadership.

Finally, there is a need for continued research and evidence building on the role of education in contributing to social cohesion. While Learning for Peace provided opportunities to develop and test methodological approaches and document select programmatic initiatives and longer-term investments in qualitative and mixed methods, participatory and locally led research is necessary to better understand what contribution education can make toward strengthening resilience and social cohesion of societies within the broader social, political, and economic transformation processes across diverse country contexts.

References

Abadzi, H. (2006, June 20). *Efficient learning for the poor: Insights from the frontier of cognitive neuroscience*. Washington, D.C.: The World Bank. Retrieved from http://documents.worldbank.org/curated/en/438221468134385073/Efficient-learning-for-the-poor-insights-from-the-frontier-of-cognitive-neuroscience

Affolter, F. W. (2004). On the absence of a 'socio-emotional enablement' discourse component in international socio-economic development thought. *Scandinavian Journal for Caring Sciences, 18*, 424–436.

Affolter, F. W. (2005). Socio-emotional enablement and the convention of the rights of the child. *International Journal of Children's Rights, 13*, 378–397.

Black, M., Walker, S. P., Fernald, L. C. H., Anderson, C. T., DiGirolamo, A. G., Lu, C., McCoy, D. M., Fink, G., Shawar, Y. R., Shiffman, J., Devercelli, A. E., Wodon, Q. T., Vargas-Barón, E., Grantham-McGregor, S., & Lancet Early Childhood Development Series Steering Committee (2017, January 7–13). Early childhood development coming of age: Science through the life course. *Lancet*, 389, 77–90.

Blair, A. H., Gerring, N., & Karrim, S. (2016, August). *Ending sexual and gender-based violence in war and peace: Recommendations for the next U.S. administration*. Washington, D.C.: United States Institute of Peace. Retrieved from https://www.usip.org/sites/default/files/PB215-Ending-Sexual-and-Gender-Based-Violence-in-War-and-Peace.pdf

Bush, K. D., & Saltarelli, D. (2000). *The two faces of education in ethnic conflict: Towards a peacebuilding education for children*. Florence, Italy: UNICEF Innocenti. Retrieved from https://www.unicef-irc.org/publications/pdf/insight4.pdf

Chigas, D., Church, M., & Corlazzoli, V. (2014, May). *Evaluating impacts of peacebuilding interventions: Approaches and methods, challenges and considerations*. London, UK: Department for International Development\[DfiD].

Dahl, R., & Suleiman, A. (2017). Adolescent brain development: Windows of opportunity. In N. Balvin & P. Banati (Eds.), *The adolescent brain: A second window of opportunity. A compendium* (pp. 21–28). Florence, Italy: UNICEF Innocenti. Retrieved from https://www.unicef-irc.org/publications/933-the-adolescent-brain-a-second-window-of-opportunity-a-compendium.html

Dawes, A., & van der Merwe, A. (2014). Structural violence and early childhood development. In J. F. Leckman, C. Panter-Brick, & R. Salah (Eds.), *Pathways to peace: The transformative power of children and families* (pp. 233–250). Cambridge, MA: The MIT Press.

El-Bushra, J., & Rees-Smith, E. (2016). Gender, education and peacebuilding. A review of selected 'learning for peace' case studies. Retrieved from https://eccnetwork.net/wp-content/uploads/Gender-Education-and-Peacebuilding-A-Review-of-Learning-for-Peace-Case-Studies.pdf

Government of Sindh. (2014). *Sindh education sector plan 2014-2018*. Karachi, Pakistan: Reform Support Unit, Education and Literacy Department. Retrieved from http://www.sindheducation.gov.pk/Contents/Menu/Final%20SESP.pdf

Human Rights Council. (2016, February 3). Promotion and protection of all human rights, civil, political, economic, social and cultural rights, including the right to development: Thirty-first session agenda item 3. *A/HRC/31/59*. Retrieved from http://undocs.org/A/HRC/31/59

Idris, I. (2016). *Youth unemployment and violence: Rapid literature review*. Birmingham, UK: GSDRC, University of Birmingham. Retrieved from http://gsdrc.org/wp-content/uploads/2016/11/YouthUnemployment_Violence.pdf

InsightShare. (2018a). Resources: Participatory video and most significant change. Retrieved from http://insightshare.org/resources/participatory-video-and-the-most-significant-change/

InsightShare. (2018b). Projects: Evaluating UNICEF peacebuilding programmes in Africa. Retrieved from http://insightshare.org/projects/evaluating-unicef-peacebuilding-programmes-in-africa/

Kirollos, M., Anning, C., Fylkesnes, G. K., & Denselow, J. (2018). *War on children*. London, UK: Save the Children International. Retrieved from https://www.savethechildren.net/waronchildren/pdf/waronchildren.pdf

Ladisch, V., & Rice, J. (2016). Addressing the recent past in schools. Reflections from Côte d'Ivoire. In C. Ramírez-Barat & R. Duthie (Eds.), *Transitional justice and education: Learning peace* (pp. 363–383). New York, NY: International Centre for Transitional Justice [ICTJ]. Retrieved at https://www.ictj.org/our-work/research/education-peacebuilding

Larsen, C. A. (2014). *Social cohesion: Definition, measurement and developments*. Aarlborg, Denmark: Institut for Statskundskab, Aalborg Universitet. Retrieved from http://www.un.org/esa/socdev/egms/docs/2014/LarsenDevelopmentinsocialcohesion.pdf

Learning for Peace. (2018). Conflict analysis. Retrieved from https://eccnetwork.net/resources/learning-for-peace/conflict-analysis/

Leckman, J. F., Panter-Brick, C. & Salah, R. (Eds.) (2014). Pathways to peace: The transformative power of children and families. Cambridge: The MIT Press.

LoBianco, J. (2016). *Language Education and Social Cohesion (LESC) Initiative in Malaysia, Myanmar and Thailand: Synthesis report*. Bangkok, Thailand: UNICEF East Asia and Pacific Regional Office. Retrieved from https://eccnetwork.net/wp-content/uploads/28-Synthesis_Report_Language_Education_andSocial_Cohesion_Initiative.pdf

Lopes Cardozo, M. T. A., Higgins, S., & Le Mat, M. L. J. (2016, February). *Youth agency and peacebuilding: An analysis of the role of formal and non-formal education. Synthesis report on findings from Myanmar, Pakistan, South Africa and Uganda.* Amsterdam, The Netherlands: Research Consortium Education and Peacebuilding, University of Amsterdam. Retrieved from: http://learningforpeace.unicef.org/partners/research-consortium/research-outputs/

McCandless, E. (2012). *Peace dividends and beyond: Contributions of administrative and social services to peacebuilding*. New York, NY: United Nations Peacebuilding Support Office. Retrieved from http://www.un.org/en/peacebuilding/pbso/pdf/peace_dividends.pdf

Menkhaus, K. (2004, July). Impact assessment in post-conflict peacebuilding challenges and future directions. Retrieved from http://3n589z370e6o2eata9wahfl4.wpengine.netdna-cdn.com/wp-content/uploads/2004/07/2004_WSP_Interpeace_Impact_Assessment_In_Post_Conflict_Peacebuilding_EN.pdf

Morgan, B., Sunar, D., Carter, C. S., Leckman, J. F., Fry, D. P., Keverne, E. B., … Olds, D. (2014). Human biological development and peace: Genes, brains, safety, and justice. In J. F. Leckman, C. Panter-Brick, & R. Salah (Eds.), *Pathways to peace: The transformative power of children and families* (pp. 95–128). Cambridge, MA: The MIT Press.

National Scientific Council on the Developing Child. (2005). *Excessive stress disrupts the architecture of the developing brain* (Working Paper No. 3). Cambridge, MA: National Scientific Council on the Developing Child. Retrieved from https://developingchild.harvard.edu/resources/wp3/

Novelli, M., Lopes Cardozo, M. T. A., & Smith, A. (2015, January). *A theoretical framework for analysing the contribution of education to sustainable peacebuilding: 4Rs in conflict-affected contexts.* Amsterdam, Sussex and Ulster: Research Consortium on Education and Peacebuilding and United Nations Children's Fund. Retrieved from http://sro.sussex.ac.uk/58005/

Office of Economic Cooperation and Development [OECD]. (2015). *States of fragility 2015: Meeting post-2015 ambitions*. Paris, France: OECD Publishing.

Omoeva, C., & Buckner, E. (2015, April). *Does horizontal education inequality lead to violent conflict? A global analysis*. Washington, D.C.: FHI360 Global Data Center.

Omoeva, C., Hatch, R., & Moussa, W. (2016). *The effects of armed conflict on educational attainment and inequality*. Washington, D.C.: FHI360 Global Data Center.

Paasonen, K., & Urdal, H. (2016). Youth bulges, exclusion and instability: The role of youth in the Arab Spring. In *Conflict Trends* (Vol. 3). Oslo, Norway: PRIO. Retrieved from https://www.prio.org/utility/DownloadFile.ashx?id=10&type=publicationfile

Pham, P. N., & Vinck, P. (2017, January). *Assessment framework for peacebuilding, education and social cohesion.* Cambridge: Harvard Humanitarian Initiative. Retrieved from https://eccnetwork.net/wp-content/uploads/19-Social-Cohesion-Assessmen-Framework_20170420-HHI.pdf

Punamäki, R. (2014). Mental health and development among children living in violent conditions: Underlying processes for promoting peace. In J. F. Leckman, C. Panter-Brick, & R. Salah (Eds.), *Pathways to peace: The transformative power of children and families* (pp. 213–231). Cambridge, MA: The MIT Press.

Ramírez-Barat, C., & Duthie, R. (2015, November). *Education and transitional justice: Opportunities and challenges for peacebuilding*. New York: International Centre for Transitional Justice [ICTJ]. Retrieved from https://www.ictj.org/sites/default/files/ICTJ-UNICEF-Report-EducationTJ-2015.pdf

Ramírez-Barat, C., & Duthie, R. (Eds.). (2016). *Education and transitional justice: Learning peace*. New York, NY: International Centre for Transitional Justice [ICTJ]. Retrieved from https://www.ictj.org/sites/default/files/ICTJ-UNICEF-Report-EducationTJ-2015.pdf

Read-Hamilton, S., & Marsh, M. (2016). The communities care programme: Changing social norms to end violence against women and girls in conflict-affected communities. *Gender and Development, 24*(2), 261–276. Available online at http://preventgbvafrica.org/wp-content/uploads/2016/07/The-Communities-Care-Programme-Changing Social-Norms-to-End-Violence-against-Women-and-Girls-in-Conflict-Affected-Communities.pdf

Renders, M., & Knezevic, N. (2017). The potential of conflict-sensitive education approaches in fragile countries: The case of curriculum framework reform and youth civic participation in Somalia. *Journal on Education in Emergencies, 3*(1), 106–128. Retrieved from https://archive.nyu.edu/bitstream/2451/39661/2/JEiE%20V3%20_%20Potential_CSE_Fragile_Countries.Jul%2017.pdf

République de Côte d'Ivoire - Ministère de l'Education Nationale. (2017, April). Plan sectoriel education/formation 2016 – 2025. Retrieved from https://www.globalpartnership.org/fr/content/plan-sectoriel-de-leducation-cote-divoire

République Démocratique du Congo. (2014, December). *Rapport d'état du système éducatif national: Pour une éducation au service de la croissance et de la paix*. Kinshasa: UNICEF, UNESCO - IIEP Pôle de Dakar. Retrieved from http://unesdoc.unesco.org/images/0023/002326/232623f.pdf

Richter, L. M., Lye, S. J., & Proulx, K. (2018). Nurturing care for young children under conditions of fragility and conflict. In J. F. Leckman & P. Britto (Eds.), *Towards a more peaceful world: The promise of early childhood development programmes. New directions for child and adolescent development* (Vol. 159, pp. 13–26). San Francisco, CA: Jossey-Bass.

Scott-Villiers, P., Wilson, S., Molu Kullu, K., Ndung'u, D., & Scott-Villiers, A. (2015). *A study of education and resilience in Kenya's arid and semi-arid lands: Final report*. Nairobi, Kenya: UNICEF UNICEF Eastern and Southern Africa Regional Office (ESARO).

Smith, A., Marks, C., Novelli, M., Valiente, O., & Scandurra, R. (2016, April). *Exploring the linkages between education sector governance, inequity, conflict, and peacebuilding in Kenya: Research report prepared for UNICEF Eastern and Southern Regional Office (ESARO)*. Nairobi: UNICEF Eastern and Southern Africa Regional Office. Retrieved from https://eccnetwork.net/wp-content/uploads/10-Equity-Education-Peacebuilding-Governance-Kenya.pdf

Staub, E. (2003). Basic human needs and their role in altruism and aggression. In E. Staub (Ed.), *The psychology of good and evil: Why children, adults and groups help and harm others* (pp. 52–67). New York, NY: Cambridge University Press.

Staub, E. (2011). *Overcoming evil: Genocide, violent conflict, and terrorism*. Oxford, MI: Oxford University Press.

UNICEF (2015a, November). Evaluation of UNICEF's Peacebuilding, Education and Advocacy Programme (PBEA). Summary. New York: UNICEF. Retrieved from https://eccnetwork.net/wp-content/uploads/Final-Learning-for-Peace-Evaluation-Summary.pdf

UNICEF. (2015b, December 17). *Press release: More than 16 million babies born into conflict this year*. New York, NY: UNICEF. Retrieved from https://www.unicef.org/media/media_86560.html

UNICEF. (2016a). *Peacebuilding, education and advocacy in conflict-affected contexts programme (PBEA): 2012–2016 programme report*. Retrieved from https://eccnetwork.net/wp-content/uploads/02-UNICEF1020_PBEA-Final-report-A4_web.pdf

UNICEF. (2016b). *Gender, education and peacebuilding brief: Emerging issues from 'Learning for Peace'*. Retrieved from https://eccnetwork.net/wp-content/uploads/PBEA-Gender_Advocacy-brief.pdf

UNICEF. (2016c, November). *Conflict sensitivity and peacebuilding: Programming guide.* Retrieved from https://eccnetwork.net/wp-content/uploads/05-Programming-Guide-Conflict-Sensitivity-and-Peacebuilding-UNICEF-Nov-2016.pdf

UNICEF. (2018). *Learning for peace narratives from the field. A compendium of programme strategies 2012/2016.* New York, NY: UNICEF. Retrieved from https://eccnetwork.net/wp-content/uploads/PBEA-case-study-compendium-online-final.pdf

UNICEF Burundi. (2016). Peacebuilding, education and advocacy in conflict-affected contexts programme: Programme report. Unpublished document.

UNICEF Pakistan. (2016). Peacebuilding, education and advocacy in conflict-affected contexts programme: Programme report. Unpublished document.

UNICEF Uganda. (2016). Peacebuilding, education and advocacy in conflict-affected contexts Programme: Programme report. Unpublished document.

United Nations. (2015). *Transforming our world: The 2030 agenda for sustainable development. A/RES/70/1.* New York, NY: United Nations. Retrieved from http://www.un.org/en/development/desa/population/migration/generalassembly/docs/globalcompact/A_RES_70_1_E.pdf

United Nations & World Bank Group. (2017). *Pathways for peace: Inclusive approaches to preventing violent conflict. Main messages and emerging policy directions.* Washington, D.C.: International Bank for Reconstruction and Development/The World Bank. Available online at https://www.openknowledge.worldbank.org/bitstream/handle/10986/28337/211162mm.pdf?sequence=2&isAllowed=y

United Nations & World Bank Group. (2018). *Pathways for peace: Inclusive approaches to preventing violent conflict.* Washington, D.C.: International Bank for Reconstruction and Development/The World Bank. Available online at https://openknowledge.worldbank.org/handle/10986/28337

United Nations General Assembly. (1989, November 20). *Convention on the rights of the child. A/RES/44/25.* New York: United Nations. Retrieved from http://www.un.org/documents/ga/res/44/a44r025.htm

United Nations General Assembly. (2016, February 3). *Report of the special rapporteur in the field of cultural rights. A/HRC/31/59.* Retrieved from http://undocs.org/A/HRC/31/59

United Nations General Assembly & United Nations Security Council (2015, June 30): Challenge of sustaining peace: Report of the advisory group of experts on the review of the peacebuilding architecture. *A/69/968 S/2015/490.* Retrieved from http://www.un.org/ga/search/view_doc.asp?symbol=A/69/968

United Nations Security Council. (2015, December 9). Resolution 2250 (2015). Adopted by the Security Council at its 7573rd meeting, on 9 December 2015. *S/RES/2250 (*2015*).* Retrieved from http://undocs.org/S/RES/2250(2015)

United Nations Security Council. (2018a, June 6). Resolution 2419 (2018). Adopted by the Security Council at its 8277the meeting on 6 June 2018. *S/RES/2418 (2018).* Available online at: http://undocs.org/S/RES/2419(2018)

United Nations Security Council. (2018b, July 9). Resolution 2427 (2018). Adopted by the Security Council at its 8305th meeting, on 9 July 2018. *S/RES/2427 (2018).* Retrieved from http://undocs.org/S/RES/2427(2018)

United Nations Women's Organization. (2015). *Preventing conflict, transforming justice, securing the peace: A global study on the implementation of United Nations security council resolution 1325.* New York, NY: UN Women. Retrieved from http://www.unwomen.org/~/media/files/un%20women/wps/highlights/unw-global-study-1325-2015.pdf

von Joeden-Forgey, E. (2016). Gender, sexualized violence and prevention. In S. P. Rosenberg, T. Galis, & A. Zucker (Eds.), *Reconstructing atrocity prevention* (pp. 125–148). New York, NY: Cambridge University Press.

World Bank Group. (2011). *World development report 2011: Conflict, security and development.* Washington, D.C.: International Bank for Reconstruction and Development.

World Economic Forum. (2018). *The global risks report 2018.* (13th ed.). Retrieved from http://www3.weforum.org/docs/WEF_GRR18_Report.pdf

Chapter 15
Educating Toward a Culture of Peace Through an Innovative Teaching Method

Silvia Guetta

15.1 Introduction to the Education Program

This chapter presents a peace education program carried out with more than 70 students in a high school in Florence, Italy, during the 2016–2017 school year. Educational activities were conducted outside the school environment and hours. Nevertheless, they were part of the curriculum and previously agreed upon with the school teachers. Liaisons for the project were the Florence UNESCO Center[1] and the Chair of Pedagogy for Conflict Management of the Department of Education and Psychology of the University of Florence. The main objectives of the program were to conduct research into the meaning of peace and to promote cultural diversity in accordance with the principles and the values endorsed by UNESCO. Therefore, we chose to follow the Peace Education Program of Prem Rawat Foundation (FPEP).

To outline the context of the program, this chapter will first present relevant models of peace education, briefly discussing the importance attributed to this type of education by the school system through which the activities took place. The education program was implemented by the school as part of their efforts to reduce the escalation of violent behaviors. It was considered an opportunity to make students take responsibility for their actions through a focus on dialogue, which is seen as a relational tool enabling the creation of a bond between personal, worldview, feelings, life plans, creativity, and individual resources. Moreover, there was a need for students to discover and understand language and behaviors related to a non-violent style of communication (Rosenberg, 1998) and to open new horizons of meaning in terms of interpersonal, intrapersonal, and intergroup relationships. The program was designed to help students explore their own and others' social and communi-

[1] www.centrounescofi.it

S. Guetta (✉)
University of Florence, Florence, Italy
e-mail: silvia.guetta@unifi.it

N. Balvin, D. J. Christie (eds.), *Children and Peace*, Peace Psychology Book Series, https://doi.org/10.1007/978-3-030-22176-8_15

cation skills and through this to discover a new lexicon and vocabulary for communicating.

The educational goals included development of a more complex perception of actions and behaviors seen in school and outside; discovery of students' innate resources such as hope, choice, and appreciation[2]; and decentering one's thoughts and emotions in order to address problems from other people's perspectives. The reflection on the circularity of one's own feelings, thoughts, and behaviors, and the capacity to view everyday problems in a positive, empathic, and creative way, was expected to help students learn to be less reactive and more proactive.

The description and explanation presented here will help readers understand how the peace education program developed by the Prem Rawat Foundation was adapted to this target audience of students and how values of cultural diversity recommended by UNESCO were integrated. Furthermore, it will clarify how students were encouraged to initiate an inner dialogue and the process of self-discovery in order to improve their sense of well-being and their relationships with others.

In this brief exposition, the author analyzes various aspects of the program and its impact. First, she considers how this contribution advances UNESCO's recommendation to foster development of a culture of peace. Second, she explains the methodological approaches used in the project. Third, she details the monitoring and evaluation criteria used to assess achievement of the educational goals, and finally, she discusses whether the students considered the experience to be truly life-changing and educational.

It should be clarified that the training pathway to peace developed in this project was part of a wider educational campaign. The project involved three target groups: 70 high school students, about 200 university students from 2 different academic programs, and about 30 teachers working in various fields and in different school grades throughout Tuscany, Italy. It was an ambitious project, supervised by the author. The program was meant to promote education for citizenship, which was considered important by Florentine politicians as part of the international event "UnityinDiversity.[3]" The contents, workshop approach, and most of the methodologies were shared by the three target groups. Locations, facilitators, and timetables were scheduled according to the training needs of the groups. The contents of the course, adapted from "Prem Rawat's Peace Education Program,"[4] was organized into ten modules, which through the use of videos, readings, and a workbook investigate the ten keywords for peace: peace, appreciation, inner strength, self-awareness, clarity, ability to understand, dignity, choice, hope, and happiness.

Three trainees with previous knowledge of the topic led activities for the high school students. The training program lasted a total of 24 hours, delivered in 2-hour meetings twice a week. The workshops took place in a social co-op with long-term

---

[2] Prem Rawat, https://www.tprf.org/wp-content/uploads/.../getting_started.pdf

[3] UnityinDiversity 2016 http://www.unityindiversity.it/conference/program; https://www.youtube.com/watch?v=4953Ilt62U8&t=0s&index=23&list=PLQwEJh6E8bRQkn7iDNcgurRL31FGrrgJY

[4] https://www.tprf.org/programs/peace-education-program/

experience in the social inclusion of people with disabilities and people from other countries and backgrounds. The education program concluded with two public events, the first organized by the university and the second held in the offices of the Municipality of Florence. The goal of the first event was to present and discuss the results of the program in terms of educational gains and outcomes realized by the three target groups. The second event was a meeting open to the public and local and national governmental authorities at which the results were presented and recommendations of best practices for peace education were made.

15.2 Peace Education in Italy: An Overview

It was only in the mid-1940s, after the catastrophe of World War II, that several Italian education specialists began wondering about the necessity of schools promoting peace education. Maria Montessori (1949) was the first to incorporate peace education into her educational activities. She based her approach on the observation that societies invest resources, time, money, research, and relationships into educating for war and conflict, even though wars do not bring wealth, success, growth, or happiness. Despite widespread awareness of this, people have not been able to abandon educational models that convey knowledge through coercion, punishment, marginalization, and discrimination.

According to Montessori, "education is the weapon of peace, which will forge men and women of peace" (Montessori, 1949, p. 43). In Italy, awareness of the necessity of a real and tangible commitment to a future based on coexistence, respect for human rights, and dialogue dates back to the 1950s and 1960s, when people not directly involved in the educational field, but associated with various disciplinary sectors, began questioning and engaging in a search to determine the deficiencies of the educational models of the time. They determined that these models were not promoting students' independence, active learning, autonomy, self-determination, or freedom of speech. Between the 1960s and 1980s, many intellectuals delivered speeches and lectures and published books and articles in order to raise awareness and influence public opinion – especially among people working in the educational field –about the importance of education based on cooperation, non-violence, and human rights. Yet, for many years, their arguments were largely ignored. The general public began recognizing the importance of peace education only toward the end of the 1990s, when Italy faced a perceived social and cultural emergency due to immigration, and political control of internal violence was achieved.

It is not possible to cover the conspicuous contributions of all of those who, in a variety of ways, outlined the educational pathways aimed at creating individuals capable of respecting human rights, avoiding all forms of violence and social or cultural oppression, and rejecting military ideals. Until recently, these contributions, while made by important and enlightened intellectuals, were exclusively expressions of the male world. Women's voices were not heard until the twenty-first century.

Peace, as the opposition to the consequence of war, has been managed by men. The syllogism was that because who go to war assume a man's duty, and implicitly their social mandate, to make peace. A reflection on the connection between peace education and gender issues remains an almost unexplored research field today. The reference models and theories are linked to a negative understanding of peace; the idea that defense and safety can be achieved only through the use of weapons is still widespread. History is the only field in which research on women's positions, attitudes, and awareness regarding wars and reconstruction processes has been well-developed. In any case, pacifist positions, and social and cultural engagements, in which women gather and support channels of dialogue and participation, have not been acknowledged to the same extent as the ones supported by male intellectuals (Bartoloni, 2017). Generally speaking, there is a parallel between the scant regard paid to women's efforts to support non-violence and to oppose war and the lack of acknowledgment of their commitment and noble resistance.

Among those who raised their voices against injustice, inequality, discrimination, exclusion, and poverty, three examples stand out: Lorenzo Milani (1923–1967), Danilo Dolci (1924–1997), and Alberto L'Abate (1931–2017). Lorenzo Milani was one of the most unusual personalities of the Catholic world. Opposed to any kind of hierarchy, which he considered meaningless and rife with abuse and oppression, he was the first intellectual to launch a debate regarding obedience, military service, and the methods used by the school system that educate students to exclude the poor and the social outcasts, rather than helping them. As a punishment for his outspokenness, Milani was forced to leave the city and was assigned to a remote school in the Tuscan hills of the Mugello area. There, he demonstrated how belief in freedom, respect for human dignity, and the right to education were the real cornerstones of knowledge that could foster emancipation. Milani established the famous popular School of Barbiana. He believed that being good men was more important than being good Christians. To him, being good men meant walking with dignity in the world, having culture, professionalism, and, especially, awareness (Milani, 1967). The school created by Milani was a real workshop of education for non-violence, in that it represented an absence of violence (Panerai, Vitaioli, & Nicola, 2012). Like Freire (1971), Milani addressed his educational work to the members of the lower-working class, in order to make them aware of their condition and of the possibility for change. He acted as a consciousness-shaping agent, creating a context that made it possible to experiment with a variety of interpersonal relationships in which the ruler-ruled hierarchy was questioned and deconstructed. He did not view the rural and mountain cultures as expressing a lower or marginalized form of knowledge. An overview of Milani's ideas, modeled on the daily educational and school experiences of the popular School of Barbiana, is outlined in the pages of two important works: *Pastoral experiences* (1958) and *Letter to a teacher* (1967).

Danilo Dolci developed Gandhi's ideas and actions of non-violence. Dolci outlined an active method of peace education: the reciprocal maieutic approach. Known as the Sicilian Gandhi, he developed his educational method inside a generic program, whose pillars were non-violent direct action to raise public awareness, such as fasting, parades, committees, protests, and popular self-analysis sessions. Dolci did not consider peace as the absence of conflict, but rather as the "capacity of renewing, building, fighting, winning in an innovative way: it is health, fullness of life [...] a different approach to life" (Dolci, 1972, p. 84).

Dolci's method is suitable for adults or children and can be used in schools and in non-formal education programs. It is based on Socratic philosophy, which focuses on stimulating learners and helping them reach their full potential. The setting is a dialogue-based workshop, in which creativity, problem-solving, and awareness of one's own knowledge are encouraged. During this dialectic educational experience, the role of the researcher/facilitator/mediator is to support the improvement of knowledge and skills of every member of the group. The goal is to develop a participatory means of defining solutions to social, economic, and environmental problems caused by violence and policies of exclusion[5] and to create a maieutic process to shape a society based on dialogue (Galeazzi, 1992).[6]

Over the years, it has become clear that only a study of the causes of wars and of the conditions for peace, supported by an accurate interdisciplinary investigation, can provide ideas, tools, and concepts necessary to train professional educators and peace operators (Panerai, Vitaioli, & Nicola, 2012). As L'Abate said, "research helps to increase our knowledge and evaluate our acts; training helps to get prepared for new tasks that might arise from research work and action helps to push forward those steps considered necessary to modify or improve the current situation" (L'Abate, 2001, p. 49). Alberto L'Abate disseminated his passion for peace to multiple generations of students through technical work, field research, and action in times of crisis and armed conflict. L'Abate strongly believed that violence is a cultural superstructure and that economies would benefit from funding and promoting peace. For this reason, he strove to reveal the political interests fostering injustices and destruction. L'Abate first introduced to Italy Galtung's ideas, research, and commitment to non-violence (Galtung, 1996). A pioneer of peace studies in Italy, L'Abate and his colleagues from various disciplines designed an original and innovative study course. In 2001, along with Giovanna Guerrieri, he founded the degree course in "Peace Operators." The course was a cooperative effort between the departments of sociology, pedagogy, medicine, and political sciences. His courses on peace research methodology illuminate the bond between theory and practice, research and intervention, and how they can support peace studies. Connecting theory and practice allows one to go beyond the abstract nature of theory, giving birth to a revolutionary and non-violent reality. He believed that the first step toward successful change was deconstructing cultural models that passively operate within

[5]Danilo Dolci's experience took place in Sicily, where he has close social bonds, especially with the disadvantaged and oppressed populations marginalized by society. Studying the ways in which people could change social, economic, and political conditions of that area in order to drive changes from the bottom, by working on people's potentiality for a democratic and social redeeming, can be considered as one of the best paths to follow if we wish to educate to peace.

[6]Many contributions paved the way to new possibilities of interpreting peace education in the 1960s and 1970s. It is not possible to mention here the copious authors that have worked and written on this theme. For further information, see Panerai, Vitaioli, and Nicola (2012) and Galeazzi (1992).

us and that we often unconsciously convey in our interpersonal relationships. For him, real revolution occurs first inside people and only afterward in social structures. All of this will be a reference point for the development of professionals working in various international peace-related fields and contexts.

15.2.1 Proposals for Peace Education

Beginning in the 1990s, the main social issues in Italian schools concerned the field of intercultural education. Scholars in the field of education and teachers in compulsory schools (for students aged 5–16) have focused on the creation of innovative educational practices, such as the inclusion of migrant children, teaching the Italian language to foreign students, ensuring educational success to those coming from other educational environments, and respecting diverse traditions, knowledge, and habits.

New fields of study regarding relationships in schools have been explored, such as tolerance, cultural integration, and inclusion. The proposal for intercultural education, which began with the inclusion of migrant children, addresses the way people deal with the "other" and those who are different, leading to a more positive image of the foreigner. In the past, foreigners were seen as needy, coming from disadvantaged, exploited areas plagued by poverty and wars. Education has encouraged a more compensative pedagogy, promoting cultural differences as an opportunity for gaining broader knowledge of the world.

Moreover, Italian pedagogy has created its own model of intercultural education from practical experience in schools. The theoretical reflection based on research, investigation, and projects came out clearly only at the end of the 1990s. At first, the presence of foreign children in schools was considered a social emergency. In particular, three socio-educational issues required a prompt solution: the migration of people from geographically, socially, and culturally different areas; a resurgence of racism and xenophobia leading to exclusion and violence; and the crisis of the models of democratization that appeared after the fall of the Berlin Wall (1989).

In the 1990s, philosophers, education specialists, anthropologists, psychologists, and intellectuals from various fields (Cambi, 2001) introduced a pedagogical paradigm of difference, addressing different types of diversity, including disability, ethnicity, culture, and gender. Recent decades have witnessed a debate on difference, starting with gender-based difference. This has allowed people to rethink education, sciences, and pedagogy, by organizing and considering education programs that address diversity. The new sociocultural mosaic outlines an "affirmation of the difference as structure and value of education in the contemporary world [that] implies the construction of a new model of *subject*, a new idea of *culture* and, finally, the theorization of a different kind of *society*. Elements characterized by structures/programs and tasks that differ from those elaborated during the historical period ruled by identity" (Cambi, 2001, p. 53).

At the beginning of the millennium, the new pedagogical issues stimulated by the debate on intercultural education partially merged into peace education. This involved the search for participatory and cooperative teaching methods that enable the creation of an inclusive learning environment. Methodological approaches, such as cooperative learning, peer education, and participatory action research, support the deconstruction of educational perspectives based on the control-based, asymmetrical relationship between teacher and student. They encourage the discovery of learning processes based on awareness, relational interdependence, self-help, and overcoming of obstacles due to linguistic differences. The relationship between native languages and teaching and learning the Italian language has been one of the primary fields of research and experimentation since Italian schools became more multicultural.

It is important to mention that in some settings, experiments have been undertaken to create experiences of active citizenship and awareness about the system of legal rights, which offer educational paths based on the reciprocal maieutic approach (Pazzi, 2018). Their goal is to provide knowledge in mediation, management, and resolution of conflicts (Novara, 2011; Sclavi, 2007).

In the last decade, a new socio-educational emergency has emerged, characterized by an increase in violence inside and outside of schools. There are numerous social and cultural causes behind these episodes, including poverty, exclusion, transmission of violent educational models, the search for simple and immediate solutions to complex and deep problems, disintegration of the social network of solidarity and ethical responsibility, and the loss of shared community values. These events have reiterated a purely "school-based" need for peace education.

Over the last few years, schools have tried various ways to address this crisis. In 2017, the Italian Ministry of Education has published the *Guidelines for peace education and glocal citizenship.*[7] The opening title of the document "Peace can be taught and learned" demonstrates how little attention is allotted to the vital maieutic dimension of feeling and experiencing peace as a life opportunity, a flourishing condition, and a personal pursuit which all people desire for themselves and their loved ones. The document clarifies that this is not a new subject or teaching area, since peace education has to be considered as "the integrating background of the whole educational process" (Italian Ministry of Education, 2017, p. 18).

This does not mean that since "everything is peace," we should not do anything differently. Peace, and especially the experience of its absence, pushes us to constantly rethink our state of mind and our teaching style (Italian Ministry of Education, 2017, p. 16). Following the perspective of *positive peace*, the guidelines state "Educating about peace means learning to live together in peace, without wars or violence, constantly promoting the respect of dignity and of every person's fundamental rights, acknowledging and appreciating differences. For these reasons, peace education covers every area of education, links them and integrates them in a constructive way" (Italian Ministry of Education, 2017, p. 16).

---

[7] Guidelines for peace education and glocal citizenship http://www.miur.gov.it; http://istruzione.umbria.it/news2017/miur/pace/LineeGuidaPaceCittadinanza.pdf

Due to the need to constrain violence in schools, there is a movement to include in the school curricula themes related to conflicts and their management, rather than their prevention. This necessitates definition of the skills required to educate individuals who live in areas of conflict, so they can prevent conflicts from becoming situations of extreme violence. Conflicts may be considered an important relational experience, since they enable people to experiment and learn verbal and nonverbal communication strategies to save a relationship between stakeholders with different goals and to find solutions to problems.

As a result of the increase of educational contributions related to understanding the evolving nature of conflicts and possible ways to mediate and manage them, a new teaching perspective has developed. This has enabled a deeper understanding of teachers' interdisciplinary and transdisciplinary perspectives but is often criticized and inaccurately portrayed in the media for its assumed fragmentation of learning and knowledge.

15.3 Peace and Peer Education: A Proposal

In view of all this, the author and her collaborators organized round table meetings with local associations, schools, and the University of Florence. There was a demonstrated need for a training program targeting high school students that provided them with the tools to express, understand, and interpret their needs and knowledge and helped them discover how to recast their needs to achieve more peaceful relationships by using appropriate language, emotions, and cooperative planning. The contribution made by theoretical reflection and new methodological approaches underlines the necessity of peace- and person-centered educational planning choices. The emphasis is on how change in thoughts, feelings, lifestyle and behavior spring from the self, rather than from external actions. The proposal advocates taking responsibility, an obligation which teenagers seldom have the chance to explore in an enriching and constructive way.

School and training programs in general tend to be based on external behavioral and communicative factors. Little room is left for investigating the inner driving force that pushes people to activate peaceful practices or actions. In this context, both the reciprocal maieutic approach and the routes toward inner peace based on Gandhi's model (Pontara, 1996) prove useful. The quest for inner peace promoted by Prem Rawat's model is appropriate for students, as it provides them with an effective yet complex path to peace rather than violence. This choice starts within oneself, the awareness of and responsibility for our actions that puts our perceptions and feelings into practice. The pathway to peace education is outlined through a search for inner peace using the key concepts suggested by Prem Rawat.[8]

Working with students aged 15–16 requires exploring patterns of reciprocal exchange and points of view. Dialogue with young people underlines their need to

[8] Rawat, PEP facilitator

find ways to protect themselves and not let the overwhelming violence in the media affect them and create a sense of disempowerment or loss of empathy. Building inner peace helps individuals identify their strengths, build a solid foundation, and avoid surrendering to those who provide quick solutions. Choosing inner awareness requires patience, empathy, and sharing and is challenged by current events and people who consider caring an outlook that cares for all humankind to be pointless.

Developing inner peace becomes a way to increase personal well-being. This kind of program helps young people realize they are increasingly responsible for their own well-being and success. Teenagers' needs for freedom, independence, and autonomy in making life-choices enhance this process. To gain an accurate idea of the described program, it is important to understand that the educational project to increase self-awareness embraces educational innovations promoted by the Italian law *La Buona Scuola* of July 13, 2015, Nr. 107.[9] Of particular relevance are the regulations outlining the compulsory design of schoolwork programs during the last 3 years of high school. Similar programs should be created based on agreements between schools and other entities (companies, firms, associations) in which students will carry out their training. Schoolwork programs can be valuable training opportunities for students, because they increase students' knowledge and shape their values, self-esteem, self-confidence, and motivation to learn. Relational and communicative relationships outside school enable them to experience previously unexplored personal skills. Schoolwork programs also provide important paths toward social inclusion for migrant students, enabling them to experience different kinds of relationships and acceptance from what they experience at school. These programs might also be positive for students at risk of leaving school early, since new relational and training opportunities encourage them to use more problem-solving techniques and in a more determined way. It also pushes them to explore creative solutions, establish mediation and negotiation procedures, and be decision-makers. In other words, it helps them to become more capable of making choices, even with only partial information, thus developing their self-esteem.[10]

15.3.1 Context and Contents of the Education Program Aimed at Peace and Cultural Diversity

The schoolwork program, *The value of cultural diversity as a key asset for human development towards a culture of peace among citizens*, is part of the regulatory framework outlined by *Buona Scuola* (whose name is translated as "good school"). Moreover, it stems from the increased interest in cross-cultural issues and conflict management in schools.

[9] https://labuonascuola.gov.it/ articles 33 to 43.

[10] Ibidem

The training program was carried out during the 2016/2017 academic year. It involved over 70 students from the Machiavelli Capponi Language High School of Florence. For the sake of adapting to the school guidelines and regulations concerning the schoolwork alternation activities, the number and length of meetings were reduced. Therefore, in line with Prem Rawat's PEP-2,[11] 12 2-hour-long workshops were designed. Each session lasted about 35 minutes and featured introductory videos. This change was made to make the program more suitable to an audience of all ages, including young people. This program is highly recommended for people who find it hard to concentrate for long periods of time and who are being introduced to these issues for the first time.[12]

In line with the PEP handbook, the activities include videos that present the topic, further readings, and the use of a notebook in which participants are encouraged to write down their thoughts, perceptions, moods, and inner experiences that are being explored. The material presented does not include any specific cultural or religious content. The thoughts and emotions that are stimulated, made explicit, and discussed allow each participant to understand how he or she feels and acts regarding peace and core life values. This process recognizes that people are diverse but the search for meaning in life is universal.

Prem Rawat says that within each one of us lies a natural tendency to be satisfied: "Within all people lies an inherent thirst to be content" (Rawat, 2015, p. 11). Despite being a deeply personal and intimate message, this is the basis for global peace. The idea that the culture of peace comes primarily from within ourselves is crucial in the speeches of Prem Rawat. However, there are several references to a highly conflicted, external social dimension, which affects the inner personal dimension. The macro dimension is represented by conflicts between people and nations. An intermediate dimension is generated in intergroup and interpersonal scenarios. The micro dimension is the conflict that arises within an individual. This is the most important conflict, as it triggers a chain reaction that leads to conflicts on the other two levels (Rawat, 2015). According to Rawat, individual responsibility is an opportunity to practice inner peace, as well as to defuse this process and create peace around ourselves.

In the videos, Prem Rawat does not diversify the content according to the environment or the audience. Prem Rawat starts from the assumption that humans are not very different from each other. Therefore, this universal message will be interpreted according to the meanings specific to each recipient. As Rawat says, building a moral base that supports peace cannot come from outside; it must come from a

[11] Http://it.theypi.net/prem-rawat.php. The aim of the Peace Education Program (PEP) is to help participants discover their own inner resources: innate instruments allowing for a better life, such as fortitude, the ability to choose, hope, and the possibility of attaining personal peace. The educational program includes ten videos, each focusing on a specific topic. This material made it possible to design individual academic modules or interactive and customized seminars for different types of participants. The topics are based on excerpts from speeches given by Prem Rawat around the world including peace, appreciation, inner strength, self-awareness, clarity, ability to understand, dignity, choice, hope, and happiness.

[12] https://www.tprf.org/programs/peace-education-program/

moral unity, shared by all human beings, that comes from listening to oneself through the so-called breath of life. Inner peace can be found in any life situation, even in the most extreme ones, such as prisons or armed conflicts. This fosters the hope that, despite living in a world threatened by weapons that could destroy us all in a matter of seconds, there is solidarity and the awareness of belonging to the same species (Balducci, 1985). All this brings us to consider a planetary perspective and a new form of humanism: *planetary humanism* (Orefice, 2003). It involves the recognition that, despite differences, we share a potential precisely because we all belong to the same species. Therefore, the first thing to do is to nourish the peace in our hearts.

From this perspective, it becomes easy to understand how every human has the right to experience peace, although in our culture this is far from obvious. Considering peace as a human right opens up areas for research and analysis on the issues of rights, duties, responsibilities, and actions. These are important learning goals for young people, who are invited to elaborate on the considerations discussed in the workshops by contextualizing the definitions through interdisciplinary sources. For example, the principle that peace is a right is linked to Article 28 of the Universal Declaration of Human Rights (United Nations, 1948), which establishes that "Everyone has the right to social and international order, one that allows the rights and freedoms stated in this Declaration to be fully realized".[13] The article does not explicitly address peace as a right, but it requires states to commit themselves to promoting the appropriate conditions, thus renouncing to the right to wage war through disarmament, educating to respect rights, establishing a Civil Peace Service, and not obtaining atomic bombs or hosting foreign military bases. In addition, UN Resolution 33/73 (1978)[14] codifies the "right of an individual to live in peace" (Milanese, 1992). In 1984, Resolution 39/11[15] (the Declaration on the Right of Peoples to Peace), with a simple text, declared the "sacred right to peace of every individual and people."

In recent years, the UN Human Rights Council has adopted the *Promotion of the right to peace* (2015) resolution, which reiterates the concept by stating that peace is a "universal, indivisible, interdependent and interrelated" right, which takes place without any kind of discrimination.

15.3.2 Cooperation in Education and Learning by Doing

After clarifying the rationale and general structure of the project, we now look at how the work was organized, the original aspects of the experience, how the program was assessed, and the strengths and weakness that emerged. As mentioned above, it was in our interest to integrate the educational models of peer education

[13] http://www.ohchr.org/EN/UDHR/Pages/Language.aspx?LangID=itn

[14] http://www.un.org/documents/ga/res/33/ares33r73.pdf

[15] http://www.ohchr.org/EN/ProfessionalInterest/Pages/RightOfPeoplesToPeace.aspx

and the educational maieutic method with the inputs and the instruments developed by Prem Rawat.

A diverse work group was created to organize the student workshops and included the author, a representative of the Prem Rawat Foundation, a PhD student, four interns, and three undergraduate students from the course for professional educators. The entire group participated in the activities prior to the completion of the course,[16] carefully studied the materials, took part in training, and joined discussions about the content. A self-training path contributed to making the group more cohesive and interdependent and enabled the design of activities that were engaging and empathetic. The group posed hypotheses about the doubts and questions the students might have and offered solutions for critical cases students might identify. It also adapted the program to the needs, motivations, and learning pace of the younger participants. Awareness of the care given to the working group was instrumental in the success of the meetings with the students. This, in turn, helped clarify the meaning of the interpersonal relationships.

The group included a range of student representatives (interns, undergraduates, and PhD students). Learning-by-doing practices were introduced to help in the construction of knowledge and educational skills. Specifically, the three interns organized the meetings with the high school students, and one of the interns was responsible for coordinating the development of the courses and arranging the final days of the program (May 19, 20, and 21). The three undergraduate students acted as activity observers, and a representative from another university involved in a similar project met with the group to compare experiences. As part of the self-education course, six meetings were devoted to sharing the proposal, training interns and facilitators, defining the observation model, and discussing the evaluation criteria. One of the strengths of the design group was to be the bearer of a multitude of contexts that allowed adoptions of a decentralized, maieutic, and inclusive education approach.

From the beginning of the collaboration, each student contributed to the project sharing their skills and opinions, in a spirit of cooperation, thus allowing for critical reflection, practicing listening skills, and strengthening of self-esteem. An exchange of ideas and opinions helped shape the operators involved in the project. The diversity of facilitators ensured that during the training and planning phases, those who participated would broaden their thinking and bridge between people. This, in turn, allowed participants to explore distant life contexts, where the meaning of peace and its related quest took on unprecedented meaning.

To better adapt the Prem Rawat program to the students' training environment, the recommendations of the facilitators were followed. The facilitators prepared for each session by familiarizing themselves with the content of the videos and readings, but the course content was at times paused to allow reflection and mutual listening and sharing of insights on issues such as diversity; social, cultural, historical, geographical, and gender identity and belonging. The facilitators gave each

[16] January–March 2017.

participant a notebook to write down their thoughts, concerns, emotions, questions, and readings that complemented their reflections.

The inputs provided by the program for peace and the trainees' commitment to train more than 70 students in a schoolwork program contributed to an understanding of how to engage in open dialogue starting from personal experiences to discussing wars, conflicts, cultural diversity, and comprehensive research to ensure everyone has a right to peace. This created daily opportunities for discussion, that are generally difficult to find in university contexts, and allowed for a firsthand assessment of how our educational environment measure up in terms of this type of thinking, feeling, and creativity.

The organizational aspect was crucial for the trainees. It required extensive synergy with daily school activities and administration and necessitated different ways of relating to students' learning. The activities included meetings and workshops, distribution of materials, arranging for use of spaces and equipment, and screening of videos. Moreover, it was important to facilitate participants' reflections and identify indicators to assess the process.

The facilitators were close in age to the students and had tangible experience in peer education. Their role as peer teachers/facilitators made the experience an open discussion, free of any reverence and fear. A dialogue began with the questions posed by the students and exchange of experiences, which at times were difficult to share. Peer education integrated with the maieutic approach and the learning-by-doing process (also useful for the trainees, who improved their educational skills) favored the building of social and empathic skills. The course content facilitated an awareness of being more attentive to one's own needs and other people's needs, as well as putting more trust in feelings and personal choices.

Workshop attendance and active participation in the discussions were monitored and served as process indicators. Participants' regular attendance was essential, partly because the PEP, by facing topics involving personal motivation and choice, calls for elaboration of a multitude of emotions and thoughts that can be better understood and contextualized if they are processed immediately.[17] At the end of the process, the facilitators also followed the PEP manual checklist and compared their findings with those of the observers.[18]

Other indicators were shared with the teachers who followed the schoolwork program, including an assessment of the ability to report what was done during the workshops and an observation of relational changes within the group. The final outputs, written materials, and questionnaires conducted during training made evaluating the process more tangible. At the end of the workshops, participants were asked to design and implement (individually or in small groups) something that expressed one or more messages of peace. There were no limits or default structures. Examples include songs or poems, video interviews, and power point presentations.[19]

---

[17] https://www.tprf.org/wp-content/uploads/.../role_facilitator.pdf, p. 3.

[18] https://www.tprf.org/wp-content/uploads/.../role_facilitator.pdf, p. 7.

[19] https://www.semidipace.space/

This final step of the process was carried out partly with the facilitators and partly at school. It consolidated the laboratory experiences, summarized and finalized the discussions, and developed awareness that when one person's ideas meet other people's ideas, the necessary strength to build new scenarios can be acquired. The creation of outputs and the presentations during days of self-assessment and local meetings[20] were not included in the Prem Rawat program. They were welcomed with interest, applause, and full approval by both local and national institutions.[21]

15.4 Conclusions

The program was evaluated according to the following indicators: observations by undergraduate students during the workshops; organization of the three final days consolidating the experience of the groups; sharing with locals the innovative concepts raised by the experiences; description of various types of outputs created by the participants; open comments on the questionnaires distributed at the end of the program; reflections and observations written by students in their notebooks; and the changes in the relationships observed by high school teachers.

The positive evaluation given by the school trainers and other professional trainers who participated in the three final days were used to assess the educational path to peace and cultural diversity. Observations made by undergraduate students suggested that the participants' attendance was regular, despite the meetings being held at a venue far from their schools. The participants made a fair contribution to the proposed topics, and their ability to elaborate on the course contents increased. Students were willing to be guided and oriented so as to know themselves better, clarify and identify their feelings, and accept new perspectives, even if they were conflicting or unusual. All observers also commended the work carried out by the facilitators.

The observations also indicated that at times the material developed by the PEP course of Prem Rawat was repetitive. Moreover, the translation hampered the understanding of the nuances of the original version. As a result, some participants appeared distracted, which required the facilitators to intervene. A review of the workbooks containing the participants' reflections required more time and needed to take place during each session of the workshop, rather than being done at the end of each module. Finally, it was noted that the students need to learn more about, and thus use more frequently, the vocabulary of emotions and feelings. Some answers given in the notebooks differed from the students' verbal communication,

---

[20] At the end of the project, two workshop presentations and assessment of products (June 19 and 20, 2017) and a presentation to the citizens were organized. The occasion was the World Day for Cultural Diversity for Dialogue and Development (May 21, 2017). The aim was to show the training work carried out by all groups (high school students, undergraduate students, and teachers).

[21] The presentation of the project, the products made by the participants, and the model of education for peace were presented at a conference organized with the City of Florence. Following this event, the students, teachers, and organizers were invited to the Senate of the Italian Republic.

indicating that the students heard and understood the message, but did not transcribe it accurately.

Those who observed the students during the workshops and at school noticed renewed interest in participating in group work, designing individual outputs, and caring for relationships. Even in this case, however, the students needed more time to design and implement their products, as well as further meetings with experts in communication and development of personal creativity. A further suggested improvement was to extend the experience to the observation of people in everyday life settings, namely, outdoors, and not limit it to a closed venue.

Everyone considered the final days of the course an important opportunity to listen, compare, share, and consolidate their reflections on how issues relating to cultural diversity and peace education (learned and processed within the peer group) offer an opportunity to prevent the radicalization of discriminatory, racist, and xenophobic prejudices and stereotypes. The training path aimed at peace and cultural diversity highlighted how adults could take steps to design educational interventions aimed at raising awareness among young people while developing their intercultural skills and peaceful coexistence, starting from a deeper knowledge of themselves.

This pilot project suggests that the methodologies of peer education and mutual maieutic dialogue are valuable and effective and can be applied in other educational contexts. This will assist in achieving the objective of educating students to develop a sense of inner peace as the first step toward managing conflict and preventing violence – something that should be included in the curricula in educational settings around the world.

References

Balducci, E. (1985). *L'uomo planetario*. Brescia, Italy: Camunia.

Bartoloni, S. (2017). *Donne di fronte alla guerra: Pace, diritti e democrazia*. Bari, Italy: Laterza.

Cambi, F. (2001). *Fondamenti interculturali*. Roma, Italy: Carocci.

Dolci, D. (1972). *Inventare il futuro*. Bari, Italy: Laterza.

Freire, P. (1971). *Pedagogy of the oppressed*. New York, NY: Herder and Herder.

Galeazzi, G. (Ed.). (1992). *L'educazione alla pace di Maria Montessori e la pedagogia della pace del '900*. Torino, Italy: Paravia.

Galtung, J. (1996). *Peace by peaceful means: Peace and conflict, development and civilization*. London, UK: Sage.

L'Abate, A. (Ed.). (2001). *Giovani e pace: Ricerche e formazione per un futuro meno violento*. Torino, Italy: Pangea.

Milanese, F. (1992). La pace come diritto umano. In *Pace, diritti dell'uomo, diritti dei popoli, IV, I* (pp. 63–77). Padova, Italy: Cedem.

Milani, L. (1967). *Lettera a una professoressa. La scuola di Barbiana*. Firenze, Italy: Libreria Editrice Fiorentina.

Montessori, M. (1949). *Educazione e Pace*. Milano, Italy: Garzanti.

Novara, D. (2011). La grammatica dei conflitti . Casale Monferrato, Italy: Edizioni Sonda.

Orefice, P. (2003). *Formazione di specie: Per la liberazione del potenziale di conoscenza del sentire e del pensare*. Milano, Italy: Guerini Editore.

Panerai, A., Vitaioli, G., & Nicola, M. (2012). *Manuale di educazione alla pace. Principi, idee, strumenti*. Bergamo, Italy: Junior.
Pazzi, A. M. (Ed.). (2018). *Luoghi di costruzione: dall'alternanza scuola – lavoro, all'alternanza scuola – comunità*. Roma, Italy: Armando.
Pontara, G. (Ed.). (1996). *M. K. Gandhi: Teoria e pratica della non-violenza*. Milano, Italy: Feltrinelli.
Rawat, P. (2015). *Splitting the arrow. Understanding the business of life*. Nagano, Japan: Nihon Hicom LTD.
Rosenberg, M. B. (1998). *Nonviolent communication*. Encinatas (CA): Puddle Dancer Press.
Sclavi, M. (2007). *Costruire una pace*. Milano, Italy: Bruno Mondadori.

Chapter 16
Experiencing Diversity: Complexity, Education, and Peace Construction

Camilla Pagani

16.1 Introduction

In this chapter I will adopt a broad definition of diversity, though I will focus especially on sociocultural diversity as experienced in the school context (e.g., Cangià & Pagani, 2014; Pagani, 2001, 2011a, 2011b, 2014a, 2014b, 2015a, 2017, 2018, 2019; Pagani & Robustelli, 2005, 2010, 2011; Pagani, Robustelli, & Martinelli, 2011). The ideas and data I will present in this chapter will draw on a number of research studies I conducted with my collaborators. For readers who wish to follow up on specific topics related to the present chapter, the following may be useful: teachers and immigrant pupils in Italian schools (Pagani & Robustelli, 2005); children's attitudes to multiculturalism (e.g., Pagani & Robustelli, 2010) (age of participants, 9–18); the relationship between these attitudes and social cohesion (Pagani, 2014a) (age of participants, 15–19); the role of emotions in children's racist attitudes (e.g., Pagani, 2011a, 2014b; Pagani & Robustelli, 2011) (age of participants, 9–18); the relationship between complex thinking and children's attitudes to multiculturalism (e.g., Cangià & Pagani, 2014; Pagani, 2015a) (age of participants, 14–18); and the relationship between complex thinking and children's empathic attitudes (Pagani, 2015a, 2018).

The concepts and ideas presented in the present chapter are based on several propositions: (1) It is necessary to adopt of a broad definition of diversity; (2) diversity and complexity are interrelated; (3) competitive patterns of living, power relations, and hierarchical structures in human societies pose a challenge to peaceful relations; and (4) the school's potential to improve children's relationship with diversity and to foster complex thinking in the interest of peace construction is enormous.

C. Pagani (✉)
Institute of Cognitive Sciences and Technologies (ISTC), National Research Council (CNR), Rome, Italy
e-mail: camilla.pagani@istc.cnr.it

N. Balvin, D. J. Christie (eds.), *Children and Peace*, Peace Psychology Book Series, https://doi.org/10.1007/978-3-030-22176-8_16

16.2 The Relationship with Diversity

The relationship with diversity is one of the basic aspects of human experience (Pagani, 2011a; Pagani, 2011b; Robustelli, 2000). Each individual is part of a reality where everything is diverse from her/him, and, indisputably, each individual's identity develops and evolves through the experience of diversity. Besides, sooner or later in the course of her/his life, each human being realizes that diversity is also *within* herself/himself. Indeed, people usually become aware of the continuous, numberless, sometimes imperceptible, physical, and psychological transformations they go through in the course of their lives.

Three points need to be clarified here: One has to do with the emotions that may be involved in our relationship with diversity, another is the context within which human relations take place, and, finally, I will touch on the question of tolerance for all kinds of diversity.

First, one of the emotions that has most often been connected with humans' relationship with diversity is fear. Some authors have maintained that fear in intergroup relations has some innate evolutionary explanation, thanks to its self-serving protective function (Kottak, 2002). In fact, in our studies on pupils' attitudes toward multiculturalism, we found that, as regards the young participants in our research, one of the emotions frequently connected with the experience of diversity is fear, which is the outcome of a perception of threat. Hence, we analyzed pupils' perceived threats and fears and developed a distinction between real and justified threats and fears (like coming across a drunk immigrant holding a knife in her/his hand late in the night) on the one hand and imaginary and unjustified threats and fears (like feeling that a group of immigrants who are talking together in their own language, which the pupil in question is unable to understand, are actually plotting something harmful against her/him) on the other hand. Thus, we did not distinguish between realistic and symbolic threats (e.g., Stephan, Ybarra, & Morrison, 2009), since we argued that, unlike the distinction between justified and unjustified threats, this specific distinction was not relevant for our research purposes.

Some authors (e.g., Magid, 2008) have pointed out that a child's experience of "secure attachment" with a caregiver can countervail this tendency toward unjustified fear of unfamiliar events and individuals. In addition, "secure attachment" can foster tolerance toward the unknown and interest in it. This means that the relationship with diversity "does not necessarily involve fear and rejection" and that "Curiosity, empathy and identification can occur instead" (Pagani et al., 2011, p. 338). And this introduces us to a second relevant issue.

Second, the main obstacle to a constructive relationship with diversity and, thus, to peace construction is the competitive life pattern, which now prevails all over the world and which is based "on a simplistic, rough, unsophisticated, coarse and unempathetic view on life" (Pagani, 2019, p. 74). In one way or another, the competitive life pattern affects all interpersonal relationships, which means that in most cases, people consider "the other" to be a rival, a competitor, an enemy, someone to be basically feared and who tries to overpower them and whom, in their turn, they may try to overpower (Miceli & Castelfranchi, 2007; Pagani, 2014c, Pagani, 2019, Pagani & Robustelli, 1998, 2005, 2010, 2011; Robustelli, 2007; Robustelli & Pagani, 1996). Fundamentally, this is because human societies are usually characterized by hierarchical structures, depending on the power each individual has over other individuals, with the weakest and/or most exploited, such as the poor, the elderly, the disabled, women, children, and animals, on the lowest rungs of the social ladder.

The role of competition in intergroup relations has been widely analyzed and debated in the social sciences. Sherif et al.'s "Realistic Conflict Theory" (1961) and Tajfel and Turner's "Integrative Theory of Intergroup Conflict" (1979) and "Social Identity Theory" (1986, 2004) have especially contributed to the debate in this field.

It goes without saying that these authors' theoretical considerations have developed in a cultural context where as a rule competition strongly affects people's thoughts, emotions, and behavior. A crucial point in complexity science is related to the role of the subject. The subject (also named the "observer," the "conceiver," or the "knower") is part of the act of observation, of conceiving, and of knowing (Morin, 2008), to which she/he participates with her/his "personal qualities in its communication with the object" (Morin, 2008, p. 107). This means that "the subject and the object are, and have to be, constitutive of each other and that the processes of observation and self-observation are integrated" (Pagani, 2019, p. xiii). In the social studies on competition in intergroup relations quoted above, this methodological perspective is not considered. In this regard, the following theoretical statements are particularly significant:

> [...] in-group bias is a remarkably omnipresent feature of intergroup relations. (Tajfel & Turner, 1979, p. 38)
>
> The aim of differentiation is to maintain or achieve superiority over an out-group on some dimensions. Any such act, therefore, is essentially competitive. (Ibid., p. 41)

Clearly, these two statements could hardly have been put forth in a Buddhist-oriented context. Conversely, when the subject acknowledges her/his role as part of the research process, she/he is more aware both of the complexity of the object of study and of the uncertainty that unavoidably characterizes scientific investigation, which is another basic principle in complexity science. In other words, the subject becomes aware of the possible limits and deficiencies of her/his point of view and of the fact that other views and realities may be possible. The consequences of this change of perspective are enormous in all human domains, including, and most significantly, education and peace issues.

Finally, as regards the nature of a specific kind of diversity and tolerance, it goes without saying that not all kinds of diversities should be accepted, for example, the diversity of a Nazi, of a racist, or of a bully. The principle that should guide actions is whether or not the actions are harmful to others. However, we should learn to deal with harmful forms of diversity. This is a very important issue especially as far as education is concerned, which I will try to address later on when I discuss the relationship between diversity and complexity.

16.3 Diversity and Complexity

The idea of diversity is at the core of complexity theory. This is indicated by the main concepts on which complexity theory is grounded (e.g., systems, networks, hierarchies, nonlinearity, emergent properties, evolution, adaptation, context, multiplicity of causes, existence of a potentially infinite number of possible solutions) (e.g., Byrne, 1998; De Toni & Comello, 2005; Johnson, 2009; Mitchell, 2009; Prigogine & Stengers, 1984, 1997), which are all founded on the existence of diversity.

Indeed, complexity is a particularly useful epistemological tool in this research area, in that, among other things, it indicates the necessity of addressing human issues – like the relationship with diversity – through newly created and multiple perspectives (Morin, 2008). In other words, complexity is inherent both in the reality of diversity and in the observer of the reality of diversity itself.

Within this context, I will not provide a general overview of complexity science. The volumes quoted above are excellent instruments for this purpose. However, for greater clarity, I will quote a very short definition provided by Neil Johnson (2009):

> [...] Complexity Science can be seen as the study of the phenomena which emerge from a collection of interacting objects [...]. (p. 3)

In order to better illustrate my point, I will quote the concluding part of a short anonymous essay written by a 10-year-old girl, who participated in our study on youths' attitudes toward multiculturalism[1] (e.g., Cangià & Pagani, 2014; Pagani, 2014a, 2014b; Pagani & Robustelli, 2005, 2010, 2011) and who declares in the first sentence of her essay that she is not a racist[2]:

> *Our immigrant classmates maltreat us and we have to put up with them and if we react against them we will be put in jail, we have to defend ourselves!*
>
> *And if we do not do it, they will conquer us!*
>
> *Here at school, they are in a privileged position; they receive snacks and sweets and do whatever they like. Pupils should come to school to study. They shouldn't come to school to eat and get warm.*
>
> *When I was in the third year, the girls in my class teased me because my father is Sardinian and is short, but not only Sardinians are short.*

If we are knowledgeable about the situation in Italian schools, we can immediately realize that the picture depicted by the girl is unrealistic. No young Italian pupil would sensibly fear that she/he should be put in jail for any reason whatsoever. Nor the idea of immigrant pupils "maltreating" and threatening "to conquer" their Italian classmates is conceivable either.

---

[1] Some of the extracts quoted in this chapter have been analyzed from partly different perspectives in Pagani (2014b); Pagani, 2019; Pagani and Robustelli (2011); and Cangià and Pagani (2014).

[2] In the quotations from participants' essays, we did not eliminate spelling, grammatical, syntactic, and lexical mistakes or any other "idiosyncratic" element in the form and in the content of the texts.

In this specific situation, a teacher might simplistically regard the girl's discontent and deep aversion to her immigrant classmates as the mere outcome of an attitude which she/he might generically define as "racist." Then the same teacher might decide, for example, to simply reprimand the pupil and, thus, close the book on the matter.

But if we look at the few sentences quoted above through a "complexity" lens, we can easily realize that the problem is multifaceted and "complex." Indeed it is a texture of many components, some of which are strongly embedded in the deep emotional substratum of the girl's story, as it has developed in the course of her life, particularly through her interactions with her family figures – notably with his father in this context – as well as with her teachers and the other pupils at school. She seems to be experiencing various intermingled emotions: fear (fear of her immigrant classmates, but also, and most notably, fear of losing her teachers' affection, on account of their supposed special attentions to immigrant pupils), anger, shame, hate, resentment, and envy. Various processes are involved in the formation of these emotions. We might even hypothesize a "hostility displacement" on the part of this pupil (from the girls in her class to her immigrant classmates[3]).

It is especially important to point out that all this complexity is displayed in the few lines of a very short essay written by a girl of 10. Indeed, even a short extract can be regarded and analyzed as a complex system, in all the various connections among its components. Moreover, in this specific system, there is a final component, which we might define as the "emergent phenomenon" – a typical concept of complexity science – that contributes to a sort of clarification, that is, to a higher-level comprehension of the essence of the situation itself, which is constituted by the interconnection of the various specific events and emotions in the girl's life. This special component is provided by the last sentence:

> *When I was in the third year, the girls in my class teased me because my father is Sardinian and is short, but not only Sardinians are short.*

In fact, these words can be regarded as a sort of climax that provides the ultimate key to the possible comprehension of the meaning of the situation itself. In brief, in our analysis, we have taken on a perspective whereby the girl's text is handled exactly as a living being, as a system in evolution, in sum as a complex system.

Interestingly, a British journalist from *The Guardian*, Richard Seymour (2014), in his considerations on popular racism in Great Britain, referred to one of the emotions I mentioned above regarding the girl's feelings, namely, resentment:

> The dominant sentiment of this racism is resentment. People are convinced that immigrants have taken something from them. Social resentment of this kind is integral to the competitive ethos of neoliberalism: given a vicious struggle for scarce resources, there is tremendous paranoia about "undeserving" people getting things unfairly.

However, we are well aware that, given its complexity, the issue of competition cannot be simply defined in terms of "a struggle for limited resources." Within this context, it is particularly important to point out that in the last few years there has

---

[3] For a deep analysis of the girl's emotions and the processes involved, see Pagani (2014b).

been an increasing interest in complexity and in the use of a "complexity lens" in the study of conflicts and in the efforts to address them constructively. Several authors (e.g., Coleman & Deutsch, 2001; Coleman & Vallacher, 2010; Kugler, Coleman, & Fuchs, 2011; Suedfeld, 2007) have addressed some of the most serious obstacles in the way of peace (like intractable conflicts, terrorism, and torture) drawing on the construct of conceptual/integrative complexity (Suedfeld, Tetlock, & Streufert, 1992) as opposed to a Manichean dogmatism (Suedfeld, 2007).

16.4 Diversity, Complex Thinking, Peace Construction, and School

Though I generally consider education in its broad sense, namely, as the sum of all the elements of reality that in one way or another affect human development (Pagani, 2000; Robustelli, 2003), here I will give a special emphasis to school. As I said above, school's potential to improve youths' relationship with diversity and to foster peace building is enormous. However, our research findings (e.g., Pagani, 2014b; Pagani et al., 2011; Pagani & Robustelli, 2010) indicate that "both teachers and pupils seldom perceive school as a place that can provide this positive and significant opportunity" (Pagani et al., 2011, p. 337). I will pick up on this point in more detail further on.

The conceptualizations regarding complex thinking, which have been especially elaborated by Morin (2008), are firmly embedded in the basic theoretical foundations of complexity theory and are particularly significant also from an educational and social point of view. In fact, in Morin's view, complex thinking is considered the essential prerequisite of humans' actions, thoughts, and emotions. More specifically, in his view, the unique possibility for mankind to survive lies in the application of complex thinking itself.

We defined complex thinking "as the combination of certain cognitive and emotional processes through which individuals try to understand themselves, the others, the world and, in general, all the aspects of reality they may be interested in" (Cangià & Pagani, 2014, p. 22). These processes include, among others, "self-awareness," "multiple perspective-taking," "acceptance of uncertainty and incompleteness," "openness to experience," "creativity," and "emotional complexity."

It is clear that the experience of diversity is at the base of these processes. Morin is not so familiar with the words "peace" or "peace construction," but in his writings on complex thinking (e.g., Morin, 2001, 2008), he firmly underlines the unique and essential role played by complex thinking in supporting the construction of a less destructive world. His view is synthesized in these words:

> Complexity is situated at a point of departure for a richer, less mutilating action. I strongly believe that the less a thought is mutilating, the less it will mutilate human beings. We must remember the ravages that simplifying visions have caused, not only in the intellectual world, but in life. Much of the suffering of millions of beings results from the effects of fragmented and one-dimensional thought. (2008, p. 57)

In our research studies, especially in those where we used pupils' anonymous open-ended essays, one of the clearest and most obvious examples of mutilating thought was provided by the presence of logical contradictions characterizing participants' attitudes toward multiculturalism, of which the pupils themselves apparently were not aware (e.g., Pagani et al., 2011; Pagani & Robustelli, 2010). The example below, where a resentful aversion to immigrants coexists with a sincere affection for an immigrant friend, is an excerpt from an anonymous essay written by a boy of 11:

> *I hate immigrants who don't want to work, who steal and come here only to wreak havoc and kill.*
>
> *I am proud to be Italian!*
>
> *But I hate, in the truest sense, gypsies* [...] *that swear at my God and despise my country.*
>
> [...] *I may be a racist, a fascist,* [...] *a rogue, a hooligan, a fool* [...].
>
> *I met a Czechoslovakian named Martin. I was in Abruzzo. With him I had a lot of fun and in order to communicate we used to speak in English.*
>
> *He was a humble kid, with no fears and very friendly.*
>
> *It was a very significant experience for me.*

Our research findings (e.g., Cangià & Pagani, 2014) indicate that the presence of good or very good levels of complex thinking is related to a deeper, more refined, and more positive representation of cultural diversity. Instead, negative, stereotyped, and prejudiced representations of cultural diversity are characterized by a relative lack of complex thinking.

This is another example of the presence of a low level of complex thinking. It is an excerpt from an anonymous essay written by a boy of 16. Interestingly, this boy attends a high school specializing in scientific subjects, a kind of school that is generally attended by higher socioeconomic class students:

> *Then the most important question is: what do all these immigrants want? Do they want a job? Do they want money? Do they want to live in peace? Or rather they want our jobs? Do they want our money? And steal our peace earned throughout centuries of wars and of our ancestors' efforts?*
>
> *Instead, why don't they stay in their country to try to change something; do you want a job → look for it do you want money → earn it do you want peace → don't make war.*
>
> *I'll make some examples: the other day I was in my car with my father and at one point a Moroccan at the traffic signal started to wash the car front window, well before the light turned green we had to give him money, well and what if I had wanted to spend that money for something else instead? I mean, it's bad enough that you come here in our country and steal our job (and don't say that they do those jobs that Italians don't do because it's bullshit) and then you even invade my freedom? My rights? How dare you; stay in your country and fight wars with bamboo canes.*
>
> *Well, I think this way, maybe it is wrong but I think this way; I won't change my opinion until someone proves me wrong.*

Just two remarks on these lines. First, the boy does not seem to be aware of the burden and of the meaning of the emotions he is experiencing – a complex system which he does not recognize – especially as far as his feelings of rage are concerned. Accordingly, his thinking is low in emotional complexity as it shows a low level of "emotional granularity" (Lindquist & Barrett, 2008), namely, of the ability to identify and describe various emotional experiences in precise and differentiated terms. It is also low in "dialecticism," a term which refers to the presence of different emotions and of their reciprocal relations within a single emotional episode (Lindquist & Barrett, 2008).

Second, his thinking is fragmented, mutilated, simplistic, dogmatic, and authoritarian. It is not open to other perspectives and to other experiences ("I won't change my opinion") and is characterized by a nonacceptance of a certain degree of uncertainty and incompleteness, by a lack of creativity, and by an almost nonexistence of self-awareness, which means it lacks those qualities that are inherent components of complex thinking.

In the closing lines of the first section of this chapter, I referred to the necessity of constructively dealing also with negative kinds of diversity and suggested, as examples, the diversity of a Nazi, of a racist, or of a bully. In this context, school should play a major role. According to some authors (e.g., Cangià & Pagani, 2014; Ezekiel, 2002), there is a sine qua non, an essential prerequisite in peace education and education against racism: pupils' mutilating and fragmented conceptualizations and emotions should be analyzed and properly discussed in class. For example, Ezekiel (2002) very clearly states:

> I would suggest that education about racism should begin with respect for the constructs and emotions that the students bring with them into the classroom. The students have ideas and emotions about race that are the product of their own lives. They have heard their parents, their neighbors, and their friends, and they have had their own experiences. To ignore their emotions and constructs around race is to ignore the sense that they make of their own experiences. (pp. 65–66)

This is equal to saying that when children's thought is mutilated, fragmented, and not sufficiently complex, this thought should be an object of attentive – and benevolent, I would say – analysis on the part of educators as well as, in my view, on the part of children themselves, in an educational context.

Now I would like to provide an example, chosen from the texts written by our research participants, which perfectly illustrates the components of complex thinking as they can be identified in a very short essay written by a boy of 14, who is presently living in Rome[4]:

> *As I came from a little town, I was scared and intrigued by a multi-ethnic city. I was scared by the rumors on immigrants and intrigued by the many cultures I was coming across. As I started living here I found out that the rumors were all wrong, instead the opposite was true* [...]. *As I was born in a big city and then moved to a little town, the people there saw me as a stranger but then, as I came here people coming from other states became the strangers, I can say that the definition of stranger depends on the perspective from which someone sees the situation so I cannot express a real opinion on this subject.*

The essay is very short, as it contains only 159 words. Interestingly, in the last line, the boy states that he is unable "to express a real opinion" on the subject. As a matter of fact, the pupil perfectly expresses his view, and he does so in a fashion that is both synthetical and analytical: only few emotions and considerations are expressed, but they are essential, deep, profoundly personal, and they are presented with great

[4] For a more detailed analysis of this essay, see Cangià and Pagani (2014).

clearness and precision. By the phrase "a real opinion," he implicitly means a "yes or no opinion," namely, a clear-cut distinction between, in this case, native and immigrant, familiar and stranger, and ingroup and outgroup. It is a fact that in the boy's view, which is a perfect example of complex system and of complex thinking, the "emergent property" is the realization on his part that in different ways, he belongs to all these categories. Thus, his identity is complex, as it embraces more than one category, and he is knowledgeable about it. Besides, he compares his view as regards immigration with the more general view in society and analyzes his own feelings and considerations on this subject as they were elaborated in different circumstances. Hence, diversity and complexity are unambiguously expressed here. Also the interconnections of his emotions contribute to producing the sense of complexity. His essay shows a high level of "dialecticism," as the presence of the two adjectives "scared" and "intrigued," both referring to the boy himself in the same context, clearly indicates. Interestingly, also Gillespie, Kadianaki, and O'Sullivan-Lago (2012) mention individuals' identity transitions from being a "local" in their home culture to being a "foreigner" and "immigrant" in a new culture, the same feelings that the young boy experienced when he moved from the big city to the little town and from the little town to the big city.

16.5 Promoting Complex Social Identities

The role played by school as far as cross-cultural relations are concerned is also indicated in this short passage from the autobiographical novel *My Place* (2006), written by the Australian writer Sally Morgan. In these lines, an Aboriginal child – Sally Morgan herself as a child – reports to her mum a request that has been made to her by her non-Aboriginal schoolmates, namely, the request to be thoroughly and precisely informed about Sally and her family's origins. Here, the concept of identity, which I mentioned above, comes to the foreground.

> The kids at school had also begun asking us what country we came from. This puzzled me because, up until then, I'd thought we were the same as them. If we insisted that we came from Australia, they'd reply, "Yeah, but what about ya parents, bet they didn't come from Australia." One day, I tackled Mum about it as she washed the dishes.
>
> "What do you mean, 'Where do we come from?'"
>
> "I mean, what country. The kids at school want to know what country we come from. They reckon we're not Aussies. Are we Aussies, Mum?"
>
> Mum was silent. Nan grunted in a cross sort of way, then got up from the table and walked outside.
>
> "Come on, Mum, what are we?"
>
> "What do the kids at school say?"
>
> "Anything. Italian, Greek, Indian."
>
> "Tell them you're Indian."
>
> I got really excited, then. "Are we really? Indian!" It sounded so exotic. "When did we come here?" I added.
>
> "A long time ago," Mum replied. "Now, no more questions. You just tell them you're Indian."

> It was good to finally have an answer and it satisfied our playmates. They could quite believe we were Indian, they just didn't want us pretending we were Aussies when we weren't. (pp. 38–39)

It goes without saying that in Sally's school, the issue of cultural diversity, not to mention the true history of the formation of the Australian state, has not been addressed during lessons. It is also clear that the opinion on Sally and her family's identity that Sally's non-Aboriginal schoolmates have elaborated is strongly affected by the social macro-context, that is, by Australian society at large, which both implicitly and explicitly has "negated" the reality of the Aboriginal culture, so that the Aboriginals are the people who come from *the outside* and who *pretend* they come from *the inside* and the British are the people who believe or pretend to believe they come from *the inside*! Consequently, Sally's sense of her own identity changes, following her classmates' questions and suggestions and her mother's brilliant solution, as she understands that an Indian, not an Aboriginal, identity can suit the other schoolchildren's expectations. Hence, the modification of Sally's sense of her own identity has occurred on account of powerful social forces, which have transformed a sense of sameness ("we are the same as them," "we are all children") into a sense of diversity.

Ezekiel (2002) has claimed that the issue of cultural identity should be thoroughly addressed in educational contexts:

> Young people, regardless of race or ethnicity, should be helped to see where their own sense of identity comes from and how it affects their own lives. And to see its many different facets. Only then can the student begin to acknowledge that other people also have a sense of identity, and that it also had multiple roots. (p. 66)

This way, the multiplicity of roots, of facets, and of dimensions that constitute an individual's identity in the course of time provides this identity with the components and characteristics of a complex system. It is an *open* system where "sameness" and "diversity" in multiple ways interact. The awareness of this complexity on the part of children should be the fundamental aim of education.

Henceforth, children should be encouraged to concretely and fully analyze and understand the various meanings which are attached to the concept of identity and which underline the importance both of sameness and of diversity. In particular, two quotations might be helpful here, the former especially focusing on the individual and the second also focusing on the role of society.

In these lines, in his presentation of the three principles of identity, Morin (2008) illustrates the second principle, which focuses on the individual:

> There is a second, and quite fascinating, principle of identity which maintains the invariance of the I-subject despite the extraordinary modifications constantly taking place at the physical, molecular, and cellular level. This is apparent not only in the fact that, every four years, the greater part of the cells that make up my organism have disappeared to be replaced by others – which is to say that, biologically speaking, I am no longer the same being that I was four years ago. There are also enormous changes which accompany the shifts from childhood through adolescence to old age. And yet, when I look at a childhood photograph of myself, I say: "That's me!" And yet, I am no longer that child, and I no longer have that

body or that face. But the occupation of this central site of the I, which abides throughout all these changes, establishes the continuity of identity. We even live in the illusion of possessing a stable identity, without really being aware of how different we are according to our moods – whether we are angry, loving, or hating – and due to the fact [...] that we are all double, triple, and multiple personalities. (pp. 74–75)

In the next quotation, the role of "external" forces is more salient:

How one identifies oneself – and how one is identified by others – may vary greatly from context to context; self- and other-identification are fundamentally situational and contextual. (Morin, 2008)

Another basic distinction is between self-identification and the identification and categorization of oneself by others. Self-identification takes place in dialectical interplay with external identification, and the two need not converge. External identification is itself a varied process. In the ordinary web and flow of social life people identify and categorize others, just as they identify and categorize themselves. But there is another key type of external identification that has no counterpart in the domain of self-identification: the formalized, codified, objectified systems of categorization developed by powerful, authoritative institutions. (Brubaker & Cooper, 2000, pp. 14–15)

16.6 Conclusions

The main assumption of this chapter is that complexity, diversity, education, and peace construction are intimately interrelated. As I said above, our research findings stress the importance of fostering the development of complex thinking so as to strengthen youths' capability of building a more personal, autonomous, and complex outlook on their relationship with cultural diversity and with diversity in general. This capability is also intimately related to the achievement of what has been defined "social identity complexity" (e.g., Brewer, 2010; Brewer & Pierce, 2005; Miller, Brewer, & Arbuckle, 2009), which implies the recognition of the diversities of the various interior and exterior components of our identity and the ability to reconcile them. This requires cognitive strategies and resources (Brewer, 2010), which school can and should provide. As I said above, our research findings show that good or very good levels of complex thinking are associated with a more elaborate and positive representation of cultural diversity, while a low level of complex thinking is correlated with negative and prejudiced representations of cultural diversity. Interestingly, Brewer et al.'s research data (Brewer, 2010; Miller, Brewer, & Arbuckle, 2009) indicate an association between high scores on complexity and "need for cognition." Accordingly, school's efforts should be especially directed toward the development of this need.

Peace construction can only rest on these bases. Indeed, the "complexity approach" – which includes both cognitive and emotional abilities – can help find more constructive solutions to conflicts and, thus, can countervail violence, which is basically grounded on an irrational and shortsighted analysis and interpretation of reality (e.g., Pagani, 2015b; Robustelli, 2005).

References

Brewer, M. B. (2010). Social identity complexity and acceptance of diversity. In R. J. Crisp & M. A. Malden (Eds.), *The psychology of social and cultural diversity* (pp. 11–33). Malden (MA): Wiley-Blackwell.

Brewer, M. B., & Pierce, K. P. (2005). Social identity complexity and outgroup tolerance. *Personality and Social Psychology Bulletin, 31*, 428–437.

Brubaker, R., & Cooper, F. (2000). Beyond "Identity". *Theory and Society, 29*, 1–47.

Byrne, D. S. (1998). *Complexity theory and the social sciences: An introduction*. London, UK: Routledge.

Cangià, F., & Pagani, C. (2014). Youths, cultural diversity, and complex thinking. *The Open Psychology Journal, 7*, 20–28.

Coleman, P., & Deutsch, M. (2001). Introducing cooperation and conflict resolution into schools: A systems approach. In D. J. Christie, R. V. Wagner, & D. D. Winter (Eds.), *Peace, conflict and violence: Peace psychology for the 21st century* (pp. 223–239). Englewood Cliffs, NJ: Prentice-Hall.

Coleman, P. T., & Vallacher, R. R. (Eds.) (2010). *Peace and Conflict: Journal of Peace Psychology, 16* (2),113–230. (Special issue devoted to dynamical models of intractable conflict).

De Toni, A. F., & Comello, L. (2005). *Prede o Ragni*. Torino, Italy: Utet.

Ezekiel, R. S. (2002). An ethnographer looks at Neo-Nazi and Klan Groups: The racist mind revisited. *American Behavioral Scientist, 46*, 51–71.

Gillespie, A., Kadianaki, I., & O'Sullivan-Lago, R. (2012). Encountering alterity: Geographic and semantic movements. In J. Valsiner (Ed.), *The oxford handbook of culture and psychology* (pp. 697–709). Oxford: Oxford University Press.

Johnson, N. F. (2009). *Simply complexity: A clear guide to complexity theory*. London, UK: Oneworld Publications.

Kottak, C. P. (2002). *Anthropology: The exploration of human diversity*. New York, NY: McGraw Hill.

Kugler, K. G., Coleman, P. T., & Fuchs, A. (2011). Moral conflict and complexity: The dynamics of constructive versus destructive discussions over polarizing issues. *SSRN Electronic Journal*. https://doi.org/10.2139/ssrn.1872654

Lindquist, K. A., & Barrett, L. F. (2008). Emotional complexity. In M. Lewis, J. M. Haviland-Jones, & L. F. Barrett (Eds.), *Handbook of emotions* (pp. 513–530). New York, NY: The Guildford Press.

Magid, K. (2008). Attachment and animal abuse. In F. R. Ascione (Ed.), *The international handbook of animal abuse and cruelty: Theory, research, and application* (pp. 335–373). West Lafayette, IN: Purdue University Press.

Miceli, M., & Castelfranchi, C. (2007). The envious mind. *Cognition and Emotion, 21*(3), 449–479.

Miller, K. P., Brewer, M. B., & Arbuckle, N. L. (2009). Social identity complexity: Its correlates and antecedents. *Group Processes and Intergroup Relations, 12*, 79–94.

Mitchell, M. (2009). *Complexity. A guided tour*. New York, NY: Oxford University Press.

Morgan, S. (2006). *My place*. London, UK: Virago Press. (Original work published 1987).

Morin, E. (2001). *Seven complex lessons in education for the future*. Paris, France: UNESCO.

Morin, E. (2008). *On complexity*. Cresskill, NJ: Hampton Press.

Pagani, C. (2000). Education and the problem of violence. In V. Scalera (Ed.), *Investigations in and for teaching. In-service teacher training and quality of education* (pp. 271–274). Milano, Italy: Franco Angeli.

Pagani, C. (2001). The cross-cultural significance of empathy as an instrument to prevent aggression. In J. M. Ramirez & D. S. Richardson (Eds.), *Cross-cultural approaches to aggression and reconciliation* (pp. 191–201). Huntington, NY: NovaScience.

Pagani, C. (2011a). Violence in cross-cultural relations as the outcome of specific cognitive and emotional processes. *The Open Psychology Journal, 4*, 21–27.

Pagani, C. (2011b). Children and adolescents who are kind to animals. In C. Blazina, G. Boyra, & D. Shen-Miller (Eds.), *The psychology of the human-animal bond: A handbook for clinicians and researchers* (pp. 289–305). New York, NY: Springer.

Pagani, C. (2014a). Diversity and social cohesion. *Intercultural Education, 25*, 300–311.

Pagani, C. (2014b). Fear, hate, anger, resentment, and envy in youths' racist attitudes toward immigrants. In J. M. Ramirez, C. Morrison, & A. Kendall (Eds.), *Conflict, violence, terrorism, and their prevention* (pp. 16–27). Newcastle upon Tyne, UK: Cambridge Scholars Publishing.

Pagani, C. (2014c). Violence in a comprehensive perspective. *Kultura i Edukacja (Culture and Education), 5*(105), 148–161.

Pagani, C. (2015a). Youth's empathy and complex thinking. In V. Wain & P. Pimomo (Eds.), *Encountering empathy: Interrogating the past, envisioning the future* (pp. 177–188). Oxford: Inter-Disciplinary Press. http://www.interdisciplinarypress.net/product/encountering-empathy-interrogating-the-past-envisioning-the-future/

Pagani, C. (2015b). Violence and complexity. *The Open Psychology Journal, 8*, 11–16.

Pagani, C. (2017). Identity, diversity, and destructive conflicts. In J. M. Ramirez & L. A. Garcia-Segura (Eds.), *XLII CICA. Conflict and transcultural dialogue, program and abstracts, Madrid 18th–20th September 2017* (pp. 43–44). Madrid, Spain: Universidad Nebrija.

Pagani, C. (2018). Empathy, complex thinking, and their interconnections. In R. J. Nelems & L. J. (Nic) Theo (Eds.), *Exploring empathy: Its propagations, perimeters and potentialities* (pp. 41–60). Leiden, The Netherlands: Brill.

Pagani, C. (2019). *Diversity and Complexity*. New York (NY): Nova Science Publishers, Inc.

Pagani, C., & Robustelli, F. (1998). Lo sviluppo dell'aggressività nel bambino [The development of childhood aggression]. *Bambini, 2*, 19–23.

Pagani, C. & Robustelli, F. (2005). *Marek a scuola. Gli insegnanti e l'inserimento degli alunni stranieri nella scuola italiana*. [Marek at School. Teachers and Immigrant Pupils' Enrolment in Italian Schools]. Milano: Franco Angeli.

Pagani, C., & Robustelli, F. (2010). Young people, multiculturalism, and educational interventions for the development of empathy. *International Social Science Journal, 200-201*, 247–261.

Pagani, C., & Robustelli, F. (2011). Youth's attitudes toward racism: A psycho-socio-cultural perspective. In B. Szegál & I. András (Eds.), *Conflicts in a society in transition* (pp. 79–95). Dunaújváros, Hungary: Dunaújváros College Press.

Pagani, C., Robustelli, F., & Martinelli, C. (2011). School, cultural diversity, multiculturalism, and contact. *Intercultural Education, 22*, 337–349.

Prigogine, I., & Stengers, I. (1984). *Order out of Chaos: Man's new dialogue with nature*. New York, NY: Bantam Books.

Prigogine, I., & Stengers, I. (1997). *The end of certainty*. New York, NY: The Free Press.

Robustelli, F. (2000). Psicologia della diversità [The psychology of diversity]. In B. M. Pirani (Ed.), *L'abbaglio dell'occidente* (pp. 189–198). Roma, Italy: Bulzoni.

Robustelli, F. (2003). Violence, rationality, education. In M. S. Dajani & A. Nadler (Eds.), *Social and psychological factors in conflict and its resolution: The mid-Eastern and European experience. Proceedings of a dialogue workshop, 7–8 June 2002* (pp. 123–124). Brussels, Belgium: European Commission.

Robustelli, F. (2005). La razionalità come alternativa alla violenza [Rationality as an Alternative to Violence]. *Prometeo, 23*, 96–101.

Robustelli, F. (2007). La competitività nella ricerca scientifica [Competitiveness in scientific research]. *A, 37*, 29–30.

Robustelli, F., & Pagani, C. (1996). L'educazione contro la violenza [Education against violence]. *Psicologia contemporanea, 136*, 4–10.

Seymour, R. (2014). Why is there so much hostility to immigrants in the UK? *The Guardian*, 14 October 2014. Retrieved from https://www.theguardian.com/commentisfree/2014/oct/14/why-hostility-immigrants-uk-racism

Sherif, M., Harvey, O. J., White, B. J., Hood, W. R., & Sherif, C. W. (1961). *Intergroup conflict and cooperation: The Robbers Cave experiment* (Vol. 10, p. 150.198). Norman, OK: University Book Exchange.

Stephan, W. G., Ybarra, O., & Morrison, K. R. (2009). Intergroup threat theory. In T. D. Nelson (Ed.), *Handbook of prejudice, stereotyping, and discrimination* (pp. 43–59). New York, NY: Psychology Press.

Suedfeld, P. (2007). Torture, interrogation, security, and psychology: Absolutistic versus complex thinking. *Analysis of Social Issues and Public Policy, 7*, 55–63.

Suedfeld, P., Tetlock, P. E., & Streufert, S. (1992). Conceptual/integrative complexity. In C. P. Smith (Ed.), *Motivation and personality: Handbook of thematic content analysis* (pp. 393–400). Cambridge, UK: Cambridge University Press.

Tajfel, H., & Turner, J. (1979). An integrative theory of intergroup conflict. In W. G. Austin & S. Worchel (Eds.), *The social psychology of intergroup relations* (pp. 33–47). Monterey, CA: Wadsworth.

Tajfel, H., & Turner, J. C. (1986). The social identity theory of intergroup behaviour. In S. Worchel & W. G. Austin (Eds.), *Psychology of intergroup relations* (pp. 7–24). Chicago, IL: Nelson-Hall.

Tajfel, H., & Turner, J. C. (2004). The social identity theory of intergroup behavior. In J. T. Jost & J. Sidanius (Eds.), *Political psychology: Key readings* (pp. 276–293). Key Readings in Social Psychology). New York, NY: Psychology Press.

Chapter 17
Developmental Trajectories of Political Engagement from Adolescence to Mid-Adulthood: A Review with Empirical Underpinnings from the German Peace Movement

Maor Shani, Daniel Horn, and Klaus Boehnke

17.1 Introduction

A politically efficacious, confident, and engaged citizenry is vital for achieving the ideals of democracy and strengthening democratic participation. The familiar observation that conventional participation in Western democracies is in decline, especially among young people (Levine, 2007; Norris, 2011), highlights the importance of engaging adolescents in politics even before they reach voting age. It is in the context of political experience and collective action that adolescents and youth take an active role as agents of social change and learn to be involved citizens in the community (Flanagan, 2013). Moreover, studies have found that an increase in political efficacy following activism is larger for youth from disadvantaged groups (Flanagan, 2009). Thus, civic and political activism among young people has the potential to facilitate political equality, by merit not only of its capacity to mobilize citizens earlier in the life course but also to do so among those segments

Klaus Boehnke's contribution to this chapter was in part prepared within the framework of the Basic Research Program at the National Research University Higher School of Economics (HSE) and supported within the framework of a subsidy by the Russian Academic Excellence Project "5-100."

M. Shani (✉)
Jacobs University Bremen, Bremen, Germany
e-mail: m.shani@jacobs-university.de

D. Horn
University of Strathclyde, Glasgow, UK

K. Boehnke
Jacobs University Bremen, Bremen, Germany

National Research University Higher School of Economics, Moscow, Russia

N. Balvin, D. J. Christie (eds.), *Children and Peace*, Peace Psychology Book Series, https://doi.org/10.1007/978-3-030-22176-8_17

typically underrepresented in political contests – precisely those segments of society which stand to benefit from increased attention from policy makers. Political science research from the "political culture" paradigm offers empirical evidence to this fact in abundance (Bogaards & Deutsch, 2015; Welzel & Deutsch, 2012).

Political socialization results from the process by which people acquire political attitudes and worldviews, as well as the patterns by which they engage in civic and political life (Easton, 1968). In political socialization theory, adolescence and youth are crucial periods. The formative years hypothesis (Jennings & Niemi, 1981) points to the importance of one's adolescent and youth years (between 15 and 25), as a period where long-term patterns of political behaviors are formed and during which individuals acquire the basic cognitive skills for political mobilization later in life.[1] Civic identity and patterns of political participation are shaped as adolescents explore their identity, seek purpose, and determine their beliefs and commitments with regard to themselves and others (Flanagan & Tucker, 1999).

It is, therefore, reasonable to expect that adolescent-age experience will be decisive in determining the formation of political identities and lifelong trajectories. Still, it is not unlikely that these patterns will change as people go through different stages of life and encounter the dynamic political world or other influences. Indeed, some have also argued that political learning is a nonlinear, lifelong process, as adults continue to craft their political perspective throughout the lifespan (Quintelier, 2015a).

17.2 Intergenerational Transmission of Political Worldviews and Participation and Their Stability Across the Lifespan

Self-identification on the left-right continuum is a prominent indicator of political worldviews. This spectrum is significant in Western political systems beyond its symbolic value, as it constitutes a framework through which citizens interpret political messages, form positions on particular issues, and participate in politics (Inglehart & Klingemann, 1976; van der Eijk, Schmitt, & Binder, 2005).

How is political orientation on the left-right dimension formed in adolescence, and how does it change throughout life? Theories on youth political engagement emphasize the importance of socialization agents, mainly family, peers, school, social organization, and mass media. More recently, emphasis has been given to the active role adolescents themselves play in their own development in the political sphere, especially during late adolescence and youth (Amnå, 2012). Since the family generally constitutes a stable base in the political socialization and identity-building of children and adolescents, ideological inclination is at least partially

[1] It is possible to distinguish adolescence and youth as overlapping stages as defined by the United Nations; www.un.org/esa/socdev/documents/youth/fact-sheets/youth-definition.pdf

molded by one's parents, through the process of *intergenerational transmission* of political traits within the family.[2] Take, for instance, a large panel study in the USA stretched over the three last decades of the twentieth century, confirming that parents play a central role in their offspring's political learning (particularly in their electoral behavior and party preference), with generally strong correlations between parents' and children's attitudes (Jennings & Niemi, 1974; Jennings, Stoker, & Bowers, 2009). More recently, Rico and Jennings (2016) analyzed data on Catalan parent-child pairs and found support for direct transmission of political worldviews from parents to children, as suggested by social learning theory. Small to moderate effects of intergenerational transmission were also found for political interests, political knowledge, and political efficacy (Jennings et al., 2009).

A more structural approach posits that political orientation may also be inherited (indirectly) through social positions and statuses (e.g., class, race, and religion), as well as shared characteristics such as social and cultural capital, all of which can independently affect adolescents' left-right location (Rico & Jennings, 2016; Vollebergh, Iedema, & Raaijmakers, 2001). Research has demonstrated, for example, that the transmission of political values is more intensive in families with more resources and where children are encouraged to participate in politics and gain political knowledge (Verba & Nie, 1972).

Whether transmission occurs directly or indirectly, individual and contextual factors also exist which facilitate or hinder political similarities between parents and children. Research has recently identified moderators of intergenerational transmission. It has been found that the association between the political identification of parents and their children increases when there is parental agreement on ideological orientation (Jennings et al., 2009); when parents demonstrate higher levels of political participation and the family has an active political climate; and when adolescents feel closeness toward their parents and there are intense and positive relationships within the family (Jennings & Niemi, 1974). Closeness plays a particularly unique role as regards gender; children are likely to embrace the political stance of the parent that is perceived as particularly competent or similar to themselves. Indeed, studies have found stronger transmission within same-sex dyads and from father to son (Boehnke, 2017; Portney, Eichenberg, & Niemi, 2009).

Still, there are reasons to assume that even if political orientations and behaviors are transmitted from parents to children during adolescence, individuals may embrace different political perspectives and patterns of engagement as they transition to adulthood. This is, to some degree, supported by trends of ideological dissimilarities recently found in studies of parent-child dyads. Corbetta, Tuorto, and Cavazza (2013), for example, report discontinuities in parent-adolescent concordance on left-right self-placement in Italy in both 1975 and 2010. Whereas in

---

[2] The theoretical foundations of intergenerational transmission of political attitudes and behaviors are rooted in social learning theory (Bandura, 1969), which asserts that owing to a lack of ability and knowledge, children and adolescents observe, imitate, internalize, and ultimately reproduce the attitudes and behaviors which are reinforced by key agents of socialization, figures who function as role models.

the mid-1970s, diverging orientations were characterized by right-wing parents and left-wing children, by the early 2010s, adolescents were found to embrace right-wing politics more than their parents.

In this context, generational replacement theory (Delli Carpini, 2006) emphasizes the importance of the sociopolitical context in which political socialization occurs. Historical events that occur during the coming of age leave a substantial formative influence on youth. Political change is partially determined by the degree to which youth adopt the view of their parents' generation or embrace distinct collective perspectives. Patterns of discontinuity in political engagement and views are therefore possible and will intersect with historical and societal changes.

Finally, political scientists have relied on developmental and rational choice models to question the persistence of early-acquired attitudes and their stability throughout life (Sears & Funk, 1999). Flanagan (2009) noted that in the transition from adolescence to adulthood, young people are characterized by a greater independence of thought and greater self-determination, and therefore their adulthood political views often divert from those of their parents. Nevertheless, common models in political science still predict persistence and relative stability in political predispositions across the lifespan. Sears and Funk (1999), for instance, examined trajectories in partisan attitudes in a large-sample longitudinal study among Americans from early adulthood to retirement age reveal substantial stability in attitudes across nearly four decades of data, alongside small but consistent changes among a considerable minority. Similarly, Becker and Saalfeld (2006) use panel data from the German Life-Course Study collected in the 1980s and 1990s to examine changes in party identification among German citizens, finding (particularly in the Western part of the country) an overall stability in party identification, despite increasing individual-level volatility over time. The debate remains as to whether and how political dispositions persist over the life course.

17.2.1 Potential Longitudinal Effect of Activism on Future Political Engagement

Political leanings are but one facet of the development of agency among adolescents and youth. Such preferences must be complemented with action. While it is common to limit such action to voting, for instance, it is also important to recognize other forms in which these preferences are actualized. In this regard, it has been hypothesized that the influence of parents on their children's political agency goes beyond the transmission of political worldviews. Although most research has focused on transmission in this area, scholars have also recently explored the effect of parental political participation on their offspring's patterns of engagement (Amnå, 2012; Jennings et al., 2009; Quintelier, 2015b). Parents shape not only the preferences of their offspring, according to this line of research, but also the engagement with the political world. For example, it has been found that children whose parents are civically involved are more likely to be politically engaged as adults (i.e., more likely to vote, volunteer, and be involved in political campaign and organization) compared to children whose parents were more disengaged from politics (McFarland & Thomas, 2006). Even children who frequently discuss politics with their parents or are exposed to political discussion at home are more likely to be politically active as they become adults (e.g., McIntosh, Hart, & Youniss, 2007). Quintelier (2015b) found that the intention to participate in politics is transmitted from parents to children indirectly, through a politicized family environment, measured by level of political discussion, more so among families of higher socioeconomic status.

However, parental effects on political engagement may be rather limited in scope and duration, since the intensity of parent-child relationship changes over the life course. Young adults elaborate their personal and social identities through multiple interactions outside the family (Erikson, 1968), in a process that weakens the influence of previously important role models. Moreover, in the framework of extended transition to adulthood that characterized youth in the late twentieth century and in our current time, other nonfamilial socialization agents often take the lead in determining political trajectories of emerging adults (Arnett, 2006). In line with this theoretical postulation, Quintelier (2015a, 2015b) explored the longitudinal effects of different agents of socialization on the development of Belgian adolescents' political participation. She found that parents and schools also contribute to political participation, although to a lesser extent than peers and voluntary associations.

In exploring diverse pathways of political socialization, scholarly attention has also been paid to the role of social networks and social media, which increasingly replace traditional social ties to families, institutions, and peers in shaping the political attitudes and engagement of young citizens (Loader, Vromen, & Xenos, 2014). Vraga et al. (2014) demonstrated how social media reinforces the role of peer relationships in political socialization during the 2008 US elections, as it encouraged civic and political talk among peers, thereby increasing their autonomy in shaping their own political orientations. Finally, Ojeda and Hatemi (2015) convincingly argue that transmission studies should also emphasize the active role offspring play in creating similarity between parents and children through influencing political convictions and behaviors of their parents.

Social psychology has traditionally focused on unraveling the psychological determinants and motives for political engagement and collective action (see Thomas & Louis, 2013) while rather neglecting the short- and long-term outcomes that may be associated with such endeavors. However, in recent years, a gradual increase in research on the psychological relationships, and benefits, of political activism and other forms of civic engagement has begun to emerge. In terms of impact on psychological and identity constructs, activism has been found to be positively related to self-esteem, physical and mental health, well-being (Boehnke & Wong, 2011), social support and cohesion, and other psychological outcomes. For example, the effect of activism on long-lasting political efficacy and empowerment has been linked to positive emotional responses to collective actions, such as pride (e.g., Drury & Reicher, 2009; Tausch & Becker, 2012). Nevertheless, the experience of failure or defeat was also found to lead to negative emotions such as upset and fear, which ultimately disempower activists and reduce their perceived efficacy (Drury & Reicher, 2005).

Youth activism has also been found to be associated with personal growth, including creative thinking (Becker, 2012), higher self-confidence (Shriver, Miller, & Cable, 2003), and lower self-derogation (Kaplan & Liu, 2000). In concordance with such positive psychological benefits, a body of research suggests that activism can have both short- and long-term effects on well-being (Boehnke & Wong, 2011; Klar & Kasser, 2009). For example, Boehnke and Wong (2011) found that political engagement among youth was negatively associated with what they called microsocial (personal) worries and positively associated with happiness in adulthood.

Activism during youth and early adulthood was also found to have biographical consequences for activists later in life. In terms of marital status and children, activists were more likely to remain single later in life and to have less children. In this domain, activism was also found to have a differential biographical impact on men and women. For example, Franz and McClelland (1994) found that women peace activists were found to choose an independent and career-pathed lifestyle, which led to higher incomes compared to non-activist women, while men activists entered the job market later and struggled occupationally.[3]

Research in recent decades has identified growing socioeconomic gaps in levels and forms of civic and political participation among youth from different social and ethnic background (e.g., Verba, Scholzman, & Brady, 1995). Evidently, young people from higher socioeconomic status encounter more institutional opportunities for activism (e.g., extracurricular activities during high school and college, community organizations, voluntary service programs) compared to youth from disadvantaged communities, who belong to institutions that provide less structural opportunities for socialization into political life (Flanagan & Levine, 2010; Settersten Jr, Furstenberg, & Rumbaut, 2008). Studies have also recently revealed the potential benefits of youth activism in resource-stressed communities. By taking a role as agents of change, whether to improve their status or in response to historical and national events (such as democratic deficits and wars), adolescents and youth from disadvantaged communities can turn negative emotions into motivation for social change, thereby increasing their political efficacy and minimizing political inequalities (Flanagan, 2013).

One additional possible outcome of activism pertains to activism itself: one's own involvement in activism may impact one's motivation and continuous involvement for civic and political engagement across the lifespan. According to this hypothesis, being active in youth may be a precursor to civic engagement in adulthood. Accordingly, Verba et al. (1995) argued that youth activism sets one on a

[3] For a review and classification of biographical consequences of activism, see Vestergren, Drury, and Chiriac (2017).

recruitment trajectory, as opportunities for sustainable engagement in organization are linked to previous engagement. The implications of this snowballing is particularly relevant for community empowerment, notably as programs aimed at addressing the basic needs of the poor are positively correlated with those constituents being active in the political arena (Verba, 2003).

The assertion of a downstream effect of activism in previous periods of life, however, still lies on thin empirical ground. Evidently, most research on activism across the lifespan is not longitudinal in its scope. Relying on cross-sectional and retrospective studies is detrimental to causal attribution: it could be that the aforementioned positive outcomes of activism merely characterize individuals who are prone to activism. In particular, longitudinal research on the impact of activism and civic engagement during adolescence on future engagement has been scarce. One such study by Verba et al. (1995) indicates that involvement in community-based organizations during adolescence predicts compatible civic engagement in adulthood. Similar results on the persistency of activism were obtained by Abramowitz and Nassi (1981) and Fendrich and Lovoy (1988).[4] In contrast, results from data collected among children and adolescents in West Germany from the mid-1980s to the early 2000s found that initial engagement with activities of the peace movement does not predict political activism in *early* adulthood.[5] Rather, it was found that cognitive involvement in political issues at an early age (e.g., factual knowledge) as well as emotional involvement (mainly being worried or stressed regarding societal conditions) predicts mobilization in early adulthood (Boehnke & Boehnke, 2005).

Although longitudinal research has yet to be sufficient, possible mechanisms underlying the long-term impact of civic and political engagement on further engagement have recently been delineated, either through qualitative research or by empirical testing in observational and even experimental research. Individual experiences in activism may feed back into intentions for continuous engagement through arousing strong emotions, altering efficacy expectations, and strengthening collective identification. Due to the psychological benefits of collective action on, for example, well-being, activists may be encouraged to continue to engage in protest where they experience positive emotions as a result of previous involvement (Ballard & Ozer, 2016).

In a series of correlational and experimental studies, Becker and Tausch (2015) have shown how psychological consequences of participation in collective action, and particularly emotions, shape and reshape motivations to engage in further actions. In particular, they argue that collective action participants can simultaneously experience positive self-directed emotions and negative outgroup-directed emotion, and both emotional orientations enhance motivation for future action. Moreover,

[4] Following 15 activists from the 1960s Berkeley free speech movement over 11 years and political engagement in adulthood among former adolescent activists in the 1960s American civil rights movement, respectively

[5] The same study as the one to be present in the second part of this chapter, but then with a larger sample, due to higher retention rates for earlier waves of the longitudinal study

they suggest that successful experiences with collective actions instill (ingroup-directed) pride among activists, while the experience of failure often breeds (outgroup-directed) anger, and both emotions increase commitment to collective action. Therefore, what determines continuous participation in collective action is not whether the preceding action was successful or not but rather how people experience, react, and frame its outcome. The long-term effect of activism on further engagement can also stem from growing identification with the group or organization and its social and political goals. Embracing collective identity, and even fusing one's self-identity to that of the group (Fischer, 2001; Kunst et al., 2018), can motivate an individual to continue acting for the collective cause through normative and nonnormative means.

One noticeable mediator of the effect of activism on future engagement is *political efficacy* – feelings of competence and motivation to engage in politics and to have an impact on the political process (Beaumont, 2010). It is mainly through political efficacy that the interplay between psychological and behavioral processes in political life is manifested. Blackwood and Louis (2012) found that peace activists' intention to engage in collective action was linked to group efficacy and perceptions of the individual benefits of participating in political activities. A successful collective action will, therefore, enhance one's efficacy and thereby one's continued engagement.

Beaumont (2010) explains that real-world political experience by youth can serve as skill-building experience for political mastery. Activism may provide young people from diverse backgrounds with models of involvement and enable them to feel connection to others. Becoming involved in collective action can also provide adolescents with social encouragement and help them build inclusive and supporting relationships and networks. By becoming active, young people can feel part of a larger community, which may increase their sense of security while engaging in political action, further strengthening bonds that themselves may seep into future policy articulation.

Finally, following collective engagement in civic or political life, adolescents were found to develop a capacity to challenge existing relations and commitment to reshaping the social world around them (Drury & Reicher, 2009). Evidence suggests activism may be an empowering experience for adolescents, instilling in them a resilient political outlook (Beaumont, 2010). Even in the face of defeat, activists who identify strongly with the movement are able to transform disempowering experiences to action motivation (Barr & Drury, 2009).

Research has also demonstrated durable effects of activism on efficacy. For example, civic and political activity in school has been found to enhance youth's belief in their individual and collective ability to bring about societal change, which may in turn stimulate long-lasting participation (Flanagan, 2013). Since the acquisition of political efficacy occurs mainly in early and mid-adolescence, we may expect early political engagement to predict continuous involvement, even all the way through early and mid-adulthood.

17.3 Examining the Relationship Between Political Orientation and Engagement Across Adolescence and Adulthood Through a German 30-Year Panel Study

The literature reviewed above highlights important yet rarely addressed questions that stem from the intersection between political socialization and developmental psychology, notably the durability and stability of political attitudes and engagement from adolescence to adulthood. To what extent does engaging in political activism as an adolescent contribute to activism into and during adulthood? To what extent does parental activism in one's adolescence uniquely influence one's own engagement in politics decades later? Finally, to what extent do political predispositions remain stable in adulthood while being affected by early-life political experiences? What is needed is data over a sufficiently long period, including items measuring variables associated with this agency.

Unique data collected in Germany allows us the opportunity to explore these questions and to examine stability and change in political engagement over more than 30 years. The longitudinal study under the title "Life under Nuclear Threat" commenced in 1985, against the background of Cold War tensions, notably the deployment of missiles in Germany in the framework of *rearmament*, and amidst fears of imminent nuclear war (Petri, Boehnke, Macpherson, & Meador, 1986). Concerned about the impact of events on children's and adolescents' mental health, a research team in West Berlin began the documentation of existential anxieties and mental health indicators among a convenience sample of young Germans (ages 8 to 23), obtained through controlled snowballing in cooperation with individuals and groups related to the peace movement. Many of the participants took part in the West German (ultimately unsuccessful) peace movement, participating in resistance activities, including mass demonstrations (for more details, see Boehnke & Boehnke, 2005; Boehnke & Wong, 2011).

Since the onset of the study, ten waves of data collection have been conducted over a period of three decades, with an interval of approximately 3.5 years between data-gathering waves. As expected, attrition has been substantial, though not particularly so compared to similar research endeavors. In the second wave of data collection, when the study "gained" its longitudinal scope, 837 individuals (of 1492 who left their addresses in Wave 1) participated. In the 10th wave in 2016/2017, 242 participants remained (a bit less than 30%). Despite this, attrition bias was not detected in previous publications (Boehnke & Wong, 2011).

Patterns of political orientation and engagement have been explored using structural equation modeling (SEM) techniques on data collected in three out of ten waves of the study: Wave 2 (W2) in 1988/1989, Wave 8 (W8) in 2009/2010, and the most recent Wave 10 (W10) in 2016/2017. Early-life engagement in politics has been selected from the second and not the initial wave of data collection, under the assumption that activism in late adolescence will reflect individual choices to a larger extent than in early adolescence (when, e.g., parents may have been "dragging" their children to demonstrations or engagement was probably more opportunistic in nature). In research addressing a similar topic, namely, the predictability of Wave 8 political engagement on the basis of several indicators from Waves 1 and 2, Boehnke, Sohr, and Stromberg (2016) showed that predictors from Wave 2 performed better as predictors of later behavior than predictors from Wave 1. Nevertheless, some of the respondents were in their early adolescence even during the second wave of data collection, and therefore age has been controlled for in all analyses. Data is then included from two recent waves in order to examine how early-life engagement predicts political orientation and engagement in adulthood. This allowed us to examine more complex longitudinal effects and thus strengthen the causal attribution of our results. Moreover, it enabled us to examine possible instabilities and trends in political orientation and engagement during the period of mid-adulthood itself.

In total, 242 respondents completed all three waves. Among them, 59.1% were female and 40.9% male. The average age of the respondents was roughly 17.5 in W2 (an age which can be referred to as "late adolescence"), 38.5 in W8 ("late 30s" mid-adulthood), and 45.5 in W10 ("mid 40s" in mid-adulthood), with age varying between 39 and 54 ($SD = 2.54$). There was no difference in the average age between men and women, $t(240) = -1.36$, $p = 0.18$. The average income of respondents in 2017, according to self-reports, was 4016 Euros per month, approximately twice the average monthly income in Germany (about 2200 Euro). Moreover, participants were also more educated on average than the wider German population, with approximately 83% holding a German *Abitur*, a certificate of tertiary education entrance qualification only held by roughly 40% of their birth cohorts (Boehnke & Boehnke, 2005).

We use two measures of political engagement from W2. One's *own activism* in adolescence is measured by a single-item, dichotomous measure "Have you been active in the peace movement since you took part in the first study (1985 and later)?" with options *yes* and *no*. To measure *parental activism*, respondents were asked to indicate whether their parents "have already been active in the peace movement" without limiting the activity to a certain period, with options *yes* and *no*.

Two single-item measures of *political orientation* and *engagement* were used both in W8 and W10. To obtain *political orientation*, participants were asked to place themselves on a discrete 10-point left-right scale (1 = *extreme left*, 10 = *extreme right*). Similar measures are frequently employed in studies of political and peace psychology to obtain general personal political preferences. Finally, to measure *political engagement* in adulthood, participants ranked their engagement on a 4-point scale with the following markers: 0 = *I have no interest in politics*; 1 = *I am not particularly interested in politics*; 2 = *I am interested in politics, but I am not active myself*; and 3 = *I am interested in politics and actively involved*. Both measures were used as continuous in the analysis.

As is common in many longitudinal studies, there was a considerable amount of missing data on single items. In order to increase the power of our analysis, and to

Table 17.1 Mean values and standard deviations (in parentheses) for political orientation and political engagement in Wave 8 and Wave 10 for all participants and by gender, orientation, and activism groups

Grouping variable		Political orientation		Political engagement	
		Wave 8	Wave 10	Wave 8	Wave 10
All participants	*N* = 242	4.02 (1.42)	4.70 (1.71)	1.80 (0.59)	1.66 (0.66)
Gender	Female (59.1%)	3.87 (1.24)	4.45 (1.46)	1.69 (0.63)	1.64 (0.66)
	Male (40.9%)	4.22 (1.63)	5.07 (1.96)	1.95 (0.47)	1.68 (0.66)
Political orientation [a]	Left (71.1%)	3.45 (1.02)	3.86 (1.07)	1.85 (0.57)	1.63 (0.69)
	Right (28.9%)	5.40 (1.31)	6.79 (1.05)	1.67 (0.61)	1.71 (0.59)
Own activism [b]	Non-active (63.2%)	4.35 (1.42)	5.18 (1.68)	1.71 (0.56)	1.62 (0.60)
	Active (36.8%)	3.45 (1.23)	3.88 (1.44)	1.97 (0.60)	1.73 (0.77)
Parental activism [b]	Non-active (57.4%)	4.48 (1.37)	5.26 (1.65)	1.73 (0.56)	1.67 (0.63)
	Active (42.6%)	3.39 (1.24)	3.96 (1.48)	1.92 (0.63)	1.64 (0.73)

Note: High scores are indicative of higher level of political engagement and more right-wing attitudes

[a]Midpoint split of Wave 10 measure

[b]Dichotomous measures in Wave 2

facilitate an analysis based on advanced statistical procedures, we impute missing data using AMOS' built-in maximum likelihood algorithm.[6]

Table 17.1 presents means and standard deviations for the study variables by gender, political orientation (median split), and self- and parental activism groups. We first examined general trends in levels of political engagement and orientation between the two recent waves. Analyses of variance revealed a significant decrease in average levels of political engagement between W8 and W10. Moreover, there is evidence of a significant main effect of gender and, more importantly, a significant interaction between gender and time. In their late 30s, men were on average more politically engaged than women (see Table 17.1). However, 7 years later, women's engagement remained stationary, while men's engagement decreased significantly. Moreover, among both men and women, there was a significant shift to the right between W8 and W10.

In order to explicate the relationship between early-life activism and adulthood political engagement and worldviews, and to examine the extent to which these relationships are different for men and women, we fitted a multiple group structural equation model. Insignificant paths in both groups were constrained to be equal to zero to achieve a parsimonious yet well-fitting model. The model integrates a cross-lagged analysis suitable for analyzing panel models with repeated measures (W8 and W10 political orientation and engagement). Finally, age is included in the model as a control variable to account for age variations among participants.

Initially, we fitted an unconstrained model. in which all structural paths were allowed to vary across groups (Fig. 17.1). The obtained model was well fitting

[6]When subsequently reporting results, we omit most statistical details for the sake of brevity and readability. A full version of the current chapter, including all statistical evidence in detail, can be obtained from the corresponding author.

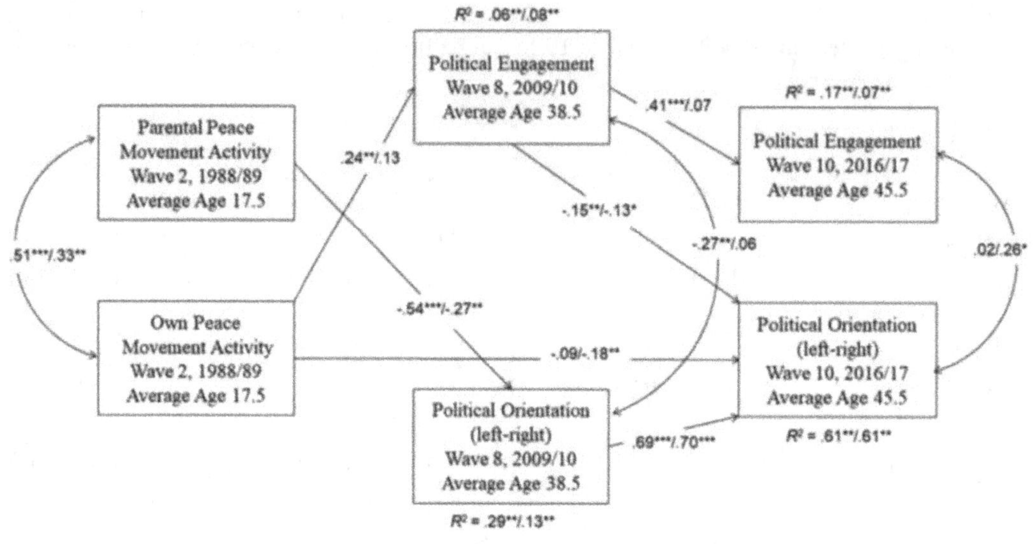

Fig. 17.1 Multiple group path model is displayed with standardized coefficients for women/men. $*p < 0.05$, $**p < 0.01$, $***p < 0.001$. Age is included in the model as a covariate of Wave 2 variable and as a predictor of Wave 8 and Wave 10 variables, but is not displayed for purposes of presentation

according to various indices of goodness of fit. Next, we constrained all regression weights to be equal for men and women. Results suggest that the model is significantly different for men and women. Consequently, we conducted a path-by-path analysis in order to find where men and women differ on specific paths.

First, we found a significant and positive relationship between adolescence-time activism in the peace movement and parallel parental activism, for both women and men. This can serve as initial evidence that political activism was intergenerationally transmitted among our peace movement sympathizers before or during late adolescence.

Second, early-life activism in the peace movement positively predicted late-30s political engagement among women, but interestingly not among their male counterparts. Third, we found that one's own peace movement activism in adolescence predicts more left-leaning attitudes at roughly mid-40s, but only among men.

Fourth, the model indicates that parental involvement in the peace movement three decades previously exhibited no significant effect on current *political engagement*. It did, however, significantly predict *political orientation* in adulthood: Among both men and women, having activist parents during adolescence is associated with being more leftist in late 30s. Furthermore, parental activism predicted political orientation in the mid-40s indirectly, via political orientation in late 30s, for both women and men. These results indicate that participants with peace activist parents increased their left-leaning orientations in adulthood.

Fifth, the cross-lagged relationship between political orientation and engagement in adulthood showed that for both men and women, higher engagement in the late 30s predicted left-leaning attitudes at mid-40s, while political orientation in late 30s had no significant effect on later engagement. Even during adulthood, sustained political interest and/or activism can buffer against the observed slip to the right side of the political spectrum.

Finally, a differential relationship pattern emerged between political orientation and political engagement within each gender group during middle adulthood. Among women, a stronger leftist orientation was associated with higher engagement in politics in their late 30s, but not in their mid-40s; the difference in W8 and W10 covariances between political orientation and engagement among women was significant. The reverse effects were found among men – i.e., no association between engagement and orientation in their late 30s, with stronger right-leaning orientation associated with higher engagement in their mid-40s. In other words, left-leaning women were more active than right-leaning women in their late 30s but not in their mid-40s, while right-leaning men were as active as left-leaning men in their late 30s, but more than the latter 7 years later.

17.4 Discussion

It is evident that literature in developmental, political, and peace psychology on processes of political socialization, with a focus on intergenerational and lifespan development on political worldviews and active participation in politics, remains an under-explored area of research. The empirical examination of the topic here, utilizing a remarkable longitudinal dataset collected over more than three decades among West Germans who were adolescents in the 1980s, provides some headway into this area of scholarship.

By employing analyses of longitudinal effects, we are able to explore potential causal effects in political attitudes and behaviors and thereby make an important contribution to a research field with a considerable and detrimental dearth of longitudinal data. Moreover, we demonstrate differential effects and trends for women and men, a potentially significant contribution to the understanding of gendered processes in political socialization and lifespan development, and one which should be explored further in future studies.

The findings offer several insights into the way early-life political engagement may be related to adulthood engagement and the way political orientation and engagement interact in adulthood. This is true both in the particular context of German peace movement sympathizers and activists and potentially in more general terms. First, we find evidence of a lasting effect of early-life activism on political engagement in adulthood: West German peace activists, especially women, maintained their commitment to political activity from late adolescence to mid-adulthood. This confirms, at least for female activists, the assertion that activism in adolescence does not only increase further political engagement in the short run but also in a sustainable way (Flanagan, 2009, 2013; Verba et al., 1995). With some caution, we can report that female adolescent activists are more likely to be adult activists compared to female adolescents who stay away from political activities.

From a policy perspective, this empowerment at early ages translates into the capacity to influence the policy agenda in ways that may have knock-on effects for future cohorts.

For the time being, we can only speculate about reasons for the "gendered" results. We find it plausible to assume that the gender difference has more to do with the participants' individual "fertility history" – that is, *when* in the life course, have participants become parents themselves? We presume this to have a gendered impact on political involvement among men and women. Men, on average, become a parent together with women, who are younger than they are. This might keep both away from politics at different times of their individual lives and with political demands that are in line with their life-course situations. Childcare traditions may also, however, have a more direct "push" effect on women than men as regards engagement in politics (e.g., topics like children's rights and even peace may carry more salience). While data on fertility histories are available from the project, they could not be analyzed for the current chapter; further research is needed to unpack potential relationships.

It is, of course, important to consider that the prediction of adulthood engagement by one's involvement as an adolescent may merely point out a selection effect. Research already suggests that volunteers and non-volunteers hold different personalities and values (Matsuba, Hart, & Atkins, 2007). Moreover, Boehnke and Wong (2011) note that active youngsters in the panel study were already characterized by better mental health than their non-active counterparts in the onset of research.

Second, the positive relationship between adolescents' own activism in the peace movement during the second half of the 1980s (assuming it was voluntary) and their parents' involvement in that movement may serve as initial evidence that political activism was directly or indirectly transmitted from parents to children. Pertaining to sustained effects, we find that parental peace activism during adolescence has a small effect on engagement in people's late 30s; however, this effect dissipates by the time participants reached their mid-40s. Nevertheless, there was no evidence of traces of intergenerational transmission of political engagement more than 30 years after the end of adolescence.

Third, we do find a positive relationship between parental activism in adolescence and adulthood *political orientation*. This may be interpreted through the framework of intergenerational transmission, as opposed to the case of engagement noted above. Although we did not include a measure of parental (or self) left-right orientation in adolescence, it is plausible that active parents leaned more to the left than non-active parents at the peak of peace activism in the 1980s. If this is true, this finding can be seen as corroborating a considerable long-term effect of intergenerational transmission on political attitudes. Moreover, it was previously found that politically engaged parents are more likely to transmit their political perceptions to their offspring (see also Jennings et al., 2009). It is therefore possible that levels of parent-child ideological continuity increased with higher parental politicization, contributing to the positive and lasting relationship between parental behavior and children's attitudes. It may also be the case that those exposed to the agency reinforcing impact of activism may internalize the possibility, and indeed desirability, of change than their counterparts.

Fourth, our analysis also revealed interesting findings regarding recent trends in political worldviews and engagement among Germans who grew up in West Germany during the Cold War and were in one way or another attached to the peace movement. Although men and women were active in the peace movement in similar proportion as adolescents, we find that, in their mid-30s, men were slightly more engaged than their female counterparts. Previous studies also find that women are, in general, less interested and active in politics compared to men (e.g., Childs, 2004). In addition, during mid-adulthood, levels of political engagements decreased among men and among participants with left-leaning orientations. Recent findings from the USA also suggest a gradual decline in civic and political engagement along the life course (e.g., Jennings & Stoker, 2004).

Quite interestingly, while women were more left-leaning than men in the beginning of the current decade, a trend of increasing right-leaning orientations is observed for both genders in the course of the decade. It is not clear to us whether the increase in rightward identification is rooted in universal lifespan or generational processes or is part of an overall conservative trend in the German society in recent years, as well as in other parts of the Western world. It is possible that this trend reflects the widely observed increasing support for far-right parties in Germany, such as *Alternative für Deutschland* (AFD), against the background of growing anti-immigration sentiments amidst recent waves of immigration into the country (Otto & Steinhardt, 2017).

That being said, we also find that (among men) adolescent activism is linked to left-leaning attitudes in adulthood, and parental activism in adolescence is consistently linked to left-leaning attitudes in adulthood for both genders. More importantly, those who were active and whose parents were active demonstrate relative resistance to the right-wing trend. These effects reveal a potentially important function of early-life activism and one which has clear policy implications: it seems possible that adolescent involvement, as well as sustained activism in adulthood, empowers individuals to maintain their beliefs amidst societal changes. This potential function remains, however, a hypothesis at this stage; future research may provide a more thorough analysis of the relationship between activism and stability in political worldviews.

Finally, the recent trends of increasing right-wing identification and decreasing engagement among men, and left-leaning adults in general, seem to have changed the relationship between political orientation and engagement between our two adulthood data-gathering waves. By 2017, left-leaning women were no longer more active than right-leaning women, while right-leaning men became more active than left-leaning men. This may also be explained by the recent decline in left-wing politics in Germany, similar to other European countries (Anheier & Weßels, 2015), or a weakening of political identities in Western democracies. This is manifested in increasing instability in political preference, growing dissatisfaction with (and lack of trust in) traditional politics, and eroding social cohesion in contrast to the growing importance of personal identities. In Germany, a gradual process of partisan dealignment was observed at the end of the twentieth century, which may also contribute to instability in self-placement along the political continuum (Becker & Saalfeld, 2006).

Some limitations of the analysis presented in this chapter must be considered. First, our data were not immune to common difficulties inherent to longitudinal endeavors, such as substantial (though not necessarily selective) attrition. Although we have attempted to expose causal relationships, we should emphasize that the study was observational and correlational in nature. We merely exposed relationships between past and present level of political engagement and were unable to point out the role of other potentially important environmental and psychological variables in determining political engagement in adulthood, as well as in intervening in the sequences between adolescence and adulthood participation. We can only hope that future research will attempt to increase the scope of our understanding of the factors that influence political participation across the lifespan.

Second, the readers must keep in mind the presumably limited external validity of the findings. The data were obtained from a population of peace-prone individuals with a high level of educational attainment at the onset of the study, thus not likely to be representative for the wider West German mid-1960s to mid-1970s cohort (see Boehnke & Boehnke, 2005). Consequently, the result must be interpreted in light of parallel results from other samples and regions. Second, one of the weaknesses of this study is the absence of potential mediators of the examined effects. More research is needed to explicate causal mechanisms which may be at work in linking early-life and adulthood engagement. Lastly, general, single-item measures of activism and engagement were utilized herein, largely ignoring length, intensity, and types of engagement with politics. One must also consider the rapidly changing multidimensional nature of political engagement (both between and within conventional and nonconventional forms) and the possible differential mechanisms and effects involving each form (see Van Deth, 2014). Future research may differentiate between those dimensions of activism, which possibly involve different motivational factors and long-term outcomes.

Concerning the implications of this research to the practice of civic and political engagement among adolescence and youth, given the partial-yet-positive associations found between early-life activism and adulthood engagement, as well as the potential function of activism in strengthening pro-peace attitudes, we can only recommend that communities involve adolescence and youth in politics. The rationale is clear: for a polity to remain vibrant and open to transformations, future generations (and especially those who traditionally had less space in the political arena) must be empowered with the experience of agency. This is particularly so for non-male, non-majority constituents.

This might, as it seems, instigate a lifetime of political involvement. It is also worth repeating the recommendation given by Flanagan (2009): to facilitate lifelong effects of civic engagement, it is not enough to engage adolescents in activism; one must also ensure that such activities enable them to explore diverse perspectives and develop efficacious attitudes toward politics. What seems of particular import is an offering that is life-course-sensitive. Such an offering should facilitate activism across life-course transitions. Transitions seem to be powerful stumbling blocks of political activism. When people leave tertiary education, enter the job market, become a parent, etc., these life events pose challenges to political activism continuance. Life-course transitions, thus, need special attention also by civil society agents.

The current findings add to the growing research on the importance of ensuring that gender equality and sustainability are supported by the voices of those most affected. Political engagement matters most for those policies which guard against adverse life-course events (e.g., social protection), and as such, empowerment is a necessary (though by no means sufficient) element of sustainable communities.

Considering future research, bridging political and peace psychology with developmental perspectives still requires longitudinal research, preferably following developmental pathways of socialization and change across the lifespan. Ideally, it would be beneficial to have data prior to the onset of political activity and partisanship in adolescence, not least to enable researchers to rule out selection effects.

References

Abramowitz, S., & Nassi, A. (1981). Keeping the faith: Psychosocial correlates of activism persistence into middle adulthood. *Journal of Youth and Adolescence, 10*, 507–523.

Amnå, E. (2012). How is civic engagement developed over time? Emerging answers from a multidisciplinary field. *Journal of Adolescence, 35*(3), 611–627.

Anheier, H. K., & Weßels, B. (2015). Political culture, political satisfaction and the rollback of democracy. *Global Policy, 6*, 93–105.

Arnett, J. J. (2006). Emerging adulthood in Europe: A response to Bynner. *Journal of Youth Studies, 9*(1), 111–123.

Ballard, P. J., & Ozer, E. J. (2016). The implications of youth activism for health and well-being. In J. Conner & S. M. Rosen (Eds.), *Contemporary youth activism: Advancing social justice in the United States* (pp. 223–243). Santa Barbara, CA: Greenwood.

Bandura, A. (1969). Social-learning theory of identifactory processes. In D. A. Goslin (Ed.), *Handbook of socialization: Theory and research* (pp. 213–261). New York, NY: Rand McNally & Company.

Barr, D., & Drury, J. (2009). Activist identity as a motivational resource: Dynamics of (dis)empowerment at the G8 direct actions, Gleneagles, 2005. *Social Movement Studies, 8*, 243–260.

Beaumont, E. (2010). Political agency and empowerment: Pathways for developing a sense of political efficacy in young adults. In L. R. Sherrod, J. Torney-Purta, & C. A. Flanagan (Eds.), *Handbook of research on civic engagement in youth* (pp. 525–558). Hoboken, NJ: Wiley.

Becker, J. C. (2012). The system-stabilizing role of identity management strategies: Social creativity can undermine collective action for social change. *Journal of Personality and Social Psychology, 103*(4), 647.

Becker, J. C., & Tausch, N. (2015). A dynamic model of engagement in normative and non-normative collective action: Psychological antecedents, consequences, and barriers. *European Review of Social Psychology, 26*(1), 43–92.

Becker, R., & Saalfeld, T. (2006). Continuity and change of party identification in Germany, 1986–2000: A contribution to construct validation using longitudinal data. Paper presented at *the ECPR Join Sessions of Workshops*, Nicosia, Cyprus, 25–29 April 2006.

Blackwood, L. M., & Louis, W. R. (2012). If it matters for the group then it matters to me: Collective action outcomes for seasoned activists. *British Journal of Social Psychology, 51*(1), 72–92.

Boehnke, K. (2017). Ist Rechtsextremismus „erblich"? Zur Ähnlichkeit rechtsextremer Verhaltenstendenzen von Studierenden und ihren Eltern [Is right-wing extremism ‚inheritable'? On the similarity of right-wing extremist behavioral tendencies among university students and their parents]. *Zeitschrift für Familienforschung, 29*(3), 340–354.

Boehnke, K., & Boehnke, M. (2005). Once a peacenik – always a peacenik? Results from a German six-wave, twenty-year longitudinal study. *Peace and Conflict: Journal of Peace Psychology, 11*, 337–354.

Boehnke, K., & Wong, B. (2011). Adolescent political activism and long-term happiness: A 21-year longitudinal study on the development of micro-and macrosocial worries. *Personality and Social Psychology Bulletin, 37*(3), 435–447.

Boehnke, K., Sohr, S., & Stromberg, C. (2016). "Politische Persönlichkeiten" – eine aussterbende Spezies? [Political personalities – an endangered species?]. In A. Gürlevik, K. Hurrelmann & C. Palentien (Eds.), *Jugend und Politik* (pp. 227–253). Wiesbaden, Germany: Springer VS.

Bogaards, M., & Deutsch, F. (2015). Deliberation by, with, and for University Students. *Journal of Political Science Education, 11*(2), 221–232.

Childs, S. (2004). A British gender gap? Gender and political participation. *The Political Quarterly, 75*(4), 422–424.

Corbetta, P. G., Tuorto, D., & Cavazza, N. (2013). Parents and children in the political socialisation process: Changes in Italy over thirty-five years. In S. Abendschon (Ed.), *Growing into politics: Context and timing of political socialization* (pp. 11–32). Colchester, UK: Ecpr Press.

Delli Carpini, M. (2006). Generational replacement. In L. Sherrod, C. A. Flanagan, R. Kassimir, & A. K. Syvertsen (Eds.), *Youth activism: An international encyclopedia* (pp. 282–284). Westport, CT: Greenwood.

Drury, J., & Reicher, S. (2005). Explaining enduring empowerment: A comparative study of collective action and psychological outcomes. *European Journal of Social Psychology, 35*(1), 35–58.

Drury, J., & Reicher, S. (2009). Collective psychological empowerment as a model of social change: Researching crowds and power. *Journal of Social Issues, 65*, 707–725.

Easton, D. (1968). The theoretical relevance of political socialization. *Canadian Journal of Political Science/Revue canadienne de science politique, 1*(2), 125–146.

Erikson, E. H. (1968). *Identity: Youth and crisis*. New York, NY: W.W. Norton.

Fendrich, J., & Lovoy, K. (1988). Back to the future: Adult behaviour of former student activists. *American Sociological Review, 53*, 780–784.

Fischer, C. (2001). *"Das gehört jetzt irgendwie zu mir." Mobilisierung von Jugendlichen aus den neuen Bundesländern zum Engagement in einem Umweltverband. Eine Fallstudie am Beispiel der BUNDjugend* ["Somehow this now belongs to me." Mobilization of adolescents towards engagement in an environmental association in the new federal states. A case study of BUNDjugend]. Chemnitz: unpublished doctoral dissertation. Retrieved from http://monarch.qucosa.de/fileadmin/data/qucosa/documents/4480/data/Index3.html

Flanagan, C. (2009). Young people's civic engagement and political development. In A. Furlong (Ed.), *International handbook of youth and young adulthood: New perspectives and agendas* (pp. 293–300). New York, NY: Routledge.

Flanagan, C., & Levine, P. (2010). Civic engagement and the transition to adulthood. *The Future of Children, 20*(1), 159–180.

Flanagan, C. A., & Tucker, C. J. (1999). Adolescents' explanations for political issues: Concordance with their views of self and society. *Developmental Psychology, 35*(5), 1198–1209.

Flanagan, C. A. (2013). *Teenage citizens: The political theories of the young*. Harvard, IL: Harvard University Press.

Franz, C., & McClelland, D. (1994). Lives of women and men active in the social protests of the 1960s: A longitudinal study. *Journal of Personality and Social Psychology, 66*(1), 196–205.

Inglehart, R., & Klingemann, H.-D. (1976). Party identification, ideological preference, and the left-right dimension among Western mass publics. In I. Budge, I. Crewe, & D. Farlie (Eds.), *Party identification and beyond* (pp. 243–273). London, UK: Wiley.

Jennings, M. K., & Niemi, R. G. (1974). *The political character of adolescence: The influence of families and schools*. Princeton, NJ: Princeton University Press.

Jennings, M. K., & Niemi, R. G. (1981). *Generations and politics*. Princeton, NJ: Princeton University Press.

Jennings, M. K., & Stoker, L. (2004). Social trust and civic engagement across time and generations. *Acta Politica, 39*, 342–379.

Jennings, M. K., Stoker, L., & Bowers, J. (2009). Politics across generations: Family transmission reexamined. *Journal of Politics, 71*(3), 782–799.

Kaplan, H., & Liu, X. (2000). Social protest and self-enhancement - a conditional relationship. *Sociological Forum, 15*(4), 595–616.

Klar, M., & Kasser, T. (2009). Some benefits of being an activist: Measuring activism and its role in psychological well-being. *Political Psychology, 30*(5), 755–777.

Kunst, J. R., Boos, B., Kimel, S. Y., Obaidi, M., Shani, M., & Thomsen, L. (2018). Engaging in extreme activism in support of others' political struggles: The role of politically motivated fusion with out-groups. *PLoS One, 13*(1), e0190639.

Levine, P. (2007). *The future of democracy: Developing the next generation of American citizens*. Medford, MA: Tufts University Press.

Loader, B., Vromen, A., & Xenos, M. (2014). *The networked young citizen: Social media, political participation and civic engagement*. New York, NY: Routledge.

Matsuba, J. K., Hart, D., & Atkins, R. (2007). Psychological and social-structural influences on commitment to volunteering. *Journal of Research in Personality, 41*, 889–907.

McFarland, D. A., & Thomas, R. J. (2006). Bowling young: How youth voluntary associations influence adult political participation. *American Sociological Review, 71*(3), 401–425.

McIntosh, H., Hart, D., & Youniss, J. (2007). The influence of family political discussion on Youth Civic Development: Which parent qualities matter? *PS: Political Science and Politics, 40*(3), 495–499.

Norris, P. (2011). *Democratic deficit: Critical citizens revisited*. New York, NY: Cambridge University Press.

Ojeda, C., & Hatemi, P. (2015). Accounting for the child in the transmission of party identification. *American Sociological Review, 80*(6), 1150–1174.

Otto, A. H., & Steinhardt, M. F. (2017). The relationship between immigration and the success of far-right political parties in Germany. *DICE Report, 15*(4), 20–23.

Petri, H., Boehnke, K., Macpherson, M. J., & Meador, M. (1986). Bedrohtheit bei Jugendlichen [The feeling of threat among adolescents]. *Psychosozial, 9*(29), 62–71.

Portney, K. E., Eichenberg, R. C., & Niemi, R. G. (2009). Gender differences in political and civic engagement among young people. *Paper presented at the Annual Meeting of the American Political Science Association*, Toronto, Canada, September 2009.

Quintelier, E. (2015a). Engaging adolescents in politics: The longitudinal effect of political socialization agents. *Youth & Society, 47*(1), 51–69.

Quintelier, E. (2015b). Intergenerational transmission of political participation intention. *Acta Politica, 50*(3), 279–296.

Rico, G., & Jennings, M. K. (2016). The formation of left-right identification: Pathways and correlates of parental influence. *Political Psychology, 37*(2), 237–252.

Sears, D. O., & Funk, C. L. (1999). Evidence of the long-term persistence of adults' political predispositions. *The Journal of Politics, 61*(1), 1–28.

Settersten, R. A., Jr., Furstenberg, F. F., & Rumbaut, R. G. (Eds.). (2008). *On the frontier of adulthood: Theory, research, and public policy*. Chicago, IL: University of Chicago Press.

Shriver, T. E., Miller, A. C., & Cable, S. (2003). Women's work: Women's involvement in the Gulf War illness movement. *The Sociological Quarterly, 44*(4), 639–658.

Thomas, E. F., & Louis, W. R. (2013). Doing democracy: The social psychological mobilization and consequences of collective action. *Social Issues and Policy Review, 7*(1), 173–200.

Van der Eijk, C., Schmitt, H., & Binder, T. (2005). Left–right orientations and party choice. In J. Thomassen (Ed.), *The European voter: A comparative study of modern democracies* (pp. 167–191). Oxford, UK: Oxford University Press.

Van Deth, J. W. (2014). A conceptual map of political participation. *Acta Politica, 49*(3), 349–367.

Verba, S. (2003). Would the dream of political equality turn out to be a nightmare? *Perspectives on Politics, 1*(4), 663–679.

Verba, S., & Nie, N. H. (1972). *Participation in America: Political democracy and social equality*. New York, NY: Harper & Row.

Verba, S., Scholzman, K. L., & Brady, H. E. (1995). *Voice and equality: Civic voluntarism in American politics*. Cambridge, MA: Harvard University Press.

Vestergren, S., Drury, J., & Chiriac, E. H. (2017). The biographical consequences of protest and activism: A systematic review and a new typology. *Social Movement Studies, 16*(2), 203–221.

Vollebergh, W. A. M., Iedema, J., & Raaijmakers, Q. A. W. (2001). Intergenerational transmission and the formation of cultural orientations in adolescence and young adulthood. *Journal of Marriage and Family, 63*(4), 1185–1198.

Vraga, E. K., Bode, L., Yang, J., Edgerly, S., Thorson, K., Wells, C., & Shah, D. V. (2014). Political influence across generations: Partisanship and candidate evaluations in the 2008 election. *Information, Communication & Society, 17*(2), 184–202.

Welzel, C., & Deutsch, F. (2012). Emancipative values and nonviolent protest: The importance of 'ecological' effects. *British Journal of Political Science, 42*(2), 465–479.

Chapter 18
Enabling Full Participation: A Community-Led Approach to Child Protection

Kathleen Kostelny, Michael Wessells, and Ken Ondoro

18.1 Introduction

Humanitarian and development work are currently of high importance, as the global burden of refugees and displaced people has reached unprecedented levels and inequalities have multiplied rapidly. Although humanitarian and development work has made significant contributions to human well-being, there is considerable room from improvement (Slim, 2015).

Peace psychology offers a useful lens for identifying and guiding some much needed improvements in the way in which humanitarian and development work are done. A cornerstone of peace psychology is the importance of social justice and the ending of the structural violence that both enables much direct, episodic violence and causes extensive suffering itself (Christie, Tint, Wanger, & Winter, 2008; Christie, Wagner, & Winter, 2001; Deutch, 1985; Galtung, 1985). From this standpoint, it is useful to use a peace psychology lens to analyze ways that humanitarian and development work may unintentionally contribute to social injustice and structural violence.

As we argue below, work on humanitarian support in emergency settings and on longer-term development in more stable settings has typically used a top-down approach in which outside experts and nongovernment organizations (NGOs) analyze a problem, identify the relevant intervention, and lead the intervention and its evaluation. This approach marginalizes local people and often imposes outside approaches that marginalize local culture (Kostelny, 2006; Wessells & Monterio, 2001). In fact, local people are actors who can bring local resources, understandings,

K. Kostelny (✉) · K. Ondoro
Child Resilience Alliance, Wilton, CT, USA

M. Wessells
Columbia University, New York, NY, USA

N. Balvin, D. J. Christie (eds.), *Children and Peace*, Peace Psychology Book Series, https://doi.org/10.1007/978-3-030-22176-8_18

and creativity into play in service of solving their own problems in ways that fit the local context (Wessells, 2015).

Even when humanitarian and development agencies have deliberately enabled participation by local people, it is often neither highly inclusive nor very deep. In the field of child protection, for example, humanitarians (the authors included) work under intense pressure for urgent results, leading to a "participation light" approach. As explained below, the most vulnerable people are often left out, and local people hold little real power.

Fortunately, current global efforts in the humanitarian sector call for a transformation in the way humanitarian assistance is provided. This proposed transformation, known as the Grand Bargain, has as one of its central pillars full participation – with voice and power – by all people, including children and people who are most vulnerable (Australian Aid et al., 2016; IASC, 2016; ICVA, 2017). This revised way of working applies to many different sectors, although this chapter attempts to show its transformative power within the field of child protection.

The purpose of this chapter is to analyze how more participatory approaches to community-based child protection can help the child protection sector achieve the high levels of inclusivity, participation, and local ownership that contribute to relevant, effective, and sustainable support for vulnerable children. The chapter begins with an analysis of the limitations of the dominant, top-down approach to community-based child protection. Next, using a case study from Kenya, it examines a bottom-up, community-led approach to child protection that places the power to make the key decisions in the hands of local people and achieves high levels of inclusivity and local ownership. It concludes with a reflection on the potential value of enabling bottom-up approaches in developing wider child protection systems.

18.1.1 The Limits of Top-Down Approaches

Top-down, expert-driven approaches are needed and effective in specific contexts, but not in all contexts. For example, in emergency situations where protective processes have been damaged or do not exist, it may make sense for agencies to use a top-down approach. Nonetheless, they have limits to enabling full participation by communities.

A first limitation is that communities are viewed as beneficiaries and thus become passive recipients of an intervention. The communities are viewed as in need of education about child protection and child rights and are seen as having harmful traditional practices and norms, such as female genital mutilation, child marriage, child labor, and corporal punishment (Wessells et al., 2015).

A second limitation is the power asymmetry between the experts and local people. Organizations hold the power, and communities have little input as to the issue to be addressed or what action will be taken. Experts analyze the situation and select the intervention according to the issue to be addressed and child protection standards. They, or a local community-based organization (CBO) partner, typically manage, guide, and train community members. They also provide most, if not all, of the resources for the intervention. The intervention often follows a manual or protocol with specific time schedules and log frames that are not part of the community's usual rhythms.

A third limitation of a top-down approach is that children's participation is often low or marginal. Though many NGOs aim to support child participation, this is seldom achieved. For example, because most children do not attend community meetings, and children are typically not given a platform to speak, they would have no input into decisions to partner with an NGO on a child protection issue. Furthermore, when children are members of an intervention such as a child welfare or child protection committee, they often are token members with little voice or influence (Wessells, 2009).

A fourth limitation is lack of inclusiveness – typically, the views of the entire community are not brought forth. At the beginning of an intervention, community meetings organized by NGOs often consist of several meetings where some subgroups of the community are not represented. These are often the most vulnerable groups, including the poorest of the poor, the disabled, and the children. The discussion usually is focused on specific categories of child protection or child rights that fit the programming approach of NGOs – such as violence against children, child marriage, and child trafficking. Typically, the discussion is not geared to deep and extensive listening about the community's main concerns about children.

The limits of a top-down approach are strikingly apparent in one of the most widely implemented child protection interventions – community child welfare committees or child protection committees (Wessells, 2009). In a comprehensive, global review of this extensively used child protection intervention, it was found that child protection and welfare committees were overwhelmingly based on NGOs' agendas. Community members played secondary roles to the roles of experts who organized, trained, and "mobilized" the communities. For the most part, the outside experts did not learn about or take into consideration the communities' traditional beliefs and practices regarding children. Not surprisingly, the community viewed these child protection committees as NGO projects, and local people felt low ownership of the projects. The child welfare committees were thus not sustainable when the NGOs finished their projects at the end of funding cycles – a finding of great concern as this review also found that community ownership was the most important factor for effectiveness and sustainability (Wessells, 2009).

Moreover, there is increasing evidence that top-down, impositional approaches, such as teaching child rights, can lead local people to view child rights as a harm to children and to even go to great lengths to continue traditional practices that clash with human rights standards under the radar to NGOs (Wessells & Kostelny, 2017; Wessells, Kostelny, & Ondoro, 2014).

18.1.2 Community-Led Approaches

Previous research has documented the effectiveness of community-driven approaches in other sectors, yet in the field of child protection, it has not been widely used. Such community-led approaches are part of a wider family of participatory action research (PAR) grounded in the work of Paulo Freire (1990). Primary tenets of community-led approaches include high levels of participation and stress equality where researchers and community members contribute equally while paying attention to issues of power, gender, and class (Minkler & Wallerstein, 2008).

Importantly, in advancing community-led approaches to child protection, communities are recognized as having social and cultural strengths, experience caring for children, concern for children's well-being, and agency. Their strengths are at the forefront, with community structures and processes built on whenever feasible. A primary tenet is that communities hold the main power. They decide the issues to be addressed on behalf of vulnerable children, plan the action, and guide and implement the work at their own pace (Wessells, 2018). The community also decides whether and how to work with NGOs, community-based organization, or government actors. For example, NGOs may have roles as facilitators who help communities engage in inclusive discussions and problem-solving, but who do not lead communities to a predetermined conclusion such as needing to engage in "child rights" or "violence against children." Also, if invited by communities, NGOs may help to build the capacities for designing and implementing the intervention.

Community-led approaches are highly inclusive as communities themselves decide how to include people who do not usually participate in full community decision-making, such as the disabled, the poorest of the poor, the marginalized ethnic groups, and the children. The entire community undertakes this work, with many community members engaging in the process. Importantly, children achieve high levels of participation as adults become more aware of the value of children's views and recognize the importance of children's leadership in addressing harms to children.

In a community-led approach, NGOs play a nondirective role. As co-learners, they listen extensively to communities and learn about children's issues and existing community mechanisms to support children's well-being. In assessments, the focus is on open-ended learning rather than on predefined questions or surveys, and local people may help to collect the data. International child rights and child protection language that are alien to the community should be avoided. Following the assessment, the findings are shared with the community in a respectful, appropriate manner.

Throughout the community action, the community monitors its work through agreed-upon processes, with room for making adjustments. Communities also evaluate their action using locally derived outcomes for children's well-being. External evaluations may also be conducted, using locally derived outcome indicators, with the findings shared in a culturally appropriate manner with community people, who discuss the implications of the findings.

Although community-led approaches have not been widely used in child protection work, they have shown promising results. In Sierra Leone, rural communities chose to address teenage pregnancy using a combination of their own locally grown approach to family planning, sexual and reproductive health, and life skills. This work was notably holistic and entailed making connections between health and child protection sectors. Before the community-led action was scuttled by the Ebola crisis, it had achieved significant reduction in the levels of teenage pregnancy. Also, it achieved high levels of community ownership, with significant leadership by children and participation by people who had been marginalized previously (Wessells, 2015). In this respect, it contributed to social justice within the community. This constellation of benefits resonates with those visible in a case study from Kenya, which is described below.

18.2 An Exemplar from Kenya: Starting with the Community

In Kenya, action research on community-based child protection mechanisms (CBCPMs) stressed the importance of learning from communities by listening to children and other community members about children's lived experiences. It then supported the communities' efforts to address their most serious child protection issue.[1] Throughout Kenya, many of the child protection risks identified by international NGOs were female genital mutilation (FGM), early marriage, and violence against children, and many organizations had specific, agency-developed interventions for these issues. This research, on the other hand, sought to learn what communities found to be the most serious harms to children and what protective factors were already there within the community. It then gave the reins to the community to plan and implement its own intervention.

The action research featured two phases: The first phase featured ethnographic processes to learn about children, child protection harms, and community responses to those harms.[2] In the second phase of the research, which took place in two rural communities in Kilifi county in Kenya, communities identified the child protection issue to address and then planned and carried out the intervention activities themselves. The planning phase took 1 year, followed by the intervention, which will be for 2 years (the intervention has been in progress 1 year at the time of writing).[3]

[1] The research was initiated by the Interagency Learning Initiative.

[2] The first research phase took place in three locations: Kilifi, Mombasa, and Kisii/Nyamira.

[3] Prior to the intervention activities, a baseline was conducted with an endline evaluation planned after 2 years.

18.2.1 Phase 1: Deep Listening Through Rapid Ethnographic Research

The research began with deep listening to children and communities through a rapid ethnographic process (Charmaz, 2004; Kostelny, Ondoro, & Wessells, 2017). It sought to learn about local conceptualizations of harms to children, protective factors, and community mechanisms for supporting vulnerable children.

The research used a mixture of narrative and participant observation methods, including in-depth interviews, group discussions, and timelines with adolescents and adults that enabled learning about children's development, and body mapping that enabled learning with young children. Recognizing that people in communities are positioned in very different ways, deliberate effort was made to learn from subgroups of young girls, older girls, young women, elder women, young boys, older boys, young men, and elder men (Kostelny, Wessells, & Ondoro, 2014).

Kenyan researchers carried out the research after extensive training in ethnographic methods by international and Kenyan researchers and after gaining permission to talk with the community from the village chiefs and elders. The national researchers lived in the communities for several weeks and were overseen by experienced Kenyan mentors. In the communities, the researchers emphasized that they were not experts, but learners, and asked communities to teach them about the situation of children in their communities as they knew best about the situation of their children.

This ethnographic process aimed to provide a rich, grounded picture of local beliefs, values, and practices regarding children, their developing activities and social relations, and the community mechanisms for their protection and well-being (Mignone, Hiremath, Sabnis, et al., 2009). It sought to identify how local people understand children and childhood, what they saw as the main harms or risks to children, what CBCPMs existed and how they were used, what protective factors enabled children's positive coping and resilience, and whether and how the CBCPMs linked with elements of the formal, government-led aspects of the national child protection system (Kostelny et al., 2014).

The researchers/learners asked simple questions to explore the actual functioning of CBCPMs, including:

- Whom do children go to when they need help?
- Who makes decisions?
- Which actions are taken?
- Which outcomes are achieved?
- How do stakeholders who occupy different social positions (such as parents, children, and community members) view the outcomes?

18.2.2 Harms to Children

Two of the main harms to children consistently raised by all subgroups in the community were early pregnancy and early sex. Early pregnancy was viewed as a harm primarily when the girl was not married, as a married girl was viewed culturally as "ready" for pregnancy. Early sex was also viewed as a major harm as girls and boys engaged in consensual sex at as early as 10 years of age, and girls became pregnant after reaching puberty, at around 14 years of age. Consensual sex frequently took place at or around video halls, dances, or *disco matangas* (funeral celebrations that raised funds for the grieved family). Also widespread was nonconsensual sex between young girls and older boys and men that was rooted in male power, economic hardship, and inability to meet basic needs. The other harms that were frequently identified – children being out of school, alcohol and drug abuse, poor parenting (e.g., parents neglecting children, not providing for children's basic needs, not sending their children to school, and not being good role models), negative influences (e.g., video halls, mobile phones, pornography), heavy labor, and child beating – overlapped and were frequently associated with causes or consequences of early pregnancy and early sex.

18.2.3 Preventive Factors

Preventive factors were identified at diverse socio-ecological levels (Bronfenbrenner, 1979) such as family, peer group, school, and community levels, and families and communities made efforts to keep their children safe and out of harm's way. For example, at the family level, in the past, parents played a key role in protecting girls from early pregnancy by teaching and advising on good behavior, though many parents were not doing this anymore. At the peer level, youth groups provided peer education about family planning. In schools, the provision of food reportedly helped to prevent children from dropping out of school and thus being more susceptible to becoming pregnant. The preventive factors, as well as the limits of preventive factors, are presented in Table 18.1. With such an approach, it should be noted that preventive factors identified by the community may clash with international child protection standards. For example, beating children who went to places where alcohol was available to children and where girls were sexually exploited was considered a preventative measure, though beating children would not be endorsed by the child protection sector.

A key finding of this research was that local people relied overwhelmingly on family and traditional community mechanisms and seldom, if ever, used the formal system (e.g., child protection officers, police, courts), even when criminal offences are involved. In this regard, there is a near total disconnect between communities and the formal child protection system. This disconnect, also reported in other studies (Bai, 2009; Thompstone, 2010; Wessells et al., 2014), owes not only to limited

Table 18.1 Protective factors, limits, and intervention activities at different social-ecological levels

	Risks and limits to preventive factors	Existing protective/ preventive factors	Intervention activities developed by community
Individual		Good behavior such as dressing modestly by girls	Life skills of "saying no" to boys and men
Family	Poor parenting (lack of knowledge and skills about talking with children about puberty and sex) Strong peer norms of consensual sex outweighed guidance and threats of punishment for engaging in early sex Girls were often coerced into sex and became pregnant as a result of sexual exploitation and abuse Poor families were unable to meet girls' basic needs, leading many girls to engage in transactional sex	Paying school fees, taking on additional work *Education:* Parents and extended family advised children and taught them good values and behavior *Discipline:* Parents did not allow children to go to night events at which drinking and sex were likely and beat children if they went *Economic support:* Parents with sufficient income met girls' basic needs for food and items such as sanitary pads	Parent training and support groups Parent-child dialogues Advising and counseling daughters
Peer	Norms of early sexual debut and consensual sex with peers, peer pressure from boys to have sex in exchange for goods, norms of having boyfriends/girlfriends and engaging in sex	Youth clubs; village soccer team for girls	Soccer teams for all girls and boys; child and adolescent messaging; peer mentoring
School	Significant numbers of children were out of school; teachers sexually abused girls	Teachers provided guidance and education about appropriate behavior, and they monitored children's behavior Provision of food at school to encourage children to attend; pregnancy tests	Life skills training

(continued)

Table 18.1 (continued)

	Risks and limits to preventive factors	Existing protective/ preventive factors	Intervention activities developed by community
Community	Older men sexually abused girls Boda boda (motorcycle taxi) drivers enticed girls with money and transportation Norms of boys and men giving girls material items in exchange for sex	*Religion:* Religious leaders counseled abstinence and taught good values and behavior. Religious groups helped to raise money to help children stay in school *Contraception:* Birth control methods such as "injections," pills, and implants were available *Discipline:* Village elders disciplined girls for inappropriate behavior *Economic support:* Community groups helped to raise or loan money that enabled children to stay in school	Sports; mentors; parenting classes and support groups; children out of school committee; theater group

access but also to cultural norms that favored traditional family and community mechanisms and mitigated against taking problems outside one's family or community.

18.2.4 Phase 2: Community Action – Selecting the Issue to Address and Developing the Intervention

At the end of the ethnographic research, a community-wide meeting in each of the two communities, with nearly the whole community in attendance – including children and the disabled – was held. This was important as the community reported that while NGOs had previously come to do surveys and research, none had ever come back to discuss the findings. After presenting the priority issues that they had learned about, the researchers invited discussion, and the communities validated the harms identified, including that early pregnancy, early sex, and children out of school were priority issues. Importantly, this meeting served as a catalyst for community members to begin their own planning of how to address these issues. In one community, an immediate action was that a "children out of school" committee was formed on the spot to address the issue of children not in school by encouraging parents to take children to school early (i.e., at age 6) and to monitor children and parents to ensure that their children are going to school regularly. In the other community, a youth group took on the issue of early pregnancy, initiating outreach to vulnerable youth and providing peer mentoring and information about contraceptives.

The next phase of the action research included identification of the issue to address, planning the intervention, and implementation of the activities. Critical to the intervention was the community-led action. To support the communities, a community facilitator was hired by the Interagency Learning Initiative. Qualities of the facilitator included being humble, patient, tolerant, and understanding. The facilitator was of the same ethnic group, spoke the same language, and was knowledgeable about local customs. Their role was to support the communities – facilitating meetings, posing reflective questions to encourage participation, and observing and documenting the process. Throughout the process, the facilitator worked to build the communities' trust. It was important that the facilitator did not identify as being affiliated with any particular NGO so as not to risk being viewed by the communities as having an NGO-driven agenda. The aim was to put the communities in the driver's seat: They would identify the child protection harm to address, develop and plan the intervention, and carry out the activities.

For example, at the first community meeting of this phase, though the meeting was well attended by adults, youth, teenagers, and children, the facilitator posed a series of reflective questions that enabled the community to start thinking about the importance of involving everyone in the process.

Facilitator: Are all the community members here?

Chorus: Yes!

Facilitator: Do all the members of the community attend meetings?

Chorus: Yes!

Facilitator: I would like us to reflect back home. Think about your house, your homestead, about your neighbors, and about the people you interact with everyday. Is there anyone that is not here?

Man: I have a neighbour who swore not to attend any meeting because he did not get the benefits that other people got who attended the meeting, like relief food.

Facilitator: Thank you. Do you have people with disabilities in this community?

Chorus: Yes.

Facilitator: Are they here?

Chorus: (Murmuring and people begin talking amongst themselves).

Woman: We have realized that there are people who are members of this community not here. People like those with disabilities, some of those who have completely shunned community meetings, some of the youth, especially the boda boda (motorcycle taxi drivers).

The dialogue continued to discuss how, in addition to the above mentioned, youth who worked as day laborers and people who lived at the far end of the village were not there. As a result of this discussion, the community made a plan for various outreach activities, including home visits by a task force committee that was formed, to invite and encourage those who do not usually come to community meetings. Many of these people attended subsequent meetings, and for those who could not attend because of disability, work, or other reasons, home visits were made to update these community members and seek their input to the planning process.

The facilitator then asked how the community would like to identify which harm to children to address. There were varied responses from different people. The adult men suggested that there should be a larger community meeting where all the community members meet for a discussion. However, women differed with men saying that they would like to have a group of their own because they would not be able to talk freely in front of their husbands. The youth, on the other hand, also felt that they needed to discuss issues in their own group because they have their own unique issues. Children also said that they would like to discuss their own issues, because when they are in a group with the adults, they cannot always talk freely, especially the girls. Thus girls wanted their own group apart from the boys. The community continued to talk among themselves and ultimately decided that they would organize subgroup meetings to make sure that everyone is free to say whatever they feel like without fear. The following subgroups were formed, and each subgroup elected their own leaders:

- Girls (aged 9–12)
- Boys (aged 9–12)
- Teenage girls
- Teenage boys
- Female youth
- Male youth
- Women
- Men

With the aid of the community facilitator, the communities organized a series of meetings of the various subgroups and larger community meetings where all community members took part. Through continuous, intensive dialogue that occurred at all levels of the community during a several-month-long process, communities ultimately chose the issue of "early sex" to address, after coming at it via discussion of the causes of early pregnancy.

After deciding on the issue to address, the community decided *how* to address the issue, taking charge of the planning process. As before, the community members created an inclusive process with all the subgroups continuing to meet to dialogue about activities for the intervention. Because communities made their own decision about which issue to address and how to address it, they saw the intervention process as their own and were highly motivated to achieving success.

In each of the two communities, each subgroup elected a representative to an Implementation Planning Task Force that coordinated all the recommendations from the various subgroups. To include marginalized people such as children with disabilities, the Task Force members made home visits on a regular basis. The recommendations from all the subgroups were fed back to the Task Force and discussed in depth at community-wide meetings, which were attended by nearly the entire community. To enable people who lived far from the meeting place to attend, the community organized transportation via the *boda boda* drivers.

An Inter-Village Implementation Task Force was also formed, with elected representatives from both communities. The Inter-Village Task Force integrated diverse inputs and helped to define viable options, which were then fed back for wider community discussion. Over several months, the Task Force developed implementation plans that outlined *what* the intervention activities would include, *who* would carry them out, and *when* and *where* they would take place. A coordinator was also elected by each community to be the focal point and oversee the intervention process.

The communities decided on multiple activities, tailored to their specific needs, avoiding the common error of taking a one-size-fits-all approach to intervention (Wessells, 2018). The activities were also constructed to reach different groups in the community. In addition to young girls, activities included parents, young boys, teenage girls and boys, and *boda boda* drivers as well as community-wide activities. The activities initiated by the community at various levels of family, peers, school, and community are aligned with the existing risks and preventive factors already identified by the community and can be viewed at various levels of the social-ecological framework (Table 18.1).

Importantly, child participation and leadership were at the forefront of the intervention as children and teenagers advocated for peer mentoring, sports activities, drama groups, and life skills training, and planned how the activities would be carried out. To help implement the intervention, the communities identified three key individuals from within their communities – a male teacher who had parenting education skills and was passionate about supporting good parenting practices; a female teacher who was a positive role model and had experience in life skills training; and a male youth activist who had experience working with a theater group – to help build capacities to address early sexual debut. The children out of school committee had already been formed with concerned community members at the community feedback session and was deemed to be an important part of the intervention.

Key elements of the intervention included:

Peer Mentoring: Older girls who were positive role models mentored younger girls about making good decisions, staying in school, and avoiding getting involved in early sex.

Life Skills: The girls' life skills facilitator is one of the few young women from the community who has gone to college and become a successful primary school teacher. A positive role model, she facilitates life skills sessions with girls that focus on critical thinking, decision-making, and problem-solving. She provides mentoring on weekends and especially during school holidays when children are idle and tend to get involved in early sex activities. Informal peer education occurred also through everyday discussions in the community.

Sports Activities: Children and teenagers identified sports activities as a channel through which they could develop leadership and life skills relating to abstaining from early sex. Girls have formed soccer teams for all girls. Recognizing that children talk in distinctive ways, children created their own messages to spread to their peers during matches and tournaments, as well as an on ongoing basis in the community. One message was *huriza ngoma, mashomo ni madzo* (avoid early sex; education is important). Older girls provide peer mentoring for younger girls on the team, and the life skills educator facilitates discussions on decision-making and critical thinking after practices and tournaments. In addition, a boy's football team was formed, and the boys are also trained on life skills including treating girls respectfully, not pressuring girls for sex, and abstinence

Theater Group: Children and teenagers reactivated a theater group as a venue for transmitting messages about early sexual debut. The theater activities include groups of 9–12-year-old and 13–15-year-old boys and girls, who also develop their own messages to pass along to their peers. They perform for adults, teens, and younger boys and girls, with discussions afterward about how to prevent early sexual debut through making good decisions.

Positive Parenting: Parents participate in workshops that cover topics such as early child development, communicating with and advising older children on puberty, sexual and reproductive health, and pregnancy prevention. Parents also formed support groups as well as shared information they learned with other parents. A well-respected local teacher, identified by the community, conducts these workshops.

Children Out of School Committee: The community identified children out of school as a critical child protection issue related to early sex. Having received feedback from the ethnographic research, the community mobilized itself and elected a "children out of school committee" that has included parents, boys, girls, village elders, pastors, and imams. Through a combination of home visits, referrals to the chief, and work with faith leaders to emphasize the importance of education, this work has reduced absenteeism and dropouts.

18.3 Conclusion

Together, these examples illustrate how work on child protection in difficult settings may be strengthened through the use of a social justice lens. By using a social justice lens, practitioners can interrogate how their engagement with communities contributes to social equity or, alternately, causes unintended harm by marginalizing particular people or subgroups. Because it promotes full participation and local ownership, the resulting community actions are more likely to be contextually appropriate, sustainable, and effective in benefitting the most vulnerable children, who too often have been marginalized in child protection work. The community-led work described in this chapter illustrates the potential value of using a social justice lens in a systematic manner to strengthen practice. The challenge for the future is to expand the use of a social justice lens throughout humanitarian and development work, enabling peace psychology to benefit highly marginalized people.

References

Austrailian Aid, The Belgian Development Corporation, Government of Canada, European Commission, Food & Agricultural Organization of the UN, German Humanitarian Assistance, World Food Program. (2016). *The grand bargain – A shared commitment to better serve people in need.* Istanbul, Turkey: Author.

Bai, J. P. (2009). *Mapping of structures for child protection in Plan Sierra Leone operational areas: Final report.* Freetown, Sierra Leone: Plan Sierra Leone.

Bronfenbrenner, U. (1979). *The ecology of human development: Experiments by nature and design*. Cambridge, MA: Harvard University Press.
Charmaz, K. (2004). Grounded theory. In S. N. Hesse-Biber & P. Leavy (Eds.), *Approaches to qualitative research* (pp. 496–521). New York, NY: Oxford University Press.
Christie, D., Tint, B., Wanger, D., & Winter. (2008). Peace psychology for a peaceful world. *American Psychologist, 63*(6), 540–552.
Christie, D. J., Wagner, R. V., & Winter, D. D. (Eds.). (2001). *Peace, conflict, and violence: Peace psychology for the 21st century*. Englewood Cliffs, NJ: Prentice-Hall.
Deutch, M. (1985). *Distributive justice: A social-psychological perspective*. New Haven, CT: Yale University Press.
Freire, P. (1990). *Pedagogy of the oppressed*. New York, NY: Continuum Publishing Company.
Galtung, J. (1985). Twenty-five years of peace research: Ten challenges and some responses. *Journal of Peace Research, 22*, 141–158.
IASC High Level Panel on Humanitarian Financing Report to the Secretary General. (2016). Too important to fail – Addressing the humanitarian financing gap. Author: Geneva.
ICVA. (2017). *The grand bargain: Everything you need to know.* ICVA briefing paper.
Kostelny, K. (2006). A culture-based, integrative approach: Helping war affected children. In N. Boothby, A. Strang, & M. Wessells (Eds.), *A world turned upside down: Social ecological approaches to children in war zones* (pp. 19–37). Bloomfield, CT: Kumarian Press.
Kostelny, K., Ondoro, K., & Wessells, M. G. (2017). What children and youth can tell us: A rapid ethnography approach to understanding harms to children in Somaliland and Puntland. In M. Denov & B. Akesson (Eds.), *Children affected by armed conflict: Theory, method & practice* (pp. 163–184). New York, NY: Columbia Press.
Kostelny, K., Wessells, M., & Ondoro, K. (2014). *Community-based child protection mechanisms in Kilifi, Kenya: A rapid ethnographic study in two rural areas*. London, UK: Interagency Learning Initiative on Community-Based Child Protection Mechanisms and Child Protection Systems.
Mignone, J., Hiremath, G., Sabnis, V., et al. (2009). Use of rapid ethnographic methodology to develop a village-level rapid assessment tool predictive of HIV infection in rural India. *International Journal of Qualitative Methods.*. Downloaded May 14, 2011 from http://ejournals.library.ualberta.ca/index.php
Minkler, M., & Wallerstein, N. (Eds.). (2008). *Community-based participatory research for health: From process to outcomes* (2nd ed.). San Francisco, CA: Jossey Bass.
Slim, H. (2015). *Humanitarian ethics: A guide to the morality of aid in war and disaster*. Cambridge: Oxford University Press.
Thompstone, G. (2010). *Mapping and analysis of the child protection system in Sierra Leone*. Hong Kong: Child Frontiers.
Wessells, M. (2009). *What are we learning about protecting children? An inter-agency review of the evidence on community-based child protection mechanisms in humanitarian and development settings*. London, UK: Save the Children.
Wessells, M. (2015). Bottom-up approaches to strengthening child protection systems: Placing children, families, and communities at the center. *Child Abuse & Neglect: The International Journal, 43*, 8–21. https://doi.org/10.1016/j.chiabu.2015.04.006
Wessells, M. (2018). Supporting resilience in war-affected children: How differential impact theory is useful in humanitarian practice. *Child Abuse & Neglect: The International Journal*.
Wessells, M., & Kostelny, K. (2017). Child rights and practitioner wrongs: Lessons from interagency research in Sierra Leone and Kenya. In M. Ruck, M. Peterson-Badali, & M. Freeman (Eds.), *Handbook of children's rights: Global and multidisciplinary perspectives* (pp. 579–595). Taylor and Francis, London: UK.
Wessells, M., Kostelny, K., & Ondoro, K. (2014). *A grounded view of community-based child protection mechanisms and their linkage with the wider child protection system in three urban and rural areas of Kenya: Summary and integrated analysis*. London, UK: Save the Children.

Wessells, M., Lamin, D., King, D., Kostelny, K., Stark, & Lilley. (2015). The limits of top-down approaches to managing diversity: Lessons from the case of child protection and child rights in Sierra Leone. *Peace and Conflict: Journal of Peace Psychology, 21*, 574–588.

Wessells, M., & Monterio, C. (2001). Psychosocial interventions and post-war reconstruction in Angola: Interweaving Western and traditional approaches. In D. Christie, R. V. Wagner, & D. Winter (Eds.), *Peace, conflict, and violence: Peace psychology for the 21st century* (pp. 262–275). Upper Saddle River, NJ: Prentice-Hall.

Chapter 19
From Research to Action and the Spaces in -Between: Experiences from Peacebuilding Programs for Young People in Cambodia and Uganda

Nikola Balvin and Tania Miletic

19.1 Introduction

In international development, the ultimate goal of conducting research is to apply its findings to improve the lives of people in need. To rephrase this into more operational language, the purpose of research, evaluation, and other evidence activities is to improve the delivery of programs, development of policies, and design of advocacy strategies that prevent or reduce harmful practices, improve health and well-being, alleviate poverty, and otherwise assist and empower people living in difficult life situations. From a peacebuilding perspective, the purpose may be oriented toward addressing structural issues and improving relationships between people affected by violent conflict. Researchers who want their work to have social or political impact have given a great deal of thought to the "packaging" of results, using policy briefs, animation, infographics, podcasts, videos, and catchy headlines on social media. Another, more long-standing and participatory approach to increasing the impact of research has been accomplished by building relationships with key stakeholders. A recent review of interventions developed to enhance the use of evidence by decision-makers found that enhancing capability, motivation, and opportunity to use evidence was key to effective evidence use (Langer, Tripney & Gough, 2016). The importance of key stakeholder participation to increase ownership does not only apply to research but also to programming and decision-making, particularly when it comes to conducting research in the interest of young people (UNICEF, 2017) and especially in conflict-affected contexts, where the building of trust and resilience is vital to recovery and healing.

N. Balvin (✉)
UNICEF Office of Research-Innocenti, Florence, Italy
e-mail: nbalvin@unicef.org

T. Miletic
Melbourne School of Government, University of Melbourne, Parkville, VIC, Australia
e-mail: tmiletic@unimelb.edu.au

N. Balvin, D. J. Christie (eds.), *Children and Peace*, Peace Psychology Book Series, https://doi.org/10.1007/978-3-030-22176-8_19

In this chapter, we present two case studies of research undertaken as part of peacebuilding programs for young people and reflect on the activities and approaches they applied to affect change. We chose these two case studies because they not only used both formal and informal education systems as platforms for change but also worked with different stakeholders, at different levels of influence and over different geopolitical contexts. The first case study is of an impact evaluation undertaken to assess a gender and peacebuilding pilot program set in the schools of Uganda's most impoverished and conflict-affected region, Karamoja. The aim of the program was to improve the status of girls in school and reduce conflict between children from different tribal backgrounds by training teachers to recognize and address gender inequality and conflict in the school setting. Despite being a small pilot, it was implemented in collaboration with influential stakeholders from the Uganda government, the United Nations Children's Fund (UNICEF), as well as local grassroots organizations. The second case study focuses on a Cambodian nongovernment organization (NGO) leading a long-term, inter-ethnic peacebuilding initiative that engaged with other local and international actors and relevant ministries within the Government of Cambodia. The research project sought to identify the problems and causes of ethnic conflicts in Cambodia and to generate empirically grounded information to inform inter-ethnic peacebuilding initiatives among youth and civil society leaders. We focus on its peace education programs in secondary schools.

Over the past decade, many funders of research have placed an increased emphasis on research uptake and impact. The UK Department for International Development (DFID) has been at the forefront of these efforts boldly stating that it "funds research in order to contribute to its overarching goal of poverty reduction" and also providing clear guidance how to communicate the findings of research and build the capacity of stakeholders to use research effectively (DFID, 2016, p. 1). Morton's (2015) Research Contribution Framework is a methodology gaining prominence for analyzing the influence of research. We borrow key concepts from Morton's (2015) framework and use them to analyze the processes and outcomes of our research to determine its observable effects on policy and practice.

Morton's (2015) methodology tracks the effects of research forward and backward: from research users to impact and from policy and practice settings backward to understand how it had been used. It collects data through key informant interviews, review of policies, media materials, relevant reports, etc. (Morton, 2012; Morton & Casey, 2017). As members of the research teams in the presented case studies, we cannot be fully objective, but our aim is not to conduct a thorough assessment of how well the research uptake activities contributed to an impact. Instead we will use the framework's concepts to *reflect* on what worked well and the biggest challenges encountered in making the research count. We end the chapter by discussing the importance and influence of the "spaces in between" research and practice, particularly in relation to the participation of key stakeholders in the research process and uptake and use of its findings.

19.2 Definition of Key Concepts

According to Morton's (2015) framework, three concepts are central to assessing research influence: (1) research uptake, (2) research use, and (3) research impact. Figure 19.1 outlines the theoretical underpinnings of the process from research uptake to impact. Much like a logic framework, impact is conceptualized as long-term behavioral change which follows a chain of events that had begun with activities engaging research users with research (Morton, 2015).

Research uptake refers to the extent that research users have engaged with the research and know that it exists. It includes common academic activities such as reading an article, report, or brief and attending a conference or a launch and also collaborative activities in which partners were involved in shaping the research in some way, through an advisory capacity, for example (Morton, 2015, p. 406). *Research use* represents a more involved engagement with the research process and findings, in which stakeholders use it to shape policy or practice, share it with others, adapt it to a particular setting, or act upon it in some other way. The last phase, *research impact*, is what most research in international development aims to achieve. It refers to changes in knowledge, attitudes, and behavior among the target population, as well as changes in policy and practice resulting from the research process

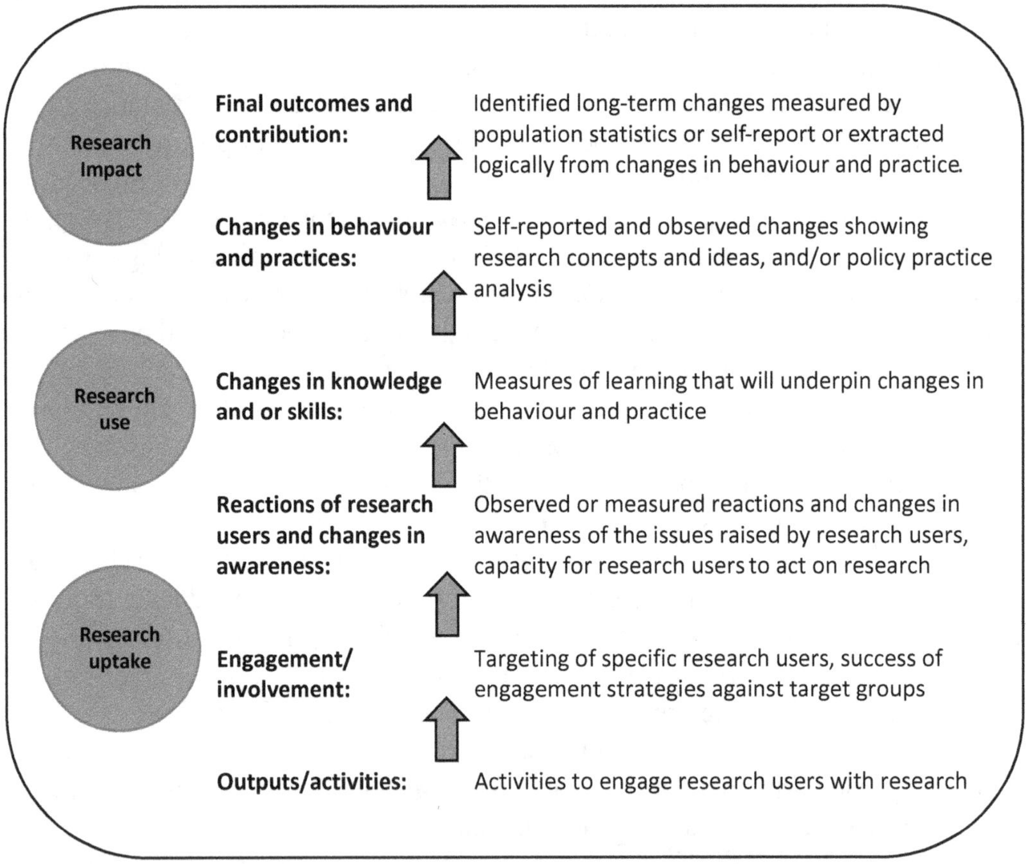

Fig. 19.1 Basic pathway to impact. (Source: Morton 2015. Reproduced with permission)

and findings (Morton, 2015, p. 406). Of course, in reality, the process from uptake to impact is not always linear, and the stages are not equal in length or effort. A policy can change long before or after a population's behavior or attitudes change, and a countless number of conference presentations may never lead to any behavioral change. The fruitfulness of these efforts is facilitated or inhibited by the socio-politico-economic environment in which they unfold. Evidence alone rarely changes the world, but when coupled with effective uptake approaches, its chances increase. Our case studies examine the uptake, use, and impact approaches of two education and peacebuilding research initiatives focused on young people. In addition, we reflect on the transitions, challenges, and opportunities encountered along the way.

19.3 Peacebuilding and Gender Equality Through Education: A Case Study from Uganda

The first case study is of an impact evaluation of a pilot program from the north-east region of Uganda, Karamoja, titled Gender Socialization in Schools and Communities. The program was part of UNICEF's wider gender, education, and peacebuilding efforts in Uganda, which were part of an even larger education and peacebuilding program called *Learning for Peace* (see Affolter and Azaryeva Valente, 2019, in this volume for details). The first author was part of the UNICEF team that commissioned the impact evaluation and coordinated the engagement of stakeholders from the government and community with the research team. Using Morton's (2015) framework, the case study reflects on how the inputs, outputs, and engagements of different stakeholders during the evaluation process contributed to the findings being noticed, understood, and acted upon.

19.3.1 The Conflict Context

Overrepresented in the country's lowest development indicators, Karamoja is one of the most disadvantaged and conflict-ridden regions of Uganda. Seventy-five percent of households in Karamoja live below the official poverty line, and child mortality is the highest in Uganda (MGLSD and UNICEF, 2015). The region has the highest proportion of girls not in school (MGLSD & UNICEF, 2015), while violence against women and girls is the highest in northern Uganda, with the practice of female genital mutilation/cutting widespread in several districts (ACCS, 2013; Datzberger et al., 2015). The education system is often considered a beacon of hope for improving opportunities for children, but in Karamoja, this comes with additional challenges. The region's limited infrastructure makes it difficult to build and maintain schools, and teachers are difficult to recruit, resulting in high pupil-to-teacher ratios.

With only one in four teachers a woman (MGLSD & UNICEF, 2015), portraying positive gender role models through the curriculum is particularly challenging. A girl's education is sometimes out of line with traditional community values, in which girls are often valued for their bride price and those with formal education are thought to attract a lower price than those who are less educated or illiterate (El-Bushra & Rees-Smith, 2016).

Gender inequality, particularly in the form of negative masculine norms and stereotypes, also has a negative impact on men and boys. Boys and younger men are subjected to initiation rituals directed by community elders (El-Bushra & Rees Smith, 2016). Inter-clan and inter-tribal violence is ongoing (ACCS, 2013). Cattle raids are often carried out to pay for a bride, a custom consistent with viewing girls as commodities. In this context, changing gender norms to achieve equality and social cohesion is difficult but nevertheless vital to addressing the drivers of conflict and working toward sustainable peace.

19.3.2 Program Overview

The main activities of the Gender Socialization in Schools and Communities pilot program took place from March to November 205, with the aim to develop a practical, school-based intervention that demonstrated the peacebuilding potential of positive masculinity and femininity models in a conflict-affected region. UNICEF worked closely with the Ugandan Ministry of Education, Science, Technology and Sport (MoESTS) and two local implementing partners – the Development Research and Training (DRT) and Forum for African Women Educationalists (FAWE) – to develop gender- and conflict-sensitive teacher training materials, including a teacher handbook with examples of lesson plans and teaching methods that addressed conflict and gender inequality. Such gender- and conflict-sensitive plans raised teachers' awareness of the number of boys and girls from different ethnic backgrounds in their classes and aimed for all students to be given equal opportunity to participate in class activities. Following the development of these materials, a "train-the-trainer" model was rolled out, in which core coordinating tutors as well as representatives from MoESTS and district inspectors were trained to become trainers who would later deliver the training to Karamojong teachers. The teacher examined gender equality and conflict through conceptual as well as practical approaches, encouraging the teachers to reflect on the issues in their lives and classrooms, including identifying gender stereotypic depictions in teaching. The core coordinating tutors continued to act as mentors to the teachers throughout the pilot, ultimately aiming for the teachers to become "agents of peace" whose new egalitarian attitudes and practices trickle down to the students.

19.3.3 The Impact Evaluation

The pilot program was evaluated by an independent research team from the American Institutes for Research (AIR), with funding and direct management from UNICEF and support from MoESTS. The impact evaluation employed a mixed-methods experimental design, with quantitative data collected at the start and end of the program and qualitative data collected in focus groups, interviews, and case studies at the end (Chinen et al., 2016). Analysis of quantitative data showed that the program succeeded in improving teachers' knowledge and changing attitudes about gender equality and conflict, but any changes in teacher practices were not statistically significant (Chinen et al., 2016). The qualitative findings mostly supported the quantitative trends, reporting teachers' correct use of relevant terms (e.g., "sex" and "gender"), knowledge of appropriate strategies for conflict resolution, ability to recognize gender-equitable practices to increase class performance and harmony, and beliefs that boys and girls should have equal responsibilities and opportunities to participate in the same activities. Some changes in teacher practices were also observed, including gender-equitable seating arrangements, dividing resources equally between boys and girls, and dividing classroom responsibilities between the two genders. Nevertheless, traditional concepts of gender roles prevailed, and more complex practices such as making lessons gender responsive and connecting gender equitable practices to peacebuilding were not observed.

The evaluation's recommendations were to (i) provide more concrete examples of the practices the program is trying to instill in materials and training; (ii) have greater involvement from the community and school governance bodies to increase their buy-in to the messages communicated by the program; (iii) ensure that teachers receive ongoing mentoring, reinforcement, and coaching; (iv) improve the training logistics, including offering teachers incentives to attend; and (v) conduct research on the impacts of the program over the long term (Chinen et al., 2016).

19.3.4 Research Uptake

The impact evaluation findings suggested that the Gender Socialization in Schools and Communities pilot yielded relatively positive outcomes in the short term, particularly given the stringent gender norms of the context. However, this chapter is not about the success of the program, but rather about how the research undertaken to evaluate it contributed (or not) to further changes following its conclusion.

Using Morton's (2015) Research Contribution Framework, Table 19.1 presents the overall "outcomes chain" or "pathway to impact," with the UNICEF-AIR impact evaluation theorized as the input that facilitated the activities and outcomes in the chain. It is important to note at the outset that the "research activity," like the rest of the pilot program, adopted a collaborative approach and engaged key stakeholders in its design and findings. The MoESTS was involved in decision-making around

Table 19.1 Research contribution analysis for the Evaluation of the Gender Socialization in Schools and Communities pilot in Karamoja, Uganda

Research impact	Final outcomes and contribution	Several impact evaluation recommendations were acted upon – including having greater involvement from the community to communicate program messages and ensuring that teachers receive ongoing mentoring – potentially contributing to the long-term goal of the evaluation/research initiative
	Changes in behavior/practices	New programs sponsored by Irish Aid were initiated to strengthen capacity in gender and peacebuilding for community members Ongoing mentoring of teachers Inclusion of some of the training materials in the national teacher curriculum
Research use	Changes in knowledge/skills	Gender unit of MoESTS strengthened and pushing scale-up of program
	Reactions of research users and changes in awareness	Increased awareness among partners and key stakeholders (e.g., MoESTS, DRT, teachers, core coordinating tutors) of gender equality as a result of the research (and program) process MoESTS keen to include teacher training in the national curriculum of teachers following presentation of findings
Research uptake	Engagement/ involvement	Launch event to disseminate research findings to government ministers, core coordinating tutors, NGOs, UN agencies, and other key stakeholders in Kampala, April 2016 Meetings between research team, UNICEF, UNESCO, and government ministers to discuss use of evidence in teacher training and policy Dissemination of findings to teachers and communities in Karamoja Presentation of research to key stakeholders at the 2016 Commission on the Status of Women (CSW) Learning for Peace event with donors Pan-African peacebuilding event
	Outputs/activities	Publications including reports on Learning for Peace and AIR websites, in *Journal on Education in Emergencies* Presentation at 4+ international conferences Engagement on topic via social media Video documenting the program
	Inputs	UNICEF-AIR impact evaluation of the Gender Socialization in Schools and Communities pilot in Karamoja, Uganda. The evaluation adapted a collaborative approach and engaged key stakeholders in its design and findings

the design and logistics of the research and acted in an advisory capacity throughout the research process. Similarly, members of the local partner organizations, DRT and FAWE, were on the research advisory committee and reviewed the research plan, baseline, midline, and final reports as they were developed. This level of engagement ensured not only that key stakeholders were aware of the research process but that they had the opportunity to have their questions answered in the design and could facilitate the understanding of findings among their peers.

To examine research uptake, Morton's (2015) framework looks at the contributions of outputs, activities, and stakeholder engagement to the overall goal of the project. Many of the activities to engage research users with the research were quite traditional or academic, including publications and conference presentations. Using the *Learning for Peace* social media platform, the findings also reached a large number of followers via Twitter and Facebook and on YouTube. Approaches to targeting key research users were less academic and drew on UNICEF's wide networks and the local partners' knowledge of the political landscape to gain traction. The results were presented at several high-profile meetings with donors, UN agencies, academics, and advocates to raise the profile of the research. MoESTS representatives contributed to the presentations at all events, strengthening their involvement with the research outside of Uganda. Other stakeholder engagements were more local and in-depth, discussing the evaluation findings in more detail, and exploring the implementation of recommendations and next steps together. The role of UNICEF as the broker between the government and the research team was particularly helpful in ensuring the independence of each party's mandate.

19.3.5 Research Use

It is difficult to untangle the impacts of the research from the impacts of the actual pilot program on the gender- and peacebuilding-related knowledge and attitudes of MoESTS staff and other stakeholders. The engagement of the MoESTS core team in the design of the teacher training materials was a powerful tool for raising awareness and improving knowledge around important gender concepts and approaches. The research outputs, including the report, presentations, and discussions, communicated these concepts to a wider audience of stakeholders and equipped core staff from the Ministry with evidence to argue that school-based approaches to tackling gender inequality and conflict can be effective. Several core coordinating tutors were invited to present at the research dissemination workshops, increasing their ownership of the program and knowledge of the findings. Finally, shortly after the launch of the research report in Kampala, the research team and representatives from UNICEF met with MoESTS decision-makers to discuss the uptake of the findings, including the possibility of including some of the training materials in the national teacher curriculum. The evaluation process and the professional and independent manner in which the findings were presented seemed an important contributor to motivating the Ministry to act on the results and recommendations.

19.3.6 Research Impact

Without the proper research/evaluation process that normally underpins a research contribution analysis and includes interviewing key stakeholders and conducting questionnaires with research partners (see Morton & Casey, 2017), it is difficult to make claims about how many of the "offshoot" initiatives were influenced by the evaluation itself. However, the evaluation recommended that the community and school governance bodies be included in future initiatives, and this approach was adopted in new programs that stemmed from the pilot. Following the evaluation, new capacity-building initiatives, sponsored by Irish Aid, were established in Karamoja to work with community members on issues of gender equality and conflict. The teacher mentoring model established during the pilot program and recommended to continue by the evaluation findings is also still in place, although it is not clear how well it is functioning without strong funding. Finally, some of the materials from the teacher training have been included in the national teacher curriculum, potentially influencing the knowledge, attitudes, and behavior of teachers around the country.

The long-term goal of the evaluation was to support equitable gender relations and social cohesion in Karamojong schools by examining what worked and what needed improvement in the pilot program. Several of the evaluation's recommendations, including to involve the community and continue mentoring, have been adopted. Others, such as adjusting the logistics of the training program, became somewhat obsolete once the decision was made not to scale the program up from its pilot format. The long-term goal of improving gender equality and peaceful relations for children in Karamoja will require ongoing, concerted efforts, of which this initiative is just one important component.

Despite being a relatively small and short-term activity, the evaluation managed to influence stakeholders in the government, UNICEF, and community, as well as external donors. Much of this influence can be attributed to the consistent and non-tokenistic involvement of key stakeholders in the design of the program and its evaluation.

19.4 Inter-ethnic Peacebuilding Initiative: A Case Study from Cambodia

The second case study reflects on a locally led peacebuilding effort involving research that informed an inter-ethnic peacebuilding program that also included a peace education component. In contrast to the former case study, the research and peacebuilding program was led by a small, local NGO called the Alliance for Conflict Transformation (ACT), which was created in 1997 by a core group of local peacebuilders to identify contemporary Cambodian conflict issues and develop mechanisms to establish sustainable, positive peace. The second author came to learn of ACT's work in 2003 and joined between 2004 and 2005 and recommenced from 2006 to 2007 as Technical Advisor on the inter-ethnic peacebuilding program. She remained engaged with the organization's board and leadership for several years afterward. The research project intended to better understand the sources of conflict between Cambodia's different ethnic groups and how this evidence base could help identify actions to reduce the identified conflict issues.

These reflections on the research and related programs are not complete, as the author recognizes there are gaps in knowledge about the various aspects of the programs development, its stakeholders, and funders over this period. Drawing on Morton's 2015 framework, this case study reflects on the research uptake, use, and impact activities that took place, highlights the importance of the engagement of key stakeholders across the research to action process, and details how these activities were used to enhance knowledge. The use of the research to influence and inform peacebuilding strategies and practice is articulated.

19.4.1 The Conflict Context

While Cambodia is a country most known for the period of the Khmer Rouge genocide, it has experienced long periods of civil conflict, intervention, and occupation. Historical conflicts and land losses from the Khmer Empire continue to influence contemporary Cambodian self-conceptualization and relationships, especially between the ethnic Khmer majority and the ethnic Vietnamese and Thai communities.

The 1991 Paris Peace Accords (PPA), negotiated by Cambodia's internal factions along with Vietnam, Thailand, China, the Soviet Union, and the USA, represented a turning point for Cambodia's transition from decades of violent conflict. The United Nations Transitional Authority (1991–1993) helped see the 1993 elections, which enabled the end of the civil and political conflict in 1998 and in turn Cambodia's post-war shift in the direction of peace (Miletic, 2016; Soth Plai & Miletic, 2009).

Under Hun Sen's continuing rule, many Cambodians have limited hope that the government will undertake necessary reforms, reduce inequalities, and entrench the rule of law. Amidst the range of international actors and international nongovernment agencies assisting Cambodia's development, its Cambodian actors have led peacebuilding efforts to help envision a peaceful future, through building relationships and adopting peace as an alternative to violence. As Cambodia looks forward, many are focused on youth (two-thirds of its population under 30 years of age) or "bamboo shoots" as the young are often called, to achieve the kind of positive peace that many Cambodians aspire to (Miletic, 2016; Soth Plai & Miletic, 2009).

19.4.2 Program Overview and the Research Activity

This case study shows how research informed and sustained an ongoing program of work affecting Cambodian society (Meas & Miletic, 2007). Given the interwoven historical, political, cultural, and economic context, the causes of prejudice, resentment, and violence in Cambodia are complex. ACT believed that these issues need to be explored and discussed with sensitivity to enable positive and useful developments for knowledge and practice. The initiative was self-described as peace research – motivated to learn about the problems with a view to promote peace, not to exacerbate the problem (Soth Plai & Miletic, 2006).

The underlying rationale of the project was that there is value in understanding the issues, concerns, and aspirations of Cambodians in relation to identity, society, and state and that these are integral to developing Cambodian society. Its main components were to identify the problems and causes of ethnic conflicts in Cambodia through research, to generate empirically grounded information, and to examine the experiences of other countries in relation to diversity and multiculturalism to inform programs, policies, and curricula. Simultaneously, the project developed the capacity of peace practitioners engaged in conflict prevention, resolution, and peacebuilding activities and facilitated youth and civil society actors to become advocates employing informed approaches to inter-ethnic peacebuilding in their own work.

The program was a locally driven peacebuilding approach, in which the people involved in, and most affected by, violent conflict work together to create and enact their own approaches to prevent, reduce, and/or transform the conflict with support from actors outside the conflict context (Purdue Peace Project, 2015). As a small, local NGO, ACT received funding by international and donor organizations who were sympathetic to and supportive of the research and the ways that research capacity and program development were occurring alongside this phase of the project.

The research team primarily involved the lead and a research assistant, along with the technical advisor. Data collection was undertaken in collaboration with partner organizations, trained in survey methods by the core research team. Partners from across the country trained by ACT project staff learned from this engagement, which provided a thorough understanding of the research and the issues it was examining. The surveys were conducted with 1100 participants across ethnic groups in 16 provinces over 47 districts, 133 communes, and 214 villages. Participants were asked about their experiences and views on ethnic tensions and relations. The responsibility for data management, transcription, and entry was the primary focus of the ACT research team.

19.4.3 Research Uptake

From the beginning, the research team engaged and collaborated with key peacebuilding actors and donors and later with government officials. The research design was developed by the research team, with input from a working group of 11 stakeholders, including donors, researchers, youth organizations, and individuals. Those selected to the Working Group on Ethnic Conflict Transformation (WG-ECT) had an interest in the topic of inter-ethnic relations and nationalism, were committed to regular meetings, and had expertise to support the project. They met monthly, provided support to deal with a range of research design considerations, and engaged to develop the research and to build a shared understanding of its purpose. The research (and subsequent initiatives) were at times seen as threatening where issues such as fear of land loss, discrimination, and concerns regarding immigration were prevalent in communities. The organization had to collaborate with staff from MoI and at the local and provincial levels to enable authorization and access for surveys to be conducted across the country. ACT staff also saw this as an opportunity to further develop understanding of the aims and purpose of the research.

Many of the traditional "output" activities to engage research users with the research such as publishing reports online, writing journal articles, and presenting at conferences were intentionally avoided. The findings relating to inter-ethnic relations and nationalism in Cambodia raised concern within the organization and stakeholders that they could be misused, and the question of their communication required sensitivity. It was decided to limit the publications to an English report intended for use by the peacebuilding community in Cambodia and to package the knowledge generated from the research into workshop and training materials to more actively engage with the findings and its users. In this way the research uptake activities begin to reflect Morton's description of research use.

Research workshops and trainings were used to disseminate key findings and promote greater understanding to targeted peacebuilding organizations and were used by ACT and the WG-ECT to develop a range of activities and initiatives that became an ongoing central program of ACT's work. Despite the report being limited in its distribution, and with targeted promotion of it within the peacebuilding community, it still had some (surprising) reach. For example, it stimulated discussions and advocacy in relation to citizenship issues within Cambodia. Another example was when the US Obama Government came into power, the author and her colleagues were asked to brief the team from the US State Department with a conflict analysis during their visit to Southeast Asia. We walked into the Embassy to find the team sitting with our 2007 research report marked full of tabs.

Table 19.2 outlines a summary of the research uptake, use, and impact following for the second case study, following the format in Table 19.1 above.

19.4.4 Research Use

As raised in relation to the first case study, it can be difficult to make claims about how many of the initiatives that followed were influenced by the research activity, especially in the case of partner organizations' activities. The research findings led ACT to consider youth and the education system as important foci for action and the peacebuilding community as requiring knowledge and skills to lead work on these issues. The IEPB project developed its program with the view that the engagement and involvement of young Cambodians was an especially important constituency for peace and the creation of a peaceful multi-ethnic society. Following the published report in 2007, and through partners who had engaged in the research workshops, ACT's IEPB launched a peace camp bringing youth from diverse ethnic groups together for a week to discover both their own prejudices, shared interests, and concerns. The research findings were also used to shape the topics discussed, though the focus on the camp was to hold an intentional space for young people to

Table 19.2 Research contribution analysis for the evaluation of the inter-ethnic peacebuilding program in Cambodia

Research impact	Final outcomes and contribution	The research directed initiatives that could contribute to more positive multi-ethnic relations, including informing ACT's IEPB Program, development of workshops and training, and motivating partner initiatives
	Changes in behavior/practices	The research provided information to better understand ethnic relations and nationalism in the Cambodian context Development of a peace education initiative in secondary schools, with support from government actors Peacebuilding actors involved in the IEPB project integrated and developed programs related to the research The education system was adapted to include peace education curriculum, and staff were trained to deliver it, with government support
Research use	Changes in knowledge/skills	Ability to engage more openly on the topic of ethnic relations and nationalism among target groups increased At ACT, the IEPB project developed from research to a focus on the promotion of a positive, inclusive vision of Cambodian national and ethnic relations through training, education programs, research, and cultural exchange The MoEYS and other related government stakeholders supported and collaborated on the integration of peace education materials and training for secondary schools Other peacebuilding and youth organizations have integrated a focus on the promotion of inter-ethnic peacebuilding into their programs Ongoing monitoring and evaluation indicated an increase in knowledge and skills to support inter-ethnic relations
	Reactions of research users and changes in awareness	Participants in IEPB-led initiatives formed a coalition that became the Council for Inter-Ethnic Peace Government stakeholders' engagement and support for initiatives became more positive over time
Research uptake	Engagement/involvement	Research users participated in ongoing workshops and training and accessed resources Collaboration between ACT and key peacebuilding actors, donors, and later government actors to better understand inter-ethnic relations and nationalism in Cambodia – primarily achieved through IEPB participatory workshops and training ACT's IEPB-developed initiatives bringing youth from diverse ethnic groups together and joined with other NGO events Engagement of government staff supported the development and implementation of Peace Education Curriculum and Teacher Trainings Materials Behavior and practices by teachers and students are monitored through reporting and roleplaying
	Outputs/activities	Publication in English targeted peacebuilding organizations Findings disseminated through workshops and seminars to raise awareness among target actors and engage with government ministries
	Inputs	Key partners from civil society, peacebuilding organizations, donors, and government participated in a Working Group for Inter-Ethnic Peace during the research design, development, and implementation phases. Training workshops held in the first 2 years to meet capacity needs (knowledge and skills and research training) extending to partners across Cambodia Research engaged local, provincial, and national government actors to support the research implementation and at later stages the implementation of initiatives

build connections and understanding. ACT partnered with another 12 NGOs (who had engaged with the research) to organize a camp that moved and was hosted across several communities. This coalition of youth-oriented NGO leaders who had participated in and organized the camps formed another coalition that became known as the Council for Inter-Ethnic Peace. The Council became a network mechanism, which for several years continued to run workshops and forums and develop activities that related to the promotion of positive multi-ethnic social relations across Cambodia.

ACT believed that building the capacity of key people, namely, "NGO community leaders, youth leaders, teachers, and MoEYS staff" was the best way to reach young people and students in the promotion of a positive, inclusive vision of Cambodian society. ACT used CDA Collaborative Learning Project's (CDA, n.d.) Reflecting on Peace Practice Matrix and methodologies to help strengthen their peacebuilding effectiveness, influencing change through their efforts by targeting "key people" to reach "more people" (CDA, n.d.) and link this with the school system and education policies at the sociopolitical level. To reach students, the project team began developing an informal peace education curriculum that specifically promotes a peaceful multi-ethnic society (ACT, n.d.). The curriculum provides teachers and students with a factual basis for forming their views, countering here-say and myth which dominates in the absence of content in the formal education system.

The peace education curriculum also demonstrated how a locally led initiative by a relatively small organization, through ongoing engagement and collaboration with key stakeholders, ultimately led to changes in the education system's policies and practices. In 2008 ACT held national workshops to bring together project staff, educators from the public education system, and trainers from peacebuilding organizations to discuss integrating research findings and peace education relating to positive inter-ethnic relations into the education system. The core components of the peace education curriculum covered 14 topics under "Conflict causes" and "Peacebuilding" that could be adapted to local contexts and needs. That year saw the commencement of teacher training delivered by ACT in cooperation with staff from the MoEYS. This included skills in facilitation and addressing challenges that may arise, such as managing rumors. Funding was sought to provide ten schools with financial and technical support to develop and deliver the curriculum. ACT conducted surveys with students, parents, local authorities, and teachers to explore changes in how communal conflict issues were perceived in the three districts where the curriculum was delivered (ACT, n.d.). ACT also engaged in regular monitoring and evaluation of the peace education project and related external processes.

19.4.5 Research Impact

The research met its internal aim to provide information to understand ethnic conflicts and nationalism in Cambodia and to identify peacebuilding initiatives that could contribute to more positive multi-ethnic relations. The research informed

ACT's IEPB Program, was used in capacity-building and awareness-raising workshops, and motivated other partner initiatives that related to inter-ethnic relations. The ability to discuss and engage constructively on the once-sensitive topic of conflicts relating to ethnicity and nationalism have transformed from latent to more open among its target groups, though the ability to "take account" for the initiatives of others is not possible. The peacebuilding actors involved in the IEPB project have integrated and developed programs that relate to the research. A focus of this chapter was how the education system was adapted to include peace education curriculum, and the training of staff to deliver it, with support from the government.

A memorandum of understanding with the Government of Cambodia was signed to have the program introduced across secondary schools in Cambodia, along with the secondment of Ministry of Education staff to help implement the curriculum development. By 2010, ACT had developed and published a Peace Education Curriculum Teacher Training Manual and Student Book. Workshops were held with MoEYS and other related ministries. Understanding the particular issues facing the diverse provinces in Cambodia also led to ACT working with provincial and commune leaders to support their capacity to manage conflicts and tensions peacefully. ACT's IEPB project is no longer resourced as a key program area. Despite the commitment of key stakeholders over the years, including the Ministry of Education and teachers engaged in the teaching of the peace education curriculum, the project is not continuing in the long term for a range of reasons, including project evolution and lack of ongoing funding.

The focus of the research process on strengthening capacity to undertake research, which was one of the perceived challenges to locally led peacebuilding initiatives, was also approached. External or technical advisors, like the author, were often brought into projects when it was perceived that technical capacity to develop and design research was needed. Beginning in 2005, the former Director of ACT, with the author, developed and delivered a course on introducing peace research methods to people working in the field who may not have a background in social sciences research (Soth Plai & Miletic, 2006). The book and practical week-long course commenced in 2006 in Cambodia and extended to run in Myanmar, Orissa (India), Kenya, and elsewhere (CPCS, n.d.). The longer-term focus on capacity building of staff also enabled the former Research Assistant at ACT to later become the IEPB Project Manager and ultimately a Co-Director of the organization.

The learnings from comparing these two research/evaluation activities of peacebuilding programs for young people have emphasized the importance of participatory approaches to increasing impact through the engagement of key stakeholders and relationship building. Morton's (2015) Research Contribution Framework allowed an examination of the research processes, in particular how the research uptake activities could be considered to have contributed to use and an impact. Of interest in the presented case studies is the emergence of a range of factors for both researching and implementing the programs that can be considered as the "spaces in between."

19.5 Discussion: The Spaces in -Between

The research to action process is not straightforward, hence our use of the term "The Spaces in -Between." In both cases the morphing of research into actions and the creation of initiatives were at times based on emergent findings as well as the need to adapt and respond to needs that arose from the research process itself. As a result, the research process became a form of "action," especially in terms of responding to capacity building that underpins these efforts.

In both cases the research process itself presented opportunities to recognize the importance of early stakeholder engagement in the uptake of research and in laying dynamic foundations for increasing participation in the use of the research. It was also important to see how the research process provided different stakeholders with the ability to use the research to influence changes at different levels of society. In the first case, the research began with high-level support by relatively powerful stakeholders and then deepened its participation with local stakeholders and research users. The second case in contrast began with local engagement, which deepened and diversified, while increasingly developing meaningful and supportive engagement with government over time. The engagement of key stakeholders at different points in the process was integral to increasing knowledge and ownership of the findings in both cases.

In the Ugandan case, the research/evaluation process was influential in facilitating change because key stakeholders from the government and community were included in shaping its objectives and research questions, facilitated data collection, and reviewed the draft reports to assist with the interpretation of findings. Their participation in shaping the program and its evaluation meant that they were familiar with the objectives and the results and could respond to them, explain them to others, and convince their peers of their significance. In the end, the pilot version of the program was not scaled up; rather some of the materials were used in the national teacher curriculum and in a community program. While this is a positive result, its caveat is that research results obtained in one setting may not translate to another.

In the Cambodian case, the research was led by ACT but was expanded through the consistent engagement of the working group and partner organizations, whose participatory engagement in the research design often ran parallel with engagement in capacity-building and awareness-raising activities. The ability to undertake the research, to extend the timeframe, and to flexibly adapt the research was enabled through the participation of key stakeholders (such as donors) throughout the process. The level of such participation was not without challenges, including managing its vast scope and decision-making along the way. The motivation to engage with the research was also evident in how a range of initiatives began during the early phases and led partner organizations to develop their own initiatives.

In both cases, developing and implementing the peace education curriculum went hand in hand with the need for ongoing teacher capacity building. The subjects of gender socialization and inter-ethnic peacebuilding were topics that the teachers needed to understand deeply and have the capacity to deliver to the students. Teachers were generally overworked and under-trained but were committed and engaged.

The importance of strategic partnerships was evident. The engagement of key stakeholders was important in the design of both programs and simultaneously enhanced decision-makers' understandings of the research, along with opportunities and motivation to use evidence. The motivation to use research was enhanced by involving key stakeholders early on in the conceptualization of the projects and throughout its implementation. A focus on relationship building with strategic partners was integral in the Cambodian context, where trust and cooperation were needed to conduct the research and support the implementation of subsequent initiatives. In the Ugandan case, it was the impact evaluation results and the impracticality of scaling up a pilot program that led to a questioning of its sustainability. In the second case, it was the lack of ongoing funding and resources, not the potential scalability, that led to the discontinuation of the program.

Given the difference in the two cases, are there reflections we can make on whether the "locally led" element was more or less valuable in either of these two peacebuilding efforts? Both cases recognize that (re)building trust, engaging in inclusive processes, and strengthening social cohesion are central to peacebuilding efforts. These elements to peacebuilding are most powerful when they are designed and driven at the local level with the commitment of those local to the context which the program seeks to influence. While local peacebuilding often costs less than peacebuilding designed from afar, the second case showed that high engagement of key local actors without adequate funding can be undermined. As CDA research (CDA, n.d.) suggests, local peacebuilding effectiveness often necessitates that certain conditions exist such as linkages between what is focused on at the local-level and national-level dynamics; local- and national-level peace work; and those approaches that target "more people" and those that target "key people." Both cases, in describing their peacebuilding education programs, try to reflect on these conditions toward peacebuilding effectiveness.

In both cases, the focus on research user engagement with key stakeholders required longer timeframes. Co-development requires time to build understanding and can influence the design and implementation of the research. The ability to avert risk and redirect efforts is an important aspect of engagement, and the timeline in both cases needed adjustment to work with perceived risks – to the feasibility or conduct of the research – or to conditions in the sociopolitical environment. Moreover, if research to action is desired for longer-term change, then longer-term commitment should be a consideration from the outset.

19.6 Conclusion

This chapter provided a reflective comparison of two programs which used education as a platform for peacebuilding. One was a UN pilot, carried out in collaboration with the government as part of an internationalized program of work. The other was a long-term, locally led peacebuilding initiative. Both allowed for the spaces in between research and practice to provide learning and adaptation; and often these led to a context-appropriate way of responding to the lessons learned from the programs.

The two case studies reflect the aspirations of the international peace and development field to conduct research to apply its findings to improve the lives of people in need. We used Morton's (2015) Research Contribution Framework to structure our reflections on how the research and practice involved in the two contexts attempted to impact on the lives of young people through peace education. Although originally developed as a rigorous methodology for assessing the impact of research, we found the framework useful as a conceptual tool for retrospective reflection on how certain outcomes and impacts were achieved as part of the research process. While a more rigorous assessment of research impact is preferable to ensure less biased conclusions, it is often not possible due to lack of time, funding, and skill to carry it out. In such instances, the reflexive approach that we adopted in this chapter may be useful for drawing out lessons and opportunities for improvement. The framework could also be adapted at the outset of research, as a planning took for research uptake activities.

The case studies also reflect the broader challenges to contributing to positive, sustained change in societies where there is or has been violent conflict. Contemporary peacebuilding theory and practice recognizes the need to work at multiple levels of society (Ramsbotham et al., 2016) and the importance of local-level peacebuilding within such efforts (Ernstorfer, Chigas & Vaughan-Lee, 2015; Lederach, 1997). Peacebuilding efforts, especially those seen as "local"- or "grassroots"-level interventions (often referred to as *Peace Writ Small*), raise questions of how and when they contribute or add up to broader society-level peace or "Peace Writ Large" (CDA, n.d.) toward collective impacts in peacebuilding (Chigas & Woodrow, 2018). Similarly, the challenges of externally led peacebuilding efforts, where meaningful and sustainable local engagement is absent, raise concerns and undermine peacebuilding effectiveness in the longer term.

The similarities of both cases are reflected in their shared approaches which emphasize linking community change focused on young people with the sociopolitical systems and structures of their contexts. While we, nor the initiatives we reflect on, suggest that these discrete projects alone "add up" to the longer-term change sought, it is likely the research processes contributed to gradual changes in policy and practice in their respective contexts. Moreover, the contextually appropriate and participatory engagement of stakeholders was central to achieving this outcome.

References

Advisory Consortium on Conflict Sensitivity (ACCS), *Northern Uganda Conflict Analysis*, ACCS, 2013.

Affolter, F., & Azaryeva Valente, A. (2019). Chapter 14: Learning for peace: Lessons learned from UNICEF's peacebuilding, education and advocacy in conflict-affected contexts programme. In N. Balvin & D. Christie (Eds.), *Children and peace: From research to action*. Springer International Publishing Switzerland.

Alliance for Conflict Transformation Cambodia (ACT). (n.d.). *Website*. https://www.act.org.kh

Centre for Peace and Conflict Studies (n.d.) Website. Retreived from: http://www.centrepeaceconflictstudies.org

CDA Collaborative Learning Projects (CDA). (n.d.). RPP methodology. Available online at http://cdacollaborative.org/cdaproject/reflecting-on-peace-practice-project/

Chigas, D., & Woodrow, P. (2018). *Adding up to peace: The cumulative impacts of peace programming*. Cambridge, MA: CDA Collaborative Learning Projects.

Chinen, M., Coombes, A., de Hoop, T., & M. Elmeski. (2016). *Evaluation of the transformative potential of positive gender socialization in education for peacebuilding*. UNICEF and American Institutes for Research (AIR). https://www.air.org/project/evaluation-transformative-potential-positive-gender-socialization-education-peace-building. Accessed 4 April 2018.

Datzberger, S., McCully, A., & Smith, A. (2015). Education and peacebuilding in Uganda. *Research Consortium on Education and Peacebuilding*, UNICEF PBEA Programme, Ulster University. https://www.ulster.ac.uk/__data/assets/pdf_file/0013/223321/uganda-country-report.pdf. Accessed 4 April 2018.

Department for International Development (DFID). (2016). *Research uptake: A guide for DFID-funded research programmes*. DFID, UK. https://assets.publishing.service.gov.uk/government/uploads/system/uploads/attachment_data/file/514977/Research_uptake_guidance.pdf. Accessed 4 April 2018.

El-Bushra, J., & Rees Smith, E. (2016). *The transformative potential of positive gender socialization in education for peacebuilding: Pilot programme and impact evaluation in Karamoja, Uganda*. UNICEF learning for peace. https://eccnetwork.net/wp-content/uploads/Gender-Socialization-in-Education-for-Peacebuilding-in-Uganda.pdf. Accessed 4 April 2018.

Ernstorfer, A., Chigas, D., & Vaughan-Lee, H. (2015). From little to large: When does peacebuilding add up. *Journal for Peacebuilding and Development, 10*(1), 72–77.

Langer, L., Tripney, J., & Gough, D. (2016). *The science of using science: Researching the use of research evidence in decision-making*. London, UK: EPPI Centre, University College.

Lederach, J. P. (1997). *Building peace: Sustainable reconciliation in divided societies*. Washington, D.C.: US Institute of Peace Press.

Meas, S., & Miletic, T. (2007). *Peace research: Understanding inter-ethnic relations and nationalism in Cambodia*. Phnom Penh, Cambodia: The Alliance for Conflict Transformation.

Miletic, T. (2016, October 26). Cambodia's peace 25 years on. *Australian Outlook*. Australian Institute of International Affairs, http://www.internationalaffairs.org.au/aiia-authors/dr-tania-miletic/

Ministry of Gender, Labour and Social Development and UNICEF Uganda. (2015). *Situation analysis of children in Uganda* (p. 59). UNICEF Uganda.

Ministry of Gender, Labour and Social Development (MGLSD) and UNICEF Uganda. (2015). *Situation analysis of children in Uganda* (p. 13).

Morton, S. (2012). Exploring and assessing research impact. In *Social policy*. Edinburgh, Scotland: University of Edinburgh.

Morton, S. (2015). Progressing research impact assessment: A 'contributions' approach. *Research Evaluation, 24*, 405–419.

Morton, S., & Casey, T. (2017). Changing national policy on violence affecting children: An impact assessment of UNICEF and partners' multi-country study on the drivers of violence affecting children in Peru. University of Edinburgh. https://www.era.lib.ed.ac.uk/bitstream/handle/1842/22063/UNICEF%20impact%20assesment%20Peru.pdf. Accessed 4 April 2018.

Purdue Peace Project. (2015, March 27). *Locally Driven Peacebuilding.* A Collective Statement. Purdue Peace Project. Available from: https://cla.purdue.edu/ppp/documents/publications/Locally.pdf

Ramsbotham, O., T. Woodhouse, and H. Miall. (2016). Contemporary Conflict Resolution. 4th ed. Cambridge: Polity Press.

Soth Plai, N., & Miletic, T. (2006). *Introduction to peace studies and research methods.* Phnom Penh, Cambodia: The Alliance for Conflict Transformation.

Soth Plai, N., & Milctic, T. (2009). Cambodia's post-war struggle for peace. Reflecting on peace practice project. Collaborative Learning Projects: Boston. Retrievable from: www.cdainc.org

UNICEF. (2017). Programming with and for adolescents: UNICEF Programme Guidance for the second decade. UNICEF Programme Division, New York, USA.

Chapter 20
Working for the Well-Being of Children: The Value and Efficacy of Adopting a Cooperative, Inter-agency Approach

Michael Wessells

Over several decades of work on behalf of vulnerable children in diverse humanitarian and long-term development settings, the author has frequently seen researchers frustrated in their efforts to use their findings to make a difference regarding policies that could support children. This challenge in impacting policies likely has diverse causes, one of which concerns researchers' mode of engaging with policy leaders. Quite often, researchers conduct research and only afterward present their findings to policy leaders together with arguments that the leaders should use the information to guide policy changes. In this approach, there is limited relationship and cooperation between the research team and the policy leaders, and policy leaders have no sense of ownership for or stake in the research. As a result, the research receives little attention from the policy leaders and has little impact on policy.

The purpose of this chapter is to offer a case study that illustrates how this challenge can be addressed by taking a more cooperative approach. A case study method (Yin, 2018) is appropriate in light of the need for initial, in-depth learning about this topic. It shows how the science of cooperation can guide a relational, cooperative approach between researchers, policy leaders, and multiple agencies engaged on children's issues. The cooperative approach generated collective ownership for the research and findings that enabled the research to contribute to policy change on behalf of children.

This chapter is written in honor of Morton Deutsch for his pioneering theory and research on cooperation.

M. Wessells (✉)
Columbia University, New York, NY, USA

N. Balvin, D. J. Christie (eds.), *Children and Peace*, Peace Psychology Book Series, https://doi.org/10.1007/978-3-030-22176-8_20

20.1 The Value of Cooperation

In work globally on humanitarian action and long-term development, inter-agency coordination, which entails cooperation, is essential for achieving effective outcomes and accountability to affected populations. Global guidelines such as the *IASC Guidelines on Mental Health and Psychosocial Support in Emergency Settings* (2007) prioritize inter-agency coordination, as do nearly all the UN NGO standards and guidelines. Calls for coordination are well founded since no agency can alone meet the totality of the needs that exist in a particular setting. It is essential to divide up the work according to a collective plan, share information, and work together for the wider good. Without coordination, different agencies may take divergent, even clashing approaches. They may also cause unintended harm by, for example, duplicating efforts, causing assessment fatigue, or concentrating efforts on the capital city, with little attention given to remote areas where the needs are greater.

Despite these considerations, coordination remains the Achilles heel of the humanitarian enterprise (Slim, 2015). Poor coordination often stems from the competition that is built into the humanitarian architecture. Since agencies compete for funding, access to information and affected populations, and status, they often keep assessment information to themselves, raise funding for themselves, and emphasize their own achievements and needs rather than collective achievements and needs (Wessells, 2009). Thus, ongoing attention is needed to enable inter-agency cooperation. In this respect, it is useful to review briefly key themes and findings from research on cooperation.

20.1.1 The Science of Cooperation

Extensive research, including studies that use quasi-experimental designs and include comparison groups, attests to the positive effects of cooperation. In both laboratory and field experiments, cooperation by members of a group frequently leads to better performance in solving diverse tasks than does competition in which group members are pitted against each other (e.g., Deutsch, 1949; Johnson, Maruyama, Johnson, Nelson, & Skon, 1981; Stanne, Johnson, & Johnson, 1999). In schools in the USA and other countries, educators have used cooperative learning strategies in which small groups work together on a learning task. Reviews of cooperative learning have reported that cooperative learning increases learning and academic achievement (Curry, Damicis, & Gilligan, 2011; Johnson & Johnson, 1989; Slavin, 1996). Also, cooperative learning strategies can improve inter-group relations (Johnson & Johnson, 1989), including relations between majority and ethnic minority groups (Slavin & Cooper, 1999). Extensive evidence indicates that intergroup cooperation is an effective means of improving group relations and reducing hostility and negative attitudes across groups that had been in competition (Deutsch, 1973; Kelman, 2002; Sherif, Harvey, White, Hood, & Sherif, 1961).

However, cooperation strategies do not work better than competitive strategies in all contexts. Even early in the study of cooperation, some findings indicated that both individual and group competition increased levels of both motivation and performance (Julian & Perry, 1967). Also, meta-analyses have found that the effects of cooperation and competition depend on the nature of the task, in particular the means interdependence of the task (Stanne et al., 1999; Tauer & Harackiewicz, 2004). A task is means interdependent when it calls for or requires individuals or groups to coordinate their efforts in completing the task. For example, when two children get to play when they have shoveled snow from the family driveway, they can complete their work by cooperating, that is, by both shoveling and not duplicating or interfering with each other's efforts. This cooperation is mutually beneficial because it enables both children to finish shoveling more rapidly, allowing more time for play. In contrast, an independent task (such as subtracting 1 from 3 or riding a bicycle) does not require individuals or groups to coordinate their efforts. In general, cooperation yields better performance on tasks that are means interdependent, whereas competitive strategies are favored on independent tasks (Stanne et al., 1999). Thus, it is very difficult to say whether cooperation or competition in general yields superior results.

Cooperative strategies can be difficult to use and may have unintended, negative effects. Cooperative strategies are difficult to use in situations such as protracted political conflict (Bar-Tal, 2000; Maoz, 2011) or strong racism. Also, the use of cooperative strategies can produce harmony across groups that differ in ethnicity and power. However, if they overemphasize harmony, cooperative strategies can serve to maintain the status quo, decrease the salience of minority identities, and reduce motivation to work for social change in patterns of inequality (Dovidio & Banfield, 2015).

20.1.2 *Implications for Cooperative Efforts to Strengthen Policies Related to Children*

The science regarding cooperation has valuable implications for developing more cooperative approaches to using research findings to influence policy. First, the cooperative strategy should emphasize the means interdependence of the task at hand—enabling children's well-being. This could be accomplished by pointing out that policies relating to children should be based on policy-relevant evidence. If the researchers and policy leaders cooperate in the development of the research, the research will more likely be seen as policy relevant by the leaders who are positioned to change policies related to children. At the same time, the researchers and policy leaders have different yet complementary roles, with the former conducting the research and the latter working to ensure that quality children's policies exist and reflect the best available evidence. These complementary roles are interdependent and reflect a common, shared commitment to children's well-being. If the roles are implemented with keen respect for interdependence and the value of joint decision-making, a spirit of collective ownership can develop that enriches and deepens the collaboration.

Second, careful attention should be given to power inequities and the humanitarian imperative Do No Harm. The voices of large, international agencies should not drown out the voices of smaller, national agencies that have less power and visibility but have a grounded understanding of children's lives and situation. Also, the emphasis should be less on harmony between the different actors and finding areas of agreement than on learning deeply about children's situation and doing what is in children's best interests. These themes, which likely apply to widcr issues of humanitarian and development coordination, will be evident in the case study presented below.

20.2 The Case Study

The case study features the cooperative, inter-agency processes around research to improve children's protection and well-being. Before discussing the cooperative processes, it is useful first to provide an overview of the research itself.

20.2.1 The Research

The research was conceptualized by the Inter-Agency Learning Initiative (ILI) on Community-Based Child Protection Mechanisms and Child Protection Systems. Save the Children (via Sarah Lilley) was selected to coordinate a global Reference Group, with one of its members—the Columbia Group for Children in Adversity (via M. Wessells)—serving as its technical arm. The ILI drew on the findings of a global review of community-level processes and mechanisms for protecting children (Wessells, 2009). The review reported that the dominant approach was non-governmental organization (NGO) led or facilitated and used a top-down approach. Frequently, NGOs led child protection assessments and then helped to establish in communities Child Welfare Committees (CWCs). The CWCs consisted of groups of local people who monitored violations against children, reported criminal violations to authorities, and took steps to prevent violations at community level. The review, however, found that such approaches tended not to be highly effective or sustainable in large part because local people did not take ownership of them (Wessells, 2009, 2015). Seeing them as NGO projects, communities tended neither to take responsibility for the CWCs nor to use their own creativity and resources to support them.

The research described below was designed to develop and test a bottom-up, community-led approach, which complements more top-down approaches (Wessells, 2015, 2018). This approach placed power in the hands of communities, enabling them to identify the key harms to children, select which one they wanted to address, plan how to address it, and then implement the community-led action while monitoring and periodically taking stock of the action. The research took place in Sierra Leone, one of the world's poorest countries. In Sierra Leone, policies regarding children's protection had placed relatively little stock in community-led action on behalf of children. Via its 2007 Child Rights Act, the emphasis had been on establishing and supporting CWCs at village level.

20.2.1.1 Design

The study consisted of action research (McIntyre, 2008) in which communities defined a problem, developed and took steps to address it, and evaluated and refined their approach. The design entailed a two-arm randomized cluster trial (see Wessells, 2015, 2018 for detailed information on the trial and the intervention). In each of two districts, there were two clusters of three villages which were approximately similar in regard to size, child protection issues, socioeconomic status, and services available. On a random basis, one cluster in each district was assigned to the intervention condition, with the other clusters serving as comparison groups. Quantitative, survey measures were taken from all young people 13–19 years of age in the communities at the baseline (pre-intervention) and midline (1.3 years after the intervention had begun). Also, narrative, qualitative data were collected before the intervention and at the midline. A planned end-line data collection was scuttled by the Ebola crisis.

20.2.1.2 Stages

The work was conducted in multiple stages, the first of which involved ethnographic learning about the communities. A key finding (Wessells et al., 2012) was that local people did not report harms to children to CWCs but overwhelmingly preferred to handle them by means of traditional mechanisms. For example, if a girl became pregnant, the girl's family developed a "compromise" with the boy's family, resulting in the boy's family paying for the girl's lost education and the boy marrying the girl. Asked whether they would report a criminal offence such as rape of a child to authorities, nearly all the participants said "No," indicating low confidence in the police or the magistrates and concerns about corruption and likely inaction. Overall, people viewed the main harms to children as teenage pregnancy out of wedlock, out of school children, heavy work, and maltreatment of children not living with their biological parents. The ethnographic findings were fed back to local collectives in a participatory manner, with space created for reflection about "What are *we* [community members] going to do about these harms to children?"

In Stage 2, the planning phase, with the help of a facilitator who enabled a slow process of dialogue and also inclusivity, the communities selected which harm they wanted to address in a manner that linked them with formal stakeholders. The communities chose to address teenage pregnancy, a third of which was owed to sexual abuse (Coinco, 2010) and which typically forced the young mothers into survival sex. With significant leadership from young girls and boys, the communities designed a community action to prevent teenage pregnancy. Broadly, the community action consisted of family planning, sexual and reproductive health, and life skills, implemented in a highly participatory manner (Wessells, 2015).

In Stage 3, the intervention communities implemented their community-led action, with ongoing monitoring and periodic reflective evaluations in which they stepped back, identified strengths and weaknesses of the community action, and made any needed adjustments. The action included activities such as collective dialogue and decision-making, child leadership and messaging via street drama and radio, peer education, support from local authorities, and linkage of communities with health services.

20.2.1.3 Results

The results at this stage were promising and featured high levels of community ownership and diverse signs of the intervention effects in addressing teenage pregnancy (Stark et al., 2014; Wessells, 2015). High levels of community ownership were evident in how many people volunteered their time and work, without material compensation, and regularly referred to the intervention as "ours," stating that NGOs and the government support them but do not lead the intervention. Many teenagers said they used contraceptives regularly, and teenage girls reported that because of the intervention, they said "No" more frequently to unwanted sex. Both girls and boys said that they had learned how to discuss and negotiate with their partners in regard to sex and also how to plan their sexual activities in light of wider, life goals.

In contrast to previous low use of health posts, many teenagers and parents in the intervention condition visited the health posts regularly for contraceptives or advice, and villages frequently invited nurses and other health staff to visit in order to educate villagers about puberty, sex, and preventing teenage pregnancy. A reduction in teenage pregnancies occurred only in the intervention condition, as confirmed by participant observations and interviews with health post staff, monitors, teenagers, and adults (Wessells, 2015). Also, the action process significantly improved communities' collaboration and linkage with the local health posts.

Unfortunately, the Ebola crisis erupted in Sierra Leone in August 2014, radically disrupting the intervention and data collection and life in general (Kostelny et al., 2016). Nevertheless, the promising results had a significant policy impact, due in no small part to the cooperative process employed.

20.2.2 The Cooperative Process and Its Policy Impact

The cooperative process was deliberately cultivated in all phases of the research as a means of influencing policy and practice. This section examines the nature of the cooperation between the research team and policy leaders at different stages and also considers how various challenges were handled through cooperative processes of dialogue, negotiation, and collective problem-solving.

20.2.2.1 Country Selection

Although the ILI had decided to conduct the action research in one country in each of West and East Africa, it had not initially chosen which countries to work in. Since the ILI recognized that achieving a national policy impact would be more likely if the United Nations Children's Fund (UNICEF) encouraged and supported it, an invitation to consider participation was sent to the UNICEF's country offices in each region. The Sierra Leone and Kenya offices of UNICEF indicated their interest in supporting the action research. Sierra Leone had emerged from a decade-long, horrific war only in 2002, whereas Kenya offered a somewhat more stable, developmental setting. The Sierra Leone case study is featured below. The references to UNICEF from here on in the paper pertain to the UNICEF country office in Sierra Leone.

20.2.2.2 The Design Phase

The broad research design expressed the common vision of the ILI for strengthening the evidence base and simultaneously developing a more community-owned and community-led approach. This vision resonated well with UNICEF, which had, as a result of a previous child protection system mapping, learned about the need for greater community involvement and deeper learning about community processes. Intentionally, however, the design was not complete and something that was imposed by outsiders. There was a need to adapt it to the particulars of the Sierra Leone context and in particular to select a limited number of sites where the work could be most illuminating. Wanting to avoid imposing outsider ideas, the ILI set out to select sites collaboratively, through open dialogue with national partners.

Appropriately, UNICEF recommended that the ILI talk initially with the National Child Protection Committee (CP Com), which was chaired by the Ministry of Social Welfare, Gender, and Children's Affairs (MSWGCA), and the members of which were international and national NGOs whose representatives were mostly Sierra Leonean. Late in 2010, M. Wessells and S. Lilley met with the CP Com, explained that they came in a spirit of co-learning, outlined the action research and its purpose, and invited discussion about two regions where the action research should be conducted. This discussion was pivotal in helping to cement a common vision that efforts to strengthen child protection practice and policy should be guided by quality evidence. Common ground for cooperation arose also from the mutual appreciation that Sierra Leonean communities have rich cultural traditions that include many practices that support children's well-being.

The discussion of priority sites for the conduct of the action research generated an initial list of many options. However, it was explained that in order to learn in depth, the action research could not be done in a large number of areas. Only two geographic regions could be included, and that one reasonable way to approach selection would be to select sites that reflect the regional, ethnic, and linguistic diversity of Sierra Leone, which remains a mostly rural, agrarian society. This explanation sparked conflict, as members of national NGOs pointed out that intensive needs existed in all districts of Sierra Leone and suggested that it would be unfair to favor some over others. Seeking to handle this conflict in a constructive, respectful manner, the action researchers affirmed the widespread needs in Sierra Leone and noted the need for evidence regarding the effectiveness of a community-led approach. The team was not suggesting that a proven approach be extended to some communities but denied to others. They suggested that if the approach worked, the approach could be taken to scale and used in many different districts. As the dialogue continued, the CP Com members came to see the benefits of learning deeply in two sites, and the Minister himself indicated that they could subsequently extend the needed support to other areas. This conversation was important substantively, and it also helped to build a norm of constructive conflict management, which itself is key in taking a cooperative approach.

The CP Com then suggested that it would be useful to conduct the action research in both the southern, Mende-speaking region and in the northern, Temne-speaking area of Sierra Leone. The agreement of the research team with this approach cemented the grounds for cooperation, and the CP Com asked to be kept updated on the site selection and to periodically meet to discuss findings as they came out. Since additional information and site visits were needed to identify the specific sites within each area, various agencies offered to help make connections with particular district offices and enable the local visits. This multilevel dialogue process led the research to select particular Chiefdoms within Moyamba and Bombali districts, respectively. A positive outcome of this site selection process was that the CP Com members began to take ownership of the research, seeing it as truly cooperative and "theirs."

20.2.2.3 The Ethnographic Phase

To strengthen a cooperative approach, an in-country Reference Group was also formed that, like the global Reference Group, was chaired by Save the Children and included UNICEF and NGOs such as Plan, World Vision, ChildFund, ActionAid, and Concern, among others. When the ethnographic research was conducted, two of the researchers came from the former agencies. David Lamin of UNICEF, who in many respects was the driving force behind the research in Sierra Leone, served as the Moyamba team leader, and a child protection worker for Save the Children became one of the researchers who lived in the villages. This arrangement deepened the cooperation between UNICEF and Save and the research team, and it marked a turning point for the researcher from Save, who said that this experience had transformed his understanding of communities and of the problems inherent in dominant NGO approaches.

A significant moment in the cooperative approach occurred when, in 2011, the ethnographic phase findings were presented to the CP Com, with the Minister of the MSWGCA as chair. In presenting the findings, the author felt apprehensive since the findings showed the limits of the approach taken over the previous 4 years by the MSWGCA, UNICEF, and CP Com. That approach was based on the 2007 Child Rights Act, which had mandated the establishment of a CWC in each village and envisioned an effective referral system for reporting violations against children to authorities. In contrast, the ethnographic findings showed that the vast majority of local people did not use the CWCs and other formal aspects of the child protection system, which they saw as embodying outsider values and approaches. Showing that people viewed child rights as harmful and preferred instead to use their traditional processes and mechanisms, the research indicated a significant disconnect between the formal and the nonformal aspects of the child protection system.

Fortunately, the Minister did not respond defensively and thanked the research team for its findings, saying that he had heard some about these kinds of problems and that the research had provided a more systematic picture of communities and the CWCs. This welcoming remark opened the door to honest group dialogue and reflection about the limits of a top-down approach, the grip of traditions on local communities, and how to engage with communities in more meaningful, effective ways. A key part of the discussion was the recognition that communities already do much to protect their children and that the agencies and workers around the table should support appropriate local efforts. In this manner, the group demonstrated its openness and commitment to learn from research findings and its willingness to reflect together about what was not working and how to improve their inter-agency approach. As people took ownership for the findings and discussed what more effective approaches might look like, the spirit of cooperation and co-learning grew richer, inviting additional action. Subsequently, UNICEF convened a workshop aimed at developing more participatory approaches to introducing child rights and ending the backlash against child rights that the ethnographic research had reported.

20.2.2.4 The Community-Led Planning and Action

Continuing the upward spiral of cooperation, the research team provided regular updates to the CP Com at regular intervals (every 6 months) as the intervention communities selected which harm to children to address, developed a plan for addressing it, and took action themselves to reduce the harm. These updates included collaborative learning about how to stimulate high levels of inclusivity and ownership via power sharing with communities and community efforts to reach out to hear the voices of the most vulnerable and marginalized children and families. These updates enabled significant problem-solving dialogue about how to achieve meaningful child participation, a priority that the global child protection sector has found difficult to achieve.

This period also saw increased cooperation with UNICEF in influencing multiple partners. UNICEF organized periodic workshops with different NGOs to help share the findings, approaches, and learnings from the community-led work. Conducted in a reflective mode, these workshops not only shared what the research team was learning and how it worked but also invited each partner agency to share about how it engaged with communities and evaluated its work. Collcctive reflection on the agency sharing increased awareness of the need for greater power sharing with communities and for increased levels of community ownership and sustainability. These workshops boosted the desire of different agencies to learn how to support a more community-led approach.

UNICEF also played a key brokering role in influencing the Government of Sierra Leone. Because UNICEF worked closely with the MSWGCA and its Minister, it knew the main power dynamics within the Ministry, understood the key leverage points, and identified when the timing was ripe for action. On a regular basis, D. Lamin organized meetings between himself, the Minister, and M. Wessells. These meetings were mostly for purposes of updating about the action research, its approach, and its key findings to date. However, they also provided a steady message of encouragement to listen more deeply to communities, build on existing community resources, and enable and learn from community action on behalf of vulnerable children. These meetings were critical in increasing the support of the Ministry, which looked to UNICEF for vision and leadership on behalf of children. With UNICEF's encouragement of a more community-led approach, the Ministry could move with confidence and without image loss in shifting direction away from the top-down approach inherent in the previous Child Rights Act.

Cooperation with UNICEF was crucial also in managing the rapid turnover (every 6 months or so) in the Minister post, which risked a loss of continuity and the shift of the MSWGCA agenda in directions away from the community action approach featured in the research. UNICEF managed this challenge effectively by cultivating strong working relationships with mid-level managers who tended to stay in posts for several years. Regular meetings between mid-level managers, D. Lamin, and M. Wessells helped to engender support for the action research at multiple levels within the MSWGCA and to avoid gaps in support that might have developed otherwise.

A similar process occurred within UNICEF, which also underwent changes in its Representative and the Chief of Child Protection posts. Regular presentations and dialogues were organized within UNICEF to update key staff, including the Representative and the Deputy Representative, on the approach, findings, and value added of the community-led approach, and also to enrich the understanding and interest of its child protection workers. The latter was vital for insuring that bottom-up approaches got included in the national efforts to strengthen the child protection system. The meetings also enabled dialogue that helped to develop a holistic vision in which top-down and bottom-up approaches were seen as complementary elements of strengthening national child protection systems.

20.2.2.5 Toward Policy Change

The inter-agency research approach and findings converged with the findings of other studies (e.g., Child Frontiers, 2010; Krueger, Thompstone, & Crispin, 2013) that highlighted the importance of community action on behalf of children. By late 2015, the MSWGCA had developed and gained Cabinet approval for a new Child Welfare Policy. Consistent with this research, the policy emphasizes the importance of the government supporting community efforts to protect children, and it cautions against the tendency to add particular structures as instruments for protecting children.

It is inherently difficult to measure whether the action research in particular significantly influenced the new national Child Welfare Policy. However, three different Ministers of the MSWGCA told the author and UNICEF that they saw the research findings as guiding the formation of a new policy that placed greater emphasis on supporting community action to protect children. Also, two mid-level managers within the MSWGCA said that this research had been pivotal because it was cooperative, systematic, and able to document using a rigorous design the effects of community-led action on behalf of children. Of interest to the author was that when MSWGCA stakeholders discussed the action research, they spoke of it as if it were their own and a rich source of co-learning. Key UNICEF stakeholders confirmed independently that the action research and its cooperative process had contributed significantly to the development of the new policy.

20.2.2.6 Limitations

The cooperative approach described here for influencing national policy is likely useful in diverse contexts, yet it is not universally applicable. If, for example, a national government was engaged in or supportive of corruption or violations against children, a cooperative approach would be inappropriate. Further, the community-led approach used in the action research would not be appropriate in zones of armed conflict that are suffused with spies and tensions. In such environments, group discussions could be misperceived as political organizing and could lead to participants being killed.

20.3 Conclusion

In concluding, it is useful to revisit the points raised earlier regarding means interdependence, attention to inequalities, and the importance of adhering to the Do No Harm principle. The cooperative approach in this case study recognized the high levels of interdependence among different agencies and stakeholders involved in policy and practice related to children's well-being. Indeed, it illustrates that the human component—relationships and processes of cooperation—can be as important as are the technical aspects of the research. Begun early on and applied in a continuous manner, a cooperative approach builds the shared vision, the spirit of interdependence, and the sense of collective ownership that enables policy leaders to take research findings on board and use them to develop more effective child protection policies. Because the process worked through the CP Com, small, national agencies had a significant voice alongside of large, international agencies. Throughout the discussions, attention was given to avoiding unintended harm and respecting children's dignity and rights.

It is important to recognize the limitations of a case study approach (Yin, 2018), which does not enable wide generalizations. It would be a mistake to assume that the kind of cooperative approach presented in this case study would apply readily to many different contexts. Still, the strategy of early and ongoing cooperation warrants further research. This case study is offered in a spirit of inviting additional work aimed at documenting and evaluating approaches to enabling research on children to actually influence policy changes.

An important challenge for the future is to enable wider use of this kind of cooperative approach for purposes of achieving a policy impact. This wider use will require a more intentional effort on the part of researchers and policy leaders to build strong relationships, explicitly recognize the interdependence of research teams and policy leaders, and do the challenging, time-consuming work of cooperation. It will also require strong "soft" skills such as listening, building trust, negotiation, and collective dialogue, reflection, and problem-solving. More thought should be devoted to developing these skills as part of the effort to prepare the next generation of researchers who can strengthen policy and practice in regard to children's protection and well-being.

References

Bar-Tal, D. (2000). From intractable conflict through conflict resolution to reconciliation: Psychological analysis. *Political Psychology, 21*(2), 351–365.

Child Frontiers. (2010). *Mapping and assessing child protection systems in West and Central Africa: A five-country analysis paper.* Bangkok, Thailand: Child Frontiers.

Coinco, E. (2010). *A glimpse into the world of teenage pregnancy in Sierra Leone.* Freetown, Sierra Leone: UNICEF.

Curry, P., Damicis, L., & Gilligan, R. (2011). *The effect of cooperative learning on inter ethnic relations in schools. ERIC no. ED519148*. Washington, D.C.: Society for Research on Educational Effectiveness.

Deutsch, M. (1949). An experimental study of the effects of co-operation and competition upon group process. *Human Relations, 2*(3), 199–232.

Deutsch, M. (1973). *The resolution of conflict: Constructive and destructive processes* (Vol. 17, p. 248). New Haven, CT: Yale University Press.

Dovidio, J. F., & Banfield, J. C. (2015). Group cooperation. In D. A. Schroeder & W. G. Graziano (Eds.), *Oxford handbook of prosocial behavior*. New York, NY: Oxford.

IASC. (2007). *IASC guidelines on mental health and psychosocial support in emergency settings*. Geneva, Switzerland: Author.

Johnson, D. W., & Johnson, R. (1989). *Cooperation and competition: Theory and research*. Edina, MN: Interaction.

Johnson, D. W., Maruyama, G., Johnson, R., Nelson, D., & Skon, L. (1981). Effects of cooperative, competitive, and individualistic goal structures on achievement: A meta-analysis. *Psychological Bulletin, 89*(1), 47–62.

Julian, J. W., & Perry, F. A. (1967). Cooperation contrasted with intra-group and inter-group competition. *Sociometry, 30*(1), 79–90.

Kelman, H. C. (2002). Interactive problem solving: Informal mediation by the scholar-practitioner. In J. Bercovitch (Ed.), *Studies in international mediation: Essays in honor of Jeffrey Z. Rubin* (pp. 167–193). New York, NY: Palgrave Macmillan.

Kostelny, K., Lamin, D., Manyeh, M., Ondoro, K., Stark, L., Lilley, S., & Wessells, M. (2016). *'Worse than the war': An ethnographic study of the impact of the Ebola crisis on life, sex, teenage pregnancy, and a community-driven intervention in rural Sierra Leone*. London, UK: Save the Children.

Krueger, A., Thompstone, G., & Crispin, V. (2013). Learning from child protection systems mapping and analysis in West Africa: Research and policy implications. *Global Policy, 5*(1), 47–55.

Maoz, I. (2011). Does contact work in protracted asymmetrical conflict? Appraising 20 years of reconciliation-aimed encounters between Israeli Jews and Palestinians. *Journal of Peace Research, 48*(1), 115–125.

McIntyre, A. (2008). *Participatory action research*. Thousand Oaks, CA: Sage.

Sherif, M., Harvey, O., White, J., Hood, W., & Sherif, C. (1961). *Inter-group conflict and cooperation: The robber's cave experiment*. Norman, OK: University of Oklahoma.

Slavin, R. (1996). Research on cooperative learning and achievement: What we know, what we need to know. *Contemporary Educational Psychology, 21*, 43–69.

Slavin, R., & Cooper, R. (1999). Improving intergroup relations: Lessons from cooperative learning programs. *Journal of Social Issues, 55*(4), 647–663.

Slim, H. (2015). *Humanitarian ethos: A guide to the morality of aid in war and disaster*. New York, NY: Oxford.

Stanne, M., Johnson, D., & Johnson, R. (1999). Does competition enhance or inhibit motor performance: A meta-analysis. *Psychological Bulletin, 125*, 133–154.

Stark, L., Macfarlane, M., King, D., Lamin, D., Lilley, S., & Wessells, M. (2014). *A community-driven approach to reducing teenage pregnancy in Sierra Leone: Midline evaluation*. London, UK: Save the Children.

Tauer, J. M., & Harackiewicz, J. M. (2004). The effects of cooperation and competition on intrinsic motivation and performance. *Journal of Personality and Social Psychology, 86*(6), 849–861.

Wessells, M. (2009). Do No Harm: Toward contextually appropriate psychosocial support in international emergencies. *American Psychologist, 64*(8), 842–854.

Wessells, M., Lamin, D., King, D., Kostelny, K., Stark, L., & Lilley, S. (2012). The disconnect between community-based child protection mechanisms and the formal child protection system in rural Sierra Leone: Challenges to building an effective national child protection system. *Vulnerable Children and Youth Studies, 7*(31), 211–227.

Wessells, M. G. (2009). *What are we learning about protecting children in the community? An inter-agency review of the evidence on community-based child protection mechanisms in humanitarian and development settings*. London, UK: Save the Children.
Wessells, M. G. (2015). Bottom-up approaches to strengthening child protection systems: Placing children, families, and communities at the center. *Child Abuse & Neglect: The International Journal, 43*, 8–21.
Wessells, M. G. (2018). *A guide for supporting community-led child protection processes*. New York, NY: Child Resilience Alliance.
Yin, R. K. (2018). *Case study research and applications: Design and methods* (6th ed.). Thousand Oaks, CA: Sage.

Part IV
Children and Survival of the Species

Chapter 21
Climate Change and Children: An Issue of Intergenerational Justice

Ann V. Sanson and Susie E. L. Burke

21.1 Introduction

The 2015 Paris Agreement reflected global acknowledgement that climate change is "an urgent and potentially irreversible threat to human societies and the planet". Scientists view it as the biggest global health threat of the twenty-first century (Costello et al., 2009). In terms of Bronfenbrenner and Morris's (2006) ecological model,[1] climate change is quintessentially a macro-system phenomenon, but its impacts are felt at every level of the system, from macro to micro. It poses substantial and escalating risks for food security, water availability, health, housing, infrastructure, agriculture and natural ecosystems (IPCC, 2014). There is a deep inequality in its causes and its impacts: disproportionately caused by the developed world, it will disproportionately affect the developing world; and children and future generations will disproportionately suffer its consequences. And yet peace psychology has been slow to consider climate change as a "peace issue". This chapter positions climate change as an urgent issue of structural violence and intergenerational justice that demands attention from psychologists, scholars, practitioners, activists and policy-makers, with particular emphasis on the needs of current and future generations of children.

[1] Bronfenbrenner and Morris's (2006) ecological model categorises influences on child development from the micro-system (the child's immediate family context) through the meso- and exo-systems (interacting social influences such as school and health care) to the macro-system (national, cultural and global factors).

A. V. Sanson (✉)
University of Melbourne, Parkville, VIC, Australia
e-mail: annvs@unimelb.edu.au

S. E. L. Burke
Australian Psychological Society, Melbourne, VIC, Australia

N. Balvin, D. J. Christie (eds.), *Children and Peace*, Peace Psychology Book Series, https://doi.org/10.1007/978-3-030-22176-8_21

After a brief outline of climate science, we examine how climate change contributes to both direct and structural violence. We then turn to the many ways in which children and youth are affected by climate change. Next we examine what a fair and just response to climate change might look like and discuss the many ways all of us can contribute towards making this a reality. We conclude by noting that, while climate change poses a dire threat, our responses to it can contribute significantly to a healthier, more equitable and more peaceful world.

21.2 The Science of Climate Change

Climate change refers to the warming of the planet caused by the build-up of greenhouse gases in the atmosphere (principally carbon dioxide, methane and nitrous oxide). As concentrations of CO_2 in the atmosphere have increased (Betts, Jones, Knight, Keeling, & Kennedy, 2016), global temperatures have risen in parallel. All of the world's ten warmest years have occurred since 1998, and the Earth has not been so warm for 115,000 years (NOAA, 2017). Climate change is responsible for increased frequency and severity of extreme weather events (EWEs) such as floods, hurricanes and bushfires, as well as slower impacts like rising sea levels, droughts and changed growing seasons.

The climate science indicates that we must act with urgency to move beyond fossil fuels and eliminate man-made emissions of greenhouse gases while at the same time drawing down the excess greenhouse gases in the atmosphere. Without such rapid change, further warming of up to 4.8 °C can be expected during the twenty-first century (IPCC, 2014). This would be catastrophic, potentially threatening the entire global ecosystem and human civilisation.

The Paris Agreement committed nations to limit the temperature increase to below 2 °C, preferably below 1.5 °C. Cooperation by all countries is needed to achieve the required deep reductions in emissions. But, although most of the technological solutions to both halting emissions and drawing down excess carbon are already available (e.g. Hawken, 2017), action is not happening nearly fast enough (The Royal Society, 2017).

21.3 Climate Change, Children and Youth

There are several reasons to focus particularly on the impact of climate change on children and young people, three of which are discussed below.

21.3.1 Children's Greater Vulnerability to Climate Change Impacts

Since climate change disrupts the basic necessities of life – shelter, food and water – it is regarded as the biggest global human health threat of the twenty-first century (Costello et al., 2009). There is clear evidence that it will exacerbate the underlying social, economic and ecological factors that cause global illness and premature death for all age groups (Watts et al., 2018). However, those most vulnerable to climate change impacts are children and youth, with the World Health Organization estimating that children will suffer more than 80% of the illnesses, injuries and deaths attributable to it (McMichael et al., 2004). Due to their immature physiological defence systems and the ways they interact with their immediate environment, they are physically more vulnerable to the *direct* effects of extreme heat, drought and natural disasters (McMichael, 2014) through injuries, environmental toxins and infectious, gastrointestinal and parasitic diseases that will become more prevalent with warmer temperatures and changed rainfall patterns (Sheffield & Landrigan, 2010). For example, comparing the year 2000 with the three decades preceding it, climate change is estimated to have increased the numbers of cases of undernutrition, diarrhoeal diseases and vector-borne diseases such as malaria by 3–10% (Confalonieri et al., 2007), a trend that is expected to accelerate (Ebi, 2014).

Children are also more susceptible to *indirect* effects of climate change, such as food shortages, intergroup conflict, economic dislocation and migration (Akresh, 2016). Particularly for younger children, their dependency on adults can lead to psychosocial consequences through the impact of climate-related extreme weather events (EWEs) on parents' physical, emotional and social well-being, family functioning and economic status (Clayton, Manning, Krygsman, & Speiser, 2017). Children also face danger in the period following EWEs when their routines and safety nets are disrupted, and they are vulnerable to physical and sexual violence, recruitment into armed groups, early marriage, trafficking and child labour (The Child Protection Working Group, 2015). There is also growing evidence of psychosocial impacts. Climate-related EWEs have been linked to consequences including post-traumatic stress disorder, depression, panic, sleep and anxiety disorders, cognitive deficits, learning problems and impaired language development (Garcia & Sheehan, 2016).

Psychosocial impacts of climate change arise not only from directly experiencing its effects but also from vicarious experience and knowledge of the threat it poses for the future. There is clear evidence of widespread emotional reactions to climate change, even in high-income countries that are not yet suffering its direct effects. Surveys have found that many young people experience fear, sadness, anger and a sense of powerlessness (Ojala, 2015; Strife, 2012; UNICEF UK, 2013). Around the world, large numbers of youth recognise that climate change poses a serious threat (e.g. 60% of Australian 16- to 17-year-olds; Tranter & Skrbis, 2014) and are worried about how it will affect their own futures (e.g. 74% of British 11- to 16-year-olds; UNICEF UK, 2013) as well as those of children and families in developing countries (63% in the British sample above). Many young people believe that the world may end during their lifetime due to climate change and other global threats (Albert, Hurrelmann, Quenzel, & Jugend, 2010). Thus there is concern about how the threat of climate change is affecting the next generation's capacity to invest in the future (Sanson, 2017).

Further, impacts on children's and youth's physical, psychological, social and cognitive development will carry sequelae right through their lifetimes and possibly beyond. They can have long-term developmental, educational and economic consequences which make it harder for them to reach their full potential (Clayton et al., 2017; Grantham-McGregor et al., 2007). This, along with likely epigenetic changes, may diminish their capacity to care for the next generation, creating a vicious intergenerational cycle of disadvantage that impedes human development.

21.3.2 Double Jeopardy for Children in Disadvantaged Circumstances

A further injustice arises from the fact that not all children and youth will suffer equally from climate change. Both physical and psychosocial impacts can be understood as the consequence of the accumulation of risk factors and the attenuation of protective factors in children's lives, along with repeated exposure to stressful situations (Sanson, Wachs, Koller, & Salmela-Aro, 2018). As discussed in Sect. 21.4, the most serious impacts of climate change are predicted in low- to-middle-income countries (LMICs), where 85% of the world's children live (UNICEF, 2014). These children, along with children in disadvantaged circumstances in developed countries, will thus experience more risk factors and fewer protective factors. Since children are already at greater risk of climate change effects than adults, children growing up in situations experiencing the worst climate change effects are in double jeopardy.

Unless We Act Now (UNICEF, 2015) clearly explains how climate change disproportionately affects the poorest children, deepening existing inequalities. Figure 21.1 graphically illustrates this with the example of drought. Those with adequate resources can safely relocate, keep families together, access health care, maintain children's education and reduce social stressors, whereas those without such resources find themselves on an escalating downwards path of long-term deprivations like poorer nutrition, limited access to safe drinking water and disruptions to schooling. For these children, intergenerational injustice is compounded with exacerbated inequalities.

21.3.3 Demands for Coping and Adaptation Placed on the Next Generation

Children and youth will need to adapt to major changes arising from climate change, which are already starting but will escalate even with speedy action to curb emissions. The direct, indirect and gradual impacts of climate change all bring obvious

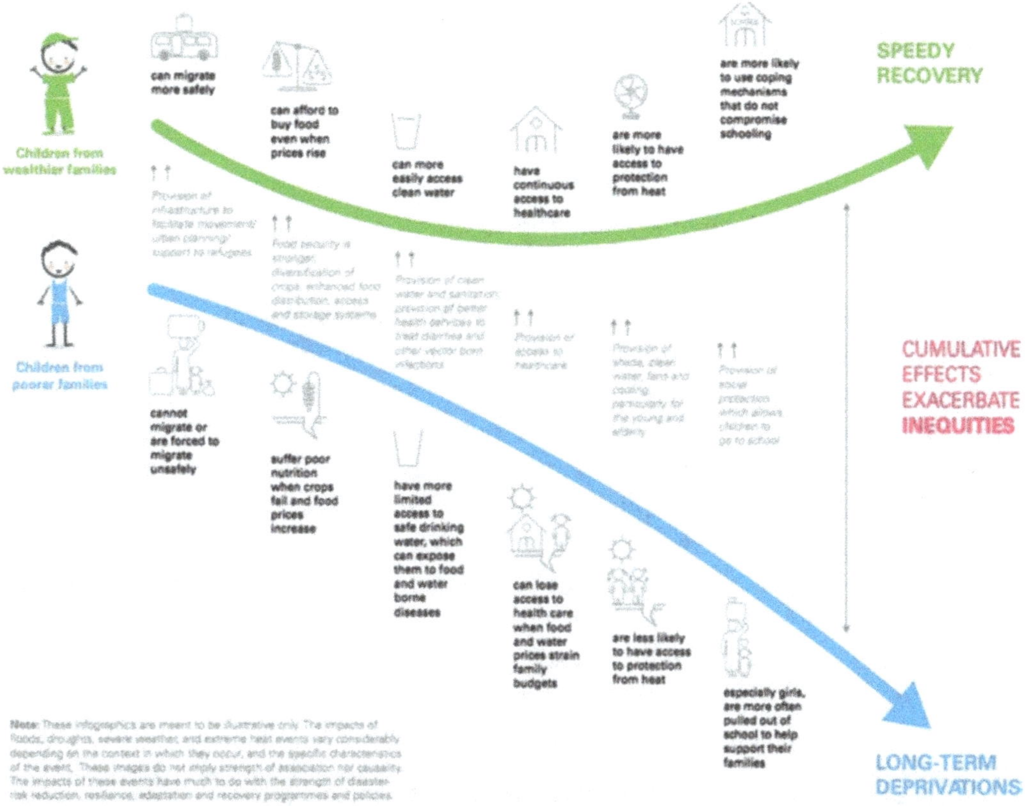

Fig. 21.1 Illustration of how climate change can exacerbate inequities, using the example of climate change-induced drought (Source: UNICEF (2015) *Unless we act now* (Fig. 7, p27))

developmental challenges for young people. Dislocation, loss of place, migration and social disruptions will be added challenges for many (see Sect. 21.4).

Additionally, restoring a safe climate requires a rapid transition to a low-carbon economy, involving major restructuring of industry, transport, energy and food production. Therefore this generation of children and youth will need to change how they live, eat, work, travel and consume.

We need to think about the knowledge, skills and attitudes that will help the next generation adapt and cope successfully with the massive changes ahead. Section 21.6 provides discussion of the role of adults in equipping children for these challenges.

21.4 Climate Change, Peace and Violence

The 2x2 matrix developed by Christie, Wagner, and Winter (2001), that differentiates between episodic (direct) violence and structural violence and episodic and structural peace-building, provides a useful framework for considering how climate change relates to peace and violence. Below we discuss how it contributes to both episodic and structural violence, while Sect. 21.5 outlines the potential for restoring a safe climate while simultaneously building more peaceful, healthy and equitable communities.

21.4.1 Climate Change's Contribution to Direct Violence

Lab-based and quasi-experiments have demonstrated a causal relationship between heat and aggression (Anderson, 2012). In a meta-analysis covering several centuries and continents, Burke, Hsiang, and Miguel (2015) found that both hotter temperatures and lower rainfall were related to increases in all forms of violence, from interpersonal to international, but particularly intergroup violence. Akresh (2016) cites evidence of links between increasing temperature and crime, community violence and civil war. As the temperature goes up, so does aggression.

Other factors often mediate the link between climate change and direct violence. Climate change effects (e.g. shortages of food and water, changed growing seasons and forced migration) can reduce social control and create social conflict, hence leading to violence (Agnew, 2011). When communities are disrupted due to EWEs or slower-acting climate change effects like droughts and rising sea levels, increasing levels of frustration in society can lead to interpersonal violence. For example, domestic abuse increased among families who experienced Hurricane Katrina in the USA (Yun, Lurie, & Hyde, 2010), and violence towards women increased in communities affected by the Australian "Black Saturday" bushfires (Molyneaux et al., 2018, submitted). When people are forced to relocate, competition for resources (like jobs and land) between existing residents and new arrivals can increase racist sentiments and behaviour as currently seen in Europe and elsewhere with the upsurge in refugees from North Africa and the Middle East. For such reasons, climate change has been described as an "accelerant" and "threat multiplier" to political instability.

21.4.2 Climate Change's Contribution to Structural Violence

Perhaps more important than its impact on direct violence, climate change worsens the root causes of violence. In this context, it is instructive to consider the United Nation's Sustainable Development Goals (SDGs) which together constitute a plan of action to "strengthen universal peace in larger freedom" (United Nations, 2015). Climate change is the focus of the 13th SDG ("Take urgent action to combat climate change and its impacts"), where it is described as the single biggest threat to development (United Nations, 2015). However, it is also relevant to most of the other SDGs – impacts on some of these are summarised in Table 21.1 (see Sanson et al., 2018, for further details). The deep asymmetry between those who have contributed

Table 21.1 Examples of how climate change will impede the achievement of selected SDGs

Sustainable Development Goal (SDG)	Examples of how climate change will compromise achievement of SDG
SDG 1: End poverty and SDG 10: Reduced inequalities	Climate change is disproportionately caused by "developed" (or "WEIRD"[a]) countries which make up 12% of the world's population. But, due to geographic position (lower latitudes and lower altitudes) and weaker infrastructure (such as transport, health, education and social welfare systems), LMICs[b] are both more susceptible to sudden EWEs and longer-term climate change effects and have less capacity to prepare for and recover from them. Hence inequalities will increase, and tackling poverty will be more challenging
SDG 2: Zero hunger	For every degree Celsius of warming, agricultural yields in Africa will diminish by 10–30%, directly threatening livelihoods (Hanna & Oliva, 2016)
SDG 3: Good health and well-being	The overall health impacts of climate change are predicted to be extremely negative (Watts et al., 2018) (see Sect. 21.3)
SDG 4: Quality education	More frequent and intense floods, wildfires, hurricanes and other EWEs will harm schooling by reducing attendance and achievement and destroying schools and, particularly in LMICs, by children leaving school to work and enhance family income (Kousky, 2016)
SDG 5: Gender equality	Girls tend to be removed from school in times of hardship more often than boys (UNICEF, 2015)
SDG 16: Peace, justice and strong institutions	Climate change will cause political and societal instability and undermine existing institutions (see Sect. 21.4.1)

[a]WEIRD stands for "Western, Educated, Industrialized, Rich and Democratic" countries which make up 12% of the world's population (Henrich, Heine, & Norenzayan, 2010)
[b]LMICs, lower- and middle-income countries

least to our warming atmosphere but will be most heavily impacted and those who contributed most but will be better protected creates a situation of fundamental injustice and a clear case of structural violence on a global scale.

21.5 A Fair and Just Response to Climate Change: Global and Community Solutions

Approaches to mitigating the severity of climate change and adapting to its impacts should also seek to reduce the deep inequalities and injustices inherent in it, thereby also protecting children's well-being. In fact, climate change may offer an opportunity for building "positive peace" (Christie et al., 2001). Here we explore some of the ways in which climate solutions can help build more peaceful and equitable societies, starting with global solutions and moving to regional and local initiatives.

21.5.1 Global Solutions

Climate change as a global problem requires global cooperation to bring about solutions. The UN Framework Convention on Climate Change (UN General Assembly, United Nations, 1994) requires nations to protect the climate system "on the basis of equity and in accordance with … common but differentiated responsibilities and respective capabilities" and has a peace-building approach at its heart. From an ethical viewpoint, it is only fair that those who contributed most to the problem, and who possess the greatest resources, should bear the greatest burden for addressing it. To date, however, fair, cooperative and systemic approaches for global burden-sharing have not emerged. The voluntary carbon reduction commitments made after the Paris Agreement are relatively weak and are insufficient to avoid dangerous climate change (Falkner, 2016). Nor is action happening fast enough.

Some argue that we should consider not only the divide between developed and developing states but also divides between affluent and poor people, wherever they live (Huntjens & Zhang, 2016). Harris, Chow, and Karlsson (2013), for example, argue that the high-carbon lifestyles of the most affluent people (the wealthiest 10% who own 87.8% of the world's wealth; Credit Suisse, 2017) and the global middle class must be regulated and taxed so that the costs of adaptation are redistributed between the world's wealthy and the poor.

Other global solutions to simultaneously address climate change and work towards climate justice rely on whole-scale changes to current economic systems. Examples include moving beyond gross domestic product (GDP) as a measure of a country's prosperity, to a broader measure of overall well-being that includes health, education and security (Stiglitz, Sen, & Fitoussi, 2010), or a measure like the Bhutanese Gross National Happiness Index which includes indicators of human well-being and environmental health. Others call for even more radical reordering of our economic and political system. According to Klein (2014), the current capitalist free market system is based on the fiction that nature is limitless. This has resulted in exploitation almost beyond the point of recovery – of the atmosphere, land, water and many species. To lower global emissions as rapidly as necessary, argues Klein, we need a completely different system: one that respects natural cycles of renewal; is sensitive to natural limits; generates plentiful, dignified work; closes deep inequalities; strengthens and transforms the public sphere; and radically reins in corporate power. Building equality and justice is deeply embedded in these types of solutions.

The discourse surrounding climate change often ignores or de-emphasises underlying structural political and economic problems, instead focusing on individualised lifestyle issues (Ojala, 2015). This is based on a neoliberal way of seeing people foremost as consumers rather than citizens, positing that people can take responsibility for global climate change by making the right consumer choices. While such individual choices are important, they will not in themselves prevent the escalation of climate change. Rather, to address the structural obstacles and injustices associated with climate change, people need to act as citizens, pressuring governments to make appropriate policy changes. "People power" will be a necessary ingredient in pushing national governments towards stronger action. Joining lobby or action groups (e.g. the Citizens' Climate Lobby) can help to overcome a sense of powerlessness and maximise the impact of individuals' actions at this level.

21.5.2 Regional, Community and Local Solutions

Proponents of climate solutions that move away from free market ideologies highlight the importance of the dispersal and devolution of power and control to regional and local communities (although strong central governments are still essential to set laws and limits to carbon-polluting activities). A worldwide movement of relocalisation seeks to build societies based on the local production of food, energy and goods and the local development of governance, currency and culture (http://www.postcarbon.org/relocalize/). Massive cuts in emissions can be achieved by localising economies so that needs are met close to home, avoiding energy-intensive transportation (Norberg-Hodge, 2003). This shift would be facilitated by government regulations to rein in corporate power, involving change at national and international levels too.

The flourishing global "transition town" movement is a good example of grassroots-led re-localised economies (Hopkins, 2009). In transition towns, local communities make plans for how to transition away from fossil fuels and build in resilience for tough times ahead. They use collective decision-making and participatory democracy to build ideas about how to strengthen their local economies with low-carbon initiatives. These efforts revitalise or create new local businesses, stimulate local jobs and help create thriving communities of people with meaningful employment in their local area. Community-owned renewable energy projects, community gardens, car-share schemes, tool libraries and repair cafes are examples of climate solutions at regional and local levels which are proliferating around the world and building fairer, safer communities (Hopkins, 2013).

Redressing climate injustice and restoring a safe climate also involve shoring up communal infrastructure to provide essential services like public transport, housing and electricity that reduce emissions and are affordable and accessible to everyone. A growing trend is for local governments to lead change. For example, in 2016, Darebin (a municipality in Melbourne, Australia) became one of the first councils in the world to declare a climate emergency and is planning and implementing changes in areas including transport, green spaces, planning, waste minimisation, energy generation and efficiency and fossil fuel divestment (https://www.yoursaydarebin.com.au/21346/documents/62558). Other municipalities are following suit; amongst the first in the USA were Hoboken County in New Jersey, Montgomery County in Maryland and the city of Los Angeles. By mid 2019, 822 jurisdictions in 16 countries had declared a climate emergency (https://climateemergencydeclaration.org/climate-emergency-declarations-cover-15-million-citizens/).

There are multiple opportunities for engagement at the community or local level for individuals and organisations. For example, to support localisation efforts, community development activities can be undertaken by practitioners and scholars from a range of disciplines as well as civic leaders, activists and involved citizens. These activities can strengthen civil society by empowering and strengthening the capacity of people as active citizens, enabling them to shape change in their communities (Craig, Gorman, & Vercseg, 2004). One among many potential roles for peace psychologists is to help build community capacity in the peace-building skills of negotiation, cooperation, conflict resolution and active communication which are vital to the successful development and operation of community-owned projects. All such initiatives seek to mitigate climate change and hence help to protect today's children and future generations from its most devastating effects.

21.6 Supporting Children in the Face of Climate Change

As noted above, individuals' actions as citizens can help mitigate climate change while simultaneously addressing inequity and injustice and building positive peace. Further, there are many ways in which children can be supported to cope with climate change that build their own capacities to take action on environmental threats. Below we start with the necessary step of overcoming denial and avoidance of the climate change problem. Then we turn to engagement of children in efforts at mitigation, followed by consideration of the skills and capacities they need to adapt to current and future climate change impacts and to be prepared for the major changes associated with a transition to a climate-changed world and low-carbon economy. We should note at the outset that virtually all the research looking at these questions has come from the "WEIRD" (developed) world, and many of the strategies we discuss are only accessible to those in developed nations or with relative wealth – who are also those with the most responsibility, and power, to act. As discussed in Sect. 21.6.3, there is a clear need for more research on how to build the resilience of children in LMIC countries.

21.6.1 Overcoming Denial and Avoidance of Climate Change

Despite most people acknowledging that climate change is a problem requiring urgent changes in human behaviour (Cook et al., 2016; Reser, Bradley, Glendon, Ellul, & Callaghan, 2012), far fewer people are taking active steps to mitigate it. Psychological factors are central to both denial of climate change and failure to act. These include cognitive biases like minimising threats which appear distant in time and space, avoidance of painful feelings, resisting change and filtering out information which conflicts with our belief systems (Centre for Research on Environmental Decisions [CRED], 2014). Psychology also provides insights into how effective action can be stimulated, by helping people (whether children or adults) come to terms with the profound implications of climate change, develop a sense of self-efficacy and collective efficacy and engage in actions which help manage their anxieties while contributing to climate mitigation (Burke, Sanson, & Keast, 2017).

Overcoming denial and avoidance involves becoming more knowledgeable about the basic facts of climate change and its implications for future peace and stability in the world. A further critical step is to break the collective silence surrounding climate change – in other words, other people's avoidance and denial. Despite its urgency, not enough people talk about climate change on a regular basis (Norgaard, 2011). For example, a 2016 survey found that only 19% of Americans hear someone they know talking about global warming at least once a month (Leiserowitz, Maibach, Roser-Renouf, Rosenthal, & Cutler, 2017). We need to find ways to bring climate change into conversations with our colleagues, institutions, professional bodies and stakeholders – including those who don't share our world-view or beliefs, seeking to find common values (like protecting children's health) which can lead to common solutions (like clean energy). The more climate change is viewed as a risk that requires action, the more it amplifies an individual's own risk perception and intention to act (van der Linden, Maibach, & Leiserowitz, 2015). Breaking the silence also includes advocating for action on climate change to politicians, policy-makers, opinion leaders and decision-makers.

We know the majority of children and youth have at least some concern about climate change, but they may not share these concerns with parents or other adults. To support children and young people in sharing their concerns and confronting the reality of climate change, important elements include providing supportive environments and opportunities for them to express their fears and concerns and have them validated; sharing your own concerns; suggesting ways to manage negative feelings; giving access to accurate information and dispelling misconceptions; and collaboratively thinking of things they can do about it (alone, with you, with peers or as part of a group) and supporting them in carrying out these ideas (Ojala & Lakew, 2017). Parents and educators, but also others such as youth and community workers, can take on these support roles.

21.6.2 Children as Active Agents in Responding to Climate Change

While it is easy to see children as victims of environmental threats like climate change, they can also be powerful protagonists for change. The Convention on the Rights of the Child states that children have the right to participate in and influence decision-making processes that may be relevant in their lives (UN General Assembly, 1989). Climate change decision-making now will determine the lives of children far into the future, so it is right that children are invited to contribute. Being given the opportunity to actively contribute to combating climate change can also provide important psychological protection, "helping them to feel more in control, more hopeful and more resilient" (Hart, Fisher, & Kimiagar, 2014, p.93). It is thus important to treat young people as active agents, to respect and support their capacities to take action, to work together and to support each other. Helping children develop effective ways of coping with climate change builds their resilience and well-being, while acknowledging the critical role that they, as the next generation of adults, will play in shaping global responses to climate change.

One effective strategy for children to use to cope with climate change is problem-focused coping which entails actively addressing an aspect of climate change (Ojala, 2012). Table 21.2 provides examples of climate change programmes illustrating different levels of child engagement, participation, co-agency and collaboration, as well as youth social action groups.

Another coping strategy is meaning-focused coping, which is particularly relevant for problems like climate change which cannot be removed or solved immediately or alone but demand active involvement over the longer term (Ojala, 2016). Meaning-focused coping involves concepts like positive reappraisal, in which the stressor is acknowledged but positive benefits are identified ("a zero-carbon world could be more healthy and fun"), and hope – recognising that big problems (like apartheid and women's voting rights) have been solved in the past and that new ways to address climate change are being developed all the time (Ojala, 2012). It thus includes a realistic appraisal of the threat, along with a positive attitude that overcomes despair and motivates action. Ojala (2012) has found that meaning-focused coping in children is related to pro-environmental behaviour, environmental efficacy, optimism and a sense of purpose. Meaning-focused coping is similar to Stoknes' (2015) concept of "authentic hope" and Macy and Johnstone's (2012) concept of "active hope".

Helping children to develop adaptive coping styles to engage with climate change can be the work of parents, carers, educators, community development workers and others and can be informed by the work of psychologists. While not much research has yet been published, climate literacy programmes for young people (e.g. http://withoneplanet.org.au; https://www.freespirit.com/pages/resource.cfm?file=1920; Kaye, 2009) and resources to assist parents (e.g. Australian Psychological Society, 2018) are being developed. Strazdins and Skeat (2011) argue that building hopeful images of a zero-carbon future encourages young people to channel their individual interests into a higher social purpose and provides a broader sense of meaning in life. Grønhøj and Thøgersen (2017) specifically examined how different parenting styles can influence young people's internalised motivation to "do something for the environment". They identified four important factors: (i) letting young people see their parents are engaging in pro-environmental behaviours; (ii) parents having their own self-determined motivation to do things for the environment; (iii) an autonomy-supporting parenting style in which parents listen to children's views and perspectives and allow them to decide things for themselves; and (iv) setting expectations for pro-environmental action.

Table 21.2 Some examples of child and youth engagement in climate change mitigation and adaptation, using categories drawn from Back, Cameron, and Tanner (2009)

Level of engagement	What is involved	Examples
Knowledge	Increasing children's knowledge and preparedness	The website www.edu4hazards.org was developed with 9- and 14-year-olds in two London schools. It uses interactive navigation in the form of labels on a suitcase to reflect different types of hazards children may experience. Children anywhere in the world can explore the site to discover how to protect themselves
Voice	Children becoming recognised as stakeholders, with greater visibility to their rights and needs, and stimulating recognition of their potential as agents of change	In Honiara, in the Solomon Islands, a Red Cross project involved training young people to become peer educators in schools and communities on issues related to climate change locally, nationally and even internationally (http://www.icicp.org/resource-library/icp-publications/global-youth-service-database/oceania/solomon-islands/)
Action to protect	Children protecting themselves and their communities, e.g. through child-led disaster drills at schools or small environmental projects	A UNICEF project in Bangladesh in 2014 built capacity, raised awareness and provided training for girls and women, resulting in improved cook stove use, reduced deforestation and respiratory problems and better family relations (https://www.unicef.org/environment/files/Bangladesh_Case_Study_2014.pdf) In the Philippines, schoolchildren skilled in disaster risk mapping and vulnerability assessments used their knowledge to successfully persuade school officials and community planners to relocate their school, previously situated in a high-risk landslide zone, to a safer area (Back et al., 2009)
Action to influence	Children influencing the actions of others, e.g. through advocating for and leading behavioural change	In 2011, over 600 children provided input to the Children's Charter for Disaster Risk Reduction calling for more commitment from governments in climate action (http://www.childreninachangingclimate.org/childrens-charted.html) National climate change strategies developed in multiple LMICs included empowering children by training them as climate change celebrity ambassadors (UNICEF, 2012)
Action to transform	Children informing or changing wider agendas and addressing the root causes of vulnerability through institutions, policies and processes beyond their community	Around the world, there has been a rise of youth social action groups such as the Australian Youth Climate Coalition (http://www.aycc.org.au), and groups of children are taking their governments to court for ruining the planet (e.g. in the Netherlands, the USA, Uganda, Pakistan, Portugal and India) (Livni, 2017)

21.6.3 Building Children's Resilience to Climate Change Impacts and a Zero-Carbon World

As well as being engaged in pro-environmental behaviours and climate actions which build just and fair solutions, children and youth will also need support to be able to adapt to faster and more wide-ranging changes than we have ever seen before. On top of increasingly negative climate impacts, they will also need to adapt to massive changes in lifestyle, consumption, work and travel as the world shifts to a zero-carbon economy – requiring flexibility, adaptability and cooperation with others.

Models of positive child and adolescent development emerging from developmental psychology can provide guidance on how to build the capacities of youth to respond effectively as individuals, community members and citizens to the changes ahead. While a range of positive development models have been proposed (e.g. Hawkins, Letcher, Sanson, Smart, & Toumbourou, 2009; Lerner, Almerigi, Theokas, & Lerner, 2005), they share a number of commonalities. They emphasise competence in (a) individual-level attitudes, values and behaviours such as self-esteem, self-efficacy, empathy and beliefs in justice and equity; (b) interpersonal spheres, reflected in healthy relationships with parents, peers and others and the capacity to cooperate and negotiate with others; and (c) at the community/social level, community involvement, civic action and engagement and trust and tolerance of others.

In general terms, these positive development attributes reflect eudaimonia (realising human potential through meaningful living) in contrast to hedonia (or pleasure-seeking) and provide foundational capacities for resilience and adaptation in the face of the changes ahead.[2] For example, to avoid violence breaking out in the face of climate-induced disruptions, skills in conflict resolution, problem-solving, intercultural understanding, empathy and acceptance and beliefs in environmental protection, equality and justice will be critical. To deal effectively with the move to a zero-carbon and more localised world, skills for cooperation and sharing, trust towards others and strong community orientation and civic engagement will be needed.

The question then is how can we build these attributes in the next generation? Hawkins et al. (2009) showed that four broad factors operating from childhood through early adolescence were related to positive development in early adulthood: self-regulation; positive and supportive relationships with parents, peers and teachers; school connectedness; and being a contributing member of their community, including volunteering and political awareness. Thus early efforts to strengthen

[2] In other climate-related literature, eudaimonic attributes are referred to as intrinsic values and contrasted with extrinsic values which are usually counterproductive in the drive to reduce greenhouse gas emissions. Intrinsic values provide a better source of motivation for engaging in bigger-than-self problems like climate change (https://valuesandframes.org/).

children's capabilities in these areas may help them to thrive and be well-prepared for responding adaptively to the changes ahead. Efforts to support positive development could also focus on helping young people to develop a sense of individual empowerment and collective efficacy by being involved in small climate action projects; talking about values like equality and compassion in age-appropriate terms; encouraging volunteering and joining community groups; encouraging a deep connection with nature; modelling responsible political action; and promoting a climate in schools that values and promotes eudaimonic attributes as much as intellectual and occupational success.

The promotion of positive development, eudaimonic/intrinsic values and meaning-focused coping thus appear to be valuable approaches for preparing young people for the realities of climate change, as well as providing them with the active citizenship skills needed to promote speedy action to mitigate climate change and adapt to the inevitable changes. However, as noted above, the available research on these concepts has been almost entirely conducted in wealthy Western countries, and it is as yet uncertain how applicable they are for the non-Western LMICs which will bear the brunt of climate change. This is clearly an important area for future research.

21.7 Summary and Conclusions

Climate change is one of the most pervasive threats to peace, development, security, health and equity around the world in the twenty-first century, involving both episodic and structural violence. However, solving climate change is also one of our best hopes for episodic and structural peace-building, resulting in a healthier, fairer and more just world.

Children are particularly at risk, being developmentally most vulnerable to many climate impacts, some lasting over their entire lifetime. Focusing on children also helps us to see the injustice and urgency of addressing climate change and encouraging the current adult generation to recognise its responsibilities and "moral duty" (Cripps, 2017) to ensure that today's children and their descendants will have the basic conditions for flourishing. We have discussed peaceful and just solutions to the problem of climate change at all the ecological levels in Bronfenbrenner and Morris's (2006) model of development – some at the macro-system (global and regional) level, some at the exo-system (local and community) level and some at the meso- and micro-system (family, school, individual) levels. Each approach provides opportunities for educators, scholars, practitioners, policy-makers and activists to make valuable contributions. Community development principles can be applied in disaster risk reduction, re-localisation and community adaptation programmes, ensuring that children are heard and fully engaged. There are multiple possibilities for programme development, evaluation and implementation around promoting coping skills, positive development and civic engagement in young people so that they can cope and thrive in a climate-changed world. Globally, there is uneven coverage of climate change in schools: the UN Decade of Education for Sustainable Development (2005–2014; see https://en.wikipedia.org/wiki/Education_for_sustainable_development) helped develop the capacity of school systems to cover sustainable development in school curricula (e.g. Mwendwa, 2017). However, climate change is more rarely a specific curriculum topic. While excellent initiatives exist such as the US Alliance for Climate Education (https://acespace.org) which reports delivering climate education to over two million students, many students across the world still receive limited information. Further, in terms of offering students opportunities to engage with climate change mitigation, it is common for schools to focus only on consumer-based actions (e.g. reduce, reuse, repair, recycle). There is typically little emphasis on active citizenship, on respecting children's rights to full participation or on helping them to develop adaptive coping strategies for the future. Schools, clubs and community groups are among potential sites for programmes to develop these skills – there are many opportunities for educators and psychologists to collaborate in this area.

In tertiary education, there needs to be a much greater integration of climate change into all disciplines and subjects. US research indicates that the majority of undergraduate students do not have an accurate understanding of climate change nor its mitigation (Huxster, Uriber-Zarain, & Kempton, 2015). Climate change, as a threat multiplier and complex global problem, affects every aspect of our lives and needs to be recognised as such. Whether thinking of the arts, architecture, planning, law or the health, social, biological or "hard" (e.g. engineering) sciences, it is difficult to think of an area of study that will not be affected by climate change but also has the potential to contribute to solutions. Within the psychology discipline specifically, climate change needs to be incorporated across all specialist areas, e.g. understanding its impacts on children's development, mental health and well-being; considering the demands on public health services that climate change impacts will entail; examining the human causes *and* solutions to climate change; and developing expertise in the peace-building skills of communication, conflict resolution and negotiation which will be so critical in the future.

Multidisciplinary collaboration to achieve effective solutions to climate change is essential. There is enormous scope for psychologists and other social scientists to work with the broader community of academics, policy-makers, scientists, community groups, activist organisations and the public in conducting climate change research and developing or implementing solutions to environmental threats and climate change. Global climate change is as much a social problem as a physical one.

In conclusion, the world is facing a dire predicament, and the challenges are massive and urgent. But we have the capacity to slow and then stop the harmful warming of our planet at the same time as building fair, just and peaceful communities. Whatever our roles in society, as today's adults, we need to accept that the future survival of our families, communities, the natural places we love and all future generations depends on the actions we take now.

References

Agnew, R. (2011). Dire forecast: A theoretical model of the impact of climate change on crime. *Theoretical Criminology, 16*, 21–42. https://doi.org/10.1177/1362480611416843

Akresh, R. (2016). Climate change, conflict, and children. *The Future of Children, 26*, 51–72.

Albert, M., Hurrelmann, K., Quenzel, G., & Jugend, G. (2010). *Eine pragmatische Generation behauptet sich. (A pragmatic generation asserts itself)*. Frankurt am Main, Germany: Fischer Taschenbuch Verlag.

Anderson, C. A. (2012). Climate change and violence. In D. Christie (Ed.), *The encyclopedia of peace psychology*. Hoboken, NJ: Wiley-Blackwell.

Australian Psychological Society. (2018, under review). *Raising children for a climate changed world: Parenting for sustainability information sheet*. Australian Psychological Society.

Back, E., Cameron, C., & Tanner, T. (2009). *Children and disaster risk reduction: Taking stock and moving forward*. UNICEF. Retrieved from: https://www.preventionweb.net/files/12085_ChildLedDRRTakingStock1.pdf

Betts, R. A., Jones, C. D., Knight, J. R., Keeling, R. F., & Kennedy, J. J. (2016). El Niño and a record CO2 rise. *Nature Climate Change, 6*, 806.

Bronfenbrenner, U., & Morris, P. A. (2006). The bioecological model of human development. In R. M. Lerner & W. Damon (Eds.), *Handbook of child psychology: Theoretical models of human development* (Vol. 1, 6th ed., pp. 793–828). Hoboken: John Wiley & Sons.

Burke, M., Hsiang, S. M., & Miguel, E. (2015). Global non-linear effect of temperature on economic production. *Nature, 527*, 235.

Burke, S., Sanson, A., & Keast, S. (2017). *The climate change empowerment handbook. Melbourne.* Melbourne, Australia: Australian Psychological Society. Retrieved from: https://www.psychology.org.au/APS/media/pdfs/Legacy/The-Climate-Change-Empowerment-Handbook.pdf

Centre for Research on Environmental Decisions [CRED]. (2014). *Connecting on climate: A guide to effective climate change communication*. Earth Institute, Columbia University. Retrieved from: http://ecoamerica.org/wp-content/uploads/2014/12/ecoAmerica-CRED-2014-Connecting-on-Climate.pdf

Christie, D. J., Wagner, R. V., & Winter, D. D. (2001). *Peace, conflict and violence. Peace psychology for the 21st century*. Englewood Cliffs, NJ: Prentice-Hall.

Clayton, S., Manning, C., Krygsman, K., & Speiser, M. (2017). *Mental health and our changing climate: Impacts, implications, and guidance*. Washington, D.C.: American Psychological Association and ecoAmerica. Retrieved from: http://ecoamerica.org/wp-content/uploads/2017/03/ea-apa-psych-report-web.pdf

Confalonieri, U. B., Menne, R., Akhtar, K. L., Ebi, M., Hauengue, R. S., Kovats, B., … Woodward, A. (2007). Human health. In M. L. Parry, O. F. Canziani, P. J. Palutikof, P. J. van der Linden, & C. E. Hanson (Eds.), *Climate change 2007: Impacts, adaptation and vulnerability. Contribution of Working Group II to the Fourth Assessment Report of the Intergovernmental Panel on Climate Change* (pp. 391–431). Cambridge, UK: Cambridge University Press.

Cook, J., Oreskes, N., Doran, P. T., Anderegg, W. R. L., Verheggen, B., Maibach, E. W., … Rice, K. (2016). Consensus on consensus: A synthesis of consensus estimates on human-caused global warming. *Environmental Research Letters, 11*, 048002. https://doi.org/10.1088/1748-9326/11/4/048002

Costello, A., Abbas, M., Allen, A., Ball, S., Bell, S., Bellamy, R., … Patterson, C. (2009). Managing the health effects of climate change. *The Lancet, 373*, 1693–1733. https://doi.org/10.1016/S0140-6736(09)60935-1

Craig, G., Gorman, M., & Vercseg, I. (2004). *The Budapest Declaration: Building European civil society through community development*. International Association for Community Development. Retrieved from: http://www.communitydevelopmentalliancescotland.org/documents/inPractice/BudapestDeclaration.pdf

Credit Suisse. (2017). *Global Wealth Report 2017*. Credit Suisse Research Institute. Retrieved from: http://publications.credit-suisse.com/index.cfm/publikationen-shop/research-institute/global-wealth-report-2017-en/

Cripps, E. (2017). Do parents have a special duty to mitigate climate change? *Politics, Philosophy & Economics, 16*, 308–325. https://doi.org/10.1177/1470594X17709038

Ebi, K. L. (2014). Childhood health risks of climate change. In *The challenges of climate change: Children on the front line* (pp. 22–25). Innocenti Insight, Florence, Italy: UNICEF Office of Research.

Falkner, R. (2016). The Paris Agreement and the new logic of international climate politics. *International Affairs, 92*, 1107–1125. https://doi.org/10.1111/1468-2346.12708

Garcia, D. & Sheehan, M. (2016). Extreme weather-driven disasters and children's health. *International Journal of Health Services, 46,* 79–105.

Grantham-McGregor, S., Cheung, Y., Cuato, S., Glewwe, P., Richter, L., Strupp, B., & International Child Development Steering Group. (2007). Developmental potential in the first 5 years for children in developing countries. *Lancet, 369*, 60–70.

Grønhøj, A., & Thøgersen, J. (2017). Why young people do things for the environment: The role of parenting for adolescents' motivation to engage in pro-environmental behaviour. *Journal of Environmental Psychology, 54*, 11–19. https://doi.org/10.1016/j.jenvp.2017.09.005

Hanna, R., & Oliva, P. (2016). Children and climate change. *The Future of Children, 26*, 115–132.

Harris, P. G., Chow, A. S. Y., & Karlsson, R. (2013). China and climate justice: Moving beyond statism. *International Environmental Agreements: Politics, Law and Economics, 13*, 291–305. https://doi.org/10.1007/s10784-012-9189-7

Hart, R., Fisher, S., & Kimiagar, B. (2014). Beyond projects: Involving children in community governance as a fundamental strategy for facing climate change. In *The challenges of climate change: Children on the frontline* (pp. 92–97). Florence, Italy: UNICEF Office of Research.

Hawken, P. (2017). *Drawdown: The most comprehensive plan ever proposed to reverse global warming*. New York, NY: Penguin Books.

Hawkins, M. T., Letcher, P., Sanson, A., Smart, D., & Toumbourou, J. W. (2009). Positive development in emerging adulthood. *Australian Journal of Psychology, 61*, 89–99. https://doi.org/10.1080/00049530802001346

Henrich, J., Heine, S. J., & Norenzayan, A. (2010). Most people are not WEIRD. *Nature, 466*, 29. https://doi.org/10.1038/466029a

Hopkins, R. (2009). *The transition handbook: From oil dependency to local resilience*. White River Junction, VT: Chelsea Green Pub.

Hopkins, R. (2013). *The power of just doing stuff: How local action can change the world*. Cambridge, UK: Green Books.

Huntjens, P., & Zhang, T. (2016). *Climate justice: Equitable and inclusive governance of climate action* (Working paper No. 16). The Hague Institute for Global Justice. Retrieved from: http://www.thehagueinstituteforglobaljustice.org/information-for-policy-makers/working-paper/climate-justice-equitable-and-inclusive-governance-of-climate-action/

Huxster, J. K., Uriber-Zarain, X., & Kempton, W. (2015). Undergraduate understanding of climate change: The influences of college major and environmental group membership on survey knowledge scores. *The Journal of Environmental Education, 46*, 149–165.

IPCC. (2014). *Climate change 2014: Synthesis report. Contribution of working groups I, II and III to the Fifth Assessment Report of the Intergovernmental Panel on Climate Change* (p. 151). Geneva, Switzerland. Retrieved from: http://www.ipcc.ch/report/ar5/syr/

Kaye, C. B. (2009). *A kids' guide to climate change and global warming: How to take action*. Minneapolis, MN: Free Spirit Pub.

Klein, N. (2014). *This changes everything*. London, UK: Penguin Books Ltd.

Kousky, C. (2016). Impacts of natural disasters on children. *The Future of Children, 26*, 73–92.

Leiserowitz, A., Maibach, E., Roser-Renouf, C., Rosenthal, S., & Cutler, M. (2017). *Climate change in the American mind: November 2016. Yale University and George Mason University*. New Haven, CT: Yale Program on Climate Change Communication.

Lerner, R., Almerigi, J. B., Theokas, C., & Lerner, J. V. (2005). Positive youth development: A view of the issues. *Journal of Early Adolescence, 25*, 10–16.

Livni, E. (2017). *Quartz*. Retrieved from: https://qz.com/1156876/juliana-vs-usa-kids-are-suing-over-climate-change/

Macy, J., & Johnstone, C. (2012). *Active hope: How to face the mess we're in without going crazy*. Novato, CA: New World Library.

McMichael, A. J. (2014). Climate change and children: Health risks of abatement inaction, health gains from action. *Children, 1*, 99–106. https://doi.org/10.3390/children1020099

McMichael, A. J., Campbell-Lendrum, D., Kovats, S., Edwards, S., Wilkinson, P., Wilson, T., … Andronova, N. (2004). Global climate change. In M. Ezzati, A. Lopez, A. Rodgers, & C. Murray (Eds.), *Comparative quantification of health risks: Global and regional burden of disease due to selected major risk factors* (pp. 1543–1649). Geneva, Switzerland: World Health Organization.

Molyneaux, R., Gibbs, L., Bryant, R. A., Humphreys, C, Hegarty, K., … & Forbes D. (2018). *Interpersonal violence and mental health outcomes following disaster*. Manuscript submitted for publication.

Mwendwa, B. (2017). Learning for sustainable development: Integrating environmental education in the curriculum of ordinary secondary schools in Tanzania. *Journal of Sustainability Education, 12*. Retrieved from: http://www.susted.com/wordpress/wp-content/uploads/2017/02/Mwendwa-JSE-Feb-2017-General-Issue-PDF.pdf

NOAA. (2017). *Global Climate Report – Annual 2016*. National Centers for Environmental Information. Retrieved from: https://www.ncdc.noaa.gov/sotc/global/201613

Norberg-Hodge, H. (2003). Globalisation: Use it or lose it. *The Ecologist, 33*, 23–25.

Norgaard, K. M. (2011). *Living in denial: Climate change, emotions, and everyday life*. Cambridge, MA: The MIT Press. https://doi.org/10.7551/mitpress/9780262015448.001.0001

Ojala, M. (2012). How do children cope with global climate change? Coping strategies, engagement, and well-being. *Journal of Environmental Psychology, 32*, 225–233. https://doi.org/10.1016/j.jenvp.2012.02.004

Ojala, M. (2015). Hope in the face of climate change: Associations with environmental engagement and student perceptions of teachers' emotion communication style and future orientation. *The Journal of Environmental Education, 46*, 133–148. https://doi.org/10.1080/00958964.2015.1021662

Ojala, M. (2016). Young people and global climate change: Emotions, coping, and engagement in everyday life. In N. Ansell, N. Klocker, & T. Skelton (Eds.), *Geographies of global issues: Change and threat* (pp. 329–346). Singapore: Springer Singapore. https://doi.org/10.1007/978-981-4585-54-5_3

Ojala, M., & Lakew, Y. (2017). Young people and climate change communication. *Oxford Research Encyclopedia of Climate Science*. https://doi.org/10.1093/acrefore/9780190228620.013.408

Reser, J. P., Bradley, G., Glendon, G. L., Ellul, M., & Callaghan, R. (2012). *Public risk perceptions, understandings and responses to climate change and natural disasters in Australia and Great Britain* (No. 17/12). National Climate Change Adaptation Research Facility (NCCARF).

Sanson, A. V. (2017). Developmental science's role in responding to the climate crisis. *ISSBD Bulletin, 1*, 10–15.

Sanson, A. V., Wachs, T. D., Koller, S. H., & Salmela-Aro, K. (2018). Young people and climate change: The role of developmental science. In S. Verma & A. Peterson (Eds.), *Sustainable Development Goals for children: Using developmental science to improve young lives globally*. (pp115-138). New York, NY: Springer.

Sheffield, P. E., & Landrigan, P. J. (2010). Global climate change and children's health: Threats and strategies for prevention. *Environmental Health Perspectives, 119*, 291–298. https://doi.org/10.1289/ehp.1002233

Stiglitz, J. E., Sen, A., & Fitoussi, J.-P. (2010). *Mismeasuring our lives: Why GDP doesn't add up*. New York, NY: New Press.

Stoknes, P. E. (2015). *What we think about when we try not to think about global warming: Toward a new psychology of climate action*. White River Junction, VT: Chelsea Green Publishing.

Strazdins, L., & Skeat, H. (2011). *Weathering the future: Climate change, children and young people, and decision making*. Canberra, Australia: Australian Research Alliance for Children and Youth. Retrieved from http://www.aracy.org.au/publicationDocuments/ARACY%20climate%20change%20report%20March%202011%20FINAL%20full1.pdf

Strife, S. J. (2012). Children's environmental concerns: Expressing ecophobia. *The Journal of Environmental Education, 43*, 37–54. https://doi.org/10.1080/00958964.2011.602131

The Child Protection Working Group. (2015). *A matter of life and death: Child protection programming's essential role in ensuring child wellbeing and survival during and after emergencies*. The Child Protection Working Group. Retrieved from: http://cpwg.net/?get=010222|2015/10/A_Matter_of_life_and_death_LowRes.pdf

The Royal Society. (2017). *Climate updates. What have we learnt since the IPCC 5th Assessment Report?* London, UK: The Royal Society. Retrieved from: royalsociety.org/climate-change

Tranter, B., & Skrbis, Z. (2014). Political and social divisions over climate change among young Queenslanders. *Environment and Planning A, 46*, 1638–1651. https://doi.org/10.1068/a46285

UN General Assembly. (1989). *Convention on the Rights of the Child* (Treaty Series No. 1577) (p. 3). United Nations. Retrieved from: http://www.refworld.org/docid/3ae6b38f0.html

UN General Assembly, United Nations. (1994). *Framework convention on climate change: Resolution adopted by the General Assembly*. Retrieved from: http://www.refworld.org/docid/3b00f2770.html

UNICEF. (2012). *Climate change adaptation and disaster risk reduction in the education sector: Resource manual*. UNICEF. Retrieved from: https://www.unicef.org/publications/index_68843.html

UNICEF. (2014). *The challenges of climate change: children on the front line*. Florence, Italy: UNICEF Office of Research – Innocenti.

UNICEF. (2015). *Unless we act now*. New York, NY: United Nations Children's Fund. Retrieved from https://www.unicef.org/publications/files/Unless_we_act_now_The_impact_of_climate_change_on_children.pdf

UNICEF UK. (2013). *Climate change: Children's challenge*. UNICEF UK. Retrieved from https://downloads.unicef.org.uk/wp-content/uploads/2013/09/unicef-climate-change-report-2013.pdf?_ga=2.115858243.495899391.1517286128-426487953.1517286128

United Nations. (2015). *Transforming our world: The 2030 agenda for sustainable development*. United Nations. Retrieved from: https://sustainabledevelopment.un.org/content/documents/21252030%20Agenda%20for%20Sustainable%20Development%20web.pdf

van der Linden, S., Maibach, E., & Leiserowitz, A. (2015). Improving public engagement with climate change: Five "best practice" insights from psychological science. *Perspectives on Psychological Science, 10*, 758–763. https://doi.org/10.1177/1745691615598516

Watts, N., Amann, M., Ayeb-Karlsson, S., Belesova, K., Bouley, T., Boykoff, M., … Costello, A. (2018). The Lancet Countdown on health and climate change: From 25 years of inaction to a global transformation for public health. *The Lancet, 391*(10120), 581–630. https://doi.org/10.1016/S0140-6736(17)32464-9

Yun, K., Lurie, N., & Hyde, P. S. (2010). Moving mental health into the disaster-preparedness spotlight. *New England Journal of Medicine, 363*, 1193–1195. https://doi.org/10.1056/NEJMp1008304

Conclusion: Peaceful Children in a Peaceful World – From Intervention to Structural and Cultural Transformation

Daniel J. Christie and Nikola Balvin

In the introduction to this book, we mentioned that the 1989 Convention on the Rights of the Child affirms children's rights to be protected and cared for in ways that ensure their safety and well-being. While the full realization of children's rights remains aspirational, this volume presents a small sample of interventions that fall within the rubric of peace psychology and point to some ways of promoting children's safety and well-being.

Interventions to improve children's lives do not take place in a vacuum. In Italy, where the 15th Symposium on the Contributions of Psychology to Peace took place, the most salient issue was migration. Peace psychologists recognize that the particular set of psychological principles and interventions that are effective in reducing violence and increasing peace vary with geohistorical context. Not surprisingly, many of the presentations that took place at the symposium highlighted concepts and principles well suited for the reduction of intergroup conflict and promotion of tolerance and harmony. Many of the presentations at the symposium were revised and edited as chapters in this book. The chapters that evaluate interventions that took place in Italy, as well as those based on research in other parts of the world, shared the objective of improving intergroup relations.

The chapters dealing with migration and multi-cultural societies offer many insights into the psychological dynamics that take place in these circumstances. Some of the main takeaways included: the valuable role that refugee men can play in promoting the well-being of their children (Veale et al., Chap. 2); the efficacy of extended, vicarious, and imagined contact on improving intergroup relations (Haji & Noguchi, Chap. 4); the effectiveness of inducing empathy toward refugees as a means of promoting more positive attitudes toward the other (Glen et al., Chap. 5);

D. J. Christie
Department of Psychology, Ohio State University, Delaware, OH, USA

N. Balvin
UNICEF Office of Research-Innocenti, Florence, Italy

N. Balvin, D. J. Christie (eds.), *Children and Peace*, Peace Psychology Book Series, https://doi.org/10.1007/978-3-030-22176-8

how civic participation can improve tolerance toward migrants (Mazzoni et al., Chap. 6); how migrants' engagement in civic life can have a desirable impact on adjustment and result in a bi-cultural identity (Marzana et al., Chap. 7); and how youth's social identity can enhance both intergroup conflict and harmony (McKeown et al., Chap. 12). Taken together, these and other chapters identified key mechanisms and conditions that promote intergroup harmony and the well-being of migrants.

Although intervention research is often beneficial for participants, the change toward sustainable peaceful relations must be systemic, which means that the structural and cultural conditions that give rise to intergroup conflict and violence must be ameliorated. Structural conditions can be conceptualized as relatively permanent arrangements in the distribution of a society's resources while culture, as Galtung (1996) puts it, refers to the symbolic sphere of our existence. Culture includes shared meanings, narratives, and norms that justify structural arrangements; together, structure and culture form an interlocking system (Noor & Christie, 2015); it is this system that we, as peace psychologists, wish to nudge in the direction of more peaceful relations.

Some glimpses of an ideal world that grapples with the difficult problem of systemic peace can be found in research on prevention and, in particular, the kind of prevention efforts that assess structural and cultural conditions that support children's safety and well-being. An example is the research presented by Milani et al., (Chap. 1) on an evidence-based assessment system designed to identify risk and protective factors that are associated with family violence. Studies on risk and protective factors are useful not only for the purposes of assessment and intervention but also because the identification of protective factors gives us insight into structural and cultural conditions associated with peace and well-being in children. Generally, these peaceful structural and cultural arrangements are found in inclusive societies where the satisfaction of "life-extending human needs" is accessible to all members of the society including people who occupy subaltern strata (Christie, 2018).

Affolter and Azaryeva Valente (Chap. 14) have demonstrated how the mitigation of structural and cultural inequities that exclude children from basic social services can not only affect their well-being but also remove some of the antecedents of conflict. Maternowska and colleagues (Chap. 9) further complicate the picture in useful ways by demonstrating that structure-based inequalities can interact with risk and protective factors to affect child outcomes. Setting aside the notion that some risk (e.g., poverty) and protective (e.g., education) factors are built into the structure of a society, another way of framing the problem is that structure-based factors represent relatively permanent arrangements in the distribution of resources that potentially enhance safety and well-being. Transient risk and protective factors operate within the context of these relatively permanent arrangements.

In an ideal world peaceful changes are not only *systemic*, they meet other criteria including *scalability*, *sustainability, measurability*, and they have *subaltern involvement*, which means the involvement and leadership of those who are directly affected by violence (Christie, 2018). For example, Guetta's (Chap. 15) educational program on nonviolent communication, while not systemic in nature, has a number of ideal qualities. First, the program is not carried out in a top-down manner; instead, it is peer-driven. Second, the program is scalable as indicated by the adoption of the program by additional schools. Third, the adoption by different schools is also one metric of success, thereby meeting the measurability criterion. Finally, the scalability of the program provides an indication that the peer education approach will be sustainable.

The criterion of sustainability, in particular, has received a great deal of attention in peace research. While interventions that yield peaceful outcomes between groups in conflict are desirable, there is no guarantee that the peace achieved will be stable and sustainable. Bigazzi and colleagues (Chap. 8) note the fragility of empowerment interventions that are not anchored in transformations of the wider structural and cultural context. This view comports with a key maxim in peace psychology; namely, the notion that sustainable forms of peace require structural and cultural transformation (Christie, 2006).

Turning to the criterion of subaltern involvement, a number of chapters featured research methodologies that were sensitive to this issue. There is a growing emphasis among peace psychologists on the value of accompaniment (Watkins, 2015), which positions researchers in a supportive role and places subalterns at the center of the change process. This discursive shift in peace psychology aligns peace psychologists with the emancipatory methodologies of critical and liberation psychology (Christie, Seedat, & Suffla, 2017). Emancipatory methodologies endorse various forms of participatory action research in which subaltern members of a society undergo a conscientization process and drive structural and cultural changes (Bretherton & Law, 2015; Montero & Sonn, 2009; Seedat, Suffla, & Christie, 2017). The involvement of subalterns as a driving force in the transformation process encourages ownership of structural change and helps ensure the sustainability of change (Ferguson, McDaid, & McAuley, 2018).

We see elements of participatory action research in several of the book's chapters. Kostelny, Wessells, and Ondoro (Chap. 18) describe a community-based participatory action research program aimed at supporting vulnerable children and enhancing child protection. As the authors suggest, it seems likely that the program will be sustainable because it was designed to promote local ownership. Similarly, the peacebuilding programs for young people in Cambodia and Uganda described by Balvin and Miletic (Chap. 19) sought to involve relevant stakeholders in various phases of the programs. Stakeholders were also involved in the research informing the programs' next steps. Engagement in the peacebuilding programs was designed to increase stakeholders' knowledge of the research and their ownership of the findings. Wessells (Chap. 20) conducted an action research program designed to engage members of multiple agencies and organizations from several communities with the purpose of developing policies in support of children's protection and well-being. The research demonstrated the value of encouraging a cooperative orientation among stakeholders that results in a sense of ownership among participants as they work on policies in support of children.

Although the prospect of an ideal world in which all children are protected and cared for in ways that ensure their survival and well-being may seem fanciful, there is not much mystery about the kind of systemic changes that are required to create a world where children's rights are fully realized. To be clear, these systemic changes require structural and cultural transformation. While structural transformations ensure a more equitable distribution of material resources and social capital, cultural transformations provide the narratives and norms that are associated with structural transformations. The problem is that there is a lack of collective will to make these changes happen on a global scale. The question is how do we get from where we are to that ideal world?

It is worth noting that the run-up to the instantiation of many human rights was prompted by the pressure of social activists, who had a sense of personal and political efficacy, combined with a skill set for organizing and building solidarity. Historically, for example, social action played an integral role in UN declarations on the rights of persons with disabilities and women's rights (Christie, Bretherton, & Lunn, in press) though some of these rights remain aspirational. Most recently, we have seen social activists take on one of the most challenging existential issues of our time: the issue of climate change (Christie et al., in press). The Human Rights Council recognizes climate change as a human rights issue in part because the known adverse impacts of climate change threaten the right to water, sanitation, food, health, housing, self-determination, and development (Knox, 2016). The issue of social justice looms large as people who live under disadvantageous conditions by dint of geography and other life circumstances are disproportionately impacted, yet they have contributed the *least* to anthropogenic climate change. Moreover, as was pointed out by Sanson and Burke (Chap. 21), there is an issue of intergenerational justice because failure to mitigate climate change leaves young people with the burden of finding a solution to its deleterious effects in the future.

Historically, peace psychologists have sought to apply psychology to the pursuit of peace. From a narrow focus on the prevention of war, peace psychologists have come to appreciate the necessity of addressing the roots of violence in a scalable and sustainable way while serving in a supportive role in which the survivors of violence and social injustices engage in direct action. Given the glacial pace in which children's rights are being realized on a global scale and the urgency of the climate crisis for all of humankind, it is timely for peace psychologists to take on the role of "emancipatory practitioners" and use their knowledge to activate the psychosocial forces necessary to create a sociocultural climate conducive to the full realization of children's rights. A strong collaboration between researchers and practitioners and a dedicated focus on research use and uptake are some of the examples this book offers on how peace psychologists can contribute to achieving this end.

References

Bretherton, D., & Law, S. F. (Eds.). (2015). *Methodologies in peace psychology: Peace research by peaceful means* (Vol. 26). Cham, Switzerland: Springer. https://books.google.co.in/books/about/Methodologies_in_Peace_Psychology.html?id=bHuBCgAAQBAJ&printsec=frontcover&source=kp_read_button&redir_esc=y#v=onepage&q&f=false.

Christie, D. J. (2006). What is peace psychology the psychology of. *Journal of Social Issues, 62*, 1–18.

Christie, D. J. (2018). The meaning and metrics of social and political transformation. *Peace and Conflict: Journal of Peace Psychology, 24*, 77–84.

Christie, D. J., Bretherton, D., & Lunn, L. (in press). Psychosocial features of movements that have advanced human rights. In N. S. Rubin & R. L. Flores (Eds.), *The Cambridge handbook of psychology and human rights*. Cambridge, UK: Cambridge University Press.

Christie, D. J., Seedat, M., & Suffla, S. (2017). Toward a socially transformative peace psychology: Overview of the symposium and proceedings. In M. Seedat, S. Suffla, & D. J. Christie (Eds.), *Enlarging the scope of peace psychology: African and world-regional contributions* (pp. 3–17). New York, NY: Springer.

Ferguson, N., McDaid, S., & McAuley, J. W. (2018). Social movements, structural violence, and conflict transformation in Northern Ireland: The role of loyalist paramilitaries. *Peace and Conflict: Journal of Peace Psychology, 24*(1), 19.

Galtung, J. (1996). *Peace by peaceful means*. London, UK: Sage.

Knox, J. H. (2016). *Report of the special rapporteur on the issue of human rights obligations relating to the enjoyment of a safe, clean, healthy and sustainable environment. Climate Change Report*. United National Human Rights Council: New York, NY.

Montero, M., & Sonn, C. C. (Eds.). (2009). *Psychology of liberation: Theory and applications*. New York, NY: Springer Science & Business Media.

Noor, N. M., & Christie, D. J. (2015). Themes in peace psychology research. In D. Bretherton & S. F. Law (Eds.), *Methodologies in peace psychology: Peace research by peaceful means* (pp. 43–70). New York, NY: Springer.

Seedat, M., Suffla, S., & Christie, D. J. (2017). *Emancipatory and participatory methodologies in peace, critical, and community psychology*. New York, NY: Springer.

Watkins, M. (2015). Psychosocial accompaniment. *Journal of Social and Political Psychology, 3*, 324–341.

Index

N. Balvin, D. J. Christie (eds.), *Children and Peace*, Peace Psychology Book Series, https://doi.org/10.1007/978-3-030-22176-8

Q

R

S

www.ingramcontent.com/pod-product-compliance
Lightning Source LLC
LaVergne TN
LVHW080013210926
848481LV00011B/3009
* 9 7 8 1 0 1 3 2 7 3 2 6 1 *